THE CHRONOLOGY OF MODERN INDIA

THE CHRONOLOGY OF MODERN INDIA

FOR FOUR HUNDRED YEARS FROM THE CLOSE OF THE FIFTEENTH CENTURY

A.D. 1494-1894

JAMES BURGESS

GYAN

Published by

Gyan Publishing House
5, Ansari Road
Daryaganj, New Delhi-110002
Phone: 011-47034999, 9811692060
E-mail: books@gyanbooks.com

Distribution Network
gyanbooks.com
India, USA, Canada, UK, Australia, France

ISBN : 978-81-212-9248-1 (PB)
First Published, 1913

2nd Impression 2023

Printed at: Gyan Press, Delhi.

THE CHRONOLOGY OF MODERN INDIA
Author: JAMES BURGESS

THE CHRONOLOGY OF MODERN INDIA

A.D. 1494—1894

THE CHRONOLOGY OF MODERN INDIA

FOR FOUR HUNDRED YEARS FROM THE CLOSE OF THE FIFTEENTH CENTURY

A.D. 1494—1894

BY

JAMES BURGESS

C.I.E., LL.D., F.R.S.E., F.R.G.S., M.R.A.S.

EDINBURGH: JOHN GRANT

31 GEORGE IV. BRIDGE

1913

PREFACE

A WORK of reference containing the principal *Fasti* of Indian History from the time when European intercourse and commercial relations began with the East, on the discovery of the Cape of Good Hope near the close of the fifteenth century, has been felt as a desideratum by students and readers. For the earlier history the excellent manual of C. Mabel Duff (Mrs W. R. Rickmers) published 1899, supplied a much felt want, and the present volume forms the complement to that work,—the two forming a continuous chronology of events in India from the earliest times till the present.

About eight years ago materials for the volume were collected from the historical works of Orme, Briggs's Ferishta, Elliot and Dowson, Mill and Wilson, Grant-Duff, Elphinstone, Marshman, Malleson, Kaye, Holmes, Danvers, Phayre, Trotter, and others—too numerous to mention. These were arranged in 1907, but laid aside. In now revising it for the press, much of it has been rewritten and considerably extended.

By writers of the eighteenth and most part of last century, Indian personal and place names were written in every variety of spelling—often in forms now scarcely recognisable. To avoid the confusion of such irregularities, proper names are here represented in general accordance with the system in use in the recent Gazetteers and Maps of the Indian Government and in several recent historical works.

The Index will be found pretty complete, and in it the

names of officers are often stated more fully than in the text, and with their subsequent ranks; to place-names are frequently added the districts in which they are; and occasional differences of spelling are corrected with a few other errata.

Differences in the dates of events are not unfrequent, occurring chiefly in translations of Muhammadan histories,—arising partly perhaps from inattention in computing the European from the Hijra reckoning,—but also from other sources,—and it is difficult to rectify such differences when they amount to a year or more. When careful research is applied to such matters, cases of the kind will in course of time be cleared up; and though none of them are of great importance, they may be corrected when a second edition of this handbook is required.

The book, it is hoped, will be found useful to all students of Indian history as well as to the general reader, and to others engaged in secretarial work.

J. BURGESS.

EDINBURGH,
September 1912.

ERRATUM

Since page 95 was printed off the story of Dr Boughton, repeated in so many works, has been investigated by Mr W. Foster, of the India Office, and the following correction is required.

Page 95, *for* lines 7-13, *read*: Jan. Mr Gabriel Boughton, surgeon of the "Hopewell," had been sent by the Surat Council to Agra as surgeon to Asālat Khān, who aids in obtaining a farmān for Surat from Shāhjahān. Later Boughton went to Shāh Shujā', Governor of Bengal, and is said to have saved the life of a favourite of his *haram*. In reward he was granted a patent to trade throughout Bengal, Bihār, and Orissa free of customs.

Page 92, lines 10-12 from bottom: the dates relative to Dr Boughton are much confused, and this event must have occurred several years later.

THE CHRONOLOGY OF INDIA

FROM THE CLOSE OF THE FIFTEENTH CENTURY.

THE purpose of the present work is to enumerate briefly, in the order of time, the historical events connected with the history of India from the closing years of the fifteenth century, when, by the discovery of the Cape of Good Hope in 1487, by Bartholomew de Diaz, and the opening of a direct sea route to the East, the Portuguese began to contend for the exclusive commerce of India. European interest in India was thus stimulated and led to the opening of all the south of Asia to the knowledge and commerce of the West. The enumeration of events is carried down in the following pages from 1492 to the Viceroyalty of the Earl of Elgin and Kincardine, 1894.*

At the commencement of the period to be dealt with, viz. 1492, the following were the leading sovereign rulers in India:—

Sikandar Shāh Lodī was Emperor or Sultān of Dehlī, having succeeded his father Bahlūl Lodī in July 1489; he ruled till 1510.

Shams-ud-dīn Muzaffar Shāh, a Habshī or Abyssinian slave, had murdered his sovereign, Mahmūd Shāh II., King of Bengal, in 1490, and ruled till 1493.

Ghiyās-ud-dīn Shāh Khaljī was ruler of Mālwa, 1475-1500.

* Where native dates are given along with the corresponding European ones, the Muhammadan lunar years from the Hijrat, 16th July 622, are indicated by "H."; the Hindu years of the Vikrama Samvat, by "V.S.," of which the epoch is 18th September 57 B.C. in Western India, but in Northern India the year begins seven months earlier—the months being the same; and the Śaka dates are marked "Ś."; its epoch is 3rd March 78 A.D.—135 years later than the Samvat era.

Mahmūd Shāh I. Baiqara or Bīgara, was the powerful King of Gujarāt, 1459-1511.

'Ādil Khān or 'Alī Shāh Fārūqī ruled in Kāndesh, 1457-1503.

Mahmūd Shāh II. was the Bahmanī King of Kulbarga, in the Dekhan, 1482-1518.

Fath Allah 'Imād Shāhī had established himself as ruler of Berār in 1485 and reigned till 1504.

Ahmad Nizām Shāh Bahrī defeated Mahmūd Shāh of Kulbarga or Ellichpur, 1490, and assumed independence at Ahmadnagar, ruling till 1508.

Yūzuf 'Ādil Shāh revolted at the same time and founded the 'Ādil Shāhī dynasty at Bijāpūr; he died in 1510.

Qāsim Barīd Shāh also assumed independence at Bīdar, 1492; he died in 1503.

In the Hindu states at the same period were:—

Bika Bhīkhaji, who founded the Bikanīr state in 1488 and ruled till 1504.

Rājamalla, ruler of Mewār, with his capital at Chitor, ruled from 1489 to 1509.

Sūrajmal, Rāja of Mārwār or Jodhpur, ruled from 1489 till 1516.

Chāma Rāja Ārberal was ruler of Mysore (Maisūr) about 1478-1513.

Of Vijayanagar, the history for more than twenty years at this period is confused and uncertain. Narasimha I. appears to have been ruler about this time.

REIGN OF SIKANDAR II. LODĪ.

A.D.	
1492	H. 897. Sikandar II. Lodī of Dehli, conquers Bihār, and dispossesses Husain Sharqī of Jaunpur. Qāsim Barīd Shāh of Bīdar rebels against Mahmūd Shāh Bahmanī of Kulbarga, and founds the Barīd Shāhī dynasty of the Dekhan.
1493	April: Rajab, H. 898. Yūsuf 'Ādil Khān defeats the Vijayanagar army under Timmarāj and the young Rāja near Raichūr. On the death of the Rāja, Timmarāj seizes the government of Vijayanagar.

A.D.

1493 Bahādur Gīlānī, Governor of the Konkan, having revolted, is repeatedly defeated by the combined forces of Mahmūd Shāh Bahmanī and Yūsuf 'Ādil Khān of Bījāpūr, and was finally slain.

Harī Nārāyan Deva succeeds his father Balrām Deva as second Rāja of Sambalpur. He settles the part now called Sonpur on his second son, Madan Gopāl.

H. 889. 'Alā-ud-dīn Husain Shāh defeats Muzaffar Shāh Habshī at Gaur, and succeeds him. 'Alā-ud-dīn concludes peace with Sikandar Lodī of Dehli.

1494 H. 899. Alaf Khān, ruler of Morāsa, rebels, but on the approach of Mahmūd Shāh Baiqara's army, flees to Ghiyās-ud-dīn Khaljī, who refuses him shelter.

June : Ramazān, H. 899. Zahīr-ud-dīn Muhammad Bābur, sixth in descent from Taimūrlang (Tamerlane), succeeds his father 'Umar Shaikh Mirzā in the government of Farghāna.

Husain Shāh Sharqī in attempting to recover his kingdom from Sikandar Lodī is defeated, and seeks refuge at the court of 'Alā-ud-dīn Pūrbī of Bengal.

1495 June: Shawwāl, H. 900. Bābur besieges the rebel Ibrāhīm Saru at the fort of Asfera in Farghāna, and receives his submission.

John Cabot seeks to discover a North-West Passage to India.

Ahmad Nizām Shāh Bahrī, first of the Nizām Shāhī dynasty of the Dekhan (1490), founds the city of Ahmadnagar as his capital, which was completed in two years.

Śaka 1417. Aniruddha wrote a commentary on the *Bhāsvatīkarana* of Satānanda.

1496 H. 901. Mahmūd Shāh Baiqara of Gujarāt marches against Īdar and Bāgar levying a heavy tribute. He pardons his revolted chief Alaf Khān.

H. 902. Muhammad, King of Kashmīr, is seized by the rebel *zamindārs* and imprisoned by his cousin, Fath Khān, who assumes the title of king.

According to Baretto de Rezende, the Portuguese now prepare for an expedition to India.

Hieronymo de Santo Stephano, a Genoese, visits Burma

A.D.

1497 H. 903. Ahmad, son of Muhammad Shāh Bahmanī, marries a daughter of Yūsuf 'Ādil Shāh of Bījāpūr.

H. 903. Bâbur succeeds to his uncle's kingdom of Samarqand, but holds it only for one hundred days.

July 8. Vasco da Gama, with three or four ships, sails from Belem. Nov. 22, doubles the Cape, and on the voyage suppresses a mutiny on board.

H. 904. Dastūr Dinār, the governor of Kulbarga, aspires to independence of Bījāpūr, but after several actions with the Bījāpūr army, is killed in battle.

Maulāna Hairāni, author of *Bahram-wa-Nahid*, the *Manāzira Arz-wa-Samā*, the *Manāzira Shama'-wa-Parmana*, and the *Manāzira Sīkh-wa-Murgh*, dies.

1498 H. 904. Yūsuf 'Ādil Khān formulates a partition treaty for the division of the Dekhan kingdoms: Kulbarga and Sāgar are brought under Bījāpūr rule.

'Ādil Khān Fārūqī of Kāndesh, refusing tribute to Gujarāt, is compelled by the army of Mahmūd Shāh to pay the arrears due.

Husain Shāh of Bengal reduces Orissa and invades Assam as far as Kāmrūp. His son Dānyāl, left to complete the settlement of the country, is cut off from supplies, and, attacked by the Rāja, perishes with his army.

Jan. 11. Vasco da Gama leaves Natal; March 2, reaches Mozambique; April 14, is hospitably received at Malindi; May 29, anchors at Kāppātt, and on the 27th at Pantalāyini Kollam, off Calicut; May 28, received in audience by the Zamorin, but harshly treated by the Moorish traders. Diogo Diaz and other Portuguese detained as prisoners in Calicut, for which Da Gama detains eighteen natives on board. The agent having been released, Da Gama sets sail (August 28) with six of the hostages still on board. He reached Lisbon in September 1499.

1499 H. 905. Budhan, a Brahman of Katāin near Lucknow, asserts that "the religions of both Muslims and Hindus, if acted upon with sincerity, are equally acceptable to God." Challenged by the Muslim doctors, he refuses to apostatise, and is forthwith executed.

A.D.

1499 Narasa, Nāyyaka of Madura—till 1500—subordinate to Narasimha, the first of the second dynasty of Vijayanagar.

Mahmūd Baiqara invades Āsīrgarh to enforce tribute from 'Ādil Khān Fārūqī, who sends the tribute.

V.S. 1555: Jan. 16. Adālaj well-inscription of the Rānī Rudadevī, wife of the Vāghela Vīrasimha of Dandahideśa.

V.S. 1556: July 21. Nāgari (near Chitor) inscription of the Guhila Rājamalla, son of Kumbhakarna of Mēdapāta (Mewār), and his wife Śringaradevī, daughter of the prince Yodha, son of Rānāmalla of Marusthali (Mārwār), dedicating a pond.

Ś. 1421: Nov. 14. An inscription in the Viśvanātha temple at Tenkāśi mentions this as the 20th year of King Jatilavarman Parākrama Pāndya Kulaśekhara.

V.S. 1556: Dec. Ahmadābād well-inscription of Bāī Hārīra, a female official in the palace of Sultān Mahmūd Baiqara.

1500 H. 905. Husain Shāh, King of Jaunpur, dies in Bengal, whither he had fled in 1494.

Aug. 27: Safar 1, H. 906. Asghar, Governor of Dehli, revolts, but submits to Sikandar Lodī at Sambhal, and is imprisoned.

Sept. 13. Pedro Alvarez Cabral, with thirteen ships and a rich cargo, arrives at Calicut; a treaty is concluded and a factory established, which was soon after destroyed by the Māppillas, and fifty persons massacred, whereupon Cabral bombards Calicut. Seizing ten of the Zamorin's ships, he sails for Cochin. December, a factory is established and a peaceful alliance made with the Cochin Rāja.

Nov. 17: Rabi II. 14, H. 906. Nāsir-ud-dīn of Mālwa puts his brother 'Alā-ud dīn to death, and assumes the government. Some days later his father Ghiyās-ud-dīn Khaljī, after a reign of thirty-two years, is found poisoned. Three provincial governors revolt, but are overpowered. He reigned till 1511.

Tenna, Nāyyaka of Madura till 1515.

Works in the Persian language now first composed by Hindus' especially a Hindu poet calling himself 'Barhaman.'

1501 March 26: Ramazān 6, H. 906. Sikandar Lodī marches from Sambhal on Dholpur and takes the fort. Entering Gwāliar he receives deputies from Rāja Mān Singh

A.D.

1501 Jan. 10. The Portuguese fleet leaves Cochin, touching at Cannanor on Jan. 15, and reaching Lisbon July 21.

March. Juan de Nueva Castilla, sent from Portugal with four vessels, arrives at Cannanor. At Cochin they sink a Moorish fleet, and depart with rich cargoes of spices and cloth.

Bihārī Lāl,—"the Thomson of India,"—a Hindi poet of the Court of Jaypur, flourished: author of *Satsaī.*

1502 Pope Alexander VI. grants to the Portuguese king a Bull constituting him "Lord of the Navigation, Conquest, and Trade of Ethiopia, Arabia, Persia, and India."

Feb. 10 (according to Correa, March 25). A fleet of ten ships under Vasco da Gama leaves Portugal. A settlement is arranged with the Kolattiri and Cochin, but the Zamorin remains hostile. Da Gama loots a Moorish pilgrim vessel and puts the crew and pilgrims to death, defeats and burns the Calicut fleet; and, Dec. 28, sails for Europe.

H. 908. A Muhammadan confederacy, under Mahmūd Shāh Bahmanī, marches towards Vijayanagar and forces the Hindus to pay tribute and surrender Raichūr and Mūdkal to Bījāpūr.

Yūsuf 'Ādil Shāh introduces the Musalman Shī'ah doctrines, but shows a wise tolerance towards those of the Sunnī persuasion.

Juan de Nueva Castilla returns to Portugal, discovering St Helena on the way, May 21, 1502.

Aug. 28: Safar 26. Husain Langāh I., King of Multān, dies. His grandson, Mahmūd Khān Langāh, succeeds.

V.S. 1559. Harivans, founder of the Rāshā Vallabhi sect, born near Mathurā, author of the *Chaurāsi Pada*, a Hindi poem, and of the *Rādhā Sudhā Nidhi* in Sanskrit.

1503 March 31. The Zamorin of Calicut, with an army of 50,000, marches to Repelim (Eddapalli) to expel the Cochin Rāja Tirumumpara who, with the resident Portuguese, retires to Vypīn or Baypīn island.

Sept. 2. Alphonso de Albuquerque arrives at Cochin. The Calicut garrison after a battle evacuates Cochin; Tirumumpara is re-established and a factory founded. This is the first European fortress in India. Factories are next established at Kollam (North Quilon) and St Thomé.

A.D.

1503 H. 909. Sultān Sikandar II. transfers the capital of the Empire from Dehli to Agra.

Sept. 6: Rabī' I. 14, H. 909. 'Ādil Khān Fārūqī (called Mīrān Ghāni), King of Kāndesh, dies. His brother, Dā'ūd Khān, succeeds, and, supported by Mālwa, provokes war with Ahmad Nizām Shāh of Ahmadnagar, who declines battle.

Ludovico di Varthema (Lewes Vertomannus) of Rome, travels from Palikat to Tenasserim, and mentions Armenian and Nestorian Christians resident at Pegu.

1504 Jan. 12. The Portuguese fleet sails from Cochin, leaving a factor and a priest. Francisco de Albuquerque concludes a treaty with the Zamorin, broken by the seizure of a Calicut boat. Jan. 25, Alphonso de Albuquerque sails. Feb. 5, his cousin Francisco sails with cargo, but is lost on the way home. Duarte Pacheco beats off an attack on the fortress by the Zamorin.

Bābur, driven from Transoxiana, invades Kābul and takes the city, which he holds for twenty-two years.

Qāsim I. of Bīdar dies, and is succeeded by his son, Amīr Barīd I. He deprives Mahmūd Shāh Bahmanī of all power, and rules till 1538. Yūzuf 'Ādil Khān also throws off allegiance to Mahmūd Shāh.

H. 910. 'Alā-ud-dīn 'Imād Shāhī succeeds his father, Fath-Allah of Berār; till about 1529.

Naroji succeeds his uncle, Bikaji or Bhīkhaji of Bikanīr; but dying the same year, is succeeded by his brother, Lankharanji.

Sept. 14. A fleet of fifteen sail under Lope Suarez, sent by King Manuel, arrives at Cochin, having intimidated the Zamorin at Calicut by a two days' bombardment.

Ś. 1427: Aug. 25. Sanskrit inscription at Devulapalli records that Imādi Nrisimha ruling at Penugonda, son of Nrisimharāya, granted the village to a Brāhman on the occasion of a lunar eclipse.

1505 June 4: Muharram 1, H. 911. Qutlugh Nigār Khānum, Bābur's mother, a descendant of Changez Khān, and who accompanied him on most of his wars, dies.

H. 911. Sikandar Lodī Afghān spoils several Hindu Rājas. His army, attacked at Chinur, is saved by the bravery of Dā'ūd Khān and Ahmad Khān.

A.D.

1505 Fath Khān of Kashmīr is defeated and driven from his capital by the ex-King, Muhammad, but returns with an army and recovers the throne.

July 6: Safar 3, H. 911. During the reign of Sikandar Shāh Lodī, Agra is devastated by a terrible earthquake.

Lope Suarez burns the town of Cranganor.

March 25. A fleet of twenty-two sail, under Dom Francisco de Almeida, leaves Portugal to consolidate the Indian and other Eastern conquests. Oct. 24, the fleet arrives at Cochin with the new Viceroy. Cochin is made the seat of government, and forts erected at Anjidīva Cannanor and Kollum. The Moors put to death all the Quilon factors, for which their ships are burnt.

H. 911. Sayyid Muhammad, son of Mīr Sayyid Khān of Jaunpur, claiming to be the "Imām Mahdī," dies. His disciples are the Ghair-Mahdvis—a sect which still exists.

1506 H. 911. Muhammadan invasion of Vijayanagar from Bīdar. In an action at Diwali the Hindus are victorious, driving back the enemy.

March 16. Lorenzo de Almeida concentrates his ships at Cannanor against the fleet of the Zamorin, and defeats the combined fleet of Turkish and Moorish allies. Lorenzo sails south, and reaches Ceylon, where a treaty is concluded.

April 18. Da Cunha leaves Lisbon with Alphonso de Albuquerque as Viceroy elect. He visits the Red Sea and Persian Gulf, where some captains mutiny and proceed straight to India. He now defeated the Zamorin, founded and fortified a settlement at Goa; then sailed to the Straits of Malacca, and took the city in Feb. 1510; reduced the Molucca and Banda islands, and in 1514 reduced Ormuz, the chief port in the Persian Gulf. Thus in twelve years he had acquired for Portugal all the chief trading ports from the Cape to China—extending to 12,000 miles of coast.

H. 912. Dilshād, vazīr of Jām Nandā of Sindh, conquers Uchh.

Jahāngir, Bābur's brother, revolts, is subdued and pardoned.

H. 912. Hanumangarh or Bhatner, reduced by Sikandar.

A.D.

1507 May 7: Zī-l hijja 24, H. 912. Mahmūd Shāh Bahmanī dies. The governors of Junnar, Bijāpūr, Berār, Bīdar, and Golkonda proclaim their independence.

In Bābar's absence Muhammad Husain Mirzā is proclaimed King of Kābul. Bābar on his return attacks and captures the Mirzā.

April 27. De Brito besieged in Cannanor by the Kolattiri, the Zamorin and the Moors, but a fleet under Da Cunha arrives from Europe and raises the siege. Peace is concluded.

May 28: Muh. 16, H. 913. Sikandar reduces Awantgarh or Ontgīr fort, and leaves for Agra.

H. 913. Narwar besieged by Sikandar Lodī, aided by Jalāl Khān, Governor of Kālpī, and taken after a year's siege; mosques and a college built.

Sept.: Jumāda II., H. 913. Bābur marches against Hindustān, drives off booty from the Afghāns, and returns to Kābul. Asked to become King of Qandahār, he is treated treacherously, but defeats the Qandahār force at Khattak.

Fath Khān is expelled a second time by Muhammad from Kashmīr.

H. 913. Ahmad Nizām Shāh supports the claims of 'Ālam Khān Fārūqī to the throne of Kāndesh, but is compelled to desist by the King of Gujarāt.

A combined fleet of Turks and Gujarātis, under Malik Ayāz, the Amīr-ul-Umarā, Governor of Dīū, attacks the Portuguese off Chaul, each side claiming the victory.

Nov. 27. Almeida, with the fleet, destroys Ponnāni, the Zamorin's port.

Dec. 6. The Portuguese fleet sails for Europe.

V.S. 1564. Rise of the Katuka sect of the Jains.

1508 March 7: Zī-l qa'da 4, 913. Humāyūn born at Kābul.

H. 914. Ahmad Nizām-ul Mulk Bahrī, Sultān of Ahmadnagar, dies. His son, Burhān Nizām Shāhī, succeeds, at the age of seven: till 1554.

Nov.: Rajab, H. 914. Mahmūd Shāh, Baiqara of Gujarāt, proceeds to Nandarbār to depose the putative 'Ādil Khān Fārūqī in favour of 'Ālam Khān, son of Hasan Khān, which is accomplished without bloodshed.

A.D.

1508 H. 914. A large fleet prepared in Egypt, under Mīr Husain, having on board 500 Mamlūks and the Zamorin's ambassador. Mayimama Mārakkār, engages the Portuguese fleet at Chaul, The Commander, Lorenzo de Almeida, and his crew are killed. Nov. 12. His father, Francisco de Almeida, in revenge, sends a fleet which burns some Calicut ships and arrives at Cannanor on Nov. 25. Dec. 12, the fleet pursues Mīr Husain and enters Dābhol on Dec. 30. He takes the town and massacres the inhabitants.

Dec. 14. Albuquerque, the Viceroy, is unable to eject Almeida. Both send despatches under this date to Dom Manuel.

1509 Jan. 5. The Portuguese fleet sails from Dābhol. Jan. 21, lands at Māhim. Feb. 3, engages and defeats the Musalmān fleet under Mīr Husain in the harbour of Dīū. March 8, Almeida enters Cochin in triumph. Albuquerque is now a prisoner. Oct. 29, Dom Fernando Coutinho arrives from Portugal with orders to instal Albuquerque as Governor-General, and (Nov. 5) he is proclaimed Viceroy at Cochin.

Feb. 24. Krishna Deva Rāya succeeds Narasa or Vīra Narasiṁha at Vijayanagar.

Rājamalla or Raimal Rānā of Mewār dies. His son, Sanga Rānā or Sangrām Singh I., succeeds.

H. 915. Bābur takes under his protection his cousin the historian, Haidar Mirzā Doghlāt, son of the Amīr of Kāshghār.

Ś. 1431. A Hampe inscription records that Krishna-deva gave the village of Singenayakanāhalli to the temple of Virupāksha.

1510 Jan. 4. Albuquerque and Coutinho arrive at Calicut, burn the Zamorin's palace, and destroy the place; but the natives rallying, Coutinho is attacked in the palace and killed, with eighty men, and Albuquerque escapes with a wound. He then withdraws with the fleet to Cochin.

Feb. 28. Goa fort rushed by Noronha, Albuquerque's nephew, and surrendered by Mīr 'Alī. March 4, the Viceroy enters Goa in state. May 20, Goa retaken by a force under Kamāl Khān, Ismā'īl 'Ādil Khān's general. The Portuguese retire till September, make another effort, and take the place again on Nov. 10.

A.D.

1510 H. 916. Yūsuf 'Ādil Khān of Bījāpur dies. Ismā'īl 'Ādil Shāh, his son, succeeds, and successfully resists the efforts of Amīr Barīd to reduce Bījāpūr. He rules till 1534.

Sikandar II. Lodī of Dehli acknowledges the independence of Gujarāt.

Aug. 6: Jumāda I. 1, H. 916. Dā'ūd Khān of Kāndesh dies. Ghazni Khān succeeds, but after two days is poisoned by the minister, Malik Hissām-ud-dīn. 'Ālam Khān, a relative, is raised to the throne, but 'Ādil Khān III. Fārūqī is everywhere acknowledged.

'Imād-ul-Mulk of Berār, induced to march on the Nizām Shāhī dominions, is defeated at Ranuri by Burhān Nizām Shāh's army.

Friar Luiz sent as ambassador to Vijayanagar, to seek help against the Zamorin.

Dec. Krishna Deva Rāya sends ambassadors to Goa on the defeat of the Bījāpūr deputy by Albuquerque.

1511 April 30: Safar 1, H. 917. Kamāl Khān plots against Ismā'īl 'Ādil Shāh. The Queen-mother discovers the plot and secures his assassination, and defeats an attack on the palace at Bijāpūr.

Bābar turns his attention to India, having lost Samarqand.

May 2: Safar 3. Nāsir-ud-dīn Khaljī dies, and Mahmūd Shah II., third son, ascends the throne of Mālwa. His eldest son heads a revolt induced by his father's scandalous conduct, but being defeated, fled to Dehli. Mahmūd ruled under various vicissitudes till 1531.

June. In order to ruin Muslim trade with China, Albuquerque strikes at Malacca, and takes the city on July 26, slaughtering the natives. A fort called "A Famosa" is erected, and rebellion crushed. Dec., Albuquerque leaves Malacca, but loses rich booty by shipwreck.

Khusru Turk, a Persian Shī'ah, invested with the estate of Belgaum and the title Azad Khān.

Nov. 23: Ramazān 2, H. 917. Mahmūd Shāh I. (Baiqara) of Gujarāt, dies after a reign of fully fifty-two years. His son succeeds as Muzaffar Shāh II., crowned at Ahmadābād, Dec. 9 (Ramazān 17), till 1526.

The Bijāpūr forces under Fūlād Khān prepare to reconquer

A.D.

1511 Goa, which is invested all winter. Help from Cochin saves the town.

V.S. 1568. Rūparshi of the Mālasavada Jaina Gotra forms the Nāgapurīya branch of the Lampāka sect.

1512 Jan. Albuquerque's return to Cochin arrests an incipient revolution.

H. 918. Qulī Qutb-ul-Mulk, Tarafdār of Talingana, assumes independence, and makes Muhammadnagar (Golkonda) his capital, taking the title of Qulī Qutb Shāh.

H. 918. Muzaffar Shāh II. of Gujarāt, on an expedition against Mālwa, is diverted from his object by the rebellion of the Bhīmrāja of Īdar, who had defeated 'Ain-ul-Mulk, Governor of Nahrwālah. On Muzaffar's arrival at Morāsa the Rāja takes flight; his lands are plundered.

Sept. 10. An expedition to reduce Makka commenced, but abandoned for an attack on Banestarim which capitulates in October. An ambassador from Goa is favourably received.

Ś. 1434. A Kuppēlūr copper-plate records that Krishnarāya gave the new village Timmalāpura or Tirmalāpura to Timmarāya, astrologer of Rattihalli and Kōd.

1513 Feb. 10. Dom Garcia de Noronha reports the Zamorin of Calicut willing to make peace. An embassy is unsuccessful, but the Zamorin is poisoned by his brother, who concludes peace and grants a site for a factory, which was at once erected.

H. 919. Muzaffar II. of Gujarāt ravages Īdar, and having made peace with Bhīmarāja continues his march into Mālwa.

Krishna Deva of Vijayanagar marches against Udayagiri, a hill fort in Nellor, and wages successful war against the King of Orissa. He is defeated at Pangul by Qulī Qutb Shāh, who takes Rājkonda, Devarkonda, Kovilkonda, and Ghanpura.

The Krishnasvāmi temple at Vijayanagar built by Krishna Deva. The temple of Hazāra Rāmasvāmi is begun.

Bettada Chāma Rāja, King of Seringapatam: till 1552.

Aug. Two attempts by the Portuguese on Aden fail, and Albuquerque returns to Goa.

Dec.: Shawwāl, H. 919. Prince Sāhib Khān of Mālwa, besieged in Mandū by Mahmūd II. of Mālwa, flees to Gujarāt,

A.D.

1513 thence to Āsīr. The Prince of Chanderi supports Mahmūd's cause against that of Shihāb-ud-dīn's son Makhsūs.

H. 919. Bābur marches on Qandahār, but concludes a peace with Shāh Beg Arghūn and returns to Kābul. Shāh Beg prepares to retreat to Sindh.

V.S. 1570. Rise of the Bijamata sect of Jains.

Sept. 20: Ś. 1435. A Sanskrit and Kanarese inscription records that Krishnarāya of Vijayanagara (1510-1529), at Sankalapura, granted the village to a temple of Ganapati.

1514 H. 920. Bhīmarāja of Īdar, who had plundered the Pātan district and defeated 'Ain-ul-Mulk at Morāsa, dies. His son, Bihār Mal, succeeds him, but is deposed by his cousin, Rāja Mal, aided by Rānā Sangrām of Mewār. Muzaffar II. of Gujarāt sends Nizām-ul-Mulk, governor of Ahmadābād, to oppose the latter.

Jan. Ambassadors from Pegu and Siam request Albuquerque for trade with Malacca. March: an embassy sent by the Portuguese to Khambay in Gujarāt, which is well received, but fails to gain permission for a fort at Dīū.

July. Attempts made by Albuquerque to plant a factory at Ormuz. He exacts tribute.

Renewed disputes arise between the Portuguese and the Bijāpūr governments.

The Bijāpūr troops defeat the combined forces of Golkonda, Ahmadnagar and Berār at Allapūr, near Bijāpūr. Mahmūd Shāh Bahmanī and his son Ahmad taken prisoners.

Dec.: H. 920. Shāh Beg Arghūn sends a force from Sūvī into Sindh, which takes the villages of Kākān and Bāghbān.

Ś. 1436. Kanarese inscription on a column at Ellamma temple at Ugargol, near Saundatti, records the finishing of the upper storey over the mandapa of west door by the Nāyyaka of Śrī Krishna.

1515 H. 921. Nizām-ul-Mulk, under orders of Muzaffar II. of Gujarāt, reinstates Bihār Mal as Rāja of Īdar, expelling the usurper Rāj Mal.

Duarte Barbosa travels in India—visits Vijayanagar, 1504-15.

A.D.

1515 April 1. The Portuguese occupy Ormuz and develop trade. Pedro de Albuquerque appointed governor.

June 23: Ś. 1437. Krishnarāya Deva's general, Sālva Timma, takes the fortress of Kondavīd, defeating the King of Orangal.

Narasa Pillai, Nāyakka of Madura: till 1519.

H. 921. Bābur again lays siege to Qandahār, but his army being weakened by fever, he again makes peace and returns to Kābul.

The Jews at Cranganor put to death many Muhammadans and lead to their own extirpation from the Malabar Coast.

V.S. 1572. Rise of the Pāśachandra sect of the Jains.

Sept. 8. Don Lope Soarez de Albergaria arrives at Goa as governor, appointed on account of slanders against Albuquerque.

Dec. 15. Alphonso de Albuquerque dies off Goa.

1516 Feb. 8. Lope Soarez conducts an expedition to Aden, but fails to reduce it; returns to Goa in September, with a loss of 800 men.

An expedition to China is undertaken by Perez, a Portuguese, who is driven by storms to Bengal.

Jorge de Brito's tyranny at Malacca causes revolts, which are put down by force.

H. 922. Sikandar Lodī promised the fortress of Ranthambhor by two plotters, fails to obtain it, and retires to Agra.

Peace and alliance concluded between Krishna Deva of Vijayanagar and the King of Orissa or Orangal.

Bābur, for the third time, besieges Qandahār, and Shāh Beg Arghūn sues for peace, agreeing to surrender the city in the following year to Bābur's officers, and Bābar returns to Kābul. In H. 923 Shāh Beg, as arranged, surrendered Qandahār.

1517 H. 923. Muzaffar II. sends an expedition against Rāja Mal who attacks Īdar and kills Zahīr-ul-Mulk, the governor. Muzaffar restores Bihār Mal.

Nov. 18: Zī-l qa'da 4, H. 923. Muzaffar Shāh lays siege to Mandū in the interests of Mahmūd Khaljī of Mālwa, who was powerless against the Hindu Medinī Rāi. Mahmūd had fled to Gujarāt.

IBRĀHĪM II. LODĪ

A.D.

1517 Nov. 21: Zī-l qa'da 7, H. 923. Sikandar II. Lodī dies. Ibrāhīm II. Husain, his eldest son, succeeds, but at the instigation of the Lodī chiefs, his brother, Jalāl Khān, to whom Jaunpur had been granted, sets up a royal establishment there.

June. Perez makes a fair voyage to the China Islands.

Fernão de Alcaceva is sent to Goa as Surveyor of Revenues. Dissensions cause him to return.

The Portuguese governor concludes a treaty with the Queen of Quilon (Kollam), and a new factory is erected.

John de Sylveyra enters the port of Chittagāon, and the Arakanese invite the Portuguese to trade with them.

H. 923. Death of Maulānā 'Abdullah of Dehlī, author of *Sharh Mīzāni-l-Mantiq*.

1518 Jan. 7: Zī-l hijja 14, H. 923 Ibrāhīm Husain Lodī imprisons his brothers in Hānsi fort for the rest of their lives. Jalāl Khān, deserted by his supporters, flees to Gwāliar and is sent a prisoner to the king, who orders his death.

H. 924. Muzaffar Shāh II. marches into Mālwa to overawe the minister Medinī Rāi who quits Dhār. On Feb. 2: Safar 2, Mandū is taken and Mālwa restored to Mahmūd Khaljī.

H. 924. Mān Singh, Rāja of Gwāliar, dies, and is succeeded by his son, Vikramājit.

Shāh Beg Arghūn prepares for the conquest of Sindh.

H. 924. Hindāl Mirzā, son of Bābur and brother of Humāyūn born.

Sept. 8. Diogo Lopes de Sequeyra arrives at Goa as governor.

Soarez makes an expedition to Ceylon, with soldiers and artizans. Sept. 18: He arrives at Point de Galle, obtains tribute and a site for a fortress, which when completed is put in charge of João de Sylveyra.

The Portuguese factory at Malacca besieged by the King of Bintang for twenty days. The Portuguese attack and take Fort Muar.

Albuquerque is recalled, and the Portuguese power in the East from this time begins to decline.

A.D.

1518 Dec. 18: Zī-l hijja 4, H. 924. Mahmūd Shāh II. Bahmanī of Kulbarga dies. His son, Ahmad II., succeeds as a mere pensioner of Amīr Barīd, and reigns two or three years.

1519 Jan.-March: Safar, H. 925. Bābar takes possession of the countries on the further side of the Indus. Overrunning the Panjāb, he chastises the Gakkhars and returns to Kābul.

H. 925. Ambassadors from Persia arrive at the Bijāpūr court.

Ismā'īl 'Ādil Shāh defeated before Raichūr by the Vijayanagar troops.

Kuru Kuru Timmappa, Nāyyaka of Madura; till 1524.

'Alā-ud-dīn Husain of Bengal dies, his son Nāsir-ud-dīn Nasrat Shāh succeeds; till 1532.

Andrea Correa concludes a treaty with the King of Pegu, and reduces the Kings of Bintang and Pacem.

Sept. Tangassēri fort at Kollam is secretly completed and fortified.

H. 925. Mahmūd Khaljī of Mālwa defeats and slays Bhīm Karan, Governor of Gāgrūn. Sangrām Singh of Mewār attacks Mahmūd and takes him prisoner, but afterwards releases him.

1520 H. 926. Bābur marches a third time on Hindustan, attacking the Afghāns on the route. Siālkot submits, Sayyidpur is taken, but hearing of an invasion from Qandahār on Kābul, Bābar returns and lays siege to Qandahār.

Rānā Sangrām defeats Mubāriz-ul-Mulk in Īdar, takes Ahmadnagar, and returns to Chitor.

War breaks out between Krishna Deva Rāya, of Vijayanagar, and Ismā'īl 'Ādil Khān, who was defeated at Raichūr, and that fort and others are captured by the Hindus. (Castanheda places this defeat 1520, Ferishta in H. 927, corresponding chiefly to 1521, Nuniz says May 1522.)

Ruy de Mello, Governor of Goa, on the defeat of 'Ādil Khān of Bijāpūr, annexes part of the mainland opposite Goa.

Fort Thomas at Tangassēri is besieged by the Muhammadans.

H. 926. Mīrān Muhammad Shāh I. succeeds 'Ādil Khān III. of Kāndesh; till 1535.

Sept.: H. 926. Muzaffar Shāh II. of Gujarāt advances against Sangrām Singh, Rānā of Chitor; encamps at Harsīl, Dec., he

A.D.

1520 appoints Malik Ayāz to the command. He then proceeds with Kiwām-ul-Mulk and defeats the Rānā at Dhamolah; afterwards Malik Ayāz and Kiwām-ul-Mulk lay siege to Mandasor.

H. 927. Shāh Beg Arghūn overruns Sindh and takes possession of Thattā, where he defeats and slays Daryā Khān, the adopted son of Jām Nandā. Jām Fīrūz flees, but afterwards submits, is pardoned and given the government of half of Sindh. Shāh Beg next takes Sīstān and then proceeds to Bhakkar.

1521 H. 927. On the death of Khān Mirzā, Bābur bestows Badakshān on Humāyūn.

Feb. 21. The Portuguese governor Sequeyra sails to attack Dīū, but fails to storm it.

March. De Brito besieged for five months in the Portuguese fortress at Colombo; a relieving force helps to rout the besiegers. Peace is arranged.

H. 927. Ahmad Shāh III. Bahmanī dies, and Amīr Barīd raises his brother, 'Alā-ud-dīn Shāh, to the throne.

Malik Ayāz, sent to avenge the depredations of the Chitor Rānā, quarrels with the Gujarāt nobles. On a threatened attack, a submissive message from Sangrām Rānā is sent to Muzaffar.

Nāsir-ud-dīn Nasrat Shāh of Bengal breaks the treaty of Bar and invades Tirhūt, kills the Rāja and appoints his son-in-law, 'Alā-ud-dīn, governor. Hājipur and Mongīr were also subdued.

Krishna Deva of Vijayanagar constructs the great dam and channel at Korragal, also the Basavanna channel.

An expedition to Sumatra undertaken by Jorge de Albuquerque, who storms Pachim, restores a friendly Rāja, and erects a fort. An attack on Bintang is repulsed, the Portuguese losing heavily.

Dec. 22. Dom Duarte de Menezes takes office as Governor at Goa, Sequeyra being recalled owing to complaints of the conduct of the Portuguese to trading vessels.

H. 927. Khondamīr begins the *Habīb-us-Siyar*, a more comprehensive history than the *Rauzat-us-Safā* of his father, Mirkhond. Born at Harāt about 1475. He left it because of the disturbed state of the country in 1527, and was patronised by Bābur, and died in 1535; he was a prolific writer.

A.D.

1522 July 18: Sha'bān 23, H. 928. Shāh Beg Arghūn leaves Pāyandah Muhammad Turkhān in charge of Bhakkar, he dies at Agham, on his way to invade Gujarāt. His eldest son, Husain Shāh, succeeds, and defeats Jām Fīrūz who had headed a rebellion in Thattā.

Dābhol is made tributary to the Portuguese; and Malik Ayāz is compelled to quit Chaul. Revolts at Ormuz are occasioned by the insolence of the Portuguese officials.

The Portuguese abandon their fort at Pacem.

1523 H. 929. 'Alā-ud-dīn Shāh Bahmanī deposed by Amīr Barīd, and soon after murdered. His brother, Walī Allah Shāh, raised to the throne; till 1525.

H. 929. Muzaffar II. of Gujarāt prepares to advance against Chitorgadh, but the Rānā's son having come with the stipulated elephants and tribute, the expedition is given up.

Saluva Timma, Krishna Deva's minister, invades the Goa mainland, but is checked at Phonda.

April. The Portuguese confirm Ismā'īl 'Ādil Shāh in possession of the Goa mainland.

H. 930. Ismā'īl 'Ādil Shāh goes to war with his brother-in-law, Burhān Nizām Shāh of Ahmadnagar, who appeals to Bīdar and Gāwilgarh for help.

Portuguese expeditions to Malacca, Pahang, Java, and Banda are attended with loss. They establish a strong fort at Cranganor, which they enlarged in 1565.

1524 H. 930. Muzaffar II. of Gujarāt rebuilds and fortifies Morāsa.

Jan. Heytor da Sylveira becomes master of Aden, which is made an open port for Portuguese vessels. The king maltreats a crew and seizes the cargo.

H. 931. The Ahmadnagar Confederacy is defeated by the Bījāpūr army.

H. 931. Prince Bahādur of Gujarāt visits Dungārpur, Chitor, and Dehlī, and takes up his residence with Ibrāhīm Lodī. A plot is formed to raise him to the imperial throne, Ibrāhīm being now in disfavour.

Bettada Chāma Rāja of Maisur dies. His three sons divide his

A.D.

1524 possessions, the youngest Chāma Rāja the Bald, obtaining Fort Puragarh, afterwards called Mahishāsur (Mysore).

Kattyama Kamayya Nāyyaka of Madurā; till 1526.

H. 931. Shāh Husain Arghūn, appointed by Bābur to the affairs of Multān, invades Multān and captures Uchh. Mahmūd Langāh marches against him, but is assassinated, and his son, Husain Langāh II., succeeds. A peace is arranged by Shaikh Bahā-ud-dīn, but Shāh Husain after a siege of fifteen months takes Multān, in H. 932.

Sept. 25. Vasco da Gama, Conde de Vidigueyra, arrives at Calicut as Viceroy, to supersede Menezes. He appoints able officers and reorganises the administration.

'Ālam Khān Lodī, a son of Sultān Bahlūl Lodī, who had taken refuge in Gujarāt (H. 930), returns to Dehlī and raises an insurrection against his nephew, Sultān Ibrāhīm, is defeated and flees to Bābur at Kābul, who made use of him in preparing to invade India.

Dec. 24. Vasco da Gama dies at Cochin. The Royal Despatch is found to appoint Dom Henrique de Menezes as successor, with Lopo Vaz de Sampayo as interim governor.

1525 H. 932. Walī-Allah Shāh is poisoned by the minister Amīr Barīd, who places his nephew, Kalīm-Allah Shāh, on the throne—the last of the Bahmanīs of Kulbarga; he dies next year.

Feb. The Zamorin attacks the Portuguese factory at Calicut, on which Menezes attacks and storms Ponnāni, burns the ships at Calicut, and destroys the native settlements and shipping at Dharmapattam and Mahé. From June 13 till Oct. 31 the Zamorin besieges the Calicut fort, which is abandoned.

Many of the Malay kings make peace with the Portuguese.

March 21: V.S. 1581. Dehli Siwālik pillar inscription of the reign of Ibrāhīm Lodī.

Nov. 17: Safar 1, H. 932. Bābur enters on the conquest of Hindustan by way of Sindh. Dec. 29, Rabī' I. 14, he reaches Siālkot.

SULTAN BĀBUR

1526 Jan.: Rabi II., H. 932. Bābur blockades and captures the fort of Malwat (Malot). April 19, at Pānīpat he totally defeats

A.D.

1526 Ibrāhīm, who was slain, and founds the Mughal dynasty in Hindustan, otherwise known as the Gurgānī Chagatai dynasty.

Feb. 21. Dom Henrique de Menezes, Governor at Goa, dies at Cannanor. Lope Vaz de Sampayo acts, pending the arrival of the next nominee. Goa, Cochin, and Cannanor are fortified against an expected Turkish invasion. At Tidor, Dom Garcia Henriques, by disarming and firing the town to settle disputes, brings the Portuguese into disrepute. On Dec. 31 a Spanish ship arrives there, and the Spaniards join the natives in expelling the Portuguese.

March 15: Jumāda II. 2, H. 932. Muzaffar Shāh II. of Gujarāt dies. April 4: His son, Sikandar Shāh, succeeds, but is murdered by 'Imād-ul-Mulk. May 26, Sha'bān 14, when his youngest brother, Nāsir Khān, ascends the throne as Mahmūd II. He in turn is deposed, and succeeded on Aug. 22, Zī-l qa'da 14, by his elder brother, Bahādur Shāh. (Firishta gives different dates.)

May 10: Rajab 28. Bābur enters Agra and takes up his residence in the palace.

H. 932. Multān is taken, after a fifteen months' siege, by Husain Arghūn of Thattā, acting for Bābur, and becomes a dependency of Dehlī.

Chinnāppa Nāyyaka of Madura, till 1530.

Jaytsinghjī of Bikhanir succeeds his father Lankaranji; till 1545.

1527 Jan. 6: Rabī' II. 3, H. 933. Humāyūn joins Bābur at Agra, and proceeds against Rānā Sangrām of Chitor: the main army following, the Rānā is defeated on March 16: Jumāda II. 13. An insurrection in the Doāb is put down by Bābur's army: Chandwār and Etāwa are captured.

Jan.: Rabī' II. Ishāq, son of Malik Ayāz, suspected of intrigue with the Portuguese, is expelled from Dīū by Bahādur Shāh.

Feb. 28. Pedro Mascarenhas, Governor-elect of Goa, returning from Malacca, is wounded at Cochin and imprisoned at Goa, Lope Vaz refusing trial. Arbitration is resorted to, and on Dec. 26 Lope Vaz de Sampayo is acknowledged governor.

H. 933. 'Alā-ud-din, 'Imād Shāh of Berār, recovers Fort Patri, which is retaken by Burhān Nizām Shāh and destroyed.

A.D.

1527 The Kāndesh and Berār armies inflict a defeat on the Ahmadnagar troops near the Godāvarī.

The Gujarāt fleet defeated by the Portuguese off Chaul.

Robert Thorne, an English merchant resident in Spain, asserts the practicability of a north-west passage to India. His attempt and six others in the succeeding reigns fail.

Chaitanya, a revivalist and mystic in Bengal, held to be an incarnation of Krishna, dies.

1528 Jan. 29: Jumāda I. 7, H. 934. Chanderī fort besieged and taken by Bābur, the Rājputs devoting themselves to death. He then crosses the Ganges in face of the Afghāns, and settles the country.

A Portuguese expedition, bound for Sanda, is driven on the Bengal coast, the leader and crew being captured and enslaved.

Sept.: Muharram, H. 935. Bābar receives the submission of Ranthambor fort from Bikramājit, Rānā Sangrām's son.

Sept. 19: Muharram 4. Bābur receives the historian Khondamīr, who henceforth accompanies the Emperor on his journeys.

Oct. 15. Lope Vaz de Sampayo takes Porca (Purakkat), defended by the natives.

The Portuguese side with Nizām-ul-Mulk against Bahādur Shāh. Chaul is strengthened and the Gujarāt fleet pursued, and in an action off Bāndra 73 out of 80 Gujarāt ships are captured.

1529 Jan.: Jumāda I. Bābur sets out to conquer Bengal. April 10: Sha'bān 1, H. 935: Mahmūd Khān, son of Sultān Sikandar, defeated by a detachment of Bābur's. May: the Bengalis, after another defeat, accept terms of peace. May 22: Ramazān 13, the Afghāns take Lucknow from Bābur's army. June 25, Bābur returns to Agra.

H. 936. Ismā'īl 'Ādil Shāh attacks and captures Amīr Barīd, minister of Bīdar, but afterwards restores him to his country. Mūdkal and Raichūr capitulate after a three months' siege.

H. 936. Bahādur Shāh destroys Ahmadnagar. Burhān Nizām Shāh of Ahmadnagar bestows the title of 'Peshwā' on a

A.D.

1529 Brāhman called Kunwar Sain; henceforward Hindus acquire great influence in the Nizām-Shāhi government.

Daryā Imād Shāh succeeds his father, 'Alā-ud-dīn, in Berār.

Nov. Nuno da Cunha arrives in India as governor with orders to send Lope Vaz de Sampayo in custody to Europe. Nov. 18: Sampayo sails from Cannanor.

The Molucca Islands transferred from Spain to Portugal for a large sum.

HUMĀYŪN

1530 Dec. 26: Jumāda I. 6, H. 937. Bābur dies near Agra, and Humāyūn, his son, succeeds at the age of twenty-two; till 1539.

1531 H. 937. War breaking out between Gujarāt and Mālwa, Bahādur captures Mandū, the capital, with Mahmūd Khaljī and his seven sons, whom he puts to death (March 28) to prevent their rescue, and annexes Mālwa. The Portuguese meanwhile attack Dīū, but are repulsed by the garrison (Feb. 16). Bahādur defeats the Dekhan forces, and concludes peace.

Achyuta Rāya succeeds Krishna Deva Rāya at Vijayanagar.

Feb. 7 With a large armament Nuno da Cunha takes Syāl or Syālbet, on the coast of Kāthiāwār, by the sword. Feb. 16, he attacks Dīū, but finds it impregnable. He leaves Antonio de Saldanha with sixty ships to plunder the Ḳhambay ports, and on the way south he destroys Balsār, Tārāpur, Kelva-Māhim, and Agāshi.

March. The Portuguese drive the natives from Mangalor and Daman. The commander of Chaul, defeated by a Gujarāt force, is deprived of office. The Portuguese are driven by the natives from Ternate.

H. 937. Turks arrive in Gujarāt, under Mustafa Rūmī, and Bahādur assigns them a dwelling at Dīū. Several Lodī chiefs find refuge at Bahādur's court, which offends the Emperor Humāyūn. Oct., Bahādur conquers and garrisons the Bāgar country.

Ratnasimha Rānā succeeds his father, Sangrām of Udaypur; till 1532.

Ayyakarai Vayyāppa, Nāyyaka of Madura; till 1535.

A.D.

1531 Tabang Shēwti ascends the throne of Burma at the age of sixteen.

H. 938. Ismā'īl 'Ādil Shāh defeats Burhān Nizām Shāh at the Bījāpūr frontier. This battle was called the victory of the sons of Rājputs and foreigners, and was the last engagement fought between Bījāpūr and Ahmadnagar.

Oct., the fort of Rīvadanda at Chaul is begun by permission of the governor.

1532 H. 938. Bahādur Shāh of Gujarāt marches into Mālwa, obtains possession of Mandū, reduces Bhilsā and restores the Muslim belief.

May 10: Ramazān 30. Raisīn fort besieged; Silhadī Purbiya agrees to become tributary and accept Islām, but his brother, Lakshman Sen, holds out; and the Rājputs put the women to the *johar* and devote themselves to death in battle.

H. 939. Humāyūn's brother, Kāmrān Mirzā, invades Kashmīr, but is repulsed with loss. Kashmīr is invaded and devastated by the Tartars.

Nasrat Shāh of Bengal sends Mulk Murjan to make a treaty with Bahādur Shāh.

Sher Khān, now master of Bihār, obtains possession of the fortresses of Chunār and Rohtās.

Ganga Rāo of Mārwār or Jodhpur dies. His son, Māldev, succeeds, and regains Ajmīr and Nāgor with other conquests; till 1584.

Ratnasimha of Mewār dies in an encounter with the Prince of Būndī. His brother, Vikramāditya, succeeds; till about 1535.

The Portuguese under Da Cunha burn all the towns from Bassein to Tārāpur, and levy contributions from Thānā and Bombay.

Nuno da Cunha takes Bassein from a garrison of 12,000 men, and razes the fortifications, and an attempt is made to take Daman.

Humāyūn's campaigns in Mālwa and Gujarāt.

1533 Jan.: H. 939. Nasrat Shāh of Bengal murdered, and Fīrūz Shāh, his son, reigns. Ghiyās-ud-dīn Mahmūd Shāh III., a son of 'Alā-ud-dīn, murders his nephew, Fīrūz, and usurps the throne.

A.D.

1533 March 24: Sha'bān 27, H. 939. Bahādur Shāh raises the siege of Chitor on payment of tribute. He withholds his allegiance to Humāyūn.

March 27: Ramazān 1, H. 939. A Kalna inscription records the building of a Jāmī' Masjid in the time of 'Alā-ud-dunya-waddīn 'Abul Muzaffar Firūz Shāh, the king, son of Nasrat Shāh, the king.

April. Orders arrive at Goa that all commanders of forts shall be sworn by the Governor-General.

Aug.: Muharram 940. Humāyūn repaired the old fort of Indraprastha, and called it Dīnpanah, making it his royal residence.

H. 940. Muhammad Zamān Mirzā, and his son, Ulugh Mirzā, revolt, and are defeated at Bhojpur.

Conspiracies occur at Ternate, ending in the murder of Gonzalo Pereira: Tristão de Ataide succeeds as governor, but no improvement in Molucca results.

1534 Farīd Khān, an Afghān chief, separates from Humāyūn, and begins an anti-Mughal movement, assuming the title of Sher Khān.

Aug. 27: Safar 16, H. 941. Ismā'īl 'Ādil Shāh of Bījāpūr dies. His son, Mallū 'Ādil Shāh succeeds, but on account of his vices is blinded and deposed after six months.

Tabeng Shwēti, the Burmese king, attacks the Peguans, takes the capital, and on the death of Takarwutbi, 1539, becomes king.

H. 941. The Portuguese obtain permission to erect a fort at Dīū. They take Swally and Daman. A treaty is made with Bahādur Shāh, also with Humāyūn, who is promised an armament against Sher Khān. The Zamorin of Calicut, after being defeated in six battles, ceases hostilities.

The *Humāyūn-nāma*, the last work of Khondamīr, written.

1535 March 25: Ramazān 20, H. 941. Bahādur Shāh, defeated by the Emperor Humāyūn's army, flees to Mandū. His followers are plundered and dispersed. Aug., Humāyūn carries the hill fort of Chāmpānīr, but his officers left in charge quarrel, and occasion the evacuation of Mālwa and Gujarāt by the Mughals.

H. 941. Mallū 'Ādil Shāh is deposed and blinded for his vices. Ibrāhīm, his younger brother, is seated on the throne; he pro-

A.D.

1535 motes Dekhanis to the exclusion of foreigners. Disputing the succession to the Vijayanagar throne, he is defeated by the Hindūs.

H. 942. Muhammad of Kashmīr dies. Prince Ibrāhīm is acknowledged king, but is expelled, the two ministers, Malik Achchi and 'Abdul Mākri, being rivals for power.

Anarchy in Mewār on the death of Vikramāditya, whose bastard brother, Banbīr, usurps authority, till 1537.

Viśvanātha Ayār, Nāyyaka of Madurā, till 1544.

The fort of Vārīvene on the Indus retaken from the Mughals by the Portuguese. Kalyān is taken from Bijāpūr.

Nuno da Cunha brings about a compact between Bahādur Shāh and Nizām-ul-Mulk; and on Oct. 25 himself concludes a treaty of peace and commerce with Bahādur.

1536 H. 943. The imperial troops in Bihār defeat a Bengal army at Bihār fort. The young king, Jalāl, flees to Gaur. Chunār fort captured by Sher Khān, who makes himself master of Bihār.

The Portuguese attack and take Cranganor, and build a fort. A citadel built at Dīū is cut off from the town by a wall erected by Bahādur.

Feb. Dom João Pereira defeats Sulaimān Āghā at Rachol, and is besieged for ten days.

March. Nuno da Cunha builds a fort at Bassein.

July. The Portuguese defeat the army of Asad Khān, the Bijāpur minister, but are besieged and accept the terms offered, viz., their lives to be spared on the demolition of the fortress.

1537 H. 943. Bahādur Shāh remonstrates against the encroachments of the Portuguese, and in the negotiations at Dīū, at an interview on the admiral's ship on Feb. 14: Ramazān 3, as he was leaving, a scuffle arises among the Gujarāt followers and Portuguese, in which both Bahādur Shāh and Manuel da Sousa are drowned. Nuno da Cunha obtains certificates from the chief men of Dīū approving his action.

Mīrān Muhammad Khān Fārūqī of Kāndesh is called to the throne of Gujarāt, but dies suddenly, Zī-l qa'da 14: April 24. The courtiers raise Bahādur's nephew, Mahmūd Shāh, son of Latīf Khān, to the throne of Gujarāt. 'Imād-ul-Mulk and Daryā Khān

A.D.

1537 act as regents and advisers. Mīrān Muhammad's brother, Mīrān Mubārak Khān II., succeeds to the government of Kāndesh.

H. 944. The Afghāns invade and capture Hājipur, the promised help from the Portuguese not arriving, Mahmud Shāh of Bengal flees to the Mughal camp at Chunār.

Uday Singh II., son of Singrām Singh, ascends the throne of Mewār in succession to the usurper Banbīr.

The Zamorin, assisted by Pate Marakkār, a wealthy merchant, makes sporadic attacks on the Portuguese and also on the King of Ceylon.

Goa is made an episcopal see by Pope Paul III., and put under the Metropolitan of Funchal. The first bishop was Dom Francisco de Mela. The Portuguese found a settlement at Hūglī near the old site of Sātgāon.

Nov. 28: Ś. 1459. An inscription on a temple of Viśvanātha a Tenkāśi shows this to be the third year of Jatilavārman Konērmaikondān Śrivallabha Pāndya.

1538 Jan. 8: Sha'bān 15, H. 944. Humāyūn lays siege to Chunār fortress and takes it from Sher Khān, who drives Mahmūd Shāh of Bengal from Gaur.

Feb. 15. Martin Affonso defeats a fleet under Pate Marakkār at Bandala, rescues Portuguese prisoners, and captures twenty-three barques. He raises the siege of Colombo, where the king's brother, Madune Pandar, was in revolt.

April 6: Zī-l qa'da 6. Gaur fort is now taken after a four days' siege, by Khawās Khān, Sher Khān obtaining Rohtās fort from the Rāja; it is afterwards invested by Humāyūn.

Rise of the Kūch Bihār kingdom under Bīsā.

H. 945. Mahmūd Shāh of Bengal dies at Khalgāon. Humāyūn leaves Jahāngir Qulī Beg as Governor of Bengal.

An attempt by the Portuguese to place a fortress at Chittagāon results in the capture of fourteen of their company, on which Nuno da Cunha burns several towns.

Sept. A Turkish expedition arrives to exterminate the Portuguese in India, and bombards Dīū for twenty days. The expected arrival of a new Viceroy and fleet causes the armada to retire on Nov. 25.

A.D.

1538 Jumāda I. 1, H. 945. A Persian inscription of Tilbegampur commemorates the erection of a wall and aqueduct in the time of Humāyūn by Mahātadittu, son of Bādshāha the Khatri, with the help and approval of Shujā-ud-dīn Amīr Faqīr 'Alī Beg Bahādur.

Sept. 24. Dom Garcia de Noronha reaches Goa as Viceroy.

Oct. Guru Nānak (born 1469), founder of the Sikh religion, dies at Kartārpur in the Jalandhar Doāb, and Angad or Lakanā, his disciple, succeeds as second Guru.

1539 Jan. Nuno da Cunha leaves India, and dies on the way to Europe.

The new Viceroy, Dom Garcia de Noronha, visits Dīū, and on Feb. 26 concludes a treaty with Khwāja Zafar, granting Mahmūd Shāh two-thirds of the revenue. The peace of Dīū causes hostilities elsewhere to cease.

June 26: Safar 9, H. 946. Humāyūn, retreating for Agra from Mongīr, is intercepted and defeated by Sher Shāh at Chapar Ghāt near Baksār. Kāmrān and Hindal reconciled with Humāyūn in face of the common enemy.

H. 946. Sher Khān proclaims himself King of Bengal and assumes the name of Farīd-ud-dīn 'Abul Muzaffar Sher Shāh.

Jahāngir Qulī Khān defeated by Jalāl Khān and Hāji Khān, and soon afterwards killed.

Pegu falls before Tabeng Shwētī, and the Talaing king is driven out.

1540 Jan. A treaty is concluded by the Portuguese with the Zamorin for thirty years. Trade facilities and support in time of war are provided. Treaties are also concluded with the Kings of Bījāpūr and Ahmadnagar.

April 3. The Viceroy, Dom Garcia de Noronha, dies. Dom Estevão da Gama succeeds. Burhān-ul-Mulk attempts to recover Bassein, but is defeated by Ruy Lorenzo de Tavora at Baylam. Da Gama treats with Mahmūd III., who had besieged Bassein but failed to take it, and Da Gama obtains half the customs receipts instead of one-third as formerly.

SHER SHĀH AFGHĀN

April: Zī-l qa'da, H. 946. Humāyūn again invades Bengal,

A.D.

1540 and on the desertion of Sultān Mirzā determines to give battle to Sher Shāh. He is defeated at Kanauj, May 17: Muharram 10, H. 947, and retires on Lāhor. Oct., he fails to assert his authority in Sindh, and escapes to Persia as an exile.

H. 947. Sher Shāh ascends the throne of Dehli, and seizes all Humāyūn's possessions. He subdivides Bengal into provinces.

Ibrāhīm of Kashmīr dies. His eldest son, after a reign of three months, is expelled by Humāyūn's general, Haidar Mirzā Doghlat, who captures Śrinagar in November.

Martaban sacked by the Burmese under Tabeng. (The record of Pinto gives 1543-4.)

Burhān Nizām of Ahmadnagar takes from Gujarāt the forts of Kanāla and Sangaza or Sānkshi.

1541 Jan. A Portuguese expedition leaves Goa for Suez, and on the way several cities are sacked, and ships captured.

July. The fleet arrives at Goa. This year a Portuguese galleon with cargo is captured by the French off the Azores.

Oct. H. 941. Hindāl Mirzā quits Humāyūn's cause, raids and takes Qandahār. Kāmrān besieges it for six months.

H. 941. Khizr Khān, Governor of Bengal, deposed by Sher Shāh at Gaur. Bengal divided into districts, each under an Amīr, under the amīn Qāzī Fazīlat.

Tabeng Shwētī defeats a Shān army and lays siege to Prome, which he captures in June following.

The *Lubbu-t Tawārīkh* of Yahyā bin 'Abd-ul Latīf written.

1542 Jan. An expedition sent from Goa to the Red Sea: meeting a hostile reception at Suakin, it returns to Goa in May.

Jan. 25. Sher Shāh at Dehli devotes himself to the establishment of unity in his dominions, dividing them into 116,000 fiscal unions, each governed by five officials.

May 6. Francis Xavier lands at Goa as the first Jesuit missionary.

June. Prome captured by Tabeng Shwētī; the royal family is massacred and a Burmese officer left in charge.

Oct. 15: Rajab 5, H. 949. Akbar born at Amarkot, in Sindh, where his father, Humāyūn, had taken refuge with Rānā Prasād.

A.D.

1542 H. 949. Burhān Nizām Shāh, taking advantage of dissensions between Ibrāhīm 'Ādil Shāh and his minister Asad Khān, invades Bijāpūr; but peace is brought about through the King of Berār

Sadāśiva succeeds Achyuta Rāya of Vijayanagar. His power is nominal, Rāma Rāya with his brothers, Tirumala and Venkatādri, ruling the state. July 27, earliest epigraphical date for his reign.

Sept. Martin Affonso da Sousa succeeds Estevão da Gama as governor. He reduces the pay of the soldiers, and compels the Queen of Bhatkal to pay tribute. The entire customs of Ormuz are relinquished by the king.

A Portuguese expedition to China discovers Japan.

1543 H. 950. Sher Khān captures Raisīn Fort; after promising the commander, Pūran Mal, the son of Silhadī, that the Hindu garrison should be allowed to march out with their arms and property, Sher Shâh attacked them, and in a desperate contest they were all slaughtered.

July 9. Humāyūn, having failed in a second attempt on Sindh, leaves for Qandahār, and thence for Persia in December, leaving Akbar with Mirzā 'Askarī at Qandahār.

Sept. 2: H. 950. Qulī Qutb Shāh of Golkondā murdered, it is supposed, at the instigation of his son Jāmshīd, who ascends the throne. Burhān Nizām Shāh enters into alliance with Vijayanagar and Golkondā against Bījāpūr, while Rāma Rāja attacks Raichūr.

1544 H. 951. Humāyūn is hospitably received by Shāh Safawī Tahmāsp of Persia, and, though forced to profess the Shī'ah religion, he obtains an army to reconquer Hindustan.

H. 951. Sher Shāh invades Mārwār, and takes Chitor, Nāgor, and Ajmir.

1545 March 21: Muharram 7, 952. Humāyūn's army reaches Qandahār, which, as promised, is given to the Persians. After the departure of the Persian army, it is retaken. Nov. 15: Ramazān 10, Kābul is taken, and Akbar recovered. Mirzās 'Askarī and Hindāl join Humāyūn, and Kāmrān flees to Sindh.

ISLĀM SHĀH

A.D.

1545 May 24: Rabī' II. 12. Sher Khān killed by an explosion at Kālinjar. Salīm or Jalāl Khān supplants his brother in the succession, and assumes the title of Islām Shāh.

H. 952. Muhammad Khān Sūr appointed Governor of Bengal and North Bihār under Salīm Shāh Sūr, but assumes royalty as Bahādur Afghān.

Mahmūd Shāh III. of Gujarāt enforces the Muhammadan law so strictly that persecution of the Hindus arises.

Prince 'Abdullah 'Ādil Khān, discovered in a plot to displace his brother, Ibrāhīm, at Bijāpūr, flees to Goa. The Portuguese take up his cause, but abandon it and return him to Ibrāhīm in exchange for Salsette and Bardes.

Sept. 1. Dom João de Castro, with a fleet of six sail, arrives at Goa to succeed Martin Affonso de Sousa.

Friar Vincent of the Franciscan Order commences a mission at Cranganor among the Syrian Christians. Failing in this, he is assisted by the Viceroy and Bishop of Goa in erecting a college, but the native Church refuses to recognise the orders of the students ordained there.

Nov. 4. By a treaty with the Spaniards, Tidor is regained for the Portuguese, the Spaniards receiving Ternate.

Nov. 20: Ramazān 17. 'Imād-ul-Mulk Malik Jīū, on a pilgrimage to Makka, is cruelly assassinated at Surat by Khudāwand Khān Rūmī.

1546 Feb. 26. Ibrāhīm 'Ādil Khān concludes a treaty with the Portuguese, providing for the custody of 'Abdullah and exemption from duty on horses and spices.

H. 952. Obstinate rebellion shown to Salīm Shāh Sūr by Khawās Khān, a partisan of his brother 'Ādil. The rebellion crushed, 'Ādil flees from Agra to Bihār.

June 24. Khwāja Zafar, defeated in a plot to seize Dīū, is killed. His son, Rūmī Khān, continues the attack till Nov. 10, when his army is routed in three actions.

Renewed incursions made by the Portuguese on the coast towns of Gujarāt, towns and ships being burnt.

A.D.

1547 April 11. The Portuguese governor, having settled Dīū, returns to Goa, and finding Salsette and Bardes still occupied by the Bijāpūr troops, proceeds to eject them. Treaties are now concluded with the Kings of Vijayanagar (Sept. 19) and Ahmadnagar (Oct. 6), constituting a triple league against Bijāpūr.

April 27. Kāmrān finally quits Kābul. He is joined at Bāmiyān by some adherents, raises an army and takes Gori.

H. 953. Shujā'at Khān, Governor of Mālwa, revolts, and is defeated by Salīm Shāh.

Many converts to Romanism made in Ceylon by Antonio del Padrou, first Commissary of St Francisco in India.

Gabriel de Ataide, a Portuguese priest, digging the foundations for a church at the little Mount, Mailapur, professed to find a cross stained with the blood of St Thomas. The place was occupied by the Order of the Pelerino about 1551.

The Portuguese defeat the King of Achīn, Sumatra, in a naval battle.

Aug. 17. Kāmrān is defeated in Badakhshān and induced to surrender. Humāyūn is reconciled to his brothers. Kāmrān consents to retire to Makka, but returns to his nobles. Oct. 5, Humāyūn returns to Kābul.

The Burmese are checked in an attack on the Siamese capital, Yuthia (Ayodhya). King Tabeng Shwētī is assassinated. Bureng Naung—"Branginoco" in the Portuguese narratives—succeeds.

1548 May 22. A large fleet arrives at Goa, with extension of office for Dom João de Castro, who, however, dies on June 6, and Garcia da Sa, third on the Succession Patent, succeeds.

Aug. 6. Eleven ships bring the first Dominican Friars to India; a convent founded at Goa.

Aug. 22. Ibrāhīm 'Ādil Khān, after his coast towns were again destroyed by the Portuguese, is constrained to make a contract with them, promising help should a Turkish fleet be sent to India.

Sept. 17. The Queen of Bhatkal agrees to pay tribute, and not to harbour pirates.

Mahmūd Shāh of Gujarāt concludes a peace with the Portuguese much in their favour.

A.D.

1548 H. 955. Shaikh 'Alai, founder of the Māhdī sect, after raising great disturbances, dies under scourging at Agra.

1549 H. 956. Humāyūn invades Balkh, but is compelled to retreat, his return to Kābul being harassed by the Usbaks.

Jan.: Muharram. Asad Khān, minister of Bijāpūr, dies.

July. Garcia da Sa dies. Aug. 11, Jorge Cabral succeeds as sixteenth governor at Goa. The Zamorin and the chief of the pepper district defeat the Portuguese and the Cochin Rāja at Bardela.

1550 H. 957. Humāyūn loses Kābul, but recovers it from Kāmrān and restores order.

Jāmshīd Qutb Shāh of Golkonda dies. His son, Ibrāhīm, succeeds.

Mirzā Haidar Doghlāt, ruler of Kashmīr, killed by conspirators.

Nov. The Zamorin, with eighteen princes, invades Cochin. The Viceroy forbids an attack, and allows the army to retreat.

Nov. Dom Affonso da Noronha arrives at Goa as Viceroy; with him the Viceroy's powers are curtailed, and a council constituted to advise and assist in the administration.

In Ceylon the Portuguese lose 800 men in defending the Kings of Kotta and Kandy. The Viceroy visits Ceylon, ostensibly to relieve the friendly King of Sitawakka, but really to capture his treasure.

1551 Jan. 14: Muh. 6, 958. Shaikh Abul-Fazl, the historian, born.

H. 958. Kashmīr is divided into three principalities, Nāzak being pageant king over all.

Khawās Khān, a partisan of 'Ādil Shāh, the brother of Salīm Shāh, is murdered by Tāj Khān Kararānī, Governor of Sambhal, in order to ingratiate himself with Salīm Shāh.

War again breaks out between Bijāpūr and Ahmadnagar. Burhān Shāh with Rāma Rāja puts to flight the Bijāpūr army. Raichūr and Mūdkal are taken from Ibrāhīm 'Ādil Shāh.

Chamba territory ravaged by the Portuguese in revenge for the detention of the homeward bound fleet. Maskat lost to the Portuguese, also Ormuz town.

Nov. 19: Zī-l qa'da 21. Hindāl Mirzā killed in a night attack

A.D.

1551 upon Humāyūn by Kāmrān, near the Khaibar pass. Hindāl's daughter, Raqia Sultāna, is given in marriage to Akbar, to whom was also given command of his uncle's troops.

1552 H. 959. Nāzak Shāh of Kashmīr deposed a second time; his son Ibrāhīm is raised to the throne, under the control of Daulat Chak, but Ghāzi Khān joined by other nobles raises civil war.

March 4. Angad, the second Sikh Guru dies, having nominated as his successor his disciple and servant, Guru Amardās. He lived at Govindvāl and built a well there, dying in 1574.

Timma Rāja Wodeyar II. Appanna succeeds to the throne of Seringapatam and province of Maisur.

Aug. 15. Gil Fernandez de Carvalho, with an expedition fitted out at his own cost, drives off the Turkish fleet from Ormuz.

Luiz de Camoens, the poet, arrives at Goa and becomes a soldier.

Dec. 2. Francis Xavier, Jesuit missionary to India, dies near Macao. Canonised at Goa 1622.

1553 The Portuguese burn the chief towns of the "Pepper Country," whereupon the chief sues for peace. The natives at Dīū are ordered to leave and the castle is demolished. Diogo de Noronha is beaten back with loss.

Aug. 26. Fernando de Noronha captures six Turkish vessels. Seven are later driven into Surat.

Sept.: Ramazān, H. 960. Kāmrān surrendered by Ādam Gakkhar to Humāyūn and blinded, on account of his repeated disturbances. He obtained permission to go to Makka, where he lived for three years, dying Oct. 1557.

MUHAMMAD SHĀH 'ĀDIL.

1554 H. 961. Islām Shāh Sūr dies at Gwāliar. His son Fīrūz is murdered by his cousin, Mubāriz Khān son of Nizām Khān Sūr, who succeeds under the title of 'Abul Muzaffar Muhammad Shāh 'Ādil, but proves a weak ruler.

Muhammad Khān Sūr Gauriah, Governor of Bengal, throws

A.D.

1554 off his allegiance to Muhammad Shāh. (The date is also given as Nov. 21, 1554: Zī-l hijja 26, H. 961.)

Burhān Nizām Shāh of Ahmadnagar dies. His son Husain, with the help of foreigners and Abyssinians succeeds, driving out the rival claimant 'Abdul-Qādir.

Feb. 16: Rabī' I. 13, H. 961. Mahmūd Shāh III., of Gujarāt, poisoned by Burhān, a menial, who, after putting the chief nobles to death, attempts to ascend the throne. He is cut down by 'Imād-ul-Mulk, and Ahmad Khān, a supposed descendant of Ahmad Shāh I., is made king.

Feb. A further fruitless Portuguese expedition to the Red Sea under Manuel de Vasconcellos.

A great earthquake in Kashmīr destroys the town of Jadra with most of its inhabitants, and changes the course of the Jailam or Vyath at Dampor.

H. 962. Sultān Haidar of Kashmīr invites Humāyūn to become king. The army refuses and Humāyūn returns to Kābul. Dec.: Safar 962, he begins his march to recover Hindustān.

Rebellions of the nobles under Muhammad Shāh 'Ādil, who divide the empire of Hindustan, and he flees to Chunār.

Sept. 23. Dom Pedro de Mascarenhas arrives at Goa as Viceroy.

IBRĀHĪM KHĀN SŪR AND SIKANDAR SHĀH III.

1555 March 29: Jumāda I. 6, H. 962. Muhammad Shāh 'Ādil of Dehli is defeated by his cousin and brother-in-law, Ibrāhīm Khān Sūr, who assumes royalty at Dehli. May: Jumāda II. Ibrāhīm Khān Sūr is defeated by Ahmad Khān, another cousin of Muhammad Shāh 'Ādil, who assumes the title of Sikandar Shāh, and obtains possession of both Dehli and Agra.

June 22. On the arrival of Humāyūn's army, under Bairām Khān, Sikandar Shāh is defeated at Sarhind.

HUMĀYŪN RESTORED.

1555 June 23: Sha'bān 3, H. 962. Humāyūn enters Dehli.

H. 962. Shāh Husain Arghūn of Sindh, who had succeeded his father Shāh Beg Arghūn, in 1524, dies childless, and with him ended the Arghūn dynasty. Mahmūd, Governor of Bhakkar,

A.D.

1555 and Mirzā 'Īsā Tarkhān, Governor of Thattā, both set up as Kings of Sindh, and are frequently at strife. Shāh 'Īsā Tarkhān died in 1567.

Ghāzi Khān and his party, having overcome in the contest with Daulat Chak, depose Ibrāhīm Khān of Kashmīr, blind him, and raise his brother Ismā'īl to the throne. Daulat Chak is seized and his eyes put out by Ghāzi Khān.

Baz Bahādur, governor of Mālwa, is crowned Sultān, and the state becomes independent.

H. 962. Muhammad Shah of Bengal is killed in an action with Muhammad 'Shāh 'Ādil of Dehli, with the help of his general, Hīmū at Chhapparghatta, near Kālpī. The Bengal army retire to Jhusi, and raise Khizr Khān to his father's throne with the title of Bahādur Shāh. Nara Nārāyan becomes Rāja of Kuch Bihār.

June 16. Dom Pedro de Mascarenhas dies at Goa, and is succeeded by Francisco Baretto as nineteenth viceroy.

The Queen of Olala (Ullāla), 2 miles south from Mangalor refuses tribute to the Portuguese; they ravage her territory and exact tribute by force.

Insurrections break out in Ceylon, many of Xavier's converts being put to death. The Portuguese attack and take Palandu.

Prince 'Abdullah ("Meale Khan"), with the Viceroy's aid, claims the title of King of Bījāpūr. He promises the Konkan to the Portuguese with one million revenue, but is defeated by Ibrāhīm 'Ādil Shāh and imprisoned.

June 1: Ś. 1477. An inscription at Gangaikondān gives this as the twenty-fourth year of King Māravarman Sundara Pāndya III.

AKBAR.

1556 Jan. 28: Rabī' I. 15, H. 963. Humāyūn dies, the result of a fall on the palace stairs. Feb. 14: Rabī' II. 2, Akbar, at the age of fourteen, succeeds; Bairām Khān exercising the regency. Sulaimān Bakhsh, Akbar's cousin, occupies Kābul, but is forced back to Badakhshān; Hakīm Mirzā, Akbar's half brother, made nominal ruler of Kābul, under the guardianship of Mun'im Khān, with his mother Mah Chuchak Begam.

A.D.

1556 May: Rajab. Shaikh Muhammad Ghaus, of Gwāliar, retires from the Dehli court.

July: Ramazān. Sikandar Sūr, after six months' siege in Mankot, sends his son 'Abdul Rahman to Akbar with terms of capitulation.

Feb. 14: Rabī' II. 2, H. 963 Akbar introduces the *Faslī* or "harvest" year—a solar year for revenue and other civil purposes, instead of the usual Muhammadan lunar year, but dating from the Hijri year 963. The Faslī year 963 began with the lunar month Āświn, Sept. 10, 1555, and corresponds to the Hindu luni-solar Samvat, from which, if 649 be subtracted, the Faslī year is found. In Orissa the era termed *Vilāyati san* commences from the 1st of the solar month Āświn, Sept. 8, 1555; hence it corresponds with the Hindu solar years of the Śaka reckoning, but beginning with Āświn. The *Bengāli san* 963 began with 1st Vaiśākh, Śaka 1479, or March 27, 1556, and follows the Śaka reckoning, with a difference of 417 years.

The Zamorin of Calicut appeals to Bījāpūr and Ahmadnagar for help against the Portuguese.

Miguel Rodrigue Coutinho carries on war with Bījāpūr, and destroys many seaports. An auxiliary force is sent to Sindh, but arriving at Thatta after peace was concluded, demands expenses. This being refused, Baretto plunders the city for eight days, returning to Chaul with the richest spoils ever captured in Asia. Dābhol is next reduced and plundered. The hill fort of Asheri and the station of Manor on the Vaitarnā river captured by the Portuguese.

Nov. 5: Muharram 2, H. 964. Akbar, with Bairām Khān, defeats Hīmū, the general of Muhammad Shāh 'Ādil, at Pānīpat, who is taken prisoner and beheaded.

H. 964. Habīb succeeds Ismā'īl on the throne of Kashmīr.

1557 H. 964. Sultān Muhammad Shāh 'Ādil, having been betrayed by his brother-in-law, Ibrāhīm Khān Sūr, had fled to Chunār, and is defeated and slain in battle at Surājgarh, near Mongīr, by Bahādur Shāh of Bengal and Sulaimān Qirānī of Orissa. He had ruled at Dehli for eleven months. 'Ādil's son assumes the title of Sher Shāh at Chunār.

A.D.

1557 Rebellion of Jagdev Rāo in Golkonda, who joins the Rāja of Vijayanagar; strenuous efforts are made by the Hindus to recover Pāngal, Kovilkonda, Ganpura Dewarkonda, Indrakonda, and Kondapalli.

H. 965. Ibrāhīm 'Ādil Shāh of Bījāpūr dies. His son, 'Alī, succeeds.

The Bījāpūr army, after several defeats by the Portuguese, sue for peace.

Pope Paul V. makes Goa a metropolitan see, promoting the second bishop, Juan de Albuquerque to be first archbishop; and at the same time sets up the Inquisition at Goa.

Dom Duarte d'Eça is deposed by the people of Ternate (Ternati), owing to his cruelty to their king and queen.

1558 H. 965. Ibrāhīm Qutb Shāh engages to assist the Bījāpūr king against Ahmadnagar, but withdraws his troops from the siege.

Akbar has now succeeded in re-establishing the Mughal power.

Baretto, requesting permission to build a fort at Chaul is refused, and brings up a force of 4,000 men. The king sues for peace, and engages not to fortify the place.

Sept. Dom Constantino de Braganza succeeds Baretto as twentieth Viceroy of Portuguese India.

H. 966. 'Alī 'Ādil Shāh and Rāma Rāja of Vijayanagar invade the Ahmadnagar territories. Husain Nizām Shāh retires to Paitan. Much land is ravaged, but peace is purchased, Sultān 'Alī 'Ādil Shāh ceding Etgir and Bagrakot, Qutb Shāh ceding Kovilkonda, Pāngal and Gantūr to Rāma Rāja.

Anthony Wilkinson, a servant of the Russia Company, crosses the Caspian into Persia, and opens a considerable trade for Eastern produce.

Viśvanātha, son of Nāgama Nāyakka of Madura, is recognised as an independent sovereign. He enforces the cession of Trichinopoly from the Chōla Rāja; died 1563.

1559 Daman fortress occupied by the Portuguese Viceroy, who confirms the customs to the neighbouring King of Sarceta.

A.D.

1559 Luiz de Mello de Silva again ravages the Malabar coast, and puts the inhabitants of Mangalor to the sword. A punitive expedition loses three ships and 400 men. A large federation of Malabar chiefs is defeated. Bahrein island attacked by the Turks, but a relieving force compels the siege to be raised.

The Portuguese become stringent in the enforcement of their pass rules, confiscating all ships and massacring crews not producing the pass. The rice trade falls into their hands.

Cochin is made a bishopric, Dom Jorge Temudo, first bishop, is afterwards translated to Goa as third archbishop.

1560 Feb. 4. A treaty signed with the inhabitants of the Laccadive islands, which become tributary to Portugal.

By this year the Portuguese entirely dominate the coast of the Konkan. Bulsār and Vypīn are also secured.

March: Jumāda II., H. 967. Akbar, tired of the tyranny of Bairām Khān, assumes the management of State. Sept., revolt of Bairām Khān, who is defeated and pardoned.

H. 968. Sher Khān II., attempting to conquer Jaunpur, is defeated by the imperial general, 'Alī Qulī Khān, Khān Zamān, who withholds the emperor's share of the spoils, and rebels but with his brother, Bahādur Khān, is afterwards defeated and slain, July 7, 1567. Adham Khān, who aspired to independence in Mālwa, submits in May.

H. 968. Bahādur Shāh of Bengal dies. Jalāl Khān, his brother, succeeds with the title of Ghiyās-ud-dīn 'Abul Muzaffar Jalāl Shāh, till H. 971.

Goa made an archbishopric; Dom Juan de Albaquerque, the second bishop, being made Metropolitan and Primate of all the Indies. The first Inquisitors also arrive to suppress the Jews.

The Viceroy lands at Jafnapatam to replace the rightful king. His usurping brother, however, is confirmed in his government, and the Viceroy barely escapes a treacherous attack.

Chingiz Khān cedes Daman fort and the coast to the Vaitarnā to the Portuguese, who send him a defending force against Adham Khān, his brother-in-law, at Surat. Daman is strongly garrisoned by the Portuguese.

A.D.

1561 Jan. 31 : Jumāda I. 14, H. 968. Bairām Khān assassinated in Gujarāt on his way to Makka by Mubārak Khān Lohānī, a private enemy.

H. 968. Bāz Bahādur, who had assumed independence in Mālwa in 963, is defeated at Sārangpur by Adham Khān. May 8 : Shāban 21, Akbar moves thither in person, and receives the tribute of the Mālwa nobles.

Akbar annexes Mulakot and Nāgor, and transfers them to another Hindu family.

April 21 : Sha'bān 5. Ahmad Shāh II. of Gujarāt is found assassinated. I'timād Khān raises to the throne a youth under the title of Muzaffar Shāh III.

Chingiz Khān is defeated at Daman, and Qadam Khān, his brother-in-law, repudiates the cession of Daman to the Portuguese. He is captured and beheaded. His successor makes peace, and is left in possession of Surat.

Sept. Dom Francisco de Coutinho Conde de Redondo succeeds Dom Constantino de Braganza as Viceroy at Goa.

1562 Bāz Bahādur collects forces and invades Mālwa but is defeated by Pīr Muhammad Khān, and flees to Mīrān Shāh of Kāndesh. Pīr Muhammad then sacks Burhānpur and massacres the inhabitants, but is defeated by Bāz Bahādur who for a time recovers his kingdom.

Feb. A large ship from Achīn is boarded by Portuguese sailors: both ships take fire and the Portuguese are saved by another vessel.

Aug. 13: Ramazān 12, H. 969. Akbar orders the death of Adham Khān for the murder of his vazīr, Shams-ud-dīn Muhammad Atgah.

H. 970. Habīb of Kashmīr is deposed by Ghāzi Chak, and civil war follows.

Husain Nizām Shāh and Ibrāhīm Qutb Shāh march against the allied forces of Bijāpūr and Vijayanagar, but lose heavily.

Ahmadnagar again besieged by Rāmrāja, but floods prevent its capture. Peace is concluded.

Sept. Renewed assaults made on Daman under Sidi Meriam, who is defeated.

A.D.

1562 Dec. The Viceroy personally ratifies the treaty with the Zamorin of Calicut.

Vasco da Sa at Amboyna estranges the goodwill of the people. They appeal for help to the neighbouring rulers, and ships are sent for their relief.

1563 H. 971. 'Abdullah Khān revolts in Mālwa; defeated by Akbar he flees to Gujarāt. The 'Uzbak nobles in the imperial army resent his fate and rise in rebellion.

H. 971. Ghāzi Chak of Kashmīr abdicates in favour of his brother, Husain Shāh Chak, but repenting, collects a force to dethrone him. This being dispersed without an action, the old king is compelled to retreat to Zainpur.

Jalāl Shāh of Bengal dies. A son succeeds, but is murdered by Ghiyās-ud-dīn, who usurps the government. Sulaimān Kararānī, governor of South Bihār, ousts the usurper with the help of his brother Tāj Khān, on whose death the seat of government is removed from Gaur to Tāndā.

Viśvanātha Nāyakka of Madura dies. His son, Periya Krishnappa, succeeds.

Bureng Naung, King of Pegu (1551-81), attacks Yuthia, the Siamese capital. Three Portuguese ships are taken and the Yuthia king surrenders and is carried away a captive, while his eldest son, in March 1564, is made a tributary king.

Revolts at Amboyna and Ceylon suppressed by the Portuguese generals Henrique da Sa and Diogo de Mello.

Cæsar Frederick, a Venetian merchant, travels *via* Persia to Kambay. He describes Kambay and Ahmadābād.

1564 Jan.: Jumāda II., H. 971. Attempted assassination of Akbar at Dehli by Koka Fūlād, a slave of Sharaf-ud-dīn Husain.

Feb. 12. The King and Grandees of the Molucca Islands execute a deed by which they cede to the King of Portugal and his successors all rights and seigniorage of the same.

Cannanor is now hostile, and the treaty broken. A protest meets with no reply, and the Malabar War begins.

Feb. 19. Francisco de Coutinho dies. João de Mendoça, from Malacca, is interim governor till September, when Dom Antonio de Noronha arrives at Goa as twenty-second Viceroy.

A.D.

1564 March: Sha'bān H. 971. 'Abul-Ma'ālī, who had taken refuge with Mirzā Muhammad Hakīm at Kābul, from Nāgor, aspires to the sovereignty of Kābul, murders the queen-regent Mah Chuchak Begam, and acts as regent. Mirzā Sulaimān of Badakhshān, Hakīm's uncle, defeats and kills him in battle, May 13: Shawwāl 1, leaving Ahmad 'Alī as vazīr at Kābul. Hakīm dismisses the latter, and is chased out of Kābul. He invades the Panjāb.

The King of Zimme flees before Bureng Naung of Pegu, who with Indians and Portuguese proceeds to Labong. (Nov.), Zimme submits.

1565 Jan. 25: Jumāda II. 20, H. 972. The Muhammadan kings of the Dekhan unite and quite overthrow the Hindu monarchy of Vijayanagar in the battle of Tālikota. Rāma Rāja is beheaded before Husain Nizām Shāh.

June 7: Zī-l qa'da 7, H. 972. Husain Nizām Shāh dies, and Murtazā Nizām Shāh I., a minor, succeeds under the guidance of his mother, Khunza Sultāna, for the first six years of his reign.

Akbar removes the *jizya* or poll-tax on Hindus instituted by Sikandar Lodī.

Vīra Chāma Rāja Wodeyar becomes independent in the province of Mysore.

H. 973. Khānuz Zamān, prime minister of Kashmīr, attacks the palace; his scheme for sovereignty being frustrated, he is subsequently executed.

Rāju, the tyrant of Ceylon, attempts to starve out Kotta and Colombo. Jorge de Mello invades the rāja's territory and discovers a planned night attack. He defeats the Singhalese, who retire to Sittawakka.

1566 H. 974. Mirzā Muhammad Hakīm, Akbar's half-brother, is incited to invade the Panjāb, and takes Lāhor. In Nov.: Jumāda I., Akbar leaves Agra with a force, whereon Hakīm returns to Kābul. The Mirzās—Ulugh Mirzā and Shāh Mirzā, nephews of Muhammad Sultān Mirzā, a kinsman of Bābar—revolt in Sambhal, and are joined by their uncles Ibrāhīm Husain Mirzā and Muhammad Husain Mirzā; they are overpowered and confined at Sambhal, but escape in 1567.

A.D.

1566 Husain Shāh Chak of Kashmīr blinds his nephew and rival, Ahmad Khān. The ex-king, Ghāzi Khān, dies.

Dec. 19: Jumāda II. 6, H. 974. Mirān Mubārak Khān of Kāndesh dies, and Mirān Muhammad Khān Fārūqī II. succeeds.

João de Souza threatened at Daman by 3,000 Mughal horse; on the arrival of a relief force they abandon their camp and treasure.

After incessant warfare and slaughter of Malabarese, the King of Cannanor sues for peace, which is granted by the Portuguese.

1567 Jan. 4. The Portuguese Viceroy, Antonio de Noronha, lands at Ullāla, whose queen is forced, after an assault, to increase her tribute and pay a sum of money. A fort "San Sebastian" there is completed in March.

The Portuguese at Amboyna are reinforced by Gonzalo Pereira with twelve ships. The inhabitants put the friendly peoples of Atire and Tavira to the sword.

Cæsar Frederick visits the court of Vijayanagar.

June 9: Zī-l hijja 1, H. 974. The Khān Zamān 'Alī Qulī Khān and his brother, Bahādur Khān, who had rebelled in Hakīm Mirzā's interest, are defeated at Mankarwāl by Akbar. They are killed in the battle and the 'Uzbak revolt quelled in July: Muharram, H. 975.

On Akbar's marching to subdue Mālwa, the Mirzās escape from Sambhal and gain Mālwa, but leave it to Akbar's generals and escape to Bharoch in Gujarāt, where they seek the protection of the governor. Chingiz Khān is assassinated: the Mirzās invade Kāndesh and Gujarāt, each securing a district.

H. 975. 'Īsa Tarkhān of Thattā dies. His son, Muhammad Bāqī, establishes himself and owns the sovereignty of Akbar; till 1585.

H. 975. Sulaimān Kararānī of Bengal and Bihār subdues Orissa and assassinates Sultān Ibrāhīm. Mukand Deva, the last King of Orissa, is defeated and killed.

'Alī 'Ādil Shāh's minister, Kishwar Khān, invades Ahmadnagar. At first successful, he is defeated with loss at Dhārur.

Tirumala Rāja, brother of Rāma Rāja of Vijayānagar, retires to Penugonda, his brother, Venkatādri, establishing himself at Chandragiri.

A.D.

1567 Aug. 22: Ś. 1489. A Tamil inscription at Tenkāsi gives this as the fifth year of King Jatilavarman Srivallabha Ativarāma.

1568 Feb. 4: Sha'bān 5, 975. The third sack of Chitorgadh, the hill fortress and capital of Mewār. Defended against Akbar's great army by the princes of the Rājput clans, headed by Pattā of Kailwā and Jaymal of Bednūr, a prolonged and brave struggle was maintained; but the walls being breached, it is said about eight thousand women of all ranks, including nine queens and five princesses, became a holocaust in *jauhar*, and the garrison flung themselves upon the besiegers, sword in hand, and perished, whilst thousands of the inhabitants were massacred by the victors, and the buildings of the city wrecked.

Taufal Khān, minister in Berār, usurps that throne from the child king, Burhān 'Imād Shāh, whom he subsequently imprisons at Parnāla.

H. 976. Feuds arise in Kashmīr between the Hanifī and Shīa'h sects.

Brāmahin, tributary King of Siam, throws off the suzerainty of Burma.

Oct. A force from Burma sacks Yuthia, which after four months' siege offers to surrender. This is refused, and the city falls in Aug. 1569.

Tirumala, the third of the "tyrant brothers," murders Sadāśiva and seizes the throne of Vijayānagar.

Oct. Dom Luiz de Ataide, Conde de Atouguia, arrives as twenty-fourth Viceroy at Goa.

The King of Ternate is treacherously murdered by Martim Affonso Pimentel, acting under the orders of his uncle Mesquita, the commander. His successor rouses the neighbouring princes against the Portuguese.

Ś. 1508. A Sanskrit and Kanarese inscription at Karkala records the charter of a Jaina temple granted by King Immādi Bhairava.

1569 March 22: Shawwāl 3, H. 976. Akbar takes the hill fort of Rantambhor from Rāja Surjan Rāī, who capitulates and is allowed to march out unmolested.

In July, Safar H. 977. Kālinjar fort capitulates.

A.D.

1569 Aug. 30: Rabī' I. 17. Birth of Prince Sultān Salīm Mirzā.

Akbar sends an embassy to Kashmīr, but executes the ambassadors on their return for instigating the murder of certain holy men. He also refuses to marry the daughter of Husain Shāh Chak, who soon after dies of grief.

'Alī Shāh Chak succeeds to the throne of Kashmīr.

Murtazā Nizām Shāh of Ahmadnagar takes over the administration of state from his mother, and marches to attack the Bījāpūr general: he attacks and takes Dhārur.

The Portuguese attack the Kolis of the Konkan, and establish a stockaded fort at Sāyvān, on the Vaitarnā river.

Rustam Khān, besieged in Bharoch by the Mughals, is relieved by the Portuguese, but refuses to become tributary. Fort Pernel captured and rased.

Luiz Camoens the poet returns to Lisbon, his friends at Goa paying his debts.

Nov. The Viceroy, Dom Luiz de Ataide, leaves Goa, reduces Honāwar, burns the town and garrisons the fort. Barcelor is next reduced, the Kings of Tolar and Cambolin are spared on promise of increased tribute.

1570 Bāz Bahādur of Mālwa is overpowered by Akbar's generals, and Mālwa becomes a province of the empire. Bāz Bahādur afterwards joined Akbar, and became an officer of 2,000 cavalry.

Jan. The Nizām sends Farhat Khān to besiege Chaul which holds out till July, when a treaty is agreed to.

From Basseīn an attack is made by the Portuguese on Kalyān, the suburbs of which are burnt.

June 7: Muharram 3, H. 978. Prince Murād, Akbar's second son, born at Sīkrī. The Rāja of Jodhpur sues for peace, his second son acting as emissary. Akbar, resenting the slight, refuses and confers Jodhpur upon Rāī Singh of Bikanir in H. 980.

A combination of native princes of Bijāpūr, Ahmadnagar, and the Zamorin formed against the Portuguese. An attack is made by the Bijāpūr army on Goa, which is besieged till Dec. 17, when a treaty is concluded between the King of Bijāpūr and the Viceroy, Dom Luiz de Ataide.

A.D.

1570 June 28. The Ahmadnagar forces attack Chaul, which was defended by Dom Francisco de Mascarenhas; after several unsuccessful attacks, a treaty is concluded.

The King of Achīn, the fourth member of the confederacy against the Portuguese, fails in his attempt upon Malacca.

1571 July 8-9: Safar 14-15, H. 979. The Zamorin of Calicut besieges the fort of Chāliyam or Jaliat, and captures it from the Portuguese on Oct. 30: Jumāda II. 10, and destroys the fort.

Chāma Rāja Wodeyar Bola succeeds Timma Rāja as Rāja of Maisur; till 1576.

Sept 6. Dom Antonio de Noronha arrives as Viceroy. Orders are sent to divide the colonies into three, the portions to be designated India, Monomotapa, and Malacca. Distraction of energies follows and wars continue till 1580.

The Portuguese attack Dābhol, but Khwāja 'Alī Shirāzi, having allowed them to land, put upwards of 150 of them to death.

Oct. The King of Achīn attacks Malacca, which is reduced to extremities, when the enemy is beaten off by Trīstão Vaz de Veiga.

Dec. A Mughal force having seized Khambay, the Portuguese defend Bassein and Daman.

1572 H. 980. The Mirzās return to Gujarāt, and make common cause against I'tmād Khān, who invites Akbar to take over Gujarāt.

Sept. 1: Rabī' II. 22. Akbar marches to Pātan, and on Rajab 14 formally receives the crown from Muzaffar III.

Rāi Singh succeeds Kalyān Singh at Bikanir, which becomes an important Mughal principality.

H. 980 'Alī Shāh Chak receives an embassy from Dehli, and proclaims Akbar Emperor of Kashmīr.

Sulaimān Shāh, Kararānī of Bengal dies. His son, Bāyazīd, succeeds, but shortly after is killed by the Afghāns; his younger brother Dā'ūd seizes the kingdom.

Further risings of the Mirzās bring Akbar to Gujarāt: he captures Bharoch and Surat. Dec., Akbar attacks Ibrāhīm Ḥusain

A.D.

1572 Mirzā at Sarnāl in a desperate encounter, and the Mirzā escapes in the darkness and flees towards Agra.

Udaysingh of Mewār dies in exile. His son, Pratāp Rānā, succeeds, and establishes himself at Komalmer.

1573 H. 980: Feb. 22, a victory over the Mirzā and Fūlādī's force is gained. April 10: Zī-l hijja 10, Akbar leaves Mirzā 'Azīz Muhammad Kokaltāsh as governor. Ahmadābād is again besieged. Akbar returns and quells the insurrection in eleven days, returning to Agra on Aug. 14: Jumāda I. H. 981.

H. 981. Dā'ūd Shāh succeeds his brother Bāyazīd as King of Bengal.

About this time Udaysingh succeeds Māldeva as Rāja of Mārwār and acknowledges Akbar's suzerainty. His sister, Jodhbāī, is married to Akbar.

Periya Krishnappa of Madura dies, and his son, Periya Virappa, succeeds.

Sept. Pereira, ordered to Malacca to crush the Queen of Joparra's army, refuses for want of adequate equipment and returns to Lisbon. Jorge de Castro, by command from Portugal, is tried for having delivered the Chāliyam fort to the Zamorin. He is found guilty and beheaded, while others equally guilty are rewarded. In 1574 a commission appointing him to another post arrives.

Tristão Vaz de Veiga appointed commander at Malacca.

1574 H. 982. Akbar having reduced the province of Bhakkar exclusive of the fort, the ruler, Mahmūd Khān, resolves at length to give it up to Akbar, but dies before the latter's emissary, Giesū Khān, arrives. Akbar thus becomes master of Upper Sindh.

May 14. Amardās, the third Sikh Guru, died, having appointed his son-in-law, Rāmdās, to the Guruship. On a site granted by Akbar, he restored an old tank which he called Amritsar, in the middle of which he built the temple of Harmandar (temple of Hari); the town was at first called Rāmdāspur—now Amritsar. He lived till 1581.

Dā'ūd Khān of Bengal takes the field against Akbar's generals. Mun'im Khān, whilst besieging Pātna, is followed by Akbar,

A.D.

1574 and they take the fort of Hājipur. Aug. 11: Rabī' II. 21, Dā'ūd Khān escapes to Orissa. Mun'im Khān receives the title of Khān Khānān, and is made Governor of Bengal and Bihār; he makes Gaur his capital, but dies Oct. 12, 1575.

Tulsi Dās, the Marāthi poet, begins his poem, the *Rāma-charita Mānas*, founded on the *Rāmāyana*.

1575 March 13: Zī-l qa'da 20, H. 982. Dā'ūd Khān is defeated at Tukharoi or Mughalmari by Todar Mal and Mun'im Khān. April 12: Muh. 1, H. 983. Peace is concluded at Katak, Dā'ūd ceding Bengal and Bihār, and Akbar acknowledging him King of Orissa.

Tirumala, King of Pennakonda, is succeeded by his second son, Śri Ranga II.

Oct. 14: Rajab 9, H. 983. Mun'im Khān Khān Khānān dies at Gaur, and most of his army is carried off by the unhealthy climate. Husain Qulī Khān, Governor of the Panjāb, is transferred to Bengal; but before he reaches his new government Dā'ūd Shāh and his Afghāns again invade Bengal.

Rāja Todar Mal sent to Gujarāt by Akbar to make a revenue settlement. Wajih-ul-Mulk appointed first minister. Mirzā Khān is second Mughal Viceroy in Gujarāt, till 1577.

The Achīnese, on the point of taking Malacca, fall into a panic and retire.

The Portuguese lose hold of the Moluccas, owing to the maladministration of their commanders. Ternate is surrendered to a combination of native powers.

1576 June 18: Rabī' I. 21, H. 984. Rānā Pratāp or Kīkā of Mewār defeated by Kunwar Mān Singh at Gogandah.

July 12: Rabī' II. 15, H. 984. Husain Qulī Khān appointed Governor of Bengal; defeats Dā'ūd Khān's army at Rājmahal. Dā'ūd is imprisoned and executed: with him ends the line of independent Bengal kings.

Mirān Muhammad Khān of Kāndesh dies. His son being a minor, his brother, Rāja 'Alī, succeeds.

H. 984. Great mosque at Fathpur Sīkrī finished.

Vīra Chāma Rāja of Maisur dies childless. Bettada Wodiyar, grandson of Chāma Rāja I., succeeds.

A.D.

1576 Portuguese affairs at Amboyna critical. Conspiracies formed against Sancho de Vasconcellos, resulting in the death of many Portuguese.

Dom Lorenço de Tavara, Viceroy-elect, dies on the voyage out. Dom Diego de Menezes, next on the Succession patent, takes office as twenty-eighth Vicroy.

Malik Tokan Thānadār of Dābhol murders the Portuguese officers at his house. Dom Hieronymo de Mascarenhas, who had absented himself, returns to Goa, where a punitive expedition is organised.

1577 March 31: Muharram 11, H. 985. Muhammad Hakīm Mirzā invests Lāhor: on Akbar's approach he returns to Kābul.

This year the Muslim creed (*kalimah*) disappears from the national coinage and liturgy.

Shihābud-dīn Ahmad Khān succeeds I'timad Khān as third Viceroy of Gujarāt till 1583.

Further efforts made against Malik Tokan of Dābhol. 'Alī 'Ādil Shāh again sues for peace.

Dec. 13. Sir Francis Drake sails from Plymouth. Having crossed the Pacific, he stops at Ternate.

1578 H. 986. 'Alī Khān Chak of Kashmīr is killed by a fall from his horse. His son, Yūsuf Khān, succeeds, and puts to death his uncle Abdāl Chak. Revolts occurring, he flees to Hindustan.

Rohtās fortress surrenders to the Khān Jahān, Governor of Bengal.

Rāja Wodeyar usurps the throne of Maisur.

Aug. 4. In an ill-fated expedition to Africa the Portuguese king, Sebastian, is defeated, and slain in the battle of Alcazar Kivēr. This event completes the downfall of Portuguese empire in the East.

Aug. Dom Luiz de Ataide arrives at Goa as Viceroy for the second time.

1579 H. 987. Husain Qulī Beg, Khān Jahān, Governor of Bengal, dies. Muzaffar Khān Turbatī is appointed his successor. During the Khān Jahān's governorship Bengal, Bihār, and Orissa with Katak were re-annexed to the empire.

A.D.

1579 Malik Tokan still troublesome at Dābhol. A Portuguese expedition defeats a Malabarese, Turkish, and Muslim fleet.

H. 987. Akbar sends a force to re-establish Yūsuf Khān on the throne of Kashmīr. Lohar Chak, son of Abdāl, the rival ruler, is blinded.

Ibrāhīm Qutb Shāh takes Kondavīd and other forts on the Vijayanagar frontier.

April 4. Thomas Stephens S.J., leaves Lisbon, and arrives at Goa, Oct. 24. He is thus the first Englishman to visit India. Died at Goa 1619.

John Huygen Linschoten, a Frieslander, arrives at Goa in the train of the archbishop: in thirteen years he amassed much information on almost every branch of inquiry. His *Voyage* was translated into English in 1598.

Sir Francis Drake landed at Ternate, and traded with the ruler of the island. Subsequently he landed in Java, and thence returns to England, *via* the Cape of Good Hope.

1580 The question of the relation of the head of the State to spiritual affairs agitated at the Mughal court. Akbar favours an eclectic theism, and the convocation decrees that the emperor may pronounce a final award in doctrinal controversy provided no opposition to the Qurān is offered.

Jan. 31. Henry I. of Portugal dies. The Eastern possessions fall into Spanish hands. Holland begins to trade directly with the East.

April: Safar, H. 988. 'Alī 'Ādil Shāh of Bījāpūr murdered. Ibrāhīm succeeds. (Ferishta dates this in 987.)

Owing to Muzaffar Khān's exactions a rebellion in Bengal breaks out under Bābā Khān Qāqshāl, who takes Gaur, and kills the governor, Muzaffar Khān, at Tāndā in April: Rabī' I. Bengal again becomes independent.

H. 988. Certain nobles of Kashmīr become disaffected, assemble in Tibet, and march on Kashmīr, but are seized, and the leaders mutilated.

July. Todar Mal disunites the rebels, and restores Bihār.

Oct. English merchants make a representation to the Lords in Council, requesting the queen's license for six ships to trade to Indian and Chinese ports.

A.D.

1581 Jan.: Zī-l hijja, H. 988. Mas'ūm Farankhūdī, Governor of Oudh, rebels, and is defeated by Todar Mal's troops.

March 3. Rāmdās, the fourth Sikh Guru, dies, and his son, Arjun-mall, succeeds, the Guruship now becoming hereditary. Arjun collected the materials of the *Granth*, the sacred code of the Sikhs; he changed the offerings to the Guru into a regular tax. He died 1606.

March: Muharram, H. 989. Mirzā Hakīm 'Askarī, defeated by Akbar, returns to Kābul. Aug. 10: Rajab 10, Akbar visits Kābul, pardons and reinstates Hakīm Mirzā.

H. 989. Yūsuf Shāh of Kashmīr receives ambassadors from Akbar, and later sends his son Ya'qūb, on a visit with presents to the Dehli court.

Muzaffar Shāh of Gujarāt, a pensioner at Akbar's court since 1573, raises a rebellion in concert with Sher Khān Fūlādi.

May 25: Rabī' II. 21, H. 989. Ibrāhīm Qutb Shāh of Golkondā dies. Muhammad Qulī succeeds.

Sept. 3. Fernão Telles de Menezes, appointed governor at Goa, administers the oath of allegiance to King Philip II. of Spain. Sept. 16, Dom Francisco de Mascarenhas Conde de Santa Cruz enters Goa as twenty-first Viceroy. Squadrons sent to Malabar, Coulete, and Capocate (Kāppātt), to put down piracy.

Daman again threatened by the Mughals, and the King of Sarceta gives trouble, but eventually offers submission.

Nov. Bweng Naung of Burma and Pegu dies. After his death, Pegu again separates from Burma.

The first Turkey and Levant Company, for purposes of trade to the East, is formed in London.

1582 H. 990. A'zam Khān, Governor of Bengal, sows dissension among the rebel chiefs and restores the emperor's authority, quietly taking possession of Tānda.

The rent-roll of Todar Mal divides Bengal into 19 Sarkārs and 682 Mahāls.

The Portuguese at Ormuz, besieged by the King of Lara, are permitted to march out, but are put to the sword by the natives.

A.D.

1582 Fernão de Miranda's marines mutiny for prize-money; proceeding to Daman, they compel the division of booty, and receive ten crowns each. Miranda next demolishes Castalette and extirpates a race of pirates. On the way home the Portuguese fleet encounters three or four English vessels.

An expedition against the Kolis in the N. Konkan results in the submission of their chief.

1583 H. 991. The Afghāns, under Qutlū Khān Lohānī, rise in Orissa. Shaikh Farīd-ud-dīn Bukhāū deputed to treat with them; he nearly perishes by Qutlū's treachery, and renews the war. The Afghāns are driven into the forests.

Feb.: Muharram. Muzaffar Shāh takes Ahmadābād, defeats the relieving army of Shihāb-ud-dīn and I'timād Khān, the new governor. He captures Baroda and Bharoch.

Mirzā Khān, Khān Khānān, fifth Viceroy of Gujarāt, till 1590.

Dom Antonio de Noronha destroys the temples in Salsette. In retaliation, the natives wreck the churches and perpetrate atrocities. Promiscuous slaughter is carried out by Gomez Yanez de Figueyredo; and new churches are erected.

March 8: John Newberie, citizen and merchant, along with Ralph Fitch, William Leedes, and James Story leave London in the "Tyger." Oct. 5, they are imprisoned at Bahrein, shipped to Goa, and liberated on Dec. 22, on bail of 2,000 ducats. Linschoten now at Goa.

1584 Jan. 29: Muharram 15, H. 992. Muzaffar Shāh defeated at Sarkhej by Mirzā Khān; he flees to Khambay and is again defeated at Rājpīpla.

H. 992. Yūsuf Shāh Chak, hearing of a proposed visit of Akbar, according to Ferishta, wishes to escort him to Kashmīr, but is prevented by his nobles. Akbar deputes a force to conquer the country, and Haidar Chak, the son of Yūsuf, is defeated by Akbar.

March: Rabī' I. Shahbāz Khān Kambū appointed Governor of Bengal.

H. 992-3. Ghafūr Khān (Kufo Khān), son of Mallu Khān of Bijāpūr, aspires to the throne. James Lopez Bayam, a

A.D.

1584 Portuguese in the service of Bijāpūr, arrives at Goa and blinds the prince, Ghafūr Khān, in conformity with an arrangement made with him at Bijāpūr.

H. 993. Mirzā Muhammad Bāqī of Thatta dies. Mirzā Jānī Beg, his grandson, succeeds, till 1592.

The Zamorin arranges terms with Dom Francisco de Mascarenhas, whereby his people can trade as far as Gujarāt.

The King of Cochin, owing to his favour for the Portuguese, causes revolts. In the tumult Giles Yanez Mascarenhas is killed.

August. Dom Duarte de Menezes appointed thirty-second Viceroy. His first official act is to effect a pacification of Cochin.

1585 Sayyid Murtazā Sabswāri and Khudāwand Khān Habshī, defeated by Salābat Khān, take refuge at Akbar's court. Hearing of the distractions at Ahmadnagar, Akbar sends Mirzā 'Azīz Koka with an army into the Dekhan.

Ibrāhīm 'Ādil Khān co-operates with the Portuguese for the reduction of the Nāyyak of Sangameśwar and his pirates. Rustam Khān and Dom Heirome de Mascarenhas constrain the Nāyyak to sue for peace. His lands are given to another Nāyyak.

April 5. Ralph Fitch and his companions escape from Goa and travel through India, reaching Fathpur Sīkrī on Sept. 28.

July 16: Sha'bān 16, H. 993. Mirzā Muhammad Hakīm, Akbar's brother, dies at Kābul, and Rāja Bhagwāndās and his son Mān Singh, are sent to Kābul to take charge of the province.

Ruy Gonçalves de Camara, uncle of the Viceroy, entrusted with an expedition to Ponnāni to erect a fort. The Zamorin delays permission, but is bribed to grant a site.

Further revolutions at Ternate and Tidor. The Portuguese fleet is also defeated at Ormuz.

1586 Feb. 25: Rabī' I. 5, H. 994. Rāja Bīrbal, who was also the *Kab-rāi* or poet laureate, and 8,000 Mughals, slain by the rebellious Yūsufzaīs in Badakhshān. Todar Mal and Mān Singh restore order, but contests are soon resumed.

A.D.

1586 Pratāp Rānā, in one campaign, recovers Mewār, exclusive of Chitor, Ajmir, and Mandalgarh. He establishes his capital at Udaypur, which gives the kingdom its name.

H. 995. Ya'qūb Shāh becomes King of Kashmīr, his father being detained at Dehli. Akbar sends another force, to which the king submits, and in 1587 he is enrolled among Akbar's nobles, and Kashmīr becomes a province of the empire.

Dom Hierome Coutinho brings orders from Portugal for the establishment of a Court of Chancery at Goa.

Aug. Rāja Singha attacks the Portuguese at Colombo: after a prolonged siege, the Portuguese assume the offensive, and plunder the cities of Balikot, Berberi, and Belligām.

The Portuguese fleet, under Pedro Vello, defeated by the Johor fleet: renewed disturbances at Malacca. The King of Achīn, his Queen, family, and nobility murdered by his general. Reinforcements from Goa and Cochin arrive in August, and Johor falls before an assault.

This year the English and Portuguese vessels engage on the high seas.

1587 H. 995. Shahbāz Khān, Governor of Bengal, superseded by Wazīr Khān, who dies the same year at Tānda.

The Jesuit missionaries, who succeeded Vincent at Cranganor, establish a Syriac college at Chennam or Ambalkotta, a few miles inland, in which the Syriac language was taught, but the Syrian Christians refused to accept their authority, and ultimately withdrew from the centres of Portuguese influence.

The Portuguese trade with India now handed to an association called "Campanha Portugueza das Indias Orientas," which proves profitless and short-lived.

Dec. The "San Philippe," a large carrack, captured by Sir Francis Drake near the Azores. Its cargo, valued at £108,049, displays the resources of India, also the type of vessel used by the Spaniards.

H. 995. Jauhar begins the *Tazkirat-ul Wāki'āt*. This history covers the period from Humāyūn's accession to his return from Persia.

A.D.

1588 Jan.: Safar, H. 996. The Shī'ah Mulla Ahmad of Thattā is murdered by Mirzā Fūlād Beg Barlās, for reviling the first three khalīfs, he is condemned to death by the emperor.

Jan. Rāja Singha makes another attack on Colombo, but is repulsed. The Portuguese devastate the west coast of Ceylon, and Colombo is strengthened.

March: Rabī' II., H. 996. Zain Khān Koka, Akbar's foster brother, appointed Governor of Zābulistān in place of Mān Singh.

May. Dom Duarte de Menezes dies, and Manoel de Sousa Coutinho, second on the succession patents, succeeds as governor.

June 5: Rajab 18. Murtazā Nizām Shāh of Ahmadnagar (according to the *Jama ul-Hind*) is poisoned by his son, Mirān Husain, who succeeds. Other accounts say he was suffocated about Rabī' I. 8, H. 997 or Jan. 15, 1589. Mirān rules with such cruelty and oppression that after ten months the minister, Mirzā Khān, secures his imprisonment.

The Raushānīas, a fanatical sect in Terah, under Jalāla Raushāni, are defeated at Bangash by Kumār Mān Singh. They continue, however, to give trouble till 1600.

1589 H. 997. Mīrzā 'Azīz Kokah, Governor of Mālwa, transferred to Gujarāt. An indecisive battle fought with the Jām of Nawānagar.

March 6. Ralph Fitch visits Ceylon from Bengal. Sails March 11.

March 28: Jumāda I. 11. Mīrān Husain Nizām Shāh of Ahmadnagar assassinated, and Ismā'īl, his nephew, is raised to the throne, the power being vested in Jamāl Khān, who defeats an army under Salābat Khān from Berār.

Oct. 2: Zī l qa'da 22, H. 997. Akbar visits Kābul. Bhagwāndās and Todar Mal die at Lāhor: the government of Kābul is conferred on Muhammad Qāsim Mīr-Bahr, and Akbar leaves, Nov. 29: Muharram 20, H. 998.

H. 998. Mān Singh, Governor of Bihār, subdues the Zamindar of Hājipur, and is appointed Governor of Bengal, with the title of Rāja.

Muhammad Qulī Qutb Shāh moves his capital from Golkonda to Haidarābād or Bhāgnagar.

A.D.

1589 The Levant Company made an expedition by land to India, and much information was obtained which proved highly useful in the subsequent establishment of Indian commerce.

A society of English merchants petition Queen Elizabeth for permission to voyage to India.

1590 Jan. 10. Four ships leave Goa, of which two are lost, and one stranded and burnt at the Azores by the English, while the fourth, the "Madre de Dios," is taken by the English, Aug. 3. Her cargo, estimated at £150,000, is "divided among the adventurers, whereof Her Majesty was the chief"; valuable information regarding Indian trade is obtained.

Feb.: Rabīʻ II., H. 999. Akbar despatches an army under Mirzā Khān, Khān Khānān, for the reduction of Sindh.

Ismāʻīl Qulī Khān, sixth Viceroy of Gujarāt for a few months. Soon succeeded by Mirzā ʻAzīz Kokaltāsh, till 1592.

Jamāl Khān, minister at Ahmadnagar, defeats the Bijāpūr army, but is killed in a battle with Burhān, father of the young king, Ismāʻīl. Burhān secures his son and ascends the throne as Burhān Nizām Shāh II., till 1594.

Portuguese authority re-established in East Africa by an expedition from Goa.

Sept. The navigator, John Davies, sails from Plymouth for India, but only reaches Madeira.

1591 Akbar orders a compilation of Muhammadan history up to the year 1000. The *Tārīkh-i-Alfī* is thereupon begun, the chief labour devolving upon Maulāna Ahmad, son of the Qāzi of Thattā.

May. Mathias de Albuquerque arrives to succeed Manoel de Sousa Coutinho as governor. The latter perishes on the way home, the ship and cargo being lost. Between 1579 and 1591, twenty-two Portuguese vessels are lost owing to extreme size or heavy cargo.

H. 1000. Muzaffar III., betrayed to the Mughals by the Rāja of Kachh, is placed in custody, but commits suicide at Dhrol.

Nov. 3: Muharram 26. Mirzā Jānī Beg of Thattā is attacked

A.D.

1591 by Akbar's general, 'Abdul Rahīm Khān, and defeated, but holds out for some months, and finally capitulates.

Rebellions break out in Kashmīr under Yādgār, nephew of the governor. The Mughal force recovers Kashmīr for Akbar.

The kings of Jafnapatam and Kandy are declared enemies by the Portuguese for their persecution of the Christians. André Furtada reduces the Coromandel coast and captures a fleet off Manār. The king and his son are put to death, a younger son being spared and restored to the kingdom.

A private mercantile expedition under James Lancaster: all ships lost.

1592 March-April: Jumāda II., H. 1000. Dilāwar Khān, having taken service with Burhān Nizām Shāh, returns to Bijāpūr on the invitation of Ibrāhīm 'Ādil Shāh, but is imprisoned and blinded.

April. The Portuguese at Chaul besieged by the troops of Ibrāhīm Nizām Shāh, and liberated only by help from Bassein and Surat.

A final revolt against Akbar's government in Kashmīr is quelled.

Mirzā Jānī Beg Tarkhān of Sindh acknowledges fealty to the emperor and is admitted a noble, and receives a command, Sindh becoming annexed to the empire.

H. 1001. Rāja Mān Singh suppresses a rebellion of Qutlugh Khān Afkān in Orissa.

Further rebellions in Ceylon result in the instalment of Vimala Dharma, a former partisan of Portugal, as King of Kandy. He holds Kandy for twelve years.

1593 March 24: Rajab 1, H. 1001. Mirzā 'Azīz Kokah, summoned from Gujarāt to court, departs without leave for Makka: Prince Murād is made Governor of Gujarāt with Sādiq Muhammad Khān as minister. Mirzā Shāhrukh is appointed Governor of Mālwa.

Some rebel chiefs of Ahmadnagar sack Burhānpur, and, dispersed by Rāja 'Alī Khān of Kāndesh, seek refuge with Akbar. Akbar prepares to invade the Dekhan, but is restrained by deputies and offerings from Rāja 'Alī.

Ibrāhīm II. of Bijāpūr invades and reduces Maisur now under Venkatādri Nāyyak.

A.D.

1593 Oct. 17: Muharram 21, H. 1002. Ambassadors from the Dekhan report the refusal of the kings to acknowledge Akbar's supremacy. Prince Dānyāl is sent south with an army which is soon transferred to Mirzā Khān, Khān Khānān.

Five ships arrive at Goa under Dom Luiz Coutinho, who brings the "Bull of the Crusade," Francisco de Faria being commissary.

The ship "Cinque Llagas" is captured by the English and burnt, twelve survivors being taken to England.

Cornelius Houtman makes inquiries in Portugal as to Indian trade.

H. 1002. Nizām-ud-dīn Ahmad Bakhshi writes the *Tabakāt-i Akbari*, a general Muhammadan history from H. 367 to 1001.

1594 H. 1002. Qulij Khān, a distinguished Persian, is appointed Governor of Kābul.

April. A Portuguese trading ship from China to Goa is blown up off the Malabar coast to prevent capture by the Malabar galliots. August 1. Furtado, in revenge, captures three Calicut ships, securing rich booty. He then defeats the entire Malabar fleet.

Sept. 4. The Portuguese defeat the Ahmadnagar army at Chaul creek and obtain the fort of Korlai ("Il Morro" in Portuguese histories).

Sept. 25. Muharram 10, H. 1003. Akbar sends Shaikh Farīd Bashi-ul-Mulk with other Amīrs to effect the conquest of Sawālik; Jammu fort is surrendered and the country is settled under Qāzi Hasan. Qandahār is subjugated and the Mughal empire consolidated over all Hindustan or north of the Vindhyas and as far as Kābul and Qandahār.

H. 1003. Bahādur, son of Muzaffar III. of Gujarāt, stirs up rebellions, but is crushed by Sūrajsingh.

Birth of Shāhjī Bhonsla, son of Māloji Bhonsla, a silahdār, or armoured soldier, in the Ahmadnagar service, and father of Śivājī.

A great meeting held at Amsterdam, when it is resolved to send a fleet to India at an early date.

Nov. 11: S. 1651. Inscription in the temple of Vādīpura-Pārsvanātha at Anhilvād, containing a *pattāvalī* or succession list of the Jaina high priests of the Brihat-Kharatara gachchha.

A.D.

1594 William Barents, a Dutchman, endeavours to discover a north-west passage to Eastern Asia.

1595 A.H. 1003. Mirzā Muzaffar Husain is prevailed upon to surrender Qandahār to Akbar. Shāh Beg Arghūn is sent to take possession of it.

April 2. Four ships under Cornelius Houtman leave from the Texel, Holland, for India *via* the Cape, and remain away two and a half years.

April 28: Sha'bān 18, H. 1003. Burhān Nizām Shāh of Ahmadnagar dies. Ibrāhīm his son and successor is killed in battle against the King of Bījāpūr in August: Zī-l hijja. Ahmad II., a reputed relative, is raised to the throne but soon after expelled, and on Sept. 30: Muharram 25, H. 1004, Bahādur Shāh, infant son of Ibrāhīm Nizām Shāh, is placed on the throne, with Chānd Bībī, widow of 'Alī 'Ādil Shāh of Bijāpūr, his great-aunt, as regent.

Kuch Bihār annexed to the Dehli empire by Lakshman Nārāyan Rāja.

Zain Khān Kokah Governor of Kābul for the second time.

Sūraj Singh Rāja of Jodhpur is appointed deputy-governor of Gujarāt.

H. 1004. Prince Murād leaves Gujarāt for the Dekhan on the invitation of Miyān Munji, the Dekhani minister of Ahmadnagar.

Oct. 14: Safar 9. Faizi, scholar, poet, and teacher of Akbar's court, dies.

Dec. 25. Prince Murād and the Mughal army appear before Ahmadnagar. The city and the town of Burhānābād are sacked, and the fort of Ahmadnagar invested but bravely defended by Chānd Bībī and the assailants compelled to raise the siege.

A fort at Salor erected by the Dominicans: plots are formed to kill the soldiers and friars, but are frustrated.

Friar Alexis de Menezes succeeds Friar Matheus as Archbishop of Goa.

1596 March 11: Rajab 1, H. 1004. Ahmadnagar fort attacked, and bravely defended by Chānd Bībī, acting for her grand-nephew, Bahādur Nizām Shāh. Overtures are made by Murād, and a treaty is signed by which Berār is ceded to the Mughals. Bahādur

A.D.

1596 is crowned and Muhammad Khān appointed minister. He acquires such power that troops from Bijāpūr are required to assert Chānd Bībī's authority. The Mughals from Berār make further incursions into the Nizām-Shāhī dominions: On Dec. 27: Jumāda I. 17, a battle is fought at the Godāvarī. The Mughals sack Ahmadnagar and Burhānābād.

The Muslims erect a fort at Pādapatam and thence attack the Portuguese at Thāna in Salsette.

John van Linschoten writes an account of his researches in India.

July 11. Cornelius Houtman lands at Sumatra, having left the Texel on Feb. 2nd.

Private venture of Sir Robert Dudley's three ships under Captain B. Wood—never again heard of.

H. 1004. 'Abdul Qādir Badāoni, author of the *Tarikh-i-Badāoni* or *Muntakhab-ut-Tawārīkh*, dies.

H. 1005. The *Tārīkh-i-Haqqī*, a Muhammadan history, is compiled by Shaikh 'Abdul Haqq—born 1551, he died 1642, H. 1052.

1597 Jan.: Jumāda II., H. 1005. The Mughal army under the Khān Khānān defeats the combined armies of the Dekhan; Prince Murād and the Khān Khānān differ regarding the campaign.

Pratāp Rānā of Udaypur dies. Amara Rānā his son succeeds.

May. Dom Francisco da Gama, Conde de Vidigueyra, assumes office as thirty-fifth Viceroy during the century at Goa.

Mar Abraham, the bishop of the Syrian Christians, dies at Angamāle.

Katula, King of Orissa, having plundered a Patani temple, the people rise and slay his son and 2,000 others. Akbar subdues Orissa.

H. 1006. Shaikh 'Abul Fazl supersedes the Khān Khānān as general.

Further coalitions are formed in Ceylon against the Portuguese. In May 1, Dom João Dharmapāla of Ceylon dies without heirs and the King of Spain is proclaimed sovereign of all Ceylon except Jafna and Kandy.

The pirate Kunhāli Marakkār, with secret support from the

A.D.

1597 Zamorin, preys upon the Malabar shipping. Dom Luiz da Gama destroys many parãos, killing the crews.

Two Dutch vessels engage with six Portuguese ships. After eight days the Dutch abandon one vessel, and the other is wrecked on the Pegu coast.

To hasten the fortifications of Bassein, Ayres de Silva de Mello is sent as superintendent.

March 14: S. 1654. An inscription at Rohtās records the repairing the palace of Māna during the governorship of Śrīdhara in the time of Mahārājadhirāja Mānasimha, the work being done by Madabala Bhatta.

1598 H. 1006. Akbar leaves the Panjāb for the Dekhan, to supervise personally the imperial army.

Alexis de Menezes, Archbishop of Goa, visits Malabar, having been commissioned by Pope Clement VIII., in a Brief of 27th Jan. 1595, to bring the Church there into conformity with the Latin rite.

The Zamorin joins the Portuguese in an attack on the Kunhāli Marakkār pirate's fortress on the Kotta or Putupattanam river mouth. A night attack is planned for May 3, but the attacking armies, failing to co-operate, are defeated in detail. A second attack also repulsed; Kunhāli is attacked by land and sea.

Strong forts are erected by the Portuguese for the conquest of Kandy and Uva: an army of 20,000 is required for the reduction of Kandy.

The Lisbon fleet is unable to sail this year, an English fleet blocking the Tagus.

The Dutch under Van Nec reach India and establish trade at Amboyna and Baroda.

April 13: S. 1654. An inscription at Sādadi of the reign of the Mahārānā Amarasimha of Mewār.

1599 May 10: Shawwāl 15, H. 1007. Sultān Murād, second son of Akbar, dies.

After further fighting the Kunhāli Marakkār surrenders to the Portuguese, on condition that his life should be spared. He is conveyed to Goa and there beheaded. His fortress is demolished.

June 20 to 26. Menezes holds the Synod of Diamper or

A.D.

1599 Udayampārūr—for which he had just previously ordained a majority of the members and had prepared the Decrees to be passed to bring the native Christian Church into entire obedience to that of Rome, whilst the Rāja of Cochin was terrorised to oblige his Christian subjects to conform to the Decrees. The union was short-lived.

H. 1008. Akbar arrives at the Narbadā, and proceeds to Burhānpur. A force is sent under Prince Dānyāl and the Khān Khānān to subdue Ahmadnagar, where Chānd Bībī was besieged by her former minister, Nihang Khān. While negotiating a peace with the Mughals Chānd Bībī is killed by the soldiery in the palace.

The stronghold of Āsīr is taken by an imperial force and Bahādur Khān Fārūqī becomes a pensioner at Dehli.

Bengal again revolts and comes almost totally under Afghān control.

Sept. 22. Merchants of London meet to discuss the Indian trade question and an "Association of Merchant Adventurers" formed. Oct. 16, Queen Elizabeth's consent signified, but political considerations with Spain prevent the immediate despatch of the expedition.

John Mildenhall is sent on an embassy to Akbar. He went by sea to Aleppo and travelled through Armenia, Persia, and Afghānistān, reaching Agra in 1603.

1600 May 13: Shawwāl 28, H. 1008. The Dekhan, Berār, Kāndesh Mālwa and Gujarāt are placed under the rule of Prince Dānyāl.

Mirzā 'Azīz Kokah is appointed Viceroy of Gujarāt for the third time.

Jalāl-ud-dīn Raushānī, the Afghān chief, defeated and slain at Ghazni by Zain Khān Kokah whom Akbar now recalls to Lāhor.

Aug.: Safar, H. 1009. Ahmadnagar stormed and captured by the Mughals, the King Bahādur Nizām Shāh and royal family being sent to Gwāliar fort as State prisoners.

The King of Jafnapatam, having assisted the King of Kandy, is brought to submit to the Portuguese without bloodshed.

Ayres de Saldanha arrives in autumn as governor at Goa.

Dec. 31. Queen Elizabeth grants the first Charter to a Corporation of "Governor and Company of Merchants of London

A.D.

1600 trading to the East Indies"—enabling them to trade for fifteen years. The Corporation is to be conducted by a chairman and twenty-four directors, to be chosen annually.

1601 Feb.: Sha'bān, H. 1009. Prince Salīm fails in an attempt to seize Agra: he takes possession of Oudh and Bihār, assumes the title of king and secures the local treasury. He returns to Allahābād and becomes reconciled to his father.

Feb. 13. Five ships under Captain Lancaster start from Woolwich and sail from Torbay, May 2. Friendly relations established at Achīn in Sumatra, and a factory at Bantam in Java, in both which places they left factors; returned to England Sept. 1603.

The Dutch are driven by André Furtado from Amboyna and Sunda.

The Portuguese obtain a footing in Arakan. The king, Meng Rājā (Salīm Shāh, the "Xilimixa" of the Portuguese), appoints Philip de Brito or Nicote his agent at Syriam. He siezes the port, defeats his former master, is chosen King of Pegu, and accepts the country in the name of the King of Portugal.

May 18. François Pyrard de Laval leaves St Maloes for Goa, where he remains many years, meeting there Spaniards, Italians, Germans, Flemings, three French, a few English—the last, prisoners of the Portuguese.

Francisco Roz, professor in the Jesuit college at Chennam, was consecrated first Romish bishop of the Syrian Church, and in 1605 styled Archbishop of Cranganor. He lived at Pārūr, and died there, Feb. 18, 1624.

S. 1523. Copper-plate inscription of Venkata I. of Vijayanagara granting the village of Vilāpāka, also named Jvaraharlingasamudra, to a Brāhman.

1602 March 29: Admiral Spilbergen arrives near Battikaloa in Ceylon with three Dutch ships, and obtains permission to build a fort, Sept. 2, he sails and captures three Portuguese vessels, which he presents to the Singhalese king.

Aug. 12: Rabī' I. 4, H. 1011. Abul Fazl, Akbar's minister, murdered at the instigation of Salīm. Akbar tacitly permits the murderer Narsing Deo's lands to be ravaged. Akbar adds the title "King of the Dekhan" to his other royal titles.

A.D.

1602 Mutta Krishnappa, Nāyyaka of Mādurā, assumes royal titles; died 1609.

The kings of Arakan and Taungu attack Syriam but are defeated by Paul del Rego Pinhero: the Taungu prince is taken prisoner—ransomed 1604.

The Dutch East India Company formed out of a number of small companies.

H. 1011. The *Rauzat-ut-Tāhirin*, a general history, is written by Tāhir Muhammad bin 'Imād-ud-dīn Hasan bin Sultān 'Alī bin Hājī Muhammad Husain Sabzwāri.

1603 Jan. 6. An expedition for the discovery of "Grand Cathay" leaves Akbar's court under B. Benedict Goes, accompanied by two Greeks and an Armenian.

The Dutch, with a large fleet, attempt to oust the Portuguese from Mozambique and blockade Goa. The struggle between the two nations begins and the Dutch gradually acquire most of the Portuguese possessions.

The English capture a Portuguese ship in Malacca: settle a "house of trade" at Bantam, and arrive home in September.

H. 1012. Disturbances in Persia enable Akbar to seize Qandahār, and Shāh Beg Arghūn is appointed governor.

Shāh Abbās sends to Golkonda an ambassador, Oghzlu Sultān, who is magnificently entertained by the king.

Mildenhall, a London merchant, reaches Agra, having left England in 1599 travelling overland. The Portuguese Jesuits traduce the English nation to Akbar, and Mildenhall remains at Akbar's court till 1606 when he obtained promises of arrangements for English trade.

1604 H. 1013. Rāja Mān Singh resigns the governorship of Bengal and comes to the capital to organise a plot in favour of the succession of his nephew, Sultān Khusro, Jahāngīr's eldest son.

March 1: Ś. 1525. A Kanarese and Sanskrit inscription on the Jaina colossus at Venūr records its dedication as Bhujabalin or Bāhubalin, by Timmarāja, brother of Prince Pāndya and son-in-law of Rāyakuvara.

The King of Arakan with the King of Taungu attack

A.D.

1604 De Brito ('Nikote'), but they are defeated. By his outrages De Brito offends the Talaings and takes prisoner Prince Meng Khamaung, son of the King of Taungu, who is carried to Syriam. A second attack is made by land and sea, and the Portuguese fleet is worsted, but they fail to capture Syriam, and the King of Arakan pays 50,000 crowns for the release of the prince.

H. 1013. Prince Dānyāl receives the submission of Malik 'Ambar, and espouses a daughter of Ibrāhīm 'Ādil Shāh.

May. Dom Martin Affonsa de Castro arrives at Goa as Viceroy.

King James I., by granting licence to Sir Edward Michelborne and others to trade in the East, encroaches on the East India Company's monopoly.

Henry IV. grants a charter to a French East India Company, but it fails and is soon after dissolved.

Second voyage of the English Company to Amboyna under Sir H. Middleton.

The Dutch establish factories in Southern India.

1605 April 20: Zī-l hijja 1, H. 1013. Prince Dānyāl dies at Burhānpur.

Mirzā 'Abdurrahīm, Khān Khānān, Governor of Ahmadnagar, unable to dispossess Miyān Manju and Malik 'Ambar, comes to an agreement with them.

Nyaung Rām Meng, King of Burma, dies, and is succeeded by his son, who takes the title of Mahādhammā Rāja. Great slaughter of the Portuguese at Dianga in Arakan.

JAHĀNGĪR.

Oct. 25: Jumāda II. 12, H. 1014. The Emperor Akbar dies after a reign of 51 lunar years 9 months, aged 64 lunar years 11 months. Prince Salīm assumes the government as Nūr-ud-dīn Muhammad Jahāngīr.

Rāja Mān Singh Kachhwāhā submits to Jahāngīr and is reappointed Governor of Bengal; but soon after (H. 1015) he is recalled and sent to quell disturbances at Rohtās in Bihār.

Nov. Husain Khān Shāmlū of Harāt, on Akbar's death,

A.D.

1605 besieges Qandahār, bravely defended by Shāh Beg Khān Arghūn, and Mirzā Ghāzī Beg is sent to relieve it, when Shāh 'Abbās ordered the siege to be raised.

1606 Feb. Ternate fort and city, held by a garrison of Dutch and natives, is besieged and taken by Da Cunha. Tidor also captured and reannexed.

April 15. Zī-l hijja 8, H. 1014. Prince Khusro with a few followers from Agra, recruits and plunders in Lāhor district, is defeated at Bhaironwāl on the Biās; and June 10: Safar 3, H. 1015, is brought captive before his father and imprisoned.

Arjun, the fifth Sikh Guru, charged with aiding in Khusro's rebellion, suffers death. He had nominated his son, Hargovind, as sixth Guru. He was the first to arm the Sikhs and took a bloody revenge on those Muhammadans whom he thought had led to his father's death. He died in 1638.

May. The Viceroy leaves Goa, and on Aug. 17 engages the Dutch, but divides his fleet into two parts, one of which—of five galleons under Nuno Pereira—is totally defeated by the Dutch on Oct. 22. The Viceroy dies of grief: again, the Dutch capture three ships and blockade Goa, to prevent the return of the Portuguese fleet to Lisbon.

Sept. 12: Jumāda I. 9, H. 1015. Qutb-ud-dīn Khān (Shaikh Khūbū) is appointed Sūbhadār of Bengal in addition to Bihār. He is ordered to send Sher Afkan 'Alī Qulī Istajlū, the husband of Nūr Jahān, to the court; Sher Afkan refuses to go, and in an encounter at Bardwān, Qutb-ud-dīn attacks Sher Afkan, who is wounded by him, and both die of their wounds.

Oct. Dom Alexis de Menezes, Archbishop of Goa, succeeds Martim Affonso as governor.

Robert de Nobilibus, a Jesuit missionary and eminent Sanskrit and Tamil scholar, preaches at Madura, and founds a mission there in 1624.

H. 1016. Qulij Khān is appointed nominal Viceroy of Gujarāt, Mirzā 'Azīz continuing to act. Shaikh Farīd-i-Bukhārī is appointed eleventh viceroy with the title of Murtazā Khān.

Third voyage of the English Company, under Keelinge, Hawkins, and D. Middleton. Hawkins goes straight to Surat,

A.D.

1606 leaving his ship with instructions to proceed to Bantam; he travels to Agra in 1609.

1607 H. 1016. Jahāngīr Qulī Khān Lālah Beg is appointed Governor of Bihār and Bengal, but dies the following year.

June 14: Safar 18, H. 1016. Jahāngīr visits Kābul and appoints Shāh Beg Khān Arghūn Governor of Kābul in addition to Qandahār, with the title of Khān Daurān, and orders him to prepare a financial settlement for the whole of Afghānistān except Harāt. He resigned the office in H. 1027, and died in 1029, aged ninety lunar years.

Malik 'Ambar, the Habshī, conciliates Murtazā Nizām Shāh of Ahmadnagar and removes the seat of government to Junnar.

H. 1016. Mahābat Khān sent with a force against Amara Singh Rānā of Udaypur; and the Khān Khānān Mirzā 'Abdur-rahīm, with Prince Parwīz as nominal commander, under the guidance of Āsaf Khān and others, are sent to settle matters in the Dekhan.

Fath Khān, an Afghān, obtains possession of Dianga, 20 miles south of Chittagāon and of Sanda, and becomes active against the Portuguese pirates.

The English fleet this year is lost on the way to India.

1608 H. 1017. Mīrza 'Azīz Kokah, Governor of Gujarāt, his son, Jahāngīr Qulī Khān, being deputy.

Shāh 'Alā-ud-dīn Islām Khān, Governor of Bengal till H. 1022.

Amara Rānā of Udaypur defeats the imperial army at Dewir.

The Burmese king, Mahādhammā Rāja, destroys Syriam and drives the Portuguese from his kingdom. Escaping to the Ganges delta, they live by piracy. Fath Khān Afghān is killed in an attempt to withstand them at Sandwīp. Prome is retaken by Mahādhammā Rāja, the Burmese king, after an investment of eight months.

Aug. Capt. William Hawkins of the "Hector" lands at Surat as envoy with letters to Jahāngīr, and proceeds to Agra.

Sept. The Portuguese Northern fleet threatens to burn the city of Surat and shipping if the English are not sent away.

Oct. 5. After losing her long-boat and twenty-seven men, the "Hector" leaves for Bantam.

A.D.

1609 H. 1018. Khān Jahān is sent to the Dekhan where the war had taken an unfavourable turn. At Mulkāpur the imperial army loses heavily in a battle with Malik 'Ambar, now virtual master of the Dekhan.

Malik 'Ambar invades Gujarāt, plunders Surat and Baroda, and retires. A force is now stationed at Rāmnagar as a protection to the Gujarāt provinces.

March. Sebastian Gonzales seizes Sandwīp and two other islands, in defiance of the Rāja of Bakla. Gaining command of the Arakanese fleet he plunders the villages on the Arakan river. A peace is concluded, but Gonzales shows such treachery that the king impales the former's nephew then a hostage.

March. André Furtado de Mendoça succeeds as governor at Goa,—the viceroy elect, the Conde de Feyra, having died on the voyage. Sept. Ruy Lourenço de Tavora succeeds as viceroy.

H. 1018. The brother of the King of Golkonda, Mirzā Muhammad Khudābanda, rebels, but is seized and imprisoned; he dies in 1611.

Muttu Vīrappa succeeds Kṛishnappa as ruler of Madura till 1623.

Captain Keelinge establishes the English factory at Bantam.

April. Capt. Hawkins arrives at Agra from Surat as envoy to Jahāngīr. He is opposed by the Portuguese Jesuits, but speaking Turki he gains the favour of the emperor, who appoints him to the command of 400 horse. The Portuguese and Muqarrab Khān of Surat, however, malign the English and their offers, and Hawkins leaves Agra, Nov. 1611.

May. A second Charter granted to the East India Company by James I., constituting them a corporate body for ever, but reserving to Government the power of dissolving them on three years' notice.

Sept 5. The English ship "Ascension" wrecked at Gandavī, her crew arriving at Surat.

Spain recognises the right of Holland to trade with India.

The Dutch build a fort at Palikat, 24 miles north of Madras, which they name Geldria, their earliest settlement in Southern India.

A.D.

1610 May 8: Safar 14, H. 1019. Pātna seized and occupied by a fictitious Sultān Khusro, at the head of a Rājput throng. The governor, Afzal Khān, marches on Pātna and defeats the pretender, who is put to death, May 15: Safar 21.

H. 1019. Malik 'Ambar, formerly minister at Ahmadnagar, founds a new capital Kharkī (now Aurangābād), and recovers the Ahmadnagar and Berār districts.

The Golkonda army unsuccessfully attempt to invade the Hindu territory of Bastar.

Rāja Wodiyar seizes Seringapatam from the Vijayanagar viceroy Tirumala, and founds the Maisur State.

Nātsheng, King of Taungu, becomes tributary to Burma, thus breaking faith with Philip de Brito (Nicote).

Troubles at Chaul occur between the native inhabitants and Portuguese. The native town is fired, but the Portuguese are driven off with heavy loss. Among the dead are Antonio Furtado de Mendoça and Gonzalo de Abreu.

Dom Hierome de Azevedo, commander at Colombo, captures and burns Kandy. The king surrenders on treaty and places two sons in the hands of the Franciscans to be brought up as Catholics.

The King of Burma subdues Nātsheng, King of Taungu, who becomes tributary, and breaks faith with De Brito.

The Dutch settle at Palikat.

1611 H. 1020. 'Abdullah Khān Bahādur Firūz Jang appointed thirteenth Viceroy of Gujarāt.

Jahāngīr marries Nūr Jahān, widow of Sher Afkan.

The Afghāns in Bengal under 'Usmān Khān rebel, and refuse obedience to the Mughal ambassador sent to conciliate them.

Capt. Hippon of the "Globe" attempts unsuccessfully to open trade at Palikat and at Peddapalli Arjampatnam, 36 miles from Masulipatam, where a factory was established ten years afterwards: the name was changed to Nizāmpatam in 1679. The "Globe" visits Masulipatam and starts an agency.

A United (second) French East India Company is formed.

Sept. 26. Sir Henry Middleton arrives off Surat. The

A.D.

1611 Portuguese obstruct his landing. Khwāja Nāsar, Governor of Surat, is deprived of office by Jahāngīr, and imprisoned on the "Peppercorn" by Middleton.

Nov. 2. Capt. Hawkins leaves Agra, after two years' residence at the Mughal court.

1612 Jan. 12. Shaikh Hassan Muqarrab Khān, the Governor of Gujarāt, alleging orders from Jahāngīr, commands the English merchants to leave Surat: Feb. 12, the ships leave Swally.

Jan. 21: Zī-l qa'da 17, H. 1020. Muhammad Qulī Qutb Shāh of Golkonda dies: his brother, 'Abdullah Qutb Shāh, succeeds.

March 12: Muharram 9, H. 1021. The imperial army under Shujā'at Khān, defeats the Afghāns in Bengal, and 'Usmān Lohānī is killed. Shujā'at Khān arrives at Dhāka (Safar 16) with prisoners.

March 12. Jahāngīr grants a *farmān* permitting the English to establish factories at Surat, Gogha, Ahmadābād, and Khambay: thus Surat forms the first established settlement of the English in India.

March. The King of Kandy makes a formal alliance with the Dutch.

The E.I. Company becomes a Joint Stock Company.

Amara Singh, Rānā of Udaypur, is defeated by Mahābat Khān; the Rānā, however, continues independent.

Malik 'Ambar forces the imperial army under 'Abdullah Khān to retreat.

Meng Rādzagyi, King of Arakan dies; his son, Meng Khamaung, succeeds, and determines to punish Sebastian Gonzales, a Portuguese pirate at Sandwīp.

De Brito, along with the King of Martaban, leads an army to Taungu, imprisons Nātsheng the vassal king, plunders the city, burns the palace and retires.

Sept. 5. The Portuguese attack two English ships off Surat and capture two men. Sept. 30. Captain Best captures a large Gujarāt ship.

Oct. 21. Treaty signed by Capt. Best and Shaikh Sufi, Governor of Ahmadābād, regulating English trade with Gujarāt,—confirmed by Mahdī Ja'far, the Governor of Gujarāt.

A.D.

1612 Oct. 28. A Portuguese fleet from Goa joins the frigates at Surat. The "Dragon" engages them on Oct. 29 and 30. Again from Nov. 22 to 27, Capt. Best gains a signal victory against superior odds, which leads to the resumption of negotiations between the English and Jahāngīr and to the final establishment of the Surat factory.

Dec. 24. Dom Hierome de Azevedo succeeds as Viceroy at Goa.

H. 1021. The *Tārikh-i-Khān Jahān Lodi* of Niāmat-ulla is completed.

The Danish East India Company formed at Copenhagen.

1613 Feb. Capt. Best leaves for Achīn, Messrs Starkey, Canning, Aldworth, Nicholas, Withington, and Kerridge remaining at Surat as factors. April 9, Paul Canning arrives at Agra with letters and presents to the emperor. May 29, Canning dies, probably poisoned by a Jesuit priest. June 22, Thomas Kerridge leaves Surat to take Canning's place.

The English establish a factory at Firando in Japan.

April. Mahādhammā Rāja, King of Burma, overlord of the King of Taungu, the victim of De Brito's violence, to punish him, blockades Syriam by sea and land, and after thirty-four days De Brito sues for peace, but receives no reply and the town is taken: he captures and impales De Brito and kills 700 defenders. A fleet on its way to assist, hearing of the disaster, returns.

The Portuguese garrison at Karanjā Fort, in revenge for the murder of their commander, put the natives to the sword. The town and district are ravaged by Sampayo e Cunha. Ruy Frière de Andrade drives off the native besiegers from Manora and Agāshi. Antonio Pinto de Fonseca arrives from Lisbon as "Visitor and Proveditor" of the forts in India.

Aug. 21: Rajab 5, H. 1022. Shaikh Islām Khān, Governor of Bengal, dies at Dhākā (Dacca). His brother, Qāsim Khān, succeeds.

Nov. The factors Aldworth and Withington start on a tour of the Gujarāt markets. Dec. 15. They leave for Lauribandar on the Indus, are imprisoned by Rājputs, and only reach Surat April 2, 1615.

A.D.

1614 A. H. 1023. Amara Singh, Rānā of Udaypur, submits to Prince Khurram, is restored to his state, and his son, Karan, is raised to a high command under Jahāngīr.

April 2: Safar 21, H. 1023. Jahān Ārā Begam, the beautiful, accomplished, and heroic daughter of Shāh Jahān, born. She shared her father's imprisonment in the fort of Agra, 1658, till his death in 1666.

Rāja Mān Singh of Amber dies at Bīdar in the Dekhan.

Venkatapati Rāya of Vijayanagar, the capital of which was now Chandragiri, dies. His nephew, Rāma Deva III., called Chikka Rāya, succeeds, but is soon deposed, and compelled to murder his family and take his own life.

The Portuguese Viceroy sends ambassadors demanding the expulsion of the Dutch from Bījāpūr. The Zamorin of Calicut with the King of Paru attempts to seize Cranganor; the King of Paru is overpowered and the Zamorin and King of Cochin conciliated.

The Portuguese Viceroy prepares a powerful fleet and armament for the destruction of four English ships which had arrived at Surat on Oct. 12. On the way Bharoch, Gogha, and Pātan are plundered and burnt. Dec. 23. The Viceroy's fleet anchors near the English vessels. Slight skirmishes occur on Dec. 27 and 28. On Dec. 29 the English fleet move to Swally.

Mildenhall, the London merchant, again in Agra. He dies by poison soon after.

The History of the Muhammadan dynasties by Muhammad Qāsim Firishta is written and called *Gulshan-i-Ibrāhīmī* and also *Nauras Nāma*.

1615 Jan. 14 and 19. The Portuguese with an augmented fleet attack the four English ships at Surat, and are again driven off. The Nawāb now refuses overtures from the Portuguese and on his departure receives Downton with respect.

Feb. 7. Mr Edwardes, the English Company's agent, presented to Jahāngīr. He obtains a general and perpetual *farmān* for trade in the Mughal dominions.

The imperial troops suppress the rebellion of Ahdād the Afghān, who had long held out in the mountains of Kābul. A victory in the Dekhan is gained by Shāh Jahān over the

A.D.

1615 united armies of Malik 'Ambar and the Kings of Bijāpūr and Golkonda.

April. Withington arrives at Ahmadābād after a fruitless attempt to reach the Indus, where English ships, he heard, were at anchor. Sir Robert Shirley's ship had sailed for Sumatra two months before Withington set out to find her.

June 7. A treaty concluded between the Portuguese and Jahāngīr, the main object being the expulsion of the English and Dutch. Spain and Portugal, hitherto separate as regards colonial commerce, unite against their rival.

July. Louis XIII. of France grants letters patent to a (third) French Company to trade to the Indies under the joint auspices of two contending parties.

Aug. Sultān Khurram appoints his favourite, Zulaqār Khān, to succeed Muqarrab Khān as Governor of Surat. Sultān Khurram avowedly favours the Portuguese. Sept. Zulfaqār Khān concludes a treaty with the Portuguese Governor of Daman.

Sept. 18. Sir Thomas Roe, ambassador from James I. to Jahāngīr, arrives at Swally Roads. Oct. 30, leaves for Agra, arriving at Ajmir on Dec. 23. He accompanies the emperor to Mandū and Gujarāt.

Oct. Aldworth, the English factor, dies at Ahmadābād: Kerridge succeeds till 1623.

Oct. 3. A Portuguese expedition for the conquest of Arakan enters the Arakan river under Dom Francisco de Menezes. Oct. 15, the Rāja, aided by some Dutch vessels, makes an indecisive attack. Nov., the pirate Gonzales of Sandwīp joins him, and on Nov. 15 a contest takes place in which Menezes is killed, and the enterprise is then abandoned.

A Portuguese squadron defeats an Achinese fleet at Malacca, but is in turn defeated by some Dutch vessels. A native settlement and fort at S. Thomé are compelled to capitulate to the Portuguese.

The finances of Portuguese India being unsatisfactory, commands and high positions are put up for sale. This causes general dissatisfaction.

The Surat factors, at the suggestion of Richard Steel, attempt to open up trade with Persia.

A.D.

1616 Jan. 10. Sir Thomas Roe, received by Jahāngīr in "Darbār," March 26, presents to Jahāngīr his nineteen articles of Amity, Commerce, and Intercourse, regarding which some concessions are granted in September, but not full assent.

Feb. Capt. Keelinge constitutes Surat as the head English factory in the Mughal's dominions.

Feb. 28. A courtmartial held on board the "Charles" in Swally Roads on Gregory Lellington for the murder of Henry Barton, gentleman—the earliest judicial proceeding on record of the English in India.

March 8. Capt. Keelinge having been invited to the Zamorin's camp at Calicut, concludes a treaty with him against the Portuguese to regain Cranganor. March 10, his ships sail, leaving ten factors who found the English settlement at Calicut, but meet with ill-treatment from the natives.

H. 1025. Prince Khurram (Shāhjahān) declared heir apparent, and sent to the Dekhan to reconquer the territory alienated by Malik 'Ambar.

April 27. Sir Thomas Roe writes to the Rev. William Lescke, chaplain at Surat factory—the earliest extant reference to a Company's chaplain. Henry Lord leaves one of the ships to be chaplain on shore. He becomes an authority on the literature, cosmogony, and mythology of the native races, and is author of "A Discoverie of the Sect of the Banians."

Rohan, one of the ten Banda isles, is ceded to the British.

In Ceylon, Manuel Mascarenhas, with a Portuguese and native army, marches against the King of Kandy, burns all in the way to Babule, and returns to Sufragam. The people at Tompane are put to the sword.

Aug. 2. Van den Broeck, first Dutchman to attempt trade at Surat, is favourably received, but not permitted to establish a factory.

Aug. Capt. Nicholas Downton dies at Bantam.

Two ships, under Beaulieu and De Nets, leave France for the Indies.

The first Danish ship arrives in India, and is wrecked off Tranquebar. Tranquebar with land 5 miles in length by 3 miles

A.D.

1616 broad is acquired at a rent of 4,000 rupees per annum, paid to the Rāja of Tanjor.

The *Ma'āsir-i-Rahīmī*, or Memoirs of 'Abdur Rahīm Khān, Khān Khānān, and of the illustrious nobles and poets of Akbar's court, completed. 'Abdul Bāqi, the author, died about 1642.

1617 March: Rabī' I., H. 1026. Prince Khurram enters the Dekhan, and detaches the Bijāpūr king from the confederacy, whereon Malik 'Ambar makes peace on the part of the Nizām Shāh, restores Ahmadnagar and the reconquered territory. On Oct. 11: Shawwāl 11, the prince returns to Mandū, where he receives the title of Shāhjahān.

March. A triple expedition from Goa to Ceylon secures submission at Sufragam, Alikur, and Butale. Peace concluded with the King of Pandar. A Singhalese, Nikapeti, personates the late king, and rallies the people, but is put to flight by the Portuguese.

Rāja Wodiyar of Maisur dies, having reunited under his rule the lands divided by Bettada Chāma Rāja. His son, Chāma Rāja, succeeds, and acquires new districts.

An ambassador from Siam offers the Portuguese Martaban port and a site for a fort. Friar Francisco returns with him to arrange terms of treaty.

Dom João de Coutinho, Conde de Redonde, succeeds Dom Hierome de Azevedo as Viceroy. War at Mangalor now in progress. The district is put under Portuguese control. Banguel fort is seized, and the town burnt by a native force. Anriques, in revenge, attacks Ullāla, but has to retire with loss.

May 24. King James I. grants to Sir James Cunningham of Glengarnock letters patent under the Great Seal of Scotland, appointing him, his heirs, and assigns to be governors, rulers, and directors of the Scottish East India Company. This patent was subsequently assigned by Sir James Cunningham to the London Company.

July 10. A Dutch ship is wrecked on the coast near Surat; the merchants are allowed to dispose of the cargo in the city. This proves the beginning of Dutch trade in Gujarāt. A factory is established also at Ahmadābād.

A.D.

1617 Second "Joint Stock" of the E. I. Company formed at London amounted to £1,600,000.

Dec. Tom Coryat, the author of "Coryate's Crudities," dies at Surat.

1618 Jan. English factories in the Mughal's dominions now number five: Agra, Ahmadābād, Burhānpur, Bharoch, and Surat. Those in East India were: Masulipatam and Peddapoli (Nizāmpatam). These were controlled from Bantam.

Luiz de Brito e Mello and Dom Francisco de Miranda Anriques, with 180 men and 60 slaves, killed by a Kanarese force under Venkata Nāyyak.

An embassy is sent by the Portuguese to Jahāngīr, who removes the disabilities on the fleet, and forbears to make war on Daman and Dīū as contemplated.

On the Tartar invasion of China, a Portuguese force is despatched from Goa to aid the Mandarins.

An expedition to Ceylon against the Madune, undertaken by Constantine da Sa e Noronha, results in the overthrow of the natives and the death of the Prince of Uva. The King of Jafnapatam, suspected of complicity, is captured, whereon the Madune also capitulates.

Aug. On the representations of a Dutchman, Marcellis de Boschhauwer, it is resolved to found a Danish colony in Ceylon. The "Oeresund" is sent under another Dutchman, Roelant Crape, to intimate to the King of Kandy that a fleet followed. Attacked on the Coromandel coast by Andrea Botelho da Costa, he is driven ashore at Tanjor, where the Nāyyak receives him. Nov., the main fleet under Gule Gjedde leaves.

Sept.: Ramazān, H. 1027. Jahāngīr leaves Gujarāt, after a sojourn of nearly a year.

Sept. Sir Thomas Roe leaves Ahmadābād for Surat, having obtained *farmāns* sufficient to set the English on a better footing in India than either the Portuguese or the Dutch.

Disputes arise between the Dutch and English companies for exclusive trade with the Spice Islands. The Dutch E.I. Co. complain to King James of England of the interference of the London Co. with the natives of Bantam and the Spice Islands. In reply the London Co. instance the violence and oppression

A.D.

1618 experienced from the Dutch at Bantam, Tidor, Polarūn, and Amboyna.

Nov. 3: Zī-l qa'da 15, 1027 H. 'Ālamgīr surnamed Abul-Zafar Muhī-ud-dīn Muhammad Aurangzīb, third son of the Emperor Shāhjahān, born at Dohad, on Jahāngīr's march from Gujarāt to Ujjain, his mother being Arjumand Bānū surnamed Mumtāz Mahall.

Nov. 19. The remaining five ships of a fleet under John Jourdain and Sir Thomas Dale arrive at Bantam and find the position of the English in the Bandas almost desperate owing to the attitude of the Dutch. Nov. 28., a large Dutch ship, the "Black Lion," captured by the English and held as a hostage for the redress of English grievances. She is accidentally destroyed by fire; and the Dutch in revenge destroy the English factory at Jakkatra (Batavia). Dec. 23., an indecisive action between the fleets takes place.

Capt. Shillinge of the "Ann" obtains a trading grant from the Governor of Mokha.

1619 H. 1028. Shāh Beg, Khān Daurān resigns the government of Afghānistān, and is appointed to Thatta, but resigns the same year owing to the ill-feeling of Āsaf Khān: he gets Khushāb Pargana as pension.

Jan. 22. Sir Thomas Dale, the English commodore, besieges the Dutch fort at Jakkatra, but abandons the siege on the intimation of the Panjaram that the fort must be delivered to him.

Feb. 17. Sir Thomas Roe returning, sails from Surat.

April 16: S. 1675. Śatruñjaya Jaina inscription of the reign of Jahāngīr.

April 22. The E. I. Co.'s fleet under Capt. Jonas Lancaster sails to Achīn and concludes a commercial treaty with the chief.

June. Dale and Pring leave Banda and anchor off Masulipatam, where Sir T. Dale dies, Aug. 18.

July 17. The "Treaty of Defence" to prevent disputes between the English and Dutch companies is ratified, by which the English are allowed to share in the pepper trade of Java and in that of Palikat, and to hold a third of the Molucca and Banda trade. But strife continues as bitterly as ever.

A.D.

1619 July 26. Capt. Jourdain with the "Hound" and "Sampson" is overmatched by three Dutch vessels under Coen, and is about to surrender when killed. Oct., Robert Bonner, whilst waiting at Tiku in the "Dragon" for Pring, is surprised and mortally wounded—the "Dragon" is taken and three other pepper-laden ships compelled to surrender. Dec. 10. Pring sails from Masulipatam for Tiku.

At Jafnapatam the Portuguese recognise the usurper Changli Kumāra, but are attacked and blockaded for a month in the church and pagoda. Luiz Texeira brings a relief force, having perpetrated revolting atrocities on the march. Nov., the Nāyyak of Tanjor attempts to gain the kingdom, but is defeated. The son of the late king adopts the Roman Catholic religion, and makes over his kingdom to the Portuguese.

Oct. 2. Three French ships under Beaulieu leave Honfleur to trade with Java.

Nov. 10. Dom João de Coutinho, Portuguese Viceroy, dies. Fernão de Albuquerque succeeds as governor.

The Danish fleet under Gyedde arrives at Ceylon, but the King of Kandy refuses to implement his promises made to the supposed ambassador Boschhauwer. They proceed to India.

Dec. Prince Khurram, afterwards Shāhjahān, leaves Kashmīr to command the imperial forces against Malik 'Ambar, the Habshī diwān of Ahmadnagar.

S. 1675. Śatrunjaya inscription of Jasvanta, son of the Yāma Śatruśālya the Jām of Nawānagar.

Sūraj Singh of Jodhpur dies in the Dekhan and is succeeded by his son Gaja Singh.

1620 H. 1029. Malik 'Ambar again revolts against the Mughals. In a battle gained by the latter, Shāhji Bhonsla Marātha distinguishes himself.

July 3. Robert Hughes, agent at Agra, arrives at Pātna to establish an agency there. Shaikh Hasan Muqarrab Khān, Governor of Bihār, receives him graciously and secures a house for him. Sept., on the arrival of John Parker trade is commenced in obtaining cotton and silk.

Nov. The Danes, Crape and Gyedde, succeed in gaining from

A.D.

1620 Raghunāth Nāyyaka of Tanjor the cession of the port of Tranquebār. A fort is built and Hendrik Hess is left in charge with twenty of a garrison.

Dec. 28. The English East India Company's ships defeat a Portuguese fleet of twenty-one sail under Admiral Ruy Frère, attacking them near Jask in Persia. The English commodore, Capt. Shillinge, is mortally wounded.

1621 The Persians seek the assistance of the English against the Portuguese aggressions: James I. writes in March to Shāh 'Abbās thanking him for past favours and requesting the continuance of protection.

H. 1030. Disturbances are renewed in the Dekhan: Shāhjahān defeats Malik 'Ambar, whereupon the Marāthās desert to the Mughals, and their leaders obtain posts of distinction.

March. Pātna is devastated by fire. The English factors with their goods are saved, but their house is burnt.

Muqarrab Khān is transferred from Bihār to Agra, and is succeeded as governor by Prince Parwīz, who evicts the factors from their house to accommodate part of his retinue. The Pātna factory, owing to the expense of transit, is relinquished and the factors move to Agra.

April 29. Dom Affonso de Noronha is appointed Viceroy at Goa. Of ten ships which leave Lisbon, nine are driven back. The Indian fleet founders, except one ship; and to resuscitate the ruined navy, large subsidies are exacted.

Karna Rānā succeeds Amara Rānā of Udaypur.

Nov. 15: Muharram 1, H. 1031. Kāngra fort capitulates to the imperial troops.

Nūr Jahān withdraws her support from Shāhjahān and betroths her daughter to Shahryār.

Nov. On the capture of Qandahār by Shāh Abbās of Persia, Shāhjahān refuses to proceed for its recapture, whereon his *jāgīrs* and troops are transferred to his brother Shahryār.

The Dutch take Bahia. In spite of an existing treaty of defence the Dutch expel the English from Bantam.

1622 Jan. 22. The English fleet anchor off Ormuz, and, for the first time, assist the Persians in expelling the Portuguese.

A.D.

1622 Jan. 26: Rabī 'I. 13, H. 1031. Sultān Khusro dies in the Dekhan—strangled, according to the *Ma'āsir Qutb Shāhī*, by a man named Raza, under orders from Shāhjahān.

Feb. 1. Ruy Frière surrenders at Kishm. Feb. 9, the English and Persians attack Ormuz, which surrenders on May 22: the Portuguese population are sent to Maskat. The English resign their share in the capture for a moiety of the customs of the port of Gombrūn and certain commercial privileges in the Persian Gulf.

May 9: Jumāda II. 27. Shāhjahān proclaims himself Emperor of Hindustān, marches on Dehli, whence, on defeat, he flees to the Dekhān. Defeated again by Parwīz and Mahābat Khān, he rallies at Golkonda and invades Orissa, whose governor, Ahmad Beg, retreats. Shāhjahān captures Bardhwān, and recruits his army.

H. 1031. Sultān Dāwar Bakhsh, son of Sultān Khusro, sixteenth Viceroy of Gujarāt, with Muhammad Safi as minister. Shāhjahān appoints 'Abdullah Khān Bahādur Firūz Jang, with Khwāja Sara 'Abdullah Khān as minister.

Shāh 'Abbās again captures Qandahār, which remains in possession of Persia till 1637.

Aug. 27. The English withdraw their factory from Palikat.

James I. authorises the E.I. Company to chastise all English persons residing in India, who should commit misdemeanours.

Sept. Dom Francisco da Gama, Conde de Vidigueira, Viceroy of Portuguese India till 1627.

Meng Khamaung of Burma dies. His son succeeds as Thiri Thudhammā Rāja, till 1638.

1623 Jan. Three English and four Dutch ships blockade Goa unopposed till March.

Feb. 17. The Dutch in Amboyna, under Harman van Speult, seize Capt. Towerson with nine Englishmen of the factory, nine Japanese, and a Portuguese sailor; they are accused of conspiring to expel the Dutch garrison—tortured at their trial, they are summarily executed. For this inhuman act the Dutch were afterwards compelled by Cromwell to pay £3,615 to the relatives of the sufferers. The two nations had jointly shared in the pepper

A.D.

1623 trade of Java, but now the Dutch monopolise the trade of the Archipelago till 1793.

H. 1032. Shājahān marches from the Dekhan for Agra. His army, under Dārāb Khān, son of 'Abdul Rahīm Khān Khānān, is defeated at Biluchpur. He then retires to Mandū, and Prince Parwīz and Mahābat Khān are sent after him, and the latter gets many of his followers to desert. Shāhjahān crosses the Narbadā, burns the boats, and occupies Āsīrgadh and Burhānpur; the Khān Khānan then deserts, and Shāhjahān escapes into Golkonda territory.

Tirumala Nāyyaka succeeds Vīrappa of Madura. He discontinues the nominal allegiance hitherto paid to Vijayanagar.

June. King James I. and the Duke of Buckingham claim a share of the prize money taken at Ormuz, and pending negotiations detain the East India fleet in arrest at Tilbury. The Company compound, by paying £10,000 to the duke, and are ordered to pay £10,000 to the king.

Thomas Rastell succeeds Kerridge as President of the Surat factory, till 1626.

Oct. 23. Tulsi Dās, Marāthi poet, dies (some say 1624).

Pietro della Valle, called "Il Pellegrino," a Roman patrician of literary attainments, visits Surat, and proceeds to Ikkeri, in Vijayanagar. He wrote sketches of his travels, published at Rome, 1650.

1624 Saif Khān (Muhammad Safi) seventeenth Viceroy of Gujarāt, acting till 1627.

July 29. Capt. Swan takes possession of Lagundi in the Sunda Straits.

The English Company obtains permission to punish its servants by martial as well as municipal law, *i.e.*, is invested with powers of government.

The English, owing to the Dutch opposition, withdraw nearly all their factories from the Eastern Archipelago, Java, Siam and the Malay peninsula. Some of the factors and agents settle on the island of Lagundi.

H. 1033. Shāhjahān invades Orissa, defeats the Governor of Bengal at Terriagarhi, and masters the province. Defeated

A.D.

1624 by the imperial army, he sends his family to Rohtās, and retreats to the Dekhan, H. 1034.

Oct.-Nov. Malik 'Ambar joins Shāhjahān in the siege of Burhānpur. The siege, however, is raised.

About this time, the Jesuits, under Robert de Nobili, establish their mission in Madura.

The Danes oppose English trade in Tanjor. Tranquebār becomes the property of the King of Denmark, to whom the Company owed money.

1625 H. 1034. Shāhjahān offers submission to his father and is pardoned. His sons, Dārā Shikoh and Aurangzīb, are sent to court as hostages.

Feb. The English obtain a grant of ground from the Rāja of Venkatagiri for a settlement at Ārmugam or Dugarājapatnam, 35 miles north of Palikāt. Dutch persecution follows them thither.

May 31. The English Company's servants abandon Lagundi Island in the Sunda Straits owing to its unhealthiness, and return to Batavia.

Kotā State is severed from Būndī, and becomes a rājaship under Mādhu Singh.

The Portuguese revenue at Goa and in Bengal is materially decreased by smuggling.

Nov. 7: Safar 6, H. 1035. Prince Parwīz dies in the Dekhan.

H. 1035. Khān Asad Khān succeeded in the government of Bengal by Mukarram Khān,—drowned 1626.

The Dutch are said to have first settled in Bengal this year, their factory being at Chinsura. Harman van Speult, Governor of Batavia, is appointed Dutch Governor at Surat.

Mahābat Khān incurs the hatred of Nūr Jahān, and is summoned to court. He complies, but arrives with 5,000 Rājputs.

1626 March: Jumāda II., H. 1035. Mahābat Khān, intrigued against by Nūr Jahān, siezes the emperor at his camp on the Jehlam. The following day Nūr Jahān, in an attempt to recover her husband, is defeated with great loss and joins him in captivity for six months.

6

A.D.

1626 H. 1035. Malik 'Ambar Habshī dies in the eightieth year of his age, and is succeeded by his son Fath Khān as minister in the Dekhan.

Sept. By means of Nūr Jahān's scheming Jahāngīr is rescued at a muster of her contingent.

Mahābat Khān is pardoned on releasing 'Asaf Khān, Nūr Jahān's brother, and is sent against Shāhjahān who is again in rebellion, and owing to desertions in his army has fled from Ajmir to Thatta. Mahābat Khān having again come to a rupture with the emperor, Shāhjahān passes through Gujarāt to the Dekhan, and is there joined soon after by Mahābat.

H. 1036. Ibrāhīm 'Ādil Shāh II. of Bijāpūr dies. Muhammad his son succeeds.

Nov. 17. Sir Thomas Herbert visits Goa. Nov. 29, touches at Swally, and is hospitably received at Surat—his "Travels" published 1634. Mr Wyld succeeds Thomas Rastell as President of the Surat factory.

H. 1036. The *Anfa'-ul-Akhbār* of Muhammad Amīn is finished.

Van Speult, Dutch general at Surat, coerces the English to join in an expedition against the Portuguese at Mokha and Bombay. Van Speult dies off Mokha, and his successor refuses assistance to form an establishment in Bombay.

1627 H. 1036. Nawāb Fidāī Khān is appointed Governor of Bengal.

May 6. Śivājī, son of Shāhjī Bhonsla, born at Śivaner, Junnar.

Dom Francisco de Brito, Bishop of Cochin, succeeds the Conde de Vidigueira as Viceroy at Goa. Vexatious charges are raised on his return against De Vidigueira.

In consequence of the necessities of the State, orders are issued limiting the appointment-dowries of Portuguese orphan girls to three years. Monastic institutions ordered to be reduced.

H. 1037. Karna Rānā of Udaypur dies. His son, Jagat Singh, succeeds.

Nov. 8: Safar 28, H. 1037. After a reign of 22 lunar years 8 months and 15 days, Jahāngir dies in camp at Rājaur on his way from Kashmīr to Lāhor, at the age of sixty. 'Asaf Khān, while favouring Shāhjahān, puts forward Dāwar Bakhsh, son of Prince Khusro. Shahryār, favoured by Nūr Jahān, is also proclaimed

A.D.

1627 king. Their forces meet near Lāhor, when Shahryār's troops are routed.

1628 Feb. Jumāda I., H. 1037. Prince Dāwar Bakhsh, his brother Garshasp, Prince Shahryār, with the sons of Prince Dānyāl, are put to death. (Elphinstone says Dāwar escaped to Persia.)

SHĀHJAHĀN.

1628 Feb. 14: Jumāda II. 8, H. 1037. Shāhjahān arrives at Agra, and ascends the throne.

March. 'Asaf Khān, their maternal grandfather, removes Dārā Shikoh and Alamgīr from the care of Nūr Jahān and sends them to their father at Lāhor.

Khān Jahān Lodi, Governor of the Dekhan, gives up Bālaghāt to the Nizām-ul-Mulk, and himself aspires to independence at Mandū. On submission, however, he is received at court.

Mahādhammā Rāja of Burma dies—the result of an obscure conspiracy. A brother of the late King Thado-dhammā Rāja overcomes a rival faction and succeeds.

The King of Kandy declares war on the Portuguese in consequence of the erection of a fort at Battikaloa. Francisco de Noronha defeats the Singhalese, and enters, burns and destroys the city.

Sept. 27. Masulipatam factory abandoned by the English, owing to the oppression of the native governor, for Dugarājapatnam where a factory built and named Armugam now mounted twelve guns.

The English president and council at Batavia move to Bantam, letters having been exchanged between King Charles I. and the King of Bantam.

Dom Francisco de Mascarenhas, viceroy-elect, is forced to return to Lisbon after sailing. The Conde de Linhares is now nominated Viceroy.

1629 April 5. Shāhjahān grants an additional *farmān* to the English at Surat, authorising them to make reprisals on the Portuguese ships within his dominions.

Oct 5. The London Company's Charter is renewed with the

A.D.

1629 additional right to export £80,000 per annum in silver and £40,000 in gold.

Nov.: Rabī' I., H. 1039. A'zam Khān, with an imperial army, pursues Khān Jahān Lodī to the Dekhan. The King of Bījāpūr holding aloof, and the King of Ahmadnagar being defeated after an unsuccessful action near Bīr, Khān Jahān takes flight to the Panjāb.

Shāhjī Bhonsla, son of Jādhav Rāi, joins A'zam Khān, and receives a command in the imperial army.

The Portuguese envoy at Achīn is imprisoned, and Malacca invested. In September a fleet leaves Goa, anchoring at Malacca, Oct. 22. After several encounters, the Portuguese rout the besiegers finally on Dec. 4. Botello, after repelling a Dutch attack, is killed by the blowing up of the enemy's vessel at Jakkatra (Batavia).

Dec. 24: Jumāda I. 8. Bāqir Khān assaults and takes Mansurgarh fort.

1630 H. 1039. The rains of 1629 having failed in the Dekhan, famine and pestilence break out, during which war is prosecuted with Murtazā Nizām Shāh of Ahmadnagar.

March 15. A Company of Commerce is established by the Portuguese in imitation of the English and Dutch, but is a total failure, not one private individual supporting it. Abolished in 1633.

Dom Constantine de Sa e Noronha, preparing to attack Uva, now the seat of the Singhalese government, is deserted by the native soldiers and killed in the rising. Colombo is besieged, and great misery suffered by the townsmen.

Sept. 30. A letter from the Surat factors to the Agra factors of this date is the earliest extant document in the Record Office.

Sept. The Portuguese fleet, under Dom Francisco Coutinho, attacks the English ships off Swally, the English having the advantage. Frequent skirmishes follow and an attempt is made to fire the English ships, which, however, succeed in landing their cargoes.

The presidency at Bantam is now reduced to an agency subordinate to Surat. Rice and sugar-cane supersede pepper as articles of cultivation.

A.D.

1630 Dec. 28: Jamāda I. 23, H. 1040. Nasīri Khān invests Kandahār in Nānder district; Telingana, is held by Sadik, son of Yāqūt Khudāwand Khān, for 4 months 19 days. Captured May 16, 1631: Shawwāl 15.

The King of Spain decrees to admit foreigners into the Portuguese Indian Service on the same terms as their own countrymen. The people of Surat object to put in force the terms of the Anglo-Spanish Treaty of Nov. 15.

The Dutch at Surat, to weaken the connection between the English and the Mughal government, depress the E.I. Co.'s stock and credit by selling the European goods at a great loss, and giving high prices for Indian goods; thus rendering the markets impracticable.

H. 1040. The *Ma'āsir-i-Jahāngīrī* of Mirzā Kāmgār Khān is begun.

1631 Feb. 3: Rajab 1, H. 1040. Khān Jahān Lodi and his followers cut to pieces 40 miles from Kālinjar by an advance guard of the imperial army under Mādhu Singh, son of the Hārā chief of Būndī.

March: Sha'bān. Two forces, under Allah Yār Khān and Bahādur Kambū, are sent by Qāsim Khān, Governor of Bengal, to extirpate the Portuguese at Hūglī.

Murtazā Nizām Shāh, threatened by 'Asaf Khān and the imperial army, liberates Fath Khān, but Nizām Shāh is put to death by the latter and Nizām Shāh's son, Husain, a lad of ten, is raised to the throne.

June 17: Zi-l qa'da 17, H. 1040. The Empress Arjumānd Bānu Begam, called Nawāb 'Aliā Begam and Mumtāz Mahall, dies at Burhānpur on the birth of a daughter.

H. 1040-1041. Muhammad 'Ādil Shāh of Bijāpūr, having thrown off his allegiance, is besieged by Yamīn-ud-daula ('Asaf Khān). The besieged hold out till distress and scarcity necessitate the withdrawal of the imperial army.

The Portuguese obtain from the Queen of Gersappa the island of Kamboli and the fort of Basrūr ("Bracalor") in South Kanara.

The Portuguese Viceroy reports on the threatening attitude of the Jesuit priests who had, at Tutikorin and Travankor,

A.D.

1631 established fortified defences at their own expense and had waged war against Portuguese sea captains, besides holding treasonable communication with Dutch and natives.

The third joint stock of the London Co. formed, amounting to £420,700.

Great famine in Gujarāt, known as the Satiāsio Kāl, or famine of Samvat 1687.

Jan. 5. Dom Jorge de Almeida renews the campaign in Ceylon: and by a series of victories by sea and land becomes master of the forts of Manieravare, Sufragam, Malvana, Kalutara, and Matara.

Feb.: Sha'bān, H. 1061. Shāhjahān orders Qāsim Yār Khān to destroy the Portuguese settlement at Hūglī, because natives were forced to Catholicism.

1632 June 19: Zī-l hijja 2. The Mughals under Qāsim's son 'Ināyat-ullah and Allah Yār Khān attack the Portuguese at Hūglī. They are hemmed in by a bridge of boats farther down the river. Sept. 30: Rabī' I. 14, H. 1042. Hūglī is carried by storm after three and a half months' siege, and 10,000 men, women, and children are killed and 4,400 of both sexes taken prisoners.

Oct.: Rabī' I., H. 1042. Qāsim Khān, Governor of Bengal, dies. A'zim Khān succeeds.

Sher Khān, Governor of Gujarāt, dies. Islām Khān is appointed nineteenth Viceroy with Khwāja Jahān as minister. The government of this province becomes lax and Bāqir Khān succeeds as twentieth Viceroy till 1633.

Rāī Singh of Bikanir dies, and Karan his son succeeds.

Gālna fort (Nāsik district) is surrendered by the governor, Mahmūd Khān, to the emperor's representatives, in expectation of a large reward. He had first intended to deliver it to Shāhujī Bhonsla.

Shāhjahān orders the destruction of Hindu temples recently begun, and seventy-six are razed at Benares.

In Portuguese India the monks flourish amid the destitution of the army. The soldiers become monks and of 1,500 men sent out only 500 are found for service.

Nov. The English factors at Armugam obtain a *farmān* from

A.D.

1632 the King of Golkonda, authorising them to re-establish their factory at Masulipatam and remitting the former heavy duties.

1633 March 13: Ramazān 1, H. 1042. Mahābat Khān, Khān Khānān invests Daulatābād fort, which in spite of several efforts of Shāhjī Bhonsla to relieve it, is finally surrendered by Fath Khān, June 28: Zī-l hijja 19. Fath Khān becomes a pensioner of the emperor and Husain Nizām Shāh is imprisoned at Gwāliar.

March 22. John Norris, agent at Masulipatam, resolves to send two merchants to Bengal to settle a factory. April 6, William Bruton with the party leaves Masulipatam, landing at Harishpurgarh. They are attacked by the Portuguese, but rescued by the natives. May 3. Permission is obtained from the Nawāb of Malkandi to trade duty free "off or on the shore in the country" of Orissa. Mr Cartwright travels on to Bālāsor, leaving a party to build a factory at Hariharpur.

April 15. The Portuguese and Singhalese conclude a treaty, dividing the kingdom into three—the Portuguese to hold Battikaloa and to decide on war and peace. The security of the Portuguese in India generally is now more uncertain than ever.

July 18: Muharram 11, H. 1043. The Christian prisoners from Hūglī brought before the emperor. Some accept Islām and are liberated; most, refusing, are cast into prison.

The Portuguese Viceroy of Goa reports to the king the arrival of French vessels in Indian seas. The Dutch obstruct Portuguese trade at Malacca.

1634 May 30: Zī-l hijja 3, H. 1043. Mahābat Khān, having failed to take Parendā (Naldurg district), is recalled, and the command vested in Khān Daurān and Khān Zamān, but they fail, and retreat.

H. 1044. Jajhār Singh Bundelā and his son, Bikramājit, rebel. The latter, defeated at Ashta by Khān Zamān, joins his father in Dhāmūnī. The imperial troops attack Ūrchhā which, on Nov. 22: Jumāda II. 2: is carried by escalade. Jajhār retreats to Chaurāgarh where, by an explosion, 'Alī Ashgar and 300 men of the imperial army perish. Jajhār again escapes, but, with his son, is subsequently killed by the Gonds.

H. 1044. The peacock throne of Dehli finished; it cost seven years' work and 100 lākhs of rupees.

A.D.

1634 Feb. 2. Shāhjahān grants a *farmān* to the English Co. to trade in Bengal, the ships to call at Pīplī alone. This is the earliest permission given to the English to enter the Ganges. Mr Norris, sent from Masulipatam to open trade at Pīplī, reports that all kinds of provisions for supplying the Coromandel factories can be purchased in Bengal.

The Bantam factory is restored to the rank of a presidency and the agencies on the Coromandel coast and in Bengal made subordinate to it.

An English factory established at Vīravāsaram, Godāvarī district. It was withdrawn in 1662, re-established in 1677 and abandoned 1702.

1635 Jan. 20. An armistice is concluded between the English and Portuguese by which the English are allowed access to the Portuguese ports in India, the agreement being made at Goa between the Conde de Linhares and Mr Methwold, president of the E.I. Co. The English plant a settlement at Cochin whence pepper is for the first time exported direct to England.

Owing to want of vessels at Goa, the English ship "London" is chartered by the Portuguese for a voyage to China, the people of Goa eagerly contributing cargo. The English contrive to do some trade on their own account and promise to return the next year.

Sept. 28. Alamgīr Aurangzīb is appointed to supreme command of the forces sent against Jajhār Singh Bundelā, chief of Ūrchhā.

Nov.: Jumāda I., H. 1045. Shāhjahān wages successful war against Ahmadnagar and Golkonda but fails to reduce Bījāpūr.

A'zam Khān appointed Viceroy of Gujarāt, defeats and makes tributary Kānji, a Koli robber.

Venkatāpati Rāya of Vijayanagar leagues with the Portuguese for the expulsion of the Dutch from Palikat, but on two occasions fails to co-operate.

Nov. Pedro da Silva arrives at Goa as Viceroy, till 1639.

Dec. 12. Charles I. gives a licence to a rival trading association under Sir William Courten and Endymion Porter, one of the Gentlemen of the Bedchamber, to trade to India for five years, in violation of the Company's charter. The E.I. Co.'s servants in India ordered not to assist the "interlopers." Captain Weddell

A. D.

1635 and Nathaniel Mounteney of Courten's Association receive permission to trade with the Portuguese.

1636 Feb. 15: Ramazān 8, H. 1045. Khān Daurān, Shāista Khān, and Khān Zamān sent to Bījāpūr, Golkonda, and Ahmadnagar to continue the subjugation of the Dekhan. March 14: Shawwāl 5. Golkonda submits to the imperial government.

March. Antonio Telles, in pursuit of thirteen Dutch vessels, is driven by storms to Bombay, the Dutch running to Dābhol. Further fights occur between Portuguese and Dutch vessels.

April 13: Zī-l qa'da 6. The Khān Zamān invests and takes Kolhāpur: other successes against Shāhji are gained.

May 10: Zī-l hijja 3. Shāhjahān having made treaties with the Dekhan kings, Prince Aurangzīb is appointed Governor of the Dekhan, and on July 25 proceeds to headquarters at Daulatābād.

June 4. Khān Daurān takes Kalyān fort. Others capitulate and 2,000 Bijāpūrīs are defeated near Bīdar, June 27. The forts of Udgīr and Usā are besieged.

June. Mr Methwold, president of the Surat factory, enters into a convention with the Portuguese Viceroy, the English being permitted to build two pinnaces at Bassein, and two at Daman for the protection of the local trade.

Sir William Courten's vessels seize and plunder five junks from Surat and Dīū. The Mughal authorities, not comprehending the distinction between these and the Company's agents, imprison the president and council of Surat. The president is released on a ransom of Rs. 170,000. Oct., five of Courten's vessels arrive at Goa.

H. 1046. Shāhjahān endeavours to introduce the revenue system of Todar Mall into Mahārāshtra, and with it the revenue or Faslī year which commenced with the current Hijra year. The year was solar, beginning when the sun enters Mārgaśīrsh, about 5th June; but it has been altered in Madras first to 13th July and in last century to 1st July.

1637 Jan.-Feb. Goa is again besieged by the Dutch, and naval fights recur. The Dutch obtain permission from the Bijāpūr government to erect a fortress at Vingorla, but the permission is soon after withdrawn.

A.D.

1637 Jan. 25. Mr Methwold, in a letter to the Viceroy at Goa, repudiates connection with Courten's Association. The Viceroy fails to comprehend the distinction and orders negotiations to be broken off. Captain Weddell, now the leading instrument of Courten's, fixes agencies at Goa and Battikaloa, obtains a grant for a factory at Achīn, and fixes one at Rājapur.

April 27: Zī-l hijja 1, H. 1046. Aurangzīb returns from the Dekhan with the Nizām-ul-Mulk of Ahmadnagar who is placed in captivity at Gwāliar, where other two Nizāms were already imprisoned.

May 19. Alamgīr Aurangzīb is married to a daughter of Shahnawāz Khān; his brother, Dārā, is married to his cousin Nādira the same day.

June. Charles I., in spite of strong representations from the London Company, issues a new grant to Courten's Association, confirming former privileges. Letters are addressed prohibiting the old Company's ships from trading at any ports where Courten or his agents had established trade.

Chāma Rāja of Maisur dies. His uncle, Immadi Rāja, succeeds, but is poisoned by the minister after eighteen months' reign.

H. 1047. 'Alī Mardān Khān, Persian Governor of Qandahār, gives up the town to Shāhjahān's army. He is appointed Amīr-ul-Umarā and subsequently made Governor of Kābul and Kashmīr.

H. 1047. A'zim Khān recalled from the government of Bengal, and censured for laxity of administration, but appointed Governor of Allahābād. Islām Khān Mashhadi appointed Governor of Bengal. Shāhjī Bhonsla, ordered by Shāhjahān, enters the Bījāpūr service and proceeds to Maisur as second under Randhula Khān.

Oct. 26. The Dutch again blockade Goa till Nov. 26, when they sail to Bassein to destroy the shipbuilding there.

Feb. 23: Newar S., 757. Inscription at Lalitapattana near Katmāndū records the dedication of a temple of Bāla Gopāla (Krishna) by Siddhinrisimhamalla, son of Hariharasimha, son of Śivasimha, son of Mahendramalla, son of Harisimha.

1638 Jan. 4. A further fight off Goa results in the loss of two Dutch ships and one Portuguese.

Jan. 8. The Dutch, requested by the Singhalese to help in

A.D.

1638 ousting the Portuguese, send three ships under Willem Jacobszoon Koster. The Portuguese are defeated near Kandy by Rāja Singha, all being killed except seventy, who are taken captive. May 11, a joint Dutch and Singhalese force attacks Battikaloa, whose commander capitulates on May 18.

S. 1694. Rāja Gaj Singh Rāthor, of Mārwār, killed in Gujarāt. Jaswant Singh, his second son, succeeds, Amara being passed over on account of his violent disposition.

H. 1047. The Magh chief of Chittagāon seeks the protection of Shāhjahān, and is acknowledged as a vassal of the empire, H. 1048. The Assamese invade Bengal, but are defeated by Islām Khān, who follows into Assam and subdues Kuchh Bihār. On his return he finds orders to return to court. Nawāb Saif Khān, deputy for Prince Shujā', succeeds him.

Feb. 25. Prince Aurangzīb, having invaded Baglāna, besieges the Rāja in Mulher, who offers terms, which are accepted, and the fort evacuated June 14. The subjugation of the district is completed July 16.

March 10. Guru Hargovind dies, having nominated his grandson, Har-rāi, as seventh Sikh Guru; he died in 1660.

Ranadhīra Kanthīrava Narasa Rāja succeeds Immadi Rāja Wodeyar in Maisur, and avenges the death of the former ruler.

The Bijāpūr army attack and take Bangalor: Kempe Gauda, the ruler, receives Magadi instead.

An English pirate, having committed acts of robbery on three Portuguese vessels at Dīū, a punitive expedition is despatched. The English at Surat refuse satisfaction, whereon English property at Goa is seized, and Portuguese cargo refused to English ships.

Nov. 15. Goa again blockaded by the Dutch ships till February, when they sail to Ceylon.

Courten's Company opens an agency at Kārwar.

William Tremlen, president of the Surat factory, till 1644.

Dec. 1: Rajab 13, 1048. 'Alī Mardān Khān received at Lāhor, and appointed Governor of Kashmīr.

1639 March. Śrī Ranga Rāyal Rāja of Chandragiri grants permission, through Ayappa Nāyyak of Chingalpat, to Francis Day, chief of the settlement at Ārmugam, to build a fort at Madraspatnam, afterwards called Chennapatnam by the natives.

A.D.

1639 April 29: Zī-l hijja 25, H. 1048. The foundations of the fort at the metropolis of Shāhjahānābād are laid—completed May 13, 1648: Rabī' I. 24, H. 1058.

H. 1049. Sultān Shujā' made Governor of Bengal; Bihār is separated and placed under command of Shāista Khān.

May. Thomas Ivy arrives from Bantam to take charge of the coast factories.

June 24. Pedro da Silva, Viceroy, dies. Dom Francisco, Archbishop of Goa, takes charge till Oct. 4, when Antonio Telles de Menezes enters office as governor.

Nine Dutch ships sail up Goa river, and burn, unopposed, three Portuguese galleons. This is the first direct attack of the Dutch.

Aug. 13. An ambassador from the Nāyyak of Madura promises the fort called "Uthear," undertakes to build churches and to aid the Portuguese.

Aug. The Dutch take Battikaloa and Trinkomalī.

Dec. 29. Muhammad Sultān, eldest son of Aurangzīb, born at Mathurā. He died at Gwāliar, 1665.

1640 Feb. Messrs Cogan and Day leave Ārmugam and arrive at Madraspatnam where on March 1 Fort St George is begun, and finished April 23, St George's Day. The settlement is called Chennapattnam, after the Nāyyak's brother.

H. 1050. The Jām of Nawānagar withholds tribute and sets up a mint. A'zam Khān forces payment with an army and orders the mint to be closed. The Jām complies.

Dr Boughton introduces two English agents to Prince Shujā', Governor of Bengal, who gives encouragement to trade and permits factories at Bālāsor and Hūglī.

Feb. 19. The combined Dutch fleets capture Fort Negambo, Ceylon, but sustain a defeat at Galle. March, joined by Rājasingha II., King of Kandy, the Dutch take Galle; the fortress of St Iago is stormed on March 13. A relieving force under Dom Antonio Mascarenhas retakes the fort on Nov. 8.

May. The Dutch, under instructions from Van Dieman of Batavia, invest Malacca. July, a fleet from the King of Johor

A.D.

1640 joins in the blockade, which continues five months. This ends the Portuguese trade in the Archipelago.

June. The chief of Gondwāna is subdued by Aurangzīb.

Sept. 20. João da Silva-Tello de Menezes, Conde de Aveiras, arrives as Viceroy. He reports home on the existing wretched state of Portuguese India.

Dec. 15. The Portuguese recover their independence at home, crowning the Duke of Braganza as João IV. at Lisbon.

Dec. 24. Manrique, an Augustinian friar, arrives at Agra and proceeds thence to Lāhor.

Charles I. compels the Company to sell to the crown on credit all their store of pepper; this he resells for ready money to merchants. These grievances make it impossible for the Company to raise a joint stock as contemplated.

1641 Jan. 14. A general assault by the Dutch on Malacca causes the final downfall of the Portuguese there.

June 12. A treaty signed between Portugal and the Netherlands for the safeguarding of Dutch and Portuguese ships bound for the East.

Aug. 13: Sha'bān 17, H. 1051. Yamīn-ud-daula, Āsaf Khān, Khān Khānān dies.

Jagat Singh, son of Vāsū, Rāja of Kāngra rebels, and an expedition is sent into his territory; Nūrpūr, Mū, and other forts are taken, and at length Tārāgarh surrenders, and Jagat Singh submits.

1642 H. 1052. A'zam Khān, having made enemies in Gujarāt, is traduced to the emperor and deprived of office. Mirzā 'Īsā Tarkhān, Governor of Surat, is appointed twenty-fourth Viceroy. He introduces the system of levying revenue in kind, called "Bhāgvatī."

Oct. 12. King Venkatāpati of Vijayanagar (or Chandragiri) dies and his nephew, Śrī Ranga Rāyal, is, after much dispute, acknowledged king, Oct. 29.

Oct. 17. The Dutch fleet again off Goa. The Portuguese are continuously molested both in India and Ceylon.

Nov. 3. Francis Day sends a letter from Bālāsor to the Company advising the retention of Bālāsor as a trading station. First direct despatch from Bengal.

A.D.

1642 Richelieu founds a new Company for trading to the Indies. This Company directs its energies to the development of Madagascar.

Dec. An edict is passed opening trade with India to all Portuguese subjects.

1643 March. The Portuguese Commissioners refuse to observe the armistice proclaimed in Europe, and hostilities with the Dutch are renewed.

June: Rabī' II., H. 1053. Aurangzīb announces his intention of withdrawing from the world as a recluse, and is deprived of his government of the Dekhan, and of his honours and income. Khān Daurān Bahādur Nasrat Jang succeeds. Later, on the intercession of his sister, Jahān Ārā Begam, he is restored to favour and to his former rank.

A commissary, Peter Borel, sent from the Dutch at Batavia to Goa to negotiate a treaty of peace with the Portuguese against the English: the cession of Ceylon to the Dutch being the basis of the projected treaty, the negotiations are broken off and the blockade of Goa renewed.

Dec. 22. A Dutch fleet appears off Galle, where the Portuguese were already besieged. An engagement results in a victory for the Dutch.

1644 Jan. 3. Negambo fortress is taken by the Dutch from the Portuguese.

H. 1054. 'Alī Mardān Khān, with Murād Bakhsh, the emperor's fourth son, makes a successful invasion to recover Balkh and Badakhshān and to chastise Tardī 'Alī Katghan. The army returns and little results from the expedition.

July 25: Jumāda I. 6. Amara Singh Rāthor, son of Gaj Singh, stabs the Mīr Bakhshi, Salābat Khān, in presence of the emperor at Agra. He is cut down at a gate of the fort.

The Bijāpūr conquest of Maisur is now complete, and a province formed out of the districts of Bangalor, Hoskot, Kolar, Dod Balapur, Chitaldurg, and Sira.

July 10. The Court of Directors institute an inquiry into the conduct of Andrew Cogan, agent at Madras, for the building of Fort St George.

A.D.

1644 Francis Breton appointed president of the Surat factory, till his death in 1649.

Nov. 10. The treaty of 1641 between the Dutch and Portuguese recognised at last at Goa. In accordance with this, Ceylon is parcelled out into provinces.

The fifth (or Colbert's) French East India Company is formed.

1645 Jan. Mr Gabriel Boughton, surgeon of the "Hopewell," sent to Agra by the Surat Council as surgeon to Shāhjahān. He succeeds in saving the life of the emperor's favourite daughter, Princess Jahān Ārā Begam, who had been severely burnt. In reward he is granted a patent for his countrymen to trade throughout the empire free of customs; this privilege was extended to the E.I. Company.

Feb. 27: Zī-l hijja 29, H. 1054. Prince Aurangzīb is appointed Viceroy of Gujarāt, Mu'izzul Mulk remaining as minister. This period is marked by disputes between the Hindus and the Musalmans.

H. 1055. Rāja Jagat Singh, brother of the Rāja of Kotā, with 14,000 Rājputs invades Badakhshān and Balkh. Prince Murād Bakhsh, with 'Alī Mardān Khān in command, is despatched thither, Zī-l hijja 30, H. 1055, Feb. 28, 1646.

Sept. 10. Dom Philippe Mascarenhas, the newly appointed Viceroy, arrives at Ceylon and remains there a year.

The Tāj Mahāl at Agra completed by Shāhjahān, as the tomb of Arjumānd Bānu Begam Mumtāz Mahal, who died in 1631.

Nov. 15. A *Kaul* is granted by Śrī Ranga to the English factors at Madras, freeing them from customs and granting them the administration of the town.

Cogan's conduct as Company's agent at Madras is vindicated.

Dec. 17: Shawwāl 29. Nūr Jahān Begam, widow of Jahāngīr, dies.

Dec. 30. Dom Philippe Mascarenhas is installed as Viceroy at Goa.

1646 Feb. 17: Zī-l hijja 29, H. 1055. Prince Murād Bakhsh, with 'Alī Mardān Khān, leaves for Balkh. June, takes Balkh, conquers the country and puts Nāzar Muhammad to flight.

A.D.

1646 The Prince insists on returning to India. Sa'dullah Khān replaces him as governor, settles the province, and returns Sept. 16: Sha'bān 5, H. 1056.

April 30. The Japanese embassy leaves Goa, and winters at Macao.

Śivājī Bhonsla obtains possession of the strong fort of Tornā, pretending to hold it for Bijāpūr, but fortifies in his own interest the neighbouring hill of Mhorbudh.

The Golkonda forces take Chandragiri and Chingalpat. Śrī Ranga Rāyal flees to the protection of Śivappa Nāyyaka of Bednūr who gives him the government of Sakrāypatna in Kadūr district of Kūrg.

July 31. Emmanuel Barradas, Ethiopian scholar, dies at Goa.

The King of Portugal orders a policy of conciliation towards the native princes who may be induced to fight the Dutch; the Maldive chief signs a treaty of vassalage to Portugal.

1647 Jan. A great famine in Madras.

Jan. 31: Zī-l hijja 24, H. 1056. Prince Aurangzīb appointed Governor of Balkh and Badakhshān provinces. Feb. 20: Muharram 15, H. 1057, he leaves for his province, then overrun by Uzbaks under 'Abdul 'Azīz. April, he reaches Kābul, and proceeds towards Balkh, is opposed by the Uzbaks and Alamāns, but arrives June 4, and defeats the armies of 'Abdul 'Azīz Khān, the son of the dispossessed King Nāzar Muhammad. Nāzar Muhammad Khān fails to get help in Persia. Shāhjahān at length abandons his conquest. Sept. 14, Aurangzīb is recalled, leaves Chalkai, and returns to Kābul pursued by attacks of the Uzbaks. Oct. 3: Ramazān 4, 1057 H., Balkh province is transferred to Nāzar Muhammad.

Shāista Khān appointed twenty-eighth Viceroy of Gujarāt, till 1648.

Śivājī usurps his father's jāgīr, and begins predatory expeditions by which he obtains possession of several forts.

Shāh Shujā' recalled from Bengal. Aitkad Khān, a younger brother of Shāista Khān, is put in his place, and Shujā' is appointed Governor of Kābul.

Courten's Company, by coining counterfeit pagodas and reals at Madagascar, brings the English in India into disrepute.

A.D.

1647 July 26. The embassy from Goa to Japan arrives at the island of Cavallos, and meets with opposition, but is allowed to depart peaceably, though with nothing accomplished.

The Dutch establish trade at Sadras.

H. 1057. The *Pādshāhnāma* or *Tārikh-i Shāh-Jahānī Dahsāla*, of Muhammad Amīn Kaswīnī, comprising the history of the first ten years of Shāhjahān's reign is finished, and dedicated to the emperor.

1648 March 3. Two Amsterdam merchants leave Genoa to trade, peaceably, if possible, in India. At Madagascar quarrels ensue as to command: a captain is put in irons, and the voyage continued. Pepper taken in at the Malay Peninsula, but not paid for.

Śivājī revolts openly against the Bijāpūr government, and takes possession of the northern Konkan, making Kalyān his capital.

Thada Dhammā, Rāja of Burma, dies. Bengtale, surnamed Grāhtāpdaraga, succeeds.

Aug. 16. The Arabs besiege and take Maskat, the last stronghold of the Portuguese on the Persian Gulf.

At Macao the Portuguese governor is put to death by the natives. His successor refuses to take up the appointment.

Bengal silk introduced into the English Company's investments. The communications of the year are kept secret: no despatches sent owing to civil war and depression of trade.

H. 1058. Sultān Dārā Shikoh is appointed twenty-seventh Viceroy of Gujarāt.

Dec. 26: Zī-l hijja 10, H. 1058. Shāh 'Abbās II. of Persia arrives before Qandahār and invests the city. Aurangzīb despatched with an army, but prevented by snowstorms from reaching it.

1649 Feb. 7-13. The Dutch under Maetsuycker land infantry at Manappadu, seize the pagoda of Tiruchendūr, eject the Portuguese from Tutikorin and sack the town.

Feb. 25: Safar 12, H. 1059. The Persians recover Qandahār from Daulat Khān the Mughal governor.

May 25: Jumāda I. 12. Aurangzīb with his army arrives

A.D.

1649 before Qandahār, but from lack of engines and provisions, after an indecisive battle with the Persians, Shāhjahān withdraws his forces and leaves for Hindustan, Oct. 26: Ramazan 8.

Prince Shujā' is again made Governor of Bengal.

The Bijāpūr government seizes Shāhjī Bhonsla as a hostage for Śivājī, who appeals to Shāhjahān. Shāhjī is released, but his son renews his policy of aggression.

July 21. Francis Breton, president of the Surat factory, dies. Capt. Jeremy Blackman succeeds, till 1655.

Oct. 28. The E.I. Co. petition the Council of State for an Act of Parliament in support of the East India trade, specifying their losses by Courten's Association. Nov. 10, the Assada Merchants propose to unite with the London Company. Nov. 2, this Union is accomplished, but only two ships are sent to India this year.

The Venetian physician Manucci arrives at Agra and resides at the court for forty-eight years, compiling memoirs of the Mughal sovereigns.

S. 769: Feb. 22. Inscription at Katmandū of Jayapratāpamalladeva, son of Lakshminrisimha, son of Hariharasimha, recording the dedication of a temple built "for the sake of" two queens, Rupāmatī and Rājāmatī.

1650 Nov. 14. The new Company, now designated "The United Joint Stock Company," petition Parliament for redress of grievances and compensation from the Dutch for their ejection from the Spice Islands.

Dec. 14. In the instructions to the Bālāsor factors, Mr Boughton, surgeon, is mentioned as likely to procure from the Prince, Shāh Shujā' a *farmān* to "outstrip the Dutch in point of privilege and freedom."

1651 The King of Golkonda and the Nawāb Mirzā Mulī cease to ask for trading passports, thus showing that the Portuguese power was no longer formidable.

May 31. The new Viceroy having died, a commission of three: Dom Francisco de Martyres, Antonio de Sousa Coutinho, and Francisco de Mello de Castro, takes office at Goa.

July 1: Rajab 12, H. 1061. An expedition is appointed to

A.D.

1651 proceed from Kashmīr to Tibet to subdue a rebel, Mīrza Jān, and to capture Fort Skhardu. Aug. 15, Sha'bān 27, intelligence of the success of this expedition received. Tibet annexed to the Dehli empire.

An English factory at Hūglī is established: Bridgeman and Stevens are the first factors.

Capt. Jeremy Blackman appointed president of the Surat factory and ordered to make a survey of all Surat dependencies. Private trade disallowed, but increased privileges obtained from the Mughal court by Mr Davidge.

The Dutch abandon St Helena, which is taken possession of by the English.

1652 May 16: Jumāda II. 3, H. 1062. Prince Aurangzīb and Jamdat-ul-Mulk Sā'adulla Khān arrive before Qandahār and invest the fortress. Shāhjahān reaches Kābul, April 14; but after a siege of two months and eight days Shāhjahān withdraws the army and retires to Hindustan.

Dārā Shikoh, Governor of Gujarāt since 1648, is succeeded by Shāista Khān.

June 14. The fort on the island of Kamboli invested by Śivāppa Nāyyak of Bednūr—a regular siege begun on Sept. 6.

August. Cromwell declares war on the Dutch for their oppression of the English Company and for other reasons.

Sept. 6. Dom Vasco de Mascarenhas, Conde de Obidos, takes office as Viceroy at Goa.

Sept. 24. Mīr Muhammad, Ardistānī, styled Mīr Jumla, takes the fort of Gandikot, in Kadapa.

Chandri Phul, ancestor of the chiefs of Patiāla, Jhind, and Nabhā, dies.

Oct. 24. A Portuguese fleet repulsed. Nov., a second fleet harasses the natives.

Mr Aaron Baker first agent for the Madras settlement.

The Council at Madras remonstrate against the Court's order to discontinue the Fort St George fortifications, as the Dutch had strengthened theirs at Palikāt.

A.D.

1653 Jan. 15. A third Portuguese fleet arrives before Kamboli, and takes on board the garrison, leaving the fort dismantled.

H. 1063. Dāra Shikoh sent with a large force against Qandahār. All efforts failing to take it, a retreat is begun, Oct. 7: Zī-lqa'da 15.

Mutiny breaks out among the Gujarāt troops.

Oct. 15. The Portuguese Viceroy is deposed by revolutionaries led by Dom Braz de Castro, who usurped the office for nearly two years.

An English factory, previously established at Lucknow, is abandoned. Trade at the other factories suspended on account of the war with the Dutch.

Fort St George, Madras, which had previously been subordinate to the chief at Bantam in Java, is raised to a presidency, though possessing only a garrison of twenty-three men. Mr Aaron Baker, the agent, is made first Governor.

The English lose four ships to the Dutch in the Persian Gulf.

H. 1064. The *Farhang-i-Rashīdī*, the first critical dictionary of the Persian language, written by Mīr 'Abdul Rashīd.

1654 March. The Dutch, defeated by the Portuguese at sea, lose Kalutara, in Ceylon, and retire upon Galle.

April 5. The war between England and Holland terminated by the Treaty of Westminster, Articles 27 and 30 of which provide that compensation be awarded for losses in the East sustained by the English. Aug., the Dutch agree to restore Polarūn, pay an indemnity of £85,000 to the London Company, and £3,615 to the heirs of the Amboyna sufferers.

Aug. 12. Muhammad 'Ādil Khān marches with an army against Goa and Bardes, but is forced to retire. Oct., a further attempt made on Salsette. Sarzora is taken, but news arriving of the Portuguese general's approach on Rachol; peace is concluded in December.

Oct. 4. Zī-l qa'da 22, H. 1064. Allāmi despatched to chastise Jagat Singh, Rānā of Udaypur, for fortifying Chitor. The Rānā sends expressions of humility, and the fort is demolished.

S. 1710. Rāja Rānā Singh succeeds his father, Jagat Singh, at Udaypur.

A.D.

1654 Murād Bakhsh appointed twenty-ninth Viceroy of Gujarāt, till 1657.

Nov. Colombo besieged by the Dutch, but not taken. Dec. 10., a similar attempt on Kalutara fails. Dec. 16., the Dutch defeat the Portuguese at Bentota.

The Syrian Christians of Malabar, having asked the Jacobite Patriarch for a Metran, Ahattala or Theodore, a Syrian, is sent. On landing at Mailapur, he is seized by the Portuguese and sent to Goa, where he is burnt as a heretic.

The civil establishment at Fort St George reduced to two factors, and its military force to ten soldiers.

The trade of India thrown open for three years. The "Merchant Adventurers' Company" formed.

1655 March. The Portuguese in Ceylon defeat Rāja Singha's troops, and drive them to Kandy.

The proprietors of the Third and Fourth Joint Stocks and of the United Stock Co. petition Cromwell, each claiming the exclusive right to Polarūn and the £85,000 claimed from the Dutch. Pending a decision, the money is vested in trustees.

H. 1065. Aurangzīb intrigues with Mīr Jumla, minister at Golkonda, for the downfall of 'Abdullah Qutb Shāh.

Aug. 23. Dom Rodrigo Sobho de Silveira, Conde de Sarzedos, assumes office as Viceroy, and apprehends the usurper, Dom Braz de Castro, together with his chief adherents.

Sept. 1. The Company's United Joint Stock stood thus:—Debit £29,271. 19s. 4d. Credit £185,589. 7s. Nathaniel Wyche is appointed president of the Surat factory in succession to Capt. Jeremy Blackman.

Job Charnock arrives in India, and obtains employment under the E.I. Co. in Bengal.

1656 Jan. 3. Dom Rodrigo da Silveira dies at Goa, perhaps from poison. Jan. 14, Manuel Mascarenhas Homem is elected Viceroy by the States. The Succession Patents added that Francisco de Mello e Castro and Antonio de Sousa Coutinho were to be joint-governors. The next Viceroy dying on the voyage out, the Commission hold office till June 14, 1661.

Jan.: Rabī' I. 20, H. 1066. Aurangzīb makes a treacherous

A.D.

1656 attack on Golkonda. 'Abdullah Qutb Shāh flees to the fortress of Golkonda, whence he agrees to the terms imposed, April 25: to give one of his daughters in marriage to Sultān Muhammad, with dowry and territory, to pay a karor of rupees, and to become tributary.

April 16: Jumāda II. 22 H. 1066. Allāmī Sa'ādulla Khān dies.

April. Shāh Shujā' grants letters patent to the English E.I. Co. to trade duty free in Bengal and Orissa.

May 7. Colombo, besieged by the Dutch, now attacked. May 12, the Portuguese evacuate the town.

Chinsura factory established by the Dutch.

Mr Revington appointed president of Surat factory.

The Koh-i-nūr diamond found at Kolhāpur on the Krishnā and presented by Mīr Jumla to Shāhjahān.

Nov.: Muharram, H. 1067. Muhammad 'Ādil Shāh of Bījāpūr dies. His son 'Alī's succession disputed, and a Mughal force sent to occupy the country.

Nov. Streynsham Master arrives at Surat with his uncle, George Oxinden.

Introduction of the *San-i-jalus*, "year of the reign," in the Southern Konkan—a solar year, though following Hijra reckoning, and running on from this date.

Pope Paul IV. having sent a commission of four Discalceat Carmelites to inquire into the Jesuits' dealings in Malabar, two of them arrive at Surat and proceed to Malabar, and after the death of the Jesuit archbishop in 1659 they were left in possession of the mission, one of them being appointed Vicar Apostolic: died 1689.

1657 Jan. 7: Rabī' I. 21, H. 1067. An expedition under the Khān Khānān leaves Khizrpur for the conquest of Eastern Bengal. Jan. 14, the city of Kuch Bihār taken.

Jan. 12-13. Job Charnock entered on the court books as junior member of council at Kāsimbazar at a salary of £20.

Jan. 27. Upon petition alleging that evil had resulted from the open trade, the Council of State in England decide that the East India trade should be carried on by the Company or a

A.D.

1657 United Joint Stock, exclusive of all others. Feb. 10, Cromwell confirms this decision, rejecting the arguments of the Merchant Adventurers for open trade, and grants a new charter for seven years. The Merchant Adventurers depress the Fort St George trade. The Company withdraw the Bengal factories. At Bantam the Dutch bribe the servants of the London Company to desert: the station, however, is kept on.

The E.I. Co. begin attempting to settle permanently at St Helena.

Jan. 11: Nepāla Sam. 778. Inscription at Kātmāndū of Mahārājādhirāja Jāyapratāpamalladeva, composed by the king himself, recording the presentation to the temple of the king's weight in gold, silver, and pearls, together with 100 horses.

April 26: Rajab 12. 'Alī Mardān Khān, Amīr-ul Umarā, dies.

April. Aurangzīb prosecutes war with Bijāpūr, reaches Zafarābād Bīdar, April 10, and Kalyānī May 14, which is captured Sept. 22, and a hasty peace with Bijāpūr is arranged.

Prince Sulaimān Shikoh and Prince Sultān Muhammad sent to Gwāliar by Aurangzīb, and killed by slow poison.

May 10: Sha'bān 6. The city of Karkalu, in Assam, taken by Khān Khānān after five months' siege.

Mokand Singh succeeds to the throne of Kotā.

May. Śivājī commits his first acts of hostility on the Mughals, plundering Junnar and partially looting Ahmadnagar.

Zī-l hijja 1067. Shahjahān's illness recalls Aurangzīb to Aurangābād. Dārā Shikoh takes the defensive against him. Shujā' marches on Agra, but is defeated by Sulaimān, Dārā's son, and returns to Bengal. Prince Morād Bakhsh proclaims himself emperor, kills 'Alī Naqi, his minister, but afterwards joins Aurangzīb, and marches against Jaswant Singh, leader of the imperial troops.

Sept. 25. Manoel Mascarenhas Homem, Governor at Goa, dies, and Francisco de Mello e Castro and Antonio de Sousa Coutinho govern by commission.

The *Rājasekhara Vilasa*, a poem by the Lingayat author, Shadakshara Deva, written.

1658 Feb. Dutch forces under Rijklof van Goens occupy Tuticorin;

A.D.

1658 Manār surrenders on Feb. 22; Jafnapatam yields on April 27, a relieving squadron being defeated on March 23.

April. Mokand Singh of Kotā and three brothers fall in defence of Shāhjahān at the battle of Ujjain. Kishor Singh survives and ascends the throne.

April 25: Rajab 22, H. 1068. Princes Aurangzīb and Murād Bakhsh defeat the imperial army under Jaswant Singh at Dharmatpur, near Ujjain, and march to meet their elder brother, Dārā Shikoh.

Khān Muhammad, minister at Bijāpūr, assassinated.

June 8: Ramazān 7, H. 1068. Aurangzīb and Murād Bakhsh defeat Dārā Shikoh at Samūgarh (Fathābād), between Agra and Dholpur, and Dārā flees by Agra and Dehli to Lāhor. Aurangzīb enters Dehli, June 11. Shāhjahān is made prisoner in the fort. June 23, Aurangzīb and Murād Bakhsh proceed after Dārā. At Mathurā, July 5, Aurangzīb proposes to celebrate Murād's accession to whom he had hitherto sworn allegiance, fills him drunk, seizes and fetters him and sends him to prison in Salīmgarh fort, but afterwards transfers him to Gwāliar where he was put to death, Dec. 25, 1660.

AURANGZĪB 'ĀLAMGIR.

1658 July 30: Zī-l qa'da 1, H. 1068. Aurangzīb openly assumes the government at Dehli and is formally proclaimed as 'Ālamgīr.

The Bengal settlements put under the Presidency of Fort St George (Madras), the agencies at Kāsimbazar Bālāsor and Pātna being subordinate to that at Hūglī. Surat the chief presidency.

Cromwell, without consulting the Company, grants a licence to Mr Rolt to export on his own account three mortars and 20,000 shells to Col. Rainsford at Surat. The Company petition the Protector to prohibit this illicit trade and direct the Surat Council to seize and dispose of the articles.

The fort and palace at Shāhjahānābād (New Dehli) completed.

Sept. Hājji Khalfa dies—author of *Fazlaka*, the *Kashf-uz-Zunān*, and a chronology.

Sept. Aurangzīb on reaching Lahor learns that Dārā had proceeded by Multān to Bhakkar in Sindh and thence to Gujarāt;

A.D.

1658 but hearing that his elder brother, Sultān Shujā', was advancing on Agra, he left an officer to besiege Bhakkar and hurried back.

Sept. A Portuguese plot to murder the Dutch and recapture Negapatam is discovered and frustrated.

Har-rāi with his Sikhs joined Dārā Shikoh when he came to the Panjāb, but when Dārā was beaten he withdrew to Kīratpur, sending his eldest son Rām-rāi with an apology to Aurangzīb, who retained him as a hostage.

1659 Jan. 15: Jumāda I. 1, H. 1069. Shāh Shujā' with his Bengal army is defeated by Aurangzīb at Khajwā about 30 miles west of Allahābād. Feb. 2, Shujā''s governor gives up Allahābād, and Shāh Shujā' returns to Bengal.

Dārā Shikoh is acknowledged emperor in Gujarat, but after a desperate contest lasting for two days, March 22 and 23, at Ajmir, he is defeated by Aurangzīb, and flees to Ahmadābād, but finds the gates shut against him. He then crosses into Sindh and seeks help from Malik Jiwān the Barozai chief of Shādar, who betrays him and his son Sipahr to Aurangzīb's foster-brother, Bahādur Khān. They were sent to Aurangzīb, and Dārā was put to death in prison, Zī-l hijja 21, 1069, by order of the emperor.

June 8: Ramazān 17. Prince Muhammad Sultān leaves Mīr Jumla at Rājmahāl, and goes over to his uncle, Shāh Shujā', but returns Feb. 19, 1660, to Mīr Jumla's camp.

Later, Sultān Shujā' flees with his family to Arakan; the king, Sanda Thudhammā, on the refusal of Shujā' to give him a daughter in marriage, attacks him, takes the prince prisoner, and drowns him in a sack. His sons are put to death, while his wife and two daughters commit suicide.

Jaswant Singh appointed thirty-second Viceroy of Gujarāt, till 1662.

Sept. A Bijāpūr army under Afzal Khān sent to Wāī. Śivājī temporises, and treacherously murders Afzal Khān. Panhālā is surrendered and thence Śivājī captures the neighbouring forts. Dec., Rustam Zamān's army from Bījāpūr is defeated at Panhālā.

Sir Thomas Chamber, Governor of Madras, gives a *kaul* to Pedda Nāyyak, who undertakes to guard Chennapatnam (Madraspatnam). Twenty peons form the force.

A.D.

1659 The forts on the Malabar coast are made subordinate to Surat.

Kanthīrava of Maisur dies childless, and Dodda Deva Rāja, grandson of Chāma Rāja Bola, succeeds. He adds to his kingdom by conquests from Madura and Bednūr.

Tirumala Nāyyak of Madura dies. His son, Vīrappa, succeeds.

1660 Jan.: Jumāda I., H. 1070. Shāista Khān, Amīr-ul-Umarā, marches from Aurangābād against Śivājī, who had plundered Rājpur and Dabhol. March 14: Rajab 1, the imperial army occupies Seogānw, where Śivājī loots their baggage. The army takes Śivapur and Poona.

Chākan is invested and taken after five months' siege. Purenda surrendered by its commander, Ghalib, without fighting.

The three powers of the Southern Konkan—Bijāpūr, the Siddis of Janjirā, and the Sāwants of Wādī—unite against Śivājī.

Sept. Śivājī, after four months' siege in Panhālā fort by the Bijāpūr army under Siddi Johār, escapes to Rāngna by a pretended surrender.

H. 1071. Mīr Jumla Mu'azzam Khān appointed Governor of Bengal, stops the English saltpetre trade, but again admits it.

The canons at Goa contest the archbishopric, and armed conflicts ensue.

July. Negapatam capitulates to the Dutch under Joan van der Laan. The Portuguese are completely expelled from Ceylon.

Nov. The States General order the Governor-General of Batavia to cede Polarūn to the London Company. The Governor of Banda under secret orders destroys all the spice trees in the island.

Guru Har-rāi, the seventh Sikh Guru, dies at Kīratpur, having nominated his second son, Harkisan, as his successor,—the eldest being kept at Dehli by Aurangzīb as a hostage. Some accounts place this at a later date. Harkisan died about 1664.

1661 Jan. 13: Jumāda I. 11, H. 1071. Sulaimān Shikoh given up to Aurangzīb by the Rāja of Śrīnagar. He with his brother, Sipahr, and the young son of Murād are put to death at Gwāliar.

Jan. 'Alī 'Ādil Shāh of Bijāpūr regains most of the forts taken by Śivājī, who, however, continues war against the Siddis

A.D.

1661 Feb. Sir Edward Winter takes office as agent at Fort St George. The factory at Hūglī is threatened by Mīr Jumla, in consequence of the agent's having seized a native junk as security for the recovery of debts.

H. 1071. 'Abdul Nabi, Governor of Mathurā, builds the great mosque in that city.

April 3. Charles II. grants a new charter "for ever," confirming former privileges and authorising the E.I. Company to make peace or war with any non-Christian prince or people, to erect fortifications, maintain armies, administer justice, and to have the right of sending unlicensed persons to England.

May. The King of Burma with his family captured by the Prince of Prome and drowned in the River Hkyengdweng. The Prome prince takes the title of Mahāpawāra Dhammā Rājā.

June 23. The marriage treaty between Charles II. of England and Catherina of Braganza is signed, by which Bombay island is ceded to the English as part of the dowry of the Infanta Catherina on her marriage with Charles II., but its occupation withheld for four years on various pretences.

June 14. A new Patent of Succession nominates Dom Manuel Mascarenhas, Luiz de Mendoza Furtado, and Dom Pedro de Lancastre to be governors at Goa. The first-named not accepting, the others assume office, till Dec. 14, 1662.

H. 1072. Mīr Jumla invades Kuch Bihār, and the Rāja taking flight, he occupies the capital, Nov. 20: Rabī' I. 27; he re-names it Alamgīrnagar and proceeds to Assam.

Dec. 14: Rabī' II. 21. Murād Bakhsh is put to death at Gwāliar.

Dec. The Dutch take Quilon or Kollam; they agree to reinstate the Cochin Rāja and afford him protection from the Portuguese, who, however, repel an attack upon the town.

1662 Jan. 15. Cranganor, after fifteen days' siege, is assaulted and taken by the Dutch in a desperate assault; most of the churches and other buildings destroyed; and the Portuguese soldiers were taken back to Europe.

Feb. The Dutch take Kollam and attack Cochin, put the Nāyars to flight and capture the queen. After a month they raise the siege, but renew it in October, when the Portuguese

A.D.

1662 surrender. Their possessions in India are now reduced to Goa and Dīū.

March 27: Sha'bān 6, H. 1072. Ghargānw, the capital of Assam, taken by Mīr Jumla. The natives harass the cavalry's movements and cut off supplies. Nov.: Rabi' I., Mīr Jumla renews the campaign in Assam and the Rāja flees to the hills.

May-Aug. Dangerous illness of Aurangzīb. Attempts are made to restore Shāhjahān. Dec. 6, Aurangzīb recovers, and departs for Kashmīr, till Oct. 1663.

H. 1072. Śivājī conquers Sāwantwādi. The Sāwants, after seeking protection at Goa, are restored by Śivājī whose tributaries they become.

Sept. 18. The English fleet, under the Earl of Marlborough and Sir Abraham Shipman, arrive at Bombay and demand the cession of the island and dependencies. The Portuguese governor raises technical difficulties, and offers to retain Bombay for the English till he should receive authority from Portugal. The troops, refused a landing at Surat, are landed at Anjidīva.

Sept. 29. Antonio de Mello e Castro arrives at Bombay as Portuguese governor.

Sir George Oxinden succeeds Mr Andrews as "president and chief director of Surat factory and all other factories" in the north parts of India. His salary to be 250 rupees per mensim, with a yearly gratuity of 2,000 rupees as a compensation for private trade: till 1669.

Oct. 6. The East India Company are forced to surrender their African trade to a new African Company.

1663 Jan. 7. A treaty between the Dutch and Portuguese at Cochin is signed, providing terms of surrender of the town, artillery, &c., disposal of the native population and the removal of unmarried Portuguese to Europe.

Jan. 16: Jumāda II. 6, H. 1073. The Rāja of Assam submits to Mīr Jumla.

March 14. Publication of the Treaty of Peace between the States General and Portugal of Aug. 6, 1661, in terms of which Cannanor and Cochin are claimed by the Portuguese, but no redress is found.

The Dutch expel all European Romish priests, and Alexander

A.D.

1663 de Campo, a native, is consecrated Bishop of the Indo-Syrian Church: he died 1676.

March 28. Charles II. of England solicits the protection of the King of Bantam for his subjects there. A fortified station ordered for Polarūn.

March 31: Ramazān 2. Mīr Jumla dies at Khizarpur in Kūch Bihār. Shāista Khān, his successor, is permitted to govern by his deputy, Dā'ūd Khān, till 1664.

April. Shāista Khān occupies Poonā, which is, however, secretly entered by Śivājī at night (April 9), when Shāista Khān is wounded and one of his sons cut to pieces.

Aug. 16. The King of Portugal issues orders to the Viceroy to cede Bombay. Nov. 23, Charles II. issues a commission to Sir Abraham Shipman to take over Bombay from the Portuguese.

The Dutch still refuse to cede Polarūn, under secret orders from Europe. British trade at Bantam suffers in consequence.

English factories attempted at Pātna, Kāsimbazar, and Bālāsor are ordered to be discontinued and purchases and sales made at Hūglī only. Major F. Willoughby appointed governor of the island of Palarūn at a salary of £50 per annum for five years.

1664 Jan. Shāhjī Bhonsla, father of Śivājī, is killed by a fall in hunting.

Jan. 15: Jumāda II. 15, H. 1074. Śivājī plunders Surat. The English hold out in the factory under Sir George Oxinden with such courage that Aurangzīb grants exemption from a portion of the customs exacted from traders of other nations.

Śivājī assumes the title of Rāja. With his reign begins the *Rāj-ābhishēk* era of the Marāthās.

Feb. 8. The King of Portugal enjoins obedience to the Bombay treaty.

On the death of Rānmalji, Jām of Nawānagar, disputes ensue, and his brother, Rāi Singh, is defeated by Qutb-ud-din; Nawānagar is captured and annexed by the Mughals.

Aug. 1. Mr Mathias Vincent, chief of the Bay of Hūglī factory, comes out as factor at £20 per annum.

Job Charnock appointed chief of Pātna factory.

A.D.

1664 Aug. Śivājī's fleet captures Mughal ships bound for Mokha: he plunders the pettah of Ahmadnagar. Oct., he defeats the Bijāpūr army, which had broken the truce of 1663.

Oct. Sir Abraham Shipman, with about 300 soldiers, perishes at Anjidīva, the Portuguese refusing to comply with the treaty, his secretary, Humphrey Cooke, is compelled to accede to a treaty drawn up by the Goa governor, by which only Bombay, without any of its dependencies, is handed to the English.

Har-kisan, the Sikh Guru, being summoned to Dehli, he died there of small-pox, but had indicated Tēg-bahādur of Bakālā as his successor. He took up his residence at Mākhovāl on the Satlaj, since called Ānandpur. He lived for a time in seclusion at Pātnā.

A French East India Company, "Compagnie des Indes," formed under the ministry of Colbert. Eight armed vessels fitted out under command of Hubert Hugo, a Dutch pirate.

1665 Jan. 17. A Commission leaves Goa to carry out the decision of the Court regarding the cession of Bombay, which takes place Feb. 18. The Portuguese levy heavy imposts on boats passing Karanjā and Thāna. Sir Humphrey Cooke, governor, resists the demand.

Gregory, the first Jacobite Metran or Bishop of the Syrian Christians, arrives in Malabar and is welcomed by the Dutch: he died 1672.

Feb. Śivājī attacks the English factory at Kārwār, and exacts a contribution of £112.

March. The survivors of the troops at Anjidīva are ordered to Fort St George.

March 25. The Dutch at length cede Polarūn to the English, but in so desolated a condition as to render it unproductive for eight years.

H. 1075. Rāja Jaysingh, Kachhwāha, sent to the Dekhan with Diler Khān, invests Rājgarh and Kondāna forts, held by Śivājī, who is induced to offer submission and is promised a *mansab*, or military rank, in the imperial army; he surrenders June 22. July, Śivājī enters the camp of Diler Khān and in Dec. co-operates with the Mughals against Bijāpūr.

Aug. Mr George Foxcroft arrives at Madras as Governor of

A.D.

1665 Fort St George. Sept. 16, the ex-governor, Sir Edward Winter, makes an armed attack, imprisons Foxcroft, his son, and Mr Jeremy Sambrooke, second in Council, under the accusation of their having uttered seditious and treasonable expressions against the king's government. He reassumes the agency and keeps the governor under restraint in the fort, till Aug. 22, 1668.

1666 Jan. 5. The Goa Viceroy complains to the King of Portugal of alleged excesses committed by the English in Bombay.

Jan. 8: Rajab 2, H. 1076. Bījāpūr invested by Rāja Jaysingh and Diler Khān with the help of Śivājī. Several forts are captured.

Feb. 2: Rajab 26, H. 1076. Shāhjahān, having lived seven years as a prisoner of Aurangzīb, attended by his daughter, Jahānārā, dies at Dehli in his seventy-fifth year.

The Mughals under Shāista Khān take Chittagāon by siege. It is annexed to Bengal and named Islāmābād. Sangrāmnagar is captured and renamed Alamgīrnagar.

Śivājī and his son, Sambhājī, are called to the Mughal Court, ungraciously received by Aurangzīb and kept in restraint. Aug. 31: Safar 29, H. 1077. Śivājī escapes, arriving at Rājgarh in December.

Sept. 2-6. The Company's saltpetre and pepper warehouses, under the Exchange, are destroyed by the Great Fire in London.

Oct. 17. João Nuno da Cunha, Conde de Vicente, takes office as Viceroy at Goa.

Nov. 5. Sir Gervase Lucas arrives at Bombay, sent out by the king, as governor, and imprisons the acting governor, Humphrey Cooke, secretary to the late Sir A. Shipman, for extortion and peculation.

The Dutch seize and reoccupy Polarūn, ceded by treaty to the English.

1667 May 21. Sir Gervase Lucas, Governor of Bombay, dies. May 22, Captain Henry Garey, Deputy-Governor of Bombay till Sept. 23, 1668.

Mr Walter Hooke chaplain at Madras.

H. 1077. Muhammad Amīn Khān, son of Mīr Jumla, appointed Governor of Kābul.

A.D.

1667 June 5: V.S. 1724. Stone inscription at Rāmnagar of King Hridayeśa and his wife Sundarīdevī, enumerating the kings of Mandala from Yādavarāya.

June 25. Sir George Oxinden obtains from Aurangzīb a *farmān* reducing the customs payable by the English at Surat from 3 to 2 per cent.

Jaysingh retires from Bijāpūr and Golkonda. July 20: Muharram 28, H. 1078, he dies at Burhānpur: said to have been killed by his son Kirat Singh, to whom Aurangzīb had promised the succession. Rām Singh succeeds to the throne of Jaypur, but is ordered to Gāwahati in Assam where he remains till 1675, H. 1086.

July 31. Polarūn ceded to the Dutch by the treaty of Breda.

Sultān Mu'azzam succeeds Jaysingh as Sūbahdār of the Dekhan and comes to terms with Śivājī, who receives, through the prince, the title of Rāja, confirmation of the *mansab* for Sambhājī, and a *jāgīr* in Berār.

Dec. 24. A French ship under M. Caron, with a Persian, Markara, on board, lands at Cochin and is well received.

1668 H. 1078. Śivājī obtains an army from 'Abdullah Qutb Shāh for the recapture of certain forts now in the hands of the Bījāpūr king. He takes Sātāra, Panhālā, and other forts, and occupies Rājgarh.

Jan. 24. The Court of Directors grant permission to the Hūglī factors to establish a factory at Dacca (Dhākā).

1078. Bahādar Khān, Khān Jahān, formerly Viceroy of Allahābād, appointed thirty-fourth Viceroy of Gujarāt, till 1671.

May 14: Zī-l hijja 1. Samaji, a town near Thatta, destroyed by earthquake.

May. 'Abd-ul Nabi, Governor of Mathurā, killed in the battle of Sahora, fought with a local rebel.

Aug. 22. Mr Foxcroft released and reinstated for one year in the governorship of Madras by a Commission under Sir William Langhorne.

Sept. 23. Bombay transferred by Charles II. to the E.I. Company "in free and common soccage, as of the manor of East Greenwich on payment of an annual rent of £10 in gold

A.D.
1668 on 30th September in each year." Sir George Oxinden first Governor of Bombay. Humphrey Cooke, ex-governor, concerts with the Goa Jesuits for an attack on Bombay, but is proclaimed a traitor.

The Court of Directors orders the agent at Bantam to send home by their ships 100 lbs. weight of the best tea: the first mention of it in their accounts.

Nov. 6. Nuno da Cunha, Viceroy, dies. The Letters Patent contain names of a Commission, viz.:—Antonio de Mello e Castro; Luiz de Miranda Henriques, commander at Dīū; Corte Real de Sampayo, councillor of State.

The French Company's president, M. Caron, founds a "Comptoir" or agency at Surat. This place being found unsuited for a head establishment, Trinkomali is seized from the Dutch but is retaken by them.

1669 Jan. 22. Twenty charges brought against Henry Young, the Company's first Deputy-Governor of Bombay. 13th Nov., he is deported to England, and Mr James Addams, with five Commissioners, succeeds.

April: Zī-l qa'da, H. 1079. Aurangzīb's persecution of Hinduism begins at Thatta, Multān, and Benares.

Aurangzīb concludes an agreement with 'Alī 'Adil Shāh of Bījāpūr. Śivājī, who has established a military government, compels Bījāpūr and Golkonda to pay tribute. The Dekhan is now tranquil for two years.

For the administration of the new presidency of Bombay, a central authority is formed at Surat, consisting of a President and Council of eight, five to reside in the presidency. Two courts of judicature established at Bombay.

July 14 Sir George Oxinden dies at Surat, and the Hon. Gerald Aungier succeeds him. Five commissioners manage affairs at Bombay till Matthew Gray is appointed Deputy-Governor.

By concession from Shāista Khān, Governor of Bengal, the E.I. Co. obtain the privilege of bringing their ships up to Hūglī for the purpose of loading. A pilot establishment is instituted at Hūglī and a pinnace built. Thus originated the Bengal Pilot Service.

A.D.

1669 Sept. 21. Monsieur C. Dellon, a French doctor, arrives at Surat—author of *A Voyage to the East Indies.*

De Graaf, a Dutch surgeon, arrives in Bengal.

St Helena regularly colonised under Captain Stringer, the captains of the twenty-two regular Indiamen touching to act as members of Council.

Dec. 5. The Persian, Markara, obtains a *farmān* from 'Abdullah Qutb Shāh, permitting the French Company to trade duty free in Golkonda, and to erect a factory at Masulipatam.

An English factory is founded at Madakkara Island near Cannanor.

The Dutch capture St Thomé from the Portuguese.

Fort St George is besieged by the local Nāyyak, but the siege is raised by command of the Nawāb.

1670 Jan. 6. Dr C. Dellon leaves Surat with orders to remove the French factory from Beliapatam (Valarpattanam) to Telicherry.

Establishment of a mint and a military establishment at Bombay sanctioned.

Sir William Langhorne, Bart., Governor of Madras, till Jan. 27, 1678.

Feb.: Ramazān, H. 1080. Aurangzīb orders the destruction of the great temple of Keśava Deva or Krishna at Mathurā, built by Bīr Singh Bundelā of Urchha, in the reign of Jahāngīr, at a cost of thirty-three lākhs,—and a mosque to be erected on the site.

H. 1080. The Afghāns defeat Muhammad Amīn Khān, son of Mīr Jumla, and proclaim their independence under a native chief.

The Dutch ships from Europe this season number fifty-two.

March. Śivājī takes Purandhar; Māhuli, Karnala, and Lohagad are captured but Janjira holds out, Siddi Yāqūt becoming a Mughal vassal.

Oct. 3. Śivājī, with 15,000 men, plunders Surat, where the English factory was successfully held by Streynsham Master; Śivājī levies tribute and returns to the Dekhan, passing through a Mughal army with his booty.

Oct. The first collision of the Portuguese and Marāthas takes

A.D.

1670 place off Daman, when a Marātha fleet captures a large Portuguese ship, losing twelve of their own vessels.

H. 1081. Aurangzīb, outwitted by Śivājī, renews the war. Diler Khān is sent to the Dekhan.

Virappa Nāyyaka of Madura dies. His son, Chokkanātha Nāyyaka, succeeds.

The King of Golkonda grants a *kaul*, by which the Company agrees to pay 1,200 pagodas (4,200 rupees) as rent for Chennapatnam (Madras) town and fort.

A second Danish East India Company formed at Copenhagen.

This year the outward investment of English bullion and goods to India is £303,500.

1671 Jan. Śivājī's general, Moro Pant Pingla, takes, with other forts, Aundha, Patta, and Sāler.

Feb. 14. The King of Kanara writes offering sites at Barcelor, Honāvar, and Mangalor for Portuguese factories, with stipulations regarding fortification and proselytising. A treaty is concluded.

H. 1081. Mahābat Khān sent to the Dekhan with 40,000 men, acting independently of Mu'azzam's authority. Bahādur Khān, Khān Jahān, sent as Viceroy.

Mahārāja Jaswant Singh, thirty-fifth Viceroy of Gujarāt, till 1674.

March 29. Mr Dacres, agent at Bantam, makes an agreement with the king that the Company should pay in lieu of all duties 4,000 rials per annum, import and export to be free.

May 22. Luiz Mendoza Furtado de Albuquerque, Conde de Lavradio, takes office at Goa as Viceroy.

Mahāpawāra Dhammā Rājā of Burma dies. His son Narawara, succeeds, but dies within the year. A junior member of the family is made king, with the title of Śri Pawāra Mahādhammā Rajā. The empire begins to decline.

Oct. M. de la Haye arrives at Surat: later is opposed in his attempt to establish a French factory, by the Dutch in the bay of Trinkomali.

Flacour, a French agent, travels from Tellicherry to Seringapatam to establish a factory.

A.D.

1671 An Englishman, Mr Boucher, captured by Kota pirates, and, refusing ransom, is killed.

1672 Jan. Sir William Langhorne, agent at Fort St George, in succession to Mr Foxcroft.

H. 1082. Diler Khān and his army lay siege to Sāler, but are defeated in the field by Śivājī. Many Mughals join the Marātha standard. Śivājī's attack on Salsette repulsed by the Portuguese.

A new Hindu sect arises, who, believing they are invulnerable, march on Dehli, causing great commotion, against whom the emperor proceeds and suppresses them.

H. 1083. 'Abdul Qutb Shāh of Golkonda dies. 'Abul Hasan, his son, succeeds.

Dodda Deva Rāja of Maisur dies. Chikka Deva Rāja succeeds. He represses feudal and quasi-independent rights, forcing his nobles to reside at Seringapatam: he also establishes a joint postal and police service in his country. His taxes on the *ra'īyat* cultivators proving vexatious, they refuse to till the fields, at the instigation of the Jangam priests, 700 of whom are entrapped and massacred at Nanjangad in one day.

June. Streynsham Master returns to England, remaining till 1676.

June 7. Gerald Aungier arrives at Bombay as governor. Dec., he makes proposals to the Portuguese Viceroy regarding friendship, observation of the international treaty and free trade. The Goa Viceroy in sending home the text of these proposals, advises the Prince Regent not to agree to them.

The French, under Admiral de la Haye, attempt unsuccessfully to plant a settlement at Point de Galle. They capture and garrison Trinkomali, which, however, immediately surrenders to the Dutch.

July 25. Meliapur (S. Thomé) is taken from the Dutch by the French.

Friar Matthew de St Joseph, a Carmelite monk, having the friendship of the Dutch governor, H. A. D. van Rheede, founds the first Carmelite establishment at Chetiata, a few miles from Cochin.

Dec. 15. 'Alī 'Ādil Shāh II. of Bījāpūr is struck with paralysis, and dies a few days after. Khawās Khān, regent, despite his

A.D.

1672 promises to the king, pursues a selfish policy. A child, Sikandar 'Ādil Shāh, succeeds.

1673 Jan.: Ramazān H. 1083. The Afghāns having set up a king, Aurangzīb sends his son, Muhammad Sultān, against them. This war is carried on for two years, after which a very imperfect settlement is made.

Feb. 20. A Dutch fleet, under Rickhoff van Goens, appears off Bombay, and remains between Bombay and Surat, but makes no demonstrations.

H. 1083. Khān Jahān defeated at Mālkhed by the Bījāpūr general Bahlūl.

March 14: 26 Zī-l qa'da. Certain insurgents of Narnal and Mewāt, called Satnāmis or Mondhis, are defeated after a fierce combat by a royal army under Ra'd-andāz Khān.

March. Śivājī assembles a force at Vishālgarh, a detachment of which, under Anāji Dattu, recovers Panhālā, the main body plundering Hubli. The English are solicited for help both by Śivājī and the Siddi, but preserve strict neutrality. May, Mr Nichols, on behalf of the English, endeavours to obtain compensation from Śivājī for losses sustained at Rājapur and Hubli, but Śivājī denies liability.

Aug. The Dutch besiege the French settlement of St Thomé. Aug. 22, the Dutch fleet of fourteen sail attacks the English Company's homeward bound ships off Pettipoly or Nizāmpatnam: takes two of the ships and sinks one: the remainder retire to Madras.

Sept. Śivājī reduces Sātāra fort. Other forts capitulate. 'Abdul Karīm, a Bījāpūr general, is intercepted by Pratāp Rāo Gujar, who grants him leave to return to Bījāpūr.

H. 1084. Kīrat Singh, son of Jaysingh of Amber, dies.

Oct. The Bombay Government, alarmed at the presence of the Siddi of Janjira at Karanjā, send a petition and presents, whereupon the Siddi withdraws his fleet.

St Helena recovered from the Dutch by Capt. Munden; Dec. 16, is granted by Charles II. to the E.I. Company. The Court appoints Capt. Field to be governor.

The outward bound fleet from England divided into three squadrons under an Admiral, Vice-Admiral, and Rear-Admiral.

A.D.

1673 M. François Caron, recalled to France, leaves Admiral de la Haye and M. Baron in charge of the French interests in the East.

1674 H. 1084. Muhammad Amīn Khān, son of Mīr Jumla, appointed thirty-sixth Viceroy of Gujarāt, till 1678.

Feb. Pratāp Rāo, Śivājī's general, is killed by the Bījāpūr army in an attack on Panhālā; but the Marātha horse, under Hasāji Mohita, Hambir Rāo, defeat the Bijāpūris immediately after.

April 6. Śivājī concludes a treaty with the English at Rāiri, agreeing to pay 10,000 pagodas (35,000 rupees) for losses inflicted at Rājapur; other clauses refer to the planting of factories, and restoration of the Company's vessels wrecked on the Malabar coast.

April. Sir Josiah Child first appointed one of the twenty-four "Committees" at the India House, subsequently obtains great influence in the direction of the E.I. Co.'s affairs.

April. The English presidency at Surat establish a factory at Dharamgāon in Kāndesh.

June 6. Śivājī is crowned Mahārāja, Mr Henry Oxinden from Bombay being present. June 12, Śivājī grants privileges of trade to the English Company. He sends Moro Pant Pingla to Kalyān to exact *chauth* from the Portuguese at Bassein.

Karna Singh of Bikanir dies. His son, Anup Singh, succeeds. This prince is also ruler of Bījāpūr and Aurangābād.

July 16. Aurangzīb arrives at Hasan Abdāl in the Panjāb to watch events on the north-west frontier, and remains a year and a half.

July 16. Gerald Aungier ratifies his Convention with the people of Bombay, who (Nov. 12, 1672) had "thought fit . . . to propose to pay 20,000 xeraphins (about £1,400) per annum to the Hon. Company," the present property-holders to be permanently secured in their possessions.

Sept. 5. The Dutch take St Thomé from the French and cede it to the King of Golkonda; the French agent, François Martin, purchases Pondicheri from Sher Khān, the Governor of Jinjī.

Oct. 21. Corporal Fake shot at Bombay for mutiny: the first court martial held in the Bombay Presidency. Capt. Shaxton,

A.D.

1674 who had encouraged the men to revolt, is deported to England. Capt. Langford succeeds as commandant.

1675 H. 1085. Rāja Jaswant Singh of Jodhpur is sent to command the Mughal forces in Afghānistān. Kābul is henceforward governed by nominees of the Dehli court.

Moro Pant, alleging aggressions by Diler Khān the Mughal general, retakes Aundha and Patta. Hasāji Mohita, Hambir Rāo, the Senāpati, levies contributions in the Bharoch district.

July 12. The English Court of Directors regulate the status and pay of their servants, with the successive titles of writers, factors, merchants, and senior merchants. The civil servants are recommended to acquire some knowledge of military duties.

Nov. 13. Tēg Bahādur, ninth Sikh Guru, captured at Rupar on the Satlaj, and imprisoned and tortured to make him become Muslim—an attendant Sikh at his request kills him. His son, Govind, becomes tenth and last Guru, and begins a religious war against Muhammadans and Aurangzīb.

Dec. Mr Nichols is appointed judge at Bombay.

The Malabar rājas so oppress the English factors on the coast that two frigates are employed to enforce the observation of treaties. The Rājapur factory is withdrawn.

A tobacco monopoly is established at Goa.

1676 April. Disputes occur between the English at Bombay and the Portuguese, originating in the protection given to a Malabar vessel pursued by Portuguese. An affray follows at Bāndra in which Sergeant Sutherland is killed. The Portuguese land a force at Bāndra but no action ensues.

Śivājī sets out for the conquest of the Karnatik and forms an alliance with Qutb Shāh at Haidarābād against the Mughals.

June 9. Siddi Qāsim, Governor of Janjira (Danda Rājpuri) and head of the armada against Śivājī, allowed to winter at Bombay.

July 7. Mr Streynsham Master arrives at Fort St George to succeed Sir William Langhorne as governor. July 31, leaves for a tour of inspection among the Bengal factories, visiting Masulipatam Bālāsor, Kāsimbazar, Hūglī (which is made head-quarters of the Bengal trade), and receives accounts of the trade

A.D.

1676 of Pātna and Mālda. At Mālda the settlement of a factory is sanctioned.

Oct. 15. The King's Letter (28 Charles II.) authorises the Company to establish a mint at Bombay to coin "rupees, pice (paisa), and budgrooks (pāī?)."

Oct. 17. The president of Surat directs the removal from Bombay of all "vagabond padrees" (monks) to Chaul or elsewhere.

Nov. Mr Streynsham Master and a Commission consult at Kāsimbazar for the better regulation of trade in Bengal.

M. Franç. Martin, French agent, obtains permission from Sher Khān to train native soldiers for defence. Three hundred are employed at Pondicheri in a combined military and industrial capacity.

Dec. 5: Shawwāl 8, H. 1087. Sultān Muhammad, eldest son of Aurangzīb, dies.

1677 Jan. 27. Mr Streynsham Master, Governor of Madras till July 3, 1681.

March. Śivājī crosses the Krishnā at Karnāl, and takes Jinjī fort. His army lays siege to Velor, which surrenders in Sept. Sivājī recovers his father's *jagīr* in Maisur and levies *chauth* and *sardesmukhī*.

Diler Khān with the Bījāpūr army under 'Abdul Karīm invades Golkonda.

March. In consequence of complaints by the British of their bad treatment by the Portuguese, Charles II. writes to the Portuguese Viceroy.

March 22. The Surat Council send instructions for the settlement on favourable terms for eminent Baniyas at Bombay.

April 21. Mr White, agent at Bantam, and the principal servants of the London Company are murdered by Javanese. Dec. 13, Charles II. writes to the king demanding that justice be done to the murderers.

H. 1087. Shāista Khān, at his own request, recalled from Bengal to Dehli, and appointed Governor of Agra. Nawāb Fidāī Khān, 'Azim Khān, succeeds as Governor of Bengal.

May 7. Siddi Sambal and Siddi Qāsim permitted by the Surat

A.D.

1677 Council to winter at Bombay on condition of giving no offence to the British Government there.

May 7. The Governor of Madras writes to Shāista Khān threatening the removal of the English from Bengal unless they receive better treatment.

The Court of Directors confers discretionary powers on President Aungier to employ force if necessary in his transactions with native princes.

June 30. Gerald Aungier, President of Surat and Governor of Bombay, dies. The Honble. Thomas Rolte, previously agent at Gombrūn, succeeds at Surat, and Mr Henry Oxinden at Bombay. Retrenchments and reduction of salaries resolved upon.

Aug. 24. Judge Niccolls suspended for abuse of office at Bombay. Mr Henry Gary appointed Chief Justice, with a seat on the Executive Council. A militia is formed at Bombay, consisting of 600 landowners.

Oct. 30. Dom Pedro de Almeida, Conde de Assumar, succeeds Luiz de Mendoza Furtado de Albuquerque, Conde de Lavradio, as Viceroy at Goa.

Dec. 14: Shawwāl 18, H. 1088. Aurangzīb, thinking his son, Muhammad Sultān, is not to be trusted, causes him to be poisoned when about thirty-eight years old.

1678 Jan. 'Abdul Karīm, regent at Bījāpūr, dies. Masa'ud Khān succeeds. Many cavalry men, dismissed from the army, join the Mughals or Marāthas.

Jan. 27. The Portuguese Viceroy, Dom Pedro de Almeida, leaves Goa for Mozambique, where he dies, March 22, 1679.

Śivājī comes to terms with his half-brother, Venkāji, who promises to pay a sum of money, to divide their father's jewels, and to share the revenue of the territory: on these conditions Śivājī allows him to retain Tanjor, and restores the *jagīr* districts.

May 1: Rabī' I. 9, H. 1089. Nawāb Fidāī Khān, 'Azim Khān, Governor of Bengal, dies. Prince Muhammad 'Azim, third son of Aurangzīb, succeeds and continues the campaign against the Assamese.

Muhammad Amīn Khān appointed thirty-seventh Viceroy of Gujarāt, till 1683.

A.D.

1678 Dec. 20: Zī-l qa'da 6. Rāja Jaswant Singh, sent as faujdār of Jamrūd in the Khaibar, dies there. His infant sons, who afterwards were plotted against by Aurangzīb, escape to Jodhpur, and are put in charge of the Rānā of Chitor.

The English factors at Dhākā receive from Sultān 'Azim, on payment of 21,000 rupees, a *nishān*, or grant of free trade in Bengal.

Sir William Langhorne recalled from Madras on a charge of having given undue advantages to a native merchant for a consideration. Streynsham Master appointed governor.

A troop of horse ordered for Bombay, the captain's pay not to exceed £120.

Dec. 15. A treaty of commerce and alliance is concluded between the Portuguese and the King of Kanara. Besides the erection of factories the king authorises the building of Roman Catholic churches at Mirzeo, Chandor, Bhatkal, and Kalyān.

1679 Jan. 3. The Court of Directors appoints Mr Job Charnock to be chief of Kāsimbazar and second in council at Hūglī.

Jan. 14: Zī-l hijja, H. 1089. Aurangzīb spends seven months in quelling Rājput revolts. Khān Jahān Bahādur is left to complete the arrangements made with the Rānā of Udaypur, who, however, again revolts. Prince Akbar, sent to chastise the Rānā, is won over to the Rājputs and leads an army against his father. Many Rājputs desert, and Akbar flees to the Marāthās.

Jan. 20. The Portuguese Viceroy writes to the Prince Regent of England complaining against the English at Bombay, for impeding navigation of the salt ships of Bassein, exacting dues, assisting Arabs with ammunition, and permitting the erection of mosques and temples, and suggesting that a nominee of each country make terms of residence more exact.

March - April: Safar, H. 1090. Aurangzīb re-enacts the imposition of the *jizya* or capitation tax on non-Muslims. A letter to Aurangzīb protesting against the tax is variously ascribed to Jaswant Singh of Jodhpur, to Subha Singh, to Rāj Singh, and to Śivājī.

March 16. Streynsham Master makes a land journey to Masulipatam *via* Palikat, Armugam, and Pettapoli (Nizāmpatam).

A. D.

1679 Aug. 1, he starts on a tour among the Bengal factories. Retrenchments are ordered.

July. Dom Fr. Antonio Brandao, Archbishop of Goa and joint-governor, dies.

Diler Khān is ordered to besiege Bījāpūr. Śivājī, to divert this army, plunders the Mughal provinces. Sept., Śivājī, defeated by the Mughals, retires to Rāiri, but, Nov.-Dec., resumes his devastations in Berār and Aurangābād.

Oct. 5: Sha'bān, 1090. Aurangzīb arrives at Ajmir to control the war in Rājputāna; and Mu'azzam is called from the Dekhan.

Oct. 12. Sultān A'zam leaves Dhākā to co-operate against the Rājputs, and is despatched with an army against Udaypur. Shāista Khān is reappointed Governor of Bengal.

Oct. 13. Great storm at Masulipatam. 20,000 persons drowned.

Oct. 18. Śivājī's admiral, Daulat Khān, takes possession of Khanderi island. The English, with the Siddi of Janjira, after attempting to dislodge them, occupy Underi.

Nov. 14. Job Charnock accepts the chiefship of Kāsimbazar, but, delaying at Pātna to supervise the saltpetre output, he inconveniences the Hūglī and Fort St George agents, and is appointed (Dec. 13) second at Hūglī.

Instructions are sent to Bombay local government to make Bombay presidency pay its expenses by levying duties on the houses in the island.

The English factory at Kārwar withdrawn in consequence of the exactions of local chiefs. It is restored in 1682.

1680 Feb. Udaypur being occupied by the imperial troops, and hundreds of temples destroyed, Aurangzīb visits the scene.

April 14: Rabī' I. 14, H. 1091. Śivājī dies at Rājgarh. May, Rāja Rām, his second son, is placed on the throne, but a faction in favour of Sambhājī, the elder son, prevails, and Rāja Rām is imprisoned in Rājgarh. June, Sambhājī makes his entry into Rājgarh and is acknowledged Rāja, with Moro Pant as Peshwā.

July 8. The English factors in Bengal, having solicited an imperial *farmān* to replace the successive orders from the governors, receive this *farmān* with much ceremony at Hūglī.

Shāista Khān enforces the payment of the *jizya* in Bengal.

A.D.

1680 The Christians refuse to pay, the Dutch and English sending a present of horses to the Nawāb.

July 15: Jumāda II. 17. Rānā Rāj Singh of Udaypur makes a treaty with Prince Muhammad A'zim. His title of Rāja is acknowledged, and he tenders the districts of Māndil, Pūr, and Badhanar in lieu of the *jizya*.

Oct. 26. The English Church of St Mary of Madras dedicated with ceremony. Mr Richard Portman, first minister.

Oct. 27. Pedda Venkatādri having been compelled to make restitution for debts due to the Madras merchants, many calico dyers go on strike and take up a mutinous attitude at S. Thomé. Nov. 29, a proclamation to the ringleaders is issued, on which, the chief Mukwais being imprisoned, the rest submit and return.

Capt. Keigwin, with a small reinforcement, is sent to Bombay at six shillings a day, and with the third place on the Council.

1681 Jan. 5. The Court of Directors orders the dismissal of Streynsham Master, Governor of Fort St George. July 3, he is succeeded by Mr William Gyfford, till July 25, 1687.

Jan. 18: Zī-l hijja 26, H. 1091. Prince Akbar, induced by Durgā Dās, revolts against his father, and an adherent attempts to assassinate Aurangzīb. Jan. 25, Akbar flees to Sambhājī for protection.

June 1. Prince Akbar arrives at Pāligarh and receives protection from Sambhājī, now at Panhālā. The faction in favour of Rām Rāja fails to win him to their cause.

Sept. 15. Aurangzīb and his army leave Ajmir, and march in three divisions against the Marāthās.

Sambhājī comes under the influence of a Brahman called Kalusha, and imprisons the Peshwā Moro Pant.

Surat again ordered to resume the rank of a presidency: Sir John Child (brother of Sir Josiah) sent out as president.

Bombay trade retarded by the occupation of Underi and Khanderi islets by Sambhājī's troops, and by the obstruction of the Portuguese. Mr Smith sent out to Bombay as Assay Master and Mint Master at a salary of £60 per annum.

Sept. 12. Francisco de Tavora, Conde de Alvor, succeeds the Commission of Three as Viceroy at Goa.

A.D.

1681 S. 1737. Rānā Rāj Singh of Udaypur dies. Jaysingh succeeds and makes a treaty with Aurangzīb, ceding three districts as mulct for having aided Akbar's rebellion.

Rāo Bhāo Singh of Būndī dies. Anurād Singh, grandson of his brother Bhīm, succeeds.

Sept. 15. Aurangzīb leaves Ajmir for the Dekhan, and reaches Burhānpur, Nov. 23, for the capture of Prince Akbar.

Nov. 14. Bengal constituted an agency separate from Fort St George. The London Company send out Mr Hedges as agent at Hūglī and governor of their settlements in Bengal.

1682 April 3: Rabī' I. 23, H. 1093. Aurangzīb arrives at Aurangābād.

April. The London Company secures from the Privy Council the continuation of their monopoly.

May 5. Foundation stone of a Portuguese fort at Anjidīva laid. Amaro Simoes appointed first governor.

July 17. The Company's Commission of Nov. 14, 1681, received, by which the Bengal agency is made a presidency, independent of Madras.

July. Great inundations of the sea threaten Madras: the Directors insist that constant expenses must be defrayed by local taxation. Mr Gyfford is compelled to levy a small monthly tax on all householders, but it is not enforced till 1686.

The Company's ship "Johanna" with £70,000 in bullion, lost.

July 24. William Hedges assumes charge of the factories at Hūglī. Oct. 14, proceeds to Dhākā to obtain redress for abuses occasioned by the native traders, but finds the Nawāb Shāista Khān indifferent to the Company's trade, and he returns to Hūglī in Dec.

Aug. The Company's settlers expelled from Bantam by the Dutch, as allies of the young king. The old king is also expelled, and the factors retire to Batavia.

Aug. Dādāji Raghunāth Deshpānde, Sambhājī's general, repulsed at Janjira. The Siddis continue to make inroads. Oct., Sambhājī, with his fleet, defeated in the Thāna river by the Siddis, and begins hostilities upon the Portuguese at Karanjā for their neutrality, and makes overtures to the English at Bombay.

A.D.

1682 S. 1738. Jagjīvandās, founder of the Satnāmī sect of Vaishnavas, born at Sardaha, 40 miles east of Lakhnow; died in 1761.

1683 H. 1094. Prince Muhammad Mu'azzam's army traverses the Konkan unopposed, but suffers severely from scarcity, Sambhājī stopping the Ghāts and intercepting the grain ships. The army retreats, fighting, to Ahmadnagar.

Feb. 1. Mr Hedges despatches personally the merchant ships from Bālāsor, visits the Nīlgiri Rāja (Orissa), and arranges for a saltpetre go-down at Bālāsor.

March 26. Mr Hedges and Council dismiss Francis Ellis on a charge of bribery: he appeals against the dismissal, as beyond their powers, he being fifth of Council at Hūglī. April 23, Rāi Bulchand, a native trader, lays information against Job Charnock before Hedges and advises his dismissal. May 28, Messrs Douglas, Nedham, and Littleton dismissed the Company's service for negotiations with "interlopers."

June. Sambhājī attacks Chaul, but fails to take it. Oct., the Portuguese Viceroy with a mixed army invades Sambhājī's territory, inflicting extreme barbarities. Nov. 10, Phonda besieged by the Portuguese who, on the arrival of Sambhājī, retire with a loss of 1,200 men, and all camp equipage and ammunition.

Mukhtār Khān appointed thirty-eighth Viceroy of Giyarāt till 1686.

Aug. 15. Charles II., by a new Charter, authorises the Company to exercise Admiralty jurisdiction in the country to enable them to seize interlopers' vessels. Dr. St John, Deputy Governor of Bombay, appointed judge with a salary of £200 per annum, and diet at the governor's table.

Aug. 23. The Company's agent and Council of Bantam, now in the possession of the Dutch, retire from Batavia to Surat. Benkūlen, in Sumatra, is fortified.

English factories established at Telicherry, also at Kadalūr Vizagapatam and at Konimer (Kunimēdu) in South Arkat.

François Martin purchases the village of Pondicheri from the Rāja of Vijayapur.

Mr Bowcher and Mr Petit, two of the English Company's servants, cause depression of trade at Surat by encouraging interlopers.

A.D.

1683 Dec. The Company's inland Bengal trade being hampered by the exactions of the native governors, a plan is formed to gain possession of Chittagāon as a sea-port.

Dec. 21. Mr Hedges dismissed from his charge at Hūglī for opening and detaining a despatch to Sir Josiah Child in London, and other misconduct. Mr Gyfford, Governor of Madras, directed to control Bengal also, and is there from Aug. 8, 1684, till Jan. 26, 1685, Mr Elihu Yale acting for him at Madras. John Beard to be agent after the termination of Mr Gyfford's visit to Bengal.

Dec. 27. Capt. Richard Keigwin, in consequence of army retrenchments at Bombay, seizes and imprisons Mr Ward, deputy governor, with some members of Council, and holds the fort in the king's name till Nov. 19, 1684. This revolt was the origin of the first Secret Committee, to inquire into the cause of the outbreak.

1684 Jan. 31. Sir John Child arrives at Bombay with three ships, but fails to reduce the revolt under Capt. Keigwin to order, his crews refusing to act against the mutineers.

March. Charles II. stops an armament about to proceed to Java to reinstate the English factors: a Commission is appointed to adjust claims, consisting of Lords Sutherland, Clarendon, Rochester, and Middleton, with Huth. Heinzius of Delf, John Goes of Leyden, Isaac Vanden Hawel, and Adrigan de Borssele Vander Hoge, Senator.

H. 1095. War with 'Abul Hasan Qutb-ul Mulk of Golkonda, carried on by Prince Mu'azzam and Khān Jahān. Haidarābād is plundered, and the king flees to Golkonda fort, whence he makes submission and peace is concluded.

May. Sir Thomas Grantham takes possession of Hippin's Island in the Straits of Sunda: he touches at Bantam, but finding the factors had left, sails for Malabar.

July. The Court of Directors intimate their desire to concentrate trade at Bombay, and to withdraw it from Surat.

July 17: Sha'bān 4, H. 1095. Aurangzīb starts for the conquest of Bījāpūr now invested by Prince A'zam. The latter is accused of treasonable negotiations with the Bījāpūrīs, and becomes estranged from his father.

July 17. Hedges is advised of his dismissal from the E.I. Co.'s

A.D.

1684 service. Beard is to succeed as agent: Gyfford of Fort St George to be made President of the Coromandel and Bengal settlements. Sept. 1, Gyfford calls an inquiry into Hedges's alleged misconduct. Sept. 23, Hedges leaves the factory and lodges in the Dutch quarter. Dec. 26, he embarks for home *via* Maskat.

Sanda Thudhammā Rāja of Arakan dies: his son, Thirī Thuriya Dhammā Rāja, succeeds. Internal disorders are prevalent during his reign, the kings of Arakan becoming the prey of their foreign guards.

Sept. 15. Capt. Keigwin having negotiated a treaty with Sambhājī for free trade in the latter's dominions, intimates his allegiance in a letter to Charles II. Nov. 11, Sir Thomas Grantham, Vice-Admiral and King's Commissioner, lands at Bombay and promises an amnesty to the rebels. Nov. 19, the fort and island formally delivered to Sir Thomas Grantham and by him transferred to Dr. St John as King's Judge. Mr Zinzan appointed deputy governor.

The Rānī of Attingal (of the Travankor family) grants a sandy spit of land at Anjengo to the English Company. She permitted the fort to be erected in 1690.

Eruma Varma Perumāl succeeds as twenty-fourth Prince of Travankor, till 1717.

1685 Ranga Krishna Muttu Virappa Nāyyak of Madura succeeds Chokanātha Nāyyak, his mother, Mangamāl, being regent.

June 4: Rajab 1, H. 1096. Aurangzīb reaches Sholāpur, in an effort to subdue the Dekhan. Bījāpūr is closely invested by Ghāzi-ud-dīn Khān.

Śivājī's troops, eluding Khān Jahān, he allies himself with Golkonda, and (Oct.) captures Bharoch,—Prince Akbar believed to be the instigator if not the leader of this expedition.

H. 1097. Shāista Khān lays further disabilities on the English in Bengal, scourges Mr Job Charnock, their agent at Kāsimbazar, boycotts the factory, and incites Aurangzīb to displeasure against them.

In consequence of Mughal exactions at Surat, the seat of British Government in India is moved to Bombay. Sir John Child appointed "Captain-General and Admiral of all the Company's Forces by Sea and Land in the north parts of India

A.D.

1685 from Cape Comorin to the Gulf of Persia"; Sir John Wyborne appointed Vice-Admiral and Deputy Governor. Martial policy is in force at Bombay and Surat till 1690. The English factory at Masulipatam is discontinued.

1686 Jan. In consequence of peremptory orders from England, Mr Littleton at Madras collects the tax of nine fanams for every great house, and six fanams for every small house, when a tumult arose and shops were closed.

April 12: King James II., by Charter, grants permission to build a mint at Madras.

July: James II., in answer to an application, issues a proclamation withdrawing British subjects from the service of native powers.

July 9: Prince Mu'azzam is sent against Golkonda; defeats the Qutb-Shāhī army at Mālkhed, and Golkonda is occupied; the king, 'Abu'l Hasan, agrees to pay a large sum in money and jewels, Oct. 29; and sacrifices his Brahman minister, putting him to death, March 26, 1686.

Prince A'zam is sent against Bījāpūr, but is reduced to great straits until Ghāzī-ud-dīn Khān succeeds in provisioning his camp.

July 13: Aurangzīb moves in person from Sholāpur on Bījāpūr, whose king, Sikandar 'Ādil Shāh, capitulates. Oct. 28: Zī-l qa'da 30, Sikandar imprisoned at Daulatābād and dies about 1700.

Shujā'at Khān, Kartalāb Khān, thirty-ninth Viceroy of Gujarāt, till 1703. A great famine prevails in Gujarāt.

Ten ships, under Admiral Nicholson, sent to check the arbitrary exercise of power of the Mughals on the English in Bengal. Oct. 28: an affray between three English soldiers and a few peons at Hūglī leads to an action in which the Nawāb's troops are defeated. Hūglī is cannonaded by the Admiral's ships and 500 houses burnt. The Nawāb seizes the Pātna factory.

Nov. 14: Aurangzīb, from Bījāpūr, reaches Sholāpur, and on Dec. 8 leaves for Kulbarga and Bidār.

Dec. 15: Francisco de Tavora leaves Goa for Portugal. Dom Rodrigue da Costa succeeds as Viceroy.

Dec. 20: The President, Mr Job Charnock, and Council quit Hūglī for Sutānatī or Chatānatī, 26 miles down the river, now the northern quarter of Calcutta.

A.D.

1686 The reduction of Chittagāon by the English squadron considered inadvisable.

1687 Jan. The Danish fleet appears off Bombay; March 24, the commander requested to draw off, trade being obstructed.

Feb. 8: Rabī' I. 25, H. 1098. Aurangzīb invests Golkonda. Many actions between the Mughals and 'Abu'l Hasan's army take place. Prince A'zam takes command of the army, and through treachery the fortress is taken. Oct. 1: Zī-l qa'da 24, 1098, 'Abul Hasan Qutb Shāh is sent a prisoner to Daulatābād, where he dies about 1114 H.

Feb. After several quarrels with Aurangzīb's officers, a Mughal army and vessels, under 'Abdul Samad Khān, are sent to expel the English from Bengal. Mr Charnock and the English retreat to Ingeli ("Hidgley" in Charnock's letters), plundering Tānna on their route. They sack and burn Bālāsor. Many die from pestilence, and after overtures for peace made by the Nawāb, a treaty is concluded Aug. 16, by which the English are allowed to return to their factories: the 3½ per cent. duty is abrogated, and factories and magazines are sanctioned at Ulubāria.

March 2: Rabī' II. 17, H. 1098. Prince Muhammad Mu'azzam is unjustly charged with treacherous conduct during the sieges of Golkonda and Bījāpūr, and is arrested with his sons. He was not released for seven years.

May 2: Sir John Child and the Surat Council arrive at Bombay, which is now constituted a presidency with extended powers, being made supreme over all the E.I. Company's establishments in India. Owing to trade obstruction, negotiations follow with the Mughal Governor of Surat. A provisional arrangement is made with Mr Harris, agent, by Mukhtār Khān, a newly appointed governor.

July 25: Mr Elihu Yale succeeds Mr Gyfford (dismissed) as Governor of Madras, till Oct. 3, 1692. The English and Portuguese compete for the possession of St Thomé.

An English settlement made at Benkūlen, in Sumatra, and a *farmān* is obtained for the sole government of it. York fort built.

Pondicheri is established by the French.

A.D.

1688 H. 1099. Aurangzīb takes possession of Bījāpūr and Golkonda, seizes Sambhājī's Mysore *jagīr* and appoints Ghāzī-ud-dīn as Governor of the Dekhan.

Feb. An army under Muhammad Sadik enters the Karnātak: the Marāthās retire from Conjivaram to Paliār. The Mughals occupy Panamali and Wandavāsh. Plundering follows, but no action between the armies.

H. 1099. Prince Akbar leaves the court of Sambhājī for Persia —dies at Garmsir 1706.

The Siddi of Janjira attacks Bombay and besieges the fort for some months.

June: By a contract with the Directors of the English Company, Armenians are encouraged to reside within the English settlement at Madras.

Oct. Capt. Heath, sent out by the Directors to intimidate the Mughals, arrives in Bengal and reopens hostilities. Nov. 29, lands at Bālāsor with the Company's servants and goods. The English factory is burnt by the governor, and two of the Company's servants taken prisoners. Heath captures a battery of thirty guns, and burns the town. Dec. 13: in spite of the Court's recommendation to the contrary the fleet sails for Chittagāon.

The French E.I. Co. acquires Chandranagar by grant from Aurangzīb.

A Mayor and Corporation are established at Madras.

Dec. 26: The new Surat governor imprisons the factors Harris and Gladman till April 4, 1690, orders the sale of the Company's goods, and offers a reward to anyone capturing Sir John Child, dead or alive.

Muhammad Qāsim writes the *Alamgīrnāma*, containing the history of the first ten years of Aurangzīb's reign.

1689 Jan. Capt. Heath of the "Resolution" finds Chittagāon too strong to take. The English state their grievances to the Nawāb at Dhākā, and attempt negotiations with the King of Arakan, but Capt. Heath does not wait an answer. Feb. 13: leaves Arakan with the Bengal Governor and Council, arriving at Madras on March 4.

The Mughals, enraged at the defiant attitude of the English,

A.D.

1689 seize and murder the English factors with Mr Stables, their chief, at Vizagapatam and Masulipatam.

H. 1100. Plague breaks out in the royal camp at Bījāpūr. The camp moves to Aklūj on the Nīrā.

Feb. 14: Siddi Yāqūt Khān lands at Sewrī and takes possession of Mazagāon fort, Māhim and Sīon, abandoned by the English. He remains till September, but the English only regain possession June 22, 1690.

March 3: Sambhājī and his Brahman minister, Kabkalās, captured (Dec. 28, 1688) by Muqarrab Khān, at his pleasure-house at Sangameshwar in the Ghāts, are brought before Aurangzīb at Talāpūr, when, refusing to accept Islām, they are cruelly tortured and put to death with Sambhājī's favourite, Kabkalās or Kālūśāh, March 14. Rāja Rām is acknowledged successor to his brother Sambhājī.

Shujā'at Khān quells a mutiny among the Ahmadābād troops.

Shāista Khān resigns the province of Bengal, and Nawāb Ibrāhīm Khān, son of 'Alī Mardān Khān, succeeds.

Oct. 28: Muharram 15, H. 1101. Rāigarh fort, invested by the imperial troops, is betrayed by a discontented Marātha, Sūryaji Piral. Sambhājī's infant son Śivaji (called Sāhu) with his mother Yesubāī, are taken to the Mughal camp.

Nov. 5: The "Chandos" arrives at Madras with news of William of Orange's accession to the English crown. The king and queen are proclaimed.

Dec. 10: Sir John Child sends Messrs Welldon and Navarro, with a merchant, Miyān Nizāmi, to Bījāpūr to solicit from Aurangzīb protection for their subjects and shipping.

The servants of the E.I. Company determine to make Calcutta their headquarters.

1690 H. 1101. Rāja Rām, Sambhājī's brother, now regent, proceeds to Jinjī, where he is proclaimed Rāja, his chief adviser being Prahlād Niraji, under the new title of Pritinidhi.

Amanat Khān, with the title of I'timad Khān, is appointed Governor of Surat.

Feb. 4: Sir John Child, Governor of Bombay, dies, and Mr Bartholomew Harris from Surat is appointed governor, and Mr Cook, deputy governor.

A.D.

1690 Feb. 27: The Bombay envoys obtain a *farmān* from Aurangzīb, which reduces the presidency to a degraded status. April: on the arrival of the *farmān* at Surat, the Company's servants are released.

June 22: In terms of the Mughal treaty, the Siddi removes his troops from Bombay. The English reoccupy Mahim, Māzagāon and Sīon. A plague left by the troops destroys the remainder of the Bombay army, only thirty-five surviving.

June 26: Miguel de Almeida succeeds Dom Rodrigue da Costa as Governor at Goa. A treaty effected by Antonio de Brito, General in the Straits, secures freedom of trade and religion at Ormus.

Aug. The Dutch and English fleets jointly attack the French fleet in Madras Roads and drive it to Bengal.

Aug. 24: Mr Charnock and Council, with factors and an escort of thirty, arrive at Chatānatī, on invitation of Nawāb Ibrāhīm Khān.

Devapattan or Tegnapatam, near Kadalūr, is purchased by Governor Mr E. Yale from Rām Rāja for the English for 32,000 rupees, and Fort St David erected there. The Rānī of Attingal permits the erection of a fort at Anjengo by the English factors.

Dec. 28: Mr Elihu Yale, Governor of Madras, having rendered service by supplying ammunition to Zulfiqār Khān, obtains a *farmān* confirming the English in possession of Vizāgapaṭam and all their settlements in Golkonda and Jinjī territory.

Rām Rāja is besieged in Jinjī by Zulfiqār Khān Nasrat Jang, and afterwards by Kām Bakhsh, who intrigues with Rām Rāja and is sent back, Zulfiqār Khān continuing the siege till 1698.

The interlopers, now banded together as an Association, apply to Parliament for trading powers: the prorogation of Parliament stops further proceedings.

H. 1100. Mūswī Khān or Fitrat, poet and critic, dies.

1691 Jan. 9: Dom Miguel de Almeida, Governor at Goa, dies. Dom Fernando Martim Mascarenhas de Lancastre and Luiz Gonçalves Cotta succeed; the latter dying in June is succeeded by the Archbishop Fra Augustinho da Annunciação.

Feb. A ship belonging to Surat is seized and plundered by a European pirate: the Surat governor in consequence places

A.D.

1691 a guard on the English factory, but removes it, the pirate proving to be a Danish vessel.

April 27: The English factors in Bengal obtain a new *farmān* from Aurangzīb, granting liberty of trade in Bengal on payment of 3,000 rupees in lieu of custom.

H. 1102. The Jāts rebel near Agra and plunder a caravan. Āghā Khān is killed in investing one of their strongholds. Khān Jahān Kokultāsh recalled for inability to quell previous riots.

Sayyid Shāhji, leader of the Matiāh and Momnā sects—followers of the Ismā'īliah Imāms—ordered to be sent to court by Aurangzīb on the charge of heterodoxy, commits suicide. His followers seize Bharoch fort and put the governor to death. The succeeding governor, Nazar 'Alī Khān, invests the fort and defeats the Momnās—most of them being slain.

Sept. The Dutch, in order to curtail their expenditure, surrender Chetwai to the Zamorin of Calicut.

Dec.: Zī-l qa'da, H. 1102. Prince Muhammad Mu'azzam Shāh Alam, is released from imprisonment and restored to favour.

The House of Commons, after hearing the claims of the London Company and those of the "Association for participating in Indian Trade," refers the matter to the king.

1692 H. 1103. Rām Rāja rescued by the Marāthās and acknowledged Rāja. Large forces under Santājī Ghorpade and Dhanāji Jādhav are gathered. Rāmchander Pant takes Wāī from the Mughal faujdār, and Parnālā fort is seized by Parshurām Trimbak.

Zulfiqār Khān, accompanied by Prince Kām Bakhsh, again lays siege to Jinjī. The Marāthās defeat the besieging army. Many Mughals take refuge at Madras. Dec., the Governor of Madras in return obtains a *kaul* from Vazīr Asad Khān and Nawāb Zulfiqār Khān for the suburbs of Egmor, Parsawākkam and Tandayārpet.

Thān, headquarters of the predatory Kāthis, stormed by the Gujarāt Viceroy, Shujā'at Khān. Disturbances break out in Mārwār under Durgadās Rāthod. The Viceroy alienates the chief landowners from their leader, who is expelled from Mārwār.

H. 1004. Aurangzīb, at the instance of the Turkish Sultān, prohibits the sale of saltpetre to Christians, its use in the manufacture of gunpowder for the destruction of Muhammadans being

A.D.

1692 objected to. The East India Company's servants in Bengal are thus kept from their chief source of commerce.

Trade at Surat and Bombay weakened by interlopers, English pirates, and "permission ships." The Mughal authorities are irritated with the Company's servants.

Oct. 11: War having been declared between the English and French, the "Elizabeth" is captured by four French sail 50 leagues from Bombay.

Oct. 13: Nathaniel Higginson succeeds as Governor of Madras, Mr Yale being dismissed for having relinquished the West Coast or Sumatra trade.

Dec. 13: Sir John Goldesborough takes office at Madras, as "Commissary General and Supervisor of the Company's affairs in India." He confirms President Higginson in the government.

An Attorney-General sent to Madras for the better regulation of the Company's interests.

1693 Jan. 10: Job Charnock, president of the Bengal factories, and founder of Calcutta, dies in the settlement at Chatānatī.

H. 1104: Santājī Ghorpade, the Marātha general, harasses the Mughal camp at Brahmapuri, also defeats Ismā'īl Khān and Rustam Khān near Sātāra. Other Mughal defeats follow.

Vijaya Ranga Chokanātha Nāyyak succeeds his father, Ranga Krishna Muttu Virappa Nāyyak at Madura; Mangamāl, grandmother of the infant Nāyyak, acts as regent.

March: Zulfiqār Khān, now before Jinjī, seeks to borrow 100,000 pagodas from the Madras Council. Mr Higginson sends a present, but declines to lend the sum asked. An attack on Madras feared.

April: A mutiny occurs at St Helena, in which the Governor, Capt. Johnson, is killed.

May 28: Dom Pedro Antonio de Noronhas, Conde de Villa Verde, succeeds as Viceroy at Goa, which had been governed by a Commission for two years.

June 13: Sir John Goldesborough proceeds to Fort St David or Tegnapatam, where the Dutch had landed ordnance and military stores. He commences the erection of works, and fixes the bounds of the English settlement. Aug. 12: he arrives at Chatānatī, and orders the transference of Mr Ellis to Fort

A.D.

1693 St George, appointing as governor Mr Eyres, chief of the Dhākā factory.

Aug. A Dutch fleet appears before Pondicheri. Sept. 8, François Martin demands a parley, and capitulation terms are wrested from him. The French quit Pondicheri. It was restored by the Treaty of Ryswick, 1697.

Governor Higginson and the Bishop of St Thomé dispute regarding the exercise of ecclesiastical authority within the English boundaries.

The Nāyyak of Punamalī disputes the cession of the villages granted in 1692. The Vazīr of Aurangzīb grants them anew.

The Company's Charter forfeited in consequence of failing in the payment of 5 per cent. levied on all Joint Stock companies.

Oct. 1: William III. grants a new Charter to the East India Company, confirming all their former privileges, but obliging them to comply with alterations the king might in future think proper to make. The Company enter into an obligation to export £150,000 of British manufactures. The right of the king to grant a Charter is denied by Parliament. Nov. 11: an additional Charter granted for augmenting the Company's stock, for defining their term, and specifying the qualifications of Proprietors to vote at the General Courts. The Court of Directors warn the presidents of the renewed activity of interlopers.

1694 H. 1105: Prince Kāmbakhsh arrested for suspected treason at Jinjī; the generals, Jumdat'ul Mulk and Zulfiqār Khān, come under Aurangzīb's displeasure.

Jan. Sir John Goldesborough, Commissary-General in India, dies. May. Sir John Gayer succeeds as General of all India. Bengal is again made subordinate to Madras.

May 10: President Harris of Surat dies. Daniel Annesley succeeds, and as Deputy-Governor of Bombay. May 17, Sir John Gayer is appointed governor.

Khāfī Khān, the Muhammadan historian, visits the English residency at Bombay.

June: The trade embargo in Bengal removed from the European nations.

June: A fortified English settlement at Anjengo is sanctioned

A.D.

1694 by the Rānī of Attingal, on payment of ground-rent. The Dutch obstruct the building of the fort.

Dr Blackwall of Fort St David bribed by the Mughals to betray the fort. This treason discovered, Blackwall is arrested and taken to Madras, where he makes full confession.

Capt. White of the interloping ship "Henry," obtains a trading pass through the Dutch and French at Surat from the Mughal governor, and so lowers the Company's credit.

Sept. 29: An additional Charter granted to the Company for rendering the application of cash subject to the orders of a general Court, and providing that any eight adventurers, possessed of £1,000 stock each, might require a general Court to be held.

1695 H. 1106: Qāsim Khān, the Mughal general, forced into Dhanderi fort and besieged a month by Santāji Ghorpade. His successor, Rūhullāh Khān, capitulates. Santāji defeats a relieving force under Himmat Khān.

The "Ganj-i Sawāī," a Mughal ship, fires on an English vessel, the "Fanny" (Capt. Avery), but is captured. Aurangzīb orders the English factors at Surat to be imprisoned, Bombay fort to be besieged by Siddi Yāqūt Khān, and Madras to be attacked by the land army. 'Īsā Qulī, the Company's vakīl, prevents the accomplishment of these orders, but the Europeans are forbidden to hoist flags, carry arms and use palanquins.

On the imprisonment of the English factors at Surat, the Dutch apply to the emperor for the exclusive trade, offering to clear the sea of pirates and convoy the pilgrims to Makka. The request is refused.

Prince Mu'azzam, Shāh 'Alam, liberated after seven years' close imprisonment.

Aug.: Muharram, H. 1107. A great flood occurs on the Bhīmā, where Aurangzīb's camp was pitched, 12,000 lives and much property lost.

Subā Singh, a zamīndār, unites with an Afghān, Rahīm Khān, for the destruction of the Rāja of Burdwān, whose son, Jagat Rāi, lays his complaint against the governor, and a force is called out against the insurgents, who take possession of Hūglī.

The Mughals continue to harass the Portuguese in all their

A.D.

1695 settlements. The Viceroy bribes the Mughal courtiers to advocate peace, by offering facilities for obtaining ammunition and cannon.

The Governor of Madras solicits the King of Burma for protection for traders, and receives encouragement to settle in the Burmese dominions.

June 26: The Parliament of Scotland passes an Act enabling the king to constitute a Scottish Company with powers to trade to Africa and the Indies, with extensive privileges.

Sir T. Cook, Chairman and Governor of the London Company, committed by the Commons to the Tower, for refusing to give an account of the money spent in bribes.

The homeward bound fleet of Indiamen is seized by the French off the coast of Galway.

The port of Calicut ravaged by the pirate, Capt. Kidd.

H. 1107: Subhān Rāī writes the *Khulāsatu-t Tawārīkh.*

1696 H. 1107: 'Alī Mardān Khān attacks Santāji Ghorpade at Kavarpāk near Jinjī, but is routed, taken captive and released on ransom. The Marāthās beat in the Mughal outposts in every direction, and make overtures to Prince Kāmbakhsh.

Anurād Singh of Būndī dies, and Budh Singh succeeds.

The English, Dutch, and French in Bengal side with the Nawāb against the Rāja of Burdwān and the rebels. The Nawāb gives the factors liberty "to defend themselves." This leads to the erection of the original Fort William at Govindpur, Calcutta. The Dutch assist in retaking Hūglī; the rebels flee to Sātgāon and make progress in Western Bengal.

Feb. Surat threatened with an attack of Marāthās, who, under Rām Rāja, had approached to Nandarbār. Active preparations ward off the assault.

June: An indecisive engagement takes place off Vingorla between seven Dutch and five French ships.

June 27: The Mughal Governor of Surat orders the release of the Surat president, Mr Annesley, and council, but trade remains restrained.

Sept. On the appearance of five pirates in the Red Sea under English colours, all European vessels are prohibited from entering Surat.

A.D.

1696 Sept. 2: The Portuguese conclude a treaty of peace with the Zamorin, providing for the erection of a church at Calicut, and the reimbursement of losses sustained through Moorish depredations. The Zamorin engages not to trade with the enemies of the Portuguese.

Sept. 30: A great storm at Bombay.

The crews of the Company's ships "Mocha" and "Josiah" mutiny, murder their officers, and turn pirates.

1697 March: The Bengali rebels capture the Dutch and English factories at Māldā. Prince 'Azīm-ush Shān, grandson of Aurangzīb, was appointed by him Governor of Bengal, Bihār, and Orissa, superseding Ibrāhīm Khān, whose son is ordered against the rebels, and defeats them at Rājmahāl in May. The prince, 'Azīm-ush Shān, assuming command, the rebels again collect.

H. 1109: Husain 'Alī Khān, a Mughal general, attacks the Marāthās near Tālner, is wounded and captured. The Marāthās extort 140,000 rupees from the people of Nandarbār and Tālner.

March: An encounter takes place between the Portuguese Indian fleet and pirates, the Viceroy stating that the crews were chiefly English. In view of the alarming increase of piracy, Sir John Gayer recommends an application to the king for authority to try and condemn pirates in India.

March 16: A Company of Commerce established at Goa, but ceases to exist in 1701, on the loss of Mombasa.

Durgādās Rāthod, in whose charge were the children of Prince Akbar, becomes reconciled to the emperor, and personally restores the children to their grandfather.

Zulfiqār Khān suspecting Prince Kāmbakhsh of intrigue with the Marāthās, sends him to the royal camp, where he is released. Zulfiqār Khān is now compelled to press the siege of Jinjī.

The Jankamīr of Vepery attempts to collect land customs on goods going to Madras.

Aug. 16: The Portuguese Viceroy concludes a treaty with the King of Sunda to regulate trade and permit the introduction of the Catholic Church into his kingdom.

The Dutch, ordered to reduce military expenditure, are no longer formidable.

A.D.

1697 The English interlopers bribe the Nawāb of Bengal to permit free trade.

Nov. The Rānī of Attingal sends a force to eject the English factors as pirates from Anjengo.

1698 Jan. 2: Mr Walsh, agent of the E.I. Co., arrives in 'Azīm-ush Shān's camp to solicit restitution of property and free trade in Bengal. In July some privileges are obtained and permission to purchase from Prince 'Azīm the villages of Govindpur, Sutānatī, and Kālikata as a zamīndārī. At Govindpur Fort William is built and becomes the seat of government.

Feb. 17: Sha'bān 6, H. 1109. Jinjī fort is taken by Zulfiqār Khān after eight years' siege, Rām Rāja's escape to Vishālgadh being connived at; thence he went to Sātāra which becomes his capital.

Santāji Ghorpade incurs the ill-will of the general Dhanājī Jādhav, is pursued and at last assassinated while bathing, by Nāgujī Manai, a former Marātha Sardār now in the imperial service. (Khāfī Khān dates this in 1105.)

April 1: The Dutch East India Company permit twelve Carmelite monks and one bishop to reside at Cochin, but exclude all other European missionaries of whatever order or nation.

Durgādās Rāthod, on the death of I'timād Khān, is made Governor of Mirtha district.

May 13: The court dismisses Samuel Annesley, president at Surat, suspecting him of obstructing the Company's trade to his own interest—recalled to the service 1709.

The Bengal rebels kill Khwāja Anwar, Prince 'Azīm's counsellor, and attack the royal camp, but are defeated with the loss of their leader, Rahīm Shāh.

Bengal is made independent of Fort St George or Madras.

July 7: Mr Thomas Pitt made Governor of Madras: to be for twelve months independent of Sir John Gayer the Commissary-General. His orders are to limit the settlements on the coast to Madras, Fort St David, and Vizāgapatam; to administer justice; and to act against interlopers.

Sept. 20: Antonio Luiz Gonçalves da Camara Coutinho

A.D.

1698 arrives at Goa as Viceroy in succession to Dom Pedro Antonio de Noronha.

Capt. Kidd, the pirate, forms the privateers into squadrons and blockades the coast. The Mughal lays an embargo on the entire European trade in Surat.

Money being required by the English Government to prosecute the war with France, the private merchants outbid the London Company in the offer of a loan; a Bill is introduced in their favour and is carried by ten votes. The new Company is called the "English Company" in contradistinction to the "London" E.I. Co.

Sept. 3: The English Company is chartered, each subscriber to be a separate trader. Sept. 5: it is incorporated as a joint stock company. The old Company avail themselves of the permission of corporations to become holders of stock, and subscribe £315,000 to the funds of the new Association.

The London Company—ordered to cease trading in three years—now allows its servants, as an encouragement, to trade privately in jewels.

Dec.: Jumāda II., H. 1110. The Mughal army arrives before Sātāra and opens a heavy fire.

In the new Charter provision is made for the maintenance of one minister in every garrison or superior factory and to instruct the "Gentoos" (Hindus) in the Protestant religion.

At Madras all the former stations are resolved to exclude the new Company's servants.

Mr Eyre, agent at Chatānatī, returns to England. Mr John Beard, jun., succeeds.

1699 Jan. Sir John Gayer is compelled by the Mughal Governor of Surat to give security to make good all future robberies by pirates. Daniel Annesley, president of Surat, dismissed, and Stephen Colt succeeds.

Jan. Commodore Warren, furnished and provisioned by the new Company, leaves Portsmouth with a fleet of four sail to extirpate the pirates in the Indian seas.

March: The English Company employ Mr Papillon to negotiate a coalition between the two Companies. This is found to be

A.D.

1699 impracticable, the English Company's funds not permitting a joint stock to be formed, nor purchase of factories in India to be made.

H. 1110: Rām Rāja leaves Sātāra at the head of a large army and marches into Berār. The Mughals make little impression on his force. Aurangzīb adopts a new plan, that of siege and pursuit combined.

Bishn Singh of Jaypur dies. Bijay Singh succeeds, receiving the name of Jaysingh II.

Chikka Deva Rāja of Maisur sends an embassy to Aurangzīb's court at Ahmadnagar to obtain recognition of his authority over his newly conquered territories. Permission is granted him to bear the title Jagat Deva Rāja, and to sit on an ivory throne.

April: The "Shrewsbury," an interloping vessel, arrives at Surat with intelligence of the establishment of the new Company.

July: Sir Edward Littleton arrives at Hūglī as President of the new Co.'s affairs and King's Consul. Mr Beard, senior councillor, intimates the intention of the London Company to maintain their position till 1701.

Sept. 5: Sir William Norris, ambassador of the new Company, arrives at Masulipatam. His authority is disavowed.

Nov. 6: Messrs Mewse and Brooke, subordinate officers of the English Company, arrive at Surat as factors.

Dec. Sir C. Eyre of the London Company, formerly agent at Chatānatī, is instructed to build a strong pentagonal fort at Calcutta, to be called Fort William, and the factory to be constituted a presidency with a council of five members.

The Danish settlement at Tranquebar attacked by the Rāja of Tanjor.

Dec. 18: Jumāda II. 25, H. 1111. Sātāra, the Marātha capital, is besieged by the Mughals, but holds out for some months.

H. 1111: 'Abdul Jalil Sayyid of Bilgrām, whose poetical name was "Wasīti," is presented to Aurangzīb, and obtains a jagīr or mansab with the offices of Bakhshi and news-writer of Gujarāt—he is author of several works. Died Rabī' I. 23, 1137.

1700 Jan. The three villages of Satānatī, Kālīkata, and Govindpur formally purchased by the London Company from Prince 'Azīm-ush Shan.

Jan. 11: Sir Nicolas Waite, formerly the old Co.'s agent at

A.D.

1700 Bantam, now King's Consul and President of the new Company, reaches Bombay where Sir John Gayer refuses to recognise him. Jan. 19: he arrives at Surat, and on the factor's refusal to strike his flag, he has it forcibly removed from the factory. These violent scenes are resented by the Mughals, and trade is again suspended.

March: Shawwāl, H. 1111. Rām Rāja of Sātāra dies of smallpox at Jinjī. His son, Karan, survives him only a few days. Seiwa, an infant son, placed on the *masnad* under guardianship of Rām Chand Pandit, and the regency of his mother Tārābāī.

April: The London Co. obtain a verdict against their rivals, Capt. Heath having seized the property of individuals on the London Co.'s ship "Neptune." April 11: the London Company obtain an Act of Parliament for continuance of their Corporation. The king recommends a union of the two interests.

May 1: Zī-l qa'da 13, H. 1111. Aurangzīb takes Sātāra fort. Parlī is immediately invested, and surrenders in June: Muharram, H. 1112.

S. 1756. Rānā Jaysingh of Udaypur dies. Amara, his revolted son, succeeds, and forms a private treaty with Shāh 'Alam (Bahādur Shāh), the Mughal heir-apparent.

At Madras, disputes occur between Consul John Pitt and President Thomas Pitt.

Dec. 10: Sir William Norris, M.P., ambassador to the Mughal, arrives at Surat and by bribes secures a public entry. Sir John Gayer disavows his authority and sends a vakīl to court.

Commodore Warren of the English Co. dies at Surat. Sir Edward Littleton succeeds. Sir Nicolas Waite accuses him of partiality to the London Company and denounces the latter to the Mughal as instigators of the piracies in India.

Mar Simon, sent by the Nestorian patriarch to Malabar as bishop, is captured by the Jesuits and taken to Pondicheri, where he was put in irons and died.

1701 Jan. Sir Charles Eyre retires from the London Company's presidency of Bengal. Mr John Beard, jun., succeeds.

Jan. The Portuguese obstruct the landing of provisions at Sīon for Bombay.

Jan. 12: Miraj is occupied by the Mughals, but retaken by the Marāthās in H. 1114.

A.D.

1701 Jan. 22: Sir N. Waite lodges a complaint with the Mughal Governor of Surat, demanding that the factors of the London Company be imprisoned for insults shown to Sir William Norris acting for the new E. India Company. The governor refusing to interfere, Sir W. Norris orders Sir John Gayer, his wife, and two members of Council to be seized.

Jan. 27: Sir W. Norris leaves Surat and on April 28 obtains an audience of Aurangzīb at Panhālā. A *farmān* is obtained for the three presidencies but no real advantage is derived. Nov. 5, he leaves for Surat but is detained on the way by Ghāzi-ud dīn Khān, the minister.

Feb. 8: The Court of Directors disapprove of the intemperate conduct of Sir Nicolas Waite, and advise commercial rivalry rather than assumption of authority. The Surat governor's son, by order of Aurangzīb, seizes Sir John Gayer, his wife, President S. Colt, and others, and imprisons and barbarously uses them at Surat.

The French leave Surat and concentrate at Pondicheri.

March 13: The Deputy-Governor of Bombay reports the capture by Marāthās of several vessels. Encounters continue between the Marāthās and the Siddis.

April 17-23: A Commission of seven appointed by a general Court to receive or make proposals for a Union between the London and the English East India Companies. Sir Basil Firebrace is empowered to adjust the terms.

H. 1112: Muhammad Hadi, son of a poor Brahman, is appointed *diwān* of Bengal with the title Kartalab Khān.

June 7: Zī-l hijja, H. 1112. Parnālā fort surrendered to Aurangzīb after a protracted siege. The forts of Vishālgarh, Singarh, Purandhar, Rājgarh, and Torna are next reduced.

Aurangzīb orders compensation to be made by the various European Companies for losses sustained by his subjects from the depredations of European pirates.

Kidd, the pirate, taken and hanged in England.

June 13: Christopher Boone appointed first coroner at Bombay.

Sept. 17: Dom Fr. Agostinho da Annunciação and Dom Vasco Luiz Coutinho take over the government at Goa, till 1703.

A.D.

1701 John Ribeiro, a Jesuit, is appointed by the King of Portugal as Bishop of Malabar. The Dutch interdict his exercise of authority in Cochin, but he settled at Ambalakāda in the Zamorin's state, whence he exercised authority till his death in 1720.

1702 Jan. At this time 109 English are in durance at Surat. The preliminaries of the union of the two Companies are settled.

Feb. 6: Mr Thomas Pitt, Governor of Madras, informs Dā'ūd Khān that Aurangzīb's demands are equivalent to a declaration of war.

Feb. Negotiations between the English in Bengal and the Mughal broken off. All the English at Kāsimbāzār, Rājmahal, and Patna are imprisoned and their goods confiscated. President Beard deters the Faujdār from further proceedings.

April: Nawāb Dā'ūd Khān invests Fort St George, but is induced to retire. July, he pays a friendly visit to Madras.

Gunpowder first manufactured at Madras.

April 12: Sir William Norris arrives at Surat from his embassy: 18th, leaves Surat. Oct. 10: dies of dysentery near Mauritius.

April 27: The two Companies approve an instrument of union and advise their servants to cease disputes.

The Bengal Council ordered to be presided over by Mr Halsey (old Company) and Mr Hedges (of the new) in alternate weeks.

H. 1113: Murshid Qulī Khān, afterwards Ja'far Khān, diwān of Bengal, accuses Prince A'zam of a plot to assassinate him and moves to Murshidābād. Aurangzīb orders the prince's removal to Bihār.

The Marāthās levy *chauth* from Surat and Burhānpur.

June 15: Muharram 19, H. 1114. Khelna or Vishālgarh, after a hard siege, is captured by the Marāthās.

June 16: Allen Catchpoole, a servant of the English Co., leaves Batavia to found a settlement on Pulo Condor, leaves some officers with Macassar slaves, revisits Chusan and returns to Pulo Condor.

July 22: An Indenture Tripartite between the queen and the two Companies, equalising the stock, passes under the Great Seal and is considered their Charter of Union. The factors of each Company to manage separately the stocks previously sent out.

A.D.

1702 The two Companies under a Court of twenty-four Managers to be allowed to trade for seven years on the Charter of the English Company, to wind up their affairs, when the Companies should be finally and completely united, taking the name of "The United Company of Merchants trading to the East Indies." The factories of the Old Company are detailed as, Bombay: Surat, Swally, Bharoch, Ahmadābād, Agra, and Lucknow. In Malabar: forts and factories of Kārwār, Telicheri, Anjengo, and Calicut. Persia: factories of Gombrūn, Shirāz, and Isfahān. Madras: Fort St George, Fort St David, Kūdalūr, Porto Novo, Pettapoli (Nizāmpatam), Masulipatam, Madhapolem, and Vizagapatam. On Sumatra: York Fort, Benkūlen, Indrapur, Tyamong, and Sellebar; also, Tonquin in Cochin China. Fort William: Chatānatī (Calcutta), Bālasor, Kāsimbāzār, Dhākā, Hūgli, Māldā, Rājmahāl, and Pātna; also, the island of St Helena. The New Company enumerate only—factories at Surat, Masulipatam, Madhapolem, and on the islands of Borneo and Pulo Condor.

The stock of the Old Company, £315,000, of the New Company, £1,662,000, and of separate trades, £23,000,—making a total of two millions sterling.

In India the opposing interests still continue to clash, especially at Surat.

Aug. 2: The English Company's ship "Norris" blown up off Dīū Point.

Nov. 2: Great storm at Bombay.

1703 H. 1114: Prince Muhammad A'zam Shāh appointed fortieth Viceroy of Gujarāt and Governor of Ajmir and Jodhpur, the minister Khwāja 'Abdul Hamid Khān to order the province till his arrival.

Aurangzīb intrigues for the death of Dargādās Rāthod, Governor of Pātan; the latter escapes a pursuing party through the devotion of his grandson and Rajput servants, who cover his retreat at the cost of their lives.

May 8: Mr John Pitt, Consul of the English Company, dies at Madras. Fort St David made subordinate to Fort St George. Gabriel Roberts appointed President.

June 4-18: The Court of Managers reappoint Sir John Gayer to be General and Governor of Bombay, Mr Burniston Deputy-

A.D.

1703 Governor, and Sir Nicolas Waite President of Surat. President Beard confirmed in his office in Bengal and a Commission of eight appointed to control all proceedings.

July 3: A defensive alliance formed between Queen Anne, the States General, and the King of Portugal, guaranteeing the safety of their respective possessions in India. Bombay to be acknowledged as an English possession, and Portuguese vessels to have the same access to Malacca as those of other European nations.

Oct. 2: Caetano de Mello de Castro, the Viceroy, succeeds the Commission at Goa.

1704 Jan. 10: The Court of the English Company censure Sir Edward Littleton at Hūglī for negligence in transmitting accounts. Secret orders are sent to four senior members of Council to report on his proceedings.

Jan. 22: An indecisive engagement between seven Portuguese and seven Arabian ships takes place off Surat.

Sir John Gayer, the London Company's servants at Surat, and the Dutch agents are imprisoned, and new security bonds extorted by the Mughal governor, in consequence of the capture of a Makka ship by a pirate. The Dutch fleet blockade Surat and obtain a promise of release from the security bond.

Feb. 17: Rājgarh Marātha fort taken by the Mughals.

Chikka Deva Rāja of Maisur dies, having established a prosperous state extending from Palni and Anemale to Midagesi, and from Baramahāl to Kūrg and Balam. Kanthirava Rāja, called Mūk-arasu (the deaf and dumb) succeeds, till 1714.

H. 1116: Murshid Qulī Ja'far Khān appointed Governor of Bengal. He founded Murshidābād as his capital; he died about 1726.

June: The Company's ship "Neptune" wrecked off Cape Comorin. The natives carry off thirty chests of treasure.

Nov. Sir Nicolas Waite, who was appointed to succeed Sir John Gayer in case of vacancy, basely contrives to prolong his detention by bribes and misrepresentations. He now takes possession of Bombay and appoints Mr Aislabie Deputy-Governor on the death of Mr Burniston.

1705 Jan. The Court of Directors formally revokes the Commission

A.D.

1705 to Sir Edward Littleton as President of Bengal and dismisses him from the service.

Jan. 19: Peace concluded between the Portuguese and the King of Kanara, the latter to pay tribute in rice, to furnish stone for a fort at Mangalor, and to recompense the state for expenses of a previous war.

The Goa Viceroy in person takes command of an expedition against Bicholim.

Jan. 29: Commodore Harland, with the queen's fleet, leaves India.

Feb. 20: Aurangzīb having moved south besieges Wākinkera, S.E. of Bijāpūr, which at length capitulates May 6.

March 2: Allen Catchpoole, factor at Pulo Condor, with nearly all the English on the island, are murdered by their Macassar garrison.

H. 1114: The Marāthās overrun Gujarāt and Kandesh, and ravage Mālwa. They defeat Safdar Khān Bābi at Ratanpur. Zulfiqār Khān and Ghāzi-ud dīn Khān sent against them. The Mughals make overtures for an accommodation, but on the increasing insolence of the Marāthās, negotiations are broken off.

Ibrāhim Khān, Viceroy of Kashmīr, appointed forty-first Viceroy of Gujarāt. Durgādās Rāthod asks for and receives pardon and secures the restoration of his lands.

Prince Muhammad Bedār Bakht forty-second Viceroy of Gujarāt till 1706. He appoints Amānat Khān Governor of Surat and Khambay.

Mar Gabriel arrives at Kollam, in an English ship, as Nestorian Bishop of Malabar; he died 1730.

1706 Jan. 31: After twenty-two years' absence Aurangzīb returns to Ahmadnagar.

Feb. 5: Prince A'zam Shāh requests permission to resign his governorship of Gujarāt and return to court. Muhammad Ibrahīm Khān is appointed governor.

A'zam Shāh procures Prince A'zim-us-Shān's recall to court, and quarrels with Prince Kām Bakhsh, the favourite son.

Ranga Krishna, Nāyakk of Madura, imprisons his grandmother, Mangamāl, and starves her to death.

A.D.

1706 H. 1118: Durgādās Rāthod and Ajīt Singh again rebel: an army is sent against them under Kunwār Mohkam Singh, whom they defeat and take Jodhpur.

The English E.I. Co. pay the diwān of Murshidābād 25,000 rupees for permission to settle a factory at Kāsimbāzār, specially for the convenience of having the European bullion coined into rupees at the mint.

March: The secret orders of the English Company counteract the instructions of the Court of Managers to the Bombay and Surat Councils. Sir John Gayer is thus left in prison and the London Company's estate exposed to Mughal extortion.

Owing to the dismissal of Sir Edward Littleton and the death of President Beard, Mr Sheldon of the London Co. and Mr Hedges of the English Co. are nominated jointly as chiefs in Bengal, and to bring up the accounts of the two Companies.

May 23: The Marātha armies, having remained in the Surat district without assaulting the town, retire, plundering the villages on their line of march.

July 9: Bartholomaeus Ziegenbalg and Plutschau, Danish missionaries, arrive at Tranquebar, where they establish the Christian Mission; they encounter much opposition. They are the first Protestant missionaries in India. Ziegenbalg died 1719.

Oct. The Dutch fleet again blockades Surat, and release is demanded from the security bonds and permission to re-establish the factory.

The islands of Sanguem and Panjem subjugated and fortified by the Portuguese: the territories of Bicholim and Sanquelim handed over to the Rāja of Sunda, who becomes tributary to the Portuguese.

Dec. 30: François Martin, Governor-General at Pondicheri, dies, and M. Dulivier succeeds.

BAHĀDUR SHĀH.

1707 March 3: Zī-l qa'da 28, H. 1118. Aurangzīb dies at Ahmadnagar in his eighty-ninth year. His third son, A'zam Shāh, crowned at Ahmadābād, March 15; but his elder brother, Muhammad Mu'azzam, assumed the crown at Kābul, and in a battle fought at Jajowan, between Agra and Dholpur, 8th June, A'zam Shāh

A.D.

1707 and his two grown-up sons were slain, and Mu'azzam reigned under the name of Bahādur Shāh, till Feb. 1712.

Dā'ūd Khān Panni appointed Deputy-Governor of the Dekhan for Zulfiqār Khān.

June: For joining Prince Bedar Bakht, Jāysingh of Jaypur is invaded: he drives out the imperial garrisons and forms a league with the Rānās of Udaypur and Jodhpur against the Muhammadans.

June 19: Rām Singh of Kotā slain at Ajaju. Bhīm Singh succeeds.

Shāhuji escapes from the Mughal camp and proclaims himself Rāja. The regent, Tārābāī, disputes his claim and sends out an army under Dhanāji Jādhav and the Pritinidhi, Parshurām Trimbak. Dhanāji is won over to Shāhuji who obtains Sātāra fort.

The Marāthās enter Gujarāt, approaching to Batvā near the Viceroy's camp. The Viceroy offers them 210,000 rupees, and Marāthās withdraw.

Khem Sāwant receives a deed from Shāhuji Rāja, confirming him in the possession of Sāwantwādi and half the revenues of the Salshi mahāl.

Murshid Quli Ja'far Khān begins a system of oppression of the zamīndārs of Bengal, depriving them of all power over their lands, and all interference with the collection.

The works at Fort William by this time were somewhat advanced, had a number of guns, and 125 soldiers, of whom half were Europeans. The Directors make Calcutta, which had been hitherto subordinate to Madras, a separate presidency.

1708 Jan. 6: Peace between the Mughal Governor of Surat and the Dutch is arranged.

Feb.: Zī-l qa'da, H. 1119. Prince Kāmbakhsh, in revolt against his brother, Bahādur Shāh, is defeated near Haidarābād, and dies of his wounds.

March: Shāhujī, or Shivājī II., released on Aurangzīb's death, formally ascends the throne of Sātāra and appoints Bhairav Pant Pingle as Peshwā. A Brahman Kulkarni of Śrīvardhan, now in charge of a village in Chaul; he is afterwards known as Bālāji Vīshvanāth Peshwā. Shāhujī prosecutes war on the party of

A.D.

1708 Tārābāī, who also claimed supremacy. Panhāla, Vishālgarh, and Rāngna forts are captured.

March: Muharram, H. 1120. The freebooter, Pāp Rāī, with a force attacks Orangal, and kills twelve or thirteen thousand people; other depredations follow: the emperor is petitioned and Pāp Rāī is besieged in Tārákandā for nine months, taken and executed.

April 20: Sir Nicolas Waite dismissed from the service of the Company as Governor of Bombay. His treachery had been disclosed by his instrument, Rustam, a native broker; but in defiance of orders from the Court he continued to retain authority. Now his Council had in January put him in confinement for maladministration. William Aislabie, deputy-governor, is appointed to succeed, Sir John Gayer being still a prisoner in the Surat factory.

Govind Singh, the last Sikh Guru, assassinated at Nander in Haidarābād districts.

The Sikhs rise in rebellion in the Panjāb and plunder extensively. Shams Khān, faujdār of the Jālandhar Duāb, defeats them with a volunteer army at Rāhūn.

Ghāzi-ud-dīn Khān Bahādur Firūz Jang appointed forty-fourth Viceroy of Gujarāt, till 1710.

The Nawāb of the Karnātak gives Uyāsarpādi and Nangābākam villages to the English. A settlement is also formed at Telicheri. The villages of Tiruvettūr, Shattankād, and Kattiwākkam (Ennūr) are granted, Sept. 25; resumed by Nawāb Sa'ādat-Ullāh Khān, 1713, but restored by the emperor, Jan. 5, 1716.

Sept. 29: Sidney, Earl of Godolphin, Lord High Treasurer of Great Britain, pronounces an award regarding the financial position of the two companies, the London Co. to pay £96,615. 4s. 9d. to the United Co., and the latter to pay £66,005. 4s. 2d. to the English Co. The London Co. to assign to the queen their home debts. The Charter is extended till March 1726, and the Companies incorporated as the United Company of Merchants of England trading to the East Indies.

The French E.I. Co., being in straits, permits private individuals to equip two vessels in the name of the Company for India, but are losers on the transaction. Le Chevalier Herbert succeeds M. Dulivier as Governor of Pondicheri.

A.D.

1708 Oct. 28: Dom Rodrigue da Costa succeeds Caetano de Mello de Castro as Viceroy at Goa.

1709 H. 1121: Religious riots break out in various cities, between the Sunnī and the Shī'ah Muhammadans on the emperor's order to introduce into the *khutba* the word *wasī* (heir), as an attribute of the Khalīf 'Alī. The *khatīb* of Ahmadābād is stabbed to death.

The Ghilzai chief, Mīr Vaīs, murders Ghurgin Khān, the Persian minister, and all the retinue at a banquet near Qandahār: the Afghāns assume the Persians' dress, enter Qandahār and master the city.

March: Muharram 1121. The Marāthās under Tārābāī, Rājārām's widow, defeat Ahmad Khān, Sūbahdār of Burhānpūr.

March 11: Samuel Annesley recalled to the service of the United Company.

March 30: Ananda Ranga Pillai, diarist, born at Perambūr, the son of Tiruvengada Pillai, merchant.

Shāhu enters into a compact with the Mughals, and so renders the reduction of Tārābāī less pressing.

Dec.: Shawwāl. Muhammad Amīn Khān attacked by Sikhs at Shāhdhara, and repulsed. Repeated battles follow, and the Sikhs are driven off to the mountains of Barfi, Rāja of Sirmūr.

Anup Singh of Bikanir dies. Sarup Singh succeeds. Phond Sāwant II. of Sāwantwādi succeeds his uncle Kham Sāwant.

April 22: Grant of perpetuity issued by writ of Privy Seal to the East India Company.

Sept. 18: Thomas Pitt is succeeded by Mr Gulston Addison, brother of Joseph Addison, as Governor of Madras; dies Oct. 17, and is succeeded by Edmond Montague, as acting Governor, till Nov. 14, when William Fraser takes office, till 1711.

The Jesuits destroy a Hindu temple at Pondicheri. Riots ensue.

A commercial agent is appointed to attend to British interests in Burma.

The exports of this year were £168,357, half as much again as those of the previous one.

1710 Sa'ādat-Ullāh Khān acknowledged Nawāb of the Karnātak.

A.D.

1710 Tārābāī, with the help of Phōnd Sāwant, recovers Panhāla from Shāhu, and fixes her court there.

The acting Governor of Harāt marches on Qandahār, and for eighteen months a campaign is carried on, ending in the complete defeat of the Persians.

Native authority restored in Arakan by Mahādanda Bo, who expels the foreign guards and supports a native chief, afterwards King Tsanda Wijāya.

The English at Surat, unable to endure the oppression of Amānat Khān, governor, close their factory for three years.

The *Ma'āsir-i 'Alamgīrī* of Muhamad Sākī Musta-idd Khān finished.

1711 H. 1123: Mun'im Khān, Khān Khanān, in disgrace for having allowed Banda, the Sikh leader, to escape, dies. He is the author of the *Ilhāmāt Muni'mī.*

Khusro Khān, nephew of Ghurgin, defeats Mīr Vaīs at the passage of the Helmand, marches on Qandahār and at once invests it. Mīr Vaīs keeps the field and harasses the besieging army.

H. 1123: On the death of Ghāzi-ud-dīn Khān, Viceroy of Gujarāt, Amānat Khān of Surat is appointed deputy with the title of Shamānath Khān.

The Marāthās again invade Gujarāt, and meeting the imperial troops at Ankleshwar sustain a defeat.

Amara II., Rānā of Udaypur, dies, and is succeeded by his son, Sangrāmasimha II.

July 11: Edward Harrison succeeds Wm. Fraser as Governor of Madras, till 1717. Raworth, Governor of Fort St David, disputes his authority, and President Harrison in person takes over the keys of the fort.

It is decided that no person be a Director of the East India Company and the Bank of England at the same time (9 Anne, c. 7).

JAHĀNDĀR SHĀH.

1712 Feb. 28: Muharram 19, H. 1124. Bahādur Shāh, Qutb-ud dīn Shāh 'Alam, of Dehli, dies at Lahor. His four sons dispute the succession, and a battle ensues in which 'Azīm-ush Shān, Rafī-ush

A.D.

1712 Shān, and Jahān Shāh are killed, and Mu'iz-ud dīn Jahāndār Shāh, the eldest son, is crowned emperor, April 20: Rabī' I. 14, H. 1124. Zulfiqār Khān appointed *vazīr*. A few months later Farrukh-siyar, son of 'Azīm-us Shān, supported by the Sayyids, 'Abdullah Khān, Governor of Pātna, and Husain 'Alī Khān, Governor of Allahābād, raises an army to oppose the new emperor.

April 7: The Portuguese conclude a treaty with Bāpu, Deśāī of Kudale to prevent the latter from waging war on Phonda.

H. 1124: Asaf-ud-daula is appointed forty-fifth Viceroy of Gujarāt, till 1713. He subdues the rebellious Kolis of the Chunwal.

Shivājī, son of Tārābāī, dies at Kolhāpur. Sambhājī, a younger son of Rāja Rām, placed in his stead. Tārābāī is imprisoned, and Shāhu's ascendancy secured.

Jaysingh of Amber invests Thun, held by Churāmani, a rebel Jāt leader; on its capture Badan Singh, brother of Jaysingh, is proclaimed at Dīg as Jāt Thākur.

Exclusive trade extended to Lady Day 1736 (10 Anne, c. 28).

Sept. 21: Vasco Fernandez César de Menezes succeeds Dom Rodrigue da Costa as Viceroy at Goa.

The French East India Company abandons direct shipping, granting its privileges to the merchants of St Malo for payment.

FARRUKH-SIYAR.

1713 Jan. 9, O.S.: Zī-l hijja 23, H. 1124. Muhammad Farrukh-siyar and the Sayyids defeat the imperial army at Khwāja, and next day Farrukh-siyar, son of 'Azim-ush Shān, ascends the throne of Dehli. Zulfiqār Khān betrays Jahāndār Shāh to the enemy, but is strangled with the emperor, Feb. 13: Muharram 17, H. 1125.

Qāzi 'Abdullah, chief of Dhākā (Dacca), elevated to the highest dignities under Farrukh-siyar.

Khusro Khān, on raising the siege of Qandahār, is attacked by Mīr Vaīs, defeated and killed.

Muhammad Farrukh-siyar intrigues against the Sayyids, sending Husain 'Alī to Mārwār with secret advice to Rāja Ajīt Singh to oppose him. Husain 'Alī, however, concludes a peace, Ajīt Singh engaging to send his son, 'Abhaya Singh, to court,

A.D.

1713 and to give his daughter in marriage to Farrukh-siyar. This marriage takes place Dec. 7, 1715: Zī-l hijja 22, 1127.

Shamānat Khān forty-sixth Viceroy of Gujarāt.

Dā'ūd Khān is transferred from the Dekhan to Gujarāt as forty-seventh Viceroy, and Chīn Qulij Khān 'Asaf Jāh appointed Viceroy in the Dekhan with the title of Nizām-ul Mulk.

Chandrasen Jādhav, the disaffected Senāpati of the Marāthās, goes over to the side of 'Asaf Jāh Nizām-ul Mulk. July, a battle ensues between the Mughals and Shāhu's party, near Purandhar, without decisive results. An accommodation is effected, and Nizām-ul Mulk withdraws to Aurangābād.

Bahiropant Pingle, Shāhu's Peshwā, proceeds against Kānhoji Āngria, is defeated and imprisoned. Āngria is met and defeated by Bālāji Vishvanāth, who makes terms, gaining Āngria to take the side of Shāhu against the Kolhāpur faction. Ruptures with the Siddis of Janjira are suppressed by Bālāji Vishvanāth.

Under Ja'far Khān the subhā of Bengal is now virtually independent of the emperor. Owing to Ja'far Khān's vexatious exactions on the English in Bengal, an embassy is sent from the settlement to protest to the emperor.

A Carmelite monk, Fr. Maurico de Santa Theresa, assumes independence in Sunda as "Bishop of the Propaganda," makes his headquarters in a temple, and resists the call of the Viceroy to leave the territories.

M. Dulivier reassumes office as Governor-General at Pondicheri.

1714 A final attempt by the Court of Isfahān to annex Qandahār results in failure.

H. 1126: Farrukh-siyar allows his palace to be occupied by the guards of the Sayyids, while a reconciliation is come to between the two state factions.

At Ahmadābād, Harīrām, a banker's agent, having used a Muhammadan roughly at the Holi, conflicts occur between the Muslims and Hindus: bankers' and jewellers' houses are pillaged.

Mūn'im Khān is appointed Governor of Surat in succession to 'Abdul Hamid Khān, and arrives in 1715.

Feb. 19: The Portuguese attack Arab ships off Surat and do much damage. Feb. 20, the Portuguese factors at Surat obtain a *farmān* limiting their duties to 2½ per cent.

A.D.

1714 Bālāji Vishwanāth is raised to the rank of Peshwā, henceforth a hereditary office in his family. Purandhar fortress is granted to him as a residence by Pant Sachiv.

Kanthirava Rāja of Maisur dies. Dodda Krishna Rāja succeeds, but proves unfit for rule. Disagreements between the Mughal governors of Sira and the Karnātak occur: finally a joint confederacy is bought off by the Maisur Rāja.

Sept. 29: The French Company gain a renewal for ten years of their privileges, though unable directly to make use of them.

Charles VI., Emperor of Germany, grants commissions for ships to trade to the East Indies. This association makes several successful experimental voyages. He afterwards founded the Ostend Company, so injurious to the interests of the English and Dutch.

A new treaty is concluded by the Portuguese with the Rāja of Sunda, making provision for the housing of Portuguese priests, and the ejection of the "Bishop of the Propaganda."

1715 Farrukh-siyar sends Husain 'Alī to govern the Dekhan, at the same time giving secret instructions to Dā'ūd Khān to oppose him in Kāndesh. Sept. 24: Ramazān 25, H. 1127: The two armies meet at the Lāl Bāgh of Burhānpur, when Dā'ūd Khān is killed. Nimāji Sindia, who had nominally joined Dā'ūd Khān's party, plunders the defeated army.

Ziyā Khān, Governor of Surat, opposes the governor-elect, Mūn'im Khān, but on the defeat of his garrison he gives way.

Ajīt Singh, Mahārāja of Jodhpur, forty-eighth Viceroy of Gujarāt, his son, Kunwar Abhaya Singh being appointed Governor of Sorath. Haidar Qulī Khān—appointed to Sorath and Gohilwār—then in charge of the Viceroy's deputy, Fath Singh Kāyat, is with difficulty installed in his office, owing to disagreements with the Viceroy.

June 19: Dr Cobbe proposes the erection of a church in Bombay, to which Governor Aislabie subscribes 1,000 rupees, and the E.I. Co. 10,000. It was completed in 1718.

July 8: A British embassy,—of Messrs Surman and Stephenson, factors from Bengal, with an Armenian as interpreter, and Wm. Hamilton, surgeon,—arrives at Dehli to solicit security from the oppression of the Mughal officers, when Surgeon Hamilton

A.D.

1715 cures the emperor and procures his favour. Dec. 7: The marriage of the emperor postpones their business for six months.

First church built in Calcutta: the steeple of which fell in 1737, and the whole church was destroyed by the Muhammadans in 1756. It was on the site of the modern St John's.

Nov. Mīr Vaīs, first acknowledged King of all Afghānistān, dies. His brother, Mīr 'Abdullah, is nominated king. A weak monarch, he sends an embassy to Persia offering conditional submission.

Stephen Strutt, Deputy-Governor, officiates as Governor of Bombay, in succession to the Honble. W. Aislabie, till 1716.

The treaty between the Siamese and the British Government in the reign of Charles II. is superseded by a second treaty.

1716 Jan. 16: The petition of the English embassy is delivered to the emperor who, in July, grants a patent conferring the right of passing commerce duty free.

Charles Boone, Governor of Bombay, till 1720.

March: Mīr Mahmūd, a young son of the late Mīr Vaīs of Afghānistān, indignant at the philo-Persian policy of his uncle, summons the chiefs, occupies the palace, kills his uncle 'Abdullah, and is proclaimed king.

Zulfiqār Beg sent to suppress the depredations of Khanderāv Dābhāde, a Marātha freebooter, is defeated and killed. A punitive party of Mughals fights an indecisive action near Ahmadnagar. Khanderāv is appointed Senāpati by Rāja Shāhu, in room of Manāji Morār, who is divested of the title.

H. 1128: Asad Khān Karam-mālū, Bahādur Shah's minister, who had been disgraced by Farrukh-siyar, dies at the age of ninety, or ninety-four lunar years.

Basālat Jang Bahādur forty-ninth Viceroy of Gujarāt. Ajīt Singh encamps at Sarkhej to resist his successor's arrival, but is persuaded to retire.

An insurrection of the Sikhs is checked by 'Abdul Samad Khān, Governor of Lāhor, who defeats and takes them prisoners, with their chief, Bānda, who is put to death with torture, and cruel persecution of his followers takes place.

Dec. 19: A treaty is concluded between the Governor of Bombay and the Portuguese general, Dom João Fernandez de

A.D.

1716 Almeida: the ships of either nationality to be allowed free access to ports and harbours of the other, only paying dues on the goods landed.

1717 Mīr Mahmūd, profiting by a revolt of the Afghān population of Harāt against their Persian Governor, Zamān Khān, marches to Zamīndāwar, attacks, defeats, and slays him. He then occupies Harāt, and declares it independent of Persia.

Jan. 6: A *farmān* is granted to the E.I. Company exempting their trade from duties, and allowing them to purchase thirty-seven towns contiguous to Calcutta, and to possess land around their factories.

Jan. 8: Joseph Collet, Governor of Madras, in succession to Edward Harrison, till Jan. 18, 1720.

Jan. 13: Dom Sebastião de Andrade Passanha, Archbishop Primate, succeeds Vasco Fernandez Cesar de Menezes as Governor at Goa. Oct. 16: Dom Luiz de Menezes, Conde de Ericeira, takes office as Viceroy.

The Ostend East India Company started for trade under the protection of the Emperor of Austria, Prince Eugene sending two forty-pound vessels to the Malabar coast under imperial colours. The Company not regularly chartered till 1723.

Husain 'Alī Khān makes peace with Rāja Shāhu, and acknowledges the latter's claim to all the territory formerly possessed by Shivāji: promises to restore all forts taken within that tract, and to allow the levy of *chauth* over the Dekhan. This treaty is not ratified by Farrukh-siyar.

Haidar Qulī Khān appointed to succeed Ajīt Singh at Ahmadābād: out of a skirmish between one of his officers and a water-carrier in Safdar Khān Bābi's retinue, a serious affray breaks out at Pitlād. Safdar Khān collects followers, and is defeated the following day. The Bābīs escape to Pālanpur.

Muhammad Amīn Khān appointed Governor of Mālwa.

Dec. 31: The people of Por-patan, *i.e.*, Prabhās-Pattan or Virāwal, refusing to pay the annual tribute, are besieged and stormed by the Portuguese Viceroy, and the town is burnt.

1718 Great famine in Gujarāt.

A.D.

1718 Murshid Qulī Khān made Governor of Bihār in addition to Bengal and Orissa.

Four of Kānhoji Āngria's vessels and two Portuguese ships engage off Anjidīva.

Daman attacked by the chiefs of 'Assarceta' and Rāmnagar. A Portuguese force pursues them to Fathpur, where they burn the place. The chief's nephews sue for peace, which is concluded.

Aug. 19: M. de la Provostière appointed *ad interim* Governor at Pondicheri.

Sept: Shawwāl, H. 1130. Farrukh-siyar is reconciled to Sayyid 'Abdullah Khān, intimidated by the threatening attitude of Husain 'Alī Khān who, later, in Nov.: Muharram, H. 1132, leaves the Dekhan for Dehli at the head of 10,000 Marāthās.

Budh Singh of Būndī, a supporter of Bahādur Shāh, is dispossessed by Jaysingh of Amber, who places Dulil Singh of Kārwar on the throne.

Oct. Rāma Kāmāti, a confidential servant of President Boone at Bombay, intrigues with Kānhoji Āngria, advising him to invade the settlement. Inquiries are carried on for two years into the charge.

An Act of Parliament passed to punish British merchants trading to India under foreign commissions.

The ex-Sultān Guelemot, of Anaksūngai, in Sumatra, raising a force, destroyed the town of Yepu (Ippoe), with the British Resident and all his people.

Dec. 25: St Thomas' Church, Bombay, formally opened: Richard Cobbe, clergyman in charge.

1719 Safī Qulī Khan defeats the Usbaks on the Harāt frontier, but is defeated by the Abdālīs whose power is now established at Harāt.

A native force obliged the English to evacuate Fort Marlborough or Benkūlen, and take refuge on their ships. Benkūlen was ceded to the Dutch in 1825.

Feb. M. Hébert, Governor of Pondicheri, is recalled in consequence of charges preferred against one Nainiya Pillai who had died in prison. M. de la Provostière succeeds.

A.D.

RAFĪ'UD DARJĀT AND RAFĪ'UD-DAULA SHĀHJAHĀN II.

1719 Feb. 25: Rabī' II. 5, H. 1131. The Bārha Sayyids, 'Abdullah Khān, Qutb-ul Mulk and his brother, Husain 'Alī Khan Amīr-ul Umrā, with Ajīt Singh of Mārwār, enter Dehli, and depose, blind, and imprison Farrukh-siyar. Feb. 28: Rabī' II. 8, they proclaim Rafī'ud Darjāt, a grandson of Bahādur Shāh. May 26: Rajab 9, Farrukh-siyar is murdered.

April 29: Jumāda II. 9. The Agra troops set up Neko-siyar, son of Prince Muhammad Akbar and grandson of Aurangzīb, as Sultān. June 25: Sha'bān 7, Haidar Qulī Khān is sent against him, and Aug. 13: Ramazān 27, the fort is captured and the prince with his supporters imprisoned.

June 7: Rajab 19. Rafī'ud Darjāt dies of consumption and his brother, Rafī'ud-daula, is raised to the throne—with the title of Shāhjahān Sānī—who dies within a few months. It is decided that these two brief reigns should be struck out of the list of Sultāns.

MUHAMMAD SHĀH.

1719 Oct. 9: Zī-l qa'da 25. The Sayyid brothers elevate to the throne Roshan Akhtar, the son of Jahān Shāh and grandson of Bahādur Shāh—a youth of seventeen—under the title of Muhammad Shāh, his reign to be reckoned from the death of Farrukh-siyar.

Pilāji Gaikwād, successor of Damāji Gaikwād, marches on Surat, defeats the imperial troops there and establishes himself at Songad.

Mahārāja Ajīt Singh fiftieth Viceroy of Gujarāt, till 1721.

The Nizām-ul-Mulk, secretly inimical to the Sayyids, is suspected and transferred from the Dekhan to Mālwa.

The English and Portuguese unite to check Āngria of Kolābā, but fail.

Aug. The Portuguese fleet, after several indecisive actions, finally routs the Arab fleet.

Dec. Jaysingh of Jaypur appointed the emperor's deputy at Agra and in Mālwa.

A.D.

1719 By Royal edict, the privileges of the French East India Company are revoked and granted to a new organisation floated by Mr Law.

A Charity School organised at Bombay, opened 1753.

Bartholemew Ziegenbalg, missionary and philologist, dies at Tranquebar, and the Danish mission is left in charge of Gründler, who survived him but a year.

1720 Jan. 18: Francis Hastings succeeds Mr Joseph Collet as Governor of Madras, till Oct. 15, 1721.

Feb. 26: The case of Rāma Kamāti and his treasonable correspondence with Āngria brought before the Bombay Council. April 11: he is found guilty and imprisoned for life.

H. 1132: Anti-Hindu disturbances break out in Kashmīr, instigated by Mahbūb Khān 'Abdul Nabī, ending in riot and pillage, in which Mahbūb and others are killed.

April: Jumāda II., H. 1132. 'Asaf Jāh, Nizām-ul-Mulk, throws off his dependence and marches into the Dekhan. June 22: Sha'bān 16, he defeats Dilāwar 'Alī Khān at Ratanpur, near Burhānpur, and Aug. 4: Shawwāl 6, defeats 'Ālam 'Alī Khān at Bālāpur. Both generals being killed, Husain 'Alī leaves Dehli to quell the revolt, but, Oct. 1: Zī-l qa'da 27, he is assassinated.

The natives of Sumatra,—fearing the Dutch more than the English, whom they had expelled, and in hope of their counteracting the intriguing activity of the Dutch, allowed them to resume their Sumatran establishments. The English now remained at peace for many years, increasing in prosperity and in influence among the natives.

The Hon. William Phipps succeeds Charles Boone as acting Governor of Bombay, till 1728.

May 16: The Italian Bishop, Don Frei Mauricio de S. Theresa, and four Carmelite priests subscribe an oath to obey the British King and Governor. May 31: the Carmelites are ordered to supersede the Portuguese priests at Bombay. July: the Portuguese Viceroy issues an edict forbidding the recognition of the Italian priests at Bombay, and in a letter to the governor insists on the recognition of the Portuguese.

July 8: Ramazān 2. A great earthquake at Dehli, nine shocks

A.D.

1720 felt, and for a month afterwards there were lesser shocks; buildings thrown down, and people killed.

H. 1133: Churāman Jāt killed in battle against Muhammad Shāh. His son, Badan Singh, succeeds.

Oct. 11: Zī-l hijja 9. 'Abdullah Khān proclaims Muhammad Ibrāhīm, son of Rafī'ush-Shān, emperor, and assembling an army, is defeated and imprisoned, Nov. 17: Muharram 14, H. 1133, at Mathurā.

Muhammad Shāh makes a triumphal entry into Dehli.

Ajīt Singh of Jodhpur possesses himself of Ajmir, and indecision on the part of the Mughal generals, Khān Daurān and Qamar-ud-dīn Khān, causes a proposed expedition against him to be abandoned. Ajīt Singh sends professions of submission to the emperor, and retains Ajmir.

Sept. 6: War proclaimed by the Bombay Council upon Āngria, for piracy.

The Conde de Ericeira, Portuguese Viceroy, erects a fort at Daman, and rebuilds the forts at Dīū and Bassein. A great influx of artisans improves the trade at these places.

Sept. 12: Dom Francisco José de Sampayo e Castro succeeds the Conde de Ericeira at Goa as Viceroy.

Oct. Bālāji Vishvanāth, Peshwā, dies. His son, Bājirāo, succeeded him as Peshwā, May 1721. In the interval Ābāji Pant Purandhare transacted the Peshwā's business.

The last Persian garrison is expelled from Afghānistān.

Murshid Qulī Ja'far Khān confirmed in his rule over Bengal.

The Company authorised to borrow money to the extent of the sums lent by them to the Government, if not exceeding five millions sterling. Dividend reduced from 5 to 4 per cent.

The French India Company offer to take up the depreciated notes of the Royal Bank, and to extinguish them at the rate of fifty millions a month for a year, provided its privileges are made perpetual. Joseph François Dupleix appointed First Councillor and Military Commissioner at Pondicheri.

1721 Jan. 5: The Conde de Ericeira leaves Goa for Portugal.

Jan. 29: Rabī' I. 29, H. 1133. Muhammad Amīn Khān, Muhammad Shāh's Vazīr, dies. 'Ināyat-ulla Khān appointed

A.D.

1721 Vazīr-Deputy, the Nizām-ul Mulk being destined for the appointment.

Anūp Singh, Deputy-Governor of Gujarāt, commits many oppressive acts. Strife arises in Ahmadābād, and Anūp Singh's and his minister Nahar Khān's houses are stormed: he is superseded by Haidar Qulī Khān.

April 15: The factor of Anjengo (in Travankor), proceeding with an escort to give the usual annual present to the Rānī of Attingal, is entrapped by stratagem and with his attendants is massacred.

May: Bājirāv Vishvanāth is formally invested with the dignity of Peshwā: Trimbakrāo Dābhāde is made Senāpati. The Nizām-ul Mulk temporises both with Sambhāji and Shāhu, and tries to evade the *chauth*, but yields on the arrival of a *farmān* from Dehli.

A Roman Catholic bishop or vicar apostolic is appointed to Ava and Pegu.

The Portuguese invite the co-operation of the English in attacking Āngria. Aug. 20: Robert Cowan concludes an agreement with the Portuguese to supply 200 men and five ships. Oct.-Dec.: skirmishes occur in which Āngria has the advantage. Dec. 30: Āngria is reinforced by 6,000 horse from Bājirāo.

Ribeiro, Bishop of Kranganor, dies, the last Romish prelate over the Syrian Church of Malabar.

Oct. 15: Nathaniel Elwich takes office as Governor of Madras, in succession to Francis Hastings, till Jan. 15, 1725. He succeeds in gaining securities for twenty-nine treasure-chests abstracted by ex-Governor Hastings.

Oct. M. de la Provostière dies at Pondicheri. M. Lenoir temporarily succeeds and, on the arrival of three richly laden ships, pays off the debts of the Company, whence poor home cargoes are returned.

Nov. 13-15: Severe storms at Madras. Bridges carried away and ships wrecked.

1722 Jan. 1: The Portuguese approached by Bājīrāv regarding a peace treaty with the Rāja Shāhu. Jan. 9: a treaty concluded with Āngria, by which all the territories of Portugal are to be regarded as exempt from tribute: mutual assistance to be looked

A.D.

1722 for with the Marāthās, intercommercial freedom in the landing of merchandise to be established—this agreement to be binding on the English also. Jan. 17: the Portuguese and English vessels leave Kolābā.

Jan. Mīr Mahmūd of Qandahār invades Persia. March 7: he defeats the Persians at Isfahān, which finally capitulates on Oct. 22. Shāh Husain is confined with his family and relations, and thus the Safavī dynasty dies out. Mahmūd Ghilzaī becomes Shāh of Persia, leaving Qandahār under Mīr Husain.

Feb. 11: Chīn Qulich Khān 'Asaf Jāh, Nizām-ul-Mulk, appointed vazīr to Muhammad Shāh.

Haidar Qulī Khān leaves Dehli for Gujarāt, and there assumes almost royal authority. Nov., he is superseded by 'Asaf Jāh, Nizām-ul Mulk, who appoints his uncle, Hamīd Khān, to act as his deputy and returns.

Rāja Jaysingh conducts an expedition against the Jāts of Bharatpur, and captures two forts.

Oct. 11: Zī-l hijja 30, H. 1134. Sayyid 'Abdullah Khān dies in prison.

An English factory is erected at Injarām, Godāvarī district; it had been founded in 1708.

Anticipating the arrival of ships, M. Lenoir prepares cargoes for return and markets for European cargo. No ships arrive, and Pondicheri is thrown into commercial straits.

Dec. 17: Charles VI. of Austria grants a deed of institution or Charter to the "Ostend East India Company," its factors and agents being chiefly persons who had served in the Dutch and English Companies.

1723 H. 1136: The Nizām-ul Mulk, in consequence of mutual aversion between the emperor and himself, resigns the office of Vazīr for that of Vakīl-i-Mutlaq, and in Oct. leaves for the Dekhan. The emperor orders Mubāriz Khān, the local Governor of Haidarābād, to assume the government of the whole Dekhan, and to raise an army against Nizām-ul Mulk.

Rustam 'Alī Khān and Shujā'at Khān, by orders from Dehli, march on Jodhpur, which they capture and plunder.

The Marāthās, for the first time, levy fixed tribute in Gujarāt. On the departure of Nizām-ul-Mulk for the Dekhan, Mubāriz-ul-

A.D.

1723 Mulk Sarbuland Khān Bahādur Dilāwar Jang is appointed fifty-third Viceroy of Gujarāt, till 1730, with Shujā'at Khān as deputy. Hamīd Khān, deputy for the Nizām, opposes his entry, but is induced by the Bābīs to withdraw to Dohad.

Hamīd Khān defeats an army under Rustam 'Alī Khān and Pilāji Gaikwād at Arās, and again at Basu where Rustam 'Alī is killed.

July 13: Francisco José de Sampayo e Castro dies. Dom Christovão de Mello assumes office for two months, when the Succession Patent names him along with Dom Ignacio de Santa Theresa, Archbishop Primate, and Christovão Luiz de Andrade, Chancellor of the State. These hold office till 1725.

A mint is erected at Fort St George, Madras.

Aug. The Emperor Charles VI., having granted Letters Patent to the Ostend East India Company, this year they establish a factory at Bānkipur, near Ichhāpur, 15 miles above Calcutta, and carry on a very successful trade until political reasons induced the emperor to destroy it. Great discontent shown by other European Companies.

Commerce revives with the arrival of ships at Pondicheri. Oct., M. Bouvallier succeeds M. Lenoir as governor.

1724 Sam. 1780: Durjan Sāl succeeds Arjun Singh on the throne of Kotā. His accession acknowledged by Muhammad Shāh.

H. 1136: Ajīt Singh retakes Ajmir and Sāmbhar as far as Narnal. An imperial army approaching, he takes flight, submits, and sends his eldest son, Dankhal Singh, to make terms. Ajīt Singh is murdered while asleep at the instigation of his son, Abhay Singh, who ascends the throne.

Shujā'-ud-dīn Khān, incensed at the English traders in Bengal for taking advantage of the emperor's grants to the Company, and passing private trade duty free, the faujdār of Hūglī stopped a boat laden with silks, which was released by a party of soldiers. For this the governor exacts a heavy fine and an apology.

May: Kānhoji Āngria desires a treaty with the English Government, when a release and exchange of prisoners is made a first condition.

The Marāthās in Gujarāt support Hamīd Khān, as the only

A.D.

1724 means of effecting a permanent footing in that province. Hamīd Khān shares the revenue with Kāntāji, Kadam Bānde and Pilāji Gaikwād. Mubāriz-ul Mulk is ordered to expel Hamīd Khān and the Marāthās.

Bājirāv, in spite of the opposition of Shrīpatrāv the Pratinidhi, makes a successful raid into Mālwa.

Oct. Muharram, H. 1137. Nizām-ul Mulk, after negotiations, defeats at Shakar-Khera, in Berār, Mubāriz Khān, who is killed Nizām-ul Mulk, now independent, establishes his court at Haidarābād.

Dom Luiz da Costa, appointed General of the North, proceeds to Bassein, which he fortifies.

Dec. 31: Rabī' II. 14, H. 1137. The emperor appoints Haidar Qulī Khān to be Mīr Ātash, superseding the Nizām-ul Mulk's nominee. The Nizām orders Hamīd Khān to resume hostilities. Sarbuland Khān, ex-Governor of Kābul, is sent against him.

1725 Feb. 7: H. 1137. Mahmūd Ghilzaī, King of Persia and Afghānistān, orders the murder of the Safavī princes, and thirty-nine of the family are barbarously slaughtered; he becomes mentally deranged and dies. His cousin, Ashraf, is elected king.

Quarrels occur between Pilāji and Kāntāji Kadam Bānde regarding the collection of *chauth.* Kāntāji finally retires to near Kairā, while Pilāji levies taxes on Khambay and Surat.

Mubāriz-ul-Mulk compels Hamīd Khān to retire, and defeats the united army of Hamīd Khān and the Marāthās at Sojitrā and again at Kāpadvanj. Antāji Bhāskar, a Marātha, lays siege to Vadnagar. The resident Nāgars purchase immunity for 400,000 rupees.

Jan. 15: James Macrae succeeds Nathaniel Elswick as Governor of Madras, till May 14, 1730.

The Madras Council sends help against a mutinous outbreak of Muhammadan soldiers at Vizāgapatam.

Mahé taken by storm by Captain Bertrand François Mahé de la Bourdonnais.

H. 1138: Murshid Qulī Khān Ja'far Khān, Nawāb of Bengal, dies. His son-in-law, Shujā'-ud-dīn, succeeds. Two Turkmān

A.D.

1725 brothers, Hāji Hamīd and Alahwardī Khān, share in his increase of power.

Two court favourites, Za'far Khān and Shāh 'Abdul Ghafūr, lose their position on a charge of embezzlement; Khān Daurān acquires great influence with the emperor.

Sept. 29: Robert Clive born.

Oct. 24: João de Saldanha da Gama arrives at Goa as Viceroy, and assumes the government.

During the five years from 1720 to 1725, the English had exported to India £578,155 of goods and £2,770,238 in bullion.

1726 Bājīrāv with a large army invades the Karnātak and levies a contribution from Seringapatam, but gains no permanent advantage.

The Sar Desāī of Kudal captures Phonda fortress from the Portuguese.

The Marāthās compel Mubāriz-ul Mulk to admit their claim for tribute. Rivalry between the Peshwā and Pilāji Gaikwād compels the latter to join Kāntāji, and together they march on Baroda, but fail to expel the Muhammadan governor from the city.

June: M. Lenoir succeeds M. de la Provostière as Governor of Pondicheri. Dec., M. Dupleix suspended from office at Pondicheri by order of the directors.

Sept. 24: A Charter granted by George I. enabling the Company to establish Courts of Record for the discharge of both civil and criminal justice, at Madras, Calcutta, and Bombay, consisting of a mayor and nine aldermen, and to hold Quarter Sessions to determine all penal causes but those of high treason. English law extended to India.

The Ostend Company are so successful that this year one-third of the original subscription of the proprietors, which remained due, was paid up from the gains alone of the trade.

The East India House erected in Leadenhall Street, London.

First Protestant Mission commenced in Madras town.

The *Nāhīd-o-Akhtar*, a poem by Prince Buland Akhtar, brother of the emperor, and whose poetical name was Achchhe, is completed.

A.D.

1727 H. 1140: Nizām-ul Mulk by hearing Sambhāji's claim, and by removing the collectors of *sardesmukhī* and Shāhu's *makāsadārs*, endeavours to revive the feud between Shāhu and Sambhāji, the former of whom, at the instigation of Bājirāv, prepares for war. Nov., Bājirāv lays waste Jālna and successfully out-manœuvres the Nizām's force, and makes a predatory expedition into Gujarāt. Pilāji and Kāntāji Kadam obtain possession of Baroda.

Muhammad Khān Bangash Ghazanfar Jang, a Rohila chief, takes Jitgarh fort from Chatrasāl who takes flight.

The English levy tribute from the Persian refugees in the islands of Zareka, &c., in the Persian Gulf, to which the Portuguese laid claim.

The Mayor's Court at Madras is recognised by Royal Charter.

The private tonnage employed in the country trade had increased during the last ten years to about 10,000 tons. Many of the Company's servants are concerned in this trade.

The Austrian or Ostend East India Company's Charter suspended for seven years by the emperor, owing to the opposition of other maritime powers. The Company is finally dissolved by the treaty of Seville, Nov. 9, 1729, but the Germans were not altogether expelled from Bānkipur till 1733. They had also a fort at Covelong (Kovalam) on the Madras coast.

1728 Bājirāv so hems in Nizām-ul Mulk's army that the latter is obliged to come to terms, Bājīrāv demanding security for payment of *chauth* and cession of fortified places; Nizām-ul Mulk refuses to give up Sambhāji. The treaty is concluded and the armies retire.

Kāntāji's foster son, Krishnaji, seizes Chāmpānīr, which becomes a permanent base for the collection of the Marātha tribute.

Momin Khān, the Gujarāt minister, dies. His brother, 'Abd'ul Ghāni Khān, succeeds.

Jaysingh's Jaypur Astronomical tables completed, constructed from his own observations for seven years.

Hon. Robert Cowan succeeds the Hon. Wm. Phipps as Governor of Bombay; dismissed the service, 1734.

The Danish East India Co. publish at Copenhagen proposals

A.D.

1728 for a new subscription, and the following year obtained extraordinary privileges from King Frederick IV.

1729 H. 1141: Sarbuland Khān Mubāriz-ul Mulk formally grants the tribute of Gujarāt to Bājīrāv, whose brother, Chimnāji Appa, extorts it from Dholkā district. Kāntāji also collects tribute with an army.

Disturbances raised in Surat by Mulla Muhammad 'Alī, Umdāb-ul-tājjār, who seizes and fortifies the island of Piram opposite Goghā. Disputes ensue with the Surat authorities, and the question is referred to the emperor.

Bājīrāv with a Marātha force assists Rāja Chatrasāl and besieges Muhammad Khān Bangash in Jitgarh for six months.

Religious disturbances break out in Agra.

Sambhāji, Rāja of Kolhāpur, is surprised and defeated by the Pratinidhi: Tārābāī and Bhawānibāī are taken prisoners to Satārā.

Vanchi Martānda Perumāl reigns at Travankor, till 1746.

The Dutch Company have their Charter extended for twenty-three years, for which they paid the republic a large consideration. Their wealth and power, particularly in Java, was at this time amazing.

Mar Thomas, the Monophisite bishop of the southern portion of the Syrian Church, dies, and is succeeded by his nephew of the same name, who charges Mar Gabriel, the Nestorian bishop of the northern diocese, with heresy and appeals to the Dutch Governor at Cochin to interfere.

1730 Jan. 15: H. 1142. Ashraf, the Ghilzaī Shāh of Persia, defeated by Tahmāsp Qulī Khān, afterwards Nādir Shāh. Ashraf escaped, but was afterwards murdered by a Biloch chief and his head sent to Shāh Tahmāsp II., son of Sultān Husain. This defeat ended Afghān rule in Persia.

On the defeat of Sambhāji, an accommodation is come to with Shāhu, and the Kolhāpur and Satārā sovereignties are defined.

May 14: George Morton Pitt succeeds Mr Jas. Macrae as Governor of Madras, till Jan. 23, 1735.

June: Āshādh S. 1786. Abhaya Singh of Mārwār appointed fifty-fourth Viceroy of Gujarāt. Mubāriz-ul-Mulk Sarbuland Khān

A.D.

1730 opposes his entry and defeats him at Adālaj. After a second engagement it is arranged that Sarbuland Khān should accept 100,000 rupees and retire to Ahmadābād.

H. 1143: Muhammad Khān Ghazanfar Jang, appointed Governor of Mālwa in order to chastise the Marāthās, connives at their proceedings, and so prolongs his period of government.

Aug. Intelligence received at Goa of invasions by Marāthās. The Fidalgos of Bassein lose Chamba fortress and defend Saibana. The English and Portuguese repulse the Marāthās in Salsette.

Āngria puts to the sword the crews of some storm-stayed Portuguese vessels at Vijayadurg.

The Bombay Government conclude an offensive and defensive alliance with Phond Sāwant of Sāwantwādi for mutual assistance against the Āngrias.

The English in Bengal, to stop the clandestine trading of the Ostend ships, block the Ganges. Of two ships one is captured.

Mar Gabriel, the Syrian Nestorian bishop at Cochin, dies: his successor from Babylon is intercepted by the Jesuits.

Dupleix's suspension order rescinded, and the post of Intendant at Chandranagar is conferred on him.

The United English East India Company's Charter again renewed till Lady Day 1769. The Company agree to accept interest at 4, instead of 5 per cent., on loan to Government of £3,200,000, and to pay a premium of £200,000. Restricted from holding lands and tenements in Britain above the value of £10,000 per annum (3 Geo. II., c. 14).

Four English ships from China arrived this year, with 1,707,000 lbs. of tea, and three other East Indiamen with 371,000 pieces of calicoes besides other valuable merchandise. From 1725 to 1730 the Company had exported £551,234 worth of goods and £2,551,872 in bullion.

1731 Nādir Shāh takes Harāt, gains the attachment of the Abdālīs, deposes Tahmāsp Shāh II. of Persia, and sets his own infant son on the throne as 'Abbās III.

Feb. The Portuguese settlement at Manor besieged by the Marāthās. March 6: they are defeated and retire. July: Rāghoji Pant and Martinho da Silveira de Menezes sign a treaty to restore the *status quo*, but on the Marātha demand for further unreason-

A.D.

1731 able terms the treaty is cancelled and hostilities resumed. Oct., the Marāthās are driven from Panhālā.

H. 1143: Trimbakrāv Dhābāde, the Marātha Senāpati, leagues with Nizām-ul Mulk against Bājīrāv, and marches for the Dekhan from Gujarāt. April 1: Bājīrāv anticipates Āsaf Jāh, and attacks Trimbakrāv Dhābāde, and defeats him and Pilāji at Bhilāpur, near Baroda. The latter is severely wounded, and the former falls in battle; Bājīrāv invests his youthful son, Yashwantrāv, with the hereditary office of Senāpati, and bestows on him the title of *Sena khās khel* in addition to his hereditary one of Shamsher Bahādur. Aug., a compact made between Bājīrāv and Nizām-ul-Mulk, allowing his claim to some possessions in Gujarāt and to countenance his sovereignty in the east of the Dekhan.

Kānhoji Āngria dies. (This date is doubtful: Grant Duff gives 1728; the Portuguese, June 20, 1729.)

Sambhāji Āngria seizes a Portuguese vessel at Dābhol. The Viceroy issues a proclamation forbidding all communication with Āngria: the Bombay Council resolves to send 300 sepoys to aid against his aggressions.

Chāma Rāja succeeds to the throne of Maisur: is imprisoned in Kabbāldurg, where he dies in 1734. Chikka or Immadi Krishna was placed on the throne by the all-powerful ministers, Deva Rāj and Nanja Rāj.

M. Dupleix takes office at Chandranagar, and restores commercial prosperity; both foreign and inland trade being carried on.

June 13: The Swedish East India Company is set on foot by the king, Frederick, for trading from Gottenborg, with a Charter for fifteen years.

King John V. forms a temporary Portuguese East India Company with *one* ship to trade to Surat.

1732 Abhay Singh schemes for the removal of Pilāji Gaikwād, Governor of Songarh and Baroda. He effects his assassination by means of a Mārwādi at the village of Dākor, occupies Baroda, and places Sher Khān Bābī in charge.

Mulla Muhammad 'Alī of Athva resists by force a demand for a lākh of rupees by Sohrāb Khān, Governor of Surat, and succeeds in driving him from the city, and the government is usurped

A.D.

1732 by Teghbakht Khān. Teghbakht afterwards imprisons the Mulla for two years and puts him to death in 1734.

Dāmājī Gaikwād succeeds his father, Pilāji, as military commander. Mādhavrāv Gaikwād, Pilāji's brother, attacks and takes Baroda from Sher Khān Bābī.

Jan. 23: The Portuguese Viceroy, João de Soldanha, hands over the government to a commission of three: Dom Ignacio de Santa Theresa, Archbishop; Dom Christovão de Mello, and Thomé Gomez Moreira.

Malhārrāv Holkar invades Mālwa, now in possession of Dia Bahādur, and at Tirella defeats the governor, who is killed.

The Siddi of Janjira defeated by the two Āngrias who become more formidable by the possession of his fleet.

Sa'ādat-ulla Khān, Nawāb of the Karnātak, dies. His nephew and adopted son, Dost 'Alī, succeeds, till 1740; on Bāqir 'Ali, a younger nephew, is conferred the government of Vellor.

John Zephaniah Holewell arrives in India as surgeon's mate in an Indiaman. Dec. 6: Warren Hastings born.

H. 1145: The *Muntakhīb ul Lubāb* of Muhammad Hāshim, Khāfī Khān, an excellent history of Hindustan from 1519 to 1718, is published.

The E.I. Company's sales this year amounted to £1,940,996, and their dividends reduced from 8 to 7 per cent., and continued so till 1744. The Dutch during a considerable part of that time realised 20 to 25 per cent. upon the capital stock, and never less than 12½.

1733 Bājīrāv, called to the help of Rāja Chatrasāl of Bundelkhand, forces Muhammad Khān Bangash into a fort. Chatrasāl confers on the Peshwā a fort and district in Jhānsi. Mālwa province transferred from Muhammad Khān to Rāja Jaysingh of Amber.

The Marāthās advance into Gujarāt to avenge the murder of Pilāji, and secure from the Ahmadābād treasury a sum of 80,000 rupees in addition to their *chauth* and *sardesmukhī* tax, Jawān Mard Khān Bābī being kept as a hostage till payment is made. At Goghā a contest for the governorship takes place between Burhān-ul-Mulk (appointed) and Sher Khān Bābī, son of the late governor, Salābat Khān Bābī.

Mr Freke's government of Fort William commenced.

A.D.

1733 The Marāthās plot against the Siddis of Janjira. The Pratinidhi gains over a pirate, Ya'qūb Khān or "Shaikhji," who was in the confidence of the Siddi. A force is sent into the Konkan, and, intrigues failing, war breaks out. The Pratinidhi is surprised and defeated at Chiplun.

Mahā Dhammā Rāja Dibata succeeds to the throne of Burma.

The Bengal Nawāb's troops blockade the German factory at Bānkipur. The agent and factors are expelled, and the factory razed to the ground.

Further ill-treatment by Tegbeg or Teghbakht Khān, the Governor of Surat, causes the English merchants to leave the factory and blockade the town in their ships. The governor yields to all their demands.

Dec. 11: Messrs Lowther and Dickson conclude a treaty with seven of the Siddis of Rājpuri.

1734 Jaysīngh, Viceroy of Mālwa, resigns his province to the Peshwā, with the tacit concurrence of the Emperor Muhammad Shāh, on whose behalf the territory is still to be held.

S. 1790: Rānā Sangrām Singh II. of Udaypur dies. During his reign most of the Mewār lost territory was regained. Rāja Jagat Singh succeeds, but fails to cope with the Marāthās.

Jawān Mard Khān Bābi attempts to take Īdar from Ānand Singh and Rāy Singh, brothers of Abhay Singh. The brothers obtain aid from Malharrāv Holkar and Rānoji Sindia, and exact 175,000 rupees from Jawān Mard Khān.

Mahādaji or Māloji Gaikwād, Dāmāji's uncle, marches on Baroda and recovers it from Sher Khān Bābi.

Under Shujā'-ud-dīn Khān, Bengal, Bihār, and Orissa greatly improve. His power is respected by the Europeans.

May 8: Dom Luiz Botelho, appointed General of the North, reaches Bassein and prepares a fleet for the subjection of Āngria.

The Siddi of Janjira dies. His eldest son, 'Abdullah, is murdered by younger brothers, and the government usurped in prejudice to Siddi Rahman, then absent from Janjira.

Chikka Krishna Rāja placed on the throne of Maisur, but the real power is in the hands of usurpers.

Ranga Krishna, Nāyyak of Madura, dies childless. His

A.D.

1734 widow, Minākshī Ammal, becomes queen-dowager; many intrigues are made to dethrone her.

Sept. 22: Mr Robert Cowan is dismissed and his place taken by John Horne as Governor of Bombay, till April 7, 1739.

Nov. The Bombay Government vote aid to Mānāji Āngria to foster his dissensions with his brother, Sambhāji. Dec. 6: Chaul fort is taken from Sambhāji.

Dec. Dharmapattanam Island and Madakkara on the Malabar coast ceded to the English, and strongly fortified.

1735 Jan. 23: Richard Benyon succeeds George Morton Pitt as Governor of Madras for nine years, till Jan. 17, 1744.

Bājīrāv joins Siddi Rahman and Ya'qūb Khān, and reduces forts Talagadh and Ghosāla in Kolābā. He besieges Janjira, but failing to take it, enters into a treaty with the besieged, which recognises Siddi Rahman's claims, and secures to the Marāthās forts Rāygarh, Tala, Ghosāla, Uchitgarh, and Birwādi.

Sambhāji Āngria takes the fortress of Chaul de Sima from the Siddi and garrisons it strongly.

Ratansingh Bandhāri and Sohrāb Khān contest the governorship of Vīramgām. The former raises an army and plunders Dholkā: he offers terms to Sohrāb Khān, and on their refusal surprises the camp at Dholi; Sohrāb Khān is killed and his forces routed.

Dāmāji Gaikwād's position as representative of Umābāī, widow of Khandherāv Dābhāde, in Gujarāt disputed by Kāntāji Gaikwād, whose rights are ignored. Kāntāji is defeated at Ānand-Mogri A peace is concluded on condition that Dāmāji should receive one-fourth share of the revenues of the country north of the Māhi.

Sept. 19: M. Benoît Dumas, Governor of Isles de France and Bourbon, takes office as Governor-General at Pondicheri. M. Bertrand de la Bourdonnais appointed Governor of the Isle de France, till 1740.

Malhārrāv Holkar overruns Mālwa and takes the fort of Sāmbhar. The city is captured and plundered, and nine hundred persons put to death.

From 1730 to 1735 the E.I. Company exported £717,854 of goods and £2,406,078 of bullion.

A.D.

1735 Chatrasāl Bundela dies, bequeathing the Peshwā the Mahāls of Kālpī, Sironj, Kūnch, Garra, Kotā, and Hirdainagar, under an express stipulation that his posterity should be protected by the Peshwā and his heirs.

1736 Jan. The Court of Directors issues a proclamation prohibiting British subjects from trading to the East Indies, contrary to the liberties and privileges granted to the Company, or from serving in or being on board any ships unlawfully trading.

The Portuguese take the part of Sambhāji Āngria against his brother, Mānāji, in an attack on Kolābā. Mānāji is taken under the Peshwā's protection.

Feb. 26: Tahmāsp Qulī Khān proclaimed and crowned with the title Nādir Shāh of Persia. With 80,000 men he marched on Qandahār, under Mīr Husain, and being refused admittance blockaded the town for two years and finally took it by successive assaults.

'Alahwardī Khān procures the title of Nawāb of Bihār, independent of Bengal.

Bājīrāv demands an extensive *jāgīr* from the emperor, who concedes the right to six sūbahs in the Dekhan. Nizām-ul Mulk, in alarm, becomes reconciled to the emperor.

March 19: Zī-l qa'da 6, H. 1148. Yādgār Khān Kashmīri deputed to mediate between the Marāthās and the emperor. He carries a patent granting to Bājīrāv Mālwa and Gujarāt, which he now held by the sword. It is stipulated that Bājīrāv should enter the imperial service.

April: The Rāja of Trichinopoly dies. Chandā Sāhib, Dost 'Alī's Diwān, profits by internal dissensions to enter into and hold the city, but still professes allegiance to the Nawāb.

The Marātha armies ravage Bhadāwar and defeat Amra Singh, who is deserted by his brother on the field. Besides plundering, the Marāthās levy a contribution of twenty lākhs of rupees.

Sept. 10: The charter of Dost 'Alī Khān from Ālambarai authorising the coining of money arrives at Pondicheri.

Ratansingh Bhandāri defeats Rangoji, Dāmāji Gaikwād's agent, at Vīramgām. The Marāthās capture Kāpadwanj.

1737 March 24: Zī-l qa'da 22, H. 1149. Sa'ādat Khān, Governor

A.D.

1737 of Audh, defeats Malhārrāv's troops on their way to plunder Sa'ādābād and Jalair; Malhārrāv joins the Peshwā at Kotal April 9: Zī-l hijja 8.

April: Zī-l hijja, H. 1149. The Marāthās besiege Shikohābād. The governor by concessions saves the town.

H. 1150. Disturbances between the Hindus and Muhammadans break out at Sāmbhar.

The Portuguese workmen at the fortress of Thāna, in desperation for food and pay, invite the Marāthās to rule Salsette island. April 6: the Marāthās occupy the fort of St Jeronym or Ghodbandar. The Portuguese governor, Dom Luiz de Botelho, hastily retires to Karanjā. May: Six forts of Salsette are captured. A force under Antonio Cardim takes Manor. Aug. An appeal to the Bombay Government for help is met with a refusal. The northern possessions of the Portuguese in India now consist only of Chaul, Karanjā Bāndra, Versova, Bassein, Māhim, Tārāpur, and Daman. Pedro de Mello now succeeds to the command of the campaign.

Bājīrāv appears before Dehli to intimidate the emperor. Retreating, he is attacked and drives back the Mughals with loss. He then marches for the Dekhan. Nizām-ul Mulk, invested with full powers to call out all the resources of state, marches on Sironj with 34,000 men.

Momin Khān, appointed fifty-fifth Viceroy of Gujarāt, is opposed by supporters of Abhay Singh, and joins the Marāthās. Ahmadābād is besieged. The Gujarāt nobles persuade the emperor to reappoint Abhay Singh Viceroy: but Momin Khān continues to besiege Ahmadābād and is joined by Dāmāji Gaikwād.

Oct. 11-12: Great hurricane and earthquake at Calcutta and up the Ganges. 300,000 lives lost and 20,000 vessels of all sizes were cast away. The steeple of the English church was thrown down and about two hundred houses destroyed.

1738 Jan. Āsaf Jāh, Nizām-ul Mulk, attacked near Bhopāl by Bājirāv, surrounded, and so harassed that on Feb. 11 he engages to cede all land between the Narbadā and Chambal rivers, and to pay fifty lākhs of rupees.

March: Qandahār capitulates to Nādir Shāh. Generous terms

A.D.

1738 are offered and accepted, and an Afghān contingent furnished for the invasion of Hindustan. June: Safar, H. 1151. Kābul is stormed and occupied. Leaving a garrison, Nādir Shāh proceeds to Peshāwar.

Phond Sāwant of Sāwantwādi dies. Rāmchandra Sāwant succeeds.

Momin Khān, with the aid of Dāmāji Gaikwād, captures Ahmadābād, half of which is handed over to the Marāthās. The latter on attempting extortion are expelled from the city. Momin Khān appointed fifty-seventh Viceroy of Gujarāt.

The Marāthās continue the campaign in the Konkan against the Portuguese, who are reinforced by contingents from Europe. Dom Antonio Cardim attacks Thāna but is repulsed by Malhār-rāv Holkar. The Marāthās sack Daman, capture several forts, and (Nov.) besiege Mahim.

Mr Freke, Governor of Fort William, is succeeded by Mr Cruttenden, who was succeeded in the following year by Mr Braddyth.

Feb. Tukāji Bhonsla dies. His son, Bāwā Sāhib, succeeds to the kingdom of Tanjor, but dies the same year. Shāhuji, the younger son, driven from the kingdom by faction, takes refuge at Chilambram and opens negotiations with Dumas at Pondicheri. Oct., the French send a mission to Tanjor, but make no impression on the usurpers.

Aug. The French send two ships to take Kārikāl and aid Shāhuji, who, however, had made friends with the Tanjor nobility and imprisoned his usurping relative Sidoji.

Chandā Sāhib, now in possession of Madura, obtains the aid of the French.

1739 Jan. 26: Ramazān 25, H. 1151. Nādir Shāh, having defeated the Mughal governor of Jalālābād, marches on Attak, crosses the river, and devastates the entire district. Jan. 21-22: Shawwāl, 10-11, the Mughal armies defeated at Shāhdaula. Lāhor by submission escapes plunder. Feb. 24: Zī-l qa'da, 15, Muhammad Shāh's army under Burhān-ul-Mulk is defeated. Deputations to the Persian camp result in a complete capitulation. March 19: Zī-l hijja 8, Muhammad Shāh enters Delhi, followed next day by Nādir Shāh. An insurrection breaks out in the city, and Nādir

A.D.

1739 Shāh orders a general massacre, in which 20,000 are said to have perished.

April 6: Zī-l hijja 26. Nāsir Mīrzā, son of the Persian emperor, marries the daughter of Murād Bakhsh. April 9: orders are issued to levy a ransom. Five divisions are made in the city, and the contribution from each paid to the Amīrs; two karors of rupees are exacted. May 16: Safar 7, H. 1152, Nādir Shāh leaves Dehli with a booty estimated at from 80 to 145 millions, in which was the famous Peacock Throne set with diamonds.

Jan. 20: Māhim capitulates to the Marāthās under Chimnāji Appa, also the forts of Kelve Katalwāda, Srīgāon, Dāhānu, Tārāpur, and Asheri. Jan. 26: the Marāthās enter Salsette, investing it on Feb. 17. May 2: the Portuguese Viceroy concludes a treaty with Bājīrāv, agreeing to cede 40 per cent. of the revenues of Salsette and Bardes. March-April: Bassein is closely invested by Chimnāji Appa and Malhārrāv Holkar, and blockaded on the sea face by Mānāji Āngria; May 16: the Portuguese capitulate.

March 28: Karañjā fort taken by Sambhāji Āngria from the Portuguese. Āngria attacks Chaul twice without success and invests it till October, when it capitulates and is formally transferred in December.

Feb. 6: Four thousand horse under Francisco Pereira are sent by Chandā Sāhib to attack Kārikāl. The fort of Kirkangarhi capitulates. Feb. 14: Kārikāl, with the adjoining country, is made over to the French, and M. Golard appointed governor.

Feb. 8: M. Dirois' appointment to the directorship of Chandranagar received at Pondicheri. He is posted temporarily at Mahé till M. Dupleix leaves for France.

March 23: Zī-l hijja 13, H. 1151. Shujā'-ud-dīn Khān, Nawāb of Bengal, dies. His son, 'Alā-ud-daula Sarfarāz Khān, succeeds.

Fidā-ud-dīn Khān, deputy viceroy in Gujarāt, is resisted in his collection of tribute by Jaitsingh of Mohanpur, whom he defeats. The Marāthās regain their share of the Ahmadābād revenues, Momin Khān being forced to sue for peace with Rangoji.

Bājīrāv, after the departure of Nādir Shāh, leagues with the Rājputs to withstand the Mughals, especially Nizām-ul Mulk He also becomes reconciled to Rāghoji Bhonsla, and secures his co-operation.

A.D.

1739 Kashmīr annexed to the kingdom of Kābul by Nādīr Shāh.

Risings take place in Pegu against the effete empire of Burma.

April 7: Stephen Law appointed Governor of Bombay in succession to Mr John Horne, till Nov. 15, 1742.

July 20: The English at Bombay conclude a treaty at Bassein with Chimnāji Appa for Bājīrāv, with a view to obtaining further commercial privileges.

Nov. 1: Sambhāji Āngria's fleet appears off Bombay. Nov. 6: he hoists his flag over Elephanta.

1740 Feb. 17: The Imām Sāhib of Golkonda pays a state visit to the French at Pondicheri.

March 31: Sinappaiyan returns to Pondicheri from Tanjor with presents from Pratāp Singh.

H. 1153: Bājirāv attacks Nāsir Jang, son of Nizām-ul Mulk, at Burhānpur, and is repulsed. The war is continued till an accommodation is come to at Munghi-Paitan, when both parties are pledged to maintain peace, and to refrain from plundering the Dekhan.

May 9: Sa'far 12. Bājīrāv Peshwā dies near the Narbadā. Rāghujī Bhonsla endeavours to prevent Bālājī Bājīrāv's appointment as Peshwā by proposing Bāpu Nāyyak, but in August Bālājī is appointed to succeed his father.

May: Rāghoji Bhonsla at the head of 50,000 Marāthās enters the Karnātak and, May 20: defeats the Nawāb's army at Dāmalcheru pass, in N. Arkat. The Nawāb Dost 'Alī, adopted son of Sa'ādat-ullāh Khān, is slain with his son, Hasan 'Alī, and most of his officers, his diwān, Mīr Asad, being taken prisoner. His son, Safdar 'Alī, succeeded him, till 1742. The country people flock to Pondicheri, as do Dost 'Alī's widow, children, and dependents, and Chandā Sāhib's wife and son.

May 20: Safar 13. Sarfarāz Khān, Nawāb of Bengal, killed at Giria in battle by Mirza Muhammad 'Alī. Alahwardī Khān, Nawāb of Bihār, usurps the government of Bengal, Bihār, and Orissā, till 1756.

Aug. Safdar 'Alī is recognised as Nawāb of the Karnātak on payment of ten million rupees to the Marāthās, and a promise to aid in expelling Chandā Sāhib from Arkat. Dumas defies the Marātha leader.

A.D.

1740 Sept. 18: In order to save Goa, the Portuguese surrender Chaul to Sambhāji Āngria.

Rāja Mārtānda Varma of Travankor unifies the country, subduing many petty chiefs, with the help of a Flemish officer, De Lanoy.

Dec. The Marāthās again invade the Karnātak. Dec. 15: Trichinopoly invested. Detachments pillage the Jinjī district. Dec. 27: a reverse is sustained by the Marāthās at Porto Nuovo. Negapatam is sacked, and the Deputy-Governor Astruc, his family and several Dutchmen taken prisoners.

From 1735 to 1740 the United East India Company exported £938,970 of goods and £2,459,470 of bullion.

1741 Jan. Revadanda, the last Portuguese possession between Goa and Daman, taken by the Marātha general, Khandoji Mānkar. Chimnāji Appa, the Peshwā's brother, dies.

March 26: Chandā Sāhib delivers Trichinopoly to the Marāthās, who after plundering the town leave Morārirāv as governor. Chandā Sāhib is made a close prisoner at Satārā.

Alahwardī Khān gives notice to Murshid Qulī Khān, brother-in-law of the late Nawāb, to quit Orissa. He refuses and is defeated near Bālāsor by Alahwardī Khān. Sayyid Ahmad, placed over the province, proves unpopular, and the people seize him and place Bāqir Khān in charge. Alahwardī Khān marches to Orissa, defeats the rebels, and appoints Muhammad Mu'azzam governor of the province.

Bhāskar Pant leads a Marātha army into Bengal and Bihār, ravages the country and demands *chauth.*

In Gujarāt, the Marāthās are defeated at Dholkā by the governor Qāim Qulī Khān. The Viceroy, Momin Khān, makes peace.

Nizām-ul Mulk leaves Dehli to crush a rebellion led by his second son, Nāsir Jang, who is defeated near Daulatābād on July 23, and carried a prisoner to Aurangābād.

Bālāji Bājīrāv II. applies to the emperor for the formal cession of Mālwa according to the treaty made with his father. No notice is taken of this appeal.

Pratāp Singh made Rāja of Tanjor instead of his half-brother

A.D.

1741 Sayajī. The latter subsequently places himself under the protection of the English.

Mināksḥī Ammal, Queen-Dowager of Madura, kills herself.

April: M. Dumas successfully diverts Rāghoji Bhonsla's demands upon Pondicheri, and a pacification is concluded. The French reputation much enhanced by this success. The Mughal confers a mansab of 45,000 horse on Dumas.

May 18: Dom Luiz de Menezes, Conde de Ericeira and first Marquis de Louriçal, takes office at Goa as Viceroy for the second time. By a victory at Bardes he regains for the Portuguese five fortresses, the province of Salsette, and the fort of Phonda.

July 28: M. Février sails from Pondicheri as administrator of Kārikāl.

Aug. 20: Mr Hubbard, Governor of Fort St David, dies.

Sept. 27: M. de la Bourdonnais, with a squadron of seven ships, arrives off Pondicheri.

Oct. 6: M. Dirois appointed Director of Chandranagar, arrives at Pondicheri. Oct. 19: M. Dumas leaves for Europe. M. Dupleix succeeds as governor, retaining his predecessor's *mansab*.

Pope Benedict XIV. by a bull forbids the prevaricating sophistry of the Jesuits in India—"inobedientes, contumaces, captiosi, et perditi homines." From this time their influence began to decline.

H. 1154. The *Tārīkh-i Hindi* of Rustam 'Alī is written.

1742 Jan. 14: M. Dupleix and suite make formal entry into Pondicheri. Presents received from Safdar 'Alī, Mīr Asad and Ghulām Husain. May 2: A flag and kettledrum for Dupleix arrive from the Emperor of Delhi.

Bālājī Bājīrāv II. masters Garah and Mandla, and through the mediation of Jaysingh and Nizām-ul-Mulk obtains a promise of the *chauth* of Mālwa province. The emperor thus secures the aid of the Peshwā against Rāghoji Bhonsla now invading Bengal. Alahwardī Khān's army is repulsed by Bhāskar Pant and driven to Katwā. Mir Habīb, former *diwān* of Murshid Qulī Khān, joins the Marāthās who are compelled to retreat before the Nawāb of Audh and the Peshwā.

Sarbuland Khān appointed Governor of Allāhābād.

A.D.

1742 Fights take place at Ahmadābād between the Marāthās and Muhammadans.

June 12: Dom Luiz de Menezes, the Portuguese Viceroy, dies. Dom Luiz de Caetano de Almeida takes over the charge of state till Dec. 20. Dom Francisco de Vasconcellos, Bishop of Cochin, goes on the commission.

Alahwardī Khān permits the English to construct a moat or ditch round their settlement at Calcutta, for protection against incursions of the Marāthās.

Oct. 2: Safdar 'Alī, Nawāb of Arkat, put to death by his brother-in-law, Murtazā 'Alī Khān of Vellor, who in November enters Arkat in triumph as Nawāb. Revolts occur in the army, the palace is surrounded and Murtazā 'Alī escapes in female disguise. Sayyid Muhammad Khān, infant son of Safdar 'Alī, is proclaimed Nawāb, under a *diwān*.

Vanchī Mārtānda Perumāl of Travankor conquers Ellayedatunād.

Sept. 11: Great cyclone off Bombay; much damage done.

Sept. 18: In a despatch, the French E.I. Co. order Dupleix to reduce the expenditure by one-half, and to stop all expense on fortifications, in view of the anticipated war with England. The sea-front at Pondicheri, however, is fortified.

Nov. 15: John Geekie, senior member of Council at Bombay, acting governor till Nov. 26, when William Wake takes office, till 1750.

Vepery, Perambur, and Puthupāk villages (now included in the city of Madras) granted to the English by the Nawāb of Arkat; Yeranavūr and Shadayankuppām villages to the south of Madras held at a peppercorn rent on *Shrotriam* tenure.

1743 Jan. Nizām-ul Mulk marches into the Dekhan, arriving at Arkat in March. His army intimidates the petty princes into submission, and by August the Karnātak is evacuated by the Marāthās. Morārirāv is acknowledged chief of Gūti. Khwāja 'Abdullah Khān, the generalissimo of the Mughal army, is appointed Nawāb of Arkat.

The Marāthās under Rāghoji Bhonsla again invade Bengal. Nawāb Alahwardī Khān succeeds in driving them back, but the

A.D.

1743 loss in revenue was immense from their plunder and the devastation they had inflicted in their raid.

Jan. 17: Mr Nicholas Morse succeeds Mr Richard Benyon as Governor of Madras, till 1746.

March 30: Dom Francisco de Vasconcellos, joint Governor of Goa, dies. May 18: Dom Lourenço de Noronha succeeds on the commission.

May: The French at Pondicheri and the English at Madras send presents to Nizām-ul Mulk, and strengthen their fortifications.

July: Jumāda I., H. 1156. The emperor grants a *farmān* to Bālājī Bājīrāv, Peshwā, ceding Mālwa nominally to be held for Prince Ahmad.

Momin Khān, Viceroy of Gujarāt, dies. Fida-ud-dīn, with Muftakhir Khān as agent, acts as viceroy. Ranghoji plots to murder these officials, but sustains a reverse. Fida-ud-dīn becomes sole master of Gujarāt.

'Abdul 'Azīz Khān of Junnar appoints himself Viceroy of Gujarāt by a forged order which names Jawān Mard Khān Bābī as deputy. Muftakhir Khān, appointed fifty-eighth Viceroy, is forced to name Jawān Mard Khān as deputy.

Rāja Jaysingh of Jaypur dies. Ishvari, his son, succeeds, but by a convention with Udaypur, Mādhav Singh, son of a Mewār princess, holds the right of succession; Holkar supports his claim.

Budh Singh of Būndī dies in exile. His son Umed, aged thirteen, levies troops and regains Pātan and Gainoli.

Rāghoji Bhonsla constitutes himself protector of the Rāja of Deogarh, in consequence of being called in to mediate in a disputed succession: all the power is taken into his hands.

Dec. 21: M. Dupleix issues an order to the effect that all officials shall build houses at Mortandi Chāvadi, henceforth to be called Dupleixpettai.

1744 'Abdul 'Azīz, Governor of Junnar, is resisted in the collection of tribute by Devāji Takpar, lieutenant of Dāmāji Gaikwād, and is defeated at Kim Kathodra, pursued and slain at the Narbadā.

Fakhr-ud-daula, Fakhr-ud-dīn Khān Shujā'at Jang Bahādur

A.D.

1744 appointed fifty-ninth Viceroy of Gujarāt: and Jawān Mard Khān Bābī as his deputy.

Feb. The East India Company agree to lend the British Government a million sterling at 3 per cent. as an equivalent for the prolongation of their charter for fourteen years to Lady-day 1783 (13 Geo. II., c. 17).

The Berār Marāthās under Bhāskarrāv Pant invade Bengal. Alahwardī Khān invites the Marāthās to a conference at Munkirru and gives the signal for the massacre of the leaders, when Bhāskar Rāv and nineteen officers are slaughtered.

March: Khwāja 'Abdullah, about to repair to Arkat to resume his command as Sūbahdār, is found dead, his body bearing traces of poison.

May 21: War declared between France and England. Their respective interests in India are henceforth maintained at the sword's point. A French fleet despatched to attack Madras. An English squadron under Commodore Barnett seizes three French ships in the straits, and another, the "Favori," at Achīn in Dec.

July 4: Sayyīd Muhammad *alias* Sa'ādat-ullah Khān II., the child Nawāb, is treacherously assassinated at a wedding-feast by a Pathān soldier. The murderer and ten accomplices are cut down. Suspicion rests on Murtazā 'Alī, who escapes to Vellor. Anwar-ud-dīn receives from Nizām-ul-Mulk a commission as Nawāb of the Karnātak.

Sept. 24: Dom Pedro Miguel de Almeida e Portugal, Conde de Assumar, takes office as Viceroy at Goa, in succession to a commission.

1745 H. 1158: The Afghāns in Alahwardī Khān's service mutiny under Mustafā Khān, plunder Rājmahāl and Monghir, march on Pātna, the governor of which defeats the rebels. Mustafā flees to Chunār, and endeavours to form a coalition with Rāghoji Bhonsla's Marāthās. Zain-ud-dīn Khān, son-in-law of Alahwardī Khān, defeats the rebels at Jagdispur, where Mustafā is killed.

Rāghoji Bhonsla again invades Bengal, reduces Katak and most of Bardhwān. He is joined by the remains of Mustafā Khān's army; they sustain a partial defeat at Katwā. Rāghoji is now obliged to return to his own territories.

A.D.

1745 March: Sa'far, H. 1158. 'Alī Muhammad, leader of the Rohila Afghāns, having possessed himself of Katir district, is besieged at Bankar and imprisoned.

Vanchi Mārtāndi Perumāl of Travankor conquers Kayankulam.

Aug. Despatches from survivors of a wrecked French vessel bring news of the French and English war to Pondicheri.

Sept. 11: Nawāb Anwar-ud-dīn Khān makes a state entry into Pondicheri, is entertained by Dupleix, and returns to camp.

The English squadron appears on the Coromandel coast, and takes three French ships. The Nawāb, appealed to by Dupleix, insists on no hostilities.

Nov. 4: Severe hurricane at Pondicheri; great damage caused. Two lesser cyclones follow on Nov. 23 and 28.

The United East India Company, from 1740 to 1745, exported £1,105,750 of goods, and £2,529,108 of bullion.

1746 Mīr Ja'far Khān, appointed to high command with a view to expelling the Marāthās and Afghāns from Katak, obtains a slight success at Midnapur, but fails to follow it up. 'Ata-ullah Khān, sent to supersede him, attempts to gain him over to a revolt. Both generals are dismissed from the army.

Sadāshiv Chimnāji Bhāu, cousin of the Peshwā, conducts an expedition to the Karnātak, where some Desmukhs had evaded tribute. He levies contributions as far as the Tungābhadrā, and reduces the fort of Bhādar Benda.

Nāsir Jang, son of Nizām-ul Mulk, marches on Seringapatam in the absence of the army, to exact tribute. A deputation meets him, tendering allegiance.

Feb. The Portuguese ship, "St Louis," pursued to Pondicheri by four English vessels, which threaten a night attack on the town. Feb. 10: Muhāfiz Khān, son of Anwar-ud-dīn, visits Dupleix in state.

March 18: In view of rumours of warlike preparations by the English at Manjakuppam, Dupleix writes to the Nawāb disclaiming responsibility should fighting occur. April 1: Dupleix receives an application for troops from a native ruler in Fort St David district.

April: A French ship, attacked by the English off Tranquebar, is run ashore and blown up to avoid capture. The Danes fire on

A.D.

1746 the assailants, but the return shot kills one and injures two of the garrison. April 12: Danish deputies from Tranquebar entertained by M. Dupleix.

April: Commodore Barnett dies at Fort St David. Mr Peyton succeeds as Admiral.

May 5: The Portuguese viceroy in person recaptures Alorna (for which he received the title Marquiz de Alorna), Tirakol, Neutim, and Rarim forts in the Dekhan.

June 25: Commodore Peyton engages with the French fleet under M. De la Bourdonnais near Negapatam. The French sustain the heavier loss and retire to refit at Pondicheri, where dissensions occur with M. Dupleix. The English refit at Trincomalī. July 24: a three days' fight begins: the English sail off.

Sept. 7: The French under De la Bourdonnais land 600 men about twelve miles south of Madras and bombard Fort St George. Sept. 10: the English garrison of 300 men submit and surrender as prisoners of war. The Nawāb of Arkat threatens to send a force to defend Madras, but is pacified by Dupleix. Oct. 10: a treaty signed by De la Bourdonnais, by which the French agree to evacuate Madras on payment of a moderate ransom in Jan. 1747. Mahfūz Khān, son of the Nawāb, invests Madras, is defeated by a sortie from the town, and again at St Thomé. Oct. 23: De la Bourdonnais leaves Madras under D'Espremesnil, a member of Dupleix's Council. Oct. 30: the ransom treaty with De la Bourdonnais declared null, and the possessions of the English seized indiscriminately. Some Englishmen escape to Fort St David, now the seat of administration under Mr John Hinde, the deputy-governor there. An attack there is repulsed by the Nawāb's natives together with the garrison.

Oct. 26: Forts Bicholim and Sanquelim, with territories, are recovered by the Portuguese from the Marāthās who swear allegiance.

1747 Jan. 6: Zī-l hijja 23, H. 1159. Amīr Khān, Umdat-ul-Mulk, ex-Governor of Allahābād, murdered by a discharged servant with the consent of Muhammad Shāh.

H. 1160. Nādir Shāh of Persia and Afghānistān, intoxicated with success, perpetrates all manner of atrocities. In distrust of the Persians he grants excessive favours to the Afghāns. June 20: Jumāda II., he is assassinated by his Persian guard. The Afghān

A.D.

1747 mercenaries, after an unsuccessful attack on the Persians, retreat. Oct., Ahmad Khān, son of Zemān Khān, the hereditary chief of the Abdālīs, repulsed in an attack upon the Persian troops, marches to Qandahār and assumes sovereignty under the name of Durānī.

Jan. 10: The French from Ariyankuppam attempt an attack by sea on Kadalūr, but are driven back by a storm. Jan. 20: the squadron from Achīn arrives, and on Feb. 19 proceeds to Goa.

March 13 N.S. The French army attacks Fort St David, but retires precipitately on the arrival of the fleet from Bengal.

April 14: Mr John Hinde dies at Fort St David prior to receipt of the Court of Directors' despatch of Jan. 24, appointing him Governor and President of Fort St David, now constituted the head settlement. April 16: Charles Floyer succeeds as governor till July 6, 1750.

At Surat factions led by Sayyid Achan, paymaster, and Safdar Muhammad, governor. The former calls in Malhārrāv Khuni and they sack the city, Sayyid Achan being elected governor. Kedarji Gaikwād, Dāmājī's cousin, obtains one-third of Surat revenues. A great famine prevails in Gujarāt.

The Peshwā concludes more specific treaties with the Rājas of Bundelkhand, by which, in addition to Orchha already ceded, one-third of the territories is made over to Bālāji Bājīrāv, with a similar share of the profits from the diamond mines at Panna.

H. 1160. Appaji, Malhārrāv and other Marātha leaders invest Dīg and Kumbher, held by Sūrajmal Jāt. The war ends several months after by the death of Khanderāv.

Ishvari Singh of Mewār, aided by Sindia, defeats the Rānā of Udaypur, who had supported the claim of Mādhu Singh, his sister's son, to the throne of Mewār.

Ānanda Ranga Pillai appointed courtier and chief *dubāsh* to M. Dupleix at Pondicheri.

Two French privateers anchor off Bombay and overmatch the East Indiaman "Anson." The home dispatches and eleven chests of treasure are landed in boats. Orders are now issued to increase the Bombay naval force.

Dec. 19: Dupleix fails in an attack upon Fort St David.

A.D.

1748 Jan. Major Stringer Lawrence arrives at Fort St David with a commission to command all the East India Co.'s forces in India, and to be major of the garrison at Fort St George. He immediately encamps the troops, which movement deters the French from their intended attack on Kadalūr.

Jan.-Feb.: Muharram, H. 1161. Ahmad Khān Durānī captures Lāhor, and wins over Zilla Khān with the whole Mughal force sent out to check him. Feb. 18: Safar 19, Prince Ahmad despatched under the direction of I'timad-ud Daula with an imposing army, which the Afghāns avoid and fire Ludhiānā. March 13: Rabī' I. 13. The armies meet at Sarhind, where Prince Ahmad repulses the Afghāns, who retire. Lāhor is re-garrisoned, and the army returns to Dehlī.

AHMAD SHĀH.

April 27: Rabī' II. 27, H. 1161. Muhammad Shāh of Dehlī dies of paralysis or of grief at the loss of his Vazīr, Qamar-ud-dīn Khān. His son, Ahmad Shāh 'Abul Nasr, succeeds till 1754, but his accession is disputed by Muzaffar Jang, the son of his deceased elder brother. Ahmad Shāh and his successor were mere pageant princes set up by the court nobles and removed at their pleasure.

Udhambāī, mother of Ahmad Shāh, in concert with Nawāb Jawād Khān, takes all administrative power out of Ahmad's hands.

June: Jumāda II. 'Asaf Jāh, Nizām-ul Mulk, dies. His second son, Nāsir Jang, succeeds as Sūbahdār of the Dekhan.

An insurrection breaks out in Bihār under Shamsher Khān and Sardār Khān, dismissed Afghān generals. Dec., the insurgents murder the Nawāb's nephew and son-in-law at a Conference at Pātna.

The Afghāns commit excesses at Pātna, and with the plunder raise new levies for the invasion of Bengal. The Nawāb, though hampered by the Marāthās, marches against the rebels.

June 28: The French attack Kadalūr, but encounter a steady resistance.

July: The English obtain a *kaul* from the Rāja of Kottayam for the monopoly of exporting pepper and cardamoms.

A.D.

1748 July 29: A fleet under Admiral Boscawen arrives at Fort St David. August: The army attacks Ariyankuppam fort, close to Pondicheri, unskilfully: the fort, however, is abandoned by the garrison, and in Oct., blown up by the English.

Sept. Pondicheri invested by Boscawen on sea and Major Stringer Lawrence on land, but they make little impression, and raise the siege, Oct. 17.

Dec.: Zī-l hijja, H. 1161. Safdar Jang, Vazīr of Audh, unsuccessfully attacks the Rohilas, who advance into Audh.

The Marāthās stop a British fleet of boats between Kāsimbāzār and Calcutta, and seize three hundred bales of raw silk.

1749 March: Alahwardī Khān defeats the Afghāns, who had been joined by Jānoji Bhonsla and his Marāthās, at Bar. He re-settles Bihār and appoints his grandson, Sirāj-ud-daula, governor.

July 23: Anwar-ud-dīn—whom Nizām-ul-Mulk had appointed Nawāb of the Karnātak during the minority of the son of Safdar 'Alī Khān of Arkat—marches to Ambūr to oppose Muzaffar Jang, son of the late Nizām-ul Mulk, and Husain Dost Khān, known as Chandā Sāhib, whom Muzaffar had made Nawāb, and who was assisted by a body of Dupleix's French troops. Anwar-ud-dīn is defeated and killed. Muzaffar Jang proclaims himself Sūbahdār at Arkat, while Chandā Sāhib is proclaimed Nawāb of the Karnātak. The French take up their cause, whilst the English side with Nazir Jang the Nizām.

The Peshwā gains complete ascendancy over Rāja Shāhu, now enfeebled; the existence of Rāma Rāja, son of the second Śivājī, is discovered, and is adopted as heir, in spite of the opposition of Shāhu's wife, Sakwārbāī, and the Pratinidhi.

Umeda Singh, chief of Būndī, after fourteen years' exile, recognised as Rāo.

At the siege of Devanhalli by the Mysoreans, Haidar 'Alī, with his brother Shahbāz, distinguishes himself and obtains a command and charge of a fort.

August: Madras restored to the English, under the treaty of Aix-la-Chapelle. St Thomé is occupied by the English, and informing priests expelled.

The English in Madras, on the promise of the territory of Devikotta, send an expedition to Tanjor to reinstate the deposed

A.D

1749 Rāja Sayaji. April: accompanied by Sayaji they fail in an attack on Devikotta. A second attempt is successful, and Pratāp Singh makes over Devikotta by treaty. The Fort St David government resolve not to become involved in native quarrels.

Oct. The French obtain the sovereignty of eighty-one villages in the vicinity of Pondicheri.

Nov. 1: Boscawen's fleet leaves Fort St David, whereupon the French and Chandā Sāhib attack Trichinopoly. They lay siege to Tanjor, and are kept before it while Pratāp Singh summons Muhammad 'Alī and Nāsir Jang. Twenty Europeans, sent by the English, effect an entrance into Tanjor. The king, however, is intimidated by an assault, and signs a treaty, Dec. 21, agreeing to pay tribute.

Dec. Rāja Shāhūjī dies, having given the Peshwā, Bālaji Bājīrāv, a deed empowering him to manage the whole government of the Marātha empire, on condition of his perpetuating the Rāja's name. Kolhāpur to be recognised as independent.

1750 Jan. The Peshwā secures Rāghoji Bhonsla in his interest. Poona becomes the seat of Marātha administration. He wins over the other chiefs by liberal concessions, and writes the emperor advising him to appoint Ghāzī-ud-dīn Viceroy of the Dekhan.

March 15: Nāsir Jang reaches Jinjī, and is joined by 600 Europeans, under Stringer Lawrence. April 4: Rabī' II. 26, H. 1163. They defeat the joint forces of Chandā Sāhib and Muzaffar Jang with their French auxiliaries.

'Alī Muhammad, Pathān Governor of Rohilkhand, restored after four years' imprisonment.

July: Rajab, H. 1163. Sirāj-ud-daula, grandson of Alahwardī Khān, summons Jhanki Rām, the Deputy-Governor of Pātna, to deliver the city to him. On receiving a refusal, he assaults the town, but fails and returns to his grandfather.

Abhisingh of Jodhpur dies. Rām Singh, his son, succeeds, but is driven from the throne by Bakht Singh, his uncle.

Ānand Rāo, founder of Dhār principality, dies. His son, Jaswant Rāo, succeeds, receiving the title Rāja of Dhār.

Lawrence attempts to warn Nāsir Jang of the treacherous designs of Dupleix, but refuses to march to Arkat, and returns to

A.D.

1750 Fort St David. Muhammad 'Alī, second son of Anwar-ud-dīn, joins Nāsir Jang, and is confirmed by him in the government. Aug., he is defeated by the French and Chandā Sāhib. Sept. 11: the French under M. Bussy take Jinjī.

Sept. 19: Mr Thomas Saunders succeeds Mr Floyer (dismissed) as Governor of Madras, till Jan. 14, 1755.

Sept. 27: Francisco de Assiz, Marquez de Tavora, succeeds the Conde de Assumar as Viceroy at Goa.

Nov. 17: Richard Bourchier appointed Governor of Bombay, till Feb. 28, 1760. Nov. 24: he arrives at a more cordial understanding with the Peshwā, who engages to aid in settling Surat affairs.

Dec. 16: Muharram 17, H. 1164. Nāsir Jang treacherously shot by Muhammad Khān, the Pathān Nawāb of Kadappa. His nephew, Muzaffar Jang, escapes from imprisonment, and with the aid of the French assumes the Viceroyalty of the six *sūbahs* of the Dekhan.

Warren Hastings arrives at Calcutta as a civil servant of the East India Co.

Chr. Frederich Schwartz arrives at Tranquebar to join the Protestant Mission there, and labours till 1798.

1751 H. 1164. Alahwardī Khān yields Katak to the Marāthās, and promises to pay annually twelve lākhs of rupees as the *chauth* of Bengal.

Mir Habīb, Governor of Orissa for the Marāthās, is killed in a skirmish. Rāmnārāyan becomes Deputy-Governor of Pātna, on the death of Jhankirām.

Rāo Lākha succeeds to the state of Kachh; Sindh, Kāthiāwār, and Pārkar are lost to this Jām.

H. 1164. Ahmad Shāh Durānī again invades the Panjāb, defeats Mu'īn-ul-Mulk and demands the cession of the Panjāb, which is yielded.

Safdar Jang, Vazīr of Audh, appeals to the Marāthās for help against the Rohilas, and allows them to levy their subsidy from the conquered territory, in consequence of which the Rohilas are reduced to the verge of destitution.

Dāmājirāv Gaikwād entrapped and imprisoned at Poona by

A.D.

1751 Bālāji Bājīrāv, and his share in the Gujarāt revenues wrested from him.

Feb. 13: 17 Rabī' I. Muzaffar Jang, Sūbadār of the Dekhan, attacks the armies of the rebel Nawābs of Karnūl, Kadapā, and Sāvanūr, who maintain their position till M. Bussy with the French army arriving gives the Nawāb the advantage, but he is killed by the Karnūl Nawāb, who is in turn slain, as also the Sāvanūr Nawāb. June: his uncle Salābat Jang, third son of 'Asaf Jāh, and brother of the late Nāsir Jang, is formally proclaimed Sūbahdār at Aurangābād. He appoints M. de Bussy, a nobleman of the empire, and sets him over the northern Jagīrs.

March: The Peshwā Bālāji Bājīrāv marches south to oppose Salābat Jang, but is bought off with a present of two lakhs of rupees, and returns to Satārā to thwart an attempt of Tārābāī to supersede his authority. Salābat Jang gives the French the villages of Nizāmpatnam, Kondavīd, Narsāpur, and Ālamanava in the Kistnā district, together with Yanun and Mahfūzbandar.

Muhammad 'Alī Khān, son of Anwar-uddīn, who had been appointed Nawāb of the Karnātak by Nāsir Jang, is opposed by Chandā Sāhib, and takes refuge in the fort of Trichinopoly. He temporises with M. Dupleix as to terms of submission to Chandā Sāhib. The latter, with a French detachment under M. d'Auteuil leaves Pondicheri to besiege Trichinopoly.

In Feb. a small English force under Capt. Cope had started to help in defending Trichinopoly, but made an unsuccessful attempt to capture Madura, held by 'Ālam Khān for Chandā Sāhib. Late in March a larger force under Capt. Gingen is sent on; joined by Cope's and Muhammad 'Alī's troops they take Vriddhāchalam; but, July 19, attacking Volkonda, the garrison and M. d'Auteuil defeated them and they fled in panic, finally reaching Trichinopoly July 28.

July: Vriddhāchalam fort, invested by neighbouring pālegārs, is relieved by troops sent from Fort St David under Capt. Clive as commissary. Clive proposes a diversion in the attack of Arkat. Aug. 30: Clive, with a detachment of 300 Sepoys, 200 Europeans and 8 officers, occupies Arkat abandoned by the enemy. Sept. 4: Clive marching out attacks the fugitive garrison, and is himself besieged fifty days in the fort, by Chandā Sāhib's superior force, but defends it with success. Nov. 24: a desperate assault is made

A.D.

1751 by Rāja Sāhib, Chandā's son, but entirely fails, and next morning Rāja Sāhib retreats on Vellāva. Trichinopoly is meanwhile besieged by M. Law.

Nov. 22, 24, and 27: Salābat Jang's army, with Bussy and his French artillery, disperse and defeat the Peshwā's troops in three engagements, when Bussy advises Salābat Jang to make peace.

Dec. Capt. Cope killed in an engagement with the French at Kistnāvaram, while on his way to aid Muhammad 'Alī, who had taken refuge in Trichinopoly, and is besieged by Chandā Sāhib's forces.

The French cause seeming triumphant, Dupleix plans the erection of a new town to be called Dupleixfathiābād, on the spot where Nāsir Jang had been killed. The erections were razed by Clive's troops in 1752.

Siddi Hāfiz Masa'ūd with his fleet seizes Surat castle and unites with the Dutch in recalling Safdar Muhammad Khān the Governor, whom the English had expelled. A plan of co-operation with the Marāthās fails, and the English factors are imprisoned and robbed. The President, Mr Lambe, makes a treaty, afterwards repudiated by the Bombay Government.

English factories are established at Bandarmalanka and Vilapuli in Godāvarī district.

1752 Jan. William Fytch appointed Governor at Fort William—died Aug. 10.

The English at Surat, by a fresh treaty with the Siddi, regain their property and receive £20,000 compensation for losses.

Ahmad Shāh Durānī again invades the Panjāb: obtains possession and demands formal cession of the province, which, with Kashmīr, he obtains.

Rānā Jagatsingh of Udaypur dies. His son, Rānā Pratāp Singh II., succeeds.

March 4: The Court of Directors appoint two additional chaplains for Anjengo and Telicheri.

April 7: Raghunāth Dās, diwān of Salābat Jang, murdered in a mutiny of his soldiery at Balki. Sayyid Lashkar Khān succeeeds as diwān. He secretly favours Ghāzī-ud-dīn.

April 13: Elmisaram taken from the French by Capt. Dalton who joins Lawrence's force, and together they enter Trichinopoly.

A.D.

1752 April 17: The seat of the Madras Government is removed from Fort St David back to Madras.

April 24: Clive marches on Uttattūr, whither d'Auteuil's detachment had retreated and, June 6, gains an advantage over d'Auteuil's troops near Volkonda, receiving the surrender of all the latter's men.

May 28: Major Lawrence unsuccessfully attempts to take Srīrangham island from M. Astruc. June 7: Chandā Sāhib's army being in straits, M. Law places Chandā Sāhib with Mānakji, the Tanjor general, who promises to connive at his escape. Mānakji puts Chandā Sāhib in irons, and on disputes occurring as to his custody, Mānakji orders his execution, June 14.

June 13: M. Law, besieged and surrounded, surrenders Trichinopoly to Major Lawrence, delivering himself with all the troops and stores. Capt. Dalton, commanding the advance guards, receives the surrender of the French troops at Jambukistna.

July 23: Major Kinnear takes the fort of Villaparum, and makes an unsuccessful attack upon Jinjī; his troops retire to Trivadi.

Aug. 18: An English and Swiss detachment under Lawrence defeats the French at Bahur. On this defeat Innis Khān, sent by Morārirāv to join the French, comes over to the English with 3,000 Marāthās.

Sept. 8: Shawwāl 27, H. 1165. Safdar Jang finding his influence at court undermined by the eunuch Jāwad Khān, invites him to an entertainment and assassinates him. The emperor now appoints Ghāzī-ud-dīn the Younger, a grandson of Nizām-ul Mulk, to be commander-in-chief, but he proves more arrogant than Safdar Jang. With the help of the Marāthās he expels the *vazīr*.

Sept. 3: The Gregorian calendar accepted in England: Sept. 3 becoming Sept. 14.

Sept. Clive takes Covelong (Kovalam) and Chingalpat, and retires on sick leave to England.

Oct. 16: Zī-l hijja 7, H. 1165. Ghāzī-ud-dīn, on his way from Dehli to regain his possessions in the Dekhan, is poisoned at Aurangābād.

Nov. 15: Salābat Jang and M. Bussy make peace with Bālāji-

A.D.

1752 rāv and Rāghuji Bhonsla at Gulbarga, and concessions are made at the expense of Salābat Jang's soldiery. This gains for Bussy the aversion of Lashkar Khān, the Nawāb's *diwān*.

1753 Jan. The French troops, joined by Morārirāv with 4,000 Marāthās, entrench on the Pennar, but fail to support their allies in several attacks made on the English lines.

Jan. M. Bussy falls ill at Gulbarga, and leaves for Masulipatam. Meanwhile, Lashkar Khān corrupts the French troops. Bussy procures the appointment of Shāh Nawāz Khān as minister, and obtains the cession of Elūr, Muzaffarnagar, Rājamandri, and Chikakol for the support of their subsidiary force.

H. 1166. Nawāb Safdar Jang, being superseded as vazīr by Intizām ud-daula, sets up a puppet emperor, and constitutes himself *vazīr*. May 9: Rajab 6, street fights occur in Dehli between the Safdar Jang's party and the emperor's.

H. 1167. Sirāj-ud-daula formally declared 'Alahwardī Khān's successor; he manifests a cruel disposition in his use of power.

Bakht Singh of Jodhpur dies by poison. Bijay Singh, his son, succeeds. Rām Singh, his cousin, contests the throne and gains it with the aid of the Marāthās, who in turn expel Rām Singh.

March: Rāghuji Bhonsla dies. His son, Jānoji, receives the title of Sena Sāhib Sabhā on the Peshwā's return from the Karnātak.

April: Jawān Mard Khān surrenders Ahmadābād to the Marāthās.

April-May: The Marāthās skirmish in Fort St David district, and a serious conflict occurs, in which Basinrāo, Morārirav's nephew, is killed, while charging the English line.

April 21: 'Abdul Wahāb, brother of Muhammad 'Alī, defeated by the troops of Murtazā 'Alī near Vellor.

July 7, N.S. M. Astruc succeeds in placing the French flag on Golden Rock, south of Trichinopoly, but his large force is completely routed in an action with Lawrence. Dissensions break out among the allies. After the victory, the Nawāb, preparing to accompany Major Lawrence to Tanjor, is detained in the city by his troops, now in arrears.

July: Brenier, Astruc's successor, sends de Cattano into Trichi-

A.D.

1753 nopoly as a spy. Capt. Dalton discovers his plans and compels him to advise an escalade. The arrival of Major Lawrence prevents the attempt.

Aug. 7: Lawrence, with his force augmented by Tanjorines under Mānakji, arrives 6 miles east of Trichinopoly and routs Brenier's force. Aug. 23: Lawrence pursues them to Waykonda, which they abandon. Sept. 1: the French encamp on Sugar-loaf Rock opposite the English at French Rock, and on the 21st are defeated by Lawrence. Waykonda forced and occupied.

Dec. 8: Dupleix, in an attempt to detach the Tanjorines from the English side, orders an attack upon Dalton's battery. The French are repulsed and trapped, and seek quarter. Dupleix sends the Marāthās to plunder Tanjor, whereupon the rāja returns to the friendship of the Nawāb.

Dec. Ava invested and taken from the Peguans by Alaunghprā, a Burmese officer who resisted the order to swear allegiance to the Talaings.

Dec. 23: Capt. Dalton beats up the Mysorean camp under Srīrangham, and posts in the island 70 Europeans and 300 sipāhis who are cut off next day. He expels from the city the Mysoreans who had been admitted as a guarantee.

A *farmān* arrives from the Dehli emperor, commanding Muzaffar Jang to aid the Governor of Pondicheri in every way.

1754 Jan. 3: A peace conference meets at Sadras to adjust the claims of the English and Muhammad 'Alī as against those of Salābat Jang and the French, the deputies being Messrs Palk and Vansittart for the English; Father Levant, M. Kirjean, and M. Bousset for the French. The French commissions from Dehli prove forgeries, and the conference leaves the international relations more strained than before.

Mānakji is reinstated as general of the Tanjor forces on the proven incompetency of Gadhu Rāo. He defeats the 1,200 Marāthās who had entered Tanjor.

Feb. 15: Morārirāv and Innis Khān rout the English convoy and grenadiers on their way to Trichinopoly. The English lose one-third of their battalion, with the convoy, provisions, and £7,000. This is the most serious British reverse in the war.

April: Mr Palk proceeds to Tanjor to recover the rāja's

A. D.

1754 loyalty to Muhammad 'Alī's interest, but that monarch is jealously watched by Sakhuji who was in treaty with the Mysoreans. A plot discovered at Trichinopoly to prejudice Muhammad Yūsuf, English sipāhi commander. The guilt is found to rest with a native interpreter named Poniapa.

May 12: Capt. Caillaud and Muhammad Yūsuf discover and defeat a body of French at Sugarloaf Rock. The latter retire to Waykonda. Major Lawrence marches to Tanjor.

MUHAMAD ĀLAMGĪR II.

June 5: Sha'bān 11, H. 1167. Ghāzī-ud-dīn with Malhārrāv Holkar seizes the persons of Ahmad Shāh and his mother, Udhambāī. Ghāzī-ud-dīn raises to the throne a son of Jahāndar Shāh with the title of 'Abūl 'Adl 'Azīz-ud-dīn Muhammad 'Ālamgīr II., Bādshāh-i-Ghāzī. Ahmad Shāh and his mother are blinded, Sept.: Zī-l hijja.

Safdar Jang dies and Ghāzī-ud-dīn becomes Vazīr.

Sūraj Mal, Jāt Chief of Bharatpur, holds out against the allied forces of Ghāzī-ud-dīn, the Marāthās, and the Rāja of Jaypur.

Mahfūz Khān, brother of Muhammad 'Alī, who had offered his services against the French, lingers at Conjivaram for money, and allows the French to take Utramalūr, in Chingalpat district. With the aid of Ensign Pichard he retakes it.

Aug. 2: Commissioners arrive from France and England to put an end to the war. The French ministry recall Dupleix, and M. Godeheu arrives as Governor of Pondicheri. He makes over the command of the French army to Maissin.

Aug. The army from Tanjor engages the French and Mysoreans at Elmiseram, and on the 22nd Mānakji takes the post and captures the French there.

Sept. 18: Dom Luiz Mascarenhas, Conde de Alva, takes office as Viceroy at Goa.

Oct. 11: M. Godeheu proposes a suspension of arms between the English and French at Madras, Trichinopoly, Pondicheri, and other places on the Coromandel coast till Jan. 11, 1755. M. Godeheu and Mr Saunders arrange terms of a treaty, securing for each nation non-interference with native powers, retention of certain places, and exchange of prisoners.

A.D.

1754 Oct. 14: Dupleix leaves for France, where he is badly received. M. Bussy is left in great power at the court of Salābat Jang, the Sūbahdār of the Dekhan.

Oct. 25: The Portuguese conclude a treaty with "the Bounsulo" (Jānoji Bhonsla). Missionaries are to be admitted into his territories. The Portuguese undertake to protect the Desāīs of Query, Sanquelim, Morly, and all who had sworn allegiance, the "Bounsulo" to pay tribute regularly and the Desāīs to recover Rarim and Neutim.

Nov. A Marātha army, sent by the Peshwā to the Karnātak, levies tribute as far as Bednūr; Raghunāthrāv, the Peshwā's brother, is entrusted with the military supervision, his cousin, Siwdāshev Chimnāji, with the civil.

The Peshwā and Tārābāī conclude an agreement by which Rām Rāja, a weak-minded prince, is kept imprisoned.

Dec. 31: The treaty between the English and French for the cessation of hostilities and the restoration to the native powers of their possessions in the Karnātak is signed at Pondicheri. Stipulations are made for the prevention of the establishment of foreign European settlements in their possessions, and to withdraw from interference in the affairs of native princes.

1755 Jan. 14: George Pigott Governor of Madras, till Nov. 14, 1763.

Feb. An English force under Lieut.-Col. Heron marches unopposed into Madura, makes alliance with the Marāvar. Heron takes Koilgadi and (March) Nelikotta by assault, and lets the countries to Mahfūz Khān. The French remonstrate, and the alliance with the Marāvar is disallowed in the interests of Tanjor. Heron is tried by court martial, found guilty and dismissed the service in June.

Feb. 15: M. Godeheu leaves for France, the governorship devolving on a secret committee of MM. Barthelemy Boileau and Gaillard pending the arrival of M. Deleyrit, who arrived on March 25th.

March: An agreement made between the Bombay governor and Rāmaji Pant for an expedition against Tulājī Āngria. Commodore James leaves in the "Protector" for the Malabar coast,

A.D.

1755 to pursue Āngria. April 2: he takes Suvarnadurg, and (April 8) Bānkot from Tulājī Āngria without the help of the Marāthās.

Rāmchandar Sāwant of Sāwantwādi abdicates in favour of his son, Khem Sāwant. Rānā Pratāp Singh of Udaypur dies. Kāma Rājsingh II. succeeds, but the Marāthās have now a firm hold upon Rājasthān.

Momin Khān recovers Goghā and Ahmadābād from the Peshwā's officers.

March: Rāghuji Bhonsla dies at Nāgpur. His eldest son, Jānoji, succeeds at Nāgpur, while Chānda and Chhatisgarh are given as an appanage to Mādhavji, a younger son.

March: Basein (Burma) occupied by Talaings, but retaken in April by the Burmese. Mr Brooke, chief of the British settlement at Negrais—begun by Mr Saunders in 1753—supplies military stores to the Burmese. Capt. Baker proceeds on an embassy from Negrais to Ava. Alaunghprā permits the establishment of factories at Rangūn and Basein.

April 14: The Maisur regent, finding his schemes against Trichinopoly futile, decamps from Srīrangam and leaves the French in camp as their representative in the Karnātak.

May: M. Maissin sent by M. Deleyrit to quell a rising in Terriūr, takes the chief town, deposes the rebellious Reddi and reinstates his predecessor.

May: The Pālegārs of Madura oppose the farming of their province by Mahfūz Khān, who in June concentrates at Tinneveli. July: he is defeated by the Pultavar's forces, and again by a Travankor army. Nov., the Pultavar cuts down two companies of English sepoys in Mahfūz Khān's army. Mahfūz Khān returns to Tinneveli.

Oct. 8: Serampur (Fredericksnagar) taken possession of by the Danes.

Oct. Clive, appointed a lieutenant-colonel in England, arrives at Bombay with a force of artillery.

The Portuguese Government nominates a procurator of the Portuguese in Pondicheri. A hundred and forty-seven Jesuit priests are apprehended at Goa and sent to Lisbon, where they were imprisoned for sixteen years.

A.D.

1755 Nov. The Peshwā's troops make incursions on Āngria's coast forts and reduce all north of Gheria or Vijayadurg.

1756 Jan. The Madura Pālegārs revolt, and are defeated, March 21st, by sipāhis under Jamāl Sāhib. Muhammad Yūsuf proceeds to Madura, reinforces the fort with sipāhis; he joins Mahfūz Khān against the rebels, who send in their submission to Chevelpetur on June 10.

Feb. 11: A second expedition against Āngria made by Rāmajī Pant and Khandoji Mānkar for the Peshwā, and Admiral Watson and Colonel Clive for the English. Rāmajī Pant plans to exclude the English from sharing the prize-money, but is anticipated; Āngria flees to the Marāthās, by whom he is held prisoner, and Vijayadurg fort surrenders to Admiral Watson, Feb. 13.

Feb. A body of Marāthās invade Sonda in Kanara, to exact tribute alleged to be due. The rāja, Imodi, offers any fortress instead, and the Marāthās occupy Phonda. An expedition sent from Goa to prevent the occupation is defeated; the Viceroy leads a second charge on June 22, when he loses his life.

Feb. Salābat Jang and Bussy march against 'Abdul Hākim Khān, Nawāb of Sāvanūr, now in league with Murārirāv of Guti. Bālājirāv at the same time reinforces Salābat Jang's army for the punishment of Murārirāv, who with the Nawāb, after three months' siege, consents to terms of a negotiation conducted by M. Bussy. Shāh Nawāz Khān, Murārirāv's deputy, instigates Salābat Jang to dismiss M. Bussy from his service, who had privately received Murārirāv's bond on the French for former services, to effect his reconciliation with the Peshwā. Bussy with his troops leaves for Masulipatam, but returns to Haidarābād in June, and becomes reconciled to Salābat Jang on Aug. 15, owing to the friendly connivance of Rāmchandar Jādaw and Jānoji Nimbālkar, who permitted M. Law to join the French with reinforcements at Chārmahal.

April 10: Rajab 9, H. 1169. Alahwardī Khān, Nawāb of Bengal, dies, and is succeeded by his grand-nephew and grandson, Mīrzā Mahmūd Sirāj-ud-daula, son of Zain-ud-dīn Mahmūd, who, by placing his favourites in the chief posts, causes several dismissed ministers to league for his removal in favour of his cousin, Shukot Jang, Governor of Purnīya. On the march against

A.D.

1756 the latter, Sirāj-ud-daula is diverted by news of the further fortification of Fort William, and, June 1, enters Kāsimbāzār. The Dutch and French at Chinsura and Chandranagar refusing help to Calcutta, messages are sent to Madras from Calcutta.

June 15: Calcutta is attacked. Mr Roger Drake, the governor, in a panic takes refuge with a few Englishmen on board a ship, and taking with them the means of defence, sails to Madras. June 19: the town capitulates. The Nawāb orders the remaining Europeans, 146 in number, to be imprisoned. Driven at the bayonet's point into a small prison in the fort, they pass the hot night without water, and only twenty-three survive, one being Mr Holwell, afterwards chosen as acting governor.

July: Alaunghprā of Arakan, after five months' blockade, takes Syriam. The Talaings escape, the Europeans remain prisoners. Many are sent up the country, and constitute the community known as the native Christians. The capital of Pegu is closely invested.

July 20: A force is despatched from Madras for the relief of Bengal.

Oct. 12: As a result of Messrs Spencer and Byfield's embassy to Poona, Bājīrāv, the Peshwā, signs a treaty providing for the exclusion of the Dutch from trade in the Marāthā dominions: the surrender to them of Vijayadurg, and, in exchange, the cession of the villages of Bānkot with Fort Victoria and Himatgarh, &c., to the E.I. Company. The Peshwā also engages to waive all claims on the Company; to give Tulājī Āngria no territory below the Ghāts; and to settle an equivalent with the Siddi for one-fourth of the customs levied by him from vessels in the Bānkot river.

Oct. 15: A squadron under Admiral Watson and Clive, with 900 Europeans and 1,500 sipāhis, leaves Madras, arriving at Falta in the Hūglī, Dec. 20. Dec. 27: the ships sail up the river to Mayapur; 500 under Clive march on Fort Busbusia, and in spite of a surprise meet and defeat Mānik Chand Seth and the Nawāb's forces. Dec. 28: the fort is found empty.

1757 Jan. 1: The English fleet take possession of Thāna and Alīgarh forts unopposed; Mānik Chand Seth, Governor of Calcutta, retires to Hūglī, and, Jan. 4: Rabī' II. 12, H. 1170,

A.D.

1757 Calcutta is reoccupied and Mr Drake restored to the government, but is afterwards dismissed from his post by the Directors. Jan. 10: Hūglī is retaken.

Jan. 24: M. Bussy, with Viziarām Rāo of Vijayanagar's assistance, attacks Bobbili, the fort of Ranga Rāo, chief Pālegār in the Vizagapatam district. After a fierce struggle the fort was taken, the garrison having burnt their women and children, and Ranga Rāo is killed. Jan. 27: Viziarām Rāo is put to death in his tent by two of the Pālegār's garrison.

Feb. 4: The Nawāb, disregarding overtures of peace, marches to Hūglī and thence to Calcutta, which he surrounds, but is defeated. Feb. 9: a treaty offensive and defensive and permitting the English to fortify Calcutta is signed, Amichand ("Omichand") and Ranjit Rāo acting as mediators.

Feb. 11: A proposed attack on Chandranagar is not found practicable by the joint army, owing to the Nawāb's shifting policy. Admiral Watson refuses to sign a proposed treaty of neutrality between the French and English in Bengal, offered by M. Renault, Governor of Chandranagar, whereon Clive attacks the town, which capitulates, March 23.

March: Capt. Caillaud marches from Trichinopoly to regain Madura and reduce the rebel Pālegārs. In conjunction with Muhammad Yūsuf he settles the Tinneveli district and regulates the affairs of the Mudali.

March: Bālājīrāv with 60,000 Marāthās appears before Seringapatam demanding two million rupees from Haidar 'Alī as arrears of tribute, and on refusal bombards the town. A smaller sum is accepted and the district of Sera occupied, Balwant Rāv being left to reduce other early Marātha possessions.

April: In the Karnātak, hostilities break out between the Nawāb Muhammad 'Alī and his brother Najibulla. The English send a force to aid the Nawāb, but recall it on its failing to take Nellor.

April 15: Mr Price on the part of the Company enters into a commercial agreement with Rām Rāja of Sātāra for the regulation of salt trade and charge of the Mahar river.

April 20: Sholavandān fort is abandoned to Muhammad Yūsuf. May 1: Caillaud is defeated in an attempt to carry Madura by escalade owing to the barking of a dog. May 26: he reaches Trichinopoly.

A.D.

1757 April: Yār Khān Lati, an officer, confers secretly with Mr Wm. Watts, English representative at Murshidābād, respecting the deposition of the Nawāb Sirāj-ud-daula: Mīr Ja'far 'Alī Khān, husband of Sirāj-ud-daula's aunt, also offers to aid. Amichand Seth ("Omichand"), however, proving mutinous, demands twenty lākhs of rupees, or 5 per cent. on the Nawāb's treasures, as the price of silence. Clive deceives "Omichand" as to the reward of his silence by a draft treaty.

H. 1170: Ahmad Shāh Durānī, to avenge Mīr Manu's son's seizure at Lāhor by Ghāzī-ud-dīn, advances into Hindustan, takes Dehli, which again becomes the scene of massacres. A detachment commanded by Sardār Jahān Khān surprises the inhabitants of Mathurā at a religious festival, and massacres them. June: Shawwāl, H. 1170, Ahmad Shāh Durānī levies money and returns to his dominions, leaving Najīb-ud-daula as Amīr-ul-'Umrā, or minister, to protect Alamgīr II. from Ghāzī-ud-dīn.

April 26: Elvasanor abandoned by the English to a French attacking force under M. d'Autueil.

May 26: The Bombay presidency send a force under Adlercron to assist at Trichinopoly. Hearing of Caillaud's arrival there they turn to Wandiwāsh, which they attack on June 6. Hearing of the French seizure of the factories at Madapollam, Bandermalanka, and Injeram, the presidency recalls the troops.

May: Alaunghprā takes the capital of Pegu: most of the leading men are put to death, and many townspeople sold as slaves. July 23: Alaunghprā grants permission to British merchants to hold the island of Negrais, also grants ground for a factory at Basein to the East India Co.

June 4: Mīr Ja'far signs a treaty with the English and explains his proposed line of assistance. June 12: Calcutta and Chandranagar troops mobilise: Mr Wm. Watts joins the army. June 15: Sirāj-ud-daula secures the neutrality of Mīr Ja'far who, however, still engages to abide by his covenant with Clive. June 16: the army encamps at Patli, west of Kāsimbāzār.

June 23: Shawwāl 5, H. 1170. The two armies engage at Plassey, when Clive's 3,000 put to flight the 18,000 horse and 50,000 infantry of Sirāj-ud-daula, Mīr Ja'far remaining inactive on the plain. The Nawāb takes flight on a camel. Mīr Ja'far is proclaimed Nawāb of Bengal, Bihār, and Orissa on June 29th.

A.D.

1757 Amichand, realising the deception practised on him, becomes insane. July 2: Sirāj-ud-daula captured and put to death by order of Mīr Ja'far's son, Mirān.

June: Utramalūr is occupied by the French; in July it is retaken by the British.

July 6: Sir Eyre Coote, dispatched to Bengal (now entered by the French, ostensibly in the late Nawāb's interests), arrives at Bāglipur. By the connivance of Rāmnārāyan, Vice-Nawāb of Bihār, the French elude Sir Eyre Coote's force. A conference is held between Coote and Rāmnārāyan, as a result of which the latter swears allegiance to Mīr Ja'far.

Aug. 16: Admiral Charles Watson dies of fever: Sir George Pococke succeeds as naval Commander-in-Chief in India.

Sept. 8: Eleven French ships, under command of the Marquis de Soupires, appear off Fort St David and disembark troops at Pondicheri, but do not attack.

Sept. Plots between the diwān Dūlab Rām and Mīr Ja'far prevent the departure of Clive from Bengal. Oct. 17: reconciliation effected by Mr Watts, but insurrections at Dhākā breaking out the Nawāb Mīr Ja'far proceeds to Rājmahāl leaving Murshidābād in charge of Mirān, who, Nov. 10: Sa'far, H. 1171, puts to death Mirzā Mehdi, the infant grandson of 'Alahwardī Khān.

Sholavandān, between Madura and Dindagal, is held by Muhammad Yūsuf to cover the French operations against Madura. Sept., Madura capitulates to Capt. Calliaud in face of certain defeat. Bussy has great influence in the Dekhan and obtains from the Sūbahdār a grant of Mustafanagar, Ellor, Rājamahendri, and Chikakol districts.

Oct. 1: M. de Soupires encamps before Chittapet in North Arkat: owing to the Nawāb Muhammad 'Alī's representations, no help is sent by the Madras presidency to the Killedār, who is shot dead in an assault. The fort falls on Oct. 13. Trinomali fort capitulates Oct. 18, and eight more forts fall before the French.

Nov. Capt. Calliaud reports the Mudali's incompetence to manage the Madura district and the necessity of removing Mahfūz Khān from the province. The latter becomes a pensioner.

Nov.-Dec. Haidar 'Alī captures the fort of Sholavandān and plunders the Madura district, though unable to take the city. Sholavandān is retaken by the British.

A.D.

1757 Dec. Clive, after ending the rebellion in Bengal, stipulates for payment, and on Dec. 20 (Rabī' II. 5, H. 1171) the twenty-four parganas are ceded to the E.I. Co. by Mīr Ja'far.

1758 Jan. 17: Jumāda II. 7, 1171. Ahmad Shāh Abdālī again invades Hindustan: he meets 'Alamgīr in the palace at Shāh Jahānābād. Oppression and severity are exercised on the inhabitants. The Abdālī sets out to coerce Sūrajmal Jāt, captures Balamgarh, despoils Mathurā and returns to Dehli. Pestilence reduces his army, and he retires, leaving Najīb-ud-daula with the titles of *amīr ul 'umarā* and *mīr bakhshi*, and Khān Jahān as commander-in-chief. Adina Beg, controlling the Duāb, fails to answer Khān Jahān's summons to court, and applies to Raghunāth Rāv (Rāghoba) the Peshwā's brother, who defeats the Abdālī governor at Sarhind and enters Lāhor as a conqueror in May: Sha'bān, H. 1171.

Feb. 4: The united armies of Clive, Dūlab Rāī, and Mīr Ja'far arrive at Pātna where the Nawāb confers the nominal nawābship of Pātna on Mīran, leaving Rāmnārāyan as deputy with full powers. Clive secures the farming of the saltpetre trade, thereby offending the Dutch East India Company. April: he leaves Pātna.

Feb. 8: A body of Marāthās under Amritrāv join Murtazā 'Alī in an attack on Tīrupati, but, on the death of Amritrāv, a sally is made and the besiegers are defeated.

Feb. 24: Commandant Pococke with the ships of war from Bengal arrives at Madras: further reinforcements from Bombay under Admiral Stevens arrive, and the squadron sails south in April.

Feb. 28: Mahfūz Khān refuses to accept the presidency's terms of reconciliation and renews his depredations in Madura. A campaign is carried on against refractory pālegārs by Muhammad Yūsuf, sipāhi commander, till April.

April 19: Jānoji Bhonsla declares war on the Portuguese, with a view to recover Tirakhol, Alorna, and Bicholim. His army is attacked and forced into three pagodas at Ammona and thence to Sanquelim. Peace is concluded soon after.

Lākhpatji Rāo of Kachh plans an expedition against Sindh, and forces Momin Khān to pay arrears of tribute amounting to Rs. 20,000.

A.D.

1758 Sher Khān Bābi dies at Junāgadh. His son, Muhammad Muhabat Khān, is acknowledged by the nobles of his court.

April 28: A French fleet under Comte d'Aché, with Count de Lally as commander-in-chief, sent by the King and Company of France for the ejection of the English from India, appears off Fort St David, and, 29th, engages the English in an undecisive combat with loss of men, inflicting, however, some damage to the English riggings. May 2: Count Lally, with his French force, lands at Pondicheri and in three hours departs for Kudalūr where he is joined by M. Soupires; Kudalūr surrenders May 4, and the French by sea and land invest Fort St David which capitulates June 1, and they raze the foundations. Lally concentrates the troops from the outposts, which are then occupied by the native garrisons. M. D'Estaign on June 4 is detached to take Devikota, which the garrison abandon on his approach.

April: M. Bussy obtains Daulatābād fort from Shāh Nawāz Khān's killadār by stratagem on behalf of Salābat Jang, whose brother, Nizām 'Alī, resents the occurrence, but simulates acquiescence and prepares to depart for his government at Haidarābād: but, May 11, invites Haidar Jang, Bussy's chief officer, to an entertainment and causes his assassination. May 12: in the confusion a Hindu sūbahdār of the French sepoys enters Shāh Nawāz Khān's tent and puts him and his son, Yeman-ud-daula, to death.

June 7: Lally returns in triumph to Pondicheri, but M. Deleyrit remonstrates regarding the empty treasury.

June 18: Lally again takes the field, reaching Kārikāl June 25. He sends proposals of alliance to the Rāja of Tanjor, and meanwhile takes Nāgor, 4 miles from Negapatam, and forces assistance from Negapatam and Tranquebar.

June 20: The "Hardwicke" arrives at Calcutta with a Commission from the Court of Directors remodelling the whole government, viz.:—a Council of ten to be appointed, the four senior members nominated as governors, each to preside in rotation for three months. Clive is not included in the nomination. The proposal is ridiculed, and Clive is unanimously elected president, June 26.

July 4: Letters are received at Calcutta from Ānand Rāo of

A.D.

1758 Rājamandri and Chikākol asking help to recover the districts taken by the French.

The Rāja of Tanjor seeks help from the presidency, which sends Muhammad Yūsuf with 500 sepoys and ten artillerymen from Trichinopoly. The French and Mānakji, the Tanjor general, remain inactive before Tanjor till Aug. 2, when Lally opens fire on the town. After a sally is made from the town, the French decamp. They arrive at Kārikāl Aug. 18.

July: M. Bussy, proceeding to Haidarābād to punish Nizām 'Alī for defection, receives imperative orders from Lally to return to Pondicheri. July 18: he quits Aurangābād with his army and reaches Nellor Sept. 4.

July 24: Dūlab Rāi is superseded as *diwān* to Mirān by Rājabullab, but ordered by Mirān to pay the troops—who surround his house. Mr Scrafton, the Resident at Murshidābād, intercedes, and Dūlab Rāi is taken to Calcutta.

Aug. 3: The French and English squadrons engage off Kārikāl, the French losing in men, the English rigging suffering damage. D'Aché decides to sail for Mauritius.

Aug. Further advices from Ānand Rāo, and similar intelligence from Mr Bristol, formerly agent at Katak, arrive at Calcutta, in view of which Clive dispatches Lieut.-Col. Francis Forde in Oct. with a force of 500 Europeans and 2,000 native troops to Vizāgapatam to create a diversion against the French in the Northern Sarkārs.

Sept. 4: Mīr Ja'far is intimidated by a seditious gathering of troops by Khwāja Hadi, the *bakhshi* of Murshidābād. A charge against Dūlab Rāi is raised, believed by Clive to be a forgery of the Nawāb and Mirān, the more so as Khwāja Hadi, the only possible witness, was killed in a fray. Clive privately warns the Nawāb.

Sept. 10: The French under M. Saubinet take Trinomali fort from Krishna Rāo's killadār, and put 500 men to the sword.

Karunguli (Carangoly) submits, and Trivatūr, under Muzaffar Beg, is taken after a field engagement.

Sept. 12: Mr Johnstone, advance agent from Bengal, arrives at Vizāgapatam, which the Rāja had taken from the French, and receives possession.

A.D.

1758 Oct. 4: Lally takes Fort St David.

Oct. 20: Col. Forde and his squadron arrive and join the Rāja Ānand Rāo's troops at Kāsimkotta, to march against the Marquis de Conflans at Rājamandri. The joint armies attack on Dec. 9 at Peddapur, where the European part of the force gains a slight success, followed by a complete victory. Conflans flees to Rājamandri, which the English occupy the following day.

Rāja Wanji Baula Perumāl succeeds Wanji Mārtānda Perumāl at Travankor. He continues the subjugation of petty chiefs by means of an army disciplined by Portuguese, Dutch, and Italian officers.

Farmāns are granted to Mr Gambier by the Rājas of Bringa and Bednūr for the purchase of pepper.

Nov. 29: Lally's army moves from Conjivaram, and on Dec. 12 commences the siege of Fort St George, Madras, held by Cols. Lawrence and Draper. Dec. 13: the French occupy Blacktown. Dec. 14: a sally is made from Madras, resulting in heavy loss for both sides. A ten weeks' cannonade is now begun, lasting till Feb. 16, 1759.

1759 Jan. 2: Lally opens fire on Madras, and continues firing on the fort for the rest of the month. Jan. 27: Capt. Preston, with Muhammad Yūsuf and 'Abdul Wahāb Khān, the Nawāb's brother, encamp at Trimliwāsh, 12 miles from Madras. Feb. 16: this force is joined by Major Calliaud with a small detachment at St Thomé, and is attacked by the French, Feb. 19, in two large bodies. Calliaud defeats them, and on the arrival of the English fleet under Admiral Pococke, Lally precipitately raises the siege of Madras, Feb. 27, N.S.

March 6: Lally's force moves to Arkat, and the English follow the French, who move to Conjivaram. Major Brereton is now vested in the command of the king's troops, and Major Calliaud succeeds Major Lawrence in the E.I.C. command.

Siddi Miyān Achan having expelled 'Alī Nawāz Khān from the government of Surat, assumes his position, but is controlled by Siddi Ahmad Khān, and trade is being ruined. Feb., Mr Spencer, chief of the factory, lands a force and takes the city, and Miyān Achan capitulates, March 4, and gives up the castle

A. D.
1759 and command of the fleet, Miyān Achan continuing as city governor or Nawāb.

During March, the Pālegārs of Madura, Najībulla, the Rāja of Tanjor, and Murtazā 'Alī declare for the English.

March 6: Col. Forde marches on Masulipatam and lays siege to it. April 1: Mr Johnstone is sent as deputy to treat with Salābat Jang, now marching on Forde's camp.

April 6: The French concentrate at Chittapet. Conjivaram is taken by the English; the commander in charge, Muzaffar Beg, sues for quarter but is decapitated as a traitor by Muhammad Yūsuf.

April 7: Col. Forde attacks Masulipatam from three quarters. The defence being dispersed, entrance is effected, and the Marquis de Conflans capitulates; 500 Europeans are taken prisoners.

April 16: Salābat Jang treats with Mr Johnstone, after the defeat of the French. May 14: a treaty is signed by which Masulipatam and eight districts, with the jurisdiction over the districts of Kondavīd, Nizāmpatam, and Akūlamannād, are granted in *inām* to the Company; Salābat Jang engages to compel the French army to pass the Krishnā within fifteen days and never to entertain French troops; he also engages not to call Ānand Rāo to account for what he had collected out of the governments belonging to the French, Ānand Rāo to pay the same tribute as his father, Vizerām Rāo; and the English engage not to assist nor give protection to Salābat Jang's enemies.

May: Major Brereton dismisses his native allies and distributes the sipāhis among the captured forts. Lally's resources are now so low that battle cannot be offered. Greater resentment than ever is shown against him by M. Deleyrit and M. Bussy for his conduct of the campaign.

Alamgīr II. appoints his son, 'Alī Gauhar, to the government of Bengal, with full powers to take possession of it, with the design of overthrowing Mīr Ja'far. Raising an army he attacked Pātna, but the Nawāb of Audh deserting the prince and treacherously seizing Allahābād in rear of the imperial army, Bengal was saved; and the prince, obliged to throw himself on Clive's protection, receives a money gratuity and retires. Mīr Ja'far in gratitude gives Col. Clive a Zamindāri as *jagīr*, said to yield £30,000 per annum.

A.D.

1759 July: Basālat Jang, fifth son of Nizām-ul Mulk, leaves his brothers and takes Polor. The Pālegārs and Najīb-ulla appeal to the Madras presidency for help.

July 7: A French detachment evacuates Covrepāk on the first summons of the English.

July: Lally appoints Rāja Sāhib, son of Chandā Sāhib, Nawāb of the Karnātak. He is crowned with ostentation at Arkat and Pondicheri. This act is tantamount to a renunciation of friendship with Salābat Jang.

July: Muhammad Yūsuf with 6,000 sipāhis carries on a campaign in Madura. Fort Kalankandan is razed. July 15: Tinneveli is reached, where Mahfūz Khān agrees to leave his allies on promise of a *jagīr*. He is sent to Madras, where some concessions secure the peace and order of Tinneveli.

July 25: Sergeant Hunterman with Krishnarāv and a garrison capitulates at Fort Tiyāgar, Volkonda, to a besieging army of 600 French: the besieged being allowed to march out with their arms.

July 26: The Portuguese Viceroy, the Conde de Ega, concludes a secret treaty with Jānoji Bhonsla by which he promises to procure from the King of Portugal the restitution of the provinces ceded in 1754.

Aug. 8: A Dutch fleet from Batavia arrives off Negapatam, bound for Bengal, the Dutch being opposed to British annexation there. Clive, previously warned of their intentions, and fearing a coalition with Mīr Ja'far, withstands them—on his asserted behalf—on land and sea, with the result that six of their fleet are captured, while of 700 troops only fourteen reach Chinsura. Dec. 8: a convention between the Bengal Government and the Dutch is signed at Calcutta.

Aug. The King of Cotiote (Kottayam) concludes an offensive alliance with the English E.I. Company.

The Marāthās under Gopāl Harī invade Maisur and after three months' siege take Channapatna. An indemnity of thirty-two lākhs is paid, and the Marāthās evacuate the pledged districts. Haidar 'Alī is accorded a splendid reception by the Rāja and saluted as Fatha Haidar Bahādur.

Aug. 30: A French fleet under D'Aché, reinforced by three

A.D.

1759 men-of-war under D'Egville, proceed from Trinkomali to Fort St David, and on Sept. 10 engage with the English fleet. Much damage done on both sides: the two fleets draw off.

Sept.: Muharram, H. 1173. Ahmad Shāh Durānī again invades the Panjāb, marching up the Indus from Shikarpur to Peshāwar, and keeping near the hills, crosses the Jamnā near Sahāranpur, in Rabī' I.: Oct.-Nov.

Sept. 26: Major Brereton with the main army marches from Conjivaram. The garrison at Tiruvattūr capitulates. Sept. 29: a triple attack made on Wandiwāsh at night, but the garrison of the French holds out. Much loss is sustained on both sides. Brereton moves for Conjivaram.

Oct. 5: Bussy arrives at Wandiwāsh, but leaves on Oct. 10 for Arkat, sending back the main body to Wandiwāsh, where they mutiny for pay, threatening to join the English. Bussy, arriving, conciliates them and they return to camp.

Oct. Alaunghprā, King of Burma, having heard that the E.I. Co. at Negrais had sold arms and ammunition to the Talaing rebels, orders the settlement to be destroyed. Oct. 5: Mr Southby the agent and other Europeans, together with 100 Indians, are murdered. All compensation refused in 1760.

Oct. 7: In answer to requests from Nārāyandīn, chief of Gānjām, for help against the French, Clive sends the "Hardwicke" to Gānjām, but Nārāyandīn being no longer anxious to expel the French, sends back the ship.

Oct.-Nov.: Rabī' I., H. 1173. The Marāthās, under Datāji Sindia, invade the Rohila country, but are surprised and cut to pieces by Ahmad Shāh 'Abdālī. Govind Pandit, one of their chiefs, is defeated by Nawāb Shujā'-ud-daula Bahādur who, with the Rohilas, proceeds to join Ahmad Shāh 'Abdālī.

Nov. M. Moracin with a small force lands at Cokanada, and failing to gain over the Rāja to the French interest, loses many of his force in fighting for food, and sails with the remaining five or six to Pondicheri.

Nov. João Lourenço Vellozo, a deserter from Goa, forges a letter in the Viceroy's name, offering to give up Goa to the French. Mr Hodges, chief of the English factory at Tellicheri, sends it with an explanation to the Viceroy, when Vellozo makes confession.

A.D.

1759 Nov. 21: Col. Coote moves on Conjivaram, while Capt. Preston takes position at Chingalpat, in readiness to move on Wandiwāsh. Major Brereton captures Tiruvattūr, and on the 26th, Wandiwāsh town. Nov. 28: Coote's detachment arrives, and on the 30th Wandiwāsh fort falls before the joint attack. M. Bussy is taken prisoner. Dec. 4: Coote's force enters Karunguli town, and the fort capitulates on Dec. 10. Dec. 13: the army goes into cantonments at Covrepāk and district.

SHAH JAHĀN II. AND SHĀH 'ALAM.

Nov. 30: Rabī' II. 20, H. 1173. Alamgīr II. murdered by order of the Vazīr Ghāzī-ud-dīn. Muhī-ul Millat, the young son of Muhī-us Sunnat, the son of Kām Bakhsh, the fifth son of Aurangzīb, is placed on the throne with the title of Shāh Jahān II., till Oct. 9. Meanwhile Mīrza 'Abdullah 'Alī Gauhar, the son of 'Alamgīr II., now in Bihār, hearing of his father's death, assumes imperial authority, Jumāda I. 4: Dec. 25, with the title of Jalāl-ud-dīn Shāh 'Alam, till 1786.

Dec. 1. Ahmad Shāh Abdālī arrived at Dehli, left a garrison there, and fell back on Anupshahr. Sadāshiv Bhāu and the Peshwā Bālāji Bājīrāv move from the Dekhan against him, are joined by Ibrāhīm Khān Gārdī (previously in the French service), by Sindia and Holkar, by Govind Pant and Sūraj Mall Jāt,—having thus an immense army. The Dehli fortifications captured in the end of Dec.

1760 Jan.: Jumāda I., H. 1173. The Afghāns and Rohilas defeat Datāji Sindia and Jankaji on the plain of Bāwali near Shāhjahānābād. Holkar's army cut to pieces by the Abdālīs at Sikandra. Holkar escapes.

Jan. 20: Against the better judgment of M. Bussy, Lally attacks Wandiwāsh, and on Jan. 22 sustains a defeat with heavy loss from the relieving force under Sir Eyre Coote. The French force defeated at Chittapet, which surrenders to Coote, Jan. 28. Lally retires to Pondicheri.

Jan. 28: Col. Clive sails for England. John Zephaniah Holwell acting Governor of Bengal, till July 27. He died Nov. 5, 1798.

Feb. The French outposts at Arkat, Devikotta, Trinomali,

A.D.

1760 Chittapet, and Ālamparai captured by the British forces; by April a chain of posts extends round Pondicheri for 70 miles.

Feb. The Prince 'Alī Gauhar again invades Bihār, proclaims himself Emperor as Shāh 'Alam II., and proceeds against Pātna. He defeats Rāja Rāmnārāyan and cuts up the detachment of British sepoys under Lieut. Cochrane. Feb. 15: defeated in turn by Calliaud and the Bengal army, he retires to Bihār. Feb. 22: doubling back on Pātna, he is again defeated. Pātna relieved by Col. Knox with a body of infantry. The Emperor next determined to push past the allied army and seize Murshidābād, but was overtaken, April 7, by Col. Calliaud, when he set fire to the imperial camp and fled.

April 3: The main army in the Madras presidency moves from Villinūr to Villupuram fort, which capitulates April 4.

April 16: Valdor, Chidambaram, Tiruvadi, and Kudālūr capitulate to the English. An attempt to recover Kudālūr is frustrated. Vridāchalam fort, captured by Major Monson, is given to the Nawāb.

May 23: The Nawāb of Purniya, who intended to join Shāh 'Alam, concentrates his troops at Rājmahāl, and on the 24th suffers defeat from Capt. Knox.

May: Alaunghprā, stricken by disease, retreats from the siege of Ayuthia and dies. His eldest son, Naungdoagyī, succeeds.

May: Lally secretly negotiates with Haidar 'Alī of Maisur for assistance at Pondicheri. The English apprised, send spies to Tiyāgar. June 4: a treaty, negotiated by the so-called Bishop of Halicarnassus, between Lally and Haidar, concluded at Pondicheri, for the expulsion of the English from Arkat. Haidar's first division under Makhdum 'Alī arrives at Tiyāgar in South Arkat. June 11: is defeated by Coote's force. July 7: a detachment of English and native troops under Major Moore is defeated by the Mysore army. July 17: Coote encamps at Villinūr and begins the siege of Pondicheri. Sept. 4: Lally attempted a surprise attack on Coote and succeeds on his right, but D'Arambure, by a false move on the left, rendered the attack futile.

July 4: Zī-l qa'da 19. Mīran, Muhammad Sādik Khān, son of Mīr Ja'far, after defeating Khādim Husain Khān near Hājīpur, is

A.D.

1760 killed by lightning at night. Col. Calliaud places his troops in cantonments for the rains.

July 24: Zī-l hijja 9. The Marātha army, under Vishvāsrāv, the son of Bālāji Bājīrāv, and Sadāshiv Bhāu, invests Dehli, which capitulates in ten days. The Bhāu defaced the palaces, tombs, and shrines for their rich ornaments, and coined the silver ceiling of the Dīwān-i-'Āmm into rupees.

The Rājputs and Jāts withdraw from the Marātha confederacy.

July 27: Henry Vansittart assumes office in succession to Clive as Governor of Bengal, till 1765.

Aug. 12: Haidar, in his camp at Darya Daulat, is treacherously fired on by his *pradhān* Khande Rāo, and escapes, owing to the non-appearance of the Marātha allies.

Aug.-Sept. Karūr fort taken from the French. The French form a treaty with Haidar 'Alī, who advances to their aid at Pondicheri; but the allies were completely beaten by the English, Sept. 4, and Haidar 'Alī soon after withdrew.

Sept. 20: Col. Monson (now invalid) succeeded by Col. Eyre Coote as commander of the Madras army.

Sept. 27: Ariangkopang fort taken and the gorges in the Pondicheri boundary hedge redoubts re-trenched. An attack of the French repulsed.

Mr Vansittart, Capt. Calliaud, and a detachment proceed to Murshidābād and request Mīr Ja'far to resign. He is deposed but to retain the title and is promised a residence at Calcutta. Sept. 27: Mīr Kāsim, son-in-law to Mīr Ja'far, is appointed Nawāb of Bengal by treaty with the English. He yields to the E.I. Co. Bardhwān, Midnapur, and Chittagāon for the support of troops. Nov. 7: Vansittart returns to Calcutta where his actions are censured by the Council not members of the Select Committee.

Oct. 1: Col. Eyre Coote and Capt. Joseph Smith capture the "Madras redoubt" at Pondicheri. Though retaken in the night it is again occupied on Oct. 2 and strongly garrisoned. Oct. 6: a naval demonstration on the French ships made by the English squadron's boats.

Oct. Lally seeks aid from the Marāthās, promising them a money payment and the cession of Jinjī fortress.

A.D.

1760 Oct. 16: Admiral Watson with stores arrives at Pondicheri. Mr Call the engineer arrives to conduct the trenches.

Oct. 26: The Portuguese Viceroy enters into a treaty with the Peshwā, who agrees to deliver Sambaulin, Supā, Sangamner, and Phonda, for which a Portuguese fleet is promised for the capture of Janjira and Kansa (44 miles south of Bombay). The Siddi of Janjira, however, privately offers these fortresses to the British at Bombay. Dec. 9: this offer is accepted and a detachment sent.

Oct. 27: Fourteen hundred natives expelled from Pondicheri but stopped at the limit by the sipāhis. They remain outside the walls till permitted by Col. Coote to pass out.

SHĀH 'ALAM II.

Oct. 9: Safar 29, H. 1174. Sadāshiv Bhāu removes Shāh Jahān II. and instals Mīrzā Jawān Bakht, grandson of 'Ālamgīr II., as Emperor, with the title of Jalāl-ud-dīn Shāh 'Alam, appointing Shujā'-ud-daula as *vazīr*. Sadāshiv captures Fort Kunjpūra, puts to death 'Abdus-Samad Khān Abdālī and Qutb Khān and imprisons other zamīndārs. Ahmad Shāh orders his troops to cross the Jumnā. Nov. 29: the Abdālīs are defeated in an action, where, however, the Marātha loss is 1,000. Dec. 23: after another conflict, in which Balwantrāv is killed, the Marāthās retire to Pānīpat.

Nov. 20: Firing resumed more continuously at Pondicheri. Major Allen at Tiyāgar is joined by Visaji Pandit the Marātha, also by a body from Tranquebar.

Dec. 4: The Rāja of Mysore enters Karūr; his forces are beaten off at Narsingpur. A revolt in Madura occurs.

Dec. 24: The Raja of Sunda (Malabar) grants a *farmān* to Robert Gambier for the purchase of pepper produced in the country.

Dec. 31: A severe hurricane at Pondicheri has serious effects on the English forces, siege-works, and ships.

Ishvari Singh, of Jaypur, dies. Mādhu Singh, his brother, succeeds.

1761 Jan. 1: Great earthquake in Arakan.

Jan. 5: A body of Marāthās issues from camp at Pānīpat in

A.D.
1761 desperation for food, but are cut to pieces by the Afghāns. A decisive battle resolved on.

Jan. 7-9: On the subsidence of the river, renewed attacks on Pondicheri are made. Fresh cannon and stores arrive from Madras. Jan. 10: Coote's aide-de-camp, Duespe, is killed while speaking to a messenger from Lally. The Hanover battery pours fire into the town. Jan. 14: a deputation advances from the town and offers terms of admission, and on Jan. 16 the English take possession. The government is vested in the Madras presidency and the fortifications demolished by order of Mr Pigot, the Governor.

Jan. 12: Ānanda Ranga Pillai, diarist and chief dobhāshi (interpreter) at Pondicheri, dies.

Jan. 12: Jumāda II. 6, H. 1174. The Marāthās advance on the Durānī camp and join battle, but sustain a terrible defeat. Sadāshiv Bhāu, Vishvāsrāv, the Peshwā's eldest son, with many other chiefs are slain; Holkar and Dāmāji Gaikwād escape. Forty thousand prisoners are said to have been slain. The Peshwā, on his way north, returns again to Poona—dies June 12: (Zī-l qa'da 9).

Jan. Jaswantrāv of Dhār having fallen at Pānīpat, Khanderāv Puār succeeds at the age of two and a half. Dhār is despoiled by Holkar and Sindia.

Claude Martin, to avoid Lally's severity, deserts to the British for whom he raises a company of French cavalry.

Jan. Major Carnac arrives at Pātna, in succession to Col. Calliaud, engages the Emperor's troops, in Mir Kāsim's interest, and defeats the imperial forces at Gayā Manpur, Jan. 15. M. Law, who had taken service with the Mughals, is taken prisoner. The Emperor gives himself up to the English.

Jan. 21: Clive, in a dispatch, intimates the dismissal by the Court of Directors from the Company's service of Messrs Holwell, Pleydell, Sumner, and Maguire.

The Sikhs assume greater power, and elect a certain Chintia as their Emperor at Lāhor; they are defeated by a Durānī invasion.

Feb. 3: Fortress of St George, to the right of Jinjī, taken by Capt. Stephen Smith. Feb. 4: Tiyāgar taken by Capt. Preston after a sixty-five days' blockade. Feb. 8: troops from England encamp at Mahé. M. Louet's allies failing, he capitu-

A.D.
1761 lates to Major Hector Munro. By April the French power in the peninsula is obliterated.

The Nawāb Mīr Kāsim 'Alī, impatient with the English, seeks to plunder the wealth of Rāmnārāyan, his deputy at Pātna, for funds to oppose them. But Rāmnārāyan solicits the help of Major Carnac, and then of Carnac's successor, Col. Eyre Coote; but they were forbidden by the Council to protect him, and he became a victim to Mīr Kāsim 'Alī's rapacity.

The Jaypur army repulsed at Kotā by the genius of Zālim Singh, Chatrsāl's prime minister.

Sūraj Mal Jāt succeeds to the absolute sovereignty of Bharatpur.

Mādhavrāv Sindia becomes ruler of Ujjain, and the ally of the regent Raghunāth against the Jāts of Bharatpur and the Rohilas; he annexes the fort of Gwaliār and consolidates his power.

March 13: Col. Eyre Coote embarks from Madras for Bengal.

June: Raghunāthrāv, as regent of the Marātha dominions, opens negotiations with the English at Bombay, in view of Nizām 'Alī's threatened invasion. Nizām 'Alī destroys the Hindu temples at Tokā, and so alienates many possible adherents; Mīr Mughal, youngest son of Nizām ul-Mulk, deserts to the Marāthās. An accommodation takes place, by which the cessions of Aurangābād and Bedar revenues are relinquished by Raghunāthrāv.

June: Haidar 'Alī enters on the government of Mysore, all power being taken out of Nanda Rāja's hands. He is invested by Basālat Jang with the Nawābship of Sira.

July 18: Nizām 'Alī imprisons Salābat Jang, and invests himself with the Sūbahdārship of the Dekhan.

Sept. Mādhavrāv, second son of the late Peshwā, invested at Sātāra as Peshwā by the nominal Rāja, who remains under the restrictions of Tārābāī.

Sept. 14: The British at Bombay come to an agreement with the Peshwā, adjusting disputes which arose from Marātha attacks on the Siddis of Janjira their allies.

Dec. Tārābāī dies at Poona. The Rāja of Sātāra's position improves, and he is allowed the town of Sātāra to live in.

Mīr Kāsim 'Alī challenges the privileges claimed by the Company's servants under the *farmān* of 1757 and the late

A.D.

1761 treaties, and begins to organise troops under Mughal officers, and removes to the fort of Mongīr.

1762 The small state of Samthar, separated from the Datiyā territory, claims independence of the Marātha suzerainty.

Jan. The Governor of Taungu rebels: his nephew, the Burmese king, blockades his city, which surrenders.

April: Great shocks of earthquake in Arakan.

April-May: Messrs Vansittart and Hastings, sent to the Nawāb at Mongīr, endeavour to modify the former treaties under which the enormities complained of from the private trade of the Company's servants were carried on. The Calcutta Council rejected the proposed terms, to the Nawāb's great annoyance.

Siddi Yāqut Khān succeeds to the regentship at Janjira, in prejudice of Siddi 'Abdul Rahim, the real heir, who, however, in 1772, receives Danda Rājpur, with the prospect of succession to Janjira on Siddi Yāqut's death: thereafter 'Abdul Rahim's second son is to be Siddi.

Rānā Gaj Singh of Udaypur dies. During his reign Marātha oppression increases. Rānā Arsi, his uncle, succeeds.

July 10: Zī-l hijja 14, H. 1175. Nizām 'Alī imprisons Salābat Jang at Bedar, and afterwards secures his assassination.

The chief of Manipur appeals to the Bengal Government for protection from the Burmese. Sept., a treaty of offensive and defensive alliance is negotiated—ratified 1763—but meanwhile Manipur is invaded.

Nov. Mīr Kāsim 'Alī renews his remonstrances against the private trade of the Company's servants. An agreement is concluded, allowing the benefits of the Company's pass to *bona fide* imports and exports, but prohibiting evasions of duty by private persons: the duties to be fixed at 9 per cent.

Mādhavrāv leads an insurrection against Raghunāthrāv, who retires to Aurangābād, but returns supported by Mughals. Mādhavrāv submits, and a reconciliation is effected.

Oct. 12: The Nawāb of the Karnātak, attempting to exact arrears of tribute from the Tanjor Rāja, appeals to the Madras Government and obtains by its mediation twenty-two lākhs as arrears, and an annual tribute of four lākhs.

A.D.

1762 The Philippine Islands taken by an expedition fitted out from Madras.

Jījībāī, widow of Sambhāji, Rāja of Kolhāpur, adopts Sivaji Bhonsla as heir, and conducts the affairs of State in his name.

Haidar 'Alī obtains the Nawābship of Sira for three lākhs of rupees, and exacts tribute from the pālegārs of Chhota Bālāpur, Raidurg, Harpanhalli, and Chittaldurg.

1763 Jan. Haidar 'Alī conquers Bednūr, which he makes his capital. The Rānī and her adopted son are taken prisoners.

Jan. 28: Mr Vansittart returns to Calcutta, where his negotiations with Kāsim 'Alī produce dissatisfaction in the Council. It is determined (Hastings and Vansittart dissenting) that the imperial farmān gives a right to internal trading duty free. March 7: it is resolved that Messrs Amyatt and Hay be sent on deputation to the Nawāb. Feb. 19: the Nawāb had seized some arms and refused to deliver them, and Mr Ellis is authorised to use force. The Nawāb's order to remit all transit dues—thus putting the British on an equal footing with the country merchants—is treated as a declaration of war. June 24: Ellis surprises and takes the Nawāb's fort at Pātna, but it was retaken next day, and all the English at Pātna were seized as prisoners.

July 7: The Calcutta Council again instal Mīr Ja'far as Nawāb, deposing Mīr Kāsim. July 10: Zī-l hijja 18, H. 1176, Mr Amyatt and several others murdered, by the Nawāb's orders, on their way to Calcutta. July 11: by a treaty with the new Nawāb, all existing treaties with the Company are confirmed and other advantages granted. Major Adams proceeds against Mīr Kāsim, whom he defeats, July 19, between Calcutta and Murshidābād. July 24: Adams storms and takes Murshidābād. Aug. 2: at Gheriā near Gaur, Mīr Kāsim's army is again defeated. Sept. 5: after another defeat at Udhā-Nālā, Mīr Kāsim flees to Mongīr and thence to Pātna, where, by means of Walter Reinhard (Samru), he murders Messrs Ellis, Hay, Lushington, and others, and 125 English prisoners. Nov. 6: Pātna taken by storm, and the Nawāb flees into Audh.

Sūrajmal Jāt of Bharatpur, now master of Agra, makes an attempt to capture Dehli: while hunting he is killed by a party of Mughals. His son, Jawāhir Singh, succeeds, and forms an

A.D.

1763 alliance with Holkar. According to the *Seir Mutakherin*, Sūrajmal was killed in battle against the Rohila Najīb-ud-daula in December.

Peace between England and France concluded by the Treaty of Paris, signed Feb. 10. All factories taken from France since 1749 to be given back. France to erect no fortifications and keep no troops in Bengal, to renounce all acquisitions on the coast of Coromandel and Orissa, and to recognise Muhammad 'Alī Khān, son of Anwar-ud-dīn Khān, as Nawāb of the Karnātak.

Muhammad Yūsuf, sipāhi commander in Madura, in consequence of having paid no tribute, is confronted with a force in August; he holds out against all their efforts.

Oct. 16: The Nawāb of the Karnātak by *sanad* confers on the English certain districts dependent on the Sūbah of Arkat, including most of the Chingalpat district.

Oct. Raghunāthrāv inflicts a severe defeat on the Mughal army, under Nizām 'Alī and his diwān, Rāja Pratāpwant, at Rākshāsbhuvan on the Godāvarī. Peace is concluded at Aurangābād.

Nov. Naungdoagyī, King of Burma, dies. His next brother, known as Hsengbyusheng, succeeds. He prepares to invade Siam.

Nov. 14: Robert Palk succeeds Mr George Pigott as Governor of Madras, till Jan. 25, 1767.

The Marāthās capture a Portuguese vessel, on which war is declared by the Portuguese, together with the King of Sunda and the Rāja of Kolhāpur, who, however, fail to co-operate. Mandangarh capitulates to a Portuguese attack.

Muhammad Reza Khān, son of Chandā Sāhib, claims and obtains Haidar's protection.

Miyān Achan, Nawāb of Surat, dies. Of four competitors, the British support Mīr Qutb-ud-dīn, who is installed as Nawāb.

Dec. The hill country of Sunda taken by Haidar 'Alī. The rāja and his family take refuge at Goa.

1764 Jan. 16: Major Adams dies when about to sail for home.

Feb. 11: The European battalion of the English army mutinous, also the sepoys, till Feb. 28, when order is restored. Major Carnac takes command. The contemplated campaign into

A.D.

1764 Audh is abandoned, and the army marched to Pātna. May 3: Nawāb Shujā'-ud-daula and the Emperor, joined by Mīr Kāsim, threaten Pātna, and are beaten off by Carnac. Major Hector Munro, who arrived from Bombay in May, superseding Major Carnac, restores discipline by severe measures.

Sept. 15: The troops leave Pātna, and, Oct. 23, completely defeat the Vazīr's army at Baksār. This leaves the English masters of Bengal. Terms are granted to Shāh 'Alam, but on Nawāb Shujā'-ud-daula's refusal to give up Mīr Kāsim and Samru, negotiations are stopped with him, and the army advanced to overrun Audh.

May 3: Clive arrives in India as an Irish viscount, and head of the Bengal Government.

Rāja Nand Kumār made Mahārāja by Shāh 'Alam, is also appointed collector of Burdhwān, Nadiya, and Hūglī.

Oct. 19: The Portuguese viceroy-elect having died on the passage, a commission, viz., Dom Antonio Taveira da Nieva, archbishop; João Vaz Pereira, Chancellor of State; and Dom João José de Mello, Comptroller-General, take office by succession patent.

Fazl Ullat Khān establishes Haidar 'Alī's posts as far north as the Krishnā. Mādhavrāv, by judicious generalship, defeats Haidar at Rattihalli, and requests Raghunāthrāv to join in command.

Oct. Muhammad Yūsuf is seized in Madura and delivered to the English attacking force. His subjection had cost the Company and their ally, the Nawāb of the Karnātak, a million of money.

Dec. Shāh 'Alam proposes to confer on the English Ghāzipur and Benares, and to retain the rest of the Vazīr of Audh's possessions. This is condemned by the Court of Directors as burdensome and profitless.

Kāsim 'Alī escapes into the Rohila country with some friends and a few jewels which he had saved from the clutches of his late ally, the Vazīr of Audh.

1765 Jan. Boundary differences between the Nawāb of the Karnātak and the Rāja of Tanjor settled in favour of the latter.

Feb. 5: Sha'bān 14, H. 1178. Mīr Ja'far 'Alī Khān dies.

A.D.

1765 His son, Mīr Phūlwārī, with the title of Najm-ud-daula appointed Nawāb. Feb. 20: a treaty with the new Nawāb commits the entire military defence of the province to the Company; a Nāib Sūbah, to be chosen by the Nawāb and approved by the Governor and Council, to have entire control of the civil government.

Feb. The Marāthās retire from the Mysore territory on the restoration of all places taken from Morārirāv of Gūtī and 'Abdul Hakim of Sāvanūr. Sira is left in Haidar's hands.

Jawāhir Singh of Dīg, the Jāt leader, defeated by the Jaypur Rāja, and murdered at Agra in 1768.

The Peshwā and the Nizām, disgusted at the treacherous vacillation of Jānoji Bhonsla, unite against him, burn Nāgpūr and force him to give up the money he had received from each for his assistance.

March 12: By a resolution of the Court of Directors Clive is reappointed President of Bengal, with command of the Company's forces in the province. He dismisses Nand Kumār, Najm-ud-daula's prime minister, and forbids him to leave Calcutta. Muhammad Reza Khān's influence now begins to be felt.

March 23: An agreement is concluded between Ravivarma, regent of the Chirakal, and the Tellicheri chiefs for the cession of the province of Randatarra (Malabar) to them.

May 3: Clive arrives at Calcutta, and on the 7th declares the Select Committee formed, with Messrs Sumner and Sykes as members. He enforces the Company's covenant against the receipt of presents.

May 3: A skirmish with the Vazīr of Audh and with the remnant of the Marātha force takes place near Korā. May 19: General Carnac receives a letter from the Vazīr, who agrees to come into the British camp, and a conference takes place, resulting in the restoration of the Vazīr's dominions. Private trade or factories in Audh not insisted on, but Allahābād and Korā were retained for the Emperor.

June 25: Clive proceeds up country to arrange with the Nawāb for the government of the province, and to conclude a treaty with the Vazīr Shujā'-ud-daula.

Aug. 12: The *farmān* of the *diwānī* of the provinces of Bengal,

A.D.

1765 Bihār, and Orissa is granted by Shāh 'Alam to the Company, and all territory previously held by the Company is confirmed to them.

Rāja Ala Singh of Patiālā dies. Amar Singh succeeds.

A British expedition dispatched to Mālwān to put down the continued plunder of the Kolhāpuris. This suppressed, the Rānī agreed to permit the establishment of a factory, with the monopoly of cloths from Europe, and to pay seven and a half lākhs of rupees. None of these promises were fulfilled.

An expedition from Bombay, under Major Gordon and Capt. John Watson, captures the fort of Yeswantgarh. It is agreed to restore it on suppression of the piracies so long practised on the British.

René Médac, a Frenchman in the service of the English at Bombay, forms a company of French and sipāhis, and leads an adventurous career, till 1777.

A dāk (postal service) established between Calcutta and Murshidābād.

1766 Jan. 1: The Select Committee issue an order that "double full batta" for the officers in Bengal, formerly paid by the Nawāb, is to cease. Much indignation felt, and in May a mutinous outbreak occurs. Almost every officer resigns. The sipāhis remain in sufficient numbers to overawe the European troops. By a court-martial some officers are cashiered — among them, Sir R. Fletcher was dismissed for not repressing the combination at first.

Jan. 20: The Burmese army encamps before Ayuthia.

Feb. 4: Negotiations entrusted by Mādhavrāv to his uncle, Raghunāthrāv, result in a treaty at Bednūr with Haidar 'Alī, who gives up all claims on Sāvanūr, and retires across the Krishnā.

Feb.: Sha'bān, H. 1178. The Nawāb of Bengal and his family retire from Lucknow to Bareilly. He fails to gain over the Rohila and Afghān chiefs.

Feb. 14: A treaty is concluded between the King of Kandy and the Government of Colombo, defining the position of the Dutch authorities in Kandy.

Feb. 16: By a secret treaty between Mādhavrāv and Haidar 'Alī, the districts ceded by the Nizām on the 4th Feb. are partially restored. Jānoji Bhonsla is compelled, on an invasion of the united armies, to sue for peace.

A.D.

1766 April: Ava reoccupied as capital by Hsengbyusheng.

May 5: Count Lally is beheaded at Paris.

May 8: Zī-l qa'da 24, H. 1179. Najm-ud-daula, Nawāb of Bengal, dies of fever. His brother, Saif-ud-daula, succeeds to the nominal office. May 19: a treaty of friendship and support between the new Nawāb and the Bengal Government is signed.

Aug. 30: Rabī' II. 13, H. 1179. Shujā'-ud-daula reinstated by the British Government as Nawāb of Audh.

Sept. 8: A Trade Committee was formed to put into execution the laws regarding private trade. Dec., letters from the Court of Directors absolutely forbid inland trade by private individuals to be carried on.

Oct. 24: The East India Company conclude a treaty with Khem Sāwant of Sāwantwādi. The fort of Vingorlā is ceded for thirteen years.

Nov. 12: Col. Calliaud, on the part of the British Government, negotiates a treaty with Nizām 'Alī, by which, for the Sarkārs of Ellur, Chikākol, Rājamandri, Muzaffarnagar, and Guntūr, the British Government agree to furnish the Nizām with a subsidiary force when required, and to pay nine lākhs a year when the assistance of their troops is not required. Two battalions join the Nizām for the reduction of the fort of Bangalor, now in possession of Haidar 'Alī.

Chikka Kishn, titular Rāja of Maisūr, dies. Nanja Rāj Udayar is placed on the throne by Haidar 'Alī, but subsequently deposed.

Malharāv's son, Khanderāv, dies. His widow, Ahilyābāī, acts as regent for her son, Malirāv, with Tukāji Holkar, a tribesman of her husband, as commander of the army.

H. 1179. Rāghoba besieges Gohad and demands tribute from Jawāhir Singh of Bharatpur, who sends two envoys to treat. These are bribed, and promise to betray Jawāhir, but their treachery is discovered.

Haidar 'Āli invaded Malabar and seized Calicut.

H. 1180. Issue of the *Jam-i-Jahān-nāma* of Muzaffar Husain, physician to Muhammad Shāh—a miscellaneous collection of historical and other facts.

A.D.
1767 Jan. 15: Lord Clive intimates his intention to resign, and leaves India. Feb. 17, Henry Verelst succeeded as Governor of Bengal, till Dec. 1769.

Jan. 25: Charles Bourchier, Governor of Madras, till Jan. 31, 1770.

Jan. 27: Thomas Hodges, Governor of Bombay, till Feb. 23, 1771.

Presents having been forbidden by the Directors, Lord Clive gave up a legacy from Mīr Ja'far of five lākhs, adding to it three lākhs from Saif-ud-daula, the successor of his brother, Najm-ud-daula, and formed "Lord Clive's Fund" for invalided officers and soldiers of the Company's service, and their widows.

Ahmad Shāh Durrānī again invades the Panjāb. He confers on Amar Singh of Patiālā the title of Rāj-i Rājgan Bahādur, and the insignia of flag and drum. He overran several Sikh districts towards Dehli, and returned to his own country.

April: The garrison at Ayuthia yield to a general attack by the Burmese besieging army. The city is destroyed by fire, and the king, Ekādatha Rāja, killed. The Burmese are at once recalled to deal with a Chinese invasion which is successfully repelled, and the eight Shān states in the basin of the Tapeng river are reunited to Burma.

Mahārāja Fath Shāhi Bahādur, ninety-ninth of the line from Bīr Sen of the Hutwa (Husainpur) Rāj, rebels against the British Government.

The Newār chief of Khātmāndū applies for aid against the Gūrkhās. Capt. Kinloch, despatched with a small force, is compelled by the deadly climate of the Terai to retire. The Gūrkhās overrun Nepāl, and their chief is eventually recognised by the British Government as Rāja.

Nizām 'Alī obtains the aid of two British battalions to aid him in the siege of Bangalūr, held by Haidar 'Alī. Haidar persuades the Nizām to desert the English alliance for his own; he also bought off the Marātha invaders by a payment of thirty-five lākhs of rupees.

Aug. 25: Haidar 'Alī's and the Nizām's forces descend the Ghāts to invade the Karnātak and attack Col. Joseph Smith, who retreats on Trinomāli till reinforced, and Sept. 26, inflicts such

A.D.

1767 loss on the enemy that they desire to negotiate, but their terms being inadmissible, Smith again defeats them, Nov. 8, near Ambūr, after which they retired above the Ghāts.

Oct. Jawāhir Singh, son of Sūrajmal Jāt, overruns the country near Ajmīr, belonging to Mādhav Singh Kachhwāhā who, declining to lead the Rājputs against him, they are headed by Dalel Sing and totally defeat Jawāhir Singh.

1768 Jan. In consequence of Nizām 'Alī's breach of the treaty of 1766, a force under Col. Peach had advanced from the Northern Sarkārs as far as Worangal, when, Feb. 26, the Nizām signed a new treaty, revoking all *sanads* granted to Haidar 'Alī by the Sūbahdārs of the Dekhan; agreeing to hand over the administration of the Karnātak above the Ghāts; not to interfere with the possessions of Muhammad 'Alī, the Nawāb of the Karnātak; and to accept a reduced payment for the Northern Sarkārs.

The Madras Government sent out two bodies of troops—one under Col. Wood to secure the fortified places in the south, and Shingarikota was taken Feb. 12, and Salem March 20; the other, under Col. Smith, entered Mysore proper, but lost much time in taking Krishnagiri, May 2; then ascended the Ghāts, took Venkatagiri, June 10; Mulbāgal, June 28; Kolār and Hosūr, July 11.

March 12: Dom João José de Mello appointed Governor at Goa. He effects several economies in Government, the governor's salary being reduced to 20,000 serafins per annum.

March 21: The King of Portugal issues an order for the expulsion of all Jesuits from India.

May: Haidar marches on Mangalor, where an insurrection had broken out. A British officer from the Bombay garrison, with 1,500 men, sent to support the town against Haidar, departs by sea, leaving 240 of the sick and wounded.

Raghunāthrāv, discontented with the power allotted him by the Peshwā, creates internal dissensions among the Marāthās, and, supported by Holkar, Jānoji Bhonsla, and Damāji Gaikwād, rebels against his nephew, but is surprised at Dhodap by Mādhavrāv, and imprisoned at Poona.

Damāji Gaikwād dies, leaving four sons. The eldest, Sayaji, being an idiot, the second, Govindrāv, secures recognition as

A. D.

1768 successor by a large *nazar* to the Peshwā, who, however, subsequently accedes to Fath Singh's representations of Sayaji's claims.

June: Safar, H. 1182. Jawāhir Singh of Bharatpur assassinated by a degraded soldier. Ratan Singh succeeds.

Aug. 4: Haidar arrives back from Malabar. The two Madras forces met at Hoskot, where a Marātha corps under Morārirāv joined them. Haidar 'Alī made a desperate but unsuccessful attempt to surprise Morāri's camp. He then went off, collected reinforcements, returned towards Kolār, and proposed terms of peace, which were refused.

An action at Mulbāgal costs Col. Wood 8 officers and 229 men killed. Nov. 14: Col. Smith is recalled to Madras: Col. Wood, his successor, twice defeated, is deprived of the command.

The Chinese with a powerful army invade Burma a fourth time.

1769 Jan. Haidar 'Alī, eluding the main British force, takes Karūr and Erod, and marches down the Kāverī. March: Haidar reaches St Thomas Mount, near Madras, with 6,000 cavalry, and proposes terms of peace, viz., mutual restoration of conquests and prisoners; assistance of each contracting party in case of the other's being attacked; the terms to be made obligatory on the Bombay presidency. March 27: this treaty concluded and ratified on April 4. This ends the First Mysore War.

April: An Act passed, allowing the territorial revenues to be held for five years by the Company, and to pay £400,000 per annum into the exchequer.

April 10: A Junta of the exchequer of Goa is created.

The exclusive privileges of the French East India Co. are suspended by the king's decree. The Company was afterwards abolished by the National Assembly of 1796.

Sept. A Commission, consisting of Messrs Scrafton, Vansittart, and Francis, appointed to inquire into Bengal affairs; these all perish in the wreck of the "Aurora."

Dec. 13: The Chinese army in Burma being defeated, and the remnant surrounded, a convention for peace, friendship, and commerce is agreed to, and signed by a Commission of fourteen Burmese and thirteen Chinese.

A.D.

1769 It was proposed to send out a naval commander-in-chief, with full political powers, on the part of the king. The measure was carried after much opposition, but proved very inconvenient during the short period it was tried.

For revenue purposes Bengal is divided into six divisions: Calcutta, Bardhwān, Rājshāhi with Murshidābād, Dhākā, Dinājpur, and Azimābād. Native officers are to be superintended by servants of the Company, called supervisors, in the collection of revenue and the administration of justice.

Warren Hastings, still in England, appointed to the second seat on the Madras Council.

Dec. 24: Mr Verelst resigned in Bengal. John Cartier succeeded as Governor of Bengal, Dec. 26, till April 13. 1772.

1770 Jan. 31: Josias Dupré succeeds Mr Charles Bourchier as Governor of Madras, till Feb. 2, 1773.

Feb.: Shawwāl, H. 1183. Great hurricane at Calcutta. This year Bengal is visited by severe plague and famine. A fifth of the population said to have perished: Mill says more than a third.

March 10: Saif-uddaula, Nawāb of Bengal, dies. His brother, Mubārik-uddaula, aged twelve, succeeds, with a stipend reduced from thirty-one lākhs odd from the Company to sixteen lākhs, during his minority.

July 26: Sir John Lindsay arrives at Madras as King's Commissioner Plenipotentiary, with powers to negotiate and conclude arrangements with Indian sovereigns in general. This appointment is made without the Company's assent, and the latter, feeling superseded, decline to co-operate. He favours the pretensions of the Nawāb of Arkat against the Company.

The East India Directors send their first expedition under Capt. Kinloch to establish trade with Nepāl. Owing to sickness and the difficult nature of the country the enterprise is abandoned

Aug. 8: A treaty of perpetual friendship concluded between the English Government and Haidar 'Alī.

Sept. A Revenue Council appointed at Murshidābād.

Oct. Najīb-uddaula, Nādir Shāh's deputy at Dehli, dies. His son, Zābita Khān, succeeds to his Indian possessions and the government of Dehli.

A.D.

1770 Nov. Mādhavrāv Peshwā sends a large body of Marātha horse, under Gopālrāv Patvardhan and Malhārrāv Rāstia, and follows himself with more troops to punish Haidar for misappropriation of tribute, and rapidly reduces forts and villages. In June 1771 he is forced by illness to return, leaving Trimbakrāv Māma to carry on the war.

A Marātha force defeats the Jāts at Bharatpur.

Nanja Rāj Udiyar, of Maisur, found intriguing with Trimbakrāv, is strangled by order of Haidar 'Alī, and his brother, Bettada Chāma, is placed on the throne.

H. 1184. The *Farhatu-n-Nāzirīn* of Muhammad Khān written.

1771 Feb. Muhammad 'Alī, Nawāb of Arkat, seeks help from Madras against the Rāja of Tanjor; being refused he dissuades the presidency from further movement. Sept. 9 to Oct. 27: Tanjor is invested by an army under General Smith and the two sons of the Nawāb. Peace is signed between the Rāja and Nawāb 'Umdat-ul-Umrā. This peace is much resented at the presidency.

Feb. 26: William Hornby succeeds Mr Thomas Hodges as Governor of Bombay, till Jan. 9, 1784.

March 5: Haidar, attempting to escape from the Marātha invaders, is attacked and defeated at Chinkulari, and flees to Seringapatam, which is invested till June, when Haidar binds himself to pay them thirty lākhs of rupees.

April 23. The British Government makes over to Momin Khān, Nawāb of Khambay, on payment of 75,000 rupees, the fort of Talāja, now taken from the piratical Kolis.

May. The Emperor Shāh 'Alam, with 16,000 troops raised by Mughal nobles, marches from Allahābād to Nabiganj, where he cantons. The Marātha vakīl, Mahādāji Sindia, presents the demands of his masters: the balance of *chauth* due from the time of Muhammad Shāh must be discharged; plunder taken to be shared equally by Mughal and Marātha troops; Marātha leaders to be confirmed in their jāgīrs; and five lākhs of rupees must be at once advanced to the Marāthās from the imperial treasury. These imperious demands being complied with, the Emperor enters Dehli in triumph on Dec. 25.

Sept. 2: Sir Robert Harland arrives at Madras, as successor

A.D.

1771 to Sir J. Lindsay, the King's commander; like his predecessor, he takes the side of the Nawāb against the presidency.

Prīthi Nārāyan, ruler of Nipāl, dies. His son, Pratāp Singh, succeeds.

Oct. 24: The Marāthās move on Bangalor, Haidar remaining at Seringapatam. He applies to the Madras presidency for help, but on the advice of the Nawāb is refused, in spite of the treaty.

The British Government sends an expedition to Bharoch to enforce the payment of arrears due to the Surat Agency. The expedition fails, but before another is sent, the Nawāb makes overtures, and a commercial and inter-political treaty is concluded, Nov. 30.

An order issued that the administration of the Custom House at Goa should be carried on for and on account of the State.

The Parliamentary restriction on the dividends ceasing in 1769, the Court in March and September again raised the dividend to 12½ per cent.

1772 Jan. The Marāthās hurry the Emperor into the field to plunder the country of the Rohilas; and they invaded the Sahāranpur jāgīr of Zābita Khān, the son of Najīb-uddaula, who was forced to escape to Shujā'-uddaula, Nawāb of Audh. The Marāthās then wholly seized the rich booty of the province.

Jan. 20: The Sūbahdār of Audh confers with General Sir Robert Barker at Faizābād regarding the Rohila persecution by the Marāthās, and the danger to Audh, with a view to the formation of an English offensive treaty. The Rohilas object to a proposed division of their territory: their lands continue to be plundered.

March: The Nawāb of the Karnātak again applies for help from Madras. A force of Europeans and Sipāhis with the Nawāb's cavalry, marches from Trichinopoly, and by June 15 all the chief forts in Great Marawar are in their hands.

April 13: Warren Hastings appointed Governor of Bengal, in succession to Mr Cartier, till Feb. 1, 1785.

The Revenue business and Treasury removed from Murshidābād to Calcutta. The law courts are also transferred, under the name of Sadr Dīwānī 'Adālat, composed of governor and two

A.D.

1772 councils for civil cases; and Sadr Nizāmat 'Adālat for criminal proceedings, composed of native law officers, exclusively subject to review of the governor and council. Under these were District Courts, and the collectors have revenue and judicial authority. These were continued till 1793.

Muhammad Razā Khān deposed from his office as Nāib Dīwān and Nāib Sūbah at Murshidābād, and arrested. Gurudās, son of Nand Kumār, succeeds as *dīwān.* The former post is abolished. Rāja Chitab Rāī, who held the same post at Pātna, is also arrested—the latter is honourably acquitted. Manī Begam, originally a dancing girl, takes charge of the young Nawāb and the control of the Murshidābād palace.

April: The Bombay Council resolve to appoint a resident envoy to the court of the Peshwā. Mr Thomas Mostyn arrives at Poona in this capacity, in Nov.—a few days before the death of Mādhavrāv.

May: After a futile attempt at an alliance with the Marāthās, the Rohilas come to terms with the Sūbahdār of Audh. July 11, a treaty is formally concluded in which the Marāthās consented to retire on a promised payment of forty lākhs of rupees by the Rohilas, and Shujā'-uddaula having made himself responsible to the Marāthās, they quitted Kuthar.

May 14: The East India Company resolve to abolish the system of dual government, and "to stand forth as *dīwān*," and to take upon themselves, by the agency of their own servants, the entire care and administration of the revenues.

In 1769 civil servants were appointed as supervisors of the native revenue officers; they were henceforth to be styled "collectors." The lands to be let for five years.

June: The Marāthās, having abandoned their designs on Bednūr and Sunda, conclude a treaty with Haidar 'Alī,—they to retain Shivaji's ancient possessions, with Mudgiri and Garamkonda, Haidar to pay thirty-six lākhs of rupees, as arrears and expenses, and fourteen as annual tribute.

War breaks out between Raghunāthrāv and Nizām 'Alī, who is compelled to give up territory, but who cajoles Raghunāthrāv into restoring the whole.

Nov. 18: H. 1186. Mādhavrāv, the Peshwā, dies at the age

A.D.

1772 of twenty-eight, having commended his brother Nārāyanrāv to the care of his uncle Raghunāthrāv.

Nov. 18: In consequence of the Nawāb's ill-treatment of the British factory agents, a British force takes Bharoch by storm.

Darendra Nārāyan, Rāja of Kuch Bihār, a minor and prisoner in the hands of the Bhutias, offers to pay half his revenue to the E.I. Co. in return for help against his oppressors.

Rānā Arsi of Udaypur is murdered: Rānā Hamīr succeeds. Six districts in each reign are severed from the kingdom.

Fath Singh Gaikwād, regent of Baroda, seeks alliance with the English, which is declined.

The Rānī of Kolhāpur dies. Plunder and mismanagement continue in her kingdom.

John Morrison, formerly a servant of the E.I. Co., takes service with Shāh 'Alam about 1772, and receives the titles of "General and Commander-in-Chief of the Great Mughal's forces," and "Ambassador and Plenipotentiary" to George III.; he went to England with a proposal to invest the King with the absolute sovereignty of Bengal, Bihār, and Orissa, in exchange for a body of troops to defend the throne of Dehli. René Madec, a French adventurer, also took service and was made a Nawāb.

The Dutch East India Company purchase Nagar from the Rājā of Tanjor. The town is surrendered.

First public courts of the Portuguese instituted in India.

Dec. 22: The Emperor, besieged by the Marāthās in Dehli, unable to resist longer, opened the gates to them. He was now entirely under their control, and they extorted from him a grant of the provinces of Korā and Allahābād.

1773 Jan. 13: The Governments of British India and Baroda enter into a short contract in which the British agree to pay the Gaikwād his share of the revenues of Bharoch captured by the English.

Feb. 2: Alexander Wynch succeeds Mr Josias Du Pré as Governor of Madras, till Dec. 11, 1775.

April 5: A treaty is signed by the Bengal Council and Darendra Nārāyan, Rāja of Kuch Bihār, by which protection is accorded by the former in return for a moiety of the Rāja's revenues.

A.D.

1773 The imperial deputy of Allahābād and Korā applies to the Company for leave to place them under British protection. The districts are sold to the Vazīr of Audh for fifty lākhs of rupees.

April 11: Raghunāthrāv again imprisoned by order of the Peshwā Nārāyanrāv, for fostering dissensions.

May 10: The E.I. Company applied to His Majesty's Government for a loan. The Government, acting on the Report of the Select Committee of the House of Commons appointed to inquire into the affairs of the Company, brought in the important "Regulating Act" (13 Geo. III., c. 63), appointing a Governor-General and four Members of Council, for five years, to Bengal: Mr Warren Hastings to be Governor; Mr Richard Barwell, senior Member; and Lieut.-General John Clavering, Colonel the Hon. George Monson, and Mr Philip Francis. To the Court of Directors, to consist of twenty-four, an annual election of six new members for four years was ordained. The nomination of Governor-General was in future to be by the Directors, subject to the approbation of Government. The other presidencies were made subordinate to Bengal. A supreme Court of Judicature was instituted at Calcutta, with judges appointed by the Crown. All territorial correspondence to be laid before the Ministry.

May: Jānoji Bhonsla dies. Mudaji's son, Rāghoji, is appointed heir. Mudaji defeated by his brother Sabaji.

May: The Marāthās in Audh return south, fearing the united armies of the Vazīr and the British.

June: Another Act of Parliament is passed lending the Company £1,400,000 at 4 per cent., restricting the dividend to 6 per cent., foregoing the annual payment of £400,000 until the debt be discharged, and continuing the retention of territorial possessions until the expiry of the Charter.

June 9: The arsenal at Goa and much shipping destroyed by fire.

June 15: Rabī' I. 25, H. 1187. Muhammad Razā Khān is acquitted, but not reinstated in the Nāibship. He joins the party of General Clavering, and is made Faujdār of Murshidābād; —dies 1785.

June. Ahmad Shāh Durānī dies. His second son, Taimūr,

A.D.

1773 succeeds by testament, but is compelled to put down the faction of his elder brother, Sulaimān Mīrza. The title of capital is removed to Kābul.

June: The Madras Government anew open war with the Rāja of Tanjor, in the interests of Muhammad 'Alī, Nawāb of Arkat, who was dissatisfied with the terms obtained in 1771. Aug., the army leaves Trichinopoly, and Tanjor falls, Sept. 16, when the Rāja Tuljāji and his family are captured. A treaty is concluded by which the Rāja binds himself to do nothing contrary to the Company's interests, to receive an English garrison, to contribute four lākhs of pagodas, and to grant to the Company 277 villages.

The English take Nagar, purchased by the Dutch from the Rāja of Tānjor.

Aug. 30: A tumult of Marātha infantry arising, Nārāyanrāv is murdered in his palace, in presence of Raghunāthrāv, who did not attempt to prevent the deed. He is proclaimed sixth Peshwā.

Aug. Warren Hastings convenes with the Nawāb of Audh. He promises aid, and makes over Allahābād and Korā to the Nawāb for £500,000; and withholds Shāh 'Alam's tribute.

Sept. 6: Jumāda II. 18, H. 1177. Nawāb Shujā'-uddaula, on compulsion by the British Government, grants a *sanad* of succession to Chait Singh, Rāja of Benares, son of Balwant Singh, who died 1770.

Oct. 4: The subject of the acquisition of the Rohila country discussed in the Council. Oct., the Nawāb of Audh drives the Rohilas across the Duāb and over the Jamnā.

Nov. 18: The Nawāb writes demanding the help promised by treaty in 1769, in the subjugation of the Rohilas. This demand is later acquiesced in.

Rām Singh of Jodhpur dies in exile. Bijay Singh succeeds—a titular sovereign—the Marāthās being virtual rulers.

Nawāb Singh of Bharatpur dies in Dīg fortress. His brother, Naval Singh, succeeds, but Ranjīt Singh, a younger brother, with Mughal aid, opposes the succession and captures Bharatpur.

A.D.

1773 The office of "Intendante da Marinha e dos Armazens" (Supervisor of Marine Dockyards) established at Goa.

In Bengal in 1773-74 the revenues were £2,481,404; and the civil and military charges £1,488,435. The army consisted of five companies of artillery; one troop of cavalry; three regiments of European infantry; twenty-three battalions of native infantry; and twenty-eight companies of invalids,—total, 27,000 men.

Madras (Fort St George) had in revenue and subsidies, £887,302; and charges £814,992. The army (1772) consisted of European infantry, 3,486; European cavalry, 68; artillery, 581; Sipāhis, 15,840,—total, 19,975.

Bombay (1773-74) had revenues, £109,163; and charges, £347,387. The army—artillery, 434; European infantry, 1,620; Sipāhis, 4,346,—total, 6,400 men.

1774 Jan. 10: Dom João de Mello, Portuguese governor, dies. Philippe de Valladares Souto Maior succeeds by Patent of Succession till Sept. 24, when Dom José Pedro de Camara takes office as "Governor and Captain-General," the title of Viceroy being now disused. The Court of Judicature at Goa is abolished.

Raghunāthrāv in the Karnātak, is obliged, for financial reasons, to come to terms with Haidar, who thus regains three of the Marātha districts. The ministers conspire against him. March 4: he gains a complete victory over Trimbakrāv Māma at Kāsigāon. He proceeds to Burhānpur, gaining men and levying contributions, when on April 18, the birth of a posthumous son of Nārāyanrāv makes his recognition as Peshwā an impossibility.

April: The English troops under General Champion enter Rohilkhand. April 23, they defeat the Rohilas at Miranpur-Katra, near Bareilly. Hāfiz Rahmat, the Protector of Rohilkhand, dies of his wounds. The Nawāb Vazīr kept aloof during the battle; but after this victory he plundered and despoiled the whole country.

April 25: A treaty of peace with Bhutān is signed at Fort William by Hastings and his Council on the representations of the Teshu Lama of Tibet. May 13: George Bogle is appointed by the Governor-General to lead an embassy to the Teshu Lama of Tibet, to open up trade and friendly relations with that country. He visits the Lama and returns, 1775.

A.D.

1774 Aug. The Nawāb of Audh and Faizulla Khān, Rohila Jāgīrdār of Rāmpūr, conclude a treaty known as that of Lāl Dang. The war with the Rohilas now terminates.

Sept. 6: The Bombay Council receive a proposal from Raghunāth for treaty and alliance, to enable him to resume the government at Poona, he promising to make over Salsette and Bassein, but they refuse this cession. Oct., the Portuguese attempt to retake Salsette. Dec. 9: the Bombay Council resolve to anticipate them by taking Thānā, which falls Dec. 28, Commodore John Watson being mortally wounded on the third day of the siege. The island of Karanjā and all Salsette reduced by Dec. 31.

Oct. Collectors' courts are abolished and Provincial Councils established at Calcutta, Bardhwān, Dhākā, Murshidābād, Dinajpur, and Pātna, to superintend the joint Departments of Revenue, Trade, and Administration of Justice,—as sanctioned in 1769.

Oct. 19: Philip Francis, Clavering, and Monson arrive in India.

WARREN HASTINGS, FIRST GOVERNOR-GENERAL.

Oct. 20: The new régime for the Government of India begins. Warren Hastings, now Governor-General, and Mr Barwell are opposed by the other three Councillors, Francis, Clavering, and Monson.

Nov. 22. Clive, under the strain of ill-health and persecution, commits suicide, aged forty-nine.

1775 Jan. 6: The Rānī of Bardhwān lodges a complaint against the English Resident, who, she said, had supported her *dīwān* in withdrawing her son from her guardianship. A compromise is effected.

Jan. 28: Zī-l qa'da 26, H. 1188. Shujā'-uddaula, the Nawāb Vazīr of Audh, dies. His son, 'Asaf-uddaula, succeeds: with him a treaty is concluded May 21, confirming him in possession of Allahābād and Korā, and ceding to the British Government Benares, Jaunpur, Ghāzipur, and the possessions of Chait Singh. Falling into arrears with the British, 'Asaf-uddaula endeavours to deprive his mother, Buhu Begam, and the mother of Shujā'-

A.D.
1775 uddaula of their property. Oct. 15: an agreement is signed, by which the Vazīr engages not to make further claims on the Begam's properties. This is guaranteed by the supreme Government.

Feb. Intelligence of the capture of Thānā reaches the Bengal Government, which had required the Bombay Council to give an account of its proceedings. Their action is censured as being inconsistent with the relations with the ruling powers at Poona.

Feb. Raghunāthrāv, deserted by Sindia and Holkar, renews negotiations with Bombay, and after many delays, on March 6, concludes "the treaty of Surat," of sixteen articles, confirming all former treaties. The Bombay Government promise help to the number of 300 men of all arms, Raghunāth making over as security for payment Amod, Hansot, Versal, and part of Anklesar, besides ceding in perpetuity Bassein and its dependencies.

March 17: Raghunāth's army, with the contingent from Bombay under Col. Keating, lands at Khambay, and after some minor actions, engages the army of the Poona regency under Haripant Phadki, when the British and their allies, after much loss, finally defeat him at Ārās on May 18. July 8: an accommodation between Fath Singh Gaikwād and Raghunāth is brought about.

March 30: A charge is preferred by Mahārāja Nand Kumār against Warren Hastings for acceptance of part of the salary of a native official. In spite of Hastings's protests against the Council's assumption of judicial power, the official is dismissed and another appointed at one-half the salary.

April: Nand Kumār is prosecuted along with Joseph Fowke, by Councillor Barwell, Mr Vansittart, and native officials for conspiracy, and Nand Kumār and Fowke are held to bail.

April: The captive King of Pegu, found guilty of inciting the Talaing people to rebellion, is publicly executed at Rangūn.

May 6: Nand Kumār was arrested under a warrant of the Supreme Court at the suit of Mohan Prasād on a charge of forgery. June 6-18: he is tried before Sir Elijah Impey, convicted, and sentenced to be hanged on Aug. 5.

June: The Bengal Government, now supreme, interfered with the Bombay Government, disapproving of their connection with any of the Marātha powers, and insisted on the cancelling at once of the treaty with Raghunāth (by which Salsette, Bassein, and

A.D.

1775 part of the revenues of Bharoch had been ceded to the Company), and on the withdrawal of all the British troops furnished for his assistance. The despatches of the Court of Directors approve of the acts of the Bombay Government, at the very time they were ordered to be annulled by the supreme authority at Calcutta.

Bettada Chāma Rāja, titular Rāja of Maisur, dies. Haidar 'Alī places a child on the throne with the title of Khasa Chāma Rāja.

Murdoch Brown, a Scotchman, arrives at Calicut as Consul for Maria Theresa of Austria, engages in trade, and in 1792 is spoken of as the most considerable of any British subject on that side of India. He lost eleven ships, each of 1,000 tons or more, in the war with France.

Sir Robert Fletcher (Commander-in-Chief 1772, but removed for obstruction) returns to Madras as Commander-in-Chief.

Dec. 11: The Right Hon. Lord Pigot, Governor of Madras till Aug. 24, 1776, is sent with powers to reinstate the Rāja of Tanjor.

Dec. 28: Lieut.-Col. John Upton sent from Calcutta as Envoy Plenipotentiary to arrange a treaty with the Marāthās, arrives at Purandhar.

1776 Jan. 22: Mr Francis enters a Minute disapproving of the quinquennial lease, and proposing the levy of a fixed land tax on the Zamīndārs.

March 1: The Treaty of Purandhar concluded by Col. Upton, supersedes the Treaty of Surat, still leaving Salsette to the Company, but not so favourable as the latter. Raghunāth is required to disband his army and retire on a pension. May 22: a supplementary agreement modifies these terms, and a despatch from the Court of Directors of April 5 confirms the Treaty of Surat, "under every circumstance." This being tantamount to a renewal of the war, Raghunāth again takes the field, no longer supported by the Bombay Government.

March: Safar, H. 1190. Sayyid Murtazā Khān, prime minister at Lucknow, killed by the eunuch Basant 'Alī Khān, who was jealous of his influence with the Nawāb 'Asaf-uddaula. Basant 'Alī is killed the same day by the Nawāb, and Īraj Khān

A.D.

1776 appointed prime minister, dies shortly after. Hasan Raza Khān succeeds, with Haidar Beg Khān as active deputy.

March: The *Tārīkh-i-Faiz Bakhsh* of Sheo Parshād finished.—Compiled at the desire of General Kirkpatrick, it forms a history of the Afghāns of Rohilkhand.

April 11: Lord Pigot reinstates the Rāja of Tanjor, thus offending the Nawāb of the Karnātak, at whose instance the President's actions are hindered. May 29: the Madras Council reject but afterwards support the claims of Paul Benfield (who had large money dealings with the Nawāb) to an assignment on the revenues of Tanjor. Lord Pigot suspends two members and orders the arrest of the Commandant, Sir Robert Fletcher.

June: Hsengbyusheng, King of Burma, dies. His son, Singgusā, succeeds.

Haidar 'Alī overruns Cochin and exacts tribute from the Rāja Verulam Tamburan: Tipū, Haidar's son, overruns Anegundi and dispossesses the chief Timmappa.

Aug. 24: Lord Pigot is arrested and imprisoned at St Thomas Mount, where he dies May 11, 1777. Four members of the Council were afterwards tried in England and fined £1,000 each. George Stratton succeeds as Governor of Madras, till Aug. 31, 1777.

Oct. 10: Mr Macleane informs the Court of Directors that Warren Hastings authorised him to tender Hastings's resignation of office. This was formally accepted by the Court, but repudiated by Hastings; and Mr Edward Wheeler appointed a member of Council to take the place of General Clavering, who, as senior member of Council, was to be Governor-General *ad interim*.

Sept. 25: By the death of Col. Monson, Hastings, with the aid of Barwell and his own casting vote, reverses the measures of the majority of the last two years.

A Roman Catholic bishop was appointed to Pondicheri.

1777 March: Lieut.-Col. Upton is recalled from Poona, and Mr Mostyn appointed as Resident Envoy. A French merchant ship arrives at Chaul with cargo, and M. St Lubin with several other Frenchmen proceed to Poona, at which the English are alarmed.

April: The quinquennial leases in Bengal expire. Neither Hastings's nor Francis's schemes being sanctioned, the annual leases are again put in force, and were continued for four years.

A.D.

1777 June 10: A Commission of the Directors restores Lord Pigot to office; he had died May 10. They then nominate Sir Thomas Rumbold to succeed him, John Whitehill to be second in Council, and Major-General Hector Munro, Commander of the Forces, to be third.

June 19: Intelligence of the reported resignation of Hastings reaches Calcutta, where great confusion arises from his disavowal of such resignation. The Supreme Court support Hastings in his resolution to retain the government.

Aug. 30: General Clavering dies. Mr Wheler succeeds on the Council. Hastings had denied his resignation, and carried all divisions by his casting vote.

Aug. 31: John Whitehill arrives at Madras, and acts as Governor till Feb. 8, 1778. George Stratton, acting Governor of Madras since Aug. 23, 1776, is suspended from the Company's service.

Oct. Mr Hornby, Governor of Bombay, in a Minute of Council, expresses the necessity for decisive action in Marātha policy, and complains of the fettered control of the Bombay Government.

Nov. In consequence of complaints from Bengal of the encroachments of the Supreme Court, who sought to extend their jurisdiction over all classes of natives, though legally restricted to the Company's servants, the Directors appeal to the Ministers for relief.

St Lubin, the French adventurer, received at the Poona court as on a mission from the King of France.

Dec. 12: Rām Rāja, the puppet prince of Sātāra, dies, and Sabū, surnamed Abba Sāheb, the adopted son of Rām Rāja, succeeds.

1778 Jan. 5: The Marāthās under Haripant Phadki and Parshurām Bhāo defeated in the Adoni district by Haidar.

Feb. 8: Sir Thomas Rumbold takes up the Governorship of Madras, till April 1780.

March 19: The Bombay Council estimate the expenses of the expedition on behalf of Raghobā or Raghunāthrāv and of money paid to him or expended on his account at rupees 22,29,652.

A.D.
1778 March: The Bengal Council consider the complaints of the Begams of Audh, against the Nawāb, who would neither pay them their maintenance allowance, nor furnish the Company's tribute.

March 24: Sir T. Rumbold proposes to bring the Zamīndārs to the seat of Government, instead of a committee visiting the Northern Sarkārs, for the settlement of business. Of the thirty-one Zamīndārs sent for, thirteen did not obey the summons. Discontent is produced by appointment of Sitarām Rāz to the *dīwānī* of his brother, the Rāja of Vizianagaram.

Moroba Phadnavis proposes to the Bombay Government the restoration of Raghunāthrāv. The Bengal Government approving, Col. Leslie is sent with a subsidiary force. Nāna Phadnavis' party retire to Purandhar, and pretend acquiescence.

June 8: With the return of Haripant Phadki and Mahādavji Sindia, the faction of Moroba is crushed. The Bombay Government, however, resolve to reinstate Raghunāth, and on Nov. 22 an advance force occupies the Bor Ghāt, and encamp at Khandāla. Mr Carnac, by his casting vote as President of the Field Committee, becomes virtual Commander of the Army. Desultory skirmishing follows till the end of the year.

July 10: The Madras Government deprecate the presence of the French in Basālat Jang's province of Guntūr.

July: Hearing that war with France was declared, the Bengal presidency capture the French settlements at Chandranagar, Masulipatam, and Kārikāl. Aug. 10: the English fleet under Sir E. Vernon and the French under M. Tronjolly engage, the French ships drawing off, and sailing away on Aug. 21. Aug. 8: Sir Hector Munro took post before Pondicheri; Aug. 21: the boundary hedge is seized; Oct. 17: in view of an assault, M. Bellecombe proposes a capitulation, and the garrison were allowed to march out with the honours of war. Oct., Mahé invested by the English, although Haidar's flag flew side by side with the French. Haidar threatens the British. Nov., Basālat Jang sends a proposal to cede Guntūr for a fixed annual payment, to dismiss the French, and to accept English troops for defence.

Rānā Hamir of Udaypur dies. Rānā Bhīm Singh, his brother, succeeds.

A.D.

1778 Rāo Srī Ghodaji II. of Kachh dies. His son, Rāo Srī Rāyadhan III. (born 1763), succeeds, till 1813.

Mādhav Singh of Jaypur dies. Pirthvi Singh, a minor, succeeds, but dies within a year. Pratāp Singh, a brother, succeeds.

Count Bénoît de Boigne joins the E.I. Co.'s service; but imagining himself neglected by them, he joins Mādhavarāv Sindia, who utilises him to train his troops.

Walter Reinhard ("Samru") dies, and is buried at Agra.

1779 Jan. 4: Capt. Stewart, leader of the advance of the British force, dies at Kārle; the army creeping forward less than a mile daily, affords Nāna Phadnavis and Mahādaji Sindia time to collect forces. Jan. 6: Col. Egerton resigns the command to Col. Cockburn. Jan. 9: the Marāthās retired from Talegāon Dābhāde when the British army arrived. Mr Carnac, with the Committee, against the opinion of the officers, now proposed to retreat, and, Jan. 11, throwing the heavy guns into a pond, and burning the stores, 2,600 British troops retreated before the Marātha forces of at least sixteen times their numbers. Next morning they were attacked, but successfully resisted, and reached Vadgāon, where, Jan. 13, Mr Carnac agreed that the British should resign to the Marāthās everything acquired since 1772 with the revenues of Bharoch and Surat, stop the advance of the Bengal army and pay 41,000 rupees to Sindia's servants. The authority to make such a treaty is repudiated by the Bombay Council, and the officers responsible are dismissed the service.

Jan. 27: A treaty is concluded with Basālat Jang confirming the cession of Guntūr; a resident is appointed, and a force under General Harpur sent to protect his territory.

Jan. 30: The British force sent from Bengal under General Thomas Goddard to aid against the Marāthās, arrives at Burhānpur after a march of nearly ten months; leaves Burhānpur Feb. 6th, and arrives at Surat 26th. He was now, Feb. 26, invested by the supreme Government with full powers to treat with the Poona ministry, but in vain endeavours to negotiate with them.

March 19: Mahé, the last of the French possessions, with its surrounding territory, surrenders, and is occupied by Col. Braithwaite and a British garrison till Nov. 29, when, on his

A.D.

1779 detachment being ordered to assist General Goddard at Surat, the fort is blown up. Haidar 'Alī had protested against the attack of a settlement in his territory: through it he drew his supplies.

March 25: Sir Eyre Coote appointed Commander-in-Chief of the Bengal army in succession to General Clavering, and member of Council in April, till April 26, 1783.

April 6: Mr Holland arrives as resident at Haidarābād from the Madras presidency: Nizām 'Alī objects to the English force with Basālat Jang, but had himself taken over the dismissed French force. The Bengal Council censure the action of the Madras presidency in the matter of Guntūr, from which province the *peshkash* (quit-rent) had been withheld.

An attack, instigated by Sindia, was made on Bānkot, to excite the English to hostilities.

June 12: Raghunāth, with his sons, Amritrāv and Bājīrāv, escapes from Sindia and arrives in General Goddard's camp, and receives from him a lavish allowance. Negotiations with Nāna Phadnavis continue, but are stopped in October, the surrender of Salsette and the person of Raghunāth being demanded as preliminaries. Goddard opens negotiations with the Gaikwād, Fath Singh of Baroda, and discovers a treacherous correspondence between Nāna Phadnavis and the Dutch factors at Surat.

June 13: The garrison at Daman, being destitute of money and clothing, revolt. The governor, anxious because of the proximity of Raghobā and the English, procures sufficient to pay them up to May 13.

The supreme Government disapproved of Sir T. Rumbold's acts at Fort St George: he indignantly repelled the interference.

The missionary Schwarz is deputed by the Madras presidency to treat with Haidar. His mission proves unsuccessful.

Haidar 'Alī and Nizām 'Alī unite to prevent Basālat Jang receiving British protection, and invade Guntūr.

Dec. 17: Peace concluded by Dom Frederico Guilherm de Sousa with the Peshwā. An offensive and defensive alliance settled.

The supreme Government notify to the Zamīndārs, &c., that they are not subject to the jurisdiction of the Supreme Court, and forbid provincial chiefs to aid them with military force.

A.D.

1780 Jan. 1: General Goddard resumes hostilities against the Marāthās, marching on Dabhoi. Mr Boddam occupies the Peshwā's districts near Surat: Mr Gambier with an irregular force, occupies Anklesar, Hansot, Desbora, and Amod. Jan. 20: Dabhoi is evacuated, and Jan. 26, Fath Singh concludes with General Goddard an offensive and defensive alliance: he was to receive the Peshwā's share of the territory north of the Māhī in lieu of his south of the Tāptī, and supply a force of 3,000 horse. Goddard marched on Ahmadābād and captured it, Feb. 15. Feb. 29: Sindia and Holkar crossed the Narbadā, but on Goddard's advance to Baroda they retired to Pāwangarh and attempted negotiation. This proving futile, Goddard surprises Sindia's camp, April 3. The Marāthās again attacked, April 19, retreat and skilfully evade a second action.

Khandirāv Puār of Dhār dies. Ānandrāv, a son born posthumously, succeeds nominally, Rangarāv Urekur, minister, acting as ruler.

Feb. Mr Gray, sent from the Madras presidency, offers renewed alliance with Haidar 'Alī,—an offer which is rejected.

Feb. Capt. Popham, sent to the assistance of the Rānā of Gohad, successfully clears the district of the Marāthās. April 21: Capt. Popham takes Lahār fort by assault.

April 11: The business of the courts at Calcutta is now divided into two parts, one relating to revenue, the other to individuals. A separate court, called the *Sadr dīwānī 'Adālat*, is established for the cognisance of disputes arising between individuals.

May 8: Col. Hartley is sent from Goddard's camp to the Konkan to prevent the Marāthās from cutting off supplies from Bombay.

June 12: The Supreme Court command the Guntūr Sarkār to be restored to Basālat Jang.

June 19: The Madras Council learn that Haidar 'Alī is on the march against Madras. A Minute presented to the Council advising active preparation is rejected by vote. June 23: Haidar enters the Karnātak.

Aug. 3: Gwāliar fort surprised and captured from Sindia's officers by Capt. Popham in a night attack, without the loss of a single life.

A.D.

1780 Aug. 17: Hastings having accused Sir Philip Francis of faithlessness and breach of trust, is challenged to a duel, in which Francis is badly wounded; he left India Dec. 9.

Aug. 25: Sir Hector Munro leaves Madras for Conjivaram. Haidar prevents Col. Baillie's junction with Munro by cutting in between the armies.

Sept. 10: Lieut.-Col. Baillie advancing from Pullalūr is overpowered at Perumbākam by an overwhelming force under Haidar and Tīpū. Of eighty-six British officers only sixteen survive. Munro, learning of the disaster, throws his guns into the tank of the temple at Chingalpat, and retreats to Madras.

Sept. 22: The Governor-General enters a Minute expressive of the inconvenience of the arrangements of the new courts.

Sept. 25: The Bengal Council determine to send relief to Madras, to suspend the Governor, Mr Whitehill, and to appoint Sir Eyre Coote to recover authority. Nov. 8: Mr Charles Smith is appointed Civil Governor at Madras, till June 22, 1781.

Oct. 24: It is passed in Council that the Chief Justice, Sir Elijah Impey, be asked to undertake the office of Judge of the Sadr Dīwānī 'Adālat.

Oct. 31: Arkat falls before Haidar's troops, and the fort surrenders Nov. 3. Haidar from this base invests the chief strongholds in the Karnātak.

Nov. 5: Sir Eyre Coote arrives at Madras.

Jas. A. Hicky's *Bengal Gazette* started—contains scurrilous attacks on Hastings and Sir Elijah Impey. Its circulation through the Post Office was stopped in Nov. He was twice arrested and punished, and in 1782 the paper ceased. Hicky, though a worthless man, was the pioneer of the English press in India.

Nov. The Vazīr of Audh, at the instance of the Council, demands 5,000 horse from Faizulla Khān, the Rohila chief, as "the quota arranged by treaty for the service of the vazīr": but the treaty having stipulated for *troops* not horse, Faizulla Khān represents his inability to comply.

The Government conclude a compact with the Rānā of Gohad. The envoys take possession of the castle.

Darindar Nārāyan, Rāja of Kuch Bihār, dies. His father,

A.D.

1780 Dhujindar Nārāyan, who had been carried off by Bhutias, succeeds till 1783.

Pierre Cuillier, afterwards known as General Perron, arrives in India as a petty officer. He deserts his ship to take military service under the Rānā of Gohad.

1781 Jan. General Goddard besieges Arnāla, a fort on a small island ten miles north of Bassein, which capitulates Jan. 18.

Jan. 17: Sir Eyre Coote marched from Madras and proceeded to Pondicheri, reoccupied by the French, where he disarmed the inhabitants. The French fleet fearing the expected English squadron, sailed, Feb. 15, to Mauritius.

Feb. 8: General Goddard's advance force penetrates the Bor Ghāt, and encamps at Khandālā. Nāna Phadnavis brings up his forces, attacks under Haripant Phadki, and sends skirmishing parties to the plains, but pretends to treat, March 15. Two corps attacked by Parshurām Bhāu Patwardhan, who sustains a reverse, but who attack the main body and drive them back with heavy loss. Goddard is obliged finally to retreat, and arrives at Pānwel with heavy loss, April 22.

Feb. 16: Col. Camac and Capt. Bruce invade Mālwa in defence of the Rānā of Gohad, take Sipri and advance on Sironj, where Mahādaji Sindia's army surrounds them. March 7: they commence a skilful retreat, followed by Sindia, whose camp they completely surprise, March 24. Sindia at first takes flight, but enters on negotiations for peace with Col. Muir, Aug. 16. Oct. 13: these culminate in a treaty by which the territory conquered on the farther side of the Jamnā is to be restored to Sindia; he is not to claim any part of the territory the English had added to Gohad, and to endeavour to effect a peace between the English and Haidar 'Alī and the Peshwā.

The English fleet attacked Haidar's new shipping, destroying it at Calicut and Mangalūr. June: Sir Eyre Coote suffered a partial repulse in attacking Chidambaram; and, July 1: Haidar risked a general engagement near Porto Novo and was completely routed. Haidar now abandoned his designs on the southern provinces; his son, Tīpū, raised the siege of Wandawāsh, and both retired to Arkat.

Mudaji Bhonsla of Nagpur sends an army into Katak. The

A.D.

1781 Governor-General purchases its retreat, detaches Mudaji from the Marātha confederacy, and turns him against both Haidar 'Alī and the Peshwā. April 6: the treaty formally concluded.

Feb. 20: Establishment of the Board of Revenue. April: Dīwānī courts increased from sixteen to eighteen. Faujdārs abolished.

April 9: Lord North brought before Parliament proposals restricting the Company, and bringing their affairs under the control of the Secretary of State. These were afterwards made the basis of three principal provisions of Mr Pitt's East India Bill. Lord North's suggestions were modified into the Act 21 Geo. III., c. 65; and all former privileges were granted to the Company till March 1, 1791. But all despatches on Revenue or Civil and Military matters were, by this Bill, to be submitted to the Minister. The Company pay down £400,000, and are allowed a dividend of 8 per cent.; three-fourths of any surplus to be paid to the Government.

June 19: Bill passed by Parliament restricting the jurisdiction of the Supreme Court in India. The Governor-General and Council, with all matters of Revenue, all Zamīndārs, Native Farmers, and Collectors of Revenue, were exempted from its jurisdiction.

June 22: Lord Macartney arrives at Madras as Governor-General. At the head of the milit a he immediately, on the breaking out of war with the Dutch, attacks their settlements at Pulikat and Sadras, which surrender.

June 26: A petition for the renewal of the East India Company's charter is presented from the Directors.

July 7: Warren Hastings leaves Calcutta for Benares and puts under arrest the Rāja Chait Singh for evasion of an increased tribute, refusal to supply three bodies of Sepoys, and alleged disrespect on the part of his people to British officers. Aug. 20: Chait Singh is rescued in a revolt of the Rāja's people, in which most of two companies of Sipāhis and their officers were destroyed. An officer is killed in an attack on the palace at Rāmnagar. The Governor-General assumes command of the province, and the Zamīndāri is bestowed on Mahīp Nārāyan Bahādur, a nephew of Chait Singh, a minor, in September.

A.D.

1781 Aug. 25: The Portuguese Captain-General captures Bicholim fort from Mudaji Bhonsla in lieu of arrears of tribute and in consideration of acts of piracy.

Aug. 27: Battle between Sir Eyre Coote and Haidar 'Alī, at the place where Baillie was defeated; the result was indecisive, but Sir Eyre Coote occupied the posts that had been taken up by Haidar. Sept. 27: Haidar suffered severe loss at the Pass of Sholangarh. Oct. 26: Haidar's fortress of Chittor capitulated to Sir Eyre Coote. Nov. 21: the Madras army returned to cantonments, having lost one-third of their force in the campaign.

Sept. 19: The Nawāb Vazīr of Audh, Asaf-uddaula, by the treaty of Chunār, is relieved of his debts to the Company, being allowed to recover the wealth illegally retained by the Begams—his mother and grandmother—who by their resources, armed followers, intrigues, pretensions, and temper were injurious to the Vazīr's government. The Begams, against Hastings's advice, had been assigned the wealth of Shujā'-uddaula amounting to about twenty million rupees; this was now paid to the Company in discharge of the debt, and the Begams received handsome pensions.

Sept. The Rāja of Benares was defeated at Latīfpur in Bundelkhand: Major Popham captured Sipri, and Patīta near Chunār. Nov. 9: his stronghold of Bijaigarh capitulated and his family are plundered. The Rānī and her attendants left treasure amounting to 23,27,813 rupees. The Rāja found an asylum at Gwāliar for twenty-nine years and died there, March 29, 1810.

In Bihār a concentration of troops is made to harass the English. Oct., Akbar 'Alī Khān of Narhat and Samoy, imprisoned at Patna for arrears, escapes and joins Chait Singh's revolt,—he is driven from his position with loss.

Nov. 12: Negapatam capitulated to Sir Hector Munro, who now commanded a force under the orders of the Governor, and with it fell all the Dutch settlements on the coast; shortly afterwards those in Ceylon shared the same fate.

Hastings founds the Muhammadan Madrasa at Calcutta: the first Government-aided educational institution in India.

The adventurer, George Thomas, lands in India as a quartermaster. He serves as a soldier among the Madras pāligārs.

A.D.

1781 Dec. 2: A treaty is concluded between the British and Muhammad 'Alī, Nawāb of the Karnātak, recognising him as the hereditary sovereign of the country. An agreement is executed by the Nawāb assigning the revenues of his country to the British Government for five years.

Col. Hartley travelled *viâ* Bāghdad to England, the journey taking about a year.

1782 Jan. 2: The English fleet, under Sir E. Hughes, sails from Negapatam, and invested Trincomali, which surrendered Jan. 14; Hughes returned to Madras, and arrived there Jan. 31.

Jan. 2: The army in the Karnātak march to relieve Vellūr. Haidar's obstructions are evaded, and Vellūr is provisioned.

Jan. 7: Major Abingdon, besieged in Tellicheri by a superior force of Haidar's army, made a sally and drove off the enemy.

Jan. 22: Detachments from England, under Col. Humberston Mackenzie, arrive at Bombay, and sail for Madras, Jan. 28.

Jan. The French fleet under M. de Suffrein arrives on the Coromandel coast. He fails to surprise Madras, and engages in four indecisive actions with Admiral Hughes.

Jan. The palace at Faizābād stormed by the Nawāb of Audh, and the resisting Begams have to surrender treasure to the value of a million sterling. Hastings recalls Mr Middleton, the Audh Resident, and appoints Mr Bristow.

Feb. 1: Fleet and troops under General Meadows arrived at Madras. Feb. 12: Major Abingdon captures Calicut from Haidar's troops. The English fleet bound for Madras joined him there, Feb. 18, and took several of Haidar's forts, returning to Calicut in May.

Feb. 16-18: Col. John Braithwaite with about 1,900 men, of whom only 100 were British, attacked at Annagudi on the Kollarun, by Tīpū at the head of 20,000 men, aided by Lally with 400 French. Brathwaite bravely and perseveringly withstood incessant attacks, but was at length forced to surrender. Tīpū treated the prisoners with humanity.

Feb. 14: The French fleet under M. Suffrein passed Madras in line of battle to the south. Sir E. Hughes followed, and on 16th he retook from the French convoy five vessels that had

A.D.

1782 been captured on the coast, and a large transport. Late on 17th an indecisive action took place. Suffrein contrived to land 2,000 men at Porto Nuovo on 19th, who were joined by part of Haidar's army.

March: Badun Meng, fifth son of Alaunghprā, by a conspiracy against Singussā, succeeds to the throne of Burma. He is known by the title of Bodoahprā. Singussā and his family are sent to the capital and burnt to death. Plots against the king give rise to indiscriminate slaughter.

April 3: Kadalūr yields to the combined forces of Lally and Tīpū Sultān.

April 8: Sir Edward Hughes, proceeding with reinforcements and stores for Trinkomalī, comes in sight of Suffrein's fleet, which follows his; on 12th, Suffrein attacks, and after a desperate action both fleets were so disabled that they lay seven days within sight of each other, preparing themselves to sail.

Haidar loses French aid, and is beaten at all points by Sir Eyre Coote. Malabar, Kūrg, and Balam revolt.

April 22: H. 1169. Mīrza Najaf Khān (Zulfiqār Khān) Amir-ul 'Umarā at Dehli dies without issue. Disputes arising as to succession between his nephew, Muhammad Beg Hamādāni, and a public servant, Afrāsyāb Khān.

All the Jāt territories, including Bharatpur, fall into Sindia's hands. Eleven districts are restored to Ranjit Singh.

May 17: A treaty is concluded at Sālbāi between the East India Company and the Poona branch of the Marāthās. Each side agrees to withhold all help from the enemies of the other. The Bombay Government retains Salsette, the Marāthās receiving back Ahmadābād and Gujarāt for Fath Singh Gaikwād, and Bharoch for Sindia.

May: Major Abingdon relieves Tellicheri, besieged by Haidar's troops, holds the place and masters the surrounding districts.

May 17: Treaty between the Government of India and the Marāthās, by which Ahmadābād, Bassein, and other acquisitions were ceded to the Marāthās, they agreeing to allow no nation but the English to have intercourse with them.

A.D.

1782 May 30: A resolution is passed in Parliament by Lord Rockingham's Ministry against Warren Hastings.

May: Haidar's force carries Permakoil before Sir Eyre Coote could relieve it.

June 2: Sir Eyre Coote marches on Arnī, but is attacked in rear by Haidar's force; a division under Tīpū dexterously carried off his treasure, and reinforced the garrison. After an indecisive skirmish, the English army retires to Madras.

June 29: Lord Macartney is informed by the Governor-General of the treaty of May 17. A negotiation was opened by Sir Eyre Coote independently with Haidar, who again out-manœuvred the general, and was only prevented from reducing Negapatam, in combined operation with M. Suffrein, who was attacked by the English admiral, July 4, and in a severe battle both fleets suffered seriously. The French proceeded to Kudalūr to refit.

Aug. 30: Admiral Suffrein takes Trinkomalī from the English. Sept. 1: Admiral Hughes arrives, and, Sept. 3, a great and well-fought action follows between the fleets, in which the French, on darkness falling, had the advantage; the proximity of Trinkomalī preventing a complete victory; and Suffrein broke six of his captains for not supporting him.

Oct. 15: The Bombay fleet, under Admiral Hughes, sails from the Coromandel coast, in spite of protests from Madras; next day a storm sunk or stranded the craft containing 30,000 bags of grain, and Madras suffers severely from famine. Twelve hundred persons said to die weekly for some weeks.

Oct. 28: The Tanjor Resident concludes a treaty with Tirumalrāv, Rānā of Maisur, for the payment of the tribute to the Mughal emperor through the British Government, and for the restoration of the ancient Hindu family to Maisur.

Nov. 22: In consequence of the representations of the India Council, the Directors order the Governor-General and Council to resume the jurisdiction of the *Sadr dīwānī 'Adālat*.

Nov. Tīpū, assisted by Lally's corps, crosses from Karūr to the Malabar coast, but is defeated in an assault on Ponnāni (Paniani) by Col. MacLeod. Nov. 29: Admiral Hughes, passing next day, left 450 men to strengthen the garrison.

A.D.

1782 Dec. 7: Haidar 'Alī dies in camp near Chittūr. His death concealed by the minister, Purnaiya, until the arrival of Tīpū from Malabar. Tīpū, in a few days, joined the main army, and was established on the throne of Maisur (Mysore).

Dec. 7: Mādhavji Bhonsla forced by the Portuguese to retire from Sanquelim.

Basālat Jang, son of Nizām-ul Mulk, dies.

H. 1196. The *Tārīkh-i-Mamālik-i Hind* compiled by Ghulām Bāsit, a former landowner, later in the service of the English.

In Parliament, Mr Dundas moved the recall of Mr Hastings: it came to no result; but, May 3: an address to the King was carried that His Majesty would be pleased to recall Sir E. Impey, to answer for his conduct in accepting a situation under the Bengal Local Government.

1783 Jan. 4: General Stuart, after undignified wrangling with the President, took the field against Tīpū, who had been joined by a strong French force from Kudalūr. Stuart marched Feb. 5, and offered battle Feb. 13, which was declined. Feb. 18: Tīpū evacuated Arkat, and withdrew his army from the Karnātak to defend Bednūr, now invested by General Mathews from Bombay.

Jan. 13: The Government of India, who had approved of the assignment of Karnātak revenues made by the Nawāb to the Madras Government in December 1781, now order the assignment to be returned; the Court of Directors had already approved of the assignment, and ordered the Supreme Government to aid that of Madras.

Feb. 16: Bednūr capitulates to General Mathews; Anantapur was carried. Feb. 14: Honāwar and Mangalūr had also fallen. General Mathews was superseded in command by Col. Macleod. April 7: Macleod, with two other officers, captured off Vijayadurg by the Marātha fleet, in defiance of the treaty of Sālbāi, and almost every man on board put to death.

March: Suffrein lands Bussy with a reinforcement of French troops at Kudalūr, and General Stuart, advised to recover possession, delays to march till April 21, and then proceeds extremely slowly.

April 9: Tīpū returns before Bednūr; takes Kavaledurg and Haidargarh, also, with another division, Anantapur.

A.D.
1783 April 28: Sir Eyre Coote dies at Madras.

April 30: Bednūr capitulates to Tīpū on honourable terms, but the officers and men are marched in irons to Seringapatam.

May 4: Tīpū invests Mangalūr.

May 10: The Burmese court moves to its new capital, Amarapura. This year a complete register of the kingdom is finished. The conquest of Arakan is determined on.

June 7: General Stuart, refusing to co-operate with General Mathews against Tīpū, attacked M. Bussy at Kudalūr, June 13, and failed with great loss. June 14: Hughes and Suffrein with their fleets arrive at Kudalūr; 20th, the fleets engage about 4 P.M., and are parted by night, and Suffrein sailed for Porto Nuovo, where the British admiral offered battle, which seems to have been declined, and then he sailed for Madras. Suffrein immediately landed reinforcements at Kudalūr. 24th: in a sally, Bernadotte (afterwards Charles XIV. of Sweden) was taken prisoner. General Stuart is recalled to Madras, and sent home under arrest by Lord Macartney for repeated acts of disobedience.

July: News of peace between France and England leads the Madras Government to propose peace to M. Bussy, who invites Tīpū to participate. Aug. 2: an armistice agreed to, but Tīpū's army remains before Mangalūr.

Aug. Reinforcements from Kudalūr are sent to reduce the pāligārs of Madura, Tinevelly, and Tanjor to obedience. Col. Fullerton, to divert the troops from Mangalūr, takes Karūr, Aravākūrchī, and Dindigal.

Pondicheri is restored to the French and Trinkomalī to the Dutch.

Nov. 4: Pālghātcheri surrounded by Fullerton's troops. Fire opened, Nov. 13, and the fort surrenders, Nov. 26. Fullerton captures Coimbatūr; marches on Seringapatam, but is ordered to treat with Tīpū and restore the captured forts.

Nov. 18: Charles James Fox introduces his Bills for the better government of India. By the first, he proposed to establish a Board of Commissioners to hold office for four years, and have absolute control over the Patronage and Government of India, with a Board of eight assistant Councillors to administer the commercial affairs of the E. I. Co. By the second, restric-

A.D.

1783 tions were imposed on the free action of the Governor-General. The first Bill passes the Commons, but on Dec. 17 is thrown out of the House of Lords.

Sir Elijah Impey recalled, at the instigation of Francis, through Burke, to answer six charges of illegality.

Samuel Turner sent to Tashilhunpo in Tibet by Warren Hastings on an embassy to congratulate the young Teshu Lama on his incarnation. He returns by Bhutān, March 1784.

Rāja Dhujendar Nārāyan of Kuch Bihār dies; his infant son, Harindar Nārāyan, succeeds, till 1839.

Mīr Fath Khān, first of the Tālpur line, establishes himself as Rais of Sindh, and obtains a *farmān* from Shāh Zamān of Qandahār for the government of Sindh by the Tālpurs. The new dynasty splits into several branches, each throwing off allegiance to the head of their house at Haidarābād.

Sir Thomas Rumbold, late Governor of Madras, was arraigned before Parliament, but the charges against him, including those of corruption and oppression, were defeated and he was acquitted.

Dec. 31: After complaints from the Vazīr of Audh, and explanations from Mr Bristow, it is determined to withdraw the resident from Audh on receiving security for the Nawāb's debt to the Company.

1784 Jan. 1: The Hon. Rawson Hart Boddam, Governor of Bombay, in succession to Hon. W. Hornby, till Jan. 9, 1788.

Jan. 8: The Queen of Kananor becomes tributary to the English.

Jan. 23: Lieut.-Col. Campbell, besieged in Mangalūr since May 23, 1783, capitulates to Tīpū, and is allowed to march with arms and the honours of war to Tellicheri: he dies Feb. 23.

Feb. 17: Warren Hastings sets out for Benares, where he imprisons the native deputy appointed on the deposition of Chait Singh, for maladministration. The Begam's jaghīrs are partially restored, and the English detachment on the Audh frontier withdrawn.

March 11: Peace concluded with Tīpū on the basis of mutual release of prisoners and restitution of conquests. No mention

A.D.

1784 being made of the treaty of Sālbāi, the Marāthās take offence. Tīpū continues to make hostile demonstrations.

April: Chimnāji Appa, posthumous son of Raghoba, born. A faction supports his claims against those of Bājīrāv, the Peshwā.

June: The "Commutation Act" passed, by which the duties on teas were reduced from 50 to 12½ per cent.

Aug. 13: Pitt's second India Bill passed. It establishes the Board of Control whereby the Home Government of India nominally passes from the Company to the Crown, large powers still remaining to the Court of Directors. Viscount Sidney is appointed President of the Board till 1790.

Oct. Afrāsyāb Khān, adopted son of Mirza Najaf Khān, Amīr-ul 'Umarā, assassinated in camp near Agra. Mahādavji Sindia receives promises of support from the chiefs, and obtains from the Emperor two patents, one nominating the young Peshwā vice-regent of the empire, and one himself as supreme deputy, with a grant of the management of Dehli and Agra provinces.

Dec. The Burmese army in three columns and flotilla occupy Sandoway and the island of Ramri. At Laungkrek the fleet is defeated, and Mahā Thannada submits.

'Abdur Rahim Siddi of Janjira dies, having bequeathed Janjira and Danda Rājpuri to his son, Bābu Mīyā. But Siddi Yāqut's will had bequeathed the estate to 'Abdur Rahim's second son, under the guardianship of his friend Siddi Johār. Bābu Mīyā and his brother flee to Poona.

1785 Jan. Zābita Khān, Amir-ul-'Umarā, dies. His son, Ghulām Qādir Khān, succeeds to the estates and position.

Jan. 6: Safar 24, H. 1199. Mīr Dard, *i.e.*, Khwāja, Muhammad Mīr of Dehli, the greatest poet of his time, dies—author of *'Ālī Nala-wa-Dard*, *Ālī Sard*, *Dard Dil*, *Ilm-ul Kitāb*, a *Diwān* in Persian, and a *Diwān* in Urdu.

Jan. M. Bussy (Charles Joseph Patissier, Marquis de Bussy Castelnau) dies at Pondicheri. Michel Raymond, his aide-de-camp, takes service with Nizām 'Alī, Sūbahdār of the Dekhan.

Feb. 8: Warren Hastings resigned the government, and embarked for England.

In 1772 the revenues under Bengal were £2,373,650; the

A.D.

1785 civil and military charges, £4,705,279; the debt in India was £1,850,166; and in England, including capital stock, &c., £12,850,166. In 1785, the receipts under Bengal had increased to £5,315,197; the expenses were £4,312,519. But the debt in 1786 was £15,443,349; and in India and China £10,464,955. During his administration he had also to provide for the charge of the other two presidencies during ruinous wars.

SIR JOHN MACPHERSON.

Sir John Macpherson, senior member of Council, becomes acting Governor-General; Lord Macartney was nominated by the Directors, but declined the appointment in June. Macpherson held office till Sept. 1786.

Mahādaji Sindia gains over Muhammad Beg Khān Humadānī's army with its leader, whom he despatches to take Rāghugarh. March 27: Agra surrenders to Rāyaji Patel, and is placed under the nominal charge of Prince Akbar. The Governor-General refuses a demand for *chauth* in Bengal, and encourages the Bombay Government to prosecute the alliance with Mādhavji Bhonsla.

March: Tīpū besieges Nargund, though his *vakīls* had been sent to Poona. A premature skirmish raises hostilities; Nargund submits and Tīpū breaks the terms of capitulation. July: Nāna Phadnavis fails to obtain co-operation from the Supreme Government against Tīpū, and believing a new alliance had been concluded between the French and Tīpū, applies to the Portuguese. Aug., he rejects a proffered force of three battalions for the defence of the boundary, and on Dec. 1, his army of conquest leaves Poona.

June 8: Lord Macartney, Governor of Madras, resigns the governorship and leaves from Calcutta for England; 18th, Mr Alexander Davidson is acting-governor till April 6, 1786.

June 28. A preliminary treaty with the Nawāb of the Karnātak concluded, assigning territory in lieu of payment of his debts due to the E. I. Co.

Sept. The Burmese army occupies Siam, the king making a heroic defence. Bodoahprā orders a retreat to Martaban.

Bābu Mahesh Datt, heir to the Hutwa Rāj, dies. A

A.D.

1785 posthumous son, Chattradhari Shāhi Bahādur, is recognised as heir.

H. 1199. Mīr Hasan, a Hindustani poet of Lucknow, dedicates the *Masnawī Mīr Hasan*, a novel in Urdu verse, to the Nawāb Āsaf-ud-daula.

1786 Jan. 9: Lord Macartney arrives in England. Feb. 13: Earl Cornwallis is appointed Governor-General and Commander-in-Chief.

April 4: First charges preferred against Warren Hastings in Parliament. Additional charges on April 28 and May 5.

April 6: Major-General Sir Archibald Campbell, K.B., Governor of Madras till Feb. 7, 1789, also Commander-in-Chief. He takes up the question of the Karnātak revenues.

May: The Marāthās under Hari Pant, with Nizām 'Alī's forces under Tohāwar Jang, attack Bādāmi and capture it, after a siege of about four weeks, on May 20. Adoni is relieved, but abandoned and re-occupied by Tīpū. Aug., Tīpū forms a junction with the Bednūr division, and crosses the Tungābhadrā. The allies retire from Sāvanūr.

Aug. 11: Penang, or Prince of Wales Island, formally taken possession of by the British, from the Rāja of Quedā, the negotiations being conducted by Capt. Francis Light. Further treaties concluded in 1791 and 1800.

EARL CORNWALLIS.

Sept. 12: Earl Cornwallis enters office as Governor-General, being also Commander-in-Chief, till Oct. 10, 1793.

Rao Rāyadhan III. of Kachh, becoming insane, is placed in confinement. A struggle for power ensued; ultimately, in 1792, a soldier, Jam'adār Fath Muhammad, succeeded to the administration.

Madras Board of Revenue instituted.

Nov. 3: Francisco de Cunha e Menezes succeeds Dom Frederico Guilherme de Souza as Governor and Captain-General at Goa, till May 22, 1794. About this time the Court of Judicature at Goa is restored.

A.D.

1786 H. 1021. The *Tārīkh-i-Ibrāhīm Khān* written—valuable for its clear account of the Marāthās.

Acts of Parliament passed (26 Geo. III., c. 16), giving to the Governor-General power of acting in opposition to his Council. Another (26 Geo. III., c. 25) giving the King the power of recalling the Governor-General. A third (26 Geo. III., c. 57), relieving servants of the Company, returning from India, from producing a statement of their fortunes. And a fourth (26 Geo. III., c. 62), enabling the Company to sell £1,207,559. 15s. of their loan of £4,200,000 to Government, and to add £800,000 to their capital.

1787 Feb. 7: Richard Brinsley Sheridan brings forward in Parliament the charge against Warren Hastings, touching the spoliation of the Begams of Audh.

Feb. 10: After prolonged negotiations the Marāthās conclude an armistice with Tīpū. April: Peace concluded, the Marāthās obtaining the retrocession of Bādāmi, Kittūr, and Nargund, with forty-five lākhs of rupees from Tīpū, who on his return treacherously seizes Harpanhalli and Rāydurg from the Pāligārs.

April: Tulāji of Tanjor dies. His half-brother, Amir Singh, succeeds, an adopted son, Sarofji, being set aside by the Madras Government through the misrepresentations of Amir Singh. April 10: Amir Singh engages to pay four lākhs of pagodas towards the defence of his country.

April 15: Lord Cornwallis secures for the Nawāb of Audh a mitigation of his grievances, the annual payment being fixed at fifty lākhs of rupees a year to cover all claims; a large part of the balance due being remitted.

The Rājas of Jaypur and Jodhpur unite against Sindia and defeat him and Muhammad Beg, in whose army De Boigne held a command, at Lālsot after three days' fighting. Muhammad Beg is killed, 14,000 of his infantry then desert to the Jaypur Rāja, Isma'īl Beg's cavalry and foot desert, and Sindia falls back on Alwar.

Ghulām Qādir, son of Zābita Khān, expels the Marātha garrison from Dehli, reduces Aligarh, and joins Isma'īl Beg before Agra.

A.D.

1787 Rājasingh succeeds his father, Gajasingh, on the throne of Bikanir. He is poisoned after thirteen days' reign. Suratsingh, another son of the late Rāja, assumes office as regent for his two nephews, but on the death of one, he strangles the other, and proclaims himself Rāja.

Vijayasingh of Jodhpur sends a gold key to Shāh 'Alam, inviting him to Ajmir, Pratāpsingh of Jaypur being a party in the invitation.

George Thomas, an Irish adventurer, arrives at Dehli, receives a commission, and subsequently the command of the army of Begam Samru of Sardanha, for whom he fights against the Sikhs.

The old city of Mysore is partially destroyed by order of Tīpū, and a new city, Nazarābād, begun.

Overland communication between England and India established with some regularity.

1788 Jan. 9: Mr Andrew Ramsay, senior member of Council, succeeds Rawson Hart Boddam as Governor of Bombay, till Sept. 6, when Sir W. Medows arrives as Governor and Commander-in-Chief, till Jan. 21, 1790.

Jan. Shāh 'Alam leaves Dehli for Ajmir, but on the way lays siege to Gokalgarh, held by Najaf Qulī Khān, who is forced to yield; Shāh 'Alam returns to Dehli on April 16.

Jan. 29: Madhuji Bhonsla agrees to cede Alorna, Bicholin, Sanquelim, and part of Purnem district in return for Portuguese aid against the Rāja of Kolhāpur. The Portuguese recover Karim, Vingorla, and Neutim for Madhuji, who endeavours to evade the terms of agreement, but is forced to sign a treaty on the terms proposed.

Feb. 13: The trial of Warren Hastings begins,—concludes April 23, 1795.

The Rāja of Chirakkal, in debt to the E.I. Co., takes possession of Randatarra, and drives away the English guard.

April 24: The Jāts, having obstructed the siege of Agra, are joined by Sindia, and defeated near Bharatpur by Isma'īl Beg and Ghulām Qādir. June 18: in a second battle, at Agra, Isma'īl Beg is defeated by De Boigne.

A.D.

1787 June: Capt. Kennaway sent to the court of Nizām 'Alī to enforce the cession of Gantūr Sarkār, which is voluntarily surrendered in September. Engagements are entered into, by a liberal construction of the treaty of Feb. 1768, to aid the Nizām with troops.

July 15: Isma'īl Beg and Ghulām Qādir enter Dehli, and set up a puppet emperor in the Prince Bedār Bakht, son of Ahmad Shāh and grandson of Muhammad Shah. Plunder and outrage are perpetrated on the royal family, and on Aug. 9: Zī-l qa'da 7, H. 1202, Ghulām Qādir blinds the emperor.

Oct. 11: Ghulām Qādir, deserted by Isma'īl Beg and threatened by Rānā Khān, fled to Mirat, whence he escapes, Dec. 21, but is captured, mutilated, and killed by Sindia.

Sept. 6: Major-General Sir William Medows arrives as Governor of Bombay, till Jan. 21, 1790.

Madhujī Bhonsla dies and is succeeded by Rāghojī II.

1789 Feb. 9: Mr John Hollond, acting Governor of Madras, in place of Sir Archibald Campbell, K.B., till Feb. 13, 1790.

June 20: Srīnivasarāv, Jagīrdār of Arni, has the estate restored, and executes an agreement engaging to fulfil the terms of the former treaty of 1762.

July 4: A treaty of offensive and defensive alliance concluded by the Supreme Government with the Nizām and the Peshwā against Tīpū Sultān, providing that they should send a contingent of 10,000 horse into Tīpū's territories to be paid for by the Company's Government; conquered lands to be divided.

The Rājā of Travankor re-purchases from the Dutch E.I. Company the forts of Kranganūr and its outpost of Ayakota, which Tīpū now claims. Dec. 14: he encamps 25 miles from Travankor territory and sends a *vakīl* demanding the surrender of refractory subjects of Mysore, the withdrawal of troops from Kranganor, and the demolition of the lines of defence crossing Kochin; these terms are rejected, and on Dec. 29, Tīpū's army breach the lines, but receive a severe repulse.

Dec. 21: Fath Singh Gaikwād, the Sena khās kheyl, dies. His brother, Mānāji, assumes charge of the Baroda Government

A.D.

1789 for Sayāji, and is recognised by the Peshwā. Sindia recognises Govind Rāo as ruler. Mānāji applies to the British Government for protection under the treaty of 1780, but interference is declined on the ground that the treaty is superseded by the treaty of Sālbāi.

De Boigne quits Sindia's service, and enters into trade at Agra.

M. Raymond, calling himself Hāji Mustafa, publishes his translation of the *Siyar-ul-Matākhirīn* of Ghulām Husain Khān Tiba Tibāī.

Lord Cornwallis's revenue reforms and decennial settlements (afterwards perpetual) are commenced.

1790 Jan. 21: Major-General Sir Robert Abercromby, K.C.B., succeeded Major-General Medows as Governor of Bombay, till Nov. 26, 1792.

Feb. 13: Edward Hollond, acting Governor at Madras. Feb. 20: Major-General Sir William Medows, Governor of Madras, till Jan. 21, 1790.

Feb. Najm Khān, Nawāb of Khambay, dies. His son, Fath 'Alī, succeeds.

Feb. Tīpū requests Commissioners to be sent to his presence. Such compliance objected to by the Madras Council. The army of General Medows, 15,000 of all arms, takes the field, and a letter from the general, April 7, declares the peace cancelled.

March: Qutb-ud-dīn of Surat dies. It is proposed to ask a *sanad* from the Emperor investing the British Government with sole administration of Surat. This is thought inexpedient, the Emperor being then in the hands of Sindia.

April 4: Dhārwār besieged, under Parashurām Bhāu Patvardhan, from Sept. 18, 1789, capitulates after a protracted blockade. The Nizām's force takes Kopāl, Kusugal, and other places.

April 15: Tīpū carries the Travankor lines.

May 4: The Supreme Government grants deeds to the Rājas of Chirakkal, Kadattanād, and Kottayam, promising to include them as allies in any treaty which the Company might make with Tīpū.

May 8: Col. Hartley, with reinforcements, having arrived at Kranganūr, dismantles the fort, and withdraws the troops to

A.D.

1790 Ālikkotta on Tīpū's flank, who busies himself demolishing the Travankor lines; May 24: he retires to the north.

May 24: General Medows takes command, and leaves Trichinopoly on 26th to march northwards; the plan of campaign being to take Koimbatūr and Palghāt with the main division, and invade Bāramahāl with another force.

June 15: General Medows takes Karūr, Dharapuram, and other places on his route to Koimbatūr.

June 20. De Boigne, now commander in Sindia's army, attacks and defeats Isma'īl Beg at Patan. The defeated infantry desert to Sindia. Aug., Sindia invades Vijaya Singh's territory, occupies Ajmir, lays siege to Tārāgarh, and on Sept. 9 defeats the Jodhpur army at Mirta. Tārāgarh capitulates, and Vijaya Singh concludes peace with De Boigne. Nov. 18: the Udaypur Rānā's capitulation renders Sindia absolute in Hindustān.

June 21: The Government of India see it necessary to resume the revenues of the Nawāb of Arkat, which had been restored by command of the Board of Control.

Sept. 13: Tīpū descends the Gajalhatti Pass, and attacks Col. Floyd's division at Satyamangala, and after much fighting retires. Col. Hartley reinforces the Koimbatūr garrison. Oct., Tīpū retakes Erod and Dhārāpuram. Oct. 24: Col. Maxwell invades Bāramahāl, and though one regiment is driven back in a defile by Tīpū's army which is baffled by Col. Maxwell's tactics.

Oct. 26: The Bombay Government conclude a treaty with Pīrarāja of Coorg, who engages to support the English against Tīpū in return for the protection of the British Government.

Dec. Tīpū invades the Karnātak, devastates Trichinopoly district, and levies contributions as far as Tiāgar, but fails to take this fort from Capt. Flint.

Dec. 10: Col. James Hartley defeats Tīpū's generals, Husain 'Alī, and Martab Khān at Tirukkallūr, near Calicut. Husain Khān, two sardārs, and 900 men are made prisoners.

Dec. 12: Lord Cornwallis arrives at Madras and takes command of the army.

Dec. 17: Kananūr surrenders to General Abercromby and a force from Bombay; and 5,000 of Tīpū's troops lay down their arms, and the Malabar coast is freed of Tīpū's troops.

A.D.

1790 'Alī Bahādur, a grandson of Bājirāv, the Peshwā, receives the investiture of Bundelkhand from Nāna Phadnavis, and, in spite of the opposition of Nāna Arjun, obtains the Rāj of Bānda and Panna.

The Rāja of Sunda, being a refugee at Goa, desirous of regaining his kingdom, promises to become a vassal of Portugal, and expresses fears lest the English or Marāthās should occupy Piro; the Portuguese hurriedly conclude a treaty with him, in which he assigned to them his rights in Phonda, Zambolim, Panchamal, &c.

Rāmmohan Rāi, in a treatise antagonistic to Hindu idolatry, lays the foundation of a prose literature in the Bengali vernacular.

1791 Jan. 6: Rāma Varma, Rāja of Kochin, executes a treaty for the payment of tribute to the British Government, in return for assistance in recovering districts seized by Tīpū.

Jan. 21: The confiscated estate of Husainpur, conferred by Government on Chattradhari Shāhi, is placed under the protection of the Court of Wards.

Jan. A Marātha army under Hari Pant leaves Poona, and at Pangal he agrees with Nizām Ali to observe the treaty with the English only so far as might humble Tīpū, without annihilating his power.

March 5: Lord Cornwallis, with the main army, having outmanœuvred Tīpū, invests Bangalor, which is carried by storm, March 21. Devanhalli and Chick Ballapur surrender, and several pāligārs tender submission.

May 1: Capt. Light concludes a treaty with the Rāja of Quedah providing for supplies from the mainland, for the payment to the Rāja of 6,000 Spanish dollars, and for the exclusion of other Europeans from the country.

May 15: Lord Cornwallis meets and defeats Tīpū at Arakere, 9 miles from Seringapatam, but the allies failing to come up, and from scarcity in camp, a retreat is begun on May 26. General Abercromby ordered to return to Malabar. May 26: on the march the Marātha armies under Parashurām Bhāu and Hari Pant join Cornwallis's force, and the combined army falls back on Bangalor, proceeding on June 6. Cross the Madūr river, 19th;

A.D.

1791 and capture Haliyardurg and destroy it. The combined army arrived at Bangalor early in July. July 16: Cornwallis takes Hosūr, and, July 22: Major Gowdie takes the double fort of Rāyakota. Oct. 13: Nandidurg was taken.

June 6: The Siddis of Janjira promise to relinquish their right and title in favour of the Peshwā to certain lands granted to 'Abdul Kharīm Khān or Bālu Mīyā in Gujarāt; but Janjira was never reduced.

Oct. 31: Extensive reinforcements having been sent from England, a detachment under Col. Maxwell arrives at Fort Pennāgaram, in Salem district, the chief retreat of predatory bands. The flag being fired on, the fort was taken, and Krishnagiri and other forts captured.

Nov. A Marātha detachment left at Madgiri is routed by a force under Kamr-ud-dīn, one of Tīpū's generals. Nov. 15: Koimbatūr, after a brave defence for five months, surrenders to Tīpū, and the garrison is marched in chains to Seringapatam in violation of the terms of capitulation.

Dec. 10: Col. Stuart proceeds against Savandurg fortress, which is stormed by Lord Cornwallis, Dec. 21. Dec. 24: Uttaradurg taken by Col. Stuart. Dec. 29: Capt. Little forces a strong position of the army near Simoga without the assistance of Parashurām Bhāu, who remains inactive, to plunder the enemy's camp.

1792 Jan. 3: Parashurām Bhāu and Capt. Little lay siege to Simoga: the garrison surrender only on obtaining the English guarantee of safety. Jan. 22: General Abercromby, under orders from headquarters, marches from the Sidasīrghāt to join the main army. Jan. 25: Lord Cornwallis leaves Haliyardurg, accompanied by the Nizām's force under his son, Sikandar Jāh, and a party of Marāthās under Hari Pant. Feb. 5: encamps 6 miles from Seringapatam. Feb. 6: attacks at night, carries the pettah of Shahar Ganjam with all redoubts and batteries. Feb. 8: Tīpū sends Lieuts. Nash and Chalmers, prisoners from Koimbatūr, with letters to the general, but at the same time directs a cavalry attack on the English rear.

Feb. 16: Abercromby joins the besieging force. The siege is continued, together with negotiations. Feb. 22: the confederacy's ultimatum is placed before Tīpū, viz., the cession to the allies, from the country adjacent to theirs, of one-half the dominions he

A.D.
1792 possessed before the war; the payment of three karors and thirty lākhs of rupees; the release of all prisoners from the time of Haidar; and the delivery of his two sons as hostages. Feb. 23: the preliminary articles signed and returned, and on Feb. 26 the two sons of Tīpū, aged ten and eight, received into the British camp. The English retain Bāramahāl, Dindigal, Malabar, and Coorg: the Marātha boundary is extended to the Tungābhadrā: Nizām 'Alī recovers his possessions north of this river, and Kadapā to the south. March 19, the treaty is signed and delivered, and the army returns to Madras.

March 1: Rajab 5, H. 1206. The Gurkhas of Nepāl open negotiations with the British Government through Jonathan Duncan, Resident at Benares, which result in a commercial treaty, the original purpose, *i.e.*, protection against the Chinese, having been frustrated by a treaty signed with the Chinese general.

April: New arrangements are made with the Nawāb of the Karnātak: in time of war the E.I. Co. to have the entire management of his revenues, and he to recover them in time of peace. July 12: a further treaty stipulates that the Nawāb should contribute nine lākhs of pagodas (31,50,000 rupees) yearly for the maintenance of a force in his territory.

June 11: Sindia arrives at Poona, and (20th to 22nd) invests with great ceremony the young Peshwā with the insignia of *Vakil-i-mutālik*, in spite of the opposition of Nāna Phadnavis.

Aug. 1: Sir Charles Oakley, Bart., succeeds General Medows as Governor of Madras, till Sept. 7, 1794.

Isma'īl Beg, preparing to revolt with Najaf Qulī Khān's widow at Kanaund, is met by Sindia's general, Col. Perron, defeated, captured, and imprisoned at Agra till his death in 1799.

Sept. 18: The Gurkha Regent of Nepāl had written to Lord Cornwallis asking military aid against the Chinese, who had invaded his country; this was refused, and Col. Kirkpatrick was sent to Nepāl, too late to be of any service, and his mission is sent back, reaching Pātna, March 1793.

Sept. 30: Holkar's army of 30,000, with four battalions under du Drenec, defeated by Sindia's general, de Boigne, at Lakhairi, after a hotly contested battle.

Nizām ud-din Khān is installed by order of the Company's

A.D.

1792 Government as Nawāb of Surat. He expresses his desire to be solely dependent on the British, declining to accept a *sanad* from Dehli.

Jam'adār Fath Muhammad makes himself master of Kachh.

George Thomas leaves Begam Samru's service, and takes office under Appa Khanderāv, who gives him the parganas of Tijāra, Tapokara, and Firuzpur in Mewāt.

An armament is prepared against the Rāja of Kolhāpur to repress continued acts of piracy, but the expedition is put off by a treaty of Nov. 25, wherein the Rāja engages to give compensation for losses sustained by British merchants, and to permit the erection of factories at Mulwān and Kolhāpur; but the system of piracy still continued, till 1812.

Sanskrit College instituted at Benares.

1793 Jan. 28: The Rāja of Travankor enters into an agreement (known as the Pepper Contract) to supply pepper for ten years to the Bombay Government, in return for arms and European goods.

Feb. 11: Lord Cornwallis, by a minute, institutes Zilā and City Courts for primary jurisdiction. Four provincial Courts of Appeal established at Calcutta, Pātna, Dhākā, and Murshidābād. A Court of last Appeal—the Sadr Dīwānī 'Adālat—is set up at Calcutta. Judges' fees abolished. Criminal Courts established, and circuits arranged. Assizes to be held at the four provincial Courts monthly, and at the Zilās twice a year. A Supreme Court of Criminal Justice, called the Nizāmat 'Adālat, is formed at Calcutta.

Feb. 25: Mr Henry Dundas defended the Government of India in favour of the renewal of the Charter of the E.I. Company. A new Charter granted for twenty years. The regulations of this Act were chiefly as before: salaries to be allowed to the Commissioners of the Board of Control, to be paid by the Company, and no longer to be taken exclusively from the Privy Council. The Company to provide 3,000 tons of shipping annually for the use of private traders.

March 16: Francisco de Menezes restores to Tīpū Sultān the fort of Piro and adjacent provinces.

May 17: Shawwāl 7, H. 1207. Taimūr Shāh of Afghānistān dies. The succession is disputed among his sons. Zamān Shāh,

A.D.

1793 his fifth son, elected at Kābul, while Humāyūn Shāh proclaims himself at Qandahār, and Mahmūd Shāh at Harāt.

June 11: A treaty is concluded with the Rāja of Tanjor, for garrisoning his country with British troops.

June-July: The E.I. Co. invested with civil and criminal jurisdiction on the Malabar coast. Small cause Courts are established in the Pālghāt, for Kongād, Mannūr, and Edattara districts.

June 22: Viscount Melville, president of the Board of Control, till April 25, 1801.

Vijaya Singh of Jodhpur dies. His grandson, Bhīm Singh, usurps the throne, defeating Zālim Singh; he poisons or assassinates his four remaining brothers. His nephew, Mān Singh, is besieged in Jhalur.

Aug. 1: Mānāji Gaikwād dies. The family quarrel among the four sons of Dāmāji is thus terminated, and the succession of Govindrāv recognised on payment of a large sum to the Peshwā.

Aug. 12: Lord Cornwallis, against the advice of Sir John Shore, carries into effect his Permanent Revenue Settlement, by which the *zamīndār* pays a fixed sum to Government, and levies this from the *rāyats* by his own agents. He also reforms the jurisdiction of Bengal, and establishes Zīlā Courts for primary cases.

Sept. 15: War having broken out between France and Britain, Col. Braithwaite besieges Pondicheri, which capitulates. The other French settlements are also taken for the third time.

A formal cession of part of northern Borneo seems to have been made to the Company by the Sultān of Sulu.

Rāja Gaurināth of Asām, deposed, appeals to Lord Cornwallis for protection. Capt. Welsh, with 1,100 sipāhis, reinstates the Rāja, who, however, is imprisoned, and a youth named Kinarām placed on the throne by the ministers.

Sept. 28. Mubārik-ud-daula, Nawāb of Bengal, dies, his eldest son, Nāzim-ul Mulk Wazīr-ud-daula, succeeds with the title of Bābar Jang.

SIR JOHN SHORE, LORD TEIGNMOUTH.

Oct. 10: Lord Cornwallis left Madras for England. Oct. 28: Sir John Shore, Lord Teignmouth, appointed Governor-General, till March 12, 1798.

A.D.

1793 George Thomas attempts to rescue Begam Samru, is defeated by the Mewātis, rallies his troops, and again offers battle, but concludes peace on favourable terms. At Appa Khanderāv's command, he reduces the rest of Begam Samru's villages.

Nov. 11: Dr William Carey, the first Baptist missionary, lands in India.

Abū Tālib Londonī writes the *Lubbus Siyar*.

1794 Jan. 1: Sir John Kennaway, Resident at Haidarābād, reports Nizām 'Alī to be ready to form engagements favourable to the English in consequence of his threatened annihilation by the Marāthās. The English offer mediation, but decline to give military assistance.

Feb. 12: Mahādāji Sindia of Gwāliar dies suddenly of fever at Wanauli. His grand-nephew and adopted son, Daulatrāv Sindia, succeeds, till March 21, 1827. The influence of Nāna Phadnavis with the Peshwā is now paramount.

March 29: Tīpū pays the war indemnity due under the treaty of 1792, and receives back his sons.

George Thomas cantons his legion at Tijara, and effects a junction with Appa Khanderāv, now a prisoner in Kuteputli fort. Thomas is adopted as Appa's son, and proceeds to his jagīrs. Appa, having visited Sindia's camp, is laid under a contribution which necessitates the mortgage of most of his property to Bāpu Phadnavis.

May 22: Francisco Antonio Vego de Cabral succeeds Francisco da Cunha e Menezes as Governor and Captain-General at Goa.

Sept.: Sa'far, H. 1209. Faizullah Khān, the Rohila chief, dies. His eldest son, Muhammad 'Alī Khān succeeds to the jagīrs at Rāmpur, but is assassinated a few days after by his brother, Ghulām Muhammad. The English Government support the cause of Ahmad 'Alī, infant son of the murdered prince. Sir Robert Abercromby at Bithaura defeats Ghulām Muhammad, who is imprisoned.

Sept. 7: Lord Hobart succeeds Sir Charles Oakley as Governor of Madras, till Feb. 20, 1798.

The Marāthās make extensive claims on Nizām 'Alī of Haidar-

A.D.

1794 ābād, who prepares to resist their demands and takes the field with a large army in Dec.

H. 1209. Sarūp Chand Khatrī compiles the *Sahīhu-'l Akhbār*, a general History of India, dealing in particular with the administration and revenue affairs of Bengal.

1795 Jan. The Peshwā leaves Poona with 130,000 troops, Marātha and Gujarāti, for Berār, with Sindia and Holkar's cavalry, to meet Nizām 'Alī, who, with 110,000, was marching from Bidar—the infantry under M. Raymond. March 11: the Marāthās defeat the Mughals in the battle of Kardā. Nizām 'Alī is surrounded in Kardā fort and capitulates on March 15, promising to cede large tracts of country, to deliver his minister, Mashir-ul-Mulk, and to pay three karors of rupees.

Ahalyābāi, widow of Khanderāv Holkar, dies, after a rule of thirty years. Tukāji Holkar now becomes sole ruler.

April 23: Warren Hastings acquitted on all charges; the proceedings had lasted seven years, and the trial had occupied 145 days, and cost him £70,000: the Company gave him a grant of money.

June: Nizām 'Alī, offended at the neutrality of the British, dismisses the battalions lent him for defence, but on the insurrection of his son, 'Alī Jāh, is compelled to recall them. M. Raymond, with the French brigade, suppresses the rebellion, and captures the prince, who, to avoid disgrace, takes poison.

Aug. 1: An expedition is fitted out by Lord Hobart, Governor of Madras, to wrest Ceylon from the Dutch.

Sept. Capt. Symes, deputed to the court of Ava, effects a treaty which leads only to permitting a British Agent to reside at Rangūn.

Oct. 12: Mr Robert Andrews concludes a preliminary treaty with the King of Kandy for friendship and alliance.

Oct. 13: Muhammad 'Alī Khān, Nawāb of the Karnātak, dies, aged seventy-eight. His son, 'Umdat-ul-Umrā, succeeds. Lord Hobart attempts to reform the abuses by assuming the collection of revenue and internal administration, but the Supreme Government refuses to consent. Tinevelly district is taken over as payment for the cavalry loan.

A.D.

1795 Oct. 20: Kochin city and Tangassēri surrendered by Mr Vanspall, the Dutch governor, to Major Petrie.

Oct. 25: Mādhavrāv II. Peshwā, wearied by the dominance of Nāna Phadnavis, throws himself from the palace roof and dies two days later, requesting that his cousin, Bājirāv, should be his successor; but Nāna suggests in council that Yashodābāi, the Peshwā's widow, should adopt a son. Bājirāv meanwhile pushes his claims with Sindia.

Nov. 17: A treaty of perpetual peace and friendship is concluded with the Rāja of Travankor, who engages to pay a subsidy for troops stationed in his country.

A squadron under Peter Ranier from Madras reduces the Dutch settlements in Ceylon, Malacca, Banda, and Amboyna, The Cape of Good Hope also falls to the English.

Rānā Bahādur of Nepāl orders his uncle, the regent, to be starved to death in prison, and reigns for five years with intolerable cruelty.

Chāma Rāja, the titular sovereign of Mysore, dies. Tīpū determines to have no more puppet kings, and despoils and imprisons his family.

Begam Samru's troops under Legois, a dismissed commander, mutiny, and take the oath of allegiance to her stepson, Zafar Yab Khān. The Begam with Levassoult, her husband and commander-in-chief of her army, in flight are overtaken, Levassoult, on a report that the Begam had killed herself, shoots himself. George Thomas obtains the release and restoration of the Begam.

Dec. 25: The Bengal officers form a Board to enforce restoration of the privileges removed by Lord Cornwallis. The commander-in-chief, Sir Robert Abercromby, proceeds to Cawnpore, and the mutiny is temporarily quelled.

Burmese troops enter Chittagāon district in pursuit of three robbers. They retire on explanations from General Erskine, and after trial and conviction the fugitives are restored.

Dec. 27: Jonathan Duncan succeeds the acting Governor, John Griffith, as Governor of Bombay, till his death, Aug. 11, 1811.

1796 Feb. 4: The British force in Ceylon takes Negambo. Feb. 12: a treaty is concluded with the King of Kandy for the erection

A.D.
1796 of forts and factories in Ceylon. Feb. 16: the Singhalese army at Colombo capitulates, and Ceylon is placed under the political control of the Madras governor.

May: New regulations for army administration arrive in Bengal, but aggravate the spirit of dissatisfaction. Sir John Shore is compelled to modify them and practically to concede the demands.

May 26: Against his will, Chimnāji Appa, Bājirāv's younger brother, is invested in camp as Chimnāji Mādhavrāv Peshwā, by Parashurām Bhāu and Bābārāv Phadke. Nāna Phadnavis, at Wai, suspects treachery and plots against the new administration, espouses the cause of Bājirāv, bribes Sindia, and, Oct. 8: arranges terms with Nizām 'Alī at Mahād, the latter engaging to send 15,000 men with a train of artillery to unite with those of the Nāna and Rāghoji Bhonsla for the restoration of Bājirāv, while Nizām 'Alī's territory and promised payments, wrested from him at Kardā, are to be restored, and his right to certain districts near Dehli confirmed, and Bājirāv to be advised to relinquish the *chauth* of Bidar.

Oct. 20: The Bībī of Kananūr executes an agreement surrendering her rights to the Company.

Oct. The Company's Government deputes Capt. Hiram Cox to be the resident at Rangūn under the supposed treaty of 1795; after a friendly reception he is neglected, and after nine months returns to Bengal.

Oct. 27: Sindia arrests Bāloba Tātya, one of Nāna Phadnavis's opponents; Chimnāji Āpa, with Parashurām Bhāu, flees to Siwneri, but is captured. Nov. 25: Nāna Phadnavis secures a declaration of friendship from Bājirāv, and returns to Poona. Dec. 4: Bājirāv is invested as Peshwā.

Sir R. Abercromby defeats the Rohila Patāns at Fathganj.

The Andaman Islands declared to be too unhealthy, and the English settlement withdrawn.

1797 Feb. 1: Lord Cornwallis re-appointed Governor-General, but does not proceed to India.

Zamān Shāh Abdālī marches on Lāhor, conciliates the Sikhs, and threatens Hindustan.

A.D.

1797 March: Sir John Shore proceeds to Lucknow to induce the Vazīr to reform his administration, and to pay part of his cavalry establishment, but with indifferent results.

Sixty Frenchmen form a Jacobin club at Seringapatam and plant a "tree of liberty" before Tīpū's palace. April: Capt. Ripaud and two Muslim envoys ordered to Mauritius, but embark only in October.

Shāmli fort capitulates to George Thomas, acting for the Marāthās. Lakhnauti is also taken. Appa Khanderāv drowns himself in the Jamnā. Fighting follows between Thomas and Vafonrāo, Appa's nephew.

Aug. 15. Tukāji Holkar dies. Anarchy begins at Indor. Malhārrāv, Tukāji's second son, assumes command of the army and state. Sept., Kāshi Rāo, the elder brother, raises an army with Sindia's aid, and attacks the army of Malhārrāv, who falls. Yaswant or Jaswantrāo Holkar, an illegitimate stepbrother, poses as the champion of Malhārrāv's infant son, and ravages Sindia's territory.

Sept. 21: Rabī' I. 28, H. 1212. 'Asaf-uddaula, Nawāb Vazīr of Audh, dies. Disputes occur between his brother, Sa'ādat 'Alī, and Mīrza Vazīr 'Alī Khān, his adopted son. The English Government recognise the latter as Nawāb, till Jan. 21, 1798.

Rāna Bahādur returns to Nepāl, but is murdered by a half-brother.

Dec. 31. Nāna Phadnavis, induced to pay a state visit to Sindia, is seized and imprisoned by Michel Filoze, a Neapolitan in Sindia's service. His retinue are attacked, and Ghātge sends soldiers to plunder the Nāna's house and those of all his adherents. Poona becomes the scene of much bloodshed. Nāna Phadnavis is imprisoned at Ahmadnagar.

Mayors' Courts abolished at Madras and Bombay, and Recorders' Courts substituted.

John Collins resident at the court of Daulatrāv Sindia till 1803.

1798 Jan. Vazīr 'Alī, on account of his conduct and alleged illegitimacy, is complained of, and Sir John Shore, after personal inquiry, deposes him, and deports him to Calcutta. Jan. 21: Sa'ādat 'Alī,

A.D.
1798 brother of 'Asaf ud-daula, is proclaimed Nawāb Vazīr. The fort of Allahābād is made over to the Company, and the permanent maintenance of 10,000 troops agreed to.

Feb. 21: Lord Harris made a lieut.-general, and appointed commander-in-chief at Madras, with a seat in Council and the right of nominating officers to military appointments, previously held by the civil power. Acting Governor in succession to Lord Hobart, till Aug. 21.

George Thomas defeats the Sikhs and concludes a treaty. Breaking with Bāpū Sindia, he aspires to independence, is checked at Kanhori, but overcomes it and occupies all Hariānā, Hissar, Hānsi, Sirsa, and Rohtak. He makes Georgegarh near Hānsi his capital.

March 25: Sir John Shore (Lord Teignmouth) leaves India: Sir Alured Clarke, the commander-in-chief, acting Governor till May 17.

March 25: Michel I. Raymond, commander of Nizām Alī's forces, dies suddenly.

March: Sindia marries Sakharām Ghātge Shirzi Rāv's daughter:—in straits for funds, Sindia appoints his father-in-law his *dīwān.* Ghātge extorts money from the people of Poona with the utmost violence and torture.

Bājirāv instigates his brother Amritrāv to murder Sindia, but when Sindia visits Bājirāv his irresolution discovers the plot.

May: The widows of Mahādaji Sindia revolt, disown Daulat Rāv, are imprisoned in Amritrāv's camp. Sindia declines the mediation of Col. Palmer, but subsequently accepts it in view of a treaty between Bājirāv and Nizām 'Alī. Sindia and Bājirāv reconciled.

May: Tīpū having sent ambassadors to the French authorities at Mauritius, the embassy returns to Mangalor, accompanied by fifty volunteers under Col. Chappuis and a naval colleague Dubac, who proceeds to Paris.

MARQUIS WELLESLEY.

May 17: The Earl of Mornington (Marquis Wellesley) arrives at Calcutta as Governor-General in succession to Lord Teignmouth, till July 29, 1805.

A.D.

1798 June 18: Lord Macartney, from the Cape of Good Hope, corroborates the fact of Tīpū's embassy to the French, and the Governor-General resolves on war against him, and to deprive him of Mangalur, his port on the coast.

Aug. 21: Lord Clive arrives at Madras to succeed Lord Hobart as Governor and Lord Harris acting Governor, till August 30, 1803.

Sept. 1: Lord Mornington concludes a treaty with Nizām 'Alī, who promises to dismiss his French officers, disband the infantry raised by M. Raymond, and maintain instead six battalions of English sepoys, paying 24,17,100 rupees annually. The exchange is effected by Sir John Malcolm without disturbance.

Oct. Zamān Shāh marches from Kābul, but is met and checked by the Sikhs near Amritsar. He makes over Lāhor to Ranjīt Singh as a fief and returns to Qandahār.

Nov. 8. The Governor-General writes to Tīpū remonstrating about his proceedings with the French, offering to depute Major Doveton to explain what might lead to a better understanding. Dec. 10: a second letter written, requesting a reply at Madras.

Dec. 31: Governor-General arrives at Madras. Tīpū's reply attempts to explain away the embassy to Mauritius, and considers further measures for preserving friendship superfluous. Warlike preparations are prosecuted at Madras.

An attempt to introduce some changes in the fiscal system into the Ceylon settlements nearly results in a revolution. The conquered settlements in Ceylon are transferred to the direct government of the Crown; the Hon. Frederick North nominated first Governor.

Great numbers of Arakanese having taken refuge in Chitagāon from the usurping Burmese, the Governor of Burma writes Lord Mornington demanding that the fugitives be given up.

1799 Jan. 8. Nawāb Nizām ud-dīn of Surat dies. The Government, compelled to interfere in order to prevent further corrupt administration of the native Darbār, recognise the Nawāb's brother, Nazīr ud-dīn. The entire administration of the city and its revenues is vested in the E.I. Company's government, the Nawāb to receive a lākh of rupees yearly and one-third of the revenues.

A.D.

1799 Jan. 14: Mr George Frederick Cherry, resident at Banares, with Capt. Conway and another Englishman, murdered by Vazīr 'Alī, who flees to Bhotwāl territory and enters Audh at the head of a band of disaffected zamīndārs. His force scattered by a British contingent, he flees to the Rajputs, but is handed over in Dec. and imprisoned at Fort William. May 1817: he died at Vellor.

Jan. 27: General Harris reaches Vellor, to command the Madras army. Feb. 3: Lord Mornington, having learnt that Tīpū Sultān had sent *vakīls* on a mission to the executive Directory of France, orders General Harris to enter the territory of Mysore. The E.I. Company intimated to be at war with Tīpū.

Feb. 21: The Bombay column, under General Stuart, reaches Kananūr. March 6: the advance guard, under General Hartley, attacked at Periyāpatna by Tīpū, but with the aid of General Stuart's force, defeats the Mysore army.

March 27: General Harris with the main army attacked at Malvalli, drives off the enemy with loss; 30th: he crosses the Kāverī at Sosile.

April 5: General Harris begins the siege of Seringapatam. April 14: Bombay army joins.

April 20: Tīpū proposes a conference, and, 22nd: is furnished with the draft of a preliminary treaty which is declined. 28th: it is determined to begin the assault of Seringapatam.

May 4: Sir David Baird leads a storming party at 1 P.M., and in seven minutes the British flag was hoisted over the walls of Seringapatam; Tīpū wounded, and finally shot by a grenadier. May 6: Fath Haidar, Tīpū's son, and Purnaya, the minister, surrender.

April 5: Col. Brown's detachment takes Karūr fortress, and, 22nd: in conjunction with Col. Reade, takes Kāverīpuram.

June 22: Partition treaty of Mysore, between the Nizām and the Government, is ratified. The Company take the southern portion and the city of Seringapatam, by which accession their territory reaches across the peninsula. The Nizām takes an equal portion on the north-east, in the districts of Gutī and the country lying along the line of the forts of Chitaldurg, Sira, Nandidurg, and Kolar, but without the forts. Districts to the

A.D.

1799 north-west—Harpanahalli, Sunda, Anagudi, and other districts—yielding from half to two-thirds the revenue of each of the other portions, are offered to the Marāthās, who refuse them, and they are divided between the Nizām and the Company's Government. The remainder formed the kingdom of Mysore under Krishna Rāja Udiyār, dependent on the British.

June: Col. Scott proceeds to Lucknow with the Governor-General's proposed scheme of army organisation for Audh. The Nawāb temporises with the resident. Nov. 12: he proposes to abdicate in favour of his son.

June 30: Krishna Rāja Udiyār, the infant descendant of the former Hindu rājas, placed on the *masnad* with Purnaya as minister.

July 8: Subsidiary treaty of Mysore, settling the arrangements between the new state of Mysore and the Indian Government.

Zamān Shāh of Afghanistān, about to invade Hindustān, is distracted by a threatened invasion from Persia, instigated by the British. A conspiracy in Afghānistān to raise Shujā Mīrza, a brother of Zamān, to the throne, is discovered to the Vazīr, who takes extreme measures for its suppression, which leads to the rebellion of the Barūkhzais.

A commercial mission is sent to Sindh, to conduct business between the Indian Government and the Tālpur Mīrs, but fails, and the agent receives orders to quit Sindh.

Oct. 4: Thanks of Parliament voted to the army for the success of the Mysore war.

Rāja Wānji Baula Perumāl of Travankor dies. Rāja Rāma-varma Perumāl succeeds.

George Thomas, now before Fathpur, is deserted by his Marātha allies, but with his own troops gains a victory over the Rajputs. Distress supervenes in his camp, when terms are offered by the Rāja and accepted. After an unsuccessful attack on Jhīnd, Thomas agrees to serve with Ambāji Inglia, and proceeds to Udaypur against Lakwa Dādā.

Oct. Dr Joshua Marshman, Baptist missionary, arrives at Serampur. Dr Carey, prevented by the E.I. Co. from establishing a mission in British territory, settles at Serampur under protection of the Danish Governor, Colonel Bie.

A.D.

1799 Oct. 25: Rāja Sarfojī of Tanjor cedes the state to the E.I. Co., receiving in return an annual income of a lākh of pagodas—about £40,000, and one-fifth of the revenue—together about £118,350, with the fort of Tanjor and a small territory.

Nov. 4: Great storm at Bombay, the shipping in the harbour —more than a hundred craft—driven ashore and shattered; the "Resolution" warship dashed to pieces; more than 500 lives lost.

Dec. 2: Lord Mornington created Marquis Wellesley.

Dec. 29: Sir John Malcolm leaves Bombay as ambassador to Persia, makes a treaty of alliance with the Shāh, and induces him to attack Zamān Shāh in order to withdraw the latter from invading the Panjāb. The Persians also agree to allow no Frenchman to remain in Persia.

1800 Jan. 5: General Perron, at Bijaigarh, defeats Lakwa Dādā and the Brahmans who had taken up the cause of the Bāīs, or ladies of the late Sindia's family. Lakwa Dādā holds out within the entrenchments, but, May 5: the works are stormed, and the confederates dispersed.

George Thomas, having established his state of Hānsi, had made inroads into Jaypur, and into the Sikh country, returning with considerable booty.

General Macdowell ordered on an embassy from Colombo to the court of Kandy: the minister Tolawē intrigues for the removal of the king. The troops are stopped and the embassy becomes formal.

Feb. The Nawāb Vazīr of Audh agrees to disband his own battalions and to accept those of the Company.

May 13: Nazir-ud-dīn, brother of the late Nizām-ud-dīn, Nawāb of Surat, receives the title with an annual revenue of one lākh of rupees and one-fifth more of the surplus revenues of the city—the entire government, civil and administrative, to vest in the Hon. E.I. Co. In 1817 he commuted the variable one-fifth for half a lākh of rupees—altogether about £15,000.

March 13: Nāna Phadnavis, ex-minister at Poona, dies. Disputes occur between the Peshwā and Sindia, over his estates. The Peshwā seizes Nāna's widow and family and imprisons them in hill forts.

A.D.

1800 Yashvantrāv (Jeswant) Holkar, son of Tukāji and brother of Kāshīrāv of Indor, increases his power in Mālwa. He is secretly encouraged by the Peshwā to oppose Sindia, whose Mālwa estates are soon attacked.

July 21: Purnem, long kept in disturbance by the Sāwants, recovered by the Portuguese.

Aug. 7: Marquis Wellesley made Captain-General and Commander-in-Chief in India.

Aug. 18: Fort William College, Calcutta, is established—abolished 1854.

Aug. 26: The Indian Government conclude an agreement with the Nawāb of the Karnātak, by which the right of collecting certain fees in Tinnevelli is ceded to the Government.

Sept. 9: Dhundia Wāgh, released on the capture of Seringapatam, having rallied some of Tīpū's troops, ravaged the Karnātak, both British and Marātha, and killed Dhondu Pant Gokhale, is pursued by Col. Wellesley and killed at Kongal.

Sept. 19: Govindrāv Gaikwād of Baroda dies. His son, Ānandrāv, of weak intellect, deposed by his half-brother Kānhoji, who is in turn ousted by a ministerial party under Rāvji Appaji.

Oct. 12: The Nizām of Haidarābād cedes to the Company the territory acquired by him from Maisur, in return for the protection in every case of a British force. Thus Kadapā, Karnūl, and Bellāri come into the Company's hands.

Oct. The Barūkhzais revolt and declare for Mahmūd, a brother of Zamān Shāh. Mahmūd's army takes Qandahār, but sustains a reverse at Ghaznī.

Oct. The Peshwā leases to the Gaikwād his share in the Gujarāt revenues for five years for five lākhs per annum.

Muhammad 'Alī Khān writes the *Tārīkh-i-Muzaffarī*.

1801 Feb. 14: Major-General Baird leaves Bengal to command forces ordered for service in Egypt. These are transported from Bombay: and arrived at Qosīr, June 8.

April 1: Vithoji Holkar, brother of Yashvantrāv, taken prisoner and cruelly executed by the Peshwā. Other executions follow at Poona.

A.D.

1801 April 4: Supreme Court instituted at Madras.

May 4: Lieut. George Bridges Bellasis, in a duel at Bombay, kills Arthur Forbes Mitchell, of Forbes & Co., for which Bellasis is sentenced to fourteen years' transportation to Sydney, Australia: pardoned June 4, 1802.

June: Sir George Leith, Governor of Prince of Wales' Island, concludes a treaty with the Rāja of Quedah for the cession of a district on the mainland, now named Wellesley Province. Treaty confirmed, Nov. 1802.

June: Holkar cuts off a detachment under Capt. M'Intyre, and then totally defeats Sindia's army under John Hessing at Ujjain. July: Holkar menaces Sindia's main force, but is checked with severe loss by Capt. Brownrigg.

July: Lord Lake, Commander-in-Chief in India, till July 1805, and again from Oct. 1805 to Oct. 1807.

July 15: 'Umdat-ul-Umarā, Nawāb of the Karnātak, dies. The Company wishes to take the government into their own hands. 'Alī Husain, the son of 'Umdat-ul-Umarā, refuses the terms offered, and 'Azim-ud-daula, the nephew of the late Nawāb, agrees to renounce the powers of government, and is raised to the nominal throne.

Aug. 15: The Governor-General sets out on a tour through the northern provinces.

Sept. 4: Supreme Court instituted at Madras, and Charter read.

Sept. Daulatrāv Sindia endeavours to secure George Thomas's co-operation with M. Perron, but Thomas refusing Perron's demand to give up Jayjar to the Marāthās, the negotiation is stopped, and a desultory campaign follows. Desertions from Thomas become frequent, and at Hānsī he capitulates to Perron.

Oct. 14: Daulatrāv Sindia sends Ghātge against Indor with a force under Col. Sutherland, who defeats Yashvantrāv Holkar at Indor, but fails to follow up his victory. Ghātge plunders mercilessly there.

Nov. 9: Brigadier-General John Carnac, the friend and associate of Clive, dies at Mangalur on a sea voyage, aged eighty-four.

Nov. 20: The Peshwā informs Sir Barry Close of his readiness

A.D.

1801 to accept part of the Governor-General's conditions of support, but refuses to part with territory or dismiss Europeans of nations not then at war with Britain.

Nov. 14: The Nawāb Vazīr of Audh cedes to the English Government lands in Rohilkhand and the Duāb in lieu of subsidy and all future expenses of defence, also providing for the reduction of troops, and the free navigation of the Ganges and other boundary rivers.

Fath 'Alī Khān of Haidarābād, Sindh, dies, leaving half his territory to his brother, Ghulām 'Alī, and half to other two brothers, Karam 'Alī and Murād 'Alī. By this arrangement Fath 'Alī's son, Sobhdār, receives no power.

Ran Bahādur of Nepāl is compelled to abdicate in favour of Gīrvānyuddha Vikrama Sāh, his son, and retires to Benares, where Capt. Knox is appointed to attend him as political agent.

Pondicheri restored to the French under the treaty of Amiens.

1802 Jan. 1: Lord Wellesley sends home his resignation of the Governor-Generalship, but on an appeal from the Court of Directors, consents to remain till 1805.

Jan. George Thomas, declining service with Sindia, is besieged, and surrenders at Hānsī to a strong combination of troops under Major Bourquin. Aug. 22: he dies at Burhānpur.

Feb. Malhārrāv Gaikwād, acting on behalf of his cousin, Kānhoji, Govindrāv's son, raises an army. Major Walker, with a small force, attempts pacific measures, but finds Malhārrāv treacherous. Many of the Gaikwād's troops desert to him. March 17: he attacks Major Walker, but is repulsed. April 12: all available troops summoned from Goa and Bombay, under Col. Sir William Clarke, land at Khambay. April 30: Kari carried by the British troops. Malhārrāv surrenders, and is settled at Nariād with an allowance of 1,25,000 rupees. The resident reorganises the civil administration, and reduces the Arab military force in Baroda.

April: Several merchants in Kandy are seized by the Prime Minister. Compensation is refused and war declared.

April 10: Hon. Sir Benjamin Sullivan is officiating Recorder at Bombay till 1804.

A.D.

1802 Ship-burning becomes prevalent in Bombay, the "Scaleby Castle" being the first case.

May 11: The Ghilzais, defeated already in three engagements, receive a final defeat at Malāh, and accept Durānī rule. June: Mahmūd Shāh Durānī, now at the height of his power, gives way to indolence and loses Khorasān. Dissensions among the chiefs follow.

Col. Symes proceeds to the court of Ava as envoy, and obtains from Bodoahprā a verbal assurance that no more demands for Arakanese fugitives will be made. He is treated with discourtesy, and returns to Bengal in Jan. 1803.

June 4: A treaty is concluded by the Nawāb of Farukhābād by which his territories are ceded to the Indian Government, a fixed sum of 1,08,000 rupees per annum being settled on the Nawāb.

July: Modified proposals again offered to Bājirāv, who refuses to pledge himself to the acceptance of the same terms as those which governed the defensive alliance with Haidarābād. He next turns to Sindia for protection.

Oct. 8: Yashvantrāv advances on Poona, and an encounter takes place. Oct. 25: Sindia's army with its European brigade under Col. Dawes is defeated by Holkar's army near Poona. The Peshwā flees to Singarh, and thence to Bassein and Bombay.

Dec. 3: Col. Close arrives at Bombay from Poona, and on the 8th advises the minister in attendance on the Peshwā that a formal treaty must not be delayed.

'Alī Bahādur, Nawāb of Bānda, dies at the siege of Kalinjār. His second son, Zulfiqār 'Alī, in violation of the title of his brother, Shamshīr Bahādur, is proclaimed Rāja, but is expelled.

Dec. 12: Col. Blair, with a native force, invests Bhagvant Singh, a rebellious zamīndār, at Sāsni in Rohilkhand. Siege operations begin Dec. 27; a sortie is repulsed, Dec. 30.

A revolution breaks out in Kachh, in which Bhāiji Bāwā, brother of Rāo Roydhan, expels Jamadār Fath Muhammad. The latter recovers part of the territory and establishes an independent state at Anjār.

Dec. In Baroda the Arab mercenaries revolt and suffer Kānhoji Gaikwād to escape. Dec. 28: Major Woodington takes Baroda after ten days' siege.

A.D.

1802 Dec. 31: The treaty of Bassein is concluded between the Peshwā and the Indian Government, represented by Sir Barry Close: the Peshwā to receive a subsidiary force of sixteen battalions with guns, and to cede territory to the value of twenty-six lākhs of rupees for their payment: to refer to the Indian Government all disputes with the Nizām and the Gaikwād, and to be restored to power at Poona.

1803 Jan. 1: A detachment under Major Holmes pursues Kānhojī Gaikwād; defeats him at Saurī, Feb. 6, and again at Kāpadvanj, March 25. He flees to Ujjain.

Jan. 3: The Sāsni garrison makes a sally on Col. Blair's force, but is driven back. Jan. 14: he unsuccessfully attacks the fort. Jan. 31: Lord Lake joins the besiegers. Feb. 8: the town is taken, and Feb. 11: Fort Sāsni evacuated, and Rāja Bhagwant Singh flees to Bijaigarh, which surrendered Feb. 28.

March 1: Col. Collins proposes to Sindia at Burhānpur to be party to an alliance similar to that concluded with the Peshwā at Bassein; but Sindia, in agreement with Perron, postpones a decisive reply.

March: Capt. Knox, ambassador at Khātmāndu, withdraws from Nepāl in consequence of the aversion of the Gurkhā Government to his presence, and evasion of the terms of treaty.

March 12: The Zamīndār of Kachaura, after continued resistance, surrenders his fort.

March 25: The Haidarābād and Madras armies, under General Wellesley, move on Poona for the reinstatement of Bājirāv as Peshwā. April 20: General Wellesley reaches Poona, and May 13, invests the Peshwā. Efforts are made to conciliate Holkar, who retires to Malwā.

June 3: Sindia receives an ultimatum from the Governor-General, intimating that (1) a march on Poona would be equivalent to a declaration of war; (2) an attack on the Nizām would be repelled; (3) that the Governor-General was prepared either to include Sindia in the treaty of Bassein, or to conclude a separate alliance with him.

June 4-6: Disturbances break out in Afghānistān between the Sunnis, under Sher Muhammad Khān, and the Shi'as, under Mahmūd Khān. July: The Amīr and his faction are driven to

A.D.
1803 the hills. July 15: Fathi Khān Barūkhzai defeated, Shujā Mirza, son of Taimūr Shāh, proclaimed Amīr, with Sher Muhammad Khān as prime minister. Shujā's haughty demeanour alienates many of his subjects.

July 4: Major Arthur Wellesley interviews Sindia and the Rāja of Berār, both of whom refuse definite alliance, proposing to depart if the Governor-General's army were disbanded. Aug. 3: Col. Collins quits the camp at Burhānpur, this being tantamount to a declaration of war.

Aug. 6: Nizām 'Alī dies at Haidarābād. His son, Mīrza Sikandar Jāh, succeeds to the Sūbah of the Dekhan.

Aug. 12: Ahmadnagar is captured and occupied by General Wellesley.

Aug. 28: General Lake defeats Sindia's force, under M. Perron, at Koil, near Aligarh, and M. Perron leaves Daulatrāv Sindia's service and retires to France. Sept. 2: a force of Marāthās, under M. Fleury, attacks the British cantonment at Shikohābād, and, after a repulse, the garrison capitulates on condition of not serving against Sindia.

Aug. 29: The Bombay army, under Lieut. Woodington, take Baroda. Sept. 17: Pawangadh taken.

Sept. 4: Aligarh fort is stormed by Col. Monson. Sept. 11: Lake's army, proceeding to Dehli, is attacked at Jeha Mala, 6 miles from Dehli, by M. Louis Berquien with a large force, who is defeated with great loss, after which M. Berquien gives himself up as a prisoner. Sept. 14: General Lake enters Dehli at the invitation of Shāh 'Alam.

Sept. 11: Pondicheri and the other French settlements are again seized.

Sept. 14: The Madras army, under Lieut.-Col. Harcourt, take Manikpatam; 18th, enter Purī without opposition. Sept. 21: Bālāsor occupied by Capt. Morgan. Oct. 3: Surang surrenders. Oct. 10: Katak taken. By the conquest of Barabati, Oct. 14, Col. Harcourt completes the conquest of Orissa. Nov. 2: Bārmūl Pass is forced by Major Forbes, and the Marāthās completely broken.

Sept. 30: Lieut.-Col. Guthrie, hemmed in at Tītīya fort in Bundelkhand, sends to Col. Dalston for assistance, who, on arriving, obliges the Marāthās to evacuate the fort.

A.D.

1803 Sept. 23: Battle of Asāi, in which General Wellesley, with only 4,500 men, attacks the armies of Sindia and Rāghoji Bhonsla of 50,000 men of all arms, and gains a complete victory, though losing one-third of his force in killed and wounded, the enemy's loss being about 12,000 men.

Oct. 15: Burhānpur is taken by General Wellesley; 21st, Asīrgarh taken.

Oct. Gosain Himmat Bahādur, with a considerable force, offers his services to the British, and joins Col. Powell, aiding in subduing the province of Bundelkhand, which is severed from the Marātha dominion.

Oct. 18: Agra fort capitulates to General Lake after a ten days' siege.

Nov. 1: At Laswāri (properly Nāswāri) Rāja Ambāji proceeds to take command of M. Perron's army, with seventeen battalions of infantry and 5,000 cavalry with artillery. General Lake, in a hardly contested battle, with less than 3,000 cavalry in the morning, aided in the afternoon by his infantry, gains a decisive victory. All Sindia's possessions north of the Chambal come under the British power.

Nov. 1: Bhīmsingh of Jodhpur dies, and is succeeded by Mānsingh, a cousin, till 1843. Feud for Krishnā Kumārī, the Udaypur princess.

Nov. 23: A truce is granted by Wellesley to Daulatrāv Sindia on condition that he should remain 20 *kos* east of Elichpur; he does not observe the terms.

Nov. 29: At Argāon, in a decisive battle, Col. Stevenson's column, co-operating with General Wellesley, attack the army of Sindia and Rāghoji Bhonsla, in which the Marāthās suffer great loss.

Dec. 15: Gāwilgadh fort, escaladed by Capt. Campbell, capitulates.

Dec. 17: By the treaty of Deogāon it is agreed that Rāghoji Bhonsla should give up Katak, including Bālāsor, with territory and shares of the revenue west of the Wardā, the forts of Gāwilgadh and Narnāla to be retained by Rāghoji, all differences between the Nizām, Peshwā, and Rāghoji to be arbitrated by the

A.D.

1803 British Government. No individual of a nation at war to be harboured without the consent of the British Government.

Dec. 16: Ambāji Inglia, having thrown off his allegiance to Sindia, joins the British forces, and agrees to surrender Gwāliar fort and certain districts to be conferred on Kirat Singh, the Rānā of Gohad.

Dec. 30: By the treaty of Surji Anjangāon, Sindia gives up to the British his territory in Hindustan and south of the Ajantā hills, except some hereditary villages; Bharoch, Ahmadnagar, and his forts in the Duāb; and resigns his claims on his former feudatory Rājas, with whom the British had made treaties.

Pratāp Singh of Jaypur dies. Jagat Singh succeeds.

Khem Sāwant of Sāwantwādi dies. Lakshmībāī acts as regent. Kolhāpur troops besiege Fort Wādi. With the aid of Viswāsrāv Ghātge and Appa Desāī the siege is raised.

Capt. Canning, envoy at Rangūn, is subjected to such ill-treatment from the officials that he has to leave in a few months.

Lallujī Lāl, by the advice of Dr John Gilchrist, writes his Prem Sāgar, in a dialect based on Urdu.

1804 Jan. Ceded districts made over to the Rānā of Gohad except the city and fort of Gwāliar.

Jan. 24: Lord Wellesley formally dissolves the alliance with the Nepalese. By the able management of the Rānī, Ran Bahādur is restored to power. The Nepalese commence a series of aggressions on the frontier.

Rāja Himmat Bahādur Gosain dies. The lands, from Allahābād to Kālpī, assigned him in 1803, are resumed, and *jagīrs* and pensions are granted to his family.

Jan. 29: Yashwantrāv Holkar called upon by the Governor-General to take away his troops, and to cease from demanding tribute in Hindustan. He refuses, except on terms which are regarded as extravagant.

Feb. 2: Shamsher Bahādur, Nawāb of Bānda, unsuccessful in attempting to re-establish his authority, accepts a provision from the Supreme Government, and permission to reside at Bānda.

Feb. 5: Yashwant (or Jashwantrāv) Holkar sends vakīls to open negotiations with Sindia.

A.D.

1804 Feb. 6: A treaty of friendship concluded by Col. Baillie with Shivrāv Bhāu, Sūbahdār of Jhānsi.

Feb. Sir James Macintosh, Recorder of Bombay, till Nov. 1811.

Feb. 27: By the treaty of Burhānpur Sindia agrees to become a party to the defensive alliance concluded at Surji Ānjangāon, and accepts a subsidiary force of 6,000 infantry with their artillery.

March 15: A treaty is entered into with Rāo Rāja Parikshit of Datiyā, according to the usual terms of protection.

April 16: The Governor-General, after several remonstrances, declares war on Holkar, and on April 23 Col. Monson drives Holkar south from Jaypur.

April 28: By the partition treaty of Haidarābād, Sikandar Jāh, Nizām of the Dekhan, receives the cession of the territories conquered from Sindia and the Rāja of Berār.

May 14: Sa'far 3, H. 1219. The treaty of Poona concluded between the British Government and the Peshwā for the partition of the territories conquered from the Rāja of Berār and Sindia.

May 16: A detachment of Lake's army, under Lieut.-Col. Don, storms and takes the fort of Tonk-Rāmpura. May 22: in Bundelkhand a detachment of British sipāhis is cut off by Amīr Khān, who is, however, attacked and routed at Kālpī by a party of horse.

July 2: Hinglājgarh fortress, in Central India, taken by a detachment under Major Sinclair, but Monson, for want of supplies and the heavy rains, is obliged to retreat. Bāpujī Sindia, with a detachment sent by Daulatrāv, deserts to Yashwant Holkar. July 10: Monson reaches Mukandwāra Pass, where Holkar summons him to surrender; refused, he attacks the force, but is repelled. July 15: Monson abandons his guns; reaches Rāmpura, 27th to 29th. Aug. 14: is reinforced, and Aug. 22, leaves, and is attacked on Aug. 24, in crossing the Bānās, when he abandons the baggage and flees to Khushalgarh, thence to Hindaun, and, Aug. 31, reaches Agra.

Aug. 24: Col. Murray, with the Gujarāt army, takes Indor, Holkar's capital in Mālwa.

Sept. The Rāja of Khurdhā in Orissa rebels and ravages Pīplī district. The rebels hold out at the fort of Khurdhā till November.

A.D.

1804 The Dutch settlement at Pālakol, Godāvarī district, transferred to the English.

Sept. Holkar takes possession of Mathurā. General Lake marches from Cawnpore to Agra; 22nd: assembles his army at Sikandara. Oct. 1: marched towards Mathurā, from which Holkar withdrew.

Oct. 8: Holkar attacks Dehli unexpectedly with an army of 20,000 men; after a siege of nine days he is repulsed by the efforts of Lieut.-Cols. Burn and Ochterlony. Oct. 18: General Lake drives Holkar to Bharatpur.

Oct. 8: Lāsalgāon fort, in Nāsik district, after a desperate resistance, is taken by a detachment of Col. Wallace's force from Farukhābād. 12th: Chāndor taken; 14th: Dhurb taken; 25th: Gālna taken, completing the reduction of Holkar's possessions in the Dekhan.

Nov. 13: Major-General H. Frazer attacks Holkar's infantry and artillery between Dīg and Govardhan, and in a severe action defeats them and takes eighty-seven guns. General Frazer mortally wounded. Nov. 17: General Lake overtakes and surprises Holkar with his cavalry at Farukhābād, and defeats them with great slaughter.

Dec. 13: Lake lays siege to Dīg, to which Holkar and his force had fled. Dec. 23: Dīg is stormed and taken by night, and the fort evacuated next night. Dīg belonged to Ranjīt Singh, Rāja of Bharatpur, who had been specially favoured by the British in Dec. 1803, yet his troops opened fire on General Frazer's troops on Nov. 13.

Bājirāv, refusing personal intercourse with the British Resident at Poona, appoints Sadāshiv Bhāu Mānkeshwar to conduct negotiations.

Umed Rāo of Būndī dies. His grandson, Bishen Singh, succeeds.

1805 Jan. 2: Lord Lake begins the siege of Bharatpur where Holkar had found protection. Insufficient forces and guns render four assaults unsuccessful.

April 2: Amīr Khān, an officer of Holkar's, is beaten by Lake near Bharatpur.

A.D.

1805 April 10: Rāja Ranjīt Singh of Bharatpur proposes terms, and agrees to pay, by instalments, a fine of twenty lākhs of rupees and cede back to the Company the additional territories granted to him in 1803, delivering up his son as a hostage. The army leaves, April 21.

April 11: Holkar, 14th, Bāpuji Sindia, and 15th, Amīr Khān join Dhaulatrāv Sindia's camp at Wer, south west of Bharatpur—Sindia had marched thither with a large army. 28th: the chiefs retire before Lake's army to Kotā, and in June towards Ajmir.

April: Shāh Shujā' of Afghānistān marches to Peshāwar, for the conquest of Kashmir, but is recalled by Barukhzāi rebellions.

April 21: By a treaty with Baroda, the auxiliary force there is made permanent, and certain territories assigned to the Company for its maintenance.

May 6: The Rāja of Travankor signs a treaty acceding to the request of the British Government for an additional regiment. The subsidy payable by the Rāja is eventually fixed at eight lākhs of rupees per annum.

LORD CORNWALLIS—SECOND VICEROYALTY.

July 30: Lord Cornwallis arrives at Calcutta as Governor-General, and he begins to reverse the "forward" policy of Lord Wellesley, and in pursuance of the new course, the alliance with the Rāja of Jaypur is ordered to be annulled.

Sept. Holkar moves from Ajmir to the Panjāb. Lord Lake stations three forces of infantry to check his movements, and with the cavalry proceeds from Mathurā to pursue Holkar's march. Sept. 19: Lord Lake receives instructions to abandon the Rājput states, but delays acting upon the instructions.

SIR GEORGE H. BARLOW—ACTING GOVERNOR-GENERAL.

Oct. 5: The Marquis Cornwallis dies at Ghāzipur. Sir George Barlow, senior member of Council, acts till July 31, 1807.

Nov. 23: A new treaty, under the immediate direction of Lord Lake, concluded with Sindia, in which the latter, renouncing all claim to tribute from Būndī, is confirmed in the sovereignty

A.D.

1805 of Gwāliar and Gohad, the Gohad Rānā to be granted an establishment.

Dec. 5: By the treaty signed at Raipur Ghāt on the Bīās, Sindia agrees to dismiss Shirji Rāv Ghātge from his councils; Ranjīt Singh is to withhold help from Holkar.

Dec. 24. Holkar signs a treaty in which he renounces all right to Tonk-Rāmpura, Būndī, and other places; engages to entertain no Europeans in his service. The British engage to refrain from interference with the possession of Holkar south of the Chambal, and to restore certain forts and districts in the Dekhan, retaining Chāndor, and the districts of Amber and Shevgāon, till his pacific intentions should be proved.

Ran Bahādur of Nepāl killed by his half-brother, Sher Bahādur, in a conspiracy. General Bhīmasena Thappa, countenanced by the chief Rānī, assumes the government as premier.

Penang is constituted a separate presidency.

1806 Jan. 6: The treaty with Holkar ratified. Sir George Barlow adds a supplementary article, leaving the allied Rājas at the mercy of Holkar and Amīr Khān.

Feb. 25: Sir George Barlow is formally appointed Governor-General. March 7: the Ministers determine to supersede Sir G. Barlow in favour of the Earl of Lauderdale. The Directors refuse to cancel the appointment, and by a warrant under the King's sign-manual Lord Minto is nominated Governor-General.

July 10: The sipāhis at Vellor, instigated by the Maisur princes, massacre the European officers and hoist Tīpū's flag. Col. Rollo Gillespie from Arkat blows open the gates, slays 500 mutineers, takes prisoners the Princes of Maisur, who are, Aug. 28, deported to Calcutta.

Aug. 24: Jumāda II. 9, H. 1221. The Government restores to the Rāja of Berār the districts of Sambhalpur and Pātna.

Holkar's army, in arrears, swears allegiance to Khande Rāv, Holkar's nephew. The sedition is crushed by the payment of arrears by means of a large sum exacted from the Rāja of Jaypur. Khande Rāv murdered by order of Holkar, who also orders the death of Khāsirāv, his stepbrother.

Oct. Ranjīt Singh crosses the Satlaj to assist the Rāja of Nabha against the Rāja of Patiāla, and dictates terms of agreement.

A.D.

1806 Nov. 19: Ramazān 7, H. 1221. Shāh 'Ālam dies. His son, Abul-Nasr Mu'īn-uddīn Muhammad, succeeds as Akbar II., as titular emperor, till Sept. 1837.

Amīr Khān of Tonk enters the service of Jagat Singh of Jaypur, but is then won over to Jodhpur.

Nov. 3: Lord Wm. Bentinck, Governor of Madras, having charged Rev. Dr R. H. Kerr, senior chaplain, to inquire into the state of the native Christians in Cochin and Travankor, Dr Kerr reports—on the St Thomé or Jacobite Christians using the Syriac language in their service, and then under Mar Dionysius as metropolitan; the Syrian Roman Catholics, using Syriac, but under the Archbishop of Krānganor and Bishop of Virappoli; and Latin Roman Catholics under the primacy of the Archbishop of Goa. Nov. 24: Dr Claudius Buchanan, patronised by the Marquis Wellesley, also visits the Syrian churches in Travankor, and meets Mar Dionysius. He collects important MSS.

1807 Jan. 29: The Rāja of Maisur enters into a treaty for the maintenance of a body of 400 horse.

Ranjīt Singh makes encroachments on cis-Satlaj territory.

Feb. The Rājas of Jaypur and Jodhpur contend for the hand of the Udaypur princess, Krishnā Kumārī, when Mān Singh of Jodhpur defeats the Jaypur Rāja, Jagat Singh. Her father poisons Krishnā.

Yashwant (Jaswant) Rāv Holkar becomes insane, and makes extravagant military preparations.

May 30: Bernardo José de Lorena, Conde de Sarzedas, succeeds Francisco Antonio da Veiga Cabral as Viceroy and Captain-General of Portuguese India.

G. ELLIOT, EARL OF MINTO.

June 20: Earl of Minto, Governor-General in succession to Sir G. Barlow, arrives at Madras, where he gives assistance in determining the disposal of the Vellor prisoners. July 31: he enters office at Calcutta, till Oct. 1813.

July 24: Mīrza Jahāngīr, the Emperor Akbar's third son, causes alarm in the palace at Dehli by his armed guards. The

A.D.

1807 Company's sipāhis take possession of the gates, and after a skirmish disperse the guards, and Mīrza Jahāngīr is sent a state prisoner to Allāhābād.

Oct. The tribute in Kāthiāwād due to the Gaikwād is levied by a military detachment under Col. Walker. The Tālukdārs engage to pay a fixed tribute to their overlords, to keep the peace toward each other, and to maintain order within their own limits. The evils of the *mulkgiri* system are thus averted. Col. Walker forms engagements with 153 states.

Sept. 11: Lord William Bentinck recalled by the Directors as partly responsible for the Vellor mutiny. Mr William Petrie becomes acting governor.

Oct. 20: Sir Edward Pellew leaves Madras with an expedition for Gresik in Java. Dec. 5: on his arrival he destroys the forts and batteries, and burns three cruisers.

Col. John Baillie, political agent in Bundelkhand, succeeds in establishing British authority there and transferring to the E.I. Co. large and valuable tracts of land.

Nov. 19: Major-General Dickens, having invested Kamonā, the fort of the rebel Dūndi Khān, in Bulandshahar district, attempts to storm it, but loses severely. Nov. 24: the fort is evacuated, and Dūndi Khān makes his escape.

Burmese intrigues with the natives of India are entered upon. A mission, ostensibly for the acquisition of books, proceeds to Benares.

Dec. 24: Sir George Hilaro Barlow succeeds Mr William Petrie, acting Governor of Madras, till May 21, 1813.

Appā Desāī Nipānikar, desiring to establish his supremacy in Sāwantwādi, with the concurrence of Lakshmibāī, widow of Khem Sāwant, and of Phond Sāwant, the next heir, causes the young prince to be strangled.

1808 Feb. 22: Col. Montresor marches against Rāja Mahīpat Rām, a minister and late favourite of Sikandar Jāh, the Nizām, now in revolt. The Rāja is pursued from Shāhpūr to Berār, and thence to Indor, where most of his followers desert. Mahīpat Rām is assassinated in camp by the party of Tulsībāī, Holkar's wife.

March 3: Sher Muhammad Khān, having proclaimed the Shāh Shūjā''s nephew king, is defeated and slain by Shāh Shūjā' on

A.D.

1808 Peshāwar plain. Later, Mahmūd Shāh, who had taken Qandahār, is defeated there.

April: Sir Harford Jones arrives at Bombay to proceed with the Company's agent, Sir John Malcolm, on an embassy to Persia. The latter, however, had left. French influence rendered these embassies unproductive.

Sir George Barlow institutes a trial of Mr Sherson, a civil servant, and Mr Smith, on a charge of fraud. They are suspended, but acquitted and restored to office.

May 3: Shāhu Rāja of Sātāra dies. His son, Pratāp Singh, succeeds.

July 18: Capt. Seton, on the part of the Bombay Government, concludes an offensive and defensive alliance with Ghulām 'Alī of Sindh. This the Bengal Council refuses to ratify, and sends Mr N. H. Smith to make new negotiations.

Aug. A mission to Lāhor is conducted by Mr Metcalfe to secure the concurrence of Ranjīt Singh. Sept., boundary questions cause Ranjīt to break up camp. A further meeting at Amritsar produces no results.

Oct. 13: Mountstuart Elphinstone leaves Dehli on an embassy to Kābul, in view of the designs of France and Russia upon India.

The Gūrkha Governor of Morung seizes the *zamīndāri* of Bhīmnagar, on the frontier of Puranīya.

The Sikhs of Sarhind send a deputation to beg the protection of the British Government against Ranjīt Singh.

A "Carnatic Commission" is appointed to inquire into the genuineness of bonds, in possession of citizens, left by the late Nawāb of the Karnātak. Reddi Rāo, late accountant, tried three times, poisons himself, and is found to be deeply implicated in the issue of fabricated securities.

The Rāja of Travankor is suddenly called on to dismiss his Karnātak Brigade in order to pay arrears of tribute, appeals to Madras and Bengal. Incited by the Diwān and assisted by the Cochin Diwān, the resident's house in Cochin is surrounded by the Nāyars, Dec. 28, and the resident, Col. Macaulay, obliged to flee to a vessel. Dec. 30: troops arrive from Malabar under Col. Chambers, and near South Kollam (Quilon); the insurgent

A.D.
1808 Travankor forces are defeated, and another body at Anjuncha, Dec. 31.

Sir John Cradock, at Madras, suggests the abolition of the Tent Contract, an allowance to officers to provide tents for the men; the abolition is approved of by Col. John Munro, Q.M.G., and by Lord Bentinck, but resented by the officers, who procure Col. John Munro's arrest, Jan. 20, and demand a court-martial.

Nov. Abū'l Qāsim Mīr 'Alam, minister at Haidarābād, dies. Munīr ul-Mulk, called Chandā Lāl, a supporter of the British, succeeds him.

A further mission from Badoahprā of Burma proceeds to India, on a greater scale than that of 1807. At Pātna they divided: most of the officers went to Bodh-gayā to make offerings, and take a complete plan of the temple, its courts and holy tree: the mission collected books at Banares, Delhi, &c., but they had probably a political object.

1809 Jan. 6: Ranjīt Singh, hearing of the approach of Col. Ochterlony, recalls his garrison from Ambālā, and proceeds to Amritsar, making promises but concluding no treaty. An apparently accidental attack by the Sikhs is vigorously repelled by the envoy's escort. In face of two British forces advancing, Ranjīt signs a treaty on April 25, in which he agrees neither to commit nor suffer encroachments on the possessions of the chiefs to the south, while the British engage to have no concern in the territories of the Rāja to the north of the Satlaj.

Jan. 15: The Travankor Diwān attacks Col. Chalmers at Anilon, but is defeated with a loss of 500. Jan. 19: 3,000 again attack Cochin and are defeated. Jan. 30: the Diwān's force commits acts of atrocity on the coast, thirty Europeans being murdered at Ālleppi. A force is at once despatched from Madras: carries by surprise the Travankor lines on Feb. 10. Feb. 18: Forts Udaygiri and Pāpanavaram surrender. Feb. 21: Col. Chalmers attacks and disperses his besiegers, and marches on Trivandram. A complete surrender follows. The "Karnātak Brigade" is dismissed, and the expenses to Government paid by the Rāja Rāma Varma.

Jan. 31: Col. John Munro, having appealed to the supreme Government, is liberated, and General Macdowall suspended

A.D.

1809 from his post as Commander-in-Chief of Madras. Major Boles suspended for having circulated the order censuring his Q.M.G.

Feb. The motion carried in the House of Commons to appoint a committee to inquire into the existence of corrupt practices in the distribution of patronage in the Court of Directors of the E.I. Co.

Feb. 11: Col. Martindell proceeds against Lakshman Dāwa, a turbulent chief holding out at Ajaygarh. Feb. 13: the commander surrenders the fort, and Lakshman, who escaped for the moment, gave himself up, and is allowed to remain on parole at Naushahr. He died in 1828.

March 5: Mountstuart Elphinstone reaches Peshāwar, and confers with Shāh Shujā'. An alliance against a possible Franco-Persian invasion is not realised, the envoy not being authorised to offer assistance against Shāh Shujā's immediate enemies.

May 1: The Madras Government by a general order suspends or supersedes a number of commanding officers who had disapproved of the actions of Government in connection with the Tent Contract abolition, among whom were Cols. St Leger, Chalmers, and Cuppage. The officers of the regiments at Jālnā and Haidarābād urge the restoration of the removed officers. July: the European regiment at Masulipatam mutinies. Aug. the Seringapatam officers occupy the fort, and seize the public treasure. Those of Chitaldurg had also seized the military treasure, and marched towards Seringapatam, but, Aug. 11, are dispersed by Col. Gibbs and his dragoons.

May 6: A treaty is concluded between the E.I. Co. and the Rāja of Cochin.

June: A British detachment sent to Bhūnnagar with orders to reduce the *zamīndāri.* The Gurkhas evacuate the lands in 1810.

June 17: Treaty between the British Government and the Shāh of Kābul.

June: An expedition leaves Madras for the protective occupation of Macao. Sept. 11: the Portuguese resist, but the English admiral, having the Goa Viceroy's sanction, lands. The Chinese Viceroy now refuses protection against the French, and on Dec. 23 the Madras division, with a detachment from Bengal, re-embarks and returns to India.

A.D.

1809 June: Vīrarāja of Kurg dies. Devamaji is recognised as Rānī, but a few months after is deposed by Lingarāja, brother of Vīrarāja.

Aug. 11: The Haidarābād officers address a penitential letter to Lord Minto, and from their example the other mutinous officers submit by Aug. 23, and sign the "Declaratory Test of Allegiance," with reference to the "Tent Contract" agitation.

Aug. 22: A treaty is concluded with the British Government by the surviving brothers of the Sindh Haidarābād family, providing for the exclusion of the French from Sindh.

Aug. 29: Reduction of the fort of Bhawānī in Hariānā, the chief of which had plundered a British settlement.

Sept. 11: Lord Minto arrives at Madras, and on Sept. 25 issues an order reprobating the officers' conduct, and in the proceedings which followed; four officers are cashiered and the rest offered the alternative of court-martial or dismissal. For their example, those of Haidarābād were pardoned.

Muhammad 'Azim Khān, Governor of Kashmīr, wrests his province from Kābul.

Aug. 4: Rodriguez island occupied by Col. Keating as a base for the conquest of the "French Islands."

Oct. Threatened by an incursion of Muhammadan fanatics, Diwān Hansrāj of Māndvi seeks protection from the British Government, engaging, Oct. 28, to pay the expenses of the military assistance, and six annas per rupee of revenue.

The Rāja of Tehri solicits admission among the protected allies of the British. This application is not entertained, in view of the policy of non-intervention.

Oct. Amīr Khān of Tonk, pretending to act for Holkar, invades Berār; a force under Col. Close marches against him; but Sādiq 'Alī, the Berār general, approached him at Jabalpur, and, his Pendhārī allies not having rejoined after the rains, Amīr Khān retreated towards Bhopāl. Nov. 17: Sādiq 'Alī following him inflicts a severe defeat on him at Jabra Ghāt. Joined by Vazīr Muhammad and the Pendhārīs, Amīr Khān follows Sādiq 'Alī back to Chaurāgarh, where he was severely defeated, and retired again into Bhopāl, and, Dec. 1, Col. Close had arrived at Amarāvatī.

A.D.

1809 Nov. 12: Rās al Khima occupied by a Bombay force sent for the suppression of piracy on the Persian Gulf. Nov. 13: at Shinas a determined resistance is made, but safety to commerce in the gulf is secured.

Nov. Gopāl Singh, usurper of Rāja Chatrasāl's lands, repulses the British force under Capt. Wilson, and plunders Tīroha. Nov. 19: he sustains a reverse at Bhāmori, and again at Killeri.

The province of Hariānā settled by the assistant Dehli Resident, the Hon. E. Gardner, who is resisted at Bhiwānī by the Bhatti chief, Khān Bahādur. Aug. 27: Bhiwānī besieged, and stormed, Aug. 29, by Col. Ball.

Ambāji Inglia dies. Daulatrāv Sindia reduces his territory in Gohad.

1810 Feb. 17: A small expedition from Madras captures Amboyna from the Dutch governor, who was shot in Java by order of Marshal d'Aendels, the governor acting for Napoleon. This capture is followed by others.

Feb. 27: Rām Singh of Rājpīpla invests his reputed son, Pratāp Singh, with the government by a *sanad* which the Bombay Government promise to guarantee; but in consequence of the death of Rām Singh the guarantee is not affixed.

March 11: The Rāja of Māndvi is reinstated in office by a British force. In consideration of the exhausted state of the country, the Rāja is released from the expenses of the expedition. as well as his arrears of tribute.

May: Sir Samuel Auchmuty arrives at Madras as Commander-in-Chief.

June: Sir John Malcolm reaches Teheran on his second embassy, but simultaneously Sir Gore Ouseley arrives from London as King's Envoy to Fath 'Alī Shāh.

June 23: The Duncan Dock, Bombay, is completed.

June 26: Gopāl Singh is surprised and defeated by Col. Brown at the Dhowāni Pass. Sept. 7: Capt. Watson carries the fort of Kshirgāon. Later (1811), Gopāl Singh tendered submission, and was granted a jagīr in the Panwārī district.

June 29: Shāh Shujā' defeated at Nimla by Mahmūd Shāh, his brother, and, driven from Afghānistān, becomes a British pensioner at Ludhiāna.

A.D.

1810 July 8: The island of Bourbon (Réunion) attacked and taken by Col. Keating.

Aug. 9: Bānda taken from the Dutch by Col. Cole. Aug. 29: Ternate captured by a detachment under Capt. Tucker.

Aug. 23: Mauritius attacked, but the British fleet is defeated with a loss of five frigates; Mauritius blockaded. Sept. 12: an action fought in which General Abercrombie's ship is captured, but retaken later in the day.

Nov. 29: A force of 12,000 landed on Mauritius. General de Caen offers a stout defence, but after an action, Dec. 9, Port Louis surrenders, and Mauritius is taken.

1811 March 4: The Chancellor of the Exchequer moves in Parliament that the East India Company's commercial privileges should cease on April 10, 1814.

March: Mountstuart Elphinstone now Resident at Poona. Exercising authority directly, he incurs the ill-will of the native agent, Khusruji, who influences Bājirāv against the Resident.

June 14: A Bill passed in the House of Commons granting to the Company a loan of a million sterling.

July: A treaty is concluded by the British Government with the Rāja of Alwar, who agrees to submit negotiations with other powers to the supreme Government.

Aug. 11: Jonathan Duncan, Governor of Bombay, dies. George Brown, senior Member of Council, is acting Governor till Aug. 12, 1812.

Aug. 4: A large expedition under Sir Samuel Auchmuty, Lord Minto accompanying it, lands at Batavia, which is occupied on Aug. 9, and on Aug. 10 Weltevreeden, an unfortified cantonment, is taken. Aug. 26: the entrenched post at Cornelis carried by assault, and 6,000 prisoners taken. Sept. 16: Auchmuty defeats Janssen near Samarang, where a treaty of surrender is signed. Mr (afterwards Sir Stamford) Raffles appointed Governor, Col. Gillespie being in charge of the military administration.

The Diwān of Travankor having usurped excessive power, Sir John Munro takes on himself the administration at the Rāja's request. Rāja Rāma Varma dies; his sister, Lakshmī Rānī, succeeds, but died in 1814; her sister, Pārvatī Rānī, succeeded, till 1829, Col. Munro still acting as resident till late in 1814.

A. D.

1811 The Peshwā makes extensive claims on the Southern Marātha *jagīrdārs*, who appeal to the British. The latter enforce the service of troops, but advise the Peshwā to guarantee them in their lands.

Capt. Canning, on an embassy to Ava, regarding an attack of the Arakanese on the Burmese conquerors of Arakan, is ordered to be detained as a hostage for the delivery of the rebels. Capt. Canning being on board a man-of-war, escapes. He left Rangūn, Sept. 1812.

For the suppression of piracy, and to afford harbour for vessels, Malwān is secured to the British from the Peshwā. Oct. the Desāi of Sāwantwādi makes over Vingorla, and agrees to allow free trade with Britain, but on his death, his widow, Durgābāī, disregards the treaty and sustains a continuous warfare till 1819.

Oct. 20: Jaswantrāv Holkar dies insane. Malhārrāv, a boy of four, adopted by Tulsibāī, succeeds under her regency at Indor.

Krishna Rāja of Maisur proclaims himself independent ruler, dismisses Purnaiya, his minister, but proves incompetent.

In consequence of Gurkha seizures in Bhotwāl and Bettīya, the first skirmish between Nepalese and British troops occurs. Encroachments taking place along the frontier, an investigation commenced by commissioners, jointly chosen, results in favour of the British, who post detachments along the frontier. These being withdrawn in the rainy season, the Nepalese make attacks on the stations, inflicting much loss.

Nov. 6: Sir Alexander Anstruther appointed Recorder at Bombay;—died July 16, 1819.

Thomas Manning reaches Lhasa by Rangpur, Bhutan, and Parijong—the first Englishman to enter Lhasa. April 12, 1812: left under orders from Pekin.

1812 The Pendhārīs come into prominence about this time; they were bodies of freebooters, who had occasionally been in the hire of Marātha chiefs, to whom they paid a sort of turbulent obedience.

Jan. A large body of Pendhārīs penetrates into Bundelkhand and Rewā, destroys villages under British protection, and menaces Mīrzapur.

Jan. 19: Kalinjār fort invested by Col. Martindell—the Killādār, Daryā Singh Chaubē, confirmed in its occupancy, Dec. 8, 1806,

A.D.

1812 having proved contumacious. The assault, though unsuccessful, leads to a surrender on Feb. 1. The fort was dismantled, 1866.

March 28: Purnaya, the aged minister at Maisur, dies. Flatterers and parasites now consume the revenues.

April 2: For conspiring with Jām Jesāji of Nawānagar to secure his own elevation to the Baroda state, Kānhoji Gaikwād is arrested; he is afterwards removed to Madras.

April 12: Rāja Sivaji of Kolhāpur dies. His elder son, Sambhu or Aba Sāhib, succeeds.

June: An application for the loan of two and a half millions to the E.I. Co. is complied with by the House of Commons.

The Rāja of Alwār seizes the forts of Dhobī and Sikrāwa, refusing to restore them till compelled by an armed force.

July 16: An engagement made between the E.I. Co. and the Rāja of Machāri or Alwār, defining the treaty of Nov. 14, 1803.

July-Aug. Mr Elphinstone, in the name of the British Government and on behalf of the Peshwā, enters into agreements with the Southern Marātha *jagīrdārs* of the Patwardhan family for their protection. This is commonly called "The Agreement of Pandharpur."

Aug. 12: Sir Evan Nepean, Bart., landed at Bombay as Governor, till Nov. 1, 1819.

Sept. Capt. Canning, Resident at Rangūn, escapes from the attempted arrest by the King of Burma.

Oct. 1: The Rāja of Kolhāpur signs a treaty by which, for the cession of certain forts, he is guaranteed against the aggression of foreign powers. He engages to abstain from hostilities with other states, and to refer all disputes with external powers to the arbitration of the Company's Government.

Oct. 3: Phond Sāwant of Sāwantwādi concludes an agreement with the Company for the suppression of piracy. He cedes Vingorla, and the battery of Gunaramo Tembe, and promises to cede Rārī and Nivti should further piracies be committed. All vessels leaving Nivti to be liable to search by the British authorities.

Oct. The Pendhārīs having entered Rewā with the Rāja's connivance, and penetrated to Mirzapur, Jaysingh Dev of Rewā agrees to a treaty with the British Government, by which, in return

A.D.

1812 for recognition of his rank and title, he will refer all disputes with neighbouring states to British arbitration.

The chiefs of Mahi Kānta bind themselves to pay the Gaikwād's dues on the average of what had been collected during the last ten years.

The Rāwal of Bānswāra offers to become tributary to the British Government in return for aid in expelling the armies of Sindia and Holkar, but no arrangement was made till 1818.

Firuz Khān, Diwān of Pāhlanpur, murdered by a faction of Sindh Jamadārs, who seize his young son, Fath Khān, and place Shamsher Khān, his uncle, in power. Through the Indian Government Fath Khān was recognised as heir, Dec. 1813.

Dec. Bikramajit Mahendar of Urchha concludes a treaty for aid against the Pendhārīs.

1813 The Peshwā forms a brigade of infantry officered by British soldiers, with Capt. John Ford as commandant.

Kusruji Modhi, being required to resign his post at the residency, or his governorship of the Marātha Karnātak, he gives up the latter, and is replaced by Trimbakjī Denglia. Kusruji has afterwards to leave Poona, but dies of poison.

June 2: Jaysingh Dev, Rāja of Rewā, having attempted to starve out a military force posted n his state, is about to be attacked by an expedition sent to compel fulfilment of the terms of treaty of 1812; he enters on a new treaty confirming the previous stipulations, and engaging to pay the expenses of military operations. He also abdicates in favour of his son, Bishnāth Singh.

Durgābāī, regent at Sāwantwādi, seizes Bharatgarh and Narsinhgarh, two forts under British protection. Sāwantwādi is declared to be in a state of war, and internal anarchy prevails.

June 4: The Governor-General in a letter to the Rāja of Nepāl demands redress for depredations of the Nepalese.

July 21: By Act of Parliament (53 Geo. III., c. 155), the Company's privileges are renewed for twenty years. Territorial and commercial affairs are now distinct, and accounts are rendered separately. The trade of India is now opened to all British subjects, that to China alone remaining exclusively in the

A.D.

1813 Company's hands. The King is empowered to create a Bishop of India and an Archdeacon for each Presidency, to be paid by the Company.

EARL OF MOIRA (MARQUIS OF HASTINGS).

1813 Oct. 4: The Earl of Moira succeeds Lord Minto as Governor-General, till Jan. 9, 1823.

Panchāyats are established for administration of justice to natives.

Oct. Bhopāl besieged by Rāghuji Bhonsla's general, Jaggu Bāpu, and defended by Vazīr Muhammad.

1814 By a third treaty with the Rāja of Rewā, the British renounce the right of interference with that state.

May: The siege of Bhopāl raised; the Marāthās canton at Sārangpur.

May 21: Sir George Barlow recalled from the Madras command,—died, Dec. 18, 1846.

May 29: The Gurkhas attack and overpower a force of police at Bhotwāl, and murder the Dārogha in cold blood. The Rāja of Nepāl disclaims responsibility, but writes threatening letters. Lord Moira demands an apology, which is refused.

July 11: Sa'ādat 'Alī, Nawāb Vazīr of Audh, dies. His son succeeds, with the title of Ghāzi-ud-dīn Haidar. The long-deferred reforms are now consummated. *Zilas* and *mahāls*, with deputy collectors, are assigned to the districts; these measures prove unpopular with the natives, and intriguing courtiers plan Major Baillie's removal from Council. Oct., the Governor-General proceeds to Audh, and in an interview with the Nawāb, some modifications in the revenue collections are arranged for.

Gangādhar Shāstri sent to Poona to adjust the claims of the Peshwā and those of the Gaikwād as to Ahmadābād. The Baroda minister, Sitarām Rāvji, prejudices the Peshwā against him, and an audience is refused. The Shāstri determines to leave the question to the arbitration of the British.

A party of merchants from British territory in Ceylon seized as spies by the King of Kandy and sent back mutilated. War is declared.

A.D.

1814 The Inquisition at Goa abolished, and the palace of the "Santa Officio" demolished.

Lakshmī Rānī, regent at Travankor, dies. Her sister, Pārvatī, is regent for the infant son of Lakshmī.

Nov. 1: War declared against Nepāl. Four divisions for service against the Gurkhas are mobilised under Major-General Ochterlony, General Sir Rollo Gillespie, Major-General John Sullivan Wood, and Lieut.-Col. Marley. Oct. 31: Gillespie is killed in an attack upon Nalapāni or Kalanga Fort, near Dehrā Dūn. Balbhadara Singh withstands two assaults—the second on Nov. 24; it was then bombarded, and the commandant with seventy men escapes. Dec. 1: Major Ludlow pursues and defeats the fugitives, and the fort is demolished. Dec. 20: Col. Marley and General Martindell occupy Nāhan, and proceed against Fort Jaitak, but the columns are overpowered in detail.

Dec. 6: General Ochterlony occupies Forts Nalagarh and Tārāgarh. Amar Singh, with a strong force, retires on Rāmgarh; he is repulsed in a desperate attack at Dibu, Dec. 28.

The Dutch cede their rights in Cochin to the British.

1815 Jan. 1: Capt. Blackney's and Capt. Sibley's detachments in the Tarai are cut up by the Gurkhas at Samanpur and Parsa respectively. Many men desert, several, with officers, are killed. Jan. 3: Major-General Sullivan Wood is beaten back at Jitgarh, near Bhotwāl, and remains on the defensive till May, when he withdraws his division into cantonments at Gorakhpur.

Jan. 31: General Marley, from near Lautan in the Tarai, retires westwards to protect Betiya.

Feb. 15: With the Jaypur irregulars, Col. William Linnæus Gardner enters Nepāl, beats back the Gurkhas in Kamāon, and concentrates at Almora, where Col. Nicholls with a column joins him, April 8.

Feb. 20: A surveying party attacked, manœuvres the Gurkhas towards their camp, when Col. Dick attacks them, kills their leader and a fourth of his men, and strikes terror into the Nepalese. They abandon the Tarai.

March 2: Vikrama Singh, King of Ceylon, is deposed for inhumanity: the island becomes a dependency of the British Crown, Sir Robert Brownrigg being first Governor.

A.D.

1815 March 20: General Martindell bombards and blockades Jaitak, in Nepāl, which capitulates in May.

April 14: General Ochterlony detaches a division for the occupation of Raila, on the Malaun ridge. April 15: Deothal fort is carried and occupied. 16th: the Gurkhas attack, but are driven from Deothal by a bayonet charge, in which 500, including their commander, Bakht Singh, are killed.

April 22: Hasti Dal, from Almora, routed by Major Paton and slain; 25th, a general attack is made on Almora stockades by Col. Gardner; 26th, the fort is surrendered, and, 27th, with Kamāon and Garhwāl, permanently annexed to the British territories.

May 8: Malaun invested by General Ochterlony, when most of the garrison gave themselves up to the British. May 10: the guns opened and Amar Singh, the chief, capitulates, and engages to surrender the Gurkha conquests west of the Jamnā. Most of the Gurkha troops take service with the British. The Khātmāndu Darbār sends commissioners to treat for peace: they agree to relinquish claims on the hill Rājas, the restoration of territory to the Sikim Rāja, and to accept a resident, but the cession of the Tarai is refused. Negotiations protracted, but treaty agreed to, Dec. 2. A Gurkha mission is despatched to the Chinese Government, asking a Chinese force. Next year, preparations for war are resumed.

Bakhtāwar Singh of Alwar dies. The succession is disputed between Bani Singh, his nephew and heir, and Balwant Singh, an illegitimate son. A compromise is effected, the former becoming titular sovereign, the latter exercising the power of the state.

July 14: Gangādhar Shāstri, the Baroda envoy at Poona, treacherously murdered by Trimbakji Denglia's hired assassins at Pandharpur. Sept. 25: The Peshwā is compelled to hand over the instigator, who is imprisoned at Thāna, but escapes, Sept. 12, 1816.

Sir William Grant, Commander-in-Chief in Java.

Oct. A band of Pendhāri freebooters carries on successful warfare against the Nizām and the British.

1816 Jan. 16: A definitive treaty concluded with the Rāo of Kachh, who agrees to pay an indemnity for recent inroads from Wāghar, and to observe the treaty of 1809. June 18: By a supplementary

A.D.

1816 treaty the Government remits all military expenses incurred in the settlement of the country, and the annual amount the Rāo had engaged to pay. The chiefs of the Okhāmandal district are brought under British authority, and their practice of piracy suppressed. May: Col. East's force returns to cantonments.

Feb. Hostilities resumed with the Gūrkhas. Sir D. Ochterlony, with four brigades supported by two columns under Nicholls and Wood, enters the hill country. Feb. 27: The Gūrkhas are driven to flight. Makwānpur fort surrenders, and, March 3: peace is concluded at Segaulī, Mr E. Gardner being appointed first Resident.

March 17: Wazīr Muhammad, Nawāb of Bhopāl, dies. His son, Nazar Muhammad Khān, succeeds him.

March 22: Rāghoji Bhonsla II. of Berār dies. His son, Parsarām, called Bālā Sāhib, succeeds, but becoming imbecile, is superseded and strangled by his cousin, Mūdojī or Apā Sāhib. May 27: Apā Sāhib admitted to the defensive alliance with the British Government.

April 16: The inhabitants of Barelly show armed resistance to the imposition of a municipal tax, and thousands gather under the Mufti, Muhammad 'Iwaz. April 21: The rebels would listen to no advice, murdered the judge's son, and had to be quelled by troops under Major Richards and Capt. Cunningham.

April: The Rāja of Jaypur solicits the protection of the Government against Amīr Khān, but on the latter's withdrawal from Jaypur, breaks off negotiations.

May 1: Treaty between the Vazīr of Audh and the E.I. Company.

June 7: Bishop Middleton, first Anglican prelate in India, dedicates the cathedral in Bombay to the memory of St Thomas.

Sept. 12: Trimbakjī Denglia escapes from Thāna fort: Bājirāv connives at his liberty, and supplies him with money to raise contingents. Sindia, Holkar, Amīr Khān, and the Pendhārīs are incited to rise against the English.

Sept. 16: A French expedition arrives at Pondicheri to enter on possession of their Indian settlements of which Pondicheri and Chandranagar are delivered Dec. 4.

A.D.

1816 Nov. 29: Dom Diogo de Sousa, Conde de Rio Pardo, succeeds Bernardo José de Lorena as Captain-General at Goa.

Severe plague of small-pox prevails in Nepāl.

Nov. 20: Rāja Gīrvānyuddha Vikrama Sāh of Nepāl dies. His son, Rājendra Vikrama Sāh, succeeds at the age of three, with Bhīmavēna Thāpā as regent.

Fath Khān of Pāhlanpur claims the interference of the British Government against the oppression of his uncle, Shamsher Khān. After a feeble defence, Pāhlanpur is taken from Shamsher Khān, and the authority of Fath Khān is confirmed.

David Hare, a watchmaker of Calcutta, in conjunction with Rāmmohan Roy, founds a Hindu College—opened Jan. 20, 1817.

Dec. The Pendhārīs invade the Northern Sarkārs, and sack Kimedi and many villages.

Sayyid Ahmad of Rāī Barelī, a freebooter, born 1786, begins to study theology at Dehli. Afterwards he goes to Makka, from which he is expelled as a Wahhābī sectary, and returns to India preaching his doctrines.

1817 Jan. 13: Treaty signed by the Rānā of Udaypur, placing his state under the protection of the British.

Jan. 15: Major Macdowall routs a band of Pendhārīs near Haidarābād. Jan. 24: The bands in Orissa are pursued and routed at Sohāgpur by Capt. Caulfield and again by Major Clarke's cavalry.

Jan. 14: After the conclusion of peace between Britain and France, Kārikāl is retransferred to the French:—Feb. 23: Mahē, and April 12: Yanāon. The conditions of restoration are regulated by a convention between the Governments of England and France, dated March 15, 1815.

Jan. 24: Capt. Caulfield, between Sohāgpur and Mandalar, attacks and disperses the Pendhārīs, who had previously left Katak.

Feb. 1: Parsarām Bhonsla of Berār found strangled in his bed. Apā Sāhib, the acting Rāja, now recognised as ruler.

Feb. 10: Treaty between the Sikkim Rāja and the E.I. Co.

Feb. 23: The Jāt chiefs of Hāthras and Mursan in Aligarh district rebel. Major-General Dyson storms Hāthras and bombards

20

A.D.

1817 the fort. March: The chief, Dāya Rām, with a few followers in armour, escape, but he is afterwards captured.

March: The Pāīks of Gūmsūr revolt under Jagabandhu, formerly a state official, march on Khurdhā, whither a detachment under Lieut. Prideaux is sent; Mr Impey, the magistrate, with a detachment, obliged to retire to Katak. April: Lieut. Faris, leading his men to Gangpara, is shot dead. Jagannāth Pūrī occupied by the rebels.

April 9: Capt. Le Fevre marches to Khurdhā, and martial law is proclaimed. May: Special commissioners inquire into the causes of the revolt, and the country is gradually settled.

April: Lieut. Dacre and a small escort murdered by Pendhārīs, who are pursued by Major Smith and routed at Pathri in Kāndesh, April 17.

May: Bājirāo informed that he must regard himself in future as a feudatory of the Company, offer a reward for Trimbakji's apprehension, resign all rights in Sāgar and Bundelkhand, abandon the reception of agents from other Marātha states, and cede Ahmadnagar and territory worth twenty-four lākhs a year. June 13: Treaty of Poona to this effect, dissolving the Marātha confederacy, signed by the Peshwā at Poona.

Shāh Khalīl-ullāh, Imām or chief of the Shī'ah Isma'īlis, is killed in a tumult at Yezd. Fath 'Alī Shāh of Persia confers on his son, Husain Husainī, Āghā Khān, the government of Kūm and Mehelati, and gives him one of his daughters to wife.

Sept. 14: The British forces muster for the suppression of the Pendhārīs, the Hindustan army in three, the Dekhan army, under Sir Thomas Hislop, in five divisions. Oct. 16: The Marquis of Hastings, as Commander-in-Chief, joins the Bengal army at Cawnpur.

Oct. 14: Mr Elphinstone interviews the Peshwā, whose attitude towards the British, while most of the British troops are absent, becomes more hostile. Oct. 28: The Marātha troops gathered in readiness to attack before the arrival of the European forces at Poona.

Nov. 1: The English brigade, with reinforcements under General Burr, removed to Kirki (Khadkī). Nov. 5: After an insolent message, the Peshwā's army of 10,000 cavalry and as many infantry with a great train of ordnance move out on Kirki.

A.D.

1817 The attack is bravely repulsed by Burr and Forde, with less than 3,000 infantry, totally defeating the Marāthās, and the Peshwā, who had been a spectator, (16th) flees from Poona. A light battalion with 1,000 auxiliary horse from General Smith joins the British camp.

Nov. 5: Daulatrāv Sindia having been proved treacherous, is bound by treaty to dispose his troops in accordance with the Governor's demand, to give up Asīrgarh and Hindia forts as security, to surrender for three years the tribute of the Rājput states.

Nov. 6: Marātha horsemen attack and rob Cornets Hunter and Morrison, and send them prisoners to the Konkan. Capt. Vaughan and his brother are robbed and seized at Wargāon, taken to Fathegāon and hanged. Lieut. Ennis and a small escort are attacked, and Ennis killed by Trimbak's men.

Nov. 6: The Governor-General concludes a treaty with Fath Singh, regent for Ānandrāv Gaikwād of Baroda, arranging an increase of the subsidiary force, the cession of the Gaikwād's rights on the Gujarāt territory of the Peshwā, with Ahmadābād, and the co-operation of the British and Baroda troops in time of war.

Nov. Great outbreak of cholera in the camp of the "Grand Army." In one week 764 soldiers and 8,000 followers perish.

Nov. 10: Amīr Khān of Tonk confirmed by treaty in all the districts bestowed on him by Holkar, on condition of his disbanding his army.

Nov. 12: Engagement made between the Rāja of Samthar and the British Government.

Nov. 15: Karauli state taken under the protection of the Company's Government; no tribute is exacted, but the Rāja, Herbakhsh Pāl, undertakes to furnish troops according to his means.

Nov. 17: Treaty between the Sūbhadār of Jhānsi and the British Government.

Nov. By the movements of the three divisions of the Madras army, the Pendhārīs are driven north and west.

Nov. 24: Apā Sāhib of Nāgpur revolts in support of the Peshwā, and with a force of about 20,000 attacks Mr Jenkins, the Resident, at Sitābaldi. Nov. 26: A severe action ensues all

A.D.

1817 night, in which the Nāgpur forces are defeated by about 1,300 men under Col. Scott. Reinforcements arrive soon after. Dec. 16: Apā Sāhib refuses submission till Dec. 24, when confronted by the whole army and a battle fought in which his guns and camp are captured. The Arabs defend themselves in the palace, but finally capitulate.

Dec 14: General Marshall at Nimghāt, in Kotā, defeats the Pendhārī cavalry with loss, as they cover the retreat of their infantry. Dec. 17: The band under Karīm Khān abandon their baggage and families at Kalana.

Dec. The Pendhārī armies of Chitu and Wāsil Muhammad enter Holkar's territories. Dec. 20: The war party put the prime minister, Ganpatrāv, under arrest, and behead Tulsībāī, the regent, to prevent a coalition with the British. Dec. 20: General Hardyman defeats a Marātha force at Jabalpur.

Dec. 21: The Indor army, with seventy guns, is attacked by the divisions under Sir John Malcolm and Sir Thomas Hislop at Mehidpur on the Siprā, and is defeated with great loss; young Holkar is carried off from the field to Alot. The leader, Raushan Beg, is severely wounded.

Dec. 26: Treaty concluded by Mr Metcalfe for the E.I. Co. with Zālim Singh, Rāja Rānā, for Umed Singh Mahārāja of Kotā, by which the Kotā state is taken under British protection; by a supplementary article the administration is vested in Zālim Singh and his descendants.

1818 Jan. 1: Capt. Staunton with one battalion, on his way to reinforce Col. Burr at Poona, encounters at Korigāon the whole of the Peshwā's forces—20,000 horse and 8,000 foot. Both parties enter the village, and a desperate all-day defence follows. Jan. 2: Hearing that General Smith was approaching, the Peshwā flees south.

Jan. 2: Lord Hastings instructs Mr Jenkins to place a grandson of Parsarām Bhonsla on the throne at Nāgpur, but conforms to terms of a treaty arranged by Mr Jenkins. Apā Sāhib is recognised, but his government is to be effectually controlled. Jan. 6: Apā Sāhib signs a treaty ceding lands in lieu of the subsidy and contingent, and engaging to govern the country in accordance with the advice of the Resident.

A.D.

1818 Jan. 6: Jodhpur is taken under British protection, the tribute to Sindia made payable to the Company's Government, and the Mahārāja engages to furnish 1,500 horse for general service when required.

Jan. 6: The treaty of Mandasor concluded between Sir John Malcolm and Tāntia Jog, Holkar's minister; it deprives Holkar of much territory, and makes him dependent on the British Government. Jan. 17: The terms of the treaty ratified.

Jan. 10: A body of Marāthās, under Raushan Beg, escaping from the field at Mehidpur, is defeated at Rāmpūra by General Browne's division.

Jan. 13: By a treaty with Bhīm Singh, the E.I. Co. agree to protect Udaypur, and to help in restoring lost territory where practicable; the Mahārānā acknowledging British supremacy, promising to refer disputes, and assigning to the supreme Government a quarter of his revenues for five years.

Jan. Nāmdār Khān, nephew of Karīm Khān, with 15,000 men is surprised and defeated at Kotri; attempts a junction with the other two Mālwa bands, but, Feb. 3: gives himself up to Col. Adams with eighty-seven followers. Feb. 15: Karīm Khān surrenders himself to Sir John Malcolm; and other Pendhārī leaders soon follow.

Jan. 17: General Pritzler overtakes Bājirāv in the Salpi Ghāt, dispersing three divisions. The Peshwā escapes with the fourth.

Jan. 25: The camp of Jaswantrāv Bhāu, who had harboured Chitu, the Pendhārī leader, is beaten in, and his town of Jāwad captured. Further reduction of forts completes the subjugation of the district.

Feb. 10: A treaty is concluded between the supreme Government and Bishan Singh of Būndi, whose state is thus freed from the rapacity of the Marāthās.

Feb. 10: Sātāra surrenders to a large force under General Smith, and next day a proclamation is issued annexing all the Peshwā's territory to the Company's, except a tract to be reserved for the restored Rāja of Sātāra. Land and religious rights to be respected, provided the claims of Bājirāv be renounced.

Feb. 15: Lord Hastings, finding his plans nearly effected, commenced his march from Rājputana.

A.D.

1818 Feb. 20: The Peshwā's forces defeated at Āshte by General Smith, the Peshwā again escaping by the devotion of Bāpu Gokhle, who is killed. The captive Rāja of Sātāra is rescued by the British troops.

Feb. 26: The Nawāb of Bhopāl requited by treaty for services rendered during the Pendhārī war.

Feb. 27: Thālner (Kāndesh) fort, held by the Killedār, resists, and is stormed by Sir Thomas Hislop, but the Arab garrison cut down the first officers who enter, whereon the British troops put the garrison of 300 Arabs to the sword, and the Killedār is hanged.

March 5: Forces concentrated in Bundelkhand by General Marshall, in consequence of Apā Sāhib's perfidy. March 11: Sāgar and Dhāmonī reduced, and, April 26: Mandala taken by storm.

March 9: Treaty between the Rāja of Bikanīr and the E.I. Company.

March 15: Apā Sāhib arrested by Mr Jenkins for having incited the Gonds to revolt, sending orders to the Killedārs to resist the surrender of the ceded forts, and intriguing with Bājirāv.

March 22: Sir T. Raffles arrives at Benkulen as Lieut.-Governor, and incurs the disfavour of the Dutch Government by interference with the native tribes. Disputes are settled by a treaty with the Bengal Government.

March 26: Kishnagarh state is taken under British protection.

April 2: Treaty between the Rāja of Jaypur and the E.I. Company.

April 6: Wāsota fort, in the Sātāra district, bombarded till April 7, when it capitulates. Cornets Hunter and Morrison, prisoners of war, are rescued, also the wives, families, and jewels of the Sātāra Rāja and his brothers.

April 11: Pratāp Singh, son of Sāhū Abba Sāheb, is placed on the throne as Rāja of Sātāra by Mr Elphinstone. Two proclamations issued: one announcing the Rāja's connection with the British Government, and one vesting the administration of the country in Mr James Cunningham Grant Duff.

April 18: Bājirāv, hemmed in on the Wardā between General

A.D.

1818 Doveton and Col. Adams, retires to Seonī, where many of his followers fall by Col. Adams's division. May 9: Chāndā, invested by Col. Adams, is stormed and carried on the 20th. The ex-Peshwā flees north with about 8,000 men, and entrenches at Asīrgarh, whence he makes overtures for peace, and after protracted negotiations, surrenders on June 3, resigning all claims to government at Poona, and receiving a pension of eight lākhs per annum, with a residence at Bithūr, near Cawnpur.

May 7: Raigarh fort surrendered by Bājirāv's wife.

May 13: Āpā Sāhib, by bribes, escapes from custody and flees to the Gonds, who protect him. With Chītu, the Pendhārī leader, he rallies the disbanded troops, and, July 20: defeats a body of troops under Capt. Sparkes.

May: All the ex-Peshwā's dominions except Kāndesh and the insurgents near Sātāra now reduced. June 13: The Arab garrison at Māligāon surrenders after a month's siege, and is shipped to Arabia.

The chiefs of Sirohi call to power Rāv Shiv Singhji and depose Udaybhanji, his brother, for tyranny and oppression. He died in confinement in 1847.

June: Fath Singh of Gujarāt dies. Sayāji Rāv, his brother, is raised to the office of *diwān*.

Fath Khān deposed from his vazīrship of Kābul and blinded by Kāmrān Mīrza.

July 31: The Rāja of Datiyā enters into treaty with the E.I. Company.

Sept. 16 and Dec. 25: Bānswāra taken under British protection.

Oct. 5: Pratāpgarh taken under British protection.

Nov. 21: A modification of the treaty of 1815 with Kandy is concluded for the better understanding between the supreme Government and the natives.

Jagat Singh of Jaypur dies. Rānā Mohan, son of Manohar Singh of Narwār, succeeds.

Nov. Bishop Middleton assumes charge of the new diocese of Calcutta.

Dec. 11 and 12: Treaties formed with Dongarpur, Jaisalmir, and Dewās, which are taken under protection by the British Government.

A.D.

1818 1818-1819: H. 1234: Munshī Sadāsukh Dehlawī writes the *Muntakhabu-t Tawārīkh.*

1819 Jan. 10: Dhār taken under British protection; and Dec. 18, 1821, by a second treaty.

Jan. A settlement made at Singapur by Sir Stamford Raffles.

Jan. 31: Fort Newa, in the Nizām's territory, reduced by Major Pitman, and the Arab garrison put to death.

Feb. 1: The French factory at Calicut with the ground formerly belonging to it is delivered to their chief of Mahē.

Feb. 4: Nivti fort in the Konkan surrendered to Sir William G. Keir. Feb. 13: Rāiri fort taken by storm.

Feb. 17: A treaty signed, by which Sāwantwādi is brought under British protection, in return for the cession of the coast-line from Kārli to the Portuguese territory. Feb. 17, 1820: confirmed.

March 6: Sir George Cooper, Recorder at Bombay, till 1820.

March 24: Sir William Kier-Grant marches on Bhuj against Bhārmalji Rāo, of Kachh, who had murdered the Prince Lāduba. March 26: Bhuj is carried by escalade. The Rāo is deposed in favour of Rāo Daisal II., his infant son, a regency being formed of Jhāreja chiefs under the superintendence of the British Resident. Oct. 13: A treaty to this effect is ratified.

April 9: Asīrgarh fort capitulates to General Doveton and Sir John Malcolm, after a siege of twenty days. Apā Sāhib, supposed to be within, is found to have escaped. Chitu Pendhārī in his escape is killed by a tiger.

April 22: A treaty of friendship concluded by Sir T. Raffles with Jauhar Shāh of Achīn.

April 25: Jay Singh III., posthumous son of Jagat Singh II. of Jaypur, born. Rānā Mohan Singh is deposed, and the infant proclaimed, and rules till 1835. Jaypur being a scene of corruption and misgovernment, a resident is appointed.

April 25: St Andrew's Presbyterian Church, Bombay, opened by Rev. James Clow, the chaplain.

May: Bodoahprā, King of Burma, dies. His grandson, Sagaing Meng, succeeds, known by the name of Hpagyidoa. He puts to death his uncles, the Governors of Prom and Taungu.

May 14: Kopāldurg taken.

A.D.

1819 Oct.: A force sent to Manipur subdues the country and leaves a garrison.

Aug. 2: 'Azīm-ud-daula, Nawāb of the Karnātak, dies. His son, 'Azīm Jāh, installed 3rd Feb. following.

Aug.: Cholera prevalent in Bombay, and for nearly a year after.

Sept. 25: Pratāp Singh, Rāja of Sātāra, agrees to hold his territory in subordinate co-operation to the British Government, the administration to be vested in the resident till 1822.

Ranjīt Singh conquers Kashmīr from Dost Muhammad.

Oct. 2: Ānandrāv Gaikwād of Baroda dies. Sayājirāv succeeds. The Gaikwād being unable to adjust the rival claims of Nahr Singh and Pratāp Singh to the government of Rājpipla, the Baroda Resident undertakes the investigation, which results in the establishment of Nahr Singh's claim.

Oct. 13: Treaty between the Rāja of Kachh and the E.I. Company. Supplemented May 21, 1822.

Oct. 30: An expedition sails from Bombay to the Persian Gulf. Dec. 9: Took the fort at Rās el-Khima, the refuge of the Joapmī pirates; and about 20th the fort and town of Zaya.

Nov. 1: Hon. Mountstuart Elphinstone takes office as Governor of Bombay, and Mr Chaplin succeeds as Commissioner for the conquered territory of the Peshwā.

1820 Jan. 8: Treaty between the Arab tribes on the Persian Gulf and the British Government.

Nazar Muhammad of Bhopāl accidentally shot by his brother-in-law, a child of eight. His widow, Qudsiā Begam, appointed regent for her nephew, Munīr Muhammad Khān, who is betrothed to the Nawāb's daughter, Sikandar Begam.

Feb. 3: 'Azim Jāh installed as Nawāb of the Karnātak,—died 1825.

Feb. Dr John Scudder, American missionary, arrives in Ceylon, where he labours for sixteen years.

March 16: An engagement mediated between Sāwantwādi and Kolhāpur darbārs, regulating the amount of revenue to be paid to the fort of Rāngna from the district of Māngāon: another fixing the amount payable to the fort of Manohargarh from the

A.D.

1820 district of Manohar. In 1822 these revenue assignments were commuted for a money payment.

The Hon. Mountstuart Elphinstone at Baroda confers with Sayājī, who agrees that all foreign affairs remain under the management of the British Government, and that internal administration be unrestrained, provided the state's financial engagements are carried out.

April 22: Rāo Sāhib Mustafa Maherban, Pant Sachiv confirmed in his jagīr. Similar grants are made to the Pratinidhi and Renukābāī Daphle of Jath, the Deshmukh of Phaltan, Shaikh Mira Wākar; and on July 3 the Company restores to Fath Singh Bhonsla, Rāja of Akalkot, the jagīrs which came into their possession with Sātāra.

May: An arrangement is made between the Resident at Haidarābād and the banking house of Palmer & Co. for the consolidation of extensive loans to the Nizām, at a reduced rate; a new loan of sixty lākhs is sanctioned by Government, but only fifty-two lākhs were to be credited to the state. Oct. The Court of Directors disapprove of the arrangement, pronouncing transactions with native princes illegal.

June 10: Sir Thomas Munro, Governor of Madras, in succession to the Right Hon. Hugh Elliot, till 1827.

Sept. 16: In consequence of revolutions in Portugal, some revolutionaries at Goa seize and depose the viceroy, and elect a "Junta," which holds office till Dec. 3rd, 1821.

Oct. 19: Sir William David Evans, Recorder of Bombay, dies Dec. 5, 1821.

Umed Singh, Rāja of Kotā, dies. His son, Kishor Singh, attempts to wrest the administrative power from Zālim Singh, the hereditary minister, is defeated by a British force, and acknowledges the minister's rights.

Nov. 9: A further treaty concluded between the British Government and the Amīrs of Sindh with a view to the exclusion of Europeans and Americans from their dominions.

Nov. 24: Troops under Lieut.-Col. Stanhope land at Dwāraka to reduce the insurgent Wāghars of Okhāmandal. The city is carried by escalade, and the district reduced to obedience.

Nov. The British resolve to take Kachār under protection

A.D.

1820 and to support Govind Chandra against the incursions of the Burmese.

Dec. 15: Bishop's College founded at Calcutta by Bishop Middleton.

Chikka Vira Rājendra Rāja succeeds Lingarāja in Kūrg. His atrocities exceed even those of his predecessors.

Dec. Mr Metcalfe, appointed Resident at Haidarābād, proceeds to inquire into the revenue question, especially with reference to the dealings of Messrs Palmer & Co.

Dec. Mahārāo Kishor Singh leaves Kotā and calls his chiefs to assist in expelling Zālim Singh the Rāj Rānā.

A Roman Catholic bishopric is established at Agra.

1821 Jan. 15: Treaty of peace and friendship concluded between the British and the Imām of Senna.

March: The capital of the Beni-Bu 'Alī tribe (Persian Gulf) taken by Col. Lionel Smith.

Mr Metcalfe, in representing the abuses in the Haidarābād revenue department, shows the complicity of Sir W. Rumbold, and is reprimanded, but subsequently receives an apology. His advice is followed: the debt to Palmer & Co. is paid off: censures from England cause Hastings to send in his resignation.

May 14: Bishan Singh of Būndī dies: his eldest son, Rām Singh, succeeds.

July 2: Āba Sāhib of Kolhāpur murdered by a Mohite chief in the palace. His infant son succeeds under a regency but dies soon after, and Shāhaji, his uncle, succeeds.

Aug. 6: 'Alī Jāh, Nawāb of Bengal, dies. His brother, Wāla Jāh, succeeds.

Sept. 16: Revolution at Goa: the Conde de Rio Pardo is deposed and a junta appointed in his place.

Sept. 23: Nāsir-ud dīn, Nawāb of Surat, dies. His son, Mīr Āfzal-ud dīn, succeeds, till 1842.

Sept. 30: Kishor Singh of Kotā, defeated at Mangrūl, and his brother killed. He flees to Nāthdwāra.

Nov. A mission leaves Bengal for Siam to secure unrestricted trade. This mission proves unsuccessful.

A.D.

1821 Nov. A general rising in Merwāra occurs. The police are massacred. A force subjugates the country in a three months' campaign. Col. Henry Hall, of the 16th Bengal N.I., is appointed first political agent.

Nov. 15: Nahr Singh of Rājpīpla being blind and incapacitated for rule, his eldest son, Verisāl, is invested with the government. The E.I. Company undertakes to manage the state, now almost bankrupt, till Verisāl's majority in 1837, thereafter exercising supervision till 1850.

Nov. 25: Dom Manoel de Camara arrives at Goa, and on Dec. 3, when the Junta is deposed, he assumes office, but is compelled to admit four colleagues in the government.

Dec. 31: Kishor Singh is restored to Kotā, with an annual allowance, but recognises the continued administration of Zālim Singh.

Carey & Marshman, of Serampur, issue from their press the first vernacular newspaper, the *Samāchār Darpan.*

Sayyid Ahmad of Rāī Barelī arrives at Calcutta with a retinue of disciples and gains many converts to his Wahhābī creed.

1822 Khem Sāwant established in his government; on his majority he proves incapable and unfit for rule.

Āba Sāhib's brother, Shāhaji, known as the Bāwa Sāhib of Kolhāpur, proves a cruel and profligate ruler.

March: Two French officers, Col. Allard and General Ventura, are taken into the army of Ranjīt Singh. Other accessions increase the efficiency of his army.

June 22: The district of Anjār restored to Kachh by treaty, in consideration of an annual payment of 88,000 rupees.

July 8: Dr T. Fanshawe Middleton, first Bishop of Calcutta, dies: Reginald Heber succeeds. He died April 3, 1826.

July: The mission to Siam, under Mr J. Crawford, proving unsuccessful, proceeds to Cochin China. No audience is granted, but permission to trade conceded. Nov. The mission leaves for India.

July: A Burmese agent arrives at Calcutta demanding the surrender of Chandra Kanta and Parindhar Singh, now refugees in Chittagāon. This request is refused, and a demonstration on the frontier made.

A.D.

1822 Aug. 21: The Native Education Society founded at Bombay.

Dec. 12: In acknowledgment of services rendered against the Pendhārīs, the Nizām of Haidarābād receives an increase of territory.

1823 Jan. 1: The Marquis of Hastings resigns office; Mr John Adam, Senior Member of Council, succeeds *ad interim*. He withdraws the license of Mr J. Buckingham, editor of the *Calcutta Journal*, for attacks on Government made in that paper.

Feb. 2: Sir Edward West, Recorder at Bombay: he is made Chief Justice, 1824.

March 4: Randhīr Singh of Bharatpur advances against Peshāwar; checked by the Yūsufzais at Naushahra, he ultimately masters the country up to the Khaibar.

May 8: Supreme Court of Judicature, Bombay, instituted, and takes the place of the Recorder's Court. Sir Edward West is made Chief Justice.

July 12: First steamship built in India, the "Diana," launched at Kidderpur.

WILLIAM PITT, LORD AMHERST.

Aug. 1: Lord Amherst assumes the Government of India till July 4, 1828.

Sept. 11: Sirohi state taken under British protection in return for acknowledgment of supremacy and government in accordance with the advice of the political resident.

Sept. 23: British guard attacked by the Burmese at the island of Shāpuri in the Nāf river. No answer is returned to the repeated demands of the British for redress.

Oct. 7: Randhīr Singh of Bharatpur dies. His brother, Baldev Singh, succeeds.

Oct. 28: Fath 'Alī, Nawāb of Kambay, dies. His brother, Bande 'Alī Khān succeeds, till 1841.

Shamshīr Bahādur of Bānda dies. His brother, Zulfiqār 'Alī succeeds.

Nov. 18: Dom Manoel de Camara, hearing of the return of the King of Portugal to power, dissolves the provisional government, and assumes sole administration.

Ava is once more made the capital of Burma.

A.D.

1823 Dec. Sayyid Ahmad the Wahhābī leaves Bombay for Upper India.

1824 Jan. Mahā Bandula, the Burmese general, leaves the capital with orders to march on Chittagāon. Feb. A British force sent into Asām, and an ultimatum issued. March 5: War with Burma is formally declared. The Burmese now claim Asām, Kachār, and Manipur.

March 10: Rāja Rām Singh of the Jaintia Hill territory puts his country under British protection, and agrees to acknowledge allegiance to the British.

March 17: A treaty, concluded between England and the Netherlands, regulates the policy of the British Government in the Malay Archipelago. Sumatra is ceded to Holland, and Malacca comes under British influence.

March: The Burmese abandon their stockades at Gauhati, in Asām, and General Richards remains there during the rains.

April 12-17: The Bengal army embarks for Rangūn.

May 11: Rangūn occupied by Col. Archibald Campbell with the Bengal and Madras armies.

May 17: The British detachment under Capt. Noton defeated at Rāmu, and driven back on Chittagāon.

May 28: An attack on two Burmese stockades successfully made. June 3: A similar attack at Kyīmyindaing fails. June 10: On again attacking the stockades, the British find Kyīmyindaing deserted.

June: The Burmese army from Manipur reappears on the Kachār frontier. Col. Innes fails to dislodge them from an entrenched post at Talain.

June 15: Zālim Singh, Rāj Rāna of Kotā, dies. His son, Mādhav Singh, succeeds in terms of the treaty of 1821, but is notoriously unfit.

July 3: The Governor of Pegu superseded by the Thunbā Wungyī, who prevents the British from further reconnaisance from Rangūn. July 8: The British storm the stockades with great loss to the Burmese. Aug. 4: The Burmese garrison expelled from Syriam. Sept. Tavoy and Mergui occupied. Nov. Martaban seized and Pegu entered without opposition.

A.D.

1824 Sept. The Desāī of Kittūr dies without issue. Mr Thackeray the agent assumes management, not recognising an adopted son of the widow. Oct. 23: The garrison at Kittūr refuse admittance to the agent, and in a sortie put him and two officers of the escort to death. Troops from Bombay and Madras bombard Kittūr, which is breached. Dec. 4: A truce forestalls the assault.

Oct. 4-7: The British destroy the stockades at Htantabeng. Col. Smith attacks the Burmese position at Kyaikkalo, is defeated and with the leading officers slain. On a further attack the stockades were found deserted.

Oct. Col. Richards drives Būra Rāja from Noagong in Asām.

No monsoon rains in Bombay, and a scarcity of water.

Nov. 1: The 47th Bengal N.I., having refused to march to Arakan, are broken at Barrackpur.

Dec. 1: Mahā Bandula concentrates his enormous force round Rangūn. Dec. 6: The besiegers are defeated by the British troops.

Bāwa Sāhib of Kolhāpur at the head of an army marches against his own feudatories of Kāgal and Ichalkaranji, plundering and devastating. British subjects suffering from his violence, a force is sent against him.

Humāyūn Jāh succeeds Wāla Jāh at Murshidābād, with the same allowance from the Company as his predecessor.

Nov. 24: The Calcutta merchants voted a lākh of rupees to the first person who would navigate a steamship to India.

Dec. 8-10: The Burmese forces occupying Kyīmindaing and Dalla driven out. Dec. 14: Rangūn fired by secret emissaries, but the magazines are untouched. Bandula retires to Danubyu, the greater part of the investing army dispersing.

1825 Jan. 22: The steamship "Enterprise," of 500 tons, launched in England to run to India, and leaves Falmouth for Calcutta, Aug. 25.

Jan. 29: Col. Richards advances on Rangpur, the capital of Upper Asām, which surrenders, completing operations in Asām.

Feb.-March: Col. Shuldham attempts to march through Kachār for Manipur, but abandons the scheme from the difficulty of transport.

A.D.

1825 Feb. 13: Sir A. Campbell moves on Prom with two divisions, one to proceed by land, the other by river under Sir Willoughby Cotton. March 7: The river force is repulsed at Danubyu by Mahā Bandula. March 25: The land army joins the river force at Danubyu and the two divisions invest the fort, which forestalls assault by capitulation on April 2. The general, Mahā Bandula, had been killed. April 4: Prom found deserted, is occupied as cantonments for the army till August.

March 29: Arakan or Myauku assaulted by General Morrison, and taken, April 1.

May: Gambhīr Singh, the expelled Rāja of Manipur, joins Capt. Pemberton, and by June Manipur district is cleared of the Burmese.

May: Sir David Ochterlony sends troops to Bharatpur to defend the claims of the young Rāja Balwant Singh against his usurping cousin, Dūrjan Sāl. Lord Amherst countermands the troops and disapproves of Ochterlony's action. Sir David Ochterlony resigns and retires to Mīrat, where he dies, July 15.

Dūrjan Sāl consolidates his power and assumes the rank and title of Rāja.

Aug. 3: The Twelve Judges decide that the limitation of the rate of interest prescribed by Act of Parliament did not apply to loans made to the subjects of native independent princes by British subjects. This finding materially affects the house of Palmer & Co. of Haidarābād.

Aug. 17: A treaty concluded with the Vazīr of Audh by which the British Government accepts a loan of a *karor* (1,000,000) of rupees at 5 per cent. from the Vazīr, he having proposed to commute part of his ceded territory for a sum of money.

Sept. 6: General Cotton comes in touch with the Burmese at Myēdē. A truce of forty days arranged, and the leaders confer at Ngyaungbengzaik, but the British demands of the cession of Arakan, Tavoy, and Mergui, and payment of two millions sterling, being rejected, hostilities are resumed.

Nov. 15: Col. MacDowall killed in an attack on Wettigan. Three converging columns forced back by the Burmese.

Dec. 2: General Campbell carries the enemy's position near Prome. Dec. 5: The river bank at Myēdē cleared. Dec. 7:

A.D.

1825 Myedē entered unopposed. The Brahman Rāj Guru, formerly a member of the mission to Bengal, sent to King Hpagyīdoa to announce the terms of peace.

The monsoon rains were almost a total failure at Bombay, and universal sickness prevailed.

Nov. 25: Sir Charles Metcalfe, now Resident at Dehli, reports on the treachery of Dūrjan Sāl of Bharatpur, who is ordered to leave the country on a provision. Dec. 5: On his refusal, an army under Lord Combermere marches on Bharatpur. Dec. 23: The siege-works and mining operations are begun.

Major Outram pacifies the Bhils in Kandesh, and from them forms the nucleus of a native corps.

Dec. 30: A treaty concluded with the Rāja of Kolhāpur by which he engages not to oppress certain jāgīrdārs, to reduce his army to the peace establishment, and not to harbour rebels.

1826 Jan. 3: The Burmese and British deputies at Malwūn agree to a treaty, and a truce for fifteen days agreed upon to allow of its ratification by the king.

Jan. 17: A treaty concluded through Capt. Henry Burney with the King of Siam to prevent his coalition with the Burmese against the British. A commercial treaty also concluded, but abrogated, its sixth article placing British subjects under Siamese law.

Jan. 18: Bharatpur attacked, mined and stormed by the Bengal army under Lord Combermere, and taken with heavy loss on both sides. Dūrjan Sāl, the usurper, imprisoned. Jan. 20: the young Rāja placed on the masnad.

Jan. 19: After fifteen days' truce, hostilities are resumed against the Burmese. Malwūn is carried, the Burmese having fled. Great stores of grain and powder obtained, also the treaty draft, which had not been forwarded to the king.

Jan. 25: The British on their march north meet Dr Price, an American missionary, a prisoner of war, sent under escort to learn the ultimatum, which is that the army would await the ratified treaty at Pugān.

Feb. 8: General Campbell defeats Nē Weng Bureng's new levies at Pugān. Feb. 24: The king, Hpagyīdoa, sends Messrs Price and Judson with the senior Wungyī and an Atwenwun,

A.D.

1826 with a fourth of the million sterling demanded, and signs the treaty of Yandabo, by which Asām, Arakan, and the Tenaserim coast, including Martaban province east of the Salwīn river, are ceded to the British, and the independence of Kachār, Jaintia, and Manipur guaranteed, with one million sterling indemnity.

Sawai Bani Singh of Alwar is required by the Supreme Government to make provision for his cousin, Balwant Singh, in territory and stipend.

The Sardār of Kapurthala, in view of Ranjīt Singh's aggressions, appeals for and receives British protection.

April 3: Bishop Heber dies at Trichinapoli. Rev. John Thomas James appointed to succeed to the see of Calcutta.

July 7: A *sanad* granted to Sivarāv Ghorpade conferring on him the *jāgīr* of Sandūr.

Nov. 3: A commercial treaty signed at Ava by John Crawford and two Atwenwuns.

Nov. Lord Amherst receives the petty chiefs of Bundelkhand at Cawnpore, and Ghāzi-ud-dīn Haidar, Vazīr of Audh. The latter secures non-interference on the part of the Supreme Government.

Nov. 30: Rāja Tirat Singh of Nungklau, chief of the dependent Khāsi states, on receiving the protection of the Government, agrees to become subject to the E.I. Company.

Dec. 21: Jumāda I. 20, H. 1242. Sayyid Ahmad, the Wahhābī, proclaims a *Jīhād* or holy war against the Sikhs, and almost every place in the Peshāwar valley is connected with the struggle; but the trained Sikh battalions at length overcome the ill-organised hordes, and defeat them at Naushahra and Bālakot.

1827 March 22: Daulatrāv Sindia dies at Gwāliar. June 18: Mukhtrāv, a boy of eleven, is placed on the throne with the title of 'Alī Jāh Jankujirāv Sindia, under the regency of Baizabāī.

July 6: Sir Thomas Munro, Governor of Madras, dies at Putakonda camp in Bellary. Mr Henry Sullivan Graeme, interim Governor of Madras, till Oct. 18.

July 9: Natives of India are permitted to sit as jurors.

Col. Welsh marches with a force into Kolhāpur, to enforce observation of the treaty of 1826, and resumes the districts of Chikodi and Manauli. Oct. A new treaty is drawn up com-

A.D.

1827 pelling the Rāja to reduce his army to 400 horse and 800 foot, and to pay compensation to those who had suffered from his lawless violence.

Oct. Lord Amherst returns to Calcutta, and effects reforms in the internal administration, viz., extended employment of native agency in the distribution of civil justice, the reduction of expenditure, and the establishment of the *Sadr Dīwānī 'Adālat*, the transference to the revenue authorities of land and boundary disputes.

Oct. 18: Stephen Rumbold Lushington takes office as Governor of Madras, till Oct. 25, 1832.

Orders from England forbid the employment of the Company's troops in preserving order in the territories of allied princes.

Oct. 30: 28 Rabī' I., H. 1243. Nāsir-uddīn Haidar succeeds his father, Ghāzi-uddīn, as King of Audh.

Oct.: Dom Manoel de Portugal e Castro succeeds the Commission at Goa as Governor.

Nov. 1: Mountstuart Elphinstone resigns the Governorship of Bombay, and is succeeded by Sir John Malcolm, till Dec. 1, 1830.

Rāja Ranjīt Singh of Samthar state, Bundelkhand, dies. Hindūpat, his posthumous son, succeeds under a regency.

Munīr Muhammad Khān, heir to the Bhopāl state, resigns his claim to the state and the hand of his cousin, Sikandar Begam, in favour of his brother, Jahāngīr Muhammad. Her mother, Qudsiā Begam, to retain the power of state, retards this marriage.

1828 Rāja Bhīm Singh of Udaypur dies. Javan Singh, his son, succeeds, till 1838.

LORD WILLIAM CAVENDISH BENTINCK.

Feb.: Lord Amherst leaves for England. Mr William Butterworth Bayley, senior member of Council, officiates till July 4, when Lord William Cavendish Bentinck takes office, till March 1835.

March: The articles of treaty of Teherān with Persia abrogated —an equivalent of 200,000 tomāns being paid to 'Abbas Mīrza to meet part of the Russian demand on their defeat of the Persians.

June: A regulation is passed to inquire into the validity of titles to freehold estates, and appointing a Special Commission of Appeal regarding rights to such estates.

June: A terrible earthquake in Kāshmīr: in Śrīnagar 1,200 houses are destroyed and 1,000 lives lost. Lesser shocks followed frequently for some weeks after.

July 30: Thomas Waghorn of the Bengal Marine, proposes to carry the mails, *viâ* the Cape in seventy days, and Mr G. Prinsep states that they might be carried from Calcutta to Kosīr in twenty-nine days and thence to London in twenty-five days.

Aug. 22: Bishop James dies on a voyage to China. Rev. John Mathias Turner, appointed to succeed,—died July 7, 1831.

Rāo Kishor Singh of Kotā dies. Bhīm Singh, his son, succeeds.

Sir John Malcolm, finding other means futile, sequestrates from the Baroda territories districts yielding twenty-seven lākhs of rupees per annum, and again others to the value of fifteen lākhs, to defray the expenses of the subsidiary force.

Nov. 9: An order issued reducing the allowance of Batta to one-half at the stations of Dinapur, Behrampur, Barrackpur, and Dam-Dam, to which Ghāzipur is afterwards added. Great discontent on the part of officers ensues.

Victor Jacquemont, the botanist, travels in India,—died Dec. 7, 1832.

Rāja Rāmmohan Roy founds the Brahmo Somāj "for the worship and adoration of the Eternal Unsearchable and Immutable Being who is the author and preserver of the universe."

1829 Jan. Lord Bentinck visits the Bengal provinces of Purnīya, Rangpur, and Dinājapur: measures are taken for the more effectual suppression of the Thags. Mr F. C. Smith, Political Commissioner in the Sāgar and Narbadā districts, is invested with full powers to bring to summary trial and conviction any apprehended criminals, and Major Sleeman appointed Commissioner for the suppression of the crime.

Lord William Bentinck makes a visit to the Straits Settlements—Penang, Singapur, Malacca, Tenaserim, and Arakan, and returns to Calcutta in April.

A.D. 1829 March 1: An Act for the relief of insolvent debtors in the East Indies is brought into operation.

Penang, with Malacca and Singapur, made subsidiary to Bengal.

April 4: The village of Nong-khlao, in the Kāsia Hills, is surrounded by armed Asamese under Tirat Singh: Lieut. Bedingfield, with Lieut. Burlton and Mr Bowman invited to a conference, are attacked and murdered, with three sepoys. Detachments from Silhat carry on retributive warfare. Tirat Singh is imprisoned for life in Dhākā jail, and the Government vested in his nephew, Rūjan Singh.

May 8: A further loan accepted by the Supreme Government from Nasīr-ud-dīn Haidar, King of Audh, the stipendiaries being the ladies of his household.

May 16: The Company enter into an agreement with the Rāja of Sātāra regarding the cession of part of the Mahābaleshwar Hills for a sanatorium in exchange for the village of Khundāla. Sept. 4: A further treaty defining the bounds of Sātāra state is concluded with Pratāp Singh.

May 23: Sikandra Jāh of Haidarābād dies. Nāsir-ud-daula succeeds, till May 1857.

Sept. 10: Rāja Diwān Singh of Cherrā-Pūnjī acknowledges British supremacy, and cedes land for a station at Cherrā-Pūnjī in exchange for an equivalent at Silhat. The Sardārs of Cherrā-Pūnjī bind themselves to be subject to Diwān Singh. The other four Kāsia states, viz., Khyrim, Nusting, Sungri, and Nongspung, receive the same treatment from the paramount power as Cherrā-Pūnjī.

Sept. 11: Sir James Dewar, Kt., chief justice at Bombay. Sir William Seymour, Kt., puisne judge at Bombay. The naval force of the East Indies is now styled the "Indian Navy" instead of the "Bombay Marines."

Mahmūd Shāh Saduzāi of Harāt dies. His son, Kāmrān Mīrza, proclaims himself King of Harāt under the suzerainty of the Shāh of Persia.

Oct. 14: Launch of the "Hugh Lindsay," the first steamer built at Bombay. Nov. 15: She starts for Suez.

Rāja Rāmavarmā invested with the government of Travankor.

A.D.

1829 Dec. 4: The Governor-General issues a regulation by which all taking part in, or abetting, cases of *Satī* should be punishable on a charge of culpable homicide.

Rev. John Wilson arrives at Bombay as missionary of the Scottish Missionary Society.

George Ramsay, ninth Earl of Dalhousie, Commander-in-Chief of the East Indies till 1832.

Col. Briggs' translation of Firishta's *Muhammadan Dynasties* published.

Major Price's translation of the *Tarīkh-i-Salim Shāhi* appears.

1830 Jan. 5: John Palmer & Co. of Calcutta fail; many of the leading houses become insolvent.

Jan. Lord William Bentinck visits Bihār, Benares, and Gorākhpur.

Col. Burney appointed British Resident in Burma.

April 17: First meeting in Bombay to promote the Red Sea route, advocated by Wm. Taylor Money.

The Rāiyats of Nagar, a division of Maisur, assemble in arms and set up Sādar Malla, a peasant Rāja. March 3: The Maisur Horse and a company under Lieut. Rochford march into the district and take Kāmandurg. March 12: The rebels are defeated at Honnali. April 6: Chandraguti is captured: Bednūr occupied, but the insurgents still hold out.

May: Rev. Alexander Duff, missionary of the Church of Scotland, arrives in Calcutta.

Lord William Bentinck establishes a system of licences for the direct conveyance of opium from the Central Provinces to Bombay.

Rāja Govind Chandra of Kachār is assassinated, and, there being no descendant, lineal or adopted, Kachār is annexed to the British dominions, except a hilly tract assigned to a successful rebel, Tulā Rām.

Oct.: Āgha Mīr Mu'tamad ud-daula is dismissed by Nasīr-ud-dīn, King of Audh, and his property demanded in repayment of sums alleged to have been stolen from the treasury. Appealing to the British Government, he is granted a residence at Cawnpur.

Nov. 30: In consequence of the irregular proceedings of the Gaikwād, the Resident at Baroda is withdrawn, and the inter-

A.D.

1830 course with Gujarāt placed in charge of a political Commissioner resident at Ahmadābād. The residency is subsequently re-established.

Nov.: Sir John Malcolm opens the Great Bor Ghāt, thus establishing communications between the Dekhan and Konkan.

Dec. 5: Sir John Malcolm, Governor of Bombay, leaves India. He died May 30, 1833. Sir T. S. Bekwith and Mr John Romer successively act as governors *ad interim*.

Rām Mohanrai visits England to advocate certain claims for the Dehli emperor. Arrived April 8, 1831; died Sept. 27, 1833.

Ishvara Chandra Gupta starts a Bengali monthly journal, named the *Sambad Prabhākar*.

1831 March 21: The Right Hon. John Fitzgibbon, Earl of Clare, Governor of Bombay till March 17, 1835.

April 13: By a Minute of Council it is resolved to abolish the provincial tribunals and vest the appellate jurisdiction in District Judges, controlled in turn by officers of greater experience.

April: Lord Bentinck censures Nasīr-ud-dīn of Audh for his conduct of affairs, and threatens to take over the internal administration and put the king on a pension; but, when Hākim Mehdi appeals to the resident for counsel and advice, the Government decide not to intervene.

May: The Wahhābīs are surprised by a Sikh army under Sher Singh at Bālakot in Hazāra, when Sayyid Ahmad is slain, and the *Jihād* ceases, the remnant settling at Polosī in Buner, on the Indus.

Col. Evans's division repulsed by the Maisur rebels at Fathpat, falls back on Simoga, and advances on Nagar, which is captured June 12. Conciliatory proclamations are issued, and the Rāiyats gain redress for many abuses.

July: Lieut. Burnes visits Ranjīt Singh, presenting him with a letter and gift of horses from King William IV.

Aug. 16: A detachment sent to Naning against 'Abdul Sayyid, the Panghulu, for his evasion of tribute and predatory incursions within the Malacca boundary, advances to Tabo, the Panghulu's residence, but fails to overawe the natives, who overrun the country.

A.D.

1831 Oct. 3: The Maisur Rāja, Krishna Udaiyār, is divested of political power, and a Commissioner, with four superintendents, placed in charge of the state.

Oct. 25: Lord Bentinck, Governor-General, and Ranjīt Singh hold a conference at Rupar on the Satlaj, when presents are exchanged and reviews held. Oct. 31: At the Mahārāja's request an assurance of perpetual friendship is executed and given to him.

Nov. 20: Insurgent outrages break out at Nārikelbāria in Bengal between Hindūs and Muhammadan Faraizis under Titu Miyān, a Wahhābi, and are suppressed after considerable bloodshed.

1832 March 2: Reinforcements from Madras move against the revolting Malays, who resist obstinately at Alorgaje. June 15: Tabo is taken after a feeble defence, and 'Abdul Sayyid having fled, the district is allocated to fifteen Panghulus, and the people settle into order.

March 20: The Bengal Government is authorised to express to the Nizām its wish that the affairs of Munīr-ul-Mulk and Palmer & Co. should be settled by arbitration. The Bengal Government and the Nizām form a joint Commission of Enquiry.

April 4: Zī-l qa'da 2, H. 1247: A treaty concluded with the Amīrs of Sindh at Haidarābād, providing for a free passage along the Indus for vessels carrying European cargoes.

April 6: The Gaikwād of Baroda, on request of the British Government, agrees to deposit with the Company ten lākhs of rupees for the payment of 3,000 horse. In consideration of this agreement, certain lands held in sequestration since 1830 are restored to the Gaikwād.

June 7: Pārsī and Hindu riots break out in Bombay owing to an order for the destruction of pariah dogs. Riots break out in Dhār on the appearance of a pretended rāja, who is joined by the Bhīls. A Koli insurrection occurs on account of the introduction of Bengali peasants to the hill districts for the cultivation of the land. The revolt is put down by the Company's troops.

The Choārs of Mānbhūm rebel, and their district is made a non-regulation province under a Commissioner.

A.D.

1832 The Rāja of Kachār dies without a legitimate heir. The Company takes over the government.

Sept. 13: A treaty concluded by the British Government with Ranjīt Singh to regulate the navigation of the Indus and the collection of duties on merchandise.

Rāja of Jaintia dies. His nephew and successor, Rājendra Singh, refusing to give up those who had carried off four native subjects to sacrifice to Kālī, declares himself unable to rule the hill tribes, and relinquishes his government for a pension of 6,000 rupees, and permission to reside in Silhat. Jaintia becomes a British province.

Oct. 25: Sir Frederick Adam, K.C.B., Governor of Madras, till March 4, 1837.

Oct. Jankojirāv Sindia flees from the tyranny of Bāizabāī, his adoptive mother, and takes refuge with the British Resident at Gwāliar.

Oct. 28: A plot to murder the European officers at Bangalor and seize the fort having been divulged, the commander-in-chief orders the punishment of the guilty; the Rāja Vīra Rājendra of Kūrg is debarred from friendship.

A Roman Catholic bishopric created for Western Madras.

1833 Jan. 15: Khem Sāwant of Sāwantwādi requests British aid to suppress disorder in his state, and binds himself not to dismiss his minister without the sanction of the British Government, and to pay for the troops required for the settlement of his affairs.

Jan. The Governor-General visits Sāgar, where the young Nawāb of Bhopāl appeals for British intervention to secure the throne from Qudsiā Begam, his aunt and prospective mother-in-law. The governor interferes, to insist on the celebration of his marriage with Sikandar Begam.

Feb. A treaty is concluded between the British Government and the Nawāb of Bahāwalpur for the free transit of European goods on the Satlaj and Indus. Supplemented Feb. 1835.

March 2: By a treaty the E.I. Co. give to Rāja Purandhar Singh the district of Upper Asām. The Rāja's government being mild but weak, he retires from the management of the country, which is resumed by the British.

A. D.

1833 Two ranges of hills between the tributaries of the Bārak river annexed to Manipur by treaty.

May: Lord William Bentinck appointed Commander-in-Chief in India, this being the third instance in which the posts of Governor-General and Commander-in-Chief are vested in the same individual.

July: Civil wars stopped in Gwāliar and Indor by British intervention. July 10: Jankoji, the young successor of Sindia, is carried off by his soldiers to camp and proclaimed Mahārāja of Gwāliar. July 13: Bāizabāī is persuaded to leave for her estates in Dholpur.

July 26: A Bill granting a renewal of the Company's Charter passes the House of Commons. Aug. 20: receives the Royal assent. Wider administrative powers conferred on the Governor-General in Council: legislative functions withdrawn from Madras and Bombay.

Aug. 28: An Act is passed requiring the Company to open the trade to India, and tea trade, &c., to China, forming a new era in British commerce; territorial management alone is continued to the Company.

Sept. 13: A treaty concluded with the Bahāwalpur Nawāb, Bahāwal Khān, which secures his independence within his own territories, and opens up traffic on the Indus and Satlaj.

Oct. Rāja Rāmchandrarāv Puār of Dhār dies; an adopted son succeeds under the name of Malhārrāv Puār.

Oct. Malhārrāv Holkar dies; an adopted son installed by the title of Mārtāndrāv Holkar, the administration remaining with Mādhavrāv Fadnavis. This succession is disputed by Harīrāv Holkar, son of Itoji, and cousin of Malhārrāv.

The Rāja of Kūrg warned against the perpetration of further atrocities, and ordered to report all cases of capital punishment to the Madras Government.

Brian Houghton Hodgson sent as Resident at Nepāl, till 1844. Made extensive researches in Buddhist literature, &c.

1834 Jan. Shāh Shujā', the exiled Afghān king, leaves his British refuge at Ludhiānā, and is defeated at Shikarpur by Dost Muhammad the *de facto* ruler at Kābul. The Shāh flees to Farrah, where his cousin, Kāmrān, plots against him. March 12:

A.D. 1834 he enters into a treaty with Ranjīt Singh for the recovery of his dominions.

Feb. 2: The partisans of Harīrāv Holkar release him from prison at Maheswar, and proclaim him at Mandlesar.

March: On the refusal of the Rāja of Kūrg to cease his cruelties and oppressive government, a force of 6,000 is sent against him in four divisions. April 2: Col. Lindsay's division disperses a body of Kūrgs, enters Madhukaira, April 6, and is joined by Lieut.-Col. Steuart. April 3: Col. Foulis' advance stubbornly resisted: he effects a junction with Steuart's force at Vīrarājendrapet. The north column, under Col. Waugh, harassed by the enemy, sustains a repulse at the Pass of Bak, and falls back on Rabata. The western auxiliary column near Belaripet forced to retire to Padanpalli.

April 10: Vīra Rājendra gives himself up to Col. Lindsay at Madhukaira. May 7: Col. Fraser, political agent, by proclamation, announces the transference of Kūrg to the government of the Company.

March: Harirāv Holkar enters Indor. April 17: he is proclaimed ruler. Mārtāndrāv and his parents are sent as British pensioners to the Dekhan.

May 1: Natives of India admitted to the magistracy.

June 29: Shāh Shujā', attacked by the army of Dost Muhammad at Abbasābād, and totally defeated. He flees to Kalāt, and thence to Sindh.

June: The Rāo Daisal of Kachh, admitted previously to the Council of Regency, is now placed in sole charge of the administration.

June: Lord Macaulay arrives at Madras as legal member of the Supreme Court at Calcutta,—till 1838.

Disputes occur between the Rānā of Kotā and his ruling minister, Madan Singh; the new principality of Jhālāvar is created as a separate provision for the descendants of Zālim Singh.

July 1: Detachments are sent to reinforce those in Ganjām, where the cultivators of Kimedi had risen against their rāja, and had defeated the first detachment sent against them.

A.D.

1834 July 10: Lord William Bentinck announces the constitution of the new Presidency of Agra. Sir Charles Metcalfe appointed first President.

Mān Singh of Jodhpur, at war with his chiefs, appeals to the British for help against a claimant to the throne, Dhokal Singh; but proving troublesome is confronted by a force under General Stevenson.

H. 1250: Amīr Khān of Tonk dies; his son, Vazīr Muhammad Khān, succeeds.

The dowager Rānī of Jaypur dies. Sanghī Jotarām, the minister, becomes virtually regent, the young Rāja's power being nominal. Dec. A force from Ajmir is sent to uphold the Rāja's authority in Shaikāwati.

Nov. 29: A treaty, supplementary to that of 1832, with Ranjīt Singh substitutes a toll on boats for duties on cargoes brought down the Indus. Dec. A similar treaty concluded with the Amīrs of Sindh.

A Roman Catholic bishopric established for Bengal at Calcutta.

1835 Jan. 7: Additional officers appointed to collect evidence against the Thags in the Narbadā, Ganges and Jamnā, Mālwa and Rajputāna districts.

Jan. Bernardo Peres da Silva (a native of India) appointed to the Portuguese government with the title of Prefect. A revolt against this officer takes place at Goa, Dom Manoel de Portugal taking office for forty-eight hours, and placing in charge Joaquim Manoel Correira da Silva e Gama. Feb. 10: a reaction in favour of Peres da Silva leads to a military revolt and the election of Col. João Casimir da Rocha Vasconello (President) and a Council of two.

Jan. 28: Lord Heytesbury sworn in as Governor-General. May 4: His appointment is revoked by a new ministry.

Feb. 1: The Rāja of Sikkim presents Darjiling to the East India Company, and receives a pension of 3000 Rs. per annum.

Feb. 25: Corporal punishment in the native army is abolished by Lord William Bentinck.

Feb. The Rāja of Jaypur, Jaysingh III., dies—poisoned, it

A.D. 1835 is thought, by Jotarām, the minister. The British Government undertakes the guardianship of Rām Singh, the infant Rāja, and appoints an agent, Major Alves, to conduct the administration. June 4: a rising in Jaypur is organised by Jotarām's friends, in which Major Alves is wounded, and his assistant, Mr M. Blake, murdered. Jotarām and his brother are imprisoned for life, and a resident appointed at Jaypur.

March 17: Sir Robert Grant, Governor of Bombay, till his death, July 9, 1838.

SIR CHARLES METCALFE.

March 20: Lord William Bentinck quits Calcutta, handing over the administration to Sir Charles Metcalfe, who acts as Governor-General from March 21 till March 1836.

April 18: Sikandar Begam of Bhopāl married to her cousin, Jahāngīr Muhammad Khān, the dowager Rānī continuing, however, to retain the management of the state.

By a judicious development of the water-supply of Mherwāra Col. Dixon brings prosperity and civilisation to the country.

The political agency is withdrawn from Bharatpur on the majority of the Rāja.

Strife between the Rājas of Bikanir and Jaisalmir necessitates the intervention of a British force. The Rājas promise to cease their ill-will.

Aug. 12: Lord Auckland appointed Governor-General for India.

Sept. 8: An armed force of Mārtāndrāv's party enters Indor, and is defeated by Harirāv's force, but the Rāv, alarmed at the conspiracy, becomes unfit to govern.

Oct. 8: Shams ud-dīn, Nawāb of Firuzpur, having caused the assassination of Mr Fraser, Political Commissioner and Agent at Dehli, is put to death along with his emissary.

Nov. The British troops occupy Gūmsur zamīndāri in Ganjām and secure payment of tribute. Mr G. Russell appointed Special Commissioner and martial law proclaimed. Two refractory zamīndārs are reduced.

A.D.

GEORGE EDEN, EARL OF AUCKLAND.

1836 March 20: Lord Auckland arrives as Governor-General, till Feb. 1842. Sir Charles Metcalfe retires to the Lieutenant-Governorship of Agra. The Court of Directors censures Sir C. Metcalfe for his liberation of the Press, and pass him over in the appointment of Governor of Madras, upon which he retires from the Company's service.

The Nawāb of Bhopāl concerts a plot to seize the power from his wife and mother-in-law, but is frustrated and put under restraint.

Mahārānā Kirat Singh of Dholpur dies. Bhagwan Singh succeeds.

Srī Drigbijai Singh succeeds his brother, Rāja Jaynārāyan Singh, as chief of Balrāmpur. Driven out of his territory by Darshan Singh, he subsequently recovers his rāj.

Bombay made a Bishop's see. Rev. Thomas Carr appointed first bishop.

A Chamber of Commerce established at Madras.

Dec. 7: Fr. Constantino de Santa Rita dies: Col. João Cabral de Estifique, Lieut.-Col. Antonio Maria de Mello, and Joaquim Antonio de Moraes Carneiro are elected as Council at Goa.

1837 Jan. 3: Bombay Bank proposed and shares subscribed for; 20th: A. S. Finlay appointed secretary; Feb. 2: the capital fixed at fifty lākhs, the chairman being Sir Charles Malcolm. It was bitterly opposed from Bengal till 1840.

March 4: Sir Frederick Adam resigns the Governorship of Madras. March 6: Lord Elphinstone succeeds, till Sept. 24, 1842.

April 30: Akbar Khān, son of Dost Muhammad of Kābul, sent against the Sikhs at Jamrūd and defeats them. Dost Muhammad sends a letter to Lord Auckland seeking alliance. His brothers seek protection from Persia and Russia. Sir Alexander Burnes sent on a mission, nominally commercial, but really political, to Dost Muhammad. He discovers the presence of a Russian agent, and advises the support of Dost Muhammad. This advice is rejected. An ambassador from the Czar, Capt. Vikovich, arrives in Qandahār.

July: Muhammad 'Alī, Shāh of Persia, sets out to besiege

A.D.

1837 Harāt, accompanied by a Russian envoy with officers and troops. Harāt is invested from Nov. 1837 to Sept. 1838; but is defended by Eldred Pottinger and the Vazīr.

Aug. 30: Capt. Burnes's mission reaches the Khaibar, and arrives at Kābul, Sept. 20. Captain Vikovich comes from Qandahār.

July 7: Nasīr-ud-dīn dies of poison at Lucknow. Col. Low assembles troops to prevent the accession of a spurious heir. July 8: the British candidate, uncle of the late king, succeeds as Muhammad 'Alī.

Sept. 28: Akbar Shāh II. of Dehli dies; his son, Muhammad Bahādur Shāh II., the last King of Dehli, succeeds as titular sovereign.

Nov. 29: Jahāngīr Muhammad Khān receives investiture as Nawāb of Bhopāl. Sikandar Begam retires to live with her mother, Qudsiā Begam.

Nov. Simão Infante de Lacerda Barão de Sabroso arrives at Goa as Governor-General.

1838 March 7: Dost Muhammad requests that the Sikh garrison be removed from Peshāwar which should be held by an Afghān, under the Mahārāja of Lāhor.

April 25: Capt. Burnes leaves Kābul. May 22: Lord Auckland declares war. The Russian Capt. Vikovich now in high favour at Kābul.

June 24: The Persians before Harāt defeated by Eldred Pottinger. Sept. 8: They are compelled to raise the siege, when the Persian sovereign returns to Persia.

Husain Husaini Āghā Khān, the Ismā'īli Imām, revolts against Muhammad 'Alī Shāh of Persia, seizes the government of Kerman, and keeps up a contest with the royal troops till 1840.

July 9: Sir Robert Grant, Governor of Bombay, dies of apoplexy at Dapurī, aged 59.

Sept. 15: The British Government, with the consent of the ruling chief, Khem Sāwant, takes over the administration of Sāwantwādi.

Oct. 1: Lord Auckland in a manifesto announces that the Barūkhzāi tribe would be replaced by the Saduzāi, Shāh Shūjā'.

A.D.

1838 The latter with Sir W. H. Macnaghten of the Bengal C.S. leaves for Shikarpur, followed in Dec. by Sir Willoughby Cotton.

Oct. 3: Humāyūn Jāh, Nawāb of Bengal, dies. His son, Mansur 'Alī, succeeds under the name Faridūn Jāh, with a stipend of sixteen lākhs of rupees.

Oct. 22: Political relations with Bahāwalpur established by a treaty which provides that the British Government protects the state, while the Nawāb is bound to act in co-operation with Government, and acknowledge its supremacy.

Nov. 29: Bāwa Sāhib of Kolhāpur dies. His son, Shivaji, succeeds under a council of regency. Misrule becomes so great that the British Government appoints as minister Dāji Krishna Pandit.

Javan Singh, Rānā of Udaypur, dies. Rānā Sardār Singh, his adopted son, succeeds.

Dec. Sir John Keane's force in Sindh, *en route* for Kābul, is obstructed by the Mīrs. After threatening to march on Haidarābād, he is able to proceed.

Dec. 26: Rāghuji Āngria of Kolāba dies.

Ludhiānā, for want of heirs, lapses to the E.I. Company.

1839 Jan. 28: A posthumous son of Rāghuji Āngria of Kolāba is born: his succession recognised under the name of Kanoji Āngria.

Jan. An army of 6,000 in the cause of Shāh Shūjā', under Mr Macnaghten, and a Panjāb force of 9,500 arrive at Rohri, crosses the Indus, seizes Bakhar and Dādar.

March 28: Sir A. Burnes negotiates a treaty with Mihrāb Khān of Kalāt in which the latter agrees to pay homage to Shāh Shūjā' of Afghānistān. The draft treaty is stolen by Mulla Husain, the hereditary minister alleging the Khān's guilt.

April 6: Sir John Keane, after detention in Sindh, arrives to take command. April 21: The force reaches Qandahār, where Shāh Shūjā' is enthroned.

Col. Sutherland marches to Jodhpur to restore quiet, and holds the capital for five months. Mān Singh now binds himself to respect the ancient usages of the country in determining the rights of the nobles, to admit a British agent, and to pay tribute and arrears.

A.D.

1839 May 31: Sir James Rivett-Carnac, Bart., succeeds the Hon. Jas. Farish, as Governor of Bombay, till April 27, 1841.

June 27: Ranjit Singh of Lāhor dies. His imbecile son, Kharag, succeeds (died 1840).

June 27: Sir John Keane, leaving his heavy guns at Qandahār, marches for Ghaznī, which surrenders on July 23. Haidar, Dost Muhammad's son, is made prisoner Aug. 2. Dost Muhammad takes flight to Bokhāra with his sons Afzal and Akbar. Aug. 7: Shāh Shujā' ul-Mulk is escorted to his palace at Kābul.

July 26: Capt. Wade forces the Khaibar Pass by taking 'Alī Masjīd.

Kalyān Singh of Kishnagar dies. Prithi Singh, his son, succeeds.

The district of Petlād is sequestered from Baroda as a punishment for continued contempt of the treaty of 1820; Sayājirāv promises compliance, and the districts are restored.

Owing to the misconduct of the Kochin Rāja the British Government takes over the administration.

Rāja Parichet of Dattiā dies. Bijai Bahādur, his adopted son, succeeds.

Bhīm Singh Thappa, the ex-minister of Nepāl, is taken from retirement, imprisoned and tortured, on which he commits suicide. Hostility to the British now becomes more active; emissaries are sent to various native states. The Government places a corps of observation on the frontier, but on the Afghān successes of the British, a change of policy takes place, resulting in an engagement to cease these intrigues.

Aug. 13: A treaty is negotiated on behalf of Lord Auckland by Major E. D'Arcy Todd, envoy to Harāt, with Kāmrān Shāh, who opens treacherous correspondence with Persia.

Sept. 5: Pratāp Singh of Sātāra deposed for persistent intrigues against the British. His brother, Shāhji, or Appa Sāhib, made chief, by order of Lord Auckland.

Nov. General Keane leaves Kābul.

Nov. General Willshire takes Kalāt. The Khān falls, his son Husain flees, while Mullā Husain is imprisoned. A youth named Shāh Nawāz Khān is set up as Khān.

Nov. 15: Dom Manoel José Mardes, Barão de Candal, takes

A.D.

1839 office at Goa as Governor-General, having come to India *via* Egypt.

Sir Colin Campbell, Governor of Ceylon, till 1847.

1840 Jan. Lord Auckland visits Sindia at Gwāliar.

April 1: The Bank of Bombay, after much opposition to its obtaining a Charter, secures premises and opens on 15th April.

April 16: The Barão de Candal dies: a Council holds office till Sept. 24, when Joaquim Lopes de Lima assumes government by appointment as interim governor.

April: The Ghilzais revolt, but are reduced to temporary submission, confirmed by the promise of a small stipend.

April: Kānhoji Āngria of Kolāba (an infant) dies. The line now being extinct, the widows of Rāghuji wish to adopt a son, but the two claimants are rejected by Government, and the state annexed to the British dominions.

May: Major Cartley's report establishes the practicability of a Jamnā canal scheme.

The Nepalese seize several villages in the Rāmnagar district, withdrawing when hostilities are threatened.

July: Kalāt occupied by a son of the deceased Khān.

Aug. The Baluchis defeat a British detachment and capture three guns. Nov. 3: General Nott recovers Kalāt and brings reinforcements from Sindh to reopen communications.

Āghā Khān Mehelati, the Imām of the Ismā'īli Khojās, is driven from Kerman by superior forces, and escapes through Baluchistān to Sindh where he is received by the Tālpūr Amīrs.

July: Dost Muhammad attempting in the north and west to regain power is repeatedly checked. Sept. 18: He is defeated by Col. Dennie near Saighān. Nov. 2: After defeating Sale at Parwāndara, Dost Muhammad gives himself up to Macnaghten at Kābul whence he is sent to Calcutta with Sir Willoughby Cotton.

Nov. 5: Rāja Kharag Singh of Lāhor dies. His son, Rāja Nau Nihāl Singh, succeeds, but on coming from his father's funeral sustains an accident from which he dies. Nov. 17: The Rānī Chand Kunwār administers the state till 1841.

A.D.

1840 Govind Rāo of Jalaun dying without issue, the state lapses to the British Government.

The British Resident is expelled from Ava.

1841 Jan. Rāja Sher Singh, second son of Rānī Chand Kunwār and of Kharag Singh, takes over the administration of Lāhor.

Jan. 12: A *sanad* is granted to Venkatrāv Ghorpade on his accession to the throne of Sundur.

Feb. Renewed risings of the Khaibaris and Ghilzais are suppressed by Cols. Nott and Wymer. Akbar Khān gains a following of 6,000 and revolts at Girishk. The Afghāns in Kohistān also rebel. Eldred Pottinger escapes to Kābul.

Oct. 9: The 35th N.I. under Col. Monteath suddenly attacked by Afghāns in camp near Kābul. Sale clears the passes and reaches Gandāmak on Oct. 30.

Nov. 2: Sir Alexander Burnes, Envoy-elect at Kābul, mobbed and murdered in his house. The British treasury is plundered. Nov. 22: Negotiations with Akbar Khān result in Eldred Pottinger with twenty others being left as hostages. Dec. 23: Sir William Macnaghten confers on the plain with Akbar Khān who murders the envoy with his own hand. Capt. Trevor is also killed.

In consequence of renewed aggressions and increasing disorganisation in the country, the whole of the Bhutān Dwārs are annexed, and a sum of 10,000 rupees allotted to the chiefs in compensation. No written agreement made. The Dwārs are formally annexed in 1865.

Harirāv Holkar adopts as heir a distant relative, Khanderāv, a boy of thirteen.

1842 Jan. 1: General Elphinstone signs a capitulation with the Afghān chiefs to retire from Afghānistān and pay 6,50,000 rupees, leaving hostages.

Jan. 6: The British force, 4,500 strong, with about 12,000 camp followers besides women and children, leave Kābul, but are attacked by tribesmen; only about 300 reach Jagdalak, where General Elphinstone is seized as a prisoner by Akbar Khān. Twenty men reach Gandāmak where they are overpowered, and

A.D.

1842 only Dr Brydon reaches Jalālābād, held by Sir Robert Sale, on Jan. 13.

Jan. 12: General Nott defeats the forces of Muhammad Akbar Khān and Safdar Jang, at Qandahār.

Jan. 15: Brigadier Wild enters the Khaibar and captures 'Alī Masjid, but for want of support abandons it and retires. 26th: General Sale and Capt. Macgregor concert with the officers for a safeconduct through the Khaibar; Capt. G. Broadfoot and two others oppose this and the reply from Shāh Shujā' being unsatisfactory, Jalālābād is put in a state of defence. Feb. 15: The Commander-in-Chief, Sir J. Nicolls, with Sir George R. Clerk, Governor-General's agent, and Capt. Henry Lawrence, authorised to relieve Jalālābād, General Pollock to carry this out and then return. Feb. 19: An earthquake shakes down much of the defences at Jalālābād and is followed by very many shocks for a month.

LORD ELLENBOROUGH.

1842 Feb. 21: Lord Ellenborough arrives at Madras as Governor-General; deals with mutinous outbreaks in the Madras army; Feb. 28: reaches Calcutta.

Feb. 22: Akbar Khān invests Jalālābād and harasses the garrison.

March 5: Col. Palmer capitulates at Ghaznī, under promise of safe-conduct by the Ghilzais: but they attack the sipāhis and massacre most of them; the officers are sent to Kābul. Aug. 19: the sipāhis are distributed as slaves.

March 7: General Nott led his troops against the Afghāns who retired before him till 10th, when the Ghāzis attack Qandahār. After a desperate struggle they are repulsed by Major Lane and Capt. H. Rawlinson. Nott returns on 12th.

April 5: Shāh Shujā' is murdered near Kābul and later his son, Fathi Jang, is set on the masnad, but Muhammad Akbar Khān, Vazīr, rules the opposition. April 7: General Sale attacks Akbar Khān's camp and gains a complete victory. April 5: General Pollock's force enters the Khaibar; 16th, reaches Jalālābād. 23rd: General Elphinstone dies, a prisoner, at Tezīn.

May 17: Rabī' II. 5, H. 1258: 'Abul Fath Muin ud-dīn

A.D.
1842 Sultān Zamān Muhammad 'Alī Shāh, King of Audh, dies. His son, Suriā Jāh-Amjad 'Alī Shāh, succeeds.

June 9: Sir George Arthur, Governor of Bombay, till Aug. 5, 1846.

June 17: Lieut.-Col. Charles Stoddard and Capt. Arthur Conolly, imprisoned by Nasr-ullah, Amīr of Bokhara, in Dec. 1841, were beheaded by the Amīr's orders.

June: Rānī Chand Kunwār of Lāhor, killed by her slave girls.

June: Two tribes of Gūmsur Kandhs place themselves under the British Government on condition of receiving its protection and justice.

Aug. 8: Mir Afzal-ud-dīn, Nawāb of Surat, dies. With him the titular dignity and office become extinct. A provision is settled on his son-in-law, Ja'far 'Alī Khān.

Aug. 7-8: General Nott evacuates Qandahār to join General Pollock at Kābul.

Aug. 20: General Pollock leaves Jalālābād for Kābul. 23rd: He defeats about 12,000 Afghans at Māmū Khel beyond Gandāmak.

Aug. 29: General Nott, at Gonīn, attacks Shams ud-dīn, Governor of Ghaznī, with about 12,000 Afghans, and completely defeats them, capturing their guns, tents, &c. Sept. 5: Nott drives Sultān Jān from Ghaznī, then blows up the walls and destroys the citadel. At Maidān he again defeats Shams ud-dīn and other chiefs, and, Sept. 17, joins General Pollock at Kābul.

Sept. 9: Sir Charles Napier arrives in Sindh and learns that Rustam Khān of Khairpur had secret correspondence with Sher Singh of Lāhor and proposes that the Amīrs should sign a treaty, in penalty. Nov. 12: The Governor-General sends a draft to be signed only if treachery be proved.

Sept. 13: General Pollock again, in a desperate fight, completely routes Muhammad Akbar Khān, Amin ullah Khān, and Muhammad Shāh in the Tazīn Pass and Haft Kotal. Sept. 15: Pollock arrives at Kābul and raises Fath Khān to the throne.

Sept. 22: The hostages arrive in the British camp. 30th: Istālif, held by Amīn ullah Khān and the murderers of Burnes, is stormed by General M'Caskill, and Charikar is destroyed. Oct.

A.D.

1842 The Kābul bāzār and a mosque are blown up; and Oct. 12: the army leaves Kābul in three divisions.

Sept. 19: Francisco Xavier da Silva Pereira, Conde des Antas, takes over the administration of Portuguese India, now disturbed by military revolts.

Sept. 24: The Marquis of Tweeddale, Governor of Madras, till Feb. 23, 1848.

Nov. 3: General Pollock's division arrives at Peshāwar. 6th: General Nott, with the rear division, arrives.

Kāmrān Shāh Abdālī of Harāt strangled by his minister, Yar Khān Alakozāi.

Dost Muhammad, liberated by Lord Ellenborough to return to his country, where he resumes his place as Amīr.

Dec. The "Hindustan," the first P. and O. steamer to India, arrives at Madras.

Dec. 17-23: Lord Ellenborough holds a pageant at Ferozpur to receive the army from Kābul.

Dec. 18: Sir Charles Napier claims the districts of Sabzalkot and Bhungbara from the Sindh Amīrs to be reannexed to Bahāwalpur.

Rānā Sardar Singh of Udaypur dies. Rānā Sarup Singh, his brother, succeeds.

Tej Singh of Urchha dies. Sarjan Singh, an adopted heir, succeeds, after opposition from the widow of Dharma Pāl.

1843 Jan. Major Outram recalled from Bombay to conduct the negotiations with the Tālpurs of Sindh.

Feb. 4: Jankaji Sindia dies without issue. His widow, aged thirteen, adopts Bhāgiratrāv, who is installed as 'Ālī Jāh Jīyajī Sindia. The Governor-General recognises Māma Sāhib, uncle of Jankaji, as regent, but the Rānī gives her support to Dādā Khāsjī, who becomes all-powerful at Gwāliar. The Resident is withdrawn to Dholpur.

Feb. 12: The old Amīr Rustam, arriving at Haidarābād, all the Amīrs, except Nasīr Khān of Khairpur, sign the treary—not, however, admitting guilt. Feb. 15: Major Outram is attacked in the Residency at Haidarābād by about 8,000 troops under Mīr Shāhdād Khān, and obliged, after a brave defence, to

A. D.
1843 abandon it, and escape on a steamer to Hālā,—joining Sir C. Napier, who marches next day to Matārī.

Feb. 17: Napier defeats the Sindh army of 22,000 troops at Mīanī, taking their camp and artillery. Six of the Amīrs give themselves up, and are afterwards sent to Bombay. Haidarābād is occupied on the 20th.

March 5: The Governor-General confirms Mīr 'Alī Murād, Khān of Khairpur, in his estates. March 13: Sir Charles Napier is appointed Governor of Sindh, and is directed to suppress the slave trade in it.

March 24: Mīr Sher Muhammad of Mīrpur, with a force of 20,000 men, is defeated at Dabo by General Napier. Mīrpur is taken, and April 4: Amarkot fortress yields to the force sent against it.

Feb. Martabar Singh, son of Bhīm Singh Thapa, the exiled minister of Nepal, is recalled from Simla, and April 17, arrives at Kathmandu along with his nephew, Kāji Jang Bahādur. Dec. 25: Martabar Singh is appointed Prime Minister.

April 25: Joaquim Garcez Palha succeeds by Patent of Succession to the administration of Portuguese India.

Mān Singh of Jodhpur dies without issue, and without adopting an heir. By choice of the widows and state officials Takht Singh of Ahmadnagar is invited to Jodhpur. Disturbances prevail in the state during his reign.

June 8: Col. Roberts engages and totally defeats the Amīr Shāh Muhammad with 2,000 men, taking their leader prisoner. June 14: Capt. Jacob, attacked by Sher Muhammad, with 4,000 Baluchis, completely routes them.

Sept. 6: Chandulāl, the Nizām's minister or Peshkār, resigns office on account of the financial disorganisation of the state and retires on a monthly pension of 30,000 rupees. He died April 15, 1845. His successor makes no effort to pay the arrears due to the supreme Government, and it demands territorial security.

The post of Resident at Maisur is abolished, and Sir Mark Cubbon made Commissioner.

Sept. 15: Sher Singh of Lāhor, and his son, Pratāp Singh, and their families massacred by Sardār Ajīt Singh. Dīlīp Singh, reputed son of Ranjīt Singh, installed as Mahārāja at the age of

A.D.

1843 six years. Sept. 16: Hīra Singh, son of Dhyān Singh, Vazīr, puts Ajīt Singh and others to death.

Oct. 24: Harirāv of Indor dies. Khanderāv, the adopted heir, succeeds by arrangement of the Resident, with the title of Tukājirāv Holkar.

Slavery is abolished throughout British India.

Dec. 26: An army under Sir Hugh Gough proceeds to Hingona in Gwāliar territory, and Lord Ellenborough requires of the Marātha vakīls the recognition of Māma Sāhib as regent and the reduction of the army. These being refused, the Governor-General with about 12,000 troops moves towards Gwāliar.

Dec. 29: At Mahārājpur, the Marāthās, with 18,000 troops and 100 guns, in an entrenched camp, are defeated with great loss. The same day, General Grey, coming from Bundelkhand with 2,000 troops, defeats a Marātha army estimated at 12,000 at Panniār. The Darbār now submits, and the army of 30,000 is reduced to 9,000, and a British contingent of seven regiments of infantry and two of cavalry is to be maintained.

1844 Jan. 13: The sovereignty at Gwāliar is secured for Jiyājī Sindia by treaty, the government during his minority to be carried on under the Resident's advice. The Rānī is pensioned off.

The misrule at Kolhāpur having become notorious, the government is taken under direct British control, the forts are dismantled and the army disbanded.

Feb. 17: Khanderāv Holkar dies. There being no lineal heir, and no person who had a right to adopt, the Resident, Sir R. Hamilton, is instructed to make a selection. He irregularly instals Tukājirāv, younger son of Bhāo Holkar, and is censured by Government.

Feb. The native infantry warned for service in Sindh refuse to march to the trans-Indus district without extra pay. At Ambālā they agree to proceed. March 4: Sir Hugh Gough disbands the 34th Infantry. Further discontent ensues. At Bombay also mutiny occurs.

May: Capt. Macpherson reports the decline of human sacrifice among the Gūmsur Kandhs.

A.D.

1844 May 20: José Ferreira Pestana succeeds Joaquim Mourão Garcez Palha as Governor at Goa. Macao and Timor sever their connection with Goa and are placed under a separate governor.

April 6: Lord Ripon informs Lord Ellenborough that the Court of Directors are inclined to recall him, but that the Cabinet refused to share the responsibility. May 5: He announces the decision.

June 15: Lord Ellenborough recalled by the Court of Directors; he left Calcutta August 1st.

July: The Gadkaris and others in Kolhāpur, displeased with the reforms of Dāji Krishna Pandit, the British agent, revolt and shut the gates of Sāmāngadh and Bhudargadh. The local militia revolt and imprison Dāji Krishna.

SIR HENRY (LORD) HARDINGE.

1844 July 23: Sir H. (Lord) Hardinge succeeds Lord Ellenborough as Governor-General till Jan. 1848.

Sept. Major G. Broadfoot, appointed Governor-General's agent for the North-West Frontier, takes charge. Nov. 1: At Lāhor the government had been vested in Rānī Jind or Jindān Kuwār, the mother of Dīlīp Singh: the minister, Hīra Singh, and Pandit Jālā conspire against the Rājā's policy.

The Rānī of Manipur, in consequence of the failure of a plot against the regent's life, flees from the country with the infant Rāja. Nur Singh, the regent, assumes government till 1850.

Oct. 8: General Delamotte proceeds to Sāmāngadh and storms and takes it on 13th. Col. Outram joins the force. 24th: The release is obtained of Dāji Pandit. Nov. 10: Bhudargadh is taken, the leader, Bābāji Ahirkar, escaping to Panhāla. Dec. 1: Panhāla is taken by storm and Bābāji killed. Rāngna and Vishālgadh forts taken by Col. Wallace and dismantled.

Oct. Tulā Rām, Senāpati of the hill district in Kachār, transfers the management of his state to his two sons, Nakalrām and Brijnāth.

Oct. 10: Sir H. Hardinge issues a resolution that in first appointments, candidates of proved competence, whether educated in Government or private schools, should have the preference.

A.D.

1844 Dec. A written address of thanks is tendered to the Governor-General by the Bābūs.

Nov. 20: The Rānī gains over the troops, and, Nov. 21: the ministers, Hīra Singh and Pandit Jālā, take to flight, are pursued and slain. The Rānī governs through her brother, Jawāhir Singh. An anti-British feeling is fostered at Lāhor.

Dec. 9: Nawāb Muhammad Jahāngīr of Bhopāl dies. His will, appointing an illegitimate son, Dustagir, his successor is set aside, and his daughter Shāh Jahān Begam, recognised by the British Government. Faujdār Muhammad Khān, her granduncle, acts as regent along with Sikandar Begam.

1845 Feb. 22: Tranquebar, Serampur, and land at Bālāsor, being the Danish possessions, are transferred to the E.I. Co. by Christian VIII. of Denmark for Rs. 12,50,000: ratified by the Court of Directors July 2.

Martabar Singh, prime minister of Nepāl, murdered at the instigation of the Rānī.

March 2-9: The Balūch robber tribes — Dūmkis, Būgtis, Khosas, Jakrānis, Mazāris, &c., on the north border of Sindh, are crushed and driven into Traki by Sir Charles Napier where they lay down their arms.

May 7: The Court of Directors inquire of the Indian Government regarding the construction of railways in India.

Sept. 21: Jawāhir Singh, brother of Jindān Kuwār, murdered by the soldiery at Lāhor. The Sikhs try to tamper with the allegiance of the Company's soldiers at Firozpur.

Dec. 3: The Governor-General arrives at Ambālā to visit the Cis-Satlaj states; 7: hears the Sikhs are preparing for a campaign; 9: that part of the army of the Khālsa was near the Satlaj; 11: requests Lord Gough, Commander-in-Chief, to move up forces from Ambālā, Mirat, &c. The Rājas, Tej Singh and Lāl Singh, had crossed the Satlaj with the Khālsa army in great force. They invested Firozpur on one side, and took up an intrenched position at Firozshāh.

Dec. 11: Sir Hugh Gough hurriedly leaves Ambālā with his army for Mūdkī; Dec. 18: The Sikhs at once attack the advance guard at Mūdkī, but are driven back three miles, losing heavily in men and seventeen guns. General Sir R. Sale mortally wounded.

A. D.

1845 Dec. 21: General Gough attacked the entrenched camp of the Sikhs under Lāl Singh at Firozshāh,—Sir H. Hardinge commanding the left wing,—carried their first line of works, and encamped for the night. Dec. 22: At daybreak the second line of the Sikhs is carried and seventy-four guns captured. Tej Singh brings up a large field of artillery and 30,000 troops and tries to regain the position, but is repulsed with great loss. Major Broadfoot and several officers killed; the loss was 694 killed and 1,721 wounded.

Dec. 27: The Sikh army recrossed the Satlaj unmolested.

For sympathy with the Sikh invaders Devendra Singh of Nābha is deposed and assigned a pension,—a fourth of his territory is given to the chiefs of Patiālā and Farīdkot. For the same reason the Sardār of Kapūrthala is deprived of his possessions on the left bank of the Satlaj.

Husain Husaini Āghā Khān, the Shī'ah Ismā'ili Imām, goes to Bombay and is received by the Khojā community as their religious head.

Roman Catholic vicariates established in Eastern Bengal, Kanara, Koimbatur, Haidarābād, Maisur, Pātna, Kollam, and the Malay Peninsula.

Dec. 31: Lord Hardinge, by proclamation, recalls all natives of Hindustan from the Panjāb.

1846 Jan. Sardār Ranjūr Singh Majīthia crosses the Satlaj at Philaur, threatening Ludhiānā, and General Sir Harry Smith, who had forced the Dharamkot garrison to surrender on 18th, is ordered to march from Dharamkot by Jagrāon to oppose him. Jan. 28: Sir H. Smith attacks the Sikh camp at Alīwāl and gains a complete victory, driving the Sikhs in confusion across the river and capturing the camp and fifty guns.

Feb. 10: General Sir H. Smith joins Sir Hugh Gough who attacks the great fortified Sikh camp opposite Sobrāon, and after a desperate struggle drives Tej Singh and the Sikhs across the river, in which many perish. Their camp and sixty-seven pieces of artillery was captured. The same day the British army began to cross into the Panjāb.

Feb. 15: Rāja Gulāb Singh, Dīwān Dinanāth, and Faqīr Nūr ud-dīn arrive at the British camp at Kasūr to treat for terms.

A.D.

1846 18th: Dīlīp Singh meets the Governor-General at Laliānā. 17th: Philaur fortress surrenders to Brigadier Wheeler. 22nd: Sir Hugh Gough with a brigade occupies the citadel of Lāhor. March 9: Treaty of peace signed; the Lāhor government to give up the territory between the Satlaj and Bīyas, and in lieu of part of the money indemnity, the hill territory of Kāshmīr and Hazāra; to pay 100 lākhs of rupees; to disband the mutinous army and reduce and reorganise a smaller force; to give up the thirty-six remaining guns that had been pointed against the British; and the Indian Government to arbitrate in all disputes. Kāshmīr and Jamu are given to Rāja Gulāb Singh on payment of seventy-five lākhs of rupees—part of the indemnity claimed.

March 2, 6: The Governor-General and Sir Hugh Gough are raised to the peerage.

Rāmavarmā of Travankor dies. Mārtāndạ Varmā succeeds.

June. Tribute from Udaypur reduced to two lākhs of rupees.

Shaikh Imām ud-dīn, Governor of Kashmīr, refuses to acknowledge the sovereignty of Gulāb Singh, and defeats his troops. Brigadier Wheeler, with Col. Henry Lawrence, the Resident, proceeds with troops to aid Gulāb Singh; Imām ud-dīn stated that he was acting under instructions from Lāl Singh, Vazīr of Lāhor, and afterwards surrenders to Col. Lawrence. His statement proving true, the Governor-General demands the exile of Vazīr Lāl Singh.

Aug. 1: Bābu Dwārkanāth Tāgor, a Hindu philanthropist, died in London.

Aug. 6: Hon. Lestock Robert Reid, officiating Governor of Bombay on the retiral of Sir George Arthur, till Jan. 28, 1847.

Sept. 14: Thirty-one influential chiefs of Nepāl put to death by Jang Bahādur, nephew of Martabar Singh. Jang Bahādur now becomes prime minister.

Dec. 16: An agreement executed at the request of the Lāhor Darbār, by which a Resident with an establishment should be appointed to have control of all matters of the state, a Council of Regency to conduct the administration; a British force to be maintained, and twenty-two lākhs of Nānakshāhi rupees to be paid for it per annum; and the Rānī to have a handsome allowance, retiring from any share in the government. This arrange-

A.D.

1846 ment to terminate 4th Sept. 1854, when Dīlīp Singh would be sixteen years of age.

In the Goa territory a system of communication by roads is begun.

A Roman Catholic vicariate or bishopric established at Madura.

1847 Jan. 13: Lāl Singh, Vazīr of Lāhor, banished for his treachery and violation of treaty.

Jan. 23: Sir George Russell Clerk, Governor of Bombay, till May 1, 1848.

March 16: Sa'far 12, H. 1263. Nasīr ud-daula Amjad 'Alī Shāh, King of Audh, dies. His son, Wajid 'Alī, succeeds, and, contrary to the advice of the Resident, he dismisses the capable minister. The minister is reinstated, but in April attacked in the palace. The offenders are arrested, but spared on the word of Col. Richmond. Nov.: The Governor-General remonstrates in person, and the king promises amendment.

Aug. 26: The Lāhor Rānī having intrigued to overthrow the Council of Regency is removed to Shaikhapura, to remain under surveillance.

Sept. 22: A *sanad* secures to the Mahārāja of Patiālā his hereditary estates and part of those taken from Nābha. A similar *sanad* issued to the Rāja of Jhīnd.

Gūmsūr Sarkār disturbed and *meriahs* or human sacrifices attempted.

The Nikobar Islands abandoned by Denmark: offered to Great Britain for £50,000—this offer not accepted. The islands are made over free of charge in 1868.

Oct. 29: A life-size statue of Alphonso de Albuquerque erected at Goa.

Dec. Satī and slavery forbidden throughout Sindia's territories also in the Panjāb, &c.

College of civil engineering founded at Rūrkī; opened 1848 under Lieut. Maclagan., R.E.

Sibindar Nārāyan of Kūch Bihār dies. His adopted son, Narindar Nārāyan, succeeds, Rājendra Nārāyan Koer, brother of the late Rāja, acts as regent.

A.D.

1847 Dec. 19: Sayājīrāv Gaikwād, of Baroda dies. Ganpatrāv, his son, succeeds.

Faujdār Muhammad Khān, regent of Bhopāl, resigns, and Sikandar Begam herself conducts the affairs of state.

A Roman Catholic vicariate established at Jafna.

Lord Hardinge reduces the native army to a peace footing.

EARL OF DALHOUSIE.

1848 Jan. 12: Earl Dalhousie arrives at Calcutta as Governor-General in succession to Lord Hardinge, who leaves Calcutta on the 18th.

Feb. 23: Lord Tweeddale leaves Madras and Mr Henry Dickinson acts as governor till April 7th, when Sir Henry Pottinger takes office, till April 24, 1854.

Col. Campbell led a brigade of sipāhis against the Rāja of Angūl, who was taken prisoner. He persuades the Bodh chiefs to give up Meria sacrifices. May: The rebel chief Chokra Bisoi, is driven out of Bodh and 135 *merias* delivered into British protection.

April 5: Shāhāji Rāja of Sātāra dies. On his deathbed he adopts a son whose succession is not acknowledged, and Sātāra is annexed by the British Government in 1849, allowances being made to Shāhāji's three widows.

April 18: Mr Vans Agnew, assistant to the Lāhor Resident, and Lieut. Anderson, having accompanied Khān Singh to Multān, murdered at the instigation of Mūlrāj, the Governor of Multān.

May 1: Lucius Bentinck, Viscount Falkland, successor to Sir G. R. Clerk as Governor of Bombay, till Dec. 26, 1853.

May 8: The Lāhor Rānī, found intriguing, is deported to Banares; and two conspirators are hanged.

May 18: A party of 300 of Lieut. Herbert Edwardes's horse at Leyā, attacked by 400 Multān horse, defeat them with the loss of their guns. 20th: Col. Cortlandt from Dera Ismail Khān having joined Edwardes, they again defeat the Sikhs with great slaughter.

June 18: Edwardes, joined by a force from Bahāwalpur, is attacked near Shujābād by the Multān force, and Col. Cortlandt

A.D.
1848 coming up with artillery, the Sikhs gave way and fled, losing six guns.

July 1 : Lieut. Edwardes, joined by a force under Imām ud-dīn, attacks the entrenched camp of Mūlrāj at Sadusām, and after a severe engagement the insurgents fled into Multān.

Aug. 18 : General Whish arrives at Multān ; and, Sept. 4, the heavy guns arrive and he lays siege to Multān. Sept. 12 : A general attack made successfully on the outworks of the town. 14th : Sher Singh with his contingent of 5,000 men went over to the enemy and the siege is raised ; Sept. 15 : the British force encamps at Sūraj-kund on the Chināb.

Sept. Chattar Singh, the father of Sher Singh, and Governor of Hazāra, revolts. Lieut. John Nicholson takes possession of Ātak fort, before Chattar Singh reaches it. Reinforcements from Hazāra sent to Jalandhar to support Capt. Abbott. Oct. Sher Singh from deserts Mūlrāj.

Nov. Major G. Lawrence and his family flee from Peshāwar to Muhammad Khān of Kohat ; they were afterwards given up as prisoners to Chattar Singh. Dec. 13 : Major Lawrence brought to Sher Singh's camp.

Nov. 7 : Mūlrāj, attempting to besiege the camp at Sūraj-kund, is defeated severely and loses six guns.

Nov. 22 : General Hugh Gough engages in a cavalry skirmish with Sher Singh's troops at Rāmnagar. Col. Havelock, General Cureton, and Capt. Fitzgerald killed.

Nov. 26 : Major Waller with John Lawrence defeats Rām Singh at Sinanagar ; Dec. 2 : he defeats the Jaswan rāja and Sikh high priest, at Unā and Aknot.

Dec. 2 : General Thackwell crossed the Chināb at Wazīrābād above Rāmnagar ; and Dec. 3rd, is cannonaded at Sadullapur by Sher Singh, with 40,000 troops and twenty-eight guns, but is repelled by a destructive artillery fire and retires Dec. 4. Dec. 28 : Lord Gough crosses the Chināb with his whole army.

Dec. 21 : The Bombay column from Sindh joins General Whish's camp, and the siege of Multān is resumed. 29th : A sortie made on the division of Major Edwardes, but is driven back. 30 : The chief magazine in the fort is blown up with 500 of the garrison.

A.D.

1849 Jan. 2: Multān town stormed and captured. 4: The citadel is invested; 21: it is breached, and 22: Mūlrāj with over 3,000 men surrenders unconditionally; he is sent to Lāhor on charges of treason and abetment of murder. The troops marched off to join Lord Gough's army.

Ātak, defended by Herbert, is taken by Chattar Singh, who advances with a large force to join his son, Sher Singh.

Jan. 13: The battle of Chiliānwāla fought by Lord Gough with Sher Singh near Rasūl, with the loss of 26 European officers killed, 66 wounded, and 2,177 men killed or wounded; the Sikh loss was much larger. March 7: The E.I. Company appoint Sir Charles Napier to supersede Lord Gough.

Feb. 12: The Sikh army decamps from Rasūl marching towards Wazīrābād. Chattar Singh joins his son, forming a force of 50,000 men with fifty-nine guns, supported by 1,500 Afghān horse under Akram Khān. 20th: They encamp at Gujarāt; Whish's division joins the main army, and 21st: Lord Gough totally defeated the Sikhs, capturing fifty-seven guns and their camp; General Gilbert pursued them beyond the Jhalam.

Feb. 25: Major G. Lawrence sent by Sher Singh to Lord Gough with proposals. March 6: Mrs Lawrence and family arrive. 8th: Sher Singh told that only unconditional surrender can be accepted. 11th: Sher Singh, Chattar Singh, and other chiefs bring in the guns captured at Chiliānwāla, and by the 14th all the officers and men had delivered up their arms, with forty-one guns.

March 17: Sir W. Gilbert pursues Akram Khān to Ātak and occupies it. 20th: He crosses the Indus and the Afghāns flee through the Khaibar pass.

March 29: A treaty is signed by Mahārāja Dīlīp Singh resigning all claim to the Panjāb which now comes under direct British control. Dīlīp Singh is pensioned with five lākhs a year. The Koh-i-nūr set aside for the Queen.

Sardār Nihal Singh, formerly holder of the Duāb estates on a life tenure, created a Rāja.

Nārāyan Singh of Sambalpur dies without heirs: his state lapses to the British Government. The new Commissioners raise the revenue assessments, and resume the land grants. The Brahmans vainly appeal.

A.D.

1849 April 6: Chand Kuwār, the intriguing mother of Dīlīp Singh, has to leave Banāras for Chunār, but escapes as a pilgrim to Nepāl.

May 7: Sir Charles Napier succeeds Lord Gough as Commander-in-Chief, till Dec. 6, 1850.

May 7: Sir Charles Napier takes over the chief command of the army from Lord Gough.

May 7: Mr Drinkwater Bethune's school for Hindu girls is opened in Calcutta.

Akbar Khān, son of Dost Muhammad, dies.

June 2-17: Mūlrāj of Multān, tried for the murder of Agnew and Anderson, is condemned to death; Sept.: commuted to banishment for life.

July. A mutiny breaks out among the sipāhis at Rāwal Pindi. Other mutinies follow; the regiment is disbanded at Govindgarh, and replaced by a regiment of Gurkhas.

Roman Catholic vicariate established at Vizagapatam.

Aug. 18-23: By a great flood of the Chināb the walls of Multān fort are undermined and fall, and many buildings wrecked.

Aug. 25: Māppillas kill three men and take post in a temple at Manjēri. Capt. Watt with a detachment tries to dislodge them, but they attack and kill Ensign Wyse on 28th. Sept. 4: The insurgents moved to a temple at Angādipuram and attack Major Dennis, and fighting savagely the whole sixty-four are destroyed.

Sept. The Sikh chiefs often violating their instructions, John Lawrence with attendants take Chattar Singh and his four sons by surprise at Atāri, and blow up the fort.

Madhu Sudan Datta publishes a poem in English—"The Captive Ladie."

Dr Hooker and Dr Campbell are detained by the Rāja of Sikkim with the object of forcing them to agree to the restoration of runaway slaves. Dec. 7: The prisoners are released. As a punishment the Rāja's pension of 6,000 rupees is stopped.

1850 Feb. 2: The Afrīdīs near Kohāt attack a fort in the pass. A brigade is sent to punish them, Sir C. Napier and Sir Colin

A.D.

1850 Campbell accompanying it. March 20: Dr Healy of the Bengal army and his attendants murdered by the Afrīdīs.

Feb. 9: A resolution of the Government of the North-West Provinces formally inaugurates the plan of visitation and superintendence of native education.

Feb. 27: The 66th Regiment Native Infantry mutiny at Govindgarh, near Amritsar, and is struck off by Sir C. Napier: their colours are given to the Nasīrī battalion.

Nūr Singh of Manipur dies. Debendra Singh, his brother, succeeds, but is expelled by Chandra Kīrti Singh, son of the late Rāja Gambhīr Singh. The British Government upholds Chandra Kīrti Singh's claim.

May 1: Explosion of a powder fleet at Banares with 3,000 barrels of gunpowder, and over 1,000 people killed.

May 25: Jang Bahādur of Nepāl visits England on an embassy, arrives at Southampton; remained till August.

July 2: Sir Charles Napier, in consequence of censure from Lord Dalhousie, resigns his post of Commander-in-Chief.

The Hindustan and Tibet road begun, starting at Kālkā.

Dec. Four Khojās murdered at Mahim by Āghā Khān's supporters, nineteen of whom are tried at Bombay, and four of them capitally sentenced and executed.

Dec. 6: Sir William Gomm sworn in as Commander-in-Chief at Calcutta. 9th: Sir Charles Napier takes a farewell review of the troops at Firozpur.

1851 Jan. 12: José Joaquim Januario Lapa, Barão (and subsequently Visconde) de Villa Nova de Ourem, succeeds José Ferreira Pestaña as Governor-General at Goa.

Feb. 28: Lieut. Cruttenden, Indian Navy, leaves Aden and visits the Sultān of Laheji. Capt. Milne murdered and Lieut. M'Pherson seriously wounded in the night at Waät.

Col. Sleeman makes a report on the abuses in the Audh administration, and advises the Government to take over the administration.

The Nizām is obliged to give up to the Resident at Haidarābād the management of territory yielding 36 lākhs of rupees to the Company, in liquidation of debt.

A.D.

1851 Sept. The mercantile community of Rangūn send intimation of the hostility of the Burmese rulers and their agents. Acts of violence are committed on British ships and seamen. The protesting naval envoys are treated with indignity and refused an apology.

Oct. The Peshāwar frontier having become disorganised owing to Mohmand raids, Sir Colin Campbell attacks the Tarakzāi and Hamilzāi clans. Sa'ādat Khān opposes and a three-months' campaign ensues.

Nov. 17: In Bombay, a lithograph of Muhammad having appeared in a Pārsī newspaper, a Muslim riot takes place and Pārsī shops are plundered and Pārsīs ill-used. Nov. 22: Another outbreak of Muhammadan bigotry is checked by armed force, many rioters wounded or taken prisoners.

1852 Jan. 3: The Madras East India Emigration Society formed.

Jan. Lieut. Boulnois, commander of a Company, constructing a fort at Michni, murdered by Mohmands. In April the Hamilzāi Mohmands are routed by Sir C. Campbell and tender submission. The Tarakzāis continue in rebellion.

Jan. Mīr 'Alī Murād of Khairpur, having forged title-deeds to lands, in place of villages of the same name, is deposed and stripped of all lands except his hereditary estates.

Jan. Lord Dalhousie sends Commodore Lambert in the "Fox" to Rangūn, to seek reparation from Pugān Meng, King of Burma, for repeated violations of the treaty of Yandabū, 1826. The Governor of Rangūn treats the officers with disrespect. Jan. 6: Commodore Lambert declares a blockade of the mouths of the river. 10th: A cannonade opened on the "Fox," but the battery is silenced by the ship's guns.

Feb. 18: The Governor-General demands reparation, stating requirements to be satisfied by 1st April, otherwise there must be war. March 28: General Godwin sailed with a force for Burma. April 5: He attacks and captures Martaban. 12th: The troops landed and repelled the Burmese, taking their stockades. 14th: Rangūn taken.

April 1: Lord Roberts arrives at Calcutta as "supernumerary second lieutenant."

A.D.

1852 Rāja Ratan Singh of Bikanir dies. Rāja Sardār Singh, his son, succeeds.

May 17: General Godwin and Commodore Lambert took Bassein. 26th: The Burmese attacked Martaban but were repulsed with much loss.

July 6: Capt. Tarleton reconnoitring the Irāwadī is opposed by a strong force at Akauk-Taong, but evades it. 9th: Reached Prom which was undefended. 27th: Lord Dalhousie arrived at Rangūn; left in a few days.

Oct. 9: General Godwin and troops arrived at Prom, and are opposed but take the place next day. Nov. 21: Pegu is captured from the Burmese, but attacked by them, Dec. 5-13, and, Dec. 14: Pegu relieved by Godwin. Dec. 20: The whole province annexed to the British Dominions.

Bahāwal Singh of Bahāwalpur dies. Sādiq Khān, the third son, succeeds. Fath Khān, the disinherited eldest son, drives him from the throne.

Sept. Rāja Nihāl Singh of Kapurthala dies. Randīr Singh, his son, succeeds.

A Wahhābi conspiracy discovered in Patna, a correspondence being traced between persons in that city and fanatics in Swāt and Sitāna.

Nakul Rām, Rāja of Kachār hill districts, is killed in an attack on the Dishomā Nāgās; and the country, which had virtually lapsed in 1830, is now formally resumed by the British Government.

Nov. General Fraser, Resident at Haidarābād, resigns. General Low, his successor, fails to persuade the Nizām to fulfil his obligations to the Supreme Government.

Dec. Bājī Rāo, ex-Peshwā, dies at Bithūr. His adopted son, Dandhu Panth (Nāna Sāhib), succeeds to his wealth, but not to the pension that Bājī Rāo had been allowed since 1818.

Narsingh Pāl, Rāja of Karauli, dies childless. Madan Pāl, son of Gardhan Pāl and cousin of Narsingh Pāl, was recognised in 1854 as chief. He died in 1869.

1853 Jan. 30: Captain Rennie defeats a force of Burmese near Lamena. Feb. 1: Rangūn and Bassein declared free ports.

A.D.

1853 Feb. Pagān Meng of Burma dethroned and imprisoned by his brother, the Prince of Mengdun, who is later crowned as King Mengdun Meng.

Feb. 19: Muhammad Hājī Khān acknowledged Rāja of Bahāwalpur.

Feb. Sir John Lawrence appointed Chief Commissioner of the Panjāb.

March 17-19: Sir John Cheape disperses the robber chief Myahtūn's force near Dānubyū. July 21: Peace with the Court of Ava proclaimed.

April 4: Burmese Commissioners arrive at Prōm. 8th: They ask to retain Bassein or some other port in Pegu. May 8: They offer to pay a large sum for the province of Pegu, but are refused; 10th: they are warned to leave Prōm within twenty-four hours.

April 16: The first Indian railway, from Bombay to Thāṇā, opened.

May 16: Ravivarmā formally installed as Rāja of Kochin.

May 21: By a treaty a revision of the Nizām's military and subsidiary obligations made. The Nizām is to retain use of the subsidiary force and contingent, but in payment of the large debt due he cedes Berār and other districts, and is released from it and from the obligation of supporting the contingent force.

Oct. 8: Bājirāv, a rebel zamīndār, defeated by Major W. Mayne near Aurangābād.

Oct. John Lawrence meets the native chiefs at Amritsar to agree on the abolition of the murder of female infants.

Nov. 7: Mr J. R. Colvin appointed Lieut.-Governor of North-Western Provinces; died at Agra, Sept. 9, 1857.

Nov. The telegraph from Calcutta to Agra begun; completed March 1855.

Nov. 21: Gangādhar Rāo, Rāja of Jhānsi, dies without heirs The state lapses to the British Government.

Dec. 11: Rāghuji Bhonsla of Nāgpur dies without heirs, and the state is annexed as the Central Provinces, and administered by a Commission.

Dec. 26: Lord Elphinstone succeeds Viscount Falkland as Governor of Bombay, till May 11, 1860.

Cheaper postage introduced.

A.D.

1854 April 8: The Ganges Canal opened at Rūrkī by Mr John R. Colvin, Lieut.-Governor of the North-Western Provinces.

April 28: Baron Harris succeeds Sir Henry Pottinger as Governor of Madras, till March 28, 1859.

April 28: Sir Frederick James Halliday, first Lieut.-Governor of Bengal, till May 1859.

May 1: The Company's Charter renewed from this date.

May 14: A new treaty concluded with the Khān of Kalāt in view of the threatened war between England and Russia. The Khān agrees to oppose all enemies of the British Government, to enter into no negotiations with other states without the consent of the Governor-General, and to receive British troops if required. He is to receive an annual subsidy of Rs. 50,000, on condition of protecting British subjects and merchants.

May. Siva Singh, Rāo of Sirohi, hands over the management of his state to the Company's Government with a view to the liquidation of his debts.

June 3: Sir Charles Wood introduces a Bill for the abolition of the patronage by the Company, which hitherto had filled the superior or covenanted posts in the service. The Charter is granted for so long only as Parliament should see fit.

Aug. The Tarakzāis under Rahīmdād Khān retreat in revolt to their hills. Sir Sidney Cotton attacks them on both sides of the Kābul river, destroying their chief villages. Their losses prove severe, and submission is made.

Aug. 8: Frontier duties between the Nizām's and British territories abolished.

Sept. 21: Brigadier Wm. Mayne's force attacked by Rohilas near Aurangābād.

Sept. 23: General Anson arrives as Commander of the Madras Army.

Tulārām Senāpati of North Kachār dies without heirs. His state therefore lapses to the British Government.

A Burmese embassy to Calcutta brings letters and presents to Lord Dalhousie.

All the privileges of the Nawāb of Bengal are repealed, including the control over the Nizāmat Deposit Fund.

A.D.

1854 A Madrasa founded at Bombay by Firuz Mulla bin Kawas for the instruction of Pārsīs in their religious lore.

A normal school and high school founded at Goa.

A Roman Catholic bishop appointed to Poona.

Dec. The Māppillas in Malabar disarmed by Mr Conolly.

1855 Jan. 31: Up to this date Mr Conolly had collected 7,561 war knives from Māppillas.

March 31: A new treaty framed at Peshāwar with Ghulām Haidar Khān for his father, Dost Muhammad of Kābul, and John Lawrence for the Government, in which each party pledges itself never to interfere in the territories of the other.

May 6: A council of five succeeds the Visconde de Villa Nova in the government of Goa till Nov. 3, when Antonio Cesar de Vasconellos Correira, Visconde de Torres Novas, takes office. The roads are much extended and improved during his administration.

Sir Arthur Phayre leads a mission to the Burmese Court at Amarapura.

July: A rising of the Sānthāls suddenly breaks out in Bengal; they commit murders and burn villages; Nov. 10: martial law is proclaimed; the raid continues till Dec.

July: Shāh Jahān Begam of Bhopāl married to Bakhshi Muhammad Khān, her husband to be Nawāb only in title. The Begam resigns her right to rule to Sikandra Begam, her mother.

Major Outram reports on the incompetency of the Audh native government, and it is resolved to take over the administration.

Sept. 11: Mr Conolly murdered in his house at Calicut in presence of his wife, by Māppilla fanatic convicts. 17: They are killed by troops after desperate resistance.

Oct. 7: Ghulām Muhammad Ghaus Khān, titular Nawāb of the Karnātak dies without heirs. His uncle, 'Azim Jāh, second son of Nawāb 'Azim Jāh (1820-1825), claims prerogatives and allowance as collateral heir. An allowance of 2,500 rupees a year is conceded, but the state is annexed.

Oct. 30: Śivaji Rāja of Tanjor, dying without heirs, the title becomes extinct.

A.D.

1855 First Bengali play, the *Kulina Kula Sarvasa*, composed by Rām Nārāyan Tarkaratna, acted in 1856 by the Oriental Seminary.

1856 Jan. Amīr Dost Muhammad regains Qandahār.

Feb. 7: Wājid 'Alī Shāh, King of Audh, refuses to sign the treaty presented by Col. Outram, vesting the administration of the civil and military administration of the state in the E.I. Company, reserving the title of King to himself and his heirs, with sovereign rights in his palace and park, and a pension of twelve lākhs, with three more for his bodyguard, and provision for all members of his family. He refuses the pension and is provided for at Calcutta. Feb. 13: The province is annexed.

LORD CANNING, FIRST VICEROY.

Feb. 29: Lord Canning succeeds Lord Dalhousie as Governor-General, and first Viceroy from Nov. 1, 1858, till March 18, 1862. March 6: Lord Dalhousie leaves Calcutta; he died Dec. 19, 1860.

March 6: First normal school opened in Madras.

Oct. 18: Tanjor fort occupied by the Company's garrison.

Oct. 28: The troops of the Nawāb of the Karnātak disbanded.

Oct. 'Īsa Khān rebels against the Saduzāi Prince of Harāt, and surrenders it to the Persian army. Nov. 1: War is declared against Persia for breach of the treaty of 1853 respecting Harāt, and Major-General Stalker is sent with a force and fleet under Sir H. Leake to the Persian Gulf. Dec. 4: The island of Kharag occupied. 10th: Bushahr is captured with sixty-five guns and warlike stores.

Ganpatrāv of Baroda grants to the British the land required for the Bombay and Baroda railway on condition that he should not suffer loss of transit duties. Nov. 19: Ganpatrāv dies. His brother, Khanderāv, succeeds.

1857 Jan. 22: The sipāhis at Damdam become uneasy about the new cartridges; and the feeling spreads to Barrackpur.

Jan. 26: Treaty with Dost Muhammad at Peshāwar, agreeing to assist him against Persia at Harāt by a monthly subsidy and a grant of arms. British officers to reside during the war at Balkh, and Qandahār.

A.D.
1857 Jan. 27: Generals Outram and Havelock with two brigades join the camp at Bushahr. Feb. 5: Outram reaches Burasjun to find the Persian army had fled.

Feb. 8: The Persians routed at Kushāb.

Feb. 26: The 19th Bengal Infantry mutiny at Bahrāmpur; March 31: the regiment is disbanded at Barrackpur.

March 20: Sir Henry Lawrence arrives at Lucknow to take the place of Mr Coverley Jackson as Chief Commissioner of Audh.

March 26: The fleet conveying Outram and Havelock's force attack the Persians at Mohamra, capture the entrenchments and find the camp deserted, but capture seventeen guns. April 1: Capt. Rennie disperses about 7,000 near Ahwāz. March 4: Treaty of peace arranged at Paris; May 2: it is ratified at Bāghdād, the Shāh renouncing all claim over Harāt or any Afghān province.

April 24: The 3rd Bengal Cavalry refuse obedience at Mīrat, and the rebels imprisoned.

May 3: The 7th Infantry mutiny at Lucknow, are disarmed and the ringleaders imprisoned.

May 10: The Mīrat prisoners released by their comrades, and the European officers and civilians are murdered on the way from church, and their houses burnt. The rebels march off to Dehli.

May 11: The sipāhis from Mīrat reach Dehli, and the Europeans are murdered, and their offices and houses burnt; the Dehli troops mutiny and murder their officers. Lieut. Willoughby and eight others resist, and at last blow up the magazine. May 16: Fifty European prisoners, men, women, and children, are butchered.

May: Nāsir-ud-daula, Nizām of Haidarābād, dies. His son succeeds with the title Afzal-uddaula.

May 13: The 45th and 57th Infantry at Firuzpur mutiny, and try to capture the magazine, but are checked by a few Europeans, and the men of the 45th are scattered—many killed: the company of the 57th disarmed and turned out of the fort. 14th: The 45th is pursued for twelve miles, and some slain and taken prisoners. May 12: The arsenal at Philaur is saved by European troops from Jalandhar. 13th: The sipāhi regiments at Lāhor disarmed. 21, 22: Sipāhis at Naushahra and Mardān mutiny, and four regiments at Peshāwar are disarmed. 25th: The mutineers of

A.D.

1857 the 55th are pursued from Naushahra and many killed or taken prisoners by Nicholson and Lind's troopers. The chiefs of Patiālā, Jhīnd, Nabhā, and Kapurthala give loyal assistance against the mutineers.

May 27: General Geo. Anson dies at Karnāl on his march from Ambālā to Dehli; Sir Henry Barnard takes command.

May 29: Two regiments at Nasīrābād mutiny and march off to Dehli with their arms. The troops at Lucknow mutiny and burn the banglas of the Europeans. May 30: Brigadier Wilson from Mīrat defeats a rebel force at Ghāziuddīnnagar. 31: He again defeats them there.

May 31: Khān Bahādur Khān, a Government pensioner, takes the lead in mutiny at Bareli, and hangs two or three Englishmen. The native regiments at Agra are disarmed.

June 7: Wilson's force joins Barnard at Alīpur.

June 1: The sipāhis at Mathurā shot some of their officers and went off to Dehli.

June 4: Neill reaches Banāras and disarms the 37th Infantry and other troops.

June 4: Nāna Sāhib captures about 130 Europeans escaping from Fathigarh and puts all to death.

June 5: The regiments at Cawnpur mutiny, plunder the treasury, and Nāna Sāhib brings them back against the Europeans.

June 5: The 12th Infantry at Jhānsi, instigated by the widow Rānī Lakshmibāi, mutiny and shoot their officers, and all others are foully murdered. 6: Mutiny at Allahābād, and many young officers slain at mess.

June 7: Two infantry and a cavalry regiment revolt at Jālandhar and march to Philaur: the sipāhis there join them, wreck Ludiānā, and proceed to Dehli.

June 8: General Sir H. Barnard defeats the rebels at Badli Sarāi, taking thirteen guns; then forces their position, the Ridge at Dehli, and thirteen guns taken. 12th: Two attacks on the British position repulsed—one of them by very heavy slaughter of the rebels. 14: The troops of the Gwāliar contingent mutiny and murder their officers and other Englishmen.

June 14: All the sipāhis at Barrackpur are disarmed. 15th:

A.D. 1857 The ex-king of Audh and his chief councillors are imprisoned in Fort William.

June 17: Majors Tombs and Reid attack the rebels constructing a battery at Īdgah Sarāi, capture a gun and destroy the battery and a magazine. 19th: A body of rebels from Nasirābād, trying to reach Dehli, are badly cut up by Brigadier Hope-Grant, but with loss. 23: On the arrival of the Jalandhar rebels another desperate attack is made on the British, but repelled with heavy loss to the rebels. 27 and 30: Attacks on Sabzi-mandi repulsed.

June 19: Wm. Tayler, Commissioner of Pātna, arrests four plotting Maulvis, and orders the citizens to give up their arms. July 3: A rising is suppressed and sixteen of the ringleaders executed.

June 6-27: Sir Hugh Wheeler holds out at Cawnpur against the incessant fire of the besiegers. 13: The hospital barrack roof is fired, and forty sick and wounded perish. 21: An assault is repulsed with great loss to the rebels. 25: 'Azim-ullah Khān, Nāna's agent, offers to give the 450 survivors English boats and provisions to go down the river. 27: On a signal from Nāna fire is opened on the boats filled with refugees. All the men taken are killed, and the women taken to Nāna's camp. One boat gets away, but is caught and brought back; and 31: the men are shot in Nāna's presence—General Wheeler, already wounded, among them. Four escaped at Fathipur—the only survivors. July 12: A boat with forty-seven refugees from Fathigarh is seized at Bithūr and is taken to Cawnpur. 15: The men are shot before Nāna, and all the women and children, about 200, left in Cawnpur are butchered, and the bodies thrown into a well.

June 30: Sir H. Lawrence's small force repulsed at Chinhat, and the native troops mostly desert. July 1: The Machhi Bhāwan blown up, and the defence confined to Lucknow Residency. 4: Sir Henry dies of a severe wound.

July 1: Holkar's troops mutiny at Indor, and kill numbers of the Christians. Col. H. Durand withdraws with the others to Sihor. The Mhau troops mutiny, kill three of their officers, and march to Indor.

July 4: The Kotā contingent mutinies, attacked by Brigadier

A.D.
1857 Polwhele, but, by blundering, his force is driven back, the cantonments fired, the city plundered, and about 5,000 Europeans and others shut up in the fort.

July 4: Rohilkhand rebels attack the British force at Dehli, but are repulsed. 5: Sir H. Barnard dies of cholera. 9: At Dehli, a charge of rebel cavalry is repulsed by Lieut. Hills; and the suburbs are cleared out by Brigadier Chamberlain.

July 9: The 9th Native Cavalry and 6th Infantry mutiny at Siālkot. 12th: General Nicholson overtakes them at Trimmu Ghāt, and puts them to flight with great loss.

July 12: General Havelock is attacked by about 3,500 of Nāna's rebels with twelve guns, and defeats them, taking all the guns and other prizes. 15: Two sharp fights at Aung and Pāndu stream, in which Havelock defeats the rebels and takes four guns. 16: About 5,000 rebels with eight guns, on the road to Cawnpur, are totally defeated by Havelock's small force. Nāna Sāhib falls back on Bithūr. 19: Nāna fled; his palace is now burnt, and the magazine blown up; twenty guns and many cattle taken.

July 20: General Neill arrives at Cawnpur. 25: takes charge of the town and district.

July 14: The mutineers attack the batteries on the Dehli ridge, are repulsed by General Showers, and followed up to 600 yards from the walls. 17: General Reed gives over the command to General A. Wilson. 18: Another attack on the Sabzi-Mandi and ridge batteries is repulsed. 23: The rebels issue from the Kashmīr gate, but are driven back with loss by Col. Showers. 31: A strong force of rebels attack through Kishenganj and a contest lasts all night, the mutineers' loss being very great.

July 20: An assault made on the Lucknow Residency is repulsed.

July 25: Three regiments mutiny at Dinapur and march off with their arms. 29th: The 12th Irregular Cavalry revolt at Sigauli, kill Major Holmes and others, and rob the treasury. A small force from Dinapur is attacked at midnight, and Capt. Dunbar and half his men cut off.

July 29: Havelock moves forward, and after two days' fighting at Onāu he repels about 12,000 rebels and takes fifteen guns. At Bashiratganj he drives the rebels off with the loss of all their guns. Aug. 4: Again drives them out of Bashiratganj, and then

A.D.

1857 retires. 12th: Attacked by an enormous force, Havelock gains another victory and returns to Cawnpur to recruit. 15: Gen. Neill routs a body of mutineers near Cawnpur. 16: Havelock attacks Nāna's army at Bithūr, and totally routs it.

July 30: Major Vincent Eyre marches from Baksār for Ārā. Aug. 2: He defeats the rebels in ambush. 3: He relieves the fifteen European civilians at Ārā and fifty Sikhs who had resisted 3,000 sipāhis with two guns for a week. 11: Eyre, with an increased force, attacks and scatters the rebels at Jagdispur. 14: At Jataura he destroys the house of the ringleader, Kūar Singh.

Aug. 10: At Lucknow a mine is burst, and another assault made by the rebels, but driven back. 17th: Another mine sprung and the enemy repulsed. 20: A sally made by the British and the neighbouring houses destroyed.

Aug. 12: The insurgents attacking Metcalfe House, Dehli, are surprised with great loss and four guns. 14th: They send a force towards Rohtak, which Hodson soon cuts up. Aug. 8: General Nicholson reached Dehli. 14: His force of fully 2,000 troops join the camp. 25th: He follows a strong rebel force from Dehli, and at Najafgarh defeats them and takes thirteen guns.

Aug. 17: Sir Colin Campbell takes over the duties of Commander-in-Chief.

Aug. 19: The 10th Native Cavalry at Firuzpur make a desperate attempt to seize the guns of a British battery.

Aug. 24: Major Montgomery from Agra routed with great slaughter a body of rebels at Aligarh.

Aug. 28: The disarmed 51st at Peshāwar make a furious rush to seize the arms of a Sikh regiment, when 150 are cut down and 400 prisoners despatched by drum-head court-martial, and others made slaves by the mountaineers.

Aug. Gulāb Singh of Kashmir dies, and is succeeded by his eldest son, Ranbīr Singh.

Sept. 3: Lord Elgin leaves Calcutta for China.

Sept. 5: The mutineers explode several mines at Lucknow, but are driven back at all points.

Sept. 9: John R. Colvin, Lieut.-Governor, North-Western Provinces, died. 30: Colonel H. Fraser, Chief Commissioner.

Sept. 14: Dehli is stormed and entered; 15: the city is

A. D.

1857 shelled; the magazine breached; a battery opened on the palace and on Salīmgarh. 16: The magazine stormed, and 170 guns obtained for use. 19: The Lāhor bastion is abandoned. 20: Hodson's horse enter from the Dehli Gate; the palace captured. 21: Hodson brings in Bahādur Shāh II., his queen Zinat Mahal, and her son, Jama Bakht, from Humāyūn's tomb. 23: He brings the two sons and grandson of the old king from the same place, but shoots them. General Nicholson dies of his wounds.

Sept. 16: Sir Jas. Outram reaches Cawnpur with reinforcements. Sept. 21: Havelock and Outram attack the rebels, driving them past Onāu and Bashiratganj, and capture four guns. 23: They attack the rebels at Ālambāgh, driving them out and taking five guns. 25: They storm their way into the Residency, losing General Neill, Col. Tytler, and in all more than 600 killed or wounded. The siege has now lasted eighty-seven days.

Sept. 18: Shankar Shāh, a Gond Rāja, and his son executed at Jabalpur. The 52nd Sipāhis mutiny and march to Damoh. Sept. 27: Col. Miller routed a band of the mutineers on his way with the English from Damoh to Jabalpur. Oct. 2: Major English at Chatra defeats the Rāmgarh rebels, taking their camp.

Sept. 23: A flying column under Col. Greathed leaves Dehli for Bulandshahr; there it defeated a body of rebels and destroyed the fort of Mālāgarh; then marched to Alīgarh and scattered a rebel force. Oct. 10: Having arrived from Hāthrās at Agra, Greathed's force is surprised by about 7,000 Indor rebels from Dholpur, but shatters their force, capturing their twelve guns. camp, and plunder, and slaughtering many.

Oct. 14: Greathed's column crosses the Jamnā, and Sir Hope Grant takes command. At Kanauj they defeat rebel troops from Dehli. 28th: Sir Hope Grant reaches Cawnpur. 30: He crossed the Ganges and took post at Banthar near Onāu.

Oct. 15: At Kotā, Dr Sadler and some others are cut down, and Major Burton and his two sons murdered. The Gwāliar contingent finally joined the rebels. Oct. 22: At Dhār Brigadier Stuart with troops of the Mālwa Field Force drove a strong rebel force before them: afterwards he captured the fort.

Nov. 1: Capt. Powell, with the Naval Brigade under Capt. Wm. Peel, defeats 4,000 rebels with heavy loss at Kājwā, 24 miles from Fathipur; Capt. Powell is killed.

A.D. 1857 Nov. 9: Sir Colin Campbell proceeds to join Sir Hope Grant; 12th: they reach Alambāgh; 14th: advance to Dil-Kushā gardens and the musketry of the rebels is met by battery firing and the Martinière College occupied. 16th: The Sikandrabāgh is carried by storm and over 2,000 rebels killed within it. The Najaf Ashraf was stormed by help of Peel's bluejackets. 17th: The Mess-house, protected by a loopholed wall and scarped ditch, attacked by Capt. Peel's sailors and Vincent Eyre's artillery, is stormed; and the enemy is driven out of the Moti Mahal. The forces now reach the Residency. 18th: The sick and wounded removed to the Dil-Kushā. 22nd: The last of the soldiers withdrawn from the Residency. 24th: General Havelock died of dysentery at Dil-Kushā. 25th: General Sir J. Outram, with the rearguard, reached Alambāgh.

Nov. 18: The 34th Infantry at Chitagāon desert, carrying off the treasure. 22: The sipāhis at Dhāka resist disarmament, but are charged by a body of sailors and many killed and taken prisoners.

Nov. 24: Col. Stuart defeats the Nimach rebels at Goraria. 25: The village is stormed. Prince Firuz Shāh, of the Dehli family, with 2,000 Afghans fled from Mandisor.

Nov. 26: General Windham attacked the Gwāliar mutineers near Cawnpur, and drove them back, capturing three guns. 27th: The rebels attack Windham's small force, outflank and defeat it. 28th: Some 20,000 rebels with forty guns, Nāna Sāhib being one of the leaders, attack Windham's position; Walpole's brigade took two guns, but owing to the strength of the rebels, the fight ended disastrously. 29th: Sir Colin Campbell arrived at the Ganges, and Hope Grant's division crosses over, followed next day by the whole force.

Dec. 3: The Lucknow garrison and other wounded sent on from Cawnpur for Calcutta.

Dec. 6: Sir Colin Campbell attacks the Gwāliar rebels and pursues them 14 miles from Cawnpur; their camp with seventeen guns and much ordnance stores taken. 9th: Hope Grant, sent to Sarāi Ghāt, defeats the rebels and takes fifteen guns, waggons, and much ammunition, without losing a man.

Dec. 15: Three of Holkar's regiments are disarmed at Indor. Col. Seaton defeated the Farukhābād Nawāb at Gangeri; and again, 18: at Patiāla, killing about 600 of them, and taking eleven

A.D.

1857 guns and camp. 19: Mainpūri recaptured by Seaton's column from the rebel rāja.

Dec. 22: Sir J. Outram from Alambāgh surprises and put to flight 5,000 rebels, capturing their four guns. 26th: At Majauli Rowcroft's small column of Sikhs, sailors, and Gurkhas attacked and routed four or five thousand followers of Muhammad Husain, a rebel Tālukdār.

The Nepāl contingent completely defeated the forces of the self-styled Nāzim of Sultānpur at Kodkua and at Chāndā on the Jaunpur frontier.

Dec. 28: Col. W. Osborne and Col. Hinde, after several times defeating the Jabalpur rebels, stormed them in Maihar, and took the citadel six days later—where the rebels made their last stand,—they capture Mohan Singh.

1858 Jan. 2: Bishop Daniel Wilson of Calcutta died; he was appointed in 1832.

Jan. 2: At Khudaganj bridge Hope Grant's force is attacked, but the rebels are driven off towards Fathigarh by Sir C. Campbell, who thus becomes master of Farukhābād. 6th: Jang Bahādur and his Gurkhas take Gorakhpur.

Jan. 12: Outram's position at Alambāgh is vigorously attacked; the enemy is routed with heavy loss. 16th: In still greater numbers their attack is again swept back with hundreds of slain.

Jan. 7 to March 9: Trial of Bahādur Shāh II. at Dehli; he was found guilty of complicity in the Mutiny. Sent to Calcutta in Oct., he was transported to Rangūn in December, and died there Nov. 7, 1862.

Jan. 16: Sir Hugh Rose marches from Indor to relieve Sāgar. 24: Colonel Holmes took Āwā, the rebels escaping by night, leaving all their guns. 26-27: Rose besieged the hill fortress of Rahātgarh; 28th: the rebels tried to escape down the rocks; the enemy outside strongly attacked the besiegers in rear, but were repulsed, and the fort taken and given to the Begam of Bhopāl.

Jan. 24: Brigadier T. H. Franks at Nasanpur defeated terribly a body of rebels. Jan. 27: Sir H. Grant surprised and defeated the Badāon rebels at Shamsābād.

Feb. 1: Sir C. Campbell left Fathigarh for Cawnpur. 4th:

A.D.

1858 Mowbray-Thompson defeats the rebels at Bhăgnipur. Part of the British army crossed the Ganges at Cawnpur.

Feb. 3. Sir H. Rose reached Săgar where English refugees had been besieged for seven months. 7th: General Whittock with the Madras troops arrived at Jabalpur. 10th: Sir H. Rose attacked Garhakot; at night the rebels stole away; are pursued and many slain. 27th: Rose left Săgar for Jhănsi.

Feb. 19: Brigadier T. H. Franks entered Audh from Badlăpur, and joined by 3,000 Gurkhas, attacked Năzim Muhammad Hasan's intrenched force at Chăndă, and took all their guns. The same day he defeated the Năzim's army. 21: He occupied Badăyan fort and pass. 23: The Năzim with 25,000 men and twenty-five guns at Bădshăhganj was totally routed and lost twenty-one of his guns.

Feb. 20: Steaming up the Ghăgră, 250 sailors landed at Naurăin, and, with 2,000 Gurkhas, took the forts guarding the road to Faizăbăd.

Feb. 21: Outram attacked at Alambăgh by 25,000, defeated them with great loss. 23: Sir H. Grant carried by storm the walled town of Miănganj, slaying or taking prisoners nearly half the garrison, and five guns.

March 1: On the way to Salīmpur Capt. Aikman defeated a body of 700 rebels and took their two guns. Gen. Franks stormed the fort of Daurăra, and reached Lucknow March 5; and 4,000 Gurkhas, under Jang Bahădur, attacked about 4,000 of the Năzim's troops at the Kăndu and utterly defeated them.

March 1: Sir C. Campbell arrives at Alambăgh. March 2: He seized the Dil-kūshă. 6: Outram crossed the Gūmti, and on 9th attacked the rebel position at Kaisar-băgh; the Martinière taken. 11: The Sikandrabăgh taken, when Capt. Hodson was mortally wounded. 12: Jang Bahădur arrived at Lucknow with 9,000 men and twenty-four guns. 14: The Imămbăra and Kaisarbăgh taken. 19: The Mūsabăgh was taken and 5,000 rebels fled. 21: The Maulvi of Faizăbăd was driven from the last rebel stronghold in Lucknow.

March 3: Col. M'Causland, to protect Kamăon, sent 200 Gurkhas to drive out some thousands of rebels from Sītăganj; the rebels fled during the night.

March 3: The Răja of Bhănpur occupies the Nărat pass

A.D.

1858 against Sir H. Rose, who attacks the Rāja of Shāhgarh with 5,000 rebels holding Madanpur pass, and drives them out. The strong pass of Māltūn, and the forts of Sarāī and Tāl Bahat fell into his hands. 10: Māraurā fort is taken. March 6: Brigadier Stuart pushed to Chanderi, and took it by storm on the 17th.

March 5: Some 10,000 or more rebels with twelve guns, under Muhammad Hasan and others, at Gorakhpur, attack Col. Rowcroft with 1,400 men and two guns; the rebels defeated and eight guns captured.

March 21: Sir H. Rose reached Jhānsi. 26-30: He laid siege to the city. April 1: With more than 20,000 men Tāntia Topi hastened from Kālpi to relieve it, but Rose with 1,500 men defeated him, captured eighteen guns, and slew about 1,500 of the rebels; more guns were taken in the retreat. 3: He stormed and entered Jhānsi, taking the palace. 4: The rest of the city taken, the Rānī escaped at night, and the rebels scatter.

March 22: General Roberts reached Kotā, and the Rāja joined his camp. 30: The rebels in the north end of the city were attacked and driven out.

March 22: Millman with a small mixed force scattered the rebels at Atrauli, but retired on hearing that Kunwar Singh's men were coming, and fell back on Azimgarh, where he was besieged. April 6: Lord Mark Kerr defeated the rebels and relieved the place.

April 14: General Sir R. Walpole attacks Narpat Singh's fort Ruiya at Rādamau, but is repulsed, and Brigadier the Hon. Adrian Hope killed. 22: Walpole defeats a large force at Sirsa near Alīganj, taking their guns and camp. With the Commander-in-Chief's division they enter Shāhjahānpur.

April 16: General Lugard's column reached Azimgarh, scattering the rebel force there. Brigadier Douglas after five days' pursuit overtook Kunwar Singh and drove his force on to Beriya in Ghāzipur. 23: Kunwar Singh defeated Capt. Le Grand with a small force from Ārā. 26: Kunwar Singh died.

April 17: Brigadier Jones crossed the Ganges below Hardwār, and in four days twice defeated the rebels in Bijnaur district with heavy loss in men and guns. May 6: He arrived at one side of Bareli as Sir C. Campbell reached it on the other. Walpole's men were attacked by a body of Ghāzis, but 133 of

A.D. 1858 them were at once bayoneted. 7: Bareli was taken, the rebel leaders having escaped.

April 19: Sir H. Rose and General Whitlock defeated the Nawāb of Bānda with 7,000 troops, who lost 500 men and seventeen guns, with his town and palace.

April 27: Sir Wm. Peel died at Cawnpur of small-pox.

May 3: About 8,000 rebels with twelve guns attacked the small garrison of Shāhjahānpur, plundered the town and drove Hall's troops into the jail. 11: Brigadier Jones with a force relieved Hall. 15: Ahmadullah Shāh, the Faizābād Maulvi, and the Begam of Audh returned to attack Jones. 18: Sir C. Campbell came to his relief and drove the rebels towards Mohamdi. 22: He followed them, but they had fled.

May 8: Lugard drove the rebels out of Jagdispur, defeated them at Dūlīpur and Chitaura, while Corfield's force hemmed them in on the opposite side.

May 8: Sir H. Rose at Kūnch defeats Tāntia Topi's strong force augmented by the Bhānpur rāja's and Begam of Audh's troops, who lost nine guns, warlike stores and 600 men. 17: Rose encamps at Golauli, five miles from Kālpi. The Bānda Nawāb joined Tāntia with 4,000 troops, who had now fully 15,000 men in a very strong position. 20: The enemy made a desperate attack on Rose but failed. 22: They sallied out against both wings of the British, but were driven back with great loss. 23: The rebel troops fled during the night, and Kālpi with all its warlike stores captured. Col. Gall pursued the rebels, and took their last guns, slaying hundreds.

May 11: The Shorapur Rāja, sentenced to transportation, shot himself on the way to Chingalpat.

May 12: Sir Hope Grant moves out of Lucknow, and at Sirsi inflicts a crushing defeat on Beni Mādhu with 17,000 followers.

May 29: Bhāskar-rāv, chief of Nargund in Dhārwār, having plotted with Bhīmrāv Nadgir of Mandārgi and other chiefs, and thinking the conspiracy known, murders Mr Manson the political agent at night, as he was resting at Suribān, and killed several attendants. Bhīmrāv attacked the treasury at Dambal, and, May 30, with 300 or 400 men, escaped to Kopaldurg.

A.D.

1858 Major Hughes from Belāri took the place, killing Bhīmrāv and 100 men. June 1: Col. Malcolm attacks Nargund and stormed it next day; the chief fled, but was captured by Mr Frank Souter of the police, tried and hanged.

May 30: Eleven thousand fugitives from Kālpi with twelve guns reached Morār outside Gwāliar, with Tāntia Topi and the Jhānsi Rānī.

June 1: The Gwāliar troops, attacked at Morār, betrayed their prince, who was defeated and fled. 16: Sir H. Rose arrived at Morār, and soon drove the enemy into the city. 18: He takes the hills to the south of the fort; the Jhānsi Rānī, fighting in male attire, is killed. 19: Everything outside the fort is taken. 20: The fort was taken by a handful of men under Lieuts. Rose and Waller. 21: Brigadier Napier pursuing Tāntia's force of 5,000 men and twenty-five guns, defeated him at Jaura Alīpur, and took all their guns.

June 2: Whitlock's column sets out for Karwī. 5: The two young chiefs yield to Whitlock, seeking pardon. 6: Karwī yields, and the enormous treasures in the palace are awarded to Whitlock's force.

June 9: Major Cox with a detachment of Col. Rowcroft's brigade drove Muhammad Hasan's rebels from Amorā in Gorakhpur. 18: With a larger force he drove 4,000 of them across the Ghāgrā.

June 12: Sir Hope Grant, with a strong brigade from Lucknow, attacked 16,000 rebels at Nawābganj who, with numerous Ghāzis, fought desperately but lost six guns and 600 men.

Fath Khān of Bhāwalpur died: Rahīm Gar Muhammad succeeded with the title of Bhāwal Khān.

July 31: Sir Hope Grant relieved Mān Singh, who was besieged by the rebels for deserting their cause.

Aug. 2: By Act 21 & 22 Victoria, c. 106, all the East India Company's territories are vested in Her Majesty, and all its powers exercised in her name.

Aug. Sir Hope Grant followed up and routed parties of rebels. At Sultānpur 14,000 of them had come together with thirteen or fourteen guns.

Sept. 2: Two regiments of Bengal infantry—about 1,500 men

A.D.

1858 —mutinied at Multān, but were overpowered, and fled, and were cut off in detail.

Sept. 13: General Sir John Michel defeated Tāntia Topi moving towards Bhopāl.

Nov. 1: The Royal Proclamation published at a grand Darbār held at Allahābād by Lord Canning transferring the Government to the Queen.

Nov. 2: Sir Colin Campbell left Allahābād, joined the army near Pratāpgarh and advanced against Lāl Mādhu Sing of Amethi, who surrendered; 12: he proceeded to Shankarpur against Beni Mādhu Bakhsh who left the fort with his troops by night. 24: Beni Mādhu was intercepted by Brigadier Horsford and his force driven in confusion across the Gūmtī. Dec. 6: Sir Colin reaches Bahramghāt, where Beni Mādhu's force across the Ghāgrā decamp and go northwards.

Nov. 25: Sir H. Grant crossed the Ghāgrā, and attacked the Rāja of Gondā, taking six guns and utterly routing his force. The general occupied Gondā.

Dec. 26: Sir C. Campbell attacked a rebel force at Bargidia, pursued them and took all their guns. 27: He took Beni Mādhu's fort of Masjidia. 30: Attacked Nānā Sāhib near Banki, and drove his force across the Rāptī. 31: The rebels escape into Nepāl or surrender.

Dec. 23: Col. Rowcroft drove Bālarāv, Nānā's brother, from Tulsipur, taking two guns.

1859 Jan. 4: Sir H. Grant follows Bālarāv through the jangal, defeated 6,000 rebels, and took fifteen guns from him. Bālarāv fled into Nepāl.

Jan. Tafazzul Husain, Nawāb Rais of Farukhābād, surrendered and was tried before a special Commission, convicted of numerous murders and sentenced to death, commuted to transportation.

Jan. 7: The rebellion in Audh reported at an end.

Jan. 9: Prince Firuz Shāh who had cut his way from Audh and crossed the Ganges, defeated the efforts of Mr Hume of Itāwā to stop him and his troops, got into Gwāliar districts and escaped with loss from General Napier, reached Indragarh in Tank, and is joined by Tāntia Topi and Mān Singh; he leaves them before the month ends.

A.D.

1859 Feb. 10: General Horsford pursued a body of rebels in the Nepāl Tarai and defeated them, taking all their fifteen guns. General Honner heavily defeated Rāo Sāhib's force.

Nāna Sāhib with his family got into Nepāl from Rohilkhand, but was informed that his women—mother, wife, and Bālarāv Sāhib's wife—with their property (jewels), would find shelter, and remained in a country palace of Jang Bahādur's, receiving a sustenance allowance; but the men of the party were refused asylum.

March 28: Sir Charles Edward Trevelyan succeeded Lord Harris as Governor of Madras, till June 8, 1860.

April 2: Mān Singh of Narwar surrendered to Major Meade at Mahūdra, and 8: enabled Meade to seize Tāntia Topi by night in the Peron jangal near Siprī. 15: Tāntia tried by court-martial and condemned for rebellion, and hanged.

April: The British Government grants the estates of Būndi and Bithauli to Randhīr Singh of Kapurthala for services rendered in Audh.

May: Sir John Peter Grant appointed Lieutenant-Governor of Bengal, till April 1862.

May: The E.I. Company's troops objected to be summarily transferred to the Crown. June 20: The Viceroy issued a fresh General Order granting discharge and a free passage home to all who claimed it, but not to enlist in any regiment in India. The 5th Bengal Europeans at Bahrampur mutiny.

July 8: Peace proclaimed throughout India; and July 28th observed as a day of thanksgiving.

Oct. 15: Lord and Lady Canning arrive at Cawnpur on a viceregal progress through the Northern Provinces; Oct. 18: proceed to Lucknow which they enter in state. Oct. 22: A grand darbār is held for the reception of the Tālukdārs. Darbārs are also held at Cawnpur (Nov. 3), Fathigarh (Nov. 15), and Agra (Dec. 21).

Nov. 20: Mountstuart Elphinstone dies.

Nov. 29: James Wilson appointed first Finance Member of the Supreme Council to reorganise the Indian finances. An income tax was imposed, and a Government paper currency created.

A.D.

1859 Dec. Sikandra Begam of Bhopal recognised as ruler by right, with succession to her daughter, for services rendered during and after the Mutiny,—died Oct. 30, 1868.

Dec. The Wāghars driven from Dwāraka and Beyt, having fortified their camp on Abhapura hill, were driven out by Col Honner, and fled to the Gīr, where Jodha Mānek, their leader, died.

1860 Jan. 24: A Concordat vests the Roman Catholic ecclesiastical patronage of the East in the crown of Portugal. British India is divided into thirty districts. Britain acknowledges no such right.

The Kūkis or Lushais from the Tipara hills on the borders of Silhat made murderous raids on neighbouring Bengali villages, killing 186 villagers and carrying off 100 captives.

Jan. 29: An industrial exhibition opened at Goa for the products of the state of the Portuguese Indies and Hindustan generally.

Jan. General Neville Chamberlain was sent on a punitive expedition against the Waziri tribes on the Panjāb frontier.

Feb. 1-22: The delimitation of the boundaries of Daman negotiated by a Commission consisting of Señor Ricardo Carlos Clarchy and Mr W. Hughes.

March: Khān Bahādur Khān of Bareli was hanged on the spot where he had raised the flag of rebellion; he had savagely murdered all the Europeans he could find.

March 30: The title of Rāja Bahādur and some territory in Sātāra was conferred on the adopted son of the late Rāja of Nāgpur.

May 3: Jwāla Prasād, who conducted the massacres for Nāna Sāhib, was hanged at the Ghāt where he directed them.

May 5: A *sanad* granted the Mahārāja of Patiāla and his successors to exercise sovereign powers within their ancestral possessions, and to exact obedience to him from all dependents and feudatories. The right of adoption conceded, the Rāja agreed to co-operate with the British forces on the appearance of an enemy, to furnish material (on payment) and land (free) for roads and railways. A similar sanad is bestowed on the Rāja of Jhīnd.

May 9: Lord Elphinstone leaves Bombay, and May 11: Sir

A.D.

1860 George Russell Clerk succeeds as Governor of Bombay, till April 24, 1862. The Local Legislative Council established.

June 8: Sir Charles E. Trevelyan was recalled, and William Ambrose Morehead acted Governor of Madras till July 5, when Sir Henry George Ward arrived and took office.

Rāo Daisal of Kachh died. Rāo Pragmal, his son, succeeded.

Martānda Rāja of Travankor died. Rāmavarmā, his nephew, succeeded.

From the continued practice of kidnapping Bengali subjects of the British Crown by the people of Sikkim, part of their territory was occupied by a force under Col. Gawler, with the Hon. Ashley Eden as envoy.

Aug. 2: Sir H. G. Ward, Governor of Madras, died there. Sir Wm. Ambrose Morehead was acting Governor for the second time, from July 5th till Feb. 18th, 1861.

Faridūn Jāh of Murshidābād memorialised the Secretary of State for India regarding his grievances.

Nov. 6: The Viceroy and Lady Canning arrive at Banāras on a tour through Upper India.

Dec. 12: Dhirāj Singh, the former chief of Udayapur, having been convicted of manslaughter, the estate is treated as a lapse, and conferred on Lāl Bandeswari Prasād Singh Deo Bahādur, a brother of the Rāja of Sargujā, in acknowledgment of his services in 1857.

Dec. 26: Treaty concluded with the Nizām by which his debt to the British Government is cancelled, and Naldrug, Dāraseo, and Raichūr, with the state of Shorapur, ceded to him.

The *Nil Darpan*, a drama satirising the indigo planters of Jessor and Nadiyā, produced by Dinabanda Mitra.

1861 Feb. 18: Sir William Thomas Denison, K.C.B., succeeds Sir H. G. Ward as Governor of Madras, till March 27, 1866.

March: The Rāja of Sikkim was obliged to make full restitution for the kidnapping of British subjects and signed a treaty securing the rights of trade, protection for travellers, and the making of roads.

July 5: A Royal Proclamation issued creating the Order of the Star of India.

A.D.

1861 Oct. 20: Āghā Khān published a demand that the Khojās should conform to the practices of the Imāmiya creed of his ancestors (the "Assassins") in respect of marriages, ablutions, and funeral ceremonies. This raised opposition again on the part of those who preferred to retain Sunnī practices.

Nov. 17: Sarup Singh, Rānā of Udaypur, died. Sambhu Singh, his nephew, a minor, succeeded under a Council of Regency aided by the political agent. Umed Singh succeeds to the throne of Sirohi.

Nov. 18: Lady Canning, wife of the Viceroy, died of jangal fever at Calcutta.

The North-West Provinces suffered extreme distress from scarcity, the State took relief measures. Half a million persons estimated to have been relieved at the expenditure by Government of three-quarters of a million sterling.

1862 Jan. 1: The Penal Code for India came into operation.

Jan. 25: The libel case in which the editor of the *Satya Prakāsh* was accused of libel by the Vallabhāchārya Mahārāja, Jadunāth Brijratanji, was begun at Bombay. The Vallabhāchārya priests accused of the most immoral practices, the charge was proven; judgment delivered April 21.

THE EARL OF ELGIN, SECOND VICEROY.

March 12: The Earl of Elgin succeeded Lord Canning as Viceroy. 18: Lord Canning left India: he died June 17th.

March: The Governor of Madras opened the South Indian railway from Negapatam to Trichinăpali.

Sanads conferring rights of adoption were given to the chiefs of Bhaganapali, Cochin, Pudukota, Sundar, and Travankor, also to the Rāja of Kashmīr.

March 28: The Rānīs of Tānjor were restored to their property.

April: Sir Cecil Beadon, Lieut.-Governor of Bengal, till April 1867.

April 24: Sir Bartle Frere succeeded Sir George R. Clerk as Governor of Bombay, till March 1867. He died May 19, 1884.

Kolhāpur restored on his majority to Sivājī, who binds him-

A.D.

1862 self to follow the advice of the British Government in all state affairs.

July 12: The High Court of Judicature, Bengal, was inaugurated.

Sept. 3: The Khojās of Bombay, under the influence of Āghā Khān, excommunicated those who continued to stand out for Sunnī marriage customs, &c., which led to the great lawsuit of 1866.

Sept. 8: Rāo Sāhib hanged for murders during the Mutiny.

Nov. 14: Mahārāja Narendra Singh of Patiāla died. His son, Mahendra Singh, succeeded.

1863 Jan. 8: Sir Charles Trevelyan, the new finance minister, arrived at Calcutta. Jan. 19-30: The first Agricultural Exhibition was held at Calcutta.

Feb. 5: Lord Elgin started on a tour of the Upper Provinces. 7: He visited Cawnpur and attended the consecration by Bishop Cotton of the grave and monument to those murdered in 1857. March 28: A great assembly held at Ambāla where the Sikh and other Panjāb chiefs were received.

March 17: The Kalāt chiefs depose Khodadād Khān and elect his cousin Sherdil Khān as ruler. The town and fort are surrendered without resistance.

April 30: The Indian Navy transferred to the Admiralty.

May: Dost Muhammad of Afghānistān takes Harāt from the Persians. June 9: He dies there. Sher 'Alī Khān, his fifth son, assumes the position of Amīr. He is acknowledged by Sir W. Denison, acting Governor-General, in Dec.

June 18: Vazīr Muhammad Khān of Tonk died, and was succeeded by his son, Muhammad 'Alī Khān.

Aug. Narendra Nārāyan of Kuch Bihār died. His infant son, Nipendra Nārāyan, succeeded, the state being managed by a British Commissioner.

Oct. 18: A force of 6,000 men under Sir Neville Chamberlain despatched to Sitāna in the Swāt country, to punish an attack on the Guides Corps made in Sept. by a band of Muhammadan fanatics, Wahhābis and escaped sipāhis. The tribes from the Indus and Kābul rivers tried to block the Ambela Pass, attacking the British force, Oct. 20; and retard the progress of the force

A.D.

1863 till Dec. 15, when the enemy's position was stormed. The village of Lālu was taken and destroyed. Dec. 16: Ambela captured and destroyed. The Buner tribes, abandoned by those of Bajaur and Swāt, submitted and joined the British in attacking the stronghold of Malka, which was burned Dec. 22. Dec. 25: The force re-enters British territory.

Nov. 9: Bhārpar Singh of Nābha dies, Bhagwān Singh, his brother, succeeds: died 1871.

Nov. 20: Lord Elgin, the Viceroy, died at Dharmsāla. Sir William Denison, Governor of Madras, acts as Governor-General, Dec. 2 till Jan. 12, 1864: Mr Edward Maltby acting as Governor of Madras.

Dec. 12: Dhālimkot fort in Bhutān taken by the British.

1864 Jan. 4: The Hon. Ashley Eden sets out as envoy on a mission to the Deb Rāja of Bhutān to seek redress for the frequent raids of the Bhutiyas on the British Dwārs bordering on that state.

SIR JOHN LAWRENCE, THIRD VICEROY.

Jan. 12: Sir John Lawrence arrived at Calcutta, and assumed office as Viceroy, till Jan. 12, 1869.

March 15: Sir Ashley Eden's mission to Bhutān reached Punākha the winter capital, but is grossly insulted both by the Deb Rāja and the Dharma Rāja, and ordered to leave. 24: Tongso Penlo, the Governor of Eastern Bhutān, demanded the cession of the Asām Dwārs; then barbarously insulted the envoy and his officers. 29: Mr Eden was compelled to sign the cession of the Dwārs.

March: Government took steps to prevent Hindus from casting their dead into the Huglī instead of burning them: this sanitary arrangement caused excitement.

March 28: Rāmavarmā succeeds Ravivarmā as Rāja of Kochin.

May: Sherdil Khān of Kalāt murdered, and Khodadād Khān re-elected chief of the state.

June 18: Wazīr-ud-daula, Nawāb of Tonk, dies. Muhammad 'Alī Khān succeeds.

A.D.

1864 July: A gold currency is proposed to be introduced at Christmas.

Sher 'Alī Khān of Afghānistān recognised by the British Government as Amīr. He treacherously imprisons his brother Afzal Khān.

Rāja Bahādur of Samtar takes over the administration of the state. His insane father, Hindupat, is removed with the Rānī to Amra.

Sept. 30: Mr Robert Davies appointed as Special Commissioner in Audh with power to direct the settlement officers and decide all questions of tenant right.

Oct. 1: The administration of Dhār transferred to the young Rāja Ānand Rāo Puār, under certain restrictions.

Oct. 5: A terrific cyclone occurs at Calcutta and Lower Bengal, with immense loss of life and damage to shipping and property; nearly 30,000 perished between Calcutta and the sea, and as many on the Madras coast.

Oct. 14: Sir J. Lawrence entered Lāhor. 18: He holds a great darbār on the plain,—604 native princes present. The Rāja of Kapurthala invested with the Star of India.

Nov. 12: The Bhutān authorities having taken no notice of the repudiation of Sir A. Eden's agreement and demand for reparation, the Viceroy issues a proclamation of war, and annexes the eleven western or Bengal Dwārs. Some 6,000 troops were sent to capture the five or six forts commanding the passes into Bhutān and all were taken next month.

Dec. 25: José Ferreira Pestaña takes office at Goa as Governor for the second time.

The *Durges Nandini*, a historical novel after the manner of Sir Walter Scott, by Benkim Chandra Chatarji, published.

1865 Jan. 29: The Bhutiyas suddenly attack the garrison of 500 sipāhis in Diwāngiri, but were finally repulsed with heavy loss. Feb. 5: The water being cut off and ammunition run short, the garrison left the fort and three guns. April 2: Brigadier H. Tombs recaptures the fort and compels the Bhutias to sue for peace, which was concluded Nov. 13, when they resigned the Bengal Dwārs and gave up the two guns, but received Rs. 25,000 yearly during good behaviour.

A.D.

1865 March 1: The Indo-European Telegraph from Karāchi, *via* Persia and Turkey, opened.

March 31: W. Massey, finance minister in succession to Sir C. Trevelyan, arrived at Calcutta. April 1: Sir C. Trevelyan announced a large deficit in the revenue.

April 23: Sir Hugh Rose retired from the command of the army and is succeeded by Sir Wm. Mansfield, Baron Sandhurst.

April 29: Ghaus Muhammad of Jaurā died; his young son, Muhammad Ismā'īl, succeeded under a regency.

Bairī Sāl appointed successor to Ranjīt Singh Mahārāwal of Jaisalmīr, having been adopted by the widow of Ranjīt Singh: installed next year.

May: Sir Chas. Trevelyan's finance plans were reversed by Sir Charles Wood.

June: The Maisur Rāja adopted a son, named Chāma Rājendra.

July: The Thākur of Lāwa complained to the British Government of the unusual demands made upon him by Muhammad 'Alī Khān of Tonk, who now assaulted Lāwa, but was repulsed with loss. A British officer settled the dispute for the time.

July 31: Jagannāth 'Sankar Seth, a prominent wealthy Hindu of Bombay, died.

Aug.: The Daudputra chiefs of Bahāwalpur rebel against their ruler.

Aug. 24: The ship "Eagle Speed" wrecked in the Hughlī and 265 coolies perished.

Aug.-Nov. The failure of the rainfall in Orissa occasions an awful famine resulting at length in the loss of 1,500,000 or a fourth of the population.

Nov. 17: Sambhu Singh, Rānā of Udaypur, attains his majority and takes over the administration.

1866 Jan. The Nawāb of Bahāwalpur, victorious over his rebel chiefs, died suddenly and suspiciously. His son, Sādiq Muhammad Khān, a child of four, succeeded. The British supported his claims, and it was subsequently decided to place the administration in British hands for reorganisation.

Jan: Famine became severe in Orissa. Feb. 1: Government

A.D.

1866 relief not supposed to be required. Mr Cecil Beadon went on a tour of investigation.

March 27: Mahārāo Rām Singh of Kotā died. The political agent prevented the performance of *satī*. Chatra Singh succeeded.

March 27: Lord Napier of Merchiston succeeds Sir Wm. Denison as Governor of Madras, till Feb. 19, 1872.

April: The question respecting the marriage of converted Hindus settled. First attempt made at a census of the North-Western and Central Provinces.

May: 'Abdul Rahman, Sher 'Alī's nephew, collects a force, regains his freedom at Shekhābād, and is proclaimed Amīr. Amīr Sher 'Alī, defeated by 'Abdul Rahman, son of Afzal Khan, near Ghaznī, fled to Qandahār—still holding it and Harāt. His brother, Afzal Khān, proclaimed Amīr at Kābul. The Viceroy refuses intervention.

April-June: The great Khojā case is tried in Bombay, the arguments and examination of witnesses occupying twenty-five days. The Khojās attached to Sunnī customs opposing Muhammad Husain Husainī, or Āghā Khān, the head of the Shī'ah-Imāmī Ismā'īlīas who claims the property and support of the Khojā community. On 12th Nov. judgment was delivered in his favour.

Aug. 4: Rāja Sivājī III. of Kolhāpur dies childless: on his deathbed he adopted his nephew Rājarām as heir.

Sept. 17: Capt. E. Jervis, tried on a charge of peculation of stores belonging to Sir Wm. Mansfield, was acquitted, but he was condemned for insubordination: his sentence of dismissal from the service was approved by Sir Wm. Mansfield, Commander-in-Chief.

Oct. 6: Dr Geo. Cotton, Bishop of Calcutta, accidentally drowned at Kushtia in Asām.

Nov. 19: Lord Lawrence held a great darbār at Agra, attended by eighty-fonr princes and chiefs from Rājputāna and Central India, and about two hundred and fifty from other provinces. The accompanying ceremonies lasted from 10th to 20th.

1867 Jan. 17: The Duke of Cambridge wrote confirming the sentence against Capt. E. Jervis, but censuring Sir W. Mansfield.

A.D.

1867 Jan. Sher 'Alī was defeated by his brother, 'Azim Khān, near Kalāt-ī-Ghilzai, and fled to Harāt which, with Balkh, was the only part of his dominions still loyal.

Feb. 12: At a public meeting in Calcutta the Viceroy appealed for help to send 27,000 tons of rice to the Orissa famine-stricken districts.

March 6: The Hon. Sir Seymour Fitzgerald arrived as Governor of Bombay, in succession to Sir Bartle Frere, till May 6, 1872.

March 10 to April 12: The great Hindu festival, held every twelfth year at Gangādwāra or Haridwār. At the close cholera broke out.

April: Sir William Gray succeeded Sir Cecil Beadon as Lieut.-Governor of Bengal, till March 1871.

Aug. 1: Muhammad 'Alī Khān of Tonk treacherously murdered Rawat Sing, uncle, and the retainers of the Thākur of Lāwa. 8: The Thākur relieved by a British officer; Muhammad 'Alī is deposed; and Lāwa made independent of Tonk.

Aug. Khem Sāwant died; his son, Anna Sāwant, succeeded, but being addicted to opium, his power was restricted.

Sept. In Orissa 270,000 people are kept alive by relief committees.

Oct. Afzal Khān of Afghanistan died. His brother, 'Azim Khān, succeeded; the British Government in India decided to maintain strict neutrality.

Nov. 1: A severe cyclone at Calcutta did much damage, ruining houses, uprooting trees, and sinking boats.

Nov. General Fytche, chief Commissioner of Burma, concluded a treaty with the king. Sir Edward Bosc Sladen also negotiated a treaty at Mandalay.

Dec. 29: The Wāghars of Okhāmandal are brought to bay at Mānaharda hill by Major Reynolds, and in the fight were almost exterminated.

1868 Jan. Muhammad Ibrāhīm 'Alī Khān placed on the throne of Tonk in room of Muhammad 'Alī Khān deposed.

Jan. 9: Major-General Sir Donald Stewart and staff leave Calcutta on the expedition to Abyssinia under General Robt. C. Napier, for the relief of Europeans imprisoned by King Theodore.

A.D.

1868 Jan. Capt. Sladen, sent on a mission to Tālifū, detained by Burmese obstructiveness at Bhamo and Momain; he returned some months later to Mandalay.

March 14: The budget surplus eight karors of rupees; the licence tax abolished; taxes on trades, &c., substituted, and 170 lākhs proposed for public works.

March 27: Krishna Rāja Udayār of Maisur died. Sept. 23: His adopted son, Chāma Rājendra, aged six, succeeded under a regency. Major Malleson appointed chief Commissioner till 1877.

March: Yā'qūb Khān, eldest son of Sher 'Alī, captures Qandahār. July: Sher 'Alī and Yā'qūb move on Ghazni and 'Azim takes to flight. Sept. 8: Sher 'Alī regained possession of Kābul and his dominions, except Balkh, where 'Azim and 'Abdul Rahman held out. Sher 'Alī receives six lākhs from the Viceroy as a donation and pledge of friendship.

April 13: Sir Robert Napier successfully attacked Magdala and released the European prisoners of King Theodore.

July: The rains failed and famine threatened in Rājputāna and Upper Provinces; timely arrangements against which Lord Lawrence made.

Oct. 3: The Hasanzai Pathāns having attacked the Panjāb police station of Oghi in Hazāra in the hot season, a punitive expedition under General Wylde started from Oghi and drove the enemy from Kun-gali. 5: The troops carried the Machai peak. 10: The headmen of the villages sued for peace, and agreed on terms including the expulsion of Indian refugees and Wahhābis.

Oct. 19: The "Panjāb Tenancy Bill" passed by the Viceroy's Council and sent to the Secretary of State for India, by whom it is finally approved next year.

Oct. 31: Sikandra Begam of Bhopal died. Her daughter, Shāh Jahān Begam, succeeded.

An attempt made by a Musalman to assassinate Sir Sālār Jang, the prime minister at Haidarābād. The would-be assassin executed, March 21st, 1869.

Nov. The Viceroy formally opened the railway joining Ambāla and Dehli.

Severe famine, 1868-69.

A.D.

1869 Jan. 3: Sher 'Alī defeated 'Azim Khān and 'Abdul Rahman at Timak Khān, near Ghazni, and established himself as sole ruler of Afghānistān. 'Abdul Rahman retired to Samarqānd, where for ten years he received an allowance from Russia.

LORD MAYO, FOURTH VICEROY.

Jan. 12: Lord Mayo arrived at Calcutta to succeed Sir John Lawrence as Viceroy of India. 19: Sir John left for England.

Feb. 25: An Imperial Edict abolished slavery in all the Portuguese dominions.

Feb. 26: Afzal ud-daula, Nizām of Haidarābād, died. March 1: Mir Mahbūb 'Alī Khān succeeded under a council of regency, headed by Sir Sālār Jang, during his minority.

March: The budget deficient by two and three-quarter karors of rupees. An income tax of 1 per cent. is applied.

March 27: Lord Mayo, in darbār at Ambāla, met Sher 'Ali. 29: In private interview, though unable to obtain all his demands, the Amīr received another six lākhs of rupees, 6,000 rifles, and some artillery. A cordial understanding established.

April 1: New divorce act came into operation.

Aug. 11: Act passed by Parliament for the better governing of India and defining the Governor-General's powers.

Aug. 22: Keshab Chandra Sen, religious Bengali teacher, opens his own Brahmo Mandir or Theistic temple in Calcutta. He died Jan. 8, 1884.

Oct. 6: 'Azim Khān, ex-Amīr of Kābul, died at Shāh Rūd.

Faridūn Jāh, Nawāb of Murshidābād, went to England to lay his grievances before Government, but met with little success.

Dec. 2: A decree is passed to reform the army of Portuguese India, and to bring it within the means and requirements of the State. The arsenal at Goa is abolished.

Dec.-April 1870: H.R.H. The Duke of Edinburgh visited India. Dec. 22-Jan. 7, 1870: At Calcutta. Great darbār held on the Maidān.

1870 Jan. 7: H.R.H. The Duke of Edinburgh left Calcutta for a tour in the Upper Provinces.

Feb. 22: In consequence of the attempted army reform,

A.D.

1870 military riots break out in Goa. The revolutionaries having gained their point, dictate to the Government.

March 1: The Prince of Wales opened at Jabalpur the completed railway from Bombay to Allahābād.

March: An embassy from Yā'qūb Beg, the conqueror of Kāshghār, reached Calcutta requesting friendly intercourse.

April 2: On the death of Ranbīr Sīngh of Kapurthala, near Aden, his son, Kharak Singh, succeeded.

April 26: Mr Douglas Forsyth started on a mission to Kāshghār, and reached Yārqand, returning in autumn.

May 6: Yā'qūb Khān rebels against his father, the Amīr Sher 'Ali, and captures Harāt.

May 7: Januario Correia de Almeida, Conde de S. Januario, takes office as Governor-General at Goa, till Dec. 10, 1871.

May: Mahārāja Ranbīr Singh of Kāshmīr made a commercial treaty with the Viceroy for the development of trade with E. Turkistān.

June 1: Sir Henry Durand succeeded Sir Donald Macleod as Lieut.-Governor of the Punjāb.

July 8—Sept. 23: The administrative duties of the Madras Presidency conducted for the first time at Uttakamand.

Oct: The great railway bridge over the Satlaj opened.

Nov. 29: Khanderāv Gaikwād of Baroda dies in a fit of passion because directed to replace his minion Dīwān by some one of character. Malhārrāv, his brother, succeeds. He had been confined at Pādra for years on suspicion of having attempted his brother Khanderāv's life.

Nov. 30: Rāja Rām of Kolhāpur dies at Florence. His successor, Mahārāja Chatrapati IV., assumes the name of Sivaji and governs under a council of regency.

Dec. 14: The Provincial Governments to receive fixed annual allotments, to be spent on cost of police, education, printing, roads and public works, &c.

1871 Jan. 1: Sir H. M. Durand, Lieut.-Governor of the Panjab, killed at Tānk,—crushed on an elephant's back under a gateway.

A.D.

1871 Jan. The Lūshais in Eastern Bengal make savage raids into Kachār, and arrangements are begun to punish them.

Volunteer system proposed for India.

Feb. The 19th Madras Native Infantry mutiny, and give trouble.

March 1: Sir George Campbell, successor to Sir Wm. Grey as Lieut.-Governor of Bengal, till April 1874.

Sir Donald Stewart, chief Commissioner in the Andaman Islands, till 1875.

Mahārāja Rājendra Pratāp Shāhi of Hasainpur died, and was succeeded by his son, Krishna Pratāp Shāhi, a minor.

June: Faramuz, the general of Amīr Sher 'Alī, assassinated by Aslam. Oct.: Aslam killed in prison.

June 14-15: Riot at Amritsar, the Hindus attack the Muhammadan butchers, killing several.

July 5: Maulvi Liakat 'Alī, a rebel who, in 1857, ruled as viceroy at Allahābād, captured.

July 8: Yā'qūb Khān reconciled to his father at Kābul through Lord Mayo; made governor of Harāt. Sept.: He again rebels.

Aug. 5: The Indian Civil Engineering College at Cooper's Hill opened by the Duke of Argyll.

Sept. 20: Chief Justice J. P. Norman, during the trial of Amīr Khān and other Wahhābis at Calcutta, stabbed by a Panjābi. 21: He died. 28: Assassin convicted, and Nov. 4: executed.

Sept. 21-24: Further rebellions in the Goa army necessitate measures for the prevention of such outbreaks; four revolutionary battalions disbanded, the military school abolished, and the force limited to one expeditionary battalion, a battery of artillery, and a police corps.

Nov. 6: Lord Mayo visiting Pālampur fair, holds a rural darbār.

Nov. 23: Military expedition under Generals Bourchier, Brownlow, and Nuttall, against the Lūshais to punish their raids. Dec. 2, and 21, 23, 26: Skirmishes. Dec. 29: They sued for peace, captives given up, and hostages taken from some tribes; others hold out.

A.D.

1871 Dec. 10: Joachim José Macedo e Conto, Governor-General at Goa, till May 10, 1875.

1872 Jan. 7-12: The King of Siam visits Calcutta.

Jan. 11: Under Rām Singh as leader, a fanatical sect of Kūkās attempt to raise an insurrection at Malair-kotlā near Ludhiāna, in the Panjāb, but it was completely suppressed by Jan. 27, and the leader deported as a state prisoner to Burma.

Jan. 15-17: A band of Kūkā fanatics rush Malodh fort in Sarhind, and another attempt to take Malair-Kotlā and seize the treasury. Deputy-Commissioner Cowan suppressed the outbreak and ordered forty-nine prisoners to be blown away from guns Others tried and executed some days later by the Commissioner T. Douglas Forsyth: Cowan dismissed and Forsyth removed from his post.

Jan. 26: Lord Mayo left Calcutta for Burma; visited Rangūn and Maulmain. Feb. 5: He left and, 8: at the convict settlement of Port Blair in the Andaman Islands, was assassinated by Sher, Alī, a transported Afghān convict. Sir J. Strachey, senior Member of Council, acts as Governor till the arrival of Lord Napier of Merchistoun from Madras, Feb. 23, who officiates.

Feb. 9: The King of Siam visited Calcutta on his return home.

Feb. 17: The Lūshai expedition reached the village of Lalbura, the Lūshai ringleader, who had fled: the force returned; March 6, reached Tipai-mukh.

Feb. 19: Alexander John Arbuthnot, acting Governor of Madras, till May 15, when Lord Hobart assumed office till his death on April 27, 1875.

Feb. 28: The Lūshais surrender unconditionally: army returning. March 7: the Khāmti tribe, while carrying off Lūshai captives, defeated, and captives rescued.

March 12: Sher 'Alī, the assassin of Lord Mayo, hanged without confessing associates. Annual pension to Lady Mayo by India of £1,000: grant of £20,000 for his children.

April: Sir Richard Temple's budget yields a surplus of about a million and three-quarters; income tax reduced.

A.D.
1872

EARL OF NORTHBROOK, FIFTH VICEROY.

May 3: Thomas George Baring, first Earl of Northbrook, arrives as Viceroy, till April 12, 1876.

May 6: Sir Philip Wodehouse succeeds Sir Vesey Fitzgerald as Governor of Bombay, till April 30, 1877.

July 26: The Bombay Government notifies that the privileges of the *firmān* under which the Portuguese goods were imported to Surat at 2½ per cent., would cease on Sept. 1, owing to the misuse made of them in underselling Bombay goods. Strong protests are made from the Portuguese minister in London.

July 27: Maulvi Liakat 'Alī, on confession, condemned to transportation for life.

July: Christian marriage bill passed.

Aug. 12: Col. Goldsmid's report on the Afghān-Persian boundary given in.

Nov. 16: The Begam of Bhopāl—Nawāb Shāhjahān—made a Knight Grand Commander of the Star of India by Lord Northbrook at Bombay.

1873 Jan. 1: Mr T. D. Forsyth sent to meet the envoy of Muhammad Yā'qūb Beg of Kāshghār.

Jan. 31: A neutral zone determines the confines of British and Russian influence in Central Asia. Only 400 miles at this time separate their boundaries.

March: Major Macdonald murdered by Bahrām Khān, Mohmand chief, at Fort Michni.

March: Col. Phayre, Resident at Baroda: Complaints made of Malhārrāv's misrule, folly, and extravagance.

March 31: Sir R. Temple's budget: the Indian Income Tax abolished.

The Khān of Khiva opposed the demands of Russia to cease slave-raids on Russian territory; his appeal to India for help refused.

May: The Khān of Kalāt or Baluchistān and his chiefs' constant quarrelling cause the withdrawal of diplomatic relations and suspension of the subsidy.

June 10: The Russians capture Khiva and impose an enormous indemnity on the Khān.

A.D.

1873 June: Sayyīd Nūr Muhammad, envoy from the Amīr Sher 'Alī, arrived at Simla. July 12-30: He convenes with the Viceroy on the Afghān and Russian Boundary question. Complete alliance requested, but friendly neutrality only conceded by the Government of India.

The Gaikwād of Baroda's government inquired into by a Commission. Malhārrāv warned that unless great improvement be manifested by the end of 1875, he will be deposed in the interest of the people, and for the peace and security of the Empire.

Aug. 18: Mr Forsyth started from Yārqand to accompany the envoy of Yā'qūb Beg to India.

Owing to claims made on the Nizāmat of Murshidābād, a Commission appointed to discharge such as are chargeable, and to exempt the Nawāb from the jurisdiction of the civil Courts.

Sept. 8: The Mullā of Tūtakkal masjid in Malabar with eight other Māppillas murdered the priest of the Hindu temple and hastened to Kulattūr where two men of the Vāriyār's family are murdered. Attacked by Capt. Vesey they charged home on the bayonets and eight of the nine were killed. The parishes concerned fined Rs. 42,000.

Nov. Messrs Bernard, Geddes, and Robinson appointed Commissioners in anticipation of famine in Bengal.

Mahārāja Kirat Singh of Dholpur dying, his grandson, Nihal Singh, succeeded.

Dec. Sher 'Alī nominates his youngest son, 'Abdullah Jān, his successor, to the great dissatisfaction of his elder son, Yāq'ūb.

1874 Jan. 11: 'Azīm Jāh Bahādur Nawāb of Arkat dies, aged seventy-four. His son, Zahir-ud-daula Bahādur, succeeds to the nominal title.

Jan. The failure of the rains causing severe famine, Sir Richard Temple appointed superintendent of relief in Bihār. Fifteen districts much distressed and eleven others affected. Temple estimates the need at a million tons of rice, and the expenditure at £6,500,000.

Jan. 24: The Mansion House relief fund begun in London for the Bengal famine. Feb. 4: £1,000 given by Queen Victoria. July 27: The fund closed; £125,000 collected.

A.D.
1874 Feb. 2: Treaty between Muhammad Yā'qūb Beg of Kāshghār and the Indian Government arranging trade and transit of goods, and appointment of representatives at Yārqand.

Feb. 13: Outbreak of Muhammadan fanatics at Bombay against the Pārsīs,—a Pārsī having published a Gujarāti translation of Irving's "Life of Mahomet:" A Pārsī temple gutted, a number of Pārsī houses plundered and wrecked and the inmates ill-used.

Feb. 21: The Marquis of Salisbury, Secretary of State for India, till March 30, 1878.

March: The revenue accounts showed a deficit of £1,807,668. March 30: A loan not exceeding ten million pounds for India Government authorised by Parliament.

March 31: A Crown Prosecutor appointed for Madras.

April 7: Sir John Strachey succeeds Sir Wm. Muir as Lieut.-Governor of N.W. Provinces, till Dec. 1876.

April 9: Sir Richard Temple, successor to Sir Geo. Campbell, as Lieut.-Governor of Bengal.

April 11: Report on the Bengal famine, stating the number of persons on the relief works reduced to 1,185,468, and 116,371 receiving free alms. June 29: Further report of the labourers having increased to 1,737,768, and those on charitable relief to 401,962. July 12: The number of labourers on relief works reduced to 895,000, but the paupers on alms increased to 525,620 individuals.

Sept. Sādan Khān, a cruel leader in the Mutiny, condemned to death.

Oct. Mahārāja Seodan Singh of Alwār dies. Mangal Singh, son of Hardeo Singh, representative of the Thāna family, succeeds.

Oct. 7: Mahārāna Sambhu Singh of Udaypur dies. Sarjun Singh, his cousin, succeeds by adoption.

Oct. 21: A man supposed to be Nāna Sāhib, captured at Gwāliar by Mahārāja Sindia: identity disproved.

Nov. 9: Attempted poisoning of Col. R. Phayre, Resident at Baroda, instigated by the Gaikwād.

Nov. 26: Poppy cultivation sanctioned under the Portuguese Government in Mozambique, for export to India and China.

Dec. 30: The Portuguese Government of India contracts with the British India Steam Navigation Co. for a steam service

A.D.

1874 from Lisbon to Goa *via* Suez, also for a service between Mozambique, Quilimane, and Lourenço Marques.

Dec. Yā'qūb Khān imprisoned by his father, Sher 'Alī.

During 1874 state emigration from Bengal to British Burma undertaken to relieve the effects of scarcity and promote cultivation of waste lands.

Dec. 23: Col. H. Browne, Dr Anderson, and Mr Ney Elias on a mission through Burma to China, received by King Mengdun Meng at Māndalé.

1875 Jan. 4: The Nāgās of Wokhā, attacking the survey party under Capt. Butler, met by a counter-attack, and the village fired. Jan. 10: Capt. Butler again attacked by 400 to 500 Nāgās drives them off with heavy loss. Later, Capt. Butler cut off and killed. About Feb. 24: Lieut. Holcombe and his surveying party, about seventy, treacherously massacred.

Jan. 14: Sir Lewis Pelly appointed Special Commissioner at Baroda, in succession to the Resident, Col. Phayre, to institute an inquiry into Malhārrāv Gaikwād's conduct and government. Malhārrāv taken to Calcutta for trial.

Jan. 15: Col. Browne reached Bhāmo. 17: A. R. Margary, from Hankau, joined the Mission. Feb. 21: Margary murdered by Chinese at Manwain. The party, attacked by the Chinese, retreated.

Jan. 29: The Daplā tribes in N.E. Āsām having raided on border villages, a body of troops was sent against them—they surrendered and paid a fine.

Feb. 23: The trial of the Gaikwād of Baroda for attempted poisoning of Sir Robert Phayre begun. The case referred to the Home Government. Lord Salisbury moves the deposal of Malhārrāv on account of his notorious misconduct and previous maladministration.

March 15-25: The Nāgā tribes severely chastised for their conduct in January.

April 23: The Viceroy, by proclamation, deposed the Gaikwād and he was deported to Madras. He died in 1882.

May 27: Gopālrāv, aged sixteen, adopted by Jamnā Bāī, widow of Khanderāv Gaikwād, installed as Siyaji Rāo III. at Baroda. During his minority a council of regency governed.

A.D.

1875 April 27: Lord Hobart died at Madras. 29: Mr William Rose Robinson acts till Nov. 23, when the Duke of Buckingham and Chandos took office as Governor, till Dec. 20, 1880.

May 10: João Tavares de Almeida succeeds as Governor of Portuguese India, till July 24, 1877.

June 15: A British embassy under Sir T. Douglas Forsyth received by King Mengdun Meng, and obtained agreement to the independence of the Western Karen-ni states; but permission for a British convoy through Burma to China refused.

Col. Duncan sent to Māndalé. Oct. Announcement that the British demands are acceded to.

Oct. Mayo College at Ajmīr for the education of native nobles opened.

Nov. 18: A conspiracy to seize the arsenal and set fire to Rangūn city discovered and defeated.

Nov. 8: His Royal Highness Edward Prince of Wales lands at Bombay. Dec. 11: He visits Madras. Dec. 23: Arrives at Calcutta. He receives the chiefs and rulers in a great encampment on the Calcutta Maidān.

Dec. 19: Mahārāo Prāgmalji Bahādur of Kachh is succeeded by his son Kengarji, a minor; the State managed by a Council till 1882.

Dec. 20: Defeat of the Malays at Kinta in the peninsula by British troops.

1876 Jan. 1: The Prince of Wales unveiled the statue of Lord Mayo at Calcutta. 7: Arrived at Lucknow; 11: at Dehli; and 18: at Lahore. Feb. 12: Reception by Sir Jang Bahādur, Prime Minister of Nepāl. March 13: Left from Bombay for England.

Feb. Lord Northbrook asks the Home Government to relieve him of the Viceroyalty.

April 3: Bill giving the title of Empress of India to the Queen is passed by the House of Lords. 28: Proclamation of Queen Victoria as "Indiæ Imperatrix," or "Empress of India." Aug. 18: It is notified by the Viceroy that the title will be officially proclaimed at a great Darbār at Dehli on 1st January 1877.

April 10: Field-Marshal Lord Robert C. Napier of Magdala, Commander-in-Chief, leaves from Bombay, and is succeeded by Sir Frederick P. Haines, till 1881.

A.D.

1876 April 12: Lord Northbrook, differing from the Home Government on Afghān policy, and having resigned office, Edward Robert, Lord Lytton, appointed his successor, arrives at Calcutta.

LORD LYTTON, SIXTH VICEROY.

April 12: The Earl of Lytton arrived, and took the oaths as Viceroy at Calcutta.

April 14: Mahendra Singh of Patiāla dies. Rājendra Singh, his infant son, succeeds under a council of regency.

April: Sir Robert Groves Sandeman negotiates a treaty with the Khān of Kalāt, and, Nov. 2: locates a strong force at Quetta, or Shālkot, to keep the unruly chiefs in subjection. Dec. 8: At an interview between the Khān and the Viceroy at Jacobābād, the treaty of 1854 renewed, with additions, and an agent is to remain at his court.

Prithvi Singh, Rāja of Jhālāvār, died without male issue; Bakht Singh adopted as heir, rules under a council of regency presided over by a British officer.

May 1: The Queen proclaimed Empress of India in London.

May 22: Sher 'Alī objects to the Viceroy's proposal to send Sir Lewis Pelly or any British envoy to Kābul.

Sept. The Amīr Sher 'Ali, being pressed to receive an envoy, offers to send his Vakīl to India to consult on matters in dispute. Oct. The Vakīl meets the Viceroy at Simla, who insists on placing British officers at Harāt and elsewhere: the conditions to be settled at a conference to be held at Peshāwar between the Amīr's minister and Sir L. Pelly.

July: At Agra Mr Fuller, a Eurasiān, had slapped a native servant for neglect, who died soon after from another cause; he was fined by a magistrate; sentence considered too light by the High Court. The Viceroy interfered with the case, censuring both the magistrate and the High Court.

Aug. 11: Deficiency through depreciation of silver currency: loss about £2,300,000: loan of £4,000,000 proposed.

Oct. 31: In a great cyclone, an enormous storm wave swept over the delta of the Ganges and Brahmaputrā, causing the loss of about 220,000 lives and immense loss of crops and property.

A.D.

1876 Oct. Famine reported in the Madras districts of Belāri, Kadapā and Nelūr, and in southern districts of Bombay and Maisūr.

Nov. Sir George Couper appointed Governor of North-West Provinces.

Nov. 20: An agricultural college is opened at Sa'idāpet, near Madras.

Dec. 31: Reception by the Viceroy at the camp of Dehli of seventy-five native princes and chiefs to be present at the proclamation of the Queen Empress next day.

1877 Jan. 1: Act 39 & 40, Victoria, proclaimed at a great Darbār at Dehli in presence of the Indian princes, by which the Queen assumed the additional title of Indiæ Imperatrix, or Empress of India. The proclamation also made at Calcutta, Bombay, and Madras.

Jan. 6: The Viceroy installed Rājendra Singh, the young son, aged five, of the late Patiāla chief.

Jan. The Hon. Ashley Eden recalled from Burma to succeed Sir Richard Temple as Lieut.-Governor of Bengal, till 1882. Jan. 19: Sir R. Temple visiting the famine-stricken districts.

Jan. 30: Sir Lewis Pelly meets Nūr Muhammad, the Afghān envoy, at Peshāwar, to secure that British officers should reside in Afghānistān. March 26: Nūr Muhammad died and negotiations ceased.

Feb. 25: Mahārāja Kunwar Rānaji Jand Bahādur of Nepāl died.

April: Raids of the Afrīdīs on the north-west frontiers suppressed.

April 29: Famine relief works organising, reports favourable.

April 30: Sir Richard Temple succeeds Sir P. Wodehouse as Governor of Bombay, till March 27, 1885.

May 1 (?): Muhammad Yā'qūb Beg of Kāshghār, defeated by the Chinese, and assassinated. Nov. Kāshghār taken and Eastern Turkistān regained by the Chinese.

July 3: Sir James Robert Longden appointed Governor of Ceylon.

July 24: João Tavares de Almeida, Portuguese governor, dies at Panjim. The archbishop, the presiding judge, the colone

A.D.

1877 of the army, and the secretary of State take charge of the administration till Nov. 12, when Antonio Sergio de Sousa, Visconde de Sergio, takes office as Governor-General.

Aug. Drought, followed by famine, visits the Central Provinces, the Panjāb and Upper Provinces. Aug. Nearly a million people reported to have died from want of food. Aug. 12: Public meeting at Madras to call for help. Aug. 15: Indian famine relief fund announced at the Mansion House. Nov. 5: £446,100 received. Fund declared closed by request of the Duke of Buckingham, Governor of Madras. Till May 20, 1878: total received £689,466. 17s.

Aug. 29: Employed on Government famine works 919,771; and 1,326,771 relieved gratuitously. Oct. 7: The crisis reported to be over.

Sept. Rāja Jagatjit Singh, a minor, succeeds his father, Kharak Singh, as Rāja of Kapurthala.

Aug. 29-30: The Jawākīs, an Afrīdī clan, having raided in British territory, are chastised by Col. J. A. H. Pollock. Oct. 21: The Jawākīs attacked Ghovizai village, killing and wounding several men. 22: Attack on Togh, near Kohat. 23: They attack Kanmer. 25: Engage a Havildār's party at Shāhkōt, near Kerat, killing five and wounding six. Nov. 9: Gen. Keyes entered their territory, and, 11th, took Paya. 14: An attack at Shādipur was repulsed. Jamu, their stronghold, taken. Dec. They are defeated and dispersed. 8: Proclamation of the Viceroy to the tribe.

Dec. Rev. Thomas Valpy appointed first Bishop of Lāhor.

Dec. Sir John Strachey's budget assigns a million and a half to be employed annually as insurance for famines; taxation raised; trade licences assessed, &c.

Dec. 31: "Imperial Order of the Crown of India" instituted for ladies.

1878 Feb. 15: The Jawākīs defeated by cavalry. 22: They surrendered unconditionally.

March 14: Bill passed in Council for the control of the Indian vernacular press.

April 17: The British ministry instructed the Government of India to send 7,000 native troops to Malta—regarded as a menace

A.D.
1878 to Russia invading Turkey. May 30: The first contingent arrives. Aug. Removed to Cyprus. Russia orders a mission to Kābul.

April 29: The Queen holds an investiture at Windsor of the Imperial Order of the Crown of India: twelve ladies invested.

May 3: The Visconde de Sergio dies at Goa. A temporary administration formed till Dec. 3, when Caetano Alexandre de Almeida e Albuquerque takes office as Governor-General.

June: General Stoletoff leads the Russian mission of three superior officers to Afghānistān. July 22: They are received in darbār at Kābul, the envoy delivering to the Amīr Sher 'Alī, a letter from the Russian Emperor.

Aug. 14: Lord Lytton writes Sher 'Alī, informing him that General Sir N. Chamberlain is to visit him as a special envoy. 17: 'Abdulla Jān, the Amīr's favourite son and designated heir, dies. 23: Lord Lytton writes offering condolences.

Sept. 2: The Governor-General decides to send a large mission to the Amīr Sher 'Alī. 21: The mission under Sir Neville Chamberlain leaves Peshāwar, with eleven British officers, 234 soldiers, and about 700 camp followers. 22: It is stopped by the Afghān officer at 'Alī Masjid, who refuses to allow the mission to pass. 26: The Governor-General orders a concentration of troops on the Afghān frontier.

Sept. 11: Mengdun Meng, King of Burma, dies, after a reign of thirty-five years. Oct. 2: The death announced. He is succeeded by Thībau (Wongyī, Prince of Thībau) as king.

Oct. 19: The Amīr sends a reply to the Indian Government, regarded as discourteous in tone; and, against the counsel of Sir John Lawrence, war is resolved upon. 31: The Viceroy informs the Amīr Sher 'Alī that, failing an apology and agreement to receive a British mission to Kābul, he would be treated as an enemy—a reply being asked before Nov. 20. Nov. 21: No reply being received, General Sir F. Roberts, with the advanced guard, crossed the Kuram and occupied the Afghān village of Kapuyan. 22: Lord Lytton's proclamation made at Lāhor of the commencement of hostilities, stating that on Sher 'Alī alone rested the responsibility of having exchanged the friendship for the hostility of the Empress of India. 22: General Sir Samuel Browne captures 'Alī Masjid, after a short bombardment. 24: Dhākā and Pishīn occupied.

A.D.

1879 Dec. 2: The British force under General Roberts totally defeated the Afghāns at the Paiwār pass. Dec. 9: Reached the Shatr-gardan pass. 11: Alikhel occupied.

Dec. 7: The Amīr's reply to the Governor-General, received at Lāhor, saying that "if the British Government should desire to send a purely friendly and temporary mission to his country, with a small escort of not more than twenty or thirty members, similar to that which attended the Russian mission, he would not oppose its progress."

Dec. 13: Sher 'Alī flees to Russian Turkistan, leaving his son Yā'qūb as recognised Amīr, to defend Kābul. The Russian mission withdrawn.

Dec. 20: The troops under command of General Sir S. Browne occupy Jalālābād. 26: At a "Darbār" held at Kuram Fort, General Roberts proclaims the annexation to the Indian empire of the Kuram district including the valleys of Khost and Dāwar. 30: The Ghwaja pass and the Khojak pass are crossed by the forces under Generals Stewart and Biddulph.

Dec. 26: A treaty of extradition and commerce between the British and Portuguese Governments in respect to their several Indian possessions is signed at Lisbon.

1879 Jan. 1: Darbār held at Jalālābād in honour of the Queen as Empress of India: General Sir Louis Cavignari explains to the Afghān chiefs the objects of the Indian Government.

Jan. 3: General Roberts with his force enters the Khost district. 6: Reaches Matūn which is surrendered by the governor: but the tribesmen attack the force. 27: Returns to Matūn and relieves the native governor, leaving the local Māliks in charge. 30: The natives attack Roberts's force but are repulsed. Feb. 2: The *Standard* correspondent expelled from General Roberts's camp.

Feb. 16: King Thībau at Māndalé, orders the assassination of eighty-six persons, being all princes of the royal family and their relations.

Feb. 21: Death of Amīr Sher 'Alī at Mazar-i-Sharif.

March: Daring Dākaītīs made by Rāmoshīs under Vāsudev Balwant Phadke in the districts round Poona

A.D.

1879 March 31: About forty-six of the 10th Hussars drowned in crossing the Kābul river.

April 2: General Gough defeats, near Fathiābād, about 5,000 Khagianis, incited to attack him by Yā'qūb Khān.

April 3: Sir Chas. U. Aitcheson, Lieut.-Governor of the Panjāb, till April 2, 1887.

April 17: Sir Alfred C. Lyall succeeds Sir George Couper as Lieut.-Governor of N.W. Provinces and Audh.

May 8: Yā'qūb Khān arrives in Sir Samuel Browne's camp at Gandāmak to negotiate. 9: Recognised as Amīr. 26: Treaty arranged by General L. Cavagnari and signed:—The British to occupy Kuram, the Khaibar pass and Pishīn valleys; to have a resident at Kābul; and an annual subsidy of six lākhs to be paid to the Amīr. 30: The treaty ratified. June 8: The British troops retire.

May 10: The Rāmoshī Dākaīts, under Daulata Rāmoshī, after plundering about Sirūr, appeared at Neri, near Pānwel in the Konkan, wounded five men and carried off Rs. 6070, and at Palaspe wounded three and plundered property valued at Rs. 60,000. Returning to the Dekhan, Major Daniell pursued them, killed Daulata and others, and recovered most of the property taken at Palaspe.

June 27: Lord Lawrence, late Viceroy (1863-68), died; buried in Westminster Abbey.

July 15: Sir Steuart C. Bailey, officiating Lieut.-Governor of Bengal, during absence of Hon. Sir Ashley Eden, till April 24, 1882.

July 21: Vāsudev Balvant Phadke, the Brāhman leader of Dākaīts, captured at Devar Navadgi by Major Daniell. He was tried at Poona and sentenced to transportation, and sent to Aden; he died there 17th Feb. 1883.

July 24: Sir Louis Cavagnari, the British envoy, and escort received at Kābul.

Aug. 11: Indian Railways Guarantee Act passed.

Aug. A rising in Rampa, the hill division of Godāvarī district, from the conduct of the Mansabdār, is put down by troops; the rebels several times defeated, and partially subdued by October.

Sept. 3: Afghān soldiery and the mob besiege the Kābul

A.D.

1879 residency; charge after charge is made by the escort, but the buildings are fired, and the defenders are massacred to a man—including Sir L. Cavagnari, Mr Wm. Jenkins, C.S., Lieut. Hamilton, and Dr Ambrose Kelly, with twenty-six cavalry and fifty infantry.

Sept. 5: Mutiny at Harāt—military and civil governors killed.

Sept. 6: General Roberts leaves Simla for Kābul: 16: He issues a proclamation from Alīkhel to the Afghān people.

Sept. 19: Attack on General Baker's entrenchments at Shatr-gardan repulsed. 22: A British convoy attacked by Mangals near Shatr-gardan: eight sipāhis and fifteen muleteers killed and mules taken. 24: General Baker's brigade advancing from Shatr-gardan occupies Kūshi. 27: General Roberts is attacked on his march from Alikhel by Mangals and Ghilzāis. 28: He arrives at Kūshi.

Sept. 27: Amīr Yā'qūb Khān arrived at General Baker's camp with his father-in-law Yahia Khān, his young son Mūsa Khān, the Commander-in-Chief Dāūd Khān, and a large escort.

Sept. 30: Lieut. Kinloch, 12th Bengal Cavalry, assassinated by Afghāns between Chapri and Mandosi in the Kuram valley.

Oct. 2: Col. Money attacked at Shatr-gardan, drives off the Afghāns, who lost severely. 5: General Roberts and his force of 6,617 in all, with eighteen guns, reach Chārasiāb about four miles from Kābul.

Oct. 6: Battle of Chārasiāb: severe contest with an army of between 8,000 and 10,000 Afghāns; the British loss, 18 killed and 70 wounded, whilst the Afghāns left 300 dead and about 98 guns. 8: The Afghān army fled. 10: General Roberts visits Sherpur, and Bala Hisār. 12: He enters Kābul.

Oct. 8: Mr St Barbe leaves the residency at Māndalé with other Europeans, and the king reported to be "drinking."

Oct. 14: Mr G. B. Damant, Political Agent in the Nāgā hills, murdered with his escort on his way to Khonoma, to seize arms stored by the Nāgās. The Nāgās then attacked Kohima, which was defended for thirteen days till relieved by Col. Johnstone from Manipur. A military expedition followed, lasting till March 1880.

Oct. 12: The Amīr Yā'qūb Khān comes to General Roberts to declare his abdication. General Roberts reads his proclama-

A.D.
1879 tion: city buildings near the Bala Hisār to be levelled to the ground; a heavy fine to be imposed; martial law in the surrounding country to a distance of ten miles; persons convicted of participating in the massacre of 3rd Sept. to be specially dealt with, and rewards offered for their capture; the populace to be disarmed within a week. General J. Hills to be military governor of Kābul, aided by Nawāb Ghulām Husain Khān.

Oct. 16: Gunpowder in the Bala Hisār exploded (supposed treacherously), and much ammunition and arms destroyed. Capt. Shafto and twenty native soldiers killed.

Oct. 17-19: Col. Money and his small force at the Shatr-gardan pass completely surrounded by a host of Ghilzāis. 19: On the approach of General H. Gough, sent from Kābul, he sallied out and dispersed them. Money then left Shatr-gardan.

Oct. New rules are issued for newspaper correspondents with the army.

Oct. 20-24: Five prisoners, Mullās and others, hanged at Kābul as murderers of Cavagnari and his attendants.

Oct. 24: General Hughes, in a sharp engagement at Shāhjui, near Qandahār, successfully defeated a strong force of Taraki Ghilzāis led by Sāhib Jān who was killed. General Hughes retired for supplies to Kalāt-i-Ghilzāi.

Oct. 28: Yā'qūb Khān informed that his abdication was accepted. Proclamation of General Roberts announcing the British occupation of Kābul.

Nov. 7: General Macpherson's brigade from Kābul gets into communication at Katasang with General Chas. Gough commanding the leading brigade of General Bright coming from Khaibar.

Nov. 12: General Roberts issues an amnesty proclamation. 14: Time-expired men and invalids sent back to India.

Nov. 15: Mr J. H. Morris, Chief Commissioner Central Provinces, till April 30, 1883.

Oct.-Nov. Of Afghān rebels, &c., 153 were tried: 87 executed as murderers, and 76 released.

Nov. 22: Khonoma besieged and taken from the Nāgā rebels. They take up a strong position on a spur of the Jāpvo. 27: Jotsoma captured, and the thirteen villages of the confederation taken or destroyed.

A.D.

1879 Nov. 24: In Maidān district the Afghān headmen refused the khālsā or government grain, and, assisted by Ghilzāis, attacked the cavalry collecting it, and murdered Sirdār Muhammad Husain Khān, the British agent. The chief Mālik's fort destroyed and his store of grain confiscated. This ends resistance.

Dec. 1: Yā'qūb Khān sent off to India by double marches. 8: Yahia Khān, Zakaria Khān, and the late Vazīr sent to India.

Dec. 8, 9: Combination of tribes under Muhammad Jān Wardak. 10: General Macpherson defeats a body of them at Paghman. 11: Attacked by 9,000 or 10,000 Afghāns, after desperate fighting all day, the Afghāns still held the Takht-i-Shāh heights.

Dec. 12: General Baker's troops take the heights between Beni-Hisār and the Bala-Hisār, the Afghāns losing heavily. 14: More Afghāns and the people from the city occupy the Koh-i-Asmāi. After desperate attacks on immense masses the troops withdraw to Sherpur.

Dec. 19: General Charles Gough advancing from Gandāmak, attacked at Jagdalak, retires into the fort. Dec. 18, 19: Indecisive conflicts.

Dec. 23: Muharram 10, H. 1297: The Afghāns—about 25,000—attack Sherpur camp, and after desperate efforts are defeated with great loss; the Ghāzīs refuse to surrender or retreat. 24: General Charles Gough's force arrived. The Afghān confederation breaks up and disperses. 26: The city and Bala Hisār reoccupied by the British.

Dec. 23: The tribesmen attack Jagdalak and are repulsed. 29: 'Azmatulla Khān, with 2,000 Ghilzāis, made a bold attack on General Francis B. Norman's position at Gandāmak.

Dec. 'Abdul Rahman, son of Afzal Khān, the eldest son of Sher Khān, fled from Turkistān to Balkh.

1880 Jan. Nāgās, from their fort above Khonoma, make a raid on Bāladhan tea-garden, in Kachār, over 80 miles distant, kill the manager, Mr Blyth, and sixteen labourers, plundered and burnt everything in the place.

Jan. 10: Ghazni is held by Muhammad Jān and other sardārs with, and on behalf of, the young Mūsa Khān as Amīr.

Jan. 15: The Mohmands, between the Khaibar and Jalālābād,

A.D.

1880 rise and attempt to cross the Kābul river with 5,000 men, but are repelled by the detachment at Dhāka.

Feb. 6: Afghān correspondence with Russia found at Kābul.

March 13: Sir R. Temple, Governor, leaves Bombay. Mr Lionel R. Ashburner, acting Governor till 28th April.

March 27: The Nāgā fort above Khonoma submitted. Khonoma destroyed, and the Nāgās have to surrender their firearms and pay fines.

March: The tribesmen attacked Fort Battye near Jalālābād: Lieut. Angelo killed.

March 30: General Sir Donald Stewart with his division leaves Qandahār for Kābul. April 19: He is attacked at Ahmadkhel by a large Ghilzāi force, and about 3,000 Ghāzīs charge home, but are successfully defeated, 1,000 dead being left on the field. 22: He arrives at Ghazni. 23: Again defeats the Ghilzāis.

March 31: Muhammad Jān defeated and killed by Hazāras.

April: Sher 'Alī, cousin of the late Amīr, made Governor of Qandahār.

April 12: King Thībau, attacked by small-pox, and to avert the anger of spirits which sent the plague, prepares a great sacrifice of human beings. Thousands of fugitives escape by steamers to Rangūn.

April 13: At a darbār at Kābul, a deputation of Sardārs from Ghazni with the Kābul and Hazāra Māliks, is informed by Mr L. Griffin that Yā'qūb Khān could not be allowed to return to Afghānistān, and that the British army would be withdrawn as soon as an Amīr had been appointed.

April 16: A camp at Duwai attacked by Pathāns and the garrison killed. 25: Col. Jenkins at Chārasiab attacked by some 4,000 Logaris; reinforced by General Macpherson, he scatters them with great loss.

April 28: Sir James Fergusson succeeds Sir Richard Temple as Governor of Bombay, till 27th March 1885. The Marquis of Hartington succeeds Viscount Cranbrook as Secretary of State for India.

May 5: Sir Donald Stewart arrived at Kābul and took over the chief command from General Roberts.

A.D.
1880 May 20: Rāmavarmā of Travankor died, and is succeeded by his brother, also named Rāmavarmā.

MARQUIS OF RIPON, SEVENTH VICEROY.

May 30: The Marquis of Ripon arrives at Bombay as successor to Lord Lytton. June 8: He is installed at Simla.

June 9: The car of Jagannāth was not, as usual, dragged through the streets of Puri on this day.

May: Prince Nyaungok, a refugee from Burma, escaping from Calcutta, organised a band on the Burmese frontier, but advancing, is defeated by the Burmese troops. June: Renewing his attempt he was again repulsed; and was made prisoner by the frontier police. June 27: He enters British territory.

June 9 (? 15): Ayūb Khān, brother of Yā'qūb Khān, leaves Harāt with an army of 7,500 for Qandahār.

July 4: General J. M. Primrose sends General J. Burrows to the Helmand to aid Wali Sher Khān against Ayūb. 11: Encamping opposite Gīrishk, Sher Khān's troops on the farther bank. 13: Sher Khān's troops deserted to Ayūb Khān; General Burrows crossed and captured the six guns they had.

July 2: Mr Charles E. Bernard succeeds Sir Chas. U. Aitcheson as Chief Commissioner of Burma, till March 2, 1883.

July 16: General Burrows retired to Khushk-i-Nakhud, half way to Qandahār. 27: At Maiwānd, Burrows, with less than 2,500 men, is attacked by about 20,000 Afghāns and totally defeated, losing 934 killed and 175 wounded and missing. The rest retreated to Qandahār. July 28: General Primrose withdrew from the cantonments into the citadel with about 4,000 men, expelled the Durānī inhabitants, and strengthened the defences.

Aug. 3: General Sir F. Roberts ordered to prepare to march to Qandahār. 9: He starts with about 10,000 men, 8,000 camp followers, and 11,000 animals. 15: Reached Ghazni, 98 miles from Kābul. 16: General Primrose made a sortie against Deh Kwāji village, but is repulsed after a severe struggle and the loss of officers and 180 men. 23: Roberts arrived at Kalāt-i-Ghilzāi. Ayūb Khān raised the siege of Qandahār and entrenched at Mazra in Arghandāb valley. 31: Roberts enters Qandahār, 313 miles from Kābul.

A.D.

1880 Aug. 10: 'Abdul Rahman, son of Muhammad Afzal Khan, the eldest brother of Sher 'Alī, finally nominated Amīr at Kābul. 11: Sir Donald Stewart, with the whole British force of 6,678 men, left Kābul; the last of them reached Peshāwar on Sept. 7.

Aug. 16: Pathān hill tribes attacking the post at Kachh Amadan, beaten off by the native troops; 180 Pathāns killed.

Sept. 1: General Sir F. Roberts attacks Ayūb Khān's army of about 20,000 at Mazra, or Bābā Wali, and after severe fighting, completely defeats them, capturing Ayūb's camp and thirty-two guns. Capt. Maclaine, taken prisoner at Maiwānd, found just murdered. 8: The troops retire by Qwetta to India.

Sept. 18: At Naini Tāl a violent storm, resulting in a great landslip, causes the death of forty-two Europeans and 105 natives, with the entire destruction of houses and much property.

Sept. 18: Siwāī Rāi Singh of Jaypur dies childless, and Khaim Singh, a descendant of Jagat Singh, is adopted as successor, under a council of regency till 1882.

Oct. General Macgregor's brigade on its way from Qandahār had to punish the Marī tribe, who had to pay a fine and submit to other penalties for their raids.

Dec. The disturbances in Rampa district continuing, the rebel leader, Chandrayya, is killed, the rebels dispersed, and the obnoxious mansabdār deported to Gopālpur.

Dec. 20: Mr William Patrick Adam, Governor of Madras, till his death, May 24, 1881.

Farīdun Jāh, Nawāb Nizām of Bengal, arranges with the Secretary of State for India to accept ten lākhs of rupees in full satisfaction of all personal claims.

1881 Jan. 1: The railway from Ahmadābād to Ajmir opened for traffic by Sir Jas. Fergusson, Governor of Bombay.

Jan. Sir Donald Martin Stewart appointed Commander-in-Chief of the Indian Army: assumed charge, 7th April.

March 12: The Bāzar Afrīdīs raided between Alī-Masjid and Landi-Kotal, are pursued and the cattle recovered. 19-21: The evacuation of the Khaibar carried out.

March 25: Sir Chas. A. Elliott succeeds Sir G. C. Bayley as Chief Commissioner of Asām, till July 8, 1883.

A.D.

1881 March 25: Mahārāja Chāma Rājendra Udayār installed by the Governor of Madras as sovereign of Maisur.

April 1: The Amīr 'Abdul Rahman's garrison for Qandahār arrives. 16: Muhammad Hāshim Khān, the new governor, arrives there. 21: General Robert Hume with the British force leaves Qandahār for the Pishīn valley *via* Chaman.

April 12: General Kennedy starts from Tānk, and General J. J. H. Gordon from Bannu, with strong forces to punish the Balozai Wazīrīs for the raid made on Tānk in Jan. 1879. The tribe gave up five of the raiding chiefs; Māshik of the Manakhel, the ringleader, escaped to Kābul, his district was despoiled; Kaniguram, the chief town, reached. May 18: General Kennedy returned to Tānk. Later Māshik was surrendered.

May 24: The Right Hon. Wm. Patrick Adam, Governor of Madras, died at Uttakamand. Mr Wm. Hudleston, acting Governor till Nov. 4.

June 3: The Amīr's governor of Girishk defeated Ayūb Khān's officers, forcing them to leave the fort. 11: At Karez-i-safīd, on the Helmand, he again defeated them.

July 26: At Karez-i-atta, close to Maiwānd, Ayūb Khān defeats the Amīr's force under Ghulām Haidar, who left his baggage and about five lākhs of rupees on the field. Ayūb at once occupied Qandahār.

Aug. 6: Ghulām Haidar holds Kalāt-i-Ghilzāi. 14: 'Abdul Rahman starts from Kābul. 21: Ghulām receives reinforcements from Kābul. Sept. 1: The Amīr reaches Kalāt-i-Ghīlzāi. Ayūb offers to negotiate, but is refused. Sept. 20: He is defeated by the Amīr at old Qandahār, chiefly through desertion of troops, and abandoning his fourteen guns and baggage, Ayūb flees to Harāt. The Amīr enters Qandahār.

Oct. 1-2: Ayūb is twice defeated by 'Abdul Kudus Khān on the way to Harāt. 2: Ayūb flees to Ghain in Persia. 4: 'Abdul Kudus enters Harāt on behalf of the Amīr.

Nov. 5: Mr Mountstuart Elphinstone Grant-Duff, Governor of Madras, till 1886.

Nov. 10: By decree of the Portuguese government Carlos Eugenio da Silva, Visconde de Paço de Arcos, appointed to succeed Caetano Alexandre de Almaida e Albuquerque as Governor-General at Goa, till Dec. 23, 1885.

A.D.
1882 Jan. Lord Ripon visited Rangūn. Government of India remonstrated against the monopolies imposed by Thībau. The monopolies condemned, but not abolished.

Feb. The Burmese foreign minister intimates to the Indian Government that the local officers on the frontier were directed to destroy the boundary marks recently made and station Burmese officials on the spot.

Feb. Afzal Khān selected by the Amīr 'Abdul Rahman, as British agent in Kābul.

April: Thībau sends an embassy to the Viceroy, received at Thyet-myo and sent to India. 30: It reached Simla. May 3: Formally received by the Viceroy. The Māndalé government refused to agree to the terms provisionally adopted, and the negotiations ceased, Aug. 21.

April 15: Mr Theodore C. Hope temporarily finance minister till May 22nd.

April 21: Political massacres said to have recommenced at Māndalė.

April 24: Sir A. Rivers Thompson installed Lieut.-Governor of Bengal, till Aug. 11, 1885.

July 10: A contingent of troops from India ordered to Egypt for the war with Arabi Pāsha. 22: The Seaforth Highlanders left Bombay; landed at Suez, Aug. 8. Aug. 5-31: Other portions of the force leave Bombay and Calcutta.

July 28: A Hindu procession at Salem stopped opposite a mosque with band and playing in defiance of custom, the Muhammadans raised a riot: two Muhammadans killed, and about 150 of both parties wounded. Aug. 16 (Muhammadan feast of 'Īd-ul-fitr): The Hindus attacked Muhammadans in a mosque, burnt it, sacked and burnt their houses and killed several, women and children included. The police and better-class Hindus sided with the rioters. Riots followed in several places in South India.

Sept. 29: Sir Muhabbat Khānjī, Nawāb of Junāgadh, died. Oct. 1: Bahādur Khānjī installed as Nawāb.

Nov. 24: The Sarhind Canal, 500 miles in length, for irrigation, opened by the Viceroy.

Dec. An earthquake in north Gujarāt and part of Rājputāna.

A.D

1882 Dec. 16: The Earl of Kimberley succeeds the Marquis of Hartington as Secretary of State for India.

1883 Jan. Ranguchārlia Diwān of Maisur died.

Jan. 17: Mānpur, Alī Rājpur, attacked by a party of Bhīls, Rohilas, &c., under Chitu a Bhīl, arising from discontentment with the Diwān or chief. The raiders dispersed by Central India Horse and Bombay local police.

Feb. 2: Mr C. P. Ilbert moves for leave to bring into Council his Criminal Procedure Amendment Bill: it excited much opposition among Europeans. Feb. 28: Great meeting in Calcutta; the opposition led to alterations.

Feb. 8: Sir Sālār Jang, minister of Haidarābād died of cholera,—greatly regretted.

March 12: Sir Steuart C. Bayley introduced into Council the Bengal Tenancy Bill.

March 29: First meeting of the European and Anglo-Indian Defence Association formed at Calcutta.

April 11: Destructive fire in Māndalé announced.

April: An Anglo-Indian Association for natives formed in London.

April: The Myingun prince, son of King Mengdun Meng, who had killed his uncle, the heir apparent, in 1866, and fled to Bengal, escapes to Chandranagar.

April 27: The Amīr, 'Abdul Rahman, from Jalālābād, summons the Shinwārīs; they decline his authority. May 8: He defeats the Shinwārīs at Pesh-Bolak. June: Peace made with them.

May 11: Bābū Surendranāth Bānarji, editor of the *Bengalee* weekly, sentenced to two months' imprisonment for gross libel against Judge Norris.

May 16: A dreadful inundation in Kachār, the town of Silchār nearly all under water, causing great distress. Food, &c., sent from Calcutta.

July 3-6: Great flood in the Tāpti river, sweeping away two miles of railway and many houses in Surat. Bombay merchants subscribed to relieve the distress.

July 21: The Indian Government sends to the Amīr of Kābul the first instalment of a monthly subsidy of a lākh of rupees.

A.D.

1883 July: Nasr ud-dīn, Shāh of Persia, sends Mīr Mausam Khān on an embassy to 'Abdul Rahman Khān. Aug. The envoy reached Quandahār. Sept. 3: The envoy received by the Amīr at Kābul. Left for Mashd about the end of October.

Aug. Major E. Baring succeeded by Sir Auckland Colvin as Finance Minister. Assumed charge, Oct. 8, till Aug. 10, 1887.

Aug. 24: Insurrection of the Ghilzāis under the Mullā Mushk-i-'Alam.

Nov. H.R.H. the Duke of Connaught arrived in Bombay to take the command of the Mīrat division of the Bengal army.

Dec. 4: The first International Exhibition held in India, opened at Calcutta by Lord Ripon in presence of H.R.H. the Duke of Connaught and Indian princes.

Dec. 21: Ilbert Bill compromise: Europeans allowed to claim a jury partly or wholly European.

Dec. The Akā tribes descend on Bālipārā, near Tezpur in Āsām, and carry off native forest officers as hostages, making demands of the forest lands. General Sale Hill sent with a force against them.

1884 Jan. 8: General Sale Hill drove back the Akās after a stubborn resistance, and advanced on Barāgāon; the prisoners given up and the head men made submission. The force returned to Tezpur, 1st Feb.

Jan. 25: The Ilbert Bill amended and passed.

March 6: Major Alikhanov requested the Turkomān elders at Merv to go to Askābād and confer with Russian authorities.

March: The Kāchīn hill tribes in North Burma revolt, and carry fire and sword half way to Māndalé. Made a partial occupation of Mogaung.

April 9: Destructive fire at Māndalé.

April: M. Ferry assures the British Ambassador that the French treaties with Burma would be only of a commercial or consular character.

April 22: The Musā Khel Pathāns in the Zhob valley, incited by the fanatic Shāh Jahān, organise an attack on road labourers near Daki or Puh, on the Thal-Chotiāli route, but are beaten off by a party of infantry. A punitive expedition ordered.

A.D.

1884 May: The Burmese again threaten to destroy the boundary marks and the Konkal British outpost.

June: The Myingun prince escapes in a French steamer to Colombo, but is returned in the same ship to Pondicheri, and detained under supervision.

June 14: The Musā Khel Pathāns made a night attack on an outpost of Thal-Chotiāli, but were repulsed.

Aug. 11: Mahārāo Kengarji Bahādur installed in the government of Kachh by Sir James Fergusson.

Aug. 24: The Amīr of Afghānistān assents to a joint Anglo-Russian Frontier Commission. Sept. 13: The British Commission, under Sir Peter Lumsden, left Quetta for the Helmand and Sarākhs.

Sept. 22: Taingda Mingyi incites the fears of King Thībau, contrives the escape of jail prisoners, and then, with other officials, leads the troops against them, sets fire to the jails and massacres the escaping prisoners; between 200 and 300 killed.

Sept. 20: Expedition under General Sir Oriel Turner to punish the Musā Khels or Kākar Pathāns of Zhob, started from Quetta for Anambar; most of the tribes at once submitted. Oct. 23: One action, in which fifty-six were killed, completed the subjugation; the leaders fled, but were captured, fined and gave hostages; Shāh Jahān escaped to the Ghilzāis. Nov. 22: The troops return.

Oct. 11: Public meeting at Rangūn memorialises the Government of India on the misgovernment and barbarity of King Thībau, and begs interference for reform or another ruler. The Chamber of Commerce also urge annexation or a change of ruler.

Dec. 3: The Marquis of Ripon retired from the government.

THE EARL OF DUFFERIN, EIGHTH VICEROY.

Dec. 13: The Earl of Dufferin installed at Calcutta as Viceroy and Governor-General.

Dec. 13: The Afghān Frontier Commission reached Balā-Murghāb, and the Russian Commissioner not having arrived, it winters there.

Dec. 27: Twelve Māppillas shoot the brother of a man who had renounced Islām; take possession of Trikkalūr temple.

A.D.

1884 28: A desperate resistance offered, and eleven killed and the twelfth mortally wounded. One private killed, and Lieut. Day and a private wounded. Three tāluks disarmed in Feb. 1885.

1885 Jan. 15: The Burmese embassy conclude a treaty at Paris, and a French consul is to reside at Māndalé. A letter from M. Ferry of same date to the Burmese foreign minister promised the transport of arms and ammunition through French Tonquin.

Feb. Alikhanov with troops from Merv tries to get possession of Panjdeh for the Russians, and occupies Aka-Tapa, Zulfiqar Pass on the Hari Rūd, and the Pul-i-Kishti. March 29: The Russian troops fix a quarrel on the Afghans and attack and kill about 500 men. The property of Capt. Charles E. Yate and his companions looted by Tekke Turkoman and other troops. General Komaroff proclaims the annexation of Panjdeh.

March 11: Bengal Tenancy Act passed by Council.

March 16: The Kachīns had retaken Bhāmo with Chinese assistance, and after a long siege the Burmese retake it.

March 27: Sir James Fergusson retires from the Governorship of Bombay, and Mr James B. Peile acts as Governor. 30: Baron Reay assumes the Governorship, till April 12, 1890.

March 31: The Amīr 'Abdul Rahman arrives at Rāwal-pindi to meet the Viceroy. April 6: He attends a parade of 17,000 troops, and is present at a state banquet. 8: Received in darbār and presented with a sword of honour. He is invested with the G.C.S.I.

April: The Bombay-Burma Trading Corporation, lessees of Ningyan teak forests, complained to Mr C. E. Bernard, the chief commissioner, of the interference by the Burmese with the terms of their contracts. He appealed to the Foreign Minister. Aug. 12: The High Court of Ava decided that the Corporation had defrauded the king of eleven lākhs, fined them double that sum, and five lākhs to be paid the foresters in the employ of the Corporation. The king refuses the arbitration of the Viceroy.

May 14: The Burmese embassy at Rome concludes a treaty with the German government negotiated by Baron von Kendell.

May 1: A gang of Māppillas in Ponnāni tāluk murdered a Cheramān and his family. 3: Having seized the house of a Nambūtiri Brahman landlord, they are all killed there by the troops.

A.D.
1885 May: A native volunteer corps formed under the Commander-in-Chief.

May: M. Haas arrived at Māndalé as French consul; he endeavoured to establish a French bank, to run a French flotilla on the Irāwadī, to work the ruby mines, to construct a French railway in Upper Burma, and to take the Ningyan forests if the Corporation's lease were cancelled.

May 30-31: Severe earthquake at Srīnagar, Kashmīr, eighty-seven killed. Successive shocks till June 20,—3,081 deaths and 70,000 dwellings reported destroyed.

June 24: Lord Randolph Churchill appointed Secretary for India.

July 8: Sir Frederick S. Roberts announced to succeed Sir Donald Stewart as Commander-in-Chief.

Aug. The Deb Rājā of Bhutān had a dispute with the Penlosor governors, and after some fighting is deposed and forced to take refuge with the Lāmas.

Aug. 28: The British Government insist that British subjects in the position of the Bombay-Burma Corporation must receive a fair trial, and request the suspension of action till this is done. Sept. 20: The Burmese stop the company's rafts. Oct. They decline any arbitration or to suspend action.

Sept. 12: Ranbīr Singh, Mahārāja of Kāshmīr, dies, and is succeeded by his son, Pratāp Singh, who proves foolish and incompetent.

Oct. M. Haas, French agent at Māndalé, announced unattached "on account of health."

Oct. 22: The Chief Commissioner of Burma sends an ultimatum to King Thibau, requiring the acceptance of a permanent Resident, the entire suspension of proceedings against the Bombay-Burma Corporation till the Resident arrived. The steamer would wait reply till 6th Nov. Nov. 7: King Thībau called upon all his officials to expel all English. 9: His reply received was tantamount to an evasion of the terms.

Oct. The Limbin prince, son of the Burman heir-apparent murdered in 1866, left British protection at Maulmein and at the head of exiled chiefs of Kengtung state sought to overthrow Thībau.

A.D.
1885 Nov. 12: The Russian and British Afghān Delimitation Commissioners meet at Zulfiqar Pass and carry the work to Maruchāk.

Nov. Three servants of the Bombay-Burma Co. massacred at Kendat on the Chindwin river.

Nov. 14: General H. Prendergast advanced with troops up the Irāwadi to Thayet-Myo, the frontier town. 17: Minhla and Gwegyaung-Kamyo forts captured after some hours' fighting. 22: Nyaungu taken and dismantled. 24: Pakokku and Myingyan taken. 26: Two ministers with a letter from Thībau offering to grant all asked in the ultimatum and requesting an armistice. Surrender only could now be listened to. 27: At Ava the Burmese troops lay down their arms and twenty-eight guns are taken. 28: The fleet reach Māndalé, and Thībau surrenders himself and his kingdom. 29: Thībau and his family sent off to Rangūn in a steamer. Dec. 14: They arrive at Madras. Finally he was interned at Ratnagiri in Western India.

Nov. 24: The Franco-Burmese convention of Jan. 15 was ratified by the President at Paris and published Nov. 26.

Dec. 2: Gwāliar citadel granted by Lord Dufferin to Mahārāja Jayaji Sindia for fifteen lākhs of rupees.

Dec. 1: Proclamation of Thībau's surrender, dethronement, and deportation, and the administration assumed by the British officers.

Dec. 18: Sir Arthur Phayre, the first Commissioner of British Burma, died.

Dec. 18: Mr C. E. Bernard, Chief Commissioner of Burma.

Dec. 19: General Prendergast with a strong force went up the river. 28: He arrived at Bhāmo, and left General Norman with a sufficient force. 29: Rebels defeated at Maulshobo by Major Williamson.

Dec. 23: Caetano Alexandre de Almaida e Albuquerque relieved of the Government of Goa. His successor, Francisco Joaquim Ferreira de Amaral, till Oct. 28, 1886.

Dec. 2: Lord Dufferin holds a darbār at Gwāliar and formally restores the fortress to Sindia, which had been held since its capture by Sir Hugh Rose in June 1858.

Dec. 25: Col. Street, Commissioner of Pegu, defeated 150 rebels marching on Pegu: twenty of them slain.

A.D.

1886 Jan. 1: Lord Dufferin proclaims the Ava territories part of the British dominions.

Jan. Dākaīts pillage outside Māndalé; sharp conflicts occur with bands of them; two pretenders to the throne appear with them; Alaunghprā, a pretender, captured: tried and shot. Taingda Mingyi, Thībau's minister, accused of murder, sent temporarily to India. Died at Rangūn, May 31, 1896.

Jan. 16: Burmese defeated at Kadol; and at Kunna; thirty-six insurgents killed. 19: The rebel chiefs flee. 27: Rebels defeated on the Mas river by Major Williamson.

Jan. 19: Grand military review held by Lord Dufferin at Dehli—35,000 troops present.

Jan. 29: Income Tax Bill passed by the Indian Council.

Feb. 7: The Earl of Kimberley succeeds Sir Randolph Churchill as Secretary of State for India (second time).

Feb. 12: The Viceroy, Lord Dufferin, along with Sir F. Roberts, arrive at Māndalé, are well received, leave 23rd.

Feb. 13: Panjdeh, given up to Russia in July 1885, is entered.

Feb 16: Lieut.-Gen. Sir Charles G. Arbuthnot, Commander-in-Chief, Bombay, till Dec. 10.

March 6: The Chief Commissioner, Mr C. E. Bernard, issues pacific proclamation to the Burmese. 12: He assumes office at a Māndalé.

March 18: At Yindowango 400 Burmese rebels surprised and defeated. A week later forty rebels killed at Zemethen. Mr St Barbe killed in Bassein district while attacking dākaīts.

March 31: General Prendergast leaves Māndalé, and General Geo. S. White takes command of the troops in Burma.

April 15: The adherents of the Myingun prince, a son of King Mengdun Meng, rushed a police station and burnt about 800 houses in the city and many more in the suburbs of Māndalé.

May: Col. Fitzgerald leads a successful expedition against the Burmese rebels; some insurgent leaders surrender.

May 15: All Burma included by decree in British India.

June 6-7: Defeat of Burmese insurgents under Bo Shwe by Mr Phayre at Neape in the Minhla jangals. 8: Mr Phayre killed. 12: Capt. Dunsford killed in a conflict with 500 dākaīts at Salem. 19: Major Hailes repulsed at Tamū.

A.D.

1886 June 21: Alī Jāh Jayajirāv Sindia of Gwāliar died; succeeded by his son, a boy, with a regency.

July: Increased dākaītī in Upper and Lower Burma. 13: The Myingaing prince offered Rs. 2,000 for the head of Sir Charles Bernard, the Chief Commissioner, and threatened to burn the Māndalé palace, used as public offices and residence of the head-quarters' staffs. 26: Lieut. Higgins defeated rebels, who lost 150 killed and wounded. Aug. 1: Several sharp skirmishes—Major Aitkinson killed.

July: The Afghānistān delimitation completed. Sept. 6: The Joint Commission dissolved. The first pillar was formally erected Nov. 12, 1885.

Aug. 4: The Right Hon. Sir Richard A. Cross appointed Secretary of State for India; created Viscount Cross, Aug. 19.

Aug. 16: A high flood of the Irāwadī bursts the embankment on the west of the suburbs of Māndalé; much destruction of property and some loss of life. 25: Inundation subsiding.

Sept. 17: General Sir Herbert Macpherson, Commander-in-Chief of Madras army, arrived at Māndalé to take charge of operations in Burma. Oct. 20: Died of fever on the Irāwadī near Prom.

Oct. 5-8: The Hindu Durgā-pujā and Muslim Muharram festivals coinciding, great riots occur at Dehli, quelled by the military.

Oct. 28: Augusto Cesar Cordoso de Carvalho, Governor-General of Goa.

Oct. Rising in Afghānistān against taxation: treasure seized in transit.

Nov. 2: Minhla burnt by Burmese insurgents. 9: Sir F. Roberts arrives at Rangūn, to pacify the country. 18: He reaches Māndalé. 23: Col. Holt captures the position at Puzan Myang: Tham-ban the rebel leader and his son killed. Expeditions against the dākaīt chiefs, Bo Shwe and Hla U, under General R. C. Low and Major Wm. P. Symons, capture their strongholds and disperse the bands.

Dec. 8: The Right Hon. Sir Robert Bourke succeeds the Right Hon. M. E. Grant Duff as Governor of Madras; created Lord Connemara, May 12, 1887.

A.D.

1886 Dec. 9: Lieut.-General Sir Charles G. Arbuthnot, Commander-in-Chief, Madras, till March 6, 1891.

Dec. 12: Col. Wm. F. Gatacre with the Bombay Lancers dispersed the rebels at Pakokku.

Dec. 31: A fire occurs in the booths at a fair at Madras: great panic, about 405 people lost their lives.

1887 Jan. 1: The Kyimyin prince—a pretender—attacked and killed, and his followers dispersed. Jan. Col. E. Stedman despatched with troops to Nyaungywé in the Shān states, to relieve Saw Maung the Sawbwa, who was attacked by the Limbin prince, son of Mendat, the brother of King Mengdun Meng. Jan. 24: Attack on the bandit Bo Shwe's camp; he escaped.

Jan. 17: The Marmagão harbour, improved to accommodate sea-going vessels, is opened. Railway from Goa opened for 47 miles, towards Hubli.

Jan. 27: Kun Saing the Sawbwa of the state of Thībaw is the first Shān chief to render allegiance.

Feb. 12: General Sir F. Roberts leaves Māndalé after organising the military and police, leaving the Upper Burma force under Gen. Sir Geo. White.

Feb. 16: The Jubilee of the Queen-Empress celebrated in India and Burma with great magnificence; schools, hospitals, and halls founded.

March 5: Wuntho Sawbwa makes his submission, but refuses to come in personally; he pays the tribute.

March 9: Bo Shwe's gang are defeated, he escapes. Oct. 1. Bo Shwe, after fifteen years' brigandage, from Minlha is pursued in Lower Burma, and killed by mounted infantry.

March 12: Mr C. H. T. Crosthwaite succeeds Sir C. E. Bernard as Chief Commissioner of Burma. March 22: Col. Dance defeats a party of dākaīts.

April 2: Mr Jas. B. Lyall succeeds Sir Ch. U. Aitcheson as Lieut.-Governor of the Punjāb, till March 5, 1892.

April: In Sagaing, the notorious bandit, Hla U, murdered by his own followers, who broke up into small bands, and terrorised the forest tracks. 20: Ōktamā in Mīnbu defeated with loss of twenty-three men.

A. D.

1887 April 19: The Amīr 'Abdul Rahman's troops defeated by the Ghilzāis. 25: Again defeated at Kalāt-i-Ghilzāi.

May 12: Meetings of Afghān Frontier Commission at St Petersburg temporarily closed. July 6: Resumed. 20: Questions settled.

May 23-24: Destructive cyclone at Calcutta: about 700 lives lost, and the "Sir John Lawrence" and tug "Retriever."

May 23: The Limbin prince, son of Prince Mindāt, having escaped from Moulmein and joined a confederacy of chiefs, attacked Saw Maung, Sawbwa of Thībau; he now surrenders and is sent a prisoner to Calcutta.

June 9: Mutiny of Ghilzāis at Harāt suppressed with much bloodshed. June 13 and 16: The Amīr's general, Ghulām Haidar, defeats them. July 26: Reinforced by 450 regular troops, deserters from Harāt garrison, they gather at Atargarh, and were attacked at Sura or Kotaldab, defeated and dispersed, the fugitives seek asylum in British territory.

June 19: Quetta with the Pishīn, Thal-Chotiāli, and Sībī districts of Baluchistān annexed to British territories; placed under Col. Sir R. G. Sandeman, appointed while on furlough.

June 21: Jubilee of the reign of Queen Victoria celebrated in Westminster Abbey, attended by the Mahārāja of Indor and many Indian princes.

July 13: Tīmūr Shāh, the leader of the Harāt mutineers, executed at Kābul.

Aug. 14: Ayūb Khān escapes from Teherān and enters Afghānistān near Harāt with a few followers; attacked by a party of Afghāns, he is driven back early in Sept. to Persia where he continues in hiding.

Aug. 31: At Mashakai a severe contest between insurgents and the Amīr's troops. Sept. 7: The rebel leader, Jalandar Khān, defeated at Makar and captured.

Sept. The Nizām of Haidarābād offered twenty lākhs of rupees annually for three years, for the defence of the north-west frontier. Oct. 10: Acknowledged with thanks.

Oct. 16: Camp near Chindwin captured; Major Kennedy and Capt. Beville killed, and about fifty dākaits.

Oct. 25: Subscriptions to Lady Dufferin's Jubilee Fund for

A.D.

1887 Native Female Medical Service in India amounted to Rs. 478,465, and in England £1,770.

Oct. 31: The Kapurthala Rāja offers his army and five lākhs of rupees for the defence of the Indian frontiers.

Nov. 6: Ayūb Khān surrenders himself to the British representative at Mashhd.

Nov. 21: Sir Auckland Colvin, Finance Minister, succeeds Sir Alfred C. Lyall as Lieutenant-Governor of the N.-Western Provinces, till Nov. 28, 1892.

Dec. 10: The Amīr of Afghānistān issues an amnesty proclamation.

1888 Jan. The Sikkim Rāja, under the influence of Tibetans, having, in contravention of his treaty, erected a fortified wall across the road over Jalāplā pass, and Tibetans occupied Lingtu, 1,000 troops are sent ostensibly to repair the road to Tibet. The Rāja and Dalai Lāma prove obstinate to the Viceroy's counsel: an expedition is prepared.

Feb. 9: Lord Dufferin announces his intention of resigning, for private reasons.

March 15: The Dalai Lāma, given till this date to withdraw his Tibetans from Lingtu, in Indian territory, took no notice of the intimation, and Col. Graham with about 2,000 men, advances. 20: The advanced stockade at Jeluk stormed and the Tibetans retired and began to fortify at Takolā and Jalāplā pass. 21: Lingtu found deserted and the fortifications ordered to be destroyed.

May 9: The Afghāns defeat a raid of Turkomāns who wished certain families of the clan to cross into Russian territory.

May: An expedition sent against Sawlapaw, chief of the Eastern Karen-ni, who had attacked Maukmé, expelling the Sawbwa, occupying the town and devastating the country. He retires before the force, but returns on their withdrawal in July.

May 22: The Tibetans, reinforced, attack General Graham's camp at Gnatong, but are repulsed.

May: Maung Po-saw raises a rebellion in Mogaung district, exciting the Kachīns to aid him; a desperate attack made on the stockaded town of Mogaung, repulsed by the Gurkha military police. The Kachīns refuse to submit, and an expedition under General Sir G. White proceeds against them in the cold season.

A.D.

1888 June 19: Major L. R. Battye and Capt. H. B. Urmistone and five sipāhis murdered by Akāzāis while exploring on the border near the Black Mountain.

Aug. Is-hāq Khān, cousin of the Amīr, and Governor of Afghān Turkistān, being summoned to Kābul, revolts. He attempted to gain the Bāmiyān pass, but the Amīr's general forestalled him. Sept. 4 (? 29): He is attacked at Tāsh-kargan by Ghulām Haidar, but defeats his left wing; Ghulām attacks with his right, and defeats Is-hāq. Is-hāq a fugitive in Russian territory.

Sept. 24: Col. Graham attacked the again reinforced Tibetans at Jalāpla pass and drove them out with great loss, and pursued them to Chumbi: the Rāja had fled. Graham's advance suspended, and the expedition recalled.

Sept. General J. W. McQueen commands "The Hazāra Field Force" of four columns to avenge the death of Major Battye and Capt. Urmistone. Oct. 4: Seizes Manakadana. General Wm. Galbraith defeats the enemy, who lose 200 men. 5: The enemy entrenched at Kotkai dislodged and a severe defeat inflicted, a body of Ghāzīs being cut off to a man. 18: General McQueen advances and burns their villages. Palosi and Maidān, the strongholds of the Hindustāni fanatics, taken. 21-30: The enemy hasten to make submission and pay fines. Nov. 2: General Channer takes Gorafar peak of the Chaila mountains, 9,500 feet. 5: Return commenced. 18: The Akāzāis, Hasanzāis, &c., finally submit.

Nov. 12: The Earl of Dufferin created Marquis of Dufferin and Earl of Ava.

THE MARQUIS OF LANSDOWNE, NINTH VICEROY.

1888 Dec. 10: Lord Dufferin departs and the Marquis of Lansdowne is installed as ninth Viceroy.

Dec. 23: Raid of the Chins on the British border.

Dec. 26: 'Abdul Rahman fired at by a soldier of the 4th Harāti regiment at Mazan-ī-Sharīf, but he missed him and was at once cut down.

1889 Jan. 1: General H. Collett, with a force from Fort Stedman (Maingthauk) to Karen-ni defeats native chiefs. 9: His and Col. J. J. Harvey's columns reach and capture the capita

A.D.

1889 Saulōn; the rebel chief, Saulapā, had fled. His nephew, Saulāwi, inducted as chief of the tributary state in subordinate alliance.

Jan. The fortress of Quetta completed.

Jan. 23: H.R.H. the Duke of Connaught with the Duchess arrived at Haidarābād on a visit to the Nizām.

Jan. 28: The Lūshai hill tribes made a raid into Tipara, destroying villages, killing about a hundred people and carrying off nearly as many prisoners.

Feb. 3: The Amīr's troops under Ghulām Haidar Khān defeated the Shinwāri insurgents. 20: Ghulām Haidar is made governor-general.

Feb. 9: Major Francis Howard stormed the dākaīt position near Mount Pōpa, south-east of Pagan.

Feb. 23: By decree Augusto Cesar Cardoso de Carvalho transferred from India to the Cape Verde Islands. April 11: Vasco Guedes de Carvalho e Menezes appointed to the Indian governorship.

Feb. 27: The Taunghu-Māndalé railway, 220 miles long, connecting Upper and Lower Burma, completed, and opened March 1 for traffic. It was sanctioned Sept. 1886.

March 9: Hkama, the capital of the Lepu Kachīns, and seventeen villages destroyed in punishment of recent raids and rebellion.

March 27: Sakkar bridge over the Indus opened. 31: There were now 13,671 miles of railway open and 1,438 miles under construction.

April 1: Sir Geo. White, at Rangūn, hands over charge of the Burma command to General Sir Benjamin Gordon, Commander-in-Chief of Madras.

April 13: General Sir George B. Wolseley leads an expedition against the Pōnkan Kachīns, south-east of Bhāmo. 18: Captures a village. May: He returns to Bhāmo.

April: Treasonable correspondence of the Mahārāja of Kashmīr and his late Diwān, Lakshman Dās, discovered by the Resident. The Mahārāja, who was notoriously unfit for rule, abdicates, and a council of state appointed.

April: The Tashōn Chins are punished for raids on Indin and Kalé, and 200 kidnapped captives recovered.

May 11: Great fire in Māndalé; about 450 houses burnt.

A.D.

1889 May: Severe famine in Ganjām, about 15,000 persons on relief works; cholera breaks out, and about 1,400 die weekly. June 18: Native chiefs aid in relief; 9,400 still on public works; 865 deaths from cholera reported in one week. July 9: Employed on works, 15,425; deaths in a week, 602.

June 2: Mr Dyson, assistant commissioner, and others killed in an attack upon Burmese dākaīts.

June: The dākaīt leader Ōktamā captured in Minbu district and most of his lieutenants and other leaders surrendered or were killed or captured.

June 29: The Government issues a resolution to borrow 200 lākhs of rupees at 4 per cent. for the public service. July 30: Subscription closed.

July 23: Lieuts. K. J. Mackenzie and H. G. Majendie with mounted infantry defeated and killed the dākaīt chief Bo Kayī Tha.

Aug. Tāntia Bhīl, a robber chief of the Central Provinces, captured. Oct. Convicted of murder in 1879. Dec. 4: Executed at Jabalpur.

Sept. 8: Mr A. P. MacDonnell officiates as Chief Commissioner of Burma for Sir C. H. T. Crosthwaite, till 8th Dec., when Sir C. Crosthwaite resumed charge as Chief Commissioner, till Dec. 10, 1890.

Nov. 9: H.R.H. Prince Albert Victor of Wales received at Bombay by Lord Reay and H.R.H. the Duke of Connaught. 15: At Haidarābād. 19: At Madras. 23: Visited Maisur. Dec. 20: Arrives at Rangūn. Dec. 24: At Māndalé.

1890 Jan. 3-13: H.R.H. the Prince of Wales received by Lord Lansdowne at Calcutta—great festivities. 14: At Banāras. 18: At Lucknow. 20: In N.W. Provinces. 25: Reaches Lāhor. 31: Visits the Khaibar pass. Feb. 9: Dehli. March 22: Returned to Bombay. 28: Embarked for home.

Jan. 10: General Wm. P. Symons, in an expedition against the Chins, receives the submission of the Yokwa Chins. March: The Tashōn tribes and the Baungshē gave up captives and paid the fines levied on them. April: At Fort White and Hāka military posts established.

Feb. 2: Sir R. G. Sandeman makes a military expedition through the Zhob valley to secure the survey and opening of a

A.D.

1890 road through the Zhob, Barhan, and Bori valleys to promote commerce.

March 13: H.R.H. the Duke of Connaught, Commander-in-Chief, Bombay army, retires and leaves; General Sir G. R. Greaves succeeds, till April 1, 1893.

March 11: A Chinese Amban from Lhāsā arrives at Calcutta. 17: A treaty that Sikkim is recognised as a British feudatory state is agreed to. The Rāja flees to Tibet. April: He is arrested in Nepāl; lives in retirement.

April 12: The Right Hon. Geo. R. Canning, Lord Harris, becomes Governor of Bombay in succession to Lord Reay,—till Feb. 16, 1895.

May 31: Major-General B. L. Gordon made over the Burma command to Brigadier-General Sir Geo. B. Wolseley.

July: The dākaīt leader, Bo Yanyun, surrenders to Mr Macdonald. Aug. He is transported for life.

Aug. 9: Great flood of the Irāwadī, Māndalé endangered.

Sept. 21-24: Takendrajit Singh, commander-in-chief of Manipur, dethroned the rāja, his elder brother, Sūra Chandra Singh, and set up his brother, Kula Chandra Dhaya Sing, the juvarāja, in his place; the Rāja Sūra Chandra retired to Calcutta.

Oct. 22: The Black Mountain expedition or demonstration under General Sir J. M. McQueen sets out; Nov. 3: returns.

Dec. 10: Sir Alexander Mackenzie succeeds Sir C. Crosthwaite as Chief Commissioner of Burma, till April 10, 1895.

Dec. 17: Sir Charles A. Elliot succeeds Sir Steuart C. Bayley as Lieut.-Governor of Bengal.

1891 Jan. 2: Punitive force sent against the Chins and other tribes reaches Theta; after a contest it is surrendered.

Jan. 8: By decree Vasco Guedes de Carvalho e Menezes is relieved of the government at Goa, and Francisco Maria da Cunha appointed 125th governor, till Feb. 4, 1892.

Jan. 12: Great fire at Poona: many houses destroyed.

Jan. 23: Beilby Lawley, Baron Wenlock, takes charge as Governor of Madras, till March 18, 1896.

Jan. Punitive expedition to Momeit, a Shān state, to punish outrages; a village burned, and rebels killed.

A.D.
1891 Feb. 15: Kanhau chiefs in Upper Burma punished for raiding; several villages destroyed; the chiefs submit, give up captives, and pay fines to Capt. F. M. Rundall.

Feb. 19: The Sawbwa of Wuntho rebels. Major O. S. Smyth with 400 Europeans reinforced. 22: The Sawbwa deposed by proclamation, and his territory annexed. 24: Wuntho, held in force by the rebels, attacked and carried after a desperate resistance, the Sawbwa flees, and his palace is burnt. Capt. A. Hutchinson defeats the rebels at Okpho. 26: General G. B. Wolseley takes command at Wuntho. March 3: He holds a darbār at Wuntho; the British flag hoisted. With Col. Macpherson he advances into the Wuntho country, and the Sawbwas of Wuntho and Kalē retreat.

March 19: The Factory Bill for the protection of women and children passed. The "Age of Consent to Marriage Bill" passed.

March 19: Expedition under General Elles to the Black Mountain: the Pioneers attacked by Ghāzīs. April 5: Sharp engagement. 7: Sappers making road attacked, fourteen sipāhis killed. 18: Machai peak ascended.

March 22: Jas. W. Quinton, Chief Commissioner of Āsām, arrived at Manipur with Col. Skene and 470 Gurkhas and officers to instal the regent and remove the Senāpati. 23: The Senāpati, Takendrajit Singh, refused to surrender. 24: His arrest resisted in a sharp struggle in the fort; the Manipuris attacked the residency; then the Senāpati invited Mr Quinton, Col. Skene, Mr Grimwood, and three others into the palace and assassinated them. At midnight the residency was again attacked; the force with Mrs Grimwood retire, taking the wounded with them. 30: They arrive at Lakhipur. 28: Lieut. C. J. W. Grant, with eighty sipāhis, started from Tamu in Burma. 31: Entrenched at Thobal, and held out against the Manipur army till April 7: only one killed.

April: The Mullās of the Miranzāi valley preach a *jihād* against the British, and are headed by Sayyid Mīr Bāsha holding the Samana heights. General Sir W. Lockhart, with 7,000 men, starts from Kohat to resist the Orakzāis, who make a sudden attack but are repulsed. 17-18: Sir W. Lockhart captures outposts. 19-20: The enemy dispersed and villages burnt: about

A.D.

1891 300 Orakzāis killed. 22: The Akhel tribe attacked: severe fighting and villages destroyed. 29: The Shaikans punished, their towers destroyed. May 3: Several tribes accept conditions and submit. May 12: The tribes seek peace and restore stolen property. 17: The troops ordered to return.

April 25: About 2,000 Manipuris driven from their entrenched camp by Col. Th. Graham's force. 26: The forces find the Manipur palace blown up and the regent, Senāpati, and other princes fled. May 8: The regent, Kula Chandra, and his minister, the Tongal general, captured; and a fortnight later the Senāpati Takendrajit Singh.

April 25: Two young Pārsī women throw themselves, or are thrown, from the University tower, Bombay—the cause not discovered.

June 9-20: The Manipur regent, the Senāpati, Angas Sena, a younger brother, and the Tongal general tried and sentenced to death. Aug. 10: The sentence on the Senāpati and Tongal general confirmed, the regent and his younger brother to be transported for life to the Andaman islands. Aug. 13: Takendrajit and the Tongal general hanged at Manipur.

Aug. Capt. Yanoff, with a military force, stops Capt. Younghusband and Lieut. Davidson travelling on the Afghān frontiers; the Russians retire on the advance of a party of Gurkhas.

Sept. 13: Chura Chand, a relative of the late Mahārāja, selected to govern Manipur as "Rāja," and being only five years old, the state to be administered during his minority by a British officer.

Oct. 23: The Viceroy visits Kashmīr: honourably received at Srīnagar. The powers of the Mahārāja increased.

Nov. General Wolseley transferred to Belgaum.

Dec. 2: The Kunza and Nāgar tribes, induced by the intrigues of Russia, attack parties making roads near Gilgit; Lieut.-Col. A. G. A. Durand, the British agent, takes Nilt fort. Dec. 20-22: Capt. Colin Mackenzie, Lieut. Manners Smith, and others force their way near Nilt, occupying other places; Ja'far Khān of Nāgar submits and the war ends.

Dec. 12: The dākaīt Bo Lē killed and his followers dispersed by Lieut. Magrath, assistant commissioner of Katha.

A.D.

1892 The revised totals of the 1891 Census of India showed a population of 287,289,783 on an area of 1,553,925 square miles. Of the population 72.28 per cent. were Hindūs, 19.97 Musalmāns, 3.24 Forest tribes, and 2.48 per cent. Buddhists almost exclusively in Burma; and there were 2,284,191 Christians, 1,907,836 Sikhs, 1,416,109 Jains, 89,887 Pārsīs, and 17,180 Jews, or together about 2 per cent.

1892 Jan. 1: General Sir Frederick S. Roberts, Commander-in-Chief, created a peer as Baron Roberts of Kandahar.

Jan. 6: Major Yule, after two days' fighting, captured Sadon. Lieut. Macnab successful in the Chin districts. Feb. 19-28: The Kachīns repulsed by Lieut. Harrison in their attack on Sadon (re-named Fort Harrison). Major Yule successfully advanced and joined Capt. Davies at Sadon; continued fighting there.

Feb. The Russian Government declares the action of Capt. Yanoff in interfering with Capt. Younghusband and Lieut. Davidson to be illegal, and apologises.

Feb. 4: Francisco Teixeira da Silva appointed Governor-General at Goa, in place of Francisco Maria da Cunha.

Jan. 29: Colonel Sir Robert G. Sandeman, Governor-General's agent in Baluchistan, died; succeeded, March 22, by Major-General Sir J. Browne, who died at Quetta, June 13, 1896.

Feb. 11: Petroleum discovered in Āsām; large quantities obtained.

March: Early in the month, 32,855 employed on relief works, chiefly in Madras. April 1: On famine relief works: 48,000 in Madras, 17,000 in Bengal, 33,000 in Rājputāna, 28,000 in Burma, and about 15,000 in Maisur and Bombay.

March: Falam, the headquarters of the Tāshons in Burma, occupied by the British.

March 14: Minlaung, a noted dākaīt, captured at Kudaung about Feb. 26, sentenced to death with others. 30: Sentence confirmed.

March 30-31: Great fire at Māndalē, destroying above 4,000 houses—a large part of the city, the telegraph office, and property valued at thirty lākhs of rupees.

March 31: The Viceroy opens the new Bombay Tansa water

A.D.

1892 works, designed by Major Tulloch, and which had cost fifteen million rupees.

April 2: Lūshais attack the tea estate of Būrūnchera and kill fifty-two labourers. Advance of Capt. J. Shakespear, superintendent of the South Lūshai hills. About 24th: Conflicts, and villages destroyed. 26: Several chiefs surrender to Mr Robt. B. M'Cabe. May: They gradually settle down.

May 2: Sir Alex. Mackenzie, Chief Commissioner of Burma, left in ill health. May 23: Sir F. W. R. Fryer officiates till May 3, 1894.

May, June: Heavy rains in Madras. May 5: 64,000 employed on famine relief works in South India. Rain in Bengal; total on relief works, 71,000.

May 22: Mahārāja Mangal Singh of Alwar dies; his heir a minor ten years old. May 25: His minister assassinated.

June: The Hazāras of Oruzghān revolt against the taxation imposed by the Amīr and defeat his troops who lose severely July: Many tribes unite to resist the Amīr's harsh rule.

June: Capt. Yanoff, with a strong military escort from Ferghāna, proceeds into Shighnān. July 24: He orders a few Afghān troops at Somatāsh near the Yeshil-kul to surrender and on their refusing his Kosāks fire on them. Sept. 14-Oct. 3: Capt. Yanoff and his force returned to Marghilan.

July: Good monsoon rains; relief works diminished.

Aug. 19: The Earl of Kimberley appointed (third time) Secretary of State for India, till March 10, 1894.

Aug. 20: The Governor of Qandahār repulsed by Hazāra insurgents. The Amīr's troops capture Kamsin from the rebels, but with heavy loss. Sept. They occupied Oruzghān.

Aug. Aman-ul-Mulk, Mehtar of Chitral, died; Oct. 17: his second son, Afzal-ul-Mulk, seized the authority, and his elder brother, Nīzām-ul-Mulk, fled to Gilgit. Nov. His uncle, Sher Afzal Khān, usurps the government, and Afzal-ul-Mulk is killed. Dec. Nizām-ul-Mulk returns and defeats Sher Afzal Khān who flees to Afghānistān.

Oct. 5: General Sir Wm. Lockhart commands the Isazai expedition against the Black Mountain tribes.

Oct. 14: The Chins rise in rebellion, and in a fight at Pombai

A.D.

1892 near Fort White they killed seven sipāhis; Lieut. Henegan arriving with fifty sipāhis, they retired; Fort White is reinforced by Lieut. Wardell.

Oct. 25: 'Abdul Khudas Khān, the Amīr 'Abdul Rahman's general, died.

1893 Jan. 6: Col. A. H. Turner occupies Bulandkhel on the Afghān frontier.

Jan. Nizām-ul-Mulk recognised as Mehtar of Chitral by the British. 28: Dr Geo. S. Robertson, agent at Gilgit, sent with a mission to Chitral. Left in June.

Jan. 17-30: The Kachīns make attacks on the police post at Sima (renamed Fort Morton) but are repulsed by Capt. Atkinson's force. Feb. 4: His force stormed and captured a stockaded fort at Palap. 12: In the Shān state of Theinni, the Kachīns encounter the military police under Lieut. Williams and gain a partial success: Lieut. Williams killed. Feb. 20-24: Major Hammans reduces to submission the Siyin and Nwengal Chins in North Theinni and about Sima.

March 4: Tribesmen from the Indus valley attack the British fort at Chilās and are repulsed with above 150 killed, but with the British loss of Major Averill Daniell, three native officers and nineteen men of the Kashmir Imperial troops.

March 8: China resists the claims of Russia in Turkistān.

March 11: Raphael Jacome Lopes de Andrade appointed Governor-General of Portuguese India.

March 13: The Chins disarmed.

April 1: General Sir G. R. Greaves resigns command of the Bombay army, and is succeeded by General Sir J. Hudson: killed by a fall from his horse, June 9.

April 2: General Sir George White, appointed to succeed Lord Roberts, arrived at Bombay. 8: Lord Roberts leaves Bombay, and Sir George White assumes office as Commander-in-Chief. 25: General Sir James C. Dormer, Commander-in-Chief, Madras, mauled by a tiger. May 3: Died at Uttakamand of injuries. Succeeded by General Mansfield Clarke.

April 9: Col. A. C. Yate arrived at Qandahār as Commissioner in the dispute about canal rights in the Kushk valley frontier. May 18: Arrived in the Kushk valley and met Lieut.-

A.D.

1893 Col. Kurapotkin, the Russian representative. Aug. An amicable settlement made. Sept. 12: Reported.

May 29: By a cyclone, sixty-four men unloading the "Germania" are drowned.

June 1: Col. Yanoff again left Marghelan with a force, moved to the Pamirs. Most of the troops remained in the Alai valley. He advanced apparently to relieve the military guards placed there throughout the winter. The expedition returned to Ferghāna in August.

June 9: Major-General C. E. Nairne succeeds Sir John Hudson as Commander-in-Chief of the Bombay army.

June 25: Serious riots at Rangūn between Hindūs and Muhammadans at the Baqr-i-'Id: several killed after an attack on the police. At Bareli the Hindūs attacked the Musalmans; and in Azamgarh district armed Hindū bands attacked them; the Lieut.-Governor, Sir Ch. Crosthwaite, took vigorous measures against the instigators.

July 30: Destructive floods in Kashmīr; part of Srīnagar destroyed, with loss of life.

Aug. 11: At the Dasara or Durga-puja, coinciding with the 10th Muharram, a great riot broke out at Bombay, and military sent to suppress it; it lasted till 15th. Deaths, 76; arrests, 1,557, 684 being Hindūs; many condemned to lengthy imprisonment.

Aug. 15: The Khān of Kalāt is deposed, who had killed 3,000 men and women in thirty-six years, and had recently put his Diwān to death. Nov. 10: Mīr Mahmūd Khān formally installed at Quetta as successor.

Sept. 18: British Mission to Kābul, under Sir H. Mortimer Durand and General E. R. Elles, started from Peshāwar. 20: Received at Dhākā by General Ghulām Haidar. 23: At Jalālābād, quartered at the Amīr's new palace. 27: Arrived at Surkh-pul. 30: At Lataband pass; and Oct 2: reached Kābul and are received with much honour and hospitality. Oct. 10: After a lengthy interview a satisfactory settlement arranged. Nov. 12: Settlement signed. The annual subsidy raised to eighteen lākhs of rupees. Nov. 13: At a darbār the mission is received by the Amīr's sons. Nov. 15: Sir H. M. Durand and the mission leave Kābul.

Oct. 20: Rioting at Yeola, Nāsik district; a Hindū procession

A.D.

1893 attacked a mosque, leading to street fighting, finally suppressed by troops.

Nov. 10: The Viceroy opens waterworks at Agra; warns Hindūs and Muhammadans against molesting one another in religious observances.

Nov. 18: Lord and Lady Lansdowne arrive at Rangūn; visit Māndalé, &c., and leave from Rangūn, Dec. 11.

1894 Jan. 2: In a skirmish with Abors at Bāmjar in Upper Āsām, seven military police killed. Dambāk and Silak captured by Capt. Maxwell's force, and villages burnt.

EARL OF ELGIN, TENTH VICEROY

Jan. 20: The Earl of Elgin and Kincardine arrives at Bombay. 23: Farewell banquet given Lord Lansdowne at Calcutta. 27: At Calcutta Lord Elgin assumed the office of Viceroy.

Feb. 20: The Opium Commission after examining witnesses and making inquiries at Pātna, Banāras, Lāhor, Agra, Dehli, Ajmīr, Indor, and Ahmadābād, the final sitting was held at Bombay. The cost of the sittings in India estimated at Rs. 20,000, and in England at £1,500.

Feb. 27: After Membo, the Abor stronghold, had been taken, the Abors surprised a party of forty-four Bengal infantry who lost thirty men and a native officer. March 6: Villages burnt by Capt. Maxwell's force. March 16: The force arrives at Sadiya.

March 24: Mr W. N. Porter leads a punitive expedition against the Kaswa Chins for their murderous raid on Naingtaung in Feb.

April 9: A party of Māppillas, after a murderous attack on Hindūs, refuse to surrender, are attacked by a detachment of the Dorset regiment and thirty-three killed and remaining two wounded.

June 1: Civil war reported in Chitral. Sher Afzal, the Mehtar's uncle, still caused trouble and had induced Umrā Khān, chief of Jāndol, to support his claims.

May: The Siyin Chins render entire submission. June: The Chins are completely disarmed and the districts quieted.

July: Serious floods in Baluchistān, Kāndesh, Gujarāt, and

A.D.

1894 other parts of Western India, doing much damage to the railways.

July 28: Rangūn High-pressure Water Supply Works opened by the Chief Commissioner.

Aug. 23: Convention ratified delimiting the frontier between China and Burma, south of latitude 25° 35′ N.

Aug. 26: In Garhwal, by a tremendous landslip near Goḥna, Sept. 6, 1893, most of the Maithāna hill fell into the Birahigangā, forming a long lake about 700 ft. deep, which now burst at midnight, carrying away bridges, buildings, animals, &c., but warnings having been sent out, no loss of life occurred.

Sept. 13: At the *Bāra Wafāt*, in memory of Muhammad's death, a Ganpati procession in Poona disturbed the Muslims in a mosque, when a riot ensued, and a Muhammadan was killed and others injured; the mob had to be charged by the police to clear the streets.

Oct. 1: Troops under Col. A. H. Turner concentrated at Dera Ismail Khān to support the political officer and protect the delimitation party against the Wazīrīs. Nov. 3: The Mahsūd Wazīrīs made an attack on his camp at Wāno with 2,000 men: they were defeated, with a loss of 330 killed.

Dec. 12: The Mahsūds refuse to comply with the terms offered and Sir Wm. Lockhart with reserves advances to carry out the demarcation and obtain reparation. The Mullā Pāwandā retreated with his followers. 21, 22: Makin destroyed and some desultory fighting.

Dec. 24-29: First medical congress at Calcutta; opened by the Viceroy.

Dec. 31: Amīr-ul-Mulk, a younger brother of Nīzām-ul-Mulk, at the instigation of Umrā Khān of Jandol, has the Mehtar of Chitral murdered and claims the succession. The Chitral war followed.

INDEX

ABĀJI Pant Purandhare, 162
  Ābā Sāhib of Kolhāpur, 315, 316
'Abbās, Shah of Persia, 63, 65, 79
  Shah III., 170
  Mirzā of Persia, 323
Abbasābād, battle, 331
Abba Sāhib—Sabū, 240
Abbott, Capt. James, 351
Abdāl Chakk of Kashmīr, 48, 49
Abdālīs, 159, 170, 187, 212, 215
'Abdul 'Azīz Khān, Afghān, 96
  Azīz Khān of Junnar, 183
  Bāqī, author, 74
  Ghafur, Shāh, 167
  Ghāni Khān, 168
  Hakim Khan of Sāvanūr, 200-202, 222
  Hamid Khān, 155
  Haqq, Shaikh, historian, 59
  Jalil Sayyid of Bilgrām, 142
  Karīm, Bījāpūr, 117, 120, 121
  Karīm Khān, "Balu Mīyā," 264
  Kudus Khān, 406, 427
'Abdullah of Janjira, 173
'Abdullah 'Ādil Khān of Bījāpūr, 30
  'Alī Gauhar, 212, 213
  Jān, Kābul, 390, 397
  Khān 'Uzbak, 40
  Khān, Sayyid, 154, 159
  Khān Bahādur, Firuz Jang, 68, 69, 79
  Khān, Qutb-ul-Mulk, 160, 162, 164
  Qutb Shāh, 69, 101, 102, 112, 114, 116
'Abdul Mākri, Kashmīr, 25
  Haqq, Shaikh, historian, 59
  Nabi, Mathura, 107, 112
  Qādir, Ahmadnagar, 34
  Qādir Badāoni, 59
  Rahīm Sidi of Janjira, 255
  Rahīm Khān (Mirzā), Khān Khānān, 47, 51, 54-56, 59, 61, 64, 66; 74, 80
  Rahman Sūr, 36
  Rahman of Kabul, 382, 384, 385, 402, 405-409, 411, 417, 419, 427
  Samad Khān of Lāhor, General, 130, 157, 162, 167
'Abdul Samad Khān Abdālī, 215
  Sayyid, Panghulu, 327, 328
  Wahāb Khān, Karnātak, 195 208
Abercromby, General Sir Robert, 261-264, 268, 270, 271, 297
Abhapura hill, 375
Abhaya Singh of Mārwār, 154, 156, 165, 169, 171, 173, 176, 190
Abingdon, Major, 249, 250
Abors, 429
Abraham, Syrian bishop, 59
Abreu, Gonzalo de, 68
'Abul Fath Mu'in-ud-dīn, Muhammad 'Alī Shāh, of Audh, 341
  Fazl, Shaikh, 32, 59, 62
  Hasan Qutb Shāh, 119, 127, 129, 130
  Ma'āli, Kābul, 41
  Qasim Mīr 'Alam, 293
  Tālib Londonī, author, 268
Abyssinia, 34
Abyssinians, Habshis, 383
Achchhē, Buland Akhtar, poet, 167
Aché, Count de, 206
Achin, Achinese, 31, 39, 45, 47, 53, 62, 70, 76, 84, 87, 90, 184
Achyuta Rāya of Vijayanagar, 22, 29
Acts of Parliament, 258, 285
Adālaj, inscription, 5; battle, 170
Adam, Sir Frederick, 329, 334
  Mr John, 317
  William Patrick, 405, 406
Ādam Khān, Gakkhar, 33
Adams, Col. John Worthington, 309, 311
  Major Thomas, 219, 220
Addams, James, 113
Addison, Gulston, 152; Joseph, 152
Adham Khān of Mālwā, 38, 39
'Aden, 12, 14, 18, 354, 386, 399
'Ādil Khān Farūqī, Mirān Ghāni, 2, 4, 7
  Khān III., Farūqī, 11, 16
  Shāh Sūr, 32
Adina Beg, 205
Adlecron, Colonel, 203
Adoni, 250, 257
adoption *sanads*, 377

Affonso, Martin, 26, 65
Afghāns, 16, 21, 26, 45, 47, 51, 61, 68, 69, 114, 117, 158, 169, 184-186, 188, 189, 212, 216, 337, 339-341, 352, 388, 390, 394, 398-404, 411, 417, 418, 424, 426, 427
Afghānistān, 61, 66, 76, 119, 157, 162, 282, 296, 339, 385, 395, 397, 415, 426
Afghān-Persian boundary, 389, 397; Afghān delimitation commission, 410, 413, 415, 417
Afrāsyāb Khān, 250, 255
African Company, 108
Afrīdī tribes, 353, 354, 395, 396, 405
Afzal Khān, 68; 105;
  Afghān, 380, 382, 383, 402, 405, 407;
  of Chitral, 426, 429
Afzal-ud-daula, Nizām, 361, 376, 385
Afzal-ud-dīn, of Surat, 315
Afzal-ul-Mulk, Chitral, 426
Agashi, 22, 70
Agham, 18
Āghā Khān, 134
  Khān Muhammad Husain Husaini, Isma'īli Imām, 306, 335, 338, 347, 354, 377, 378, 382
  Mīr Mutāmad-ud-daula, 326
Agnew, Patrick A. Vans, 350, 353
Agra, 7, 8, 20, 22, 27, 30, 32, 34, 41, 46, 61-63, 65-67, 69-72, 75, 77, 78, 80, 83, 93-95, 98, 103-105, 120, 134, 146, 149, 160, 169, 219, 222, 242, 255, 256, 258, 259, 261, 357, 362, 365, 366, 374, 382, 394; Waterworks, 429
Agricultural exhibition, 378
Ahatalla or Theodore, Syrian bishop, 101
Ahdād, an Afghān, 71
Ahalyā-bāī, of Indor, 224, 269
Ahmad II. Bahmanī, of Ahmadnagar, 58
  'Alī, of Kābul, 41
  'Alī, Rohila, 268
  Beg, Orīssa, 79
  Khān, 7
  Khān, Ahmad Shāh II. of Gujarāt, 34; Ahmad III., 39
  Khān, Kashmīr, 42
  Khān of Burhānpur, 152
  Khān, Abdālī, 187
  'Abul Nasr, Sultān, 183, 188, 196, 197, 260
  Shāh Abdālī, 205, 211, 212, 215
  Shāh III., Bahmanī, 17
  Nizām Shāh Bahrī of Ahmadnagar, 2, 3, 7, 9
Ahmad Shāh Durānī, 191, 193, 203, 211, 225, 233
  Sayyid, Wahhābi, 327
Ahmadābād, 40, 46, 51, 69, 72, 74, 75, 105, 132, 146, 149, 155, 158, 170, 172, 176-178, 181, 195, 199, 244, 250, 301, 307, 327; khatīb of, 152
Ahmadkhel, 403
Ahmadnagar, 3, 16, 18, 21, 23, 27, 28, 31, 33, 36, 37, 39, 42, 44, 52, 54-59, 61, 64, 68, 74, 84, 88-90, 103, 110, 126, 142, 148, 149, 157, 272, 283, 285, 306
Ahmadulla, Faizābād Maulvī, 369, 371
Ahwāz, 361
Aikman, Captain, 369
Aislabie, William, 147, 151, 156, 157
Aitchison, Sir Charles U., 399, 404, 416
Aitkad Khān, Bengal, 96
Aitkinson, Major, 415
Aix-la-Chapelle, treaty, 189
Ajaju, battle, 150
Ajaygarh, 294
Ajīt Singh, of Mārwār, 149, 154, 156 158, 160, 162
  Singh, Sardār, Lāhor, 343, 344
Ajmīr, 23, 29, 52, 72, 82, 105, 123-125, 162, 165, 226, 259, 262, 288, 293, 405
Akā tribes, 409
Akā-Tapa, 411
Akauk-Taung, 356
Akāzāī clan, 419
Akbar, Sultān, 28, 29, 33, 35, 36, 38-64, 74
Akbar II., Abul-Nasr Mu'in-ud-dīn Muhammad, 256, 290, 335
  Prince, son of 'Alamgīr, 122, 124, 125, 128, 139
  'Alī Khān of Narhat, 248
  Khān of Kābul, 334, 339-341, 353
Akhel tribe, 424
Akluj, 132
Aknot, battle, 351
Akram Khān, Afghān, 352
Akūlamannād district, 209
Alaf Khān of Morāsa, 3
Alahwardī or Allahwīrdī Khān, 167, 175, 179-182, 184, 189, 191, 195, 200, 204
'Alā Singh of Patiāla, 223
'Alā-ud-daula, Sarfarāz Khān, 178
'Alā-ud-dīn II., Bahmanī, 17, 18, 20
  Husain of Bengal, 3, 4, 16
  'Imād Shāhī, 7, 20, 22
  Islām Khān of Bengal, 66
  Khalji, 5
  Muzaffar Firuz Shāh of Bengal, 24

Alai, Shaikh, of Māhdī sect, 32
Alai valley, 428
'Ālam 'Alī Khān, 161
 Khān, 192
 Khān Lodī, 19
 Khān Fārūqī, 9, 11
Alamanava, village, 192
Alamāns, 96
Ālambāgh, 366-369
Alambarai, 175
'Ālamgīr Sultān, 104-169, *see* Aurangzīb
'*Alamgīr-nāma*, history, 131
Alamgīrnar-Kuch Bihār, 107
Ālamparai, 213
Alaunghprā of Burma, 196, 199, 201, 203, 211, 213, 250; 414
Albert Victor, H. R. H. Prince of Wales, 421
Albuquerque, Alphonso, 7, 10-15
 Francisco, 7
 Jorge de, 17
 Juan de, 37, 38
 Ferdnão de, 77
 Alphonso de, 349
 Caetano Alexandre de, 397, 406, 413
 Luiz Mendoza Furtado de, 115, 121
 Mathias de, 55
 Pedro de, 14
Alcaceva, Fernão, 15
Alcazar Kivīr, battle, 48
Aldworth, Mr, factor, 70, 72
Alexander VI., Pope, 6
'Alī 'Ādil Shāh I. of Bījāpur, 37, 42, 48, 49
'Alī Ādil Shāh II., 102, 106, 113, 116
 Ashgar, 87
 Bahādur of Bānda, 281
 Gauhar, prince, 209
 Husain of Arkāt, 279
 Jāh, Haidarābād, 269
 Jāh of Bengal, 315
 Jāh Jankujirāv Sindia, 322
 Jāh Jayajīrāv Sindia, 415
 Jāh Jiyajī Bhāgiratrāv Sindia, 342
 Khān Fārūqī of Kāndesh, 47, 56
 Khān Chakk, of Kashmīr, 44, 45, 48
 Mardan Khān, 90, 91, 94, 95, 103, 132, 138
 Muhammad, Rohila, 185, 190
 Murād, Mīr, of Khairpur, 355
 Naqi, 103
 Nawāz Khān, Surat, 208
 Qulī Khān, Khān Zamān, 38
Aliganj, 209
Aligarh, 201, 258, 283, 305, 365, 366
Alikhanov, Major, 409, 411
Alīkhel, 398, 400
Ālikotta, 262
Alikūr, Ceylon, 74
'Alī-Masjid, 337, 340, 397, 405
Alīpur, 362
Alīwāl battle, 347
Allah Yār Khān, 85, 86
Allahābād, 61, 62, 90, 105, 112, 209, 222, 229, 232-234, 236, 273, 291, 362, 373, 386, 387
Allāmi, Sa'ādullah Khān, 100, 102
Allapur, battle, 13
Allard, Col. Jean Francois, 316
Allegiance, Declaratory test of, 295
Allen, Major, 215
Ālleppey, 293
Almeida, Francisco de, 8, 10
 Januario Correia de, 386
 João Fernandes de, 157, 158
 João Tavares de, 393, 395
 Jorge de, 86
 Lorenzo de, 8-10
 Luiz de Caetano de, 182
 Miguel de, 133
 Pedro de, 121
Almora, 302, 303
Alorgaje, Malacca, 328
Alorna fort, 186, 205, 259
Alot, 308
Alves, Major, 333
Alvor, Conde de, 124
Alwar, 258, 297, 299
Aman-ul-Mulk of Chitral, 426
Amānat Khān, I'tmād Khān, 132, 140 148, 153
Amara Singh I. of Udaypur, 59, 60, 69, 71, 78; Amara II., 143, 153
 Singh Rāthor, of Jodhpur, 91, 94
 Singh of Patiāla, 223, 225
 Singh, Gurkha, 302, 303
Amaral, Francisco Joaquim Ferreira de, 413
Amarapura, Burma, 253, 359
Amarāvatī, 295
Amardās, 3rd Sikh Guru, 33, 46
Amarkot, 28, 343
Amaro, Simoes, 125
Ambāji Inglia, 276, 284, 285, 296
Ambālā, 293, 344, 346, 378, 384, 385
Ambalakāda, 145
Ambalkotta or Chennam, 53, 62
Ambela Pass, 378, 379
Amber, 154
Amboyna, 40, 42, 48, 60, 62, 64, 76, 79, 100, 101, 270, 296
Ambūr, 189, 226
Amherst, William Pitt, Lord, 317, 322, 323
Amichand ("Omichund") Seth, 202-204

Amiens, Treaty of, 280
Amin-ullah Khān, 341
Amīr Barīd I., of Bīdar, 7, 11, 16-19, 21
    Khān of Tonk, 286-290, 295, 304, 307, 332
    Khān, Wahhābi, 387
    Khān, Umdat-ul-Mulk, 186
    Rustam of Sindh, 342
    Singh of Tanjor, 258
Amīr-ul-Mulk, Chitral, 430
Amjad 'Alī Shāh of Audh, 349
Ammona, 205
Amod, 237, 244
Amorā, 372
Amra, 380
Amritrāv of Poona, 205, 243, 273
Amritsar, 46, 274, 292, 293, 354, 357, 387
Amsterdam merchants, 97
Amyatt, Mr, 219
Ānandrāv Puār of Dhār, 190, 244, 380
    of Rājmandrī, 207-209
    Gaikwād, 278, 307, 313
    of Īdar, 173
Ānand-Mogri, battle, 174
Anantapur, 252
Andaman islands, 271, 387, 388, 424
Andrade, Christovão Luiz de, 165
    Raphael Jacome Lopes de, 427
    Ruy Frière de, 70
Anderson, Lieut., 350, 353
    Dr John, 392
Andrews, Matthew, 108
    Robert, 269
Anegundi, 239, 276
Angad, 2nd Sikh Guru, 27, 33
Angādipuram, 353
Angedīva island. *See* Anjidīva
Angelo, Lieut., 403
Anglo-Spanish treaty, 85
Āngria, 160-163, 170-173
Angūl, rāja of, 350
Anhilawāda inscription, 57
Anilon battle, 293
Aniruddha, author, 3
Anjār, 281, 316
Anjengo, 128, 136, 140, 146, 163, 193
Anjidīva, Angedīva island, 8, 108, 110, 125, 159
Anjuncha, battle, 293
Ankleshwar, Anklesar, 153, 237, 244
Annagudi, 249
Anna Sāwant, 383
Anne, Queen, 147
Annesley, Daniel, 136, 141
    Samuel, 138, 140, 152
Annunciação, Archbp. Fra Augustinho da, 133, 144
Anriques, Francisco da Miranda, 74, 75
Anson, General George, 358, 362
Anstruther, Sir Alexander, 298
Antāji Bhāskar, Marātha, 166
Anup Singh of Bikhanir, 118, 152, 163
Anupshahr, 212
Anurād Singh of Būndī, 125, 138
Anwar-ud-dīn, Nawāb 184, 185, 189, 191, 192, 220
Apā Sāhib or Mudoji of Berār, 304, 305, 307-312
Appa Desāi Nipānkar, 285, 291
    Khanderāv, 266, 268, 272
Appanna Timma II. Udayār, 33, 45
Ārā, 365, 370
Arabs, 97, 122, 280, 281, 310-313
Arabi Pāshā, 407
Arakan, 62-64, 67, 72, 105, 128, 131, 153, 253, 274, 281, 298, 319, 320-322
Arakan or Myauku, 320
Arakere, 263
Ārās, 165, 237
Aravākūrchī, 253
Arbuthnot, Alexander John, 388
    General Sir Chas. C., 414, 416
Argāon, battle, 284
Arghandāb, 404
Arghūn, Shāh Beg, 35
Argyll, Duke of, 387
Ariyankuppam fort, 187, 189, 214
Arjumand Bānū Begam, 76, 85, 95
Arjun-mal, 5th Sikh Guru, 50, 65
Arjun Sing of Kotā, 165
Arkat, 126, 182, 184, 186, 190, 192, 204, 208, 210-213, 220, 228, 229, 234, 245, 246, 252, 262, 289
Armenia, 61; Armenians, 131
Ārmugam, 81, 83, 86, 91, 92, 122
Arnāla, 246
Arsi, Rānā of Udaypur, 218, 232
Arthur, Sir George, 341, 348
Asad Khān, Bījāpūr, 25, 29
    Khān Karam-mālū, 157
'Asaf Jāh. *See* Nizām-ul-Mulk
    Khān, Mirzā Ja'far, 66, 76, 82, 83, 85
'Asaf-ud-daula, 154; 236-238, 245, 248, 249, 254, 257, 272, 273
Asāi, battle, 284
Āsām, 4, 9, 103, 107, 108, 112, 121, 267, 318, 319, 322, 325, 329, 392, 409, 425, 429
"Ascension," ship, 67
Ashburner, Lionel R., 403
Asheri, 36, 178
Ashraf, Ghilzaī of Persia, 166, 169
Āshta, 87, 310

Asirgarh fort, 5, 13, 61, 80, 284, 307, 311, 312
Askābād, 409
Askarī, Mirzā, 29
Aslam, 387
Assada merchants, 98
Assarceta chiefs, 159
Assassins, 377
Assiz, Francisco de, Marquez de Tavora, 191
Assumar, Conde de, 121, 191
Astruc, M., 180, 194, 195
Ataide, Gabriel de, 31
  Luiz de, 43-45, 48
  Tristão de, 24
Atak,—Attock, 177, 352
Atargarh, 417
Atāri, 353
'Ata-ullah-Khān, 185
Atire, 42
Atkinson, Capt., 427
Atrauli, 370
Attingal, Rānī, 128, 137, 140, 163
Auchmuty, Sir Samuel, 296, 297
Auckland, George Eden Lord, 333-335, 337, 338
Audh, 50, 62, 184, 209, 219, 221, 222, 224, 230, 231, 233-236, 241, 258, 275, 276, 301, 304, 320, 322, 325, 354, 363, 369, 371, 373, 374, 380, 399
Aundha fort, 115, 119
Aurangābād (Karkī), 68, 103, 106, 118, 123, 155, 180, 192, 194, 207, 217, 218, 220, 357, 358
Aurangzib, Alamgir, 76, 77, 81, 83, 85-97, 99, 101, 103-106, 108, 109, 111-115, 117-125, 127-134, 136-138, 142-146, 148-150, 160, 212
Auteuil M. d', 192, 194, 203
Ava, 163, 196, 199, 224, 261, 281, 298, 317, 322, 339, 357, 368, 413, 414
Avery, Capt., 137
Awantgarh—Ontgir, 9
Ayakota, 260
Ayappa Nāyyak, Chengalpat, 91
Ayūb Khān, 404-406, 417, 418
Ayudhya—Ayuthia, Yuthia, 31, 213, 223, 225
Ayyakarai Vayyāppa Nāyyaka, 22
'Azam, Prince, Sātāra, 127, 129, 130, 140, 143, 145
  Shāh, 149
  Khān of Bengal, 50
Azevido, Hierome de, 68, 70, 74
'Azim Khān, Bengal, 84, 86, 88, 92, 93
  Khān, Kābul, 383-385
'Azim Jāh, 313, 357, 390
'Azim-ud-daula, 279, 313
'Azim-ullah Khān, 363
Azimābād, 228
Azimgarh, 370, 428
'Azim-ush-Shan, prince, 139, 140, 142, 148, 153, 154
'Azīz (Mirzā) Kokaltāsh, 46, 52, 54-56, 61, 65, 66
'Azmatulla Khān, Afghān, 402
Azores, 28, 53, 55

BĀBUR, emperor, 3, 4, 7-11, 13-17, 19-22, 41
Bābā Khān Qaqshāl, 49
Bābā-Walī or Mazra, battle, 405
Bābāji Ahirkar, 345
Bābārāv Phadke, 271
Bābar Jang of Bengal, 267
Bābī family, 165
Bābu Mīya of Janjira, 255
Babule, Ceylon, 73
Badakhshān, 17, 35, 52, 94-96
Bādāmi, 257, 258
Badan Singh, Jāt, 154, 162
Badāyan fort, 369
Badhanar, 124
Badlāpur, 369
Badli Sarāi, battle, 362
Badoahprā of Burma, 293
Bādshāha, Khatri, 27
Bādshāhganj, battle, 369
Badun Meng of Burma, 250
Bāgar, 22
Bāghdād, 361
Baglāna, 91
Bāglipur, 204
Bāgrakot, 37
Bahādur, Gilāni, 3
  Chattra Singh of Samtar, 380
  Gujarāt, 57
  Kambū, 85
  Khān, 38, 42
  Khān, Khān Jahān, 105, 112, 115
  Khān Bareli, 375
  Khānji of Junāgarh, 407
  Nizām Shāh, 58, 61
  Khān Farūqī, 61
  Salīm Shāh Sūr, 30
  Shāh of Bengal, 36, 38
  Shāh I., Shāh 'Ālam, 143, 149-153, 157, 159, 160; *see* Muhammad Mu'azzam
  Shāh II., 335, 366, 368
  Shāh of Gujarāt, 18, 20-25
Bahā-ud-dīn, Shaikh, 19
Bahāwal Singh of Bahāwalpur, 330, 356

Bahāwalpur, 329, 330, 336, 342, 350, 356, 357, 381
Bahiropant Pingle, Peshwa, 155
Bahlūl Lodī, Sultān, 1, 19
Bahlūl, Bījāpūr, 117
Bahmanī kings, 19
Bahram Khān, Mohmand, 389
Bahram, Ghāt, 373, 374
Bahrampur, 324, 361
Bahrein, 38, 51
Bahūr, 194
Bailey, Sir Steuart C., 399, 408
Baillie, Col. John, 286, 291, 301
Col. William, 245, 248
Bairam Khān, 34-36, 38, 39
Baird, Gen. Sir David, 275, 278
Bairī Sāl of Jaisalmir, 381
Baizābāī Sindia, 322, 329, 330
Bajaur, 379
Bājirāv I., 2nd Peshwa, 162, 163, 165, 167-169, 171, 172, 174-176, 178, 179; 263
II., 9th Peshwa, 243, 270, 271, 273, 281, 282, 287, 297, 304, 306, 309, 310, 356
Zamindār, rebel, 357
Bak pass, battle 331
Bakāla, Panjāb, 110
Baker, Aaron, 99, 100
Gen. Sir Thos. D., 400, 402
Bakhar, 336
Bakht Singh of Jodhpur, 190, 196
of Jhālāvar, 394
Gurkha, 303
Bakhtāwar Singh, Alwar, 303
Bakla, 67
Baksār, 27, 221, 365
Bālā Sāhib, Parasharām Bhonsla, 304
Bala Hisār, Kābul, 400-402
Bala-Murghāb, 410
Bāladhan tea-garden, 402
Bālāghāt, 83
Bālāji Bajīrāv, 3rd Peshwa, 179-181, 183, 187, 190, 192, 194, 200, 202, 212, 214, 217
Vishvanāth, 1st Peshwa, 150, 155, 156, 162
Bālākot, battle, 322; 327
Balam, 147, 250
Bālāpur, battle, 161
Bālārāv (Nānā Sāhib's brother), 373, 374
Bālāsor, 87, 92, 93, 98, 104, 109, 119, 126, 130, 131, 146, 283, 284, 340
Balbhadra Singh, 302
Baldev Singh of Bharatpur, 317
Bālikot, 53
Bālipārā, 409
Balkh, 32, 94-96, 360, 383, 384, 402
Ball, Col. George, 296
Bāloba Tātya, 271
Balozāi Wazīrīs, 406
Balram Deva, Sambalpur, 3
Balrāmpur, 334
Balsār, 22, 38
Baluchīs, Baluchistān, 338, 343, 346, 417, 425, 429
Balwantrāv, 202, 215
Balwant Singh of Banāras, 234
Singh of Alwar, 303, 322
Singh of Bharatpur, 320
Bāmiyān, 31, 419
Bāmjar, 429
Banāras — Benares 86, 113, 221, 236, 247, 248, 254, 266, 275, 280, 291, 293, 326, 350, 353, 354, 362, 376, 421
Banās river, 286
Banbīr of Mālwā, 25, 26
Bānda islands, 8, 18, 73, 76, 106, 270, 297
Bānda state, 263, 271
Banda, Sikh leader, 153, 157
Bandala, 26
Bandarmalanka, 193, 203
Bānde 'Alī Khān, 317
Bāndra, 21, 119, 176
Banestarim, 12
Bangalor or Bengalūr, 91, 94, 224, 225, 230, 263, 329
Bangash, battle, 54
Banguel fort, 74
Bani Singh, 303, 322
Baniyās, merchants, 120
Bankar, 185
Bankāpur, 165, 168, 173
Bānkot, 199, 201, 243
Bannu, 406
Bānswāra, 300, 311
Bantam, 62, 63, 66, 67, 73, 75, 76, 78, 83, 84, 92, 100, 103, 109, 113, 115, 120, 125-127, 143
Bāpu Gokhale, 310
Phadnavis, 268
Bāpuji Sindia, 273, 277, 286, 288, 289
Nāyyak Bārāmatikar, 179
Bāqir 'Alī, Vellor, 172
Bāqir Khān, Gujarāt, 84, 86
Khān, Orissa, 180
Bar, 17, 89
Bārak riv., 330
Bārāmahāl, 147, 262, 265
Bāra wafāt riot, 430
Barbosa, Duarte, 13
Barcelor,—Basrūr, 44, 115
Bardes, 30, 31, 100, 101, 178, 181
Bardhwān, 65, 79, 137, 138, 184, 214, 221, 228, 236

Barēli,—Bareilly, 223, 235, 304, 362, 371, 428
Barents, William, 58
Baretto, Francisco, 35-37
Barfi, Sirmūr, 152
Bargidia, battle, 373
Barhaman, poet, 5
Barīd Shāhī dynasty, 2
Baring, Major, E., 409
Barker, Gen. Sir Robert, 230
Barlow, Sir Geo. H., 288-292, 301
Bārmūl pass, 283
Barnard, Gen. Sir Henry Wm., 362, 364
Barnett, Commodore, 184, 186
Baroda, 51, 60, 67, 167, 168, 171-173, 232, 244, 281, 288, 299, 300, 313, 314, 324, 326, 328, 337, 392
Baron, M., 118
Barrackpur, 313. 324, 360-362
Barradas, Emmanuel, 96
Barton, Henry, 73
Barūkhzāīs, 276, 278, 288, 335
Barwell, Richard, 233, 234, 237, 239
Basālat Jang, 157; 210, 217, 241-244, 252
Basant 'Alī Khān, Lucknow, 238
Basein, Burma, 199, 203
Basain (Bassein), 23, 25, 27, 44, 45, 56, 60, 89, 90, 118, 122, 162, 166, 170, 173, 176, 178, 179, 236, 237, 281, 282, 356, 357, 414
Bashiratganj, 364, 366
Basrūr,—'Bracalor,' 85
Bastar, 68
Basu, battle, 165
Batavia, 81, 83, 91, 93, 106, 125, 126, 145, 297
batta, 324
Battikaloa, 62, 83, 87, 90-92
Battye, Major L. R., 419; Fort, 403
Batvā, 150
Baungshe, tribe, 421
Bāwā Sāhib of Tanjor, 177; of Kolhāpur, 316, 319, 336
Bāwali, battle, 212
Bayam, James Lopez, 51
Bāyazīd bin Sulaimān, 45, 46
Baylam, battle, 27
Bayley, Sir Steuart Colvin, 405, 422
William Butterworth, 323
Bāz Bahādur, 35, 39, 44
Beadon, Sir Cecil, 377, 382, 383
Beard, John, 127, 128, 142, 145, 149; jun., 141, 143
Beaulieu, Capt., 73, 77
Beckwith, Sir Thos. S., 327
Bedar Bakht, 260
Bedingfield, Lieut., 325
Belāri—Bellary, 278, 322, 372, 395
Belgaum, 424
Beliapatam,—Valarpattanam, 114
Bellasis, Lieut. Geo. Bridges, 279
Bellcombe, Mons., 241
Belligām, 53
Benares, *see* Banāras
Benedict XIV., 181
Benfield, Paul, 239
Bengal, 21, 27, 30, 33, 40, 42, 45-49, 54, 61, 63, 66, 68, 69, 81, 87-91, 93, 96-98, 101-104, 111, 113, 114, 119-123, 125, 127-136, 139, 140, 143-145, 147, 150, 155, 156, 165, 170, 173, 179-182, 184, 187, 188, 191, 201, 202, 204, 205, 207, 209, 210, 217, 220-223, 228, 232-234, 239, 240, 242, 243, 255, 256, 267, 269, 271, 315, 334, 358, 375, 390, 392, 407, 408
Bengal Tenancy Bill, 408, 411
Bengal Pilot service, 113
"Bengalee" newspaper, 408
'Bengāli San' years, 36
Bengtale Grāhtāpdaraga of Burma, 97
Beni-bu 'Alī, tribe, 315
Beni Mādhu, rebel, 371, 373
Benkim Chandra Chattarji, author, 380
Benkulen, 126, 130, 146, 159, 310
Bentinck, Lord Wm. Cavendish, 290, 291, 293, 323, 324, 326-330, 332, 333; *see* Falkland.
Bentota, battle, 101
Benyon, Richard, 174, 183
Berār, 20-22, 29, 43, 54, 58, 61, 68, 112, 123, 142, 166, 269, 283, 286, 289, 291, 295, 357
Bernadotte, John B. Julius (Charles XIV. of Sweden), 253
Bernard, Sir Charles E., 390, 404, 413-416
Berquien, M. Louis, 283
Best, Capt., 69, 70
Bethune, John E. Drinkwater, 353
Bettada Chāma Rāja of Maīsur, 12, 18; 74
Chāma, 229, 238
Bettīya, 298, 302
Beyt, island, 375
Bhādar Benda, fort, 185
Bhadāwar district, 175
Bhāgnagar or Haidarābād, 54, *see* Haidarābad
Bhagnipur, battle, 369
Bhagwān Singh of Dholpur, 334
Singh of Nābha, 379
Bhagwāndās Kachhwaha, Rāja, 52, 54
Bhagwant Singh, 281, 282
'Bhāgvati' tax, 93

Bhaiji Bāwā, Kachh, 281
Bhairāv Pant Pingle, 150
Bhaironwāl, battle, 65
Bhakkar, 17, 18, 35, 104, 105
Bhāmo, 384, 392, 411, 413, 420
Bhāmori, 296
Bhānpur, 369, 371
Bharatgarh, 300
Bharatpur, 217, 219, 229, 234, 250, 259, 287, 288, 317, 320, 321, 333
Bhārmal of Kachh, 312
Bharoch, 44-46, 51, 71, 75, 119, 128, 134, 146, 230, 232, 238, 242, 250, 285
Bhārpar Singh, 379
Bhāskar Pant, 180, 181, 184
Bhāskar-rāv of Nargund, 371
Bhātkal, 29, 31, 122
Bhau Holkar, 344
 Singh of Būndī, 125
Bhāwal Khān, 372
Bhawānī fort, 295, 296
Bhawānībāī of Kolhāpur, 169
Bhilāpur battle, 171
Bhīls, 321, 328, 408
Bhilsā, 23
Bhīmā riv., 137
Bhīm Karan, 16
 Singh of Būndī, 125
 Singh of Udaypur, 241, 323
 Singh of Kotā, 150; 324
 Singh of Jodhpur, 267, 284
 Singh Thāpā, 337, 343
Bhīmavēna Thāpā, 305
Bhīmnagar, 292, 294
Bhīmrāja, 12, 13
Bhīmrāv Nadgir, 371, 372
Bhojpur, battle, 24
Bhopāl, 176, 295, 301, 310, 323, 329, 333-335, 346, 368, 373
Bhotwāl, 275, 298, 301, 302
Bhudargadh fort, 345
Bhuj, 312
Bhungbāra, 342
Bhutan, Bhūtīas, 232-235, 246, 254, 339, 379, 380
Bicholim, 148, 149, 186, 205, 248, 259
Bie, Col., Serampur, 276
Bīdar, 18, 21, 71, 89, 129, 217, 218, 299, 271
Biddulph, General Sir Michael A. S., 398
Bihār, 25, 30, 40, 42, 47-49, 54, 62, 64-66, 78, 92, 139, 145, 173, 179, 180, 188, 189, 212, 213, 248, 326, 390
Bihārī Mal of Idar, 13, 14
 Lāl, poet, 6
Bijamata, Jaina sect, 13
Bījāpur, 2, 6, 11, 13, 16, 18, 23-25, 27-29, 31, 36, 37, 39, 44, 49, 51, 55, 56, 58, 59, 71, 72, 74, 84, 88-90, 94, 96-98, 102-106, 110-113, 118, 120, 121, 123, 127-132, 148
Bijay Bahādur, 337
 Singh, 162, 195, 234
Bijaigarh, 248, 277, 282
Bijnaur, 370
Bika Bhikaji, 2, 7
Bikanir, 2, 7, 20, 44, 45, 118, 259, 333
Bikramājit of Mewār, 21
 Bundela, 87
 Mahendra, 300
Bilgrām, 142
Biluchpur, battle, 80
Bintang island, 15-17
Bīr, 84
Bīr Sen, 225
 Singh, Bundela, 114
Birahigangā riv., 430
Bīrbal, Rāja, "Kab-rai," 52
Bīrwādi fort, 174
Bīsā of Kuch Bihār, 26
Bishan Singh, of Jaypur, 142
 Singh of Būndī, 287, 309, 315
Bishnāth Singh, 300, 301
bishops, 301
Bishop's College, 315
Bīthauli, 374
Bithūr, Cawnpur, 311, 356, 363-365
Biyās riv., 289, 348
Black Mountain, 419, 422, 423, 426
Blackman, Capt. Jeremy, 98, 99, 101
Blackney, Capt., 302
Blackwall, Dr, 137
Blair, Col. Sir Robert, 281, 282
Blake, Mr M., 333
Bobbili fort, 202
Boddam, Hon. Rawson Hart, 244, 254, 259
Bodh, 350
Bodh-Gayā, 293
Bodoahprā of Burma, 250, 256, 281, 312
Bogle, George, 235
Boileau, M. Barthelemy, 198
Bo Kayī Tha, dākait, 421; Bo La, 424; Bo Shwe, 414-416; Bo Yanyun, 422
Bokhāra, 337
Boles, Major Thos., 294
Bombay, 23, 82, 89, 107-114, 118-125, 127-131, 133, 135-137, 139, 143, 144, 146, 147, 149, 156, 159, 161, 167, 170, 171, 174, 179, 182, 187, 199, 205, 217, 221, 223, 225, 237, 238, 240, 241, 249, 252, 256, 272, 277-281, 292, 299, 304, 312,

Bombay (*continued*)—
317-319, 325, 326, 328, 334, 338, 342-344, 347, 354, 355, 357, 359, 375, 383, 386, 389, 391, 393, 395, 403, 404, 407-409, 414, 421, 427-429
Bombay-Burma trading company, 411-413
Bonner, Robert, 77
Boone, Charles, 157, 159, 161
Christopher, 144
Borel, Peter, 94
Bōr Ghāt, 241, 246, 327
Borneo, 146, 267
Boscawen, Admiral Edward, 189, 190
Boschauwer, Marcellis de, 75, 77
Botelho, Luis, 173, 176
Botello, Capt., 84
Boucher, Mr, 116
Boughton, Dr, 92, 98, and erratum p. vi
Boulnois, Lieut., 355
Bourbon,—Réunion, island, 174, 297
Bourchier, Charles, 225, 228
General Sir George, 387
Richard, 191
Bourdonnais, Bertrand Fr. Mahé De la, 166, 174, 181
Bourke, Rt. Hon. Sir Robt. Lord Connemara, 415
Bourquien, Major Louis, 280
Bousset, Mons., 196
Bouvalier, Mons., 165
Bowcher, Mr, 126
Bowman, Mr, 325
Braddyth, Mr, 177
Braganza, Constantino de, 37, 39
Duke of, 93
Catherina de, 107
Brāmahin, k. of Siam, 43
Brahmapuri, 135
Brahmaputrā riv., 394
Brahmo Somāj, 324
Brandas, Fr. Antonio, 123
Brathwaite, Col. Sir John, 242, 249, 267
Breda, treaty, 112
Brenier, Mons., 195, 196
Brereton, Major, 208, 209, 211, 212
Breton, Francis, 95-98
Bridgeman, Mr, 99
Briggs, Col. John, 326
Bright, General Sir Robert O., 401
Brijnāth Rām, 345
Bringa, 208
Bristol, Mr, 207
Bristow, John, 249, 254
British Government, 225, 228-230, 234, 288, 337-339, 345, 350, 352, 354, 356, 357, 374, 378, 381, 383, 398, 412
British India Steam Navigation Co., 391
Brito, Antonio de, 133
Francisco de, Bishop, 82
Jorge de, 14, 17
e Mello, Luis de, 75
Philipe de, or 'Nicote,' 62, 64, 68-70
Broadfoot, Major George, 340, 345, 347
Broeck, Van den, 73
Brooke, Mr, 199
Brown, Col., 275, 296
George, 297
Murdoch, 238
Browne, General, 309
Col. H., 392
General Sir James, 425
General Sir Samuel, 397-399
Brownlow, General Sir Charles, 387
Brownrigg, Capt., 279
Sir Robert, 302
Bruce, Capt., 246
Bruton, William, 87
Brydon, Dr William, 340
Buchanan, Rev. Dr Claudius, 290
Buckingham, Duke of, 80
and Chandos, Duke of, 393, 396
Buckingham, James Silk, 317
budgets, 384, 385, 388, 389, 391, 396
Budhan, of Katain, fanatic, 4
Būgtī Baluchīs, 346
Buhu Begam of Audh, 236, 237
Bulānd Akhtar, prince, 167
Bulāndkhel, 427
Bulāndshahr, 366
Bundelkhand, 187, 248, 263, 283, 284, 286, 291, 298, 306, 310, 322, 323
Būndī, 23, 81, 85, 288, 289, 315, 374
Būner, 327, 379
Būra Rāja of Naugong, 319
Bureng Naung, 'Branginoco,' of Burma, 31, 40, 41, 50
Burhān, usurper, 34
Burhān 'Imād Shah, 43
Nizām Shāh I, 9, 11, 18, 20, 23, 29, 33
Nizām Shāh II, 55, 56, 58
Burhān-ul-Mulk, 27, 28; 172, 177
Burhānpur, 39, 56, 61, 64, 75, 80, 81, 85, 112, 125, 145, 152, 156, 161, 179, 235, 242, 280, 282-284, 286
Burke, Edmund, 254
Burlton, Lieut. Philip Bowles, 325
Burma, 23, 43, 50, 64, 68, 97, 138, 152, 173, 179, 225, 227, 250, 274, 317, 318, 326, 355, 383, 388, 392, 393, 395, 397, 404, 409, 410, 412, 414, 416, 420, 422-425, 430

Burmese, 291, 298, 315-320, 355-358, 384, 411, 415, 421
Burn, Lieut.-Col., 287
Burnes, Sir Alexander, 327, 334-336, 339, 341
Burney, Col. Henry, 321, 326
Burniston, Mr, 146, 147
Burr, General, 306-308
Burrows, General J., 404
Burton, Major, 366
Būrūnchera tea estate, 426
Busbusia fort, 201
Bushahr—'Abushahr, 360, 361
Bussy, Charles Joseph Patissier, 191-195, 198, 200, 202, 204, 206, 208, 209, 211, 212, 253, 255
Butale, 74
Butler, Capt., 392
Byfield, Mr, 201

CABOT, John, 3
Cabral, Francisco Ant. Vego de, 268
Cabral Ant. da Vaiga, 290
Pedro Alvarez, 5
Caillaud, Lieut.-Col. John, 197, 202-204, 208, 213, 214, 216, 224
Calcutta, 129, 132, 138, 140, 142, 150, 157, 158, 165, 167, 176, 182, 189, 191, 201-203, 206, 207, 210, 214, 219, 222, 223, 228, 230, 236, 238, 240, 247, 256, 266, 272, 289, 290, 311, 315-317, 323, 324, 332, 333, 338, 340, 344, 350, 353-355, 357, 358, 360, 365, 367, 377-381, 383, 385-388, 392-395, 404, 407-410, 417, 421, 422, 429, 430
Calicut,—Kolikōtta, 4-6, 10, 19, 36, 40, 44, 45, 57, 73, 138, 139, 146, 224, 238, 246, 249, 262, 312, 359
Call, John, 215
Camara, Coutinho Antonio Luiz Gonçalves da, 140
Gonçalves de, 52
Jose Pedro de, 235
Manaet de, 316, 317
Cambolin, 44
Cambridge, H.R.H. Duke of, 382
Camoens, Luiz de, 33, 44
Campbell, Gen. Sir Archibald, 257, 260, 318, 320, 321
Capt. Sir Colin, 284, 338
General Sir Colin, Lord Clyde 353, 355, 365, 367-371, 373
Sir George, 387, 391
Lieut.-Col. John, 254
Major-General Sir John, 350
Campbell, Dr, 353
Cannanore, *see* Kannanūr
Canning, Paul, 70
Capt., 285, 298, 299
Charles John, Earl, 360, 373, 374, 376, 377
Lady, 376, 377
Capocate, 50
Cardim, Antonio, 176, 177
Carey, Rev. Dr Wm., 268, 276; and Rev. Dr Joshua Marshman, 316
Carmelites, 102, 116, 140, 161
Carnac, Major John, 216, 217, 220, 221, 241, 242, 279
Caron François, 112, 113, 118
Carr, Thomas, bishop, 334
Cartier, John, 228, 230
Cartley, Major, 338
cartridge scare, 360
Cartwright, Mr, 87
Carvalho, Augusto Cesar, Cordoso de, 415, 420
Gil Fernandez de, 33
Castilla, Juan de Nueva, 6
Castro, Antonio de Mello e, 108, 113
Braz de, 100, 101
Caetano de Mello e, 147, 152
Franciso de Mello e, 98, 101, 103
João de, 30, 31
Jorge de, 46
Manoel de Portugal e, 323
Martin Affonsa de, 64
Catchpoole, Allen, 145, 148
Caulfield, Capt., 305
Cavagnari, General Sir Louis, 398-401
Cavallos, island, 97
Cawnpur — Kānhpur, 270, 306, 322, 326, 362-369, 371, 374, 398
census of India, 425
Ceylon, 15, 26, 32, 35, 40, 41, 53, 54, 56, 59, 73-75, 77, 86, 93-95, 100, 101, 106, 248, 269-271, 274, 302, 313
Chagataī, Gurgānī, dynasty, 20
Chaila, mount, 419
Chait Singh, 234, 236, 254
Chaitanya, reformer, 21
Chākan, 106
Chāliyam or Jaliat fort, 45, 46
Chalmers, Maj.-General Sir John M., 264, 293, 294
Chāma, Rāja rberal, 2
Rāja Udayār Bola, 45, 106
Rāja II., 74, 90
Rāja III., 171
Rājendra, 381, 384
Rājendra II., Udayār, 406
Chambā dist , 32
Chambā fort, 170

Chambal river, 176, 284, 289
Chamber, Sir Thomas, 105
Chamberlain, General Sir Neville, 364, 375, 378, 397
Chambers, Col., 292
Chāmpānīr fort, or Pawangadh, 24, 168
Champion, General Alexander, 235
Chānd Bībī, 58, 61
Chand Kunwar Rānī, 338, 339, 341, 350, 353
Chāndā, 199, 311, 368, 369
Chanda Sāhib, 175; 177-180, 189-194, 210, 220
Chanderi fort, 21, 370
Chāndor, 122, 287
Chandra Kānta, 316
Kīrtī Singh, 354
Chandragiri, 43, 71, 96
Chandraguti, 326
Chandranagar, 131, 170, 171, 178, 181, 201-203, 241, 304, 408
Chandrasen Jādhav, 155
Chandrayya, Rampa, 405
Chandri Phul, 99
Chandu Lāl, Peshkar, 293, 328, 343
Changli Kumāra, Jafnapattam, 77
Channer, General, 419
Channapatna, 91, 92, 210
Chapar Ghāt, 27, 35
Chaplin, Mr, 313
Chappuis, Col., 273
Chārasiāh,—Chārasiāb, 400, 403
Charikar, 341
Charity school, Bombay, 161
Charles I., 83, 88, 90, 93
II., 107, 109, 112, 117, 120, 124, 127, 128, 157
VI. of Austria, 155, 164, 165
Chārmahal, 200
Charnock, Job, 101, 102, 109, 122, 123, 126, 128-130, 133, 135
charters of E.I. Co., 61-62, 67, 126, 129, 136, 137, 141, 145, 151, 152, 167, 168, 170, 247, 266, 330, 358
charter of United E.I. Co., 170
of Dutch Company, 169
Chatānatī or Satānatī, Calcutta, 133, 135, 141, 142, 146
Chatra, battle, 366
Chatrapati IV., Mahārāja, 386
Chatra Singh, 382
Chatrasāl, 168, 169, 172, 175; 296
Chatrgardan pass, 398, 400, 401
Chattar Singh, Sikh, 351-353
Chattradhari Shāhi of Hatwā, 257, 263
Chaul, 9, 10, 18, 21-23, 36, 37, 44, 45, 56, 57, 68, 120, 126, 150, 174, 176, 178, 179
Chaul de Sima, 174
Chaurāgarh, 87, 295
Cheape, Sir John, 357
Chennam, *see* Ambalkotta
Chennapatnam, Madras, 105, 115
Cherrā-Punji,—Sohra-pungi, 325
Cherry, Geo. Frederick, 275
Chetiata, 116
Chetwai, 134
Chevelpetur, 200
Chattīsgarh, 199
Chhota Bālāpur pālegārs, 219
Chidambaram or Chilambaram, 177, 213, 246
Chikākul, 195, 204, 224
Chikka Rāya, 71
Deva Rāja, 116; 142, 147
Krishna, 171, 173; 224
Vīra Rājendra of Kurg, 315
Chikodi district, 322
Chilās fort, 427
Child, Sir Joshua, 118, 124, 127, 128, 130-132
Chilianwālā, battle, 352
Chīmnāji Appa, 169, 178-180; 255, 271
Mādhavrāv, 8th Peshwa, 271
Chin Qulij Khān, 'Asaf Jāh, 155, 164, 166, 168
Chināb river, 351, 353
Chindwin, 413, 417
Chinese, 226, 227, 265, 303, 392, 395, 411, 422
Chingalpat, 96, 194, 197, 212, 220, 245, 371
Chingiz Khān, 38, 39
Chinhat, 363
Chinkulari battle, 229
Chinnappa Nāyyaka, 20
Chins, 419, 421, 422, 425-427, 429
Chinsura, 81, 102, 201, 210
Chintia, Sikh, 216
Chinūr, battle, 7
Chiplun, battle, 173
Chirakkal, 222, 259, 261
Chitaura, battle, 371
Chitaldurg, 94, 219, 275
Chitor, Chitorgadh, 16-18, 20, 24, 29, 43, 53, 100, 122
Chitral, 427, 429, 430
Chittagāon, 26, 66, 91, 111, 127, 130, 131, 214, 270, 274, 316, 318, 367
Chittapet, 204, 209, 212, 213
Chittūr, Arkat district, 248, 252
Chitu, Pendhārī, 308, 309, 311, 312
Bhil, 408
Chokkanāth Nāyyaka, 115, 128
Chokra Bisoi, Bodh rebel, 350
Chola Rāja, Trichinapalli, 37
cholera, 307, 313
Christian VIII. of Denmark, 346

Christians, 20, 290, 389, 425
Chumbī, 419
Chunār, 23, 25, 26, 34, 36, 37, 184, 248, 353
Churā Chand of Manipur, 424
Churāmanī, Jāt, 154, 162
Churchill, Lord Randolph, 412, 414
Chusan, 145
Clarchy, Ricardo Carlos, 375
Clare, John Fitzgibbon, Earl of, 327
Clarendon, Lord, 127
Clarke, Sir Alured, 273
 Major, 305
 General Sir Chas. Mansfield, 427
 Col. Sir William, 280
Clavering, Col. John, 233, 236, 239, 240, 243
Clement VIII., Brief of, 60
Clerk, Sir George Russell, 340, 349, 350, 376, 377
Clive, Lord Robert, 167, 192, 194, 199-205, 207, 209-212, 214, 216, 221, 222, 225, 236
 second Lord, 274, 279
 fund, 225
Close, Col. Sir Barry, 279, 281, 282, 295
Clow, Rev. James, 312
Cobbe, Rev. Dr Richard, 156, 159
Cochin—Kochin, Kochhi, 5-8, 10, 12, 19, 20, 32, 38, 52, 53, 61, 71, 88, 107, 108, 112, 140, 145, 169, 182, 239, 260, 270, 290, 292-294, 302, 337, 357, 379
Cochin-China, 146, 316
Cockburn, Col. Sir William, 242
Cochrane, Lieut., 213
Coen, Capt., 77
Cogan, Andrew, 92, 94, 95
Coimbatur—Koyamuttūr, 253, 262, 264
Colbert, Jean Baptiste, 110
Cole, Commander Sir Christopher, 297
Collet, General Sir Henry, 419
 James, 161
 Joseph, 158, 161
Collins, Col. John, 272, 282, 283
Colombo, 17, 26, 41, 53, 54, 68, 84, 101, 102, 223, 271, 277, 410
Colt, Stephen, 141, 144
Colvin, Sir Auckland, 409, 418
 John Russell, 357, 358, 365
Combermere, Stapleton Cotton, Lord, 321
Commutation Act, 255
Comorin—Kumāri, Cape, 147
"Companie des Indes," 110
"Company of Commerce," 84, 139
Conflans, Marquis de, 208, 209
Conjivaram, 131, 197, 208, 209, 211, 212, 245
Connaught, H.R.H. Duke of, 420-422
Conolly, Capt. Arthur, 341
 Henry Valentine, 359
Convention, Bombay, 118
Conway, Capt., 275
Cook, Mr, 132
 Sir T., 138
Cooke, Humphrey, 110, 111, 113
Cooper, Sir George, 312
Cooper's Hill Engineering College, 387
Coorg, Kurg (Kudag), 265
Coote, Sir Eyre, 204, 212-217, 243, 245, 246, 248, 250, 251, 253
Cope, Capt., 192, 193
Corfield, Col., 371
Cornelis, Java, 297
Cornwallis, Charles Marquis, 257, 258, 261-267, 270, 271, 288
Correa, Andrea, 16
Cortlandt, Col., 350
Cossaks—Kosāks, 426
Costa, Andrea Botelho da, 75
 Luiz da, 166
 Rodrique da, 129, 133, 152, 154
Cotiote—Kottayam, 210
Copenhagen, 70, 168
Cotta, Luis Gonçalves, 133
Cotton, Bishop Edward L., 320, 336, 338
 Sir Willoughby, 336
Couper, Sir George, 396, 399
Courten, Sir William, 88-91, 96
courts, 167, 168, 233, 247, 266, 267, 272, 378
Court-marshal, 73
Coutinho, Antonio de Sousa, 98, 101, 103
 Fernando, 10
 Francisco de, 39-41
 Dom Francisco, 84
 Hierome, 53
 Dom João de, 74, 77
 Luiz, 57
 Manoel de Sousa, 54, 55
 Miguel Rodriques, 36
 Dom Vasco Luiz, 144
Couta, Joachim José Macedo e, 388
Covrepak, 210, 212
Cowan, Hon. Robert, 168, 174
 Mr, 388
Cox, Capt. Hiram, 271
Cox, General Charles Vyvyan, 372
Cradock, Sir John, 293
Cranbrook, Cathorne Hardy, Earl of, 403
Cranganor or Kranganūr, *see* Kodungallūr.
Crape, Capt. Roelant, 75, 77
Crawford, John, 316, 322

cremation, 379
criminal procedure Bill, 408, 409
Cromwell, Oliver, 79, 99, 101, 103, 104
Cross, Sir Richard Assheton, 415
Crosthwaite, Sir Chas. H. Todd, 416, 421, 422, 428
Crown of India, Imperial Order of, 396, 397
Crusade—Bill of, 57
Cruttenden, Mr, 177
 Lieut., 354
Cubbon, Sir Mark, 343
Cuddalore, *see* Kūdalūr.
Cunha, Francisco Maria da, 422, 424
 João Nuno da, 111
 Nunez da, 22, 23, 25-27
 Nuno da, 113
 Sampayo e, 70
Cunningham, Sir Jas., 74
 Capt., 304
Cuppage, Col., 294
Cureton, General Chas. Robert, 351
cyclones, 380, 383, 394, 397, 417, 428
Cyprus, 397

DABHOI, 244
 Dābhol, 10, 18, 36, 48, 106, 174
Dabo, battle, 343
De Caen, General, 297
D'Aché, Comte, 207, 210
Dacre, Lieut., 306
Da Cunha, 65, *see* Cunha
Dacres, Mr, 116
Dādā Khāsji, Gwāliar, 342
Dādāji Raghunāth Deshpānde, 125
Dādar, 336
D'Aendels, Marshal, 296
Dāhānu, 178
Daisal II., Rāv of Kachh, 312, 331, 376
Dājī Krishna Pandit, 336, 345
dākāīts, 398, 399, 414
Dākor, 171
Dalai Lama, 418
Dale, Sir Thomas, 76
Dalel Singh, Rājput, 226
Dalhousie, Earl of, 350, 354-356, 358, 360
Dalston, Col., 283
Dalton, Capt. John, 193, 194, 196
Dāmāji Gaikwād I., 160; Dāmāji II., 172-177, 183, 187, 191, 216, 226; 267
Dāmalcheru pass, 179
Damān, 22-24, 38-42, 45, 50, 72, 75, 114, 159, 162, 176, 177, 180, 243, 375
Damant, G. Henry, 400
Dambāk, 429
Dambal, 371
Damdam, 324
Damoh, 366
Dampor, 34
Dance, Col., 416
Danda-Rājpuri, 119, 218, 255
Danes, 77, 81, 185, 199, 346, 349
Daniell, Major, 399, 427
Danish East India Company, 70, 115, 168
Dankhal Singh, Mārwār, 165
Danubyu, 319, 320, 357
Dānyāl, of Bengal, 4
 Prince, 61, 64, 83
Daplā tribes, 392
Dāpurī, 335
D'Arambure, Mons., 213
Dārā Shikoh, Prince, 81, 83, 90, 97, 99, 100, 103-105
Darbārs, 373, 374, 380, 385, 387, 393-395, 398, 411
Dard, Mīr—Khwāja Muhammad Mīr, author, 255
Darnidar Nārāyan, Kuch Bīhār, 232, 245
Darshan Singh, Balrāmpur, 334
Darjiling, 332
Darya Khān, Sindh, 17; of Gujarāt, 25
 'Imād Shāh, 22
 Singh Chaube, 298
Dastūr Dīnār, Kulbarga, 4
Datāji Sindia, 211, 212
Datiyā, 218, 286, 311, 337
Dā'ūd Khān, Shāh, Bengal, 46, 47
 Khān, Karnātak, 145, 155, 156
 Khān Panni, 150
 Khān, Afghān, 400
Daulatābād, 87, 129, 130, 180, 206
Daulat Chakk, 33, 35
Daulata Rāmoshi, 399
Daulatrāv Sindia, 268, 272, 273, 279, 283, 284, 286, 307, 322
Daurāra fort, 369
d'Autueil, M., 203
Davidge, Mr, 99
Davidson, Col. John, 424, 425
Davies, John, 55
 Robert, 380
 Lieut.-Col. Thos. A. Harkness, 425
Dāwar Bakhsh, Prince, 79, 82, 83
Dāwar valley, 398
Dawes, Col., 281
Day, Francis, 91-93
 Lieut., 411
Deb Rāja of Bhutān, 379, 412
Debendra Singh, Manipur, 354

De Boigne, Count Benoit, 242, 249, 258, 259, 261, 262, 265
de Brito, *see* Brito
D'Eça, Daurte, 37
Defence, Treaty of, 76
De Graaf, Surgeon, 114
D'Egville, Commander, 211
Deh Kwāji, battle, 404
Dehli, 7, 18-20, 28, 34-37, 40, 58, 79, 99, 104, 116, 119, 120, 153-156, 160-164, 176-178, 180, 188, 194, 195, 203, 205, 212, 214, 219, 225, 228, 229, 232, 255, 258-260, 266, 271, 283, 287, 290, 292, 293, 305, 321, 327, 333, 361-368, 384, 393, 395, 414, 415, 421
Dekhan, Dakhan, 22, 41, 52, 56-61, 66, 67, 71, 73, 74, 78, 80-84, 89, 90, 94, 113, 123, 128, 131, 155, 156, 158-161, 164, 171, 175, 176, 179, 182, 191, 194, 204, 289, 399
De la Bourdonnais, Capt. Bertrand Fr. Mahé, 166, 174, 181
De La Haye, Admiral, 115, 116, 118
De Laval, François Pyrard, 62
Delamotte, General, 345
Deleyrit, Mons., 198, 199, 206, 209
Dellon, Mons. C., 114
De Nets, Capt., 73
Denison, Sir Wm. Thomas, 376, 378, 379, 382
Dennie, Col. Wm. Henry, 338
Dennis, Major, 353
Deogāon, treaty, 284
Deogarh, 183
Deothal fort, 303
Dera Ismail Khān, 350, 430
De Sousa, Dom Diogo, Conde de Rio Pardo, 306, 315
D'Espremesnil, Mons., 186
D'Estaign, Mons., 206
Deva Rāja, Maisur, 171
Devāji Takpar, 183
Devamaji of Kurg, 295
Devanhalli, 189, 263
Devendra Singh of Nābha, 347
Devikotta, 189, 190, 206, 212
Dewar, Sir James, 325
Dewarkonda, 37
Dewās, 311
Dewir, battle, 66
Dhākā, Dacca, 69, 70, 112, 122, 123, 125, 131, 136, 146, 154, 204, 228, 236, 266, 367
Dhākā, Afghānistān, 397, 403, 428
Dhaki or Pulı, 409
Dhālimkot fort, 379
Dhamolā, 17
Dhanāji Jādav, 134, 140, 150
Dhanderi fort, 137
Dhār, 15, 190, 312, 328, 366, 380
Dharamgāon factory, 118
Dharamkot, 347
Dhārāpuram, 262
Dhāraseo or Dhārasinva, 376
Dharma Pāl, Urchha, 342
Dharmapāla, João, 59
Dharmapattanam island, 19, 174
Dharma Rāja of Bhutān, 379
Dharmasāla, 379
Dharmatpur battle, 104
Dharūr, 42, 44
Dhaulatrāv Sindia, 288, 296
Dhiraj Singh, Chhota Udayapur, 376
Dhobī fort, 299
Dhokal Singh, Jodhpur, 332
Dholī, battle, 174
Dholkā, 169, 174, 180
Dholpur, 5, 149, 330, 342, 366
Dhrol, 55
Dhujindar Nārāyan, 246, 254
Dhunda Pant Gokhale, 278
Dhundūpant, *see* Nāna Sāhib
Dhundia Wāgh, 278
Dhurb, or Dhorap, fort, 287
Dhyān Singh, Vazīr, 344
Dīn Bahādur, 172
Diamper — Udayampārūr, Synod of, 60
Dianga, Arakan, 64, 66
Dibu, attack on, 302
Dick, Col., 302
Dickens, Major-General, 291
Dickenson, Henry, 350
Dickson, Mr, 173
Dīg, 154, 187, 234, 287
Dilāwar Khan, 56
'Alī Khān, 161
Dīler Khān, 110, 111, 115, 116, 119, 120, 123
Dīlīp Singh of Lāhor, 343, 345, 348, 349, 352, 353
Dīl-kusha, Lucknow, 367, 369
Dilshād Vazīr, 8
Dinabanda Mitra, author, 376
Dinājpur, 228, 236, 324
Dinanāth, Dīwān, Lāhor, 347
Dinapur or Dānāpur, 324, 364
Dindagal, 204, 253, 265
Dionysius, Mar, Jacobite bishop, 290
Dīnpanah fort, Dehli, 24
Dirois, Mons., 178, 181
Dishomā Nāgās, 356
Dīū, 10, 13, 17, 20, 22, 24-27, 30, 31, 33, 75, 89, 91, 108, 113, 146, 162
Divorce Act, 385
Divali battle, 8

Dīwāngiri fort, 380
Dixon, Col., 333
Dodda Deva Rāja of Maisur, 106, 116
  Krishna Rāja, 156
Dohad, 76, 165
Don, Lieut.-Col., 286
Dormer, General Sir Jas. Charlemagne, 427
Dost 'Alī, Karnātak, 172, 175, 179
Dost Muhammad, 313, 330, 331, 334, 335, 337, 338, 342, 353, 359-361, 378
Douglas, Mr, 126
  Brigadier, 370
Doveton, General Sir John, 274, 311, 312
Downton, Capt. Nicholas, 71, 73
Drake, Sir Francis, 48, 49, 53
  Roger, 201, 202
Draper, Col. Sir William, 208
Dubac, Mons., 273
Drigbijai Singh of Balrampur, 334
Dudley, Sir Robert, 59
Du Drenec, Mons., 265
Duespe, Mons., 216
Duff, Rev. Dr Alexander, 326
Dufferin, Earl of, 410, 413, 414, 418, 419
  Lady, Female Medical Service Fund, 417, 418
Dugarājapatnam, 81, 83
Dulāb Rām Rāī, 204, 205, 207
Dulil Singh, Kārwar, 159
Dulīpur, battle, 371
Dulivrier, Mons., 149, 151, 155
Dumas, M. Benoît, 174, 177, 179, 181
Dunbar, Capt., 364
Duncan, Col., 393
Duncan, Jonathan, 265, 270, 279
Duncan Dock, Bombay, 296
Dundas, Henry, 252, 266
Dundi Khān, rebel, 291
Dungārpur, 18, 311
Dunsford, Capt., 414
Dupleix, Marquis Joseph François, 162, 167, 170, 171, 178, 181-183, 185-187, 189, 190, 192, 193, 196-198
Dupleixpettai, 183; Dupleixfathiābād, 193
Dupré, Josias, 228, 232
Durand, Sir Henry M., 363, 386
  Sir H. Mortimer, 428
  Lieut.-Col. A. G. A., 424
Durānīs, 187, 188, 216
Durgābāī, Sāwantwādi, 298, 300
Durgādās, Rāthod, 124, 134, 139, 140, 146, 148, 149
Durjan Sāl of Kotā, 165
  of Bharatpur, 320, 321
Dustagir, Bhopāl, 346
Dutch, 62, 64, 67, 71, 73, 78-81, 84-96, 100, 102, 103, 105, 107-109, 112-114, 118, 133, 136, 150, 155, 156, 159, 161, 172, 193, 201, 234, 243, 247, 248, 253, 269, 270, 287, 297, 302, 318
Dutch East India Company, 63, 75, 140, 169, 205, 232, 260
Duwai, 403
Dwārkā,—Dwārakā, 314, 375
Dwārs, Bhutān and Bengal, 379, 380
Dyson, Major-General, 305
  Mr, 421

EARTHQUAKES, 34, 112, 161, 216, 218, 324, 407, 408, 412
East, Col., 304
East India Company, 61, 62, 64, 69, 75, 76, 78, 79, 85, 88, 95, 98, 101-104, 107, 108, 112, 113, 117, 118, 127, 128, 130, 132, 135, 136, 140, 144, 149, 153, 156, 158, 172, 174, 184, 188, 191, 201, 203, 205, 210, 211, 214, 218, 221-224, 231-234, 238, 242, 250, 253, 256, 259, 265, 267, 271, 274-277, 291, 294, 297, 299, 304, 305, 308-311, 313, 315, 322, 329, 332, 336, 346, 360, 372, 374
East India Co.'s charters, *see* charters.
  India House, 167
Edattara dist, 267
Eden, Sir Ashley, 376, 379, 380, 395, 399
Edinburgh, H.R.H. Duke of, 385, 386
Education, 354, 360
Edwards, Mr, 71
  Sir Herbert B., 350-352
Egerton, Col. Charles, 242
Egypt, 278, 407
Ekādatha of Siam, 225
Elephanta, 179
Elgin, James Bruce, Eighth Earl of, 365, 377-379
  Victor A., Ninth Earl of, 429
Elias, Ney, 392
Elichpur, 284
Elizabeth, Queen, 55, 61
Ellayedatunād, 182
Ellenborough, Lord, 340, 342, 344, 345
Elles, General Sir Wm. Kidston, 423, 428

Elliot, Sir Charles A., 406, 422
George, Earl of Minto, 290
Rt. Hon. Hugh, 314
Ellis, Francis, 126
Mr, 219
Elmisaram, 193, 197
Elphinstone, John Lord, 334, 358, 375
Mountstuart, 292, 294, 297, 299, 306, 310, 313, 314, 323, 374
General Wm. Geo. Keith, 339, 340
Elwick, Nathaniel, 163, 166
Elūr,—Ellur, 195, 204, 224
Elvasanor, 203
English Company, 64, 88, 97, 141, 145, 151
Refugees, 369
English, Major Frederick, 366
Ennis, Lieut., 307
Ennūr, 151
Ericeira, Conde de, 158, 162
Erod,—Īrōd, 227, 262
Erskine, General, 270
Eruma-varmā Perumāl, 128
Estifique, Col. Ioão Cabral de, 334
Etāwā,—Itāwā, 20, 373
Etgīr, 37
Eugene, Prince, 158
European Anglo-Indian defence Association, 409
Evans, Sir William David, 314
Col., 327
Exhibition, Indian International, 409
Eyre, Sir Charles, 136, 141-143
General Sir Vincent, 365, 367

FACTORIES, 70, 75, 126, 131, 146
Factory Bill, 423
Faizābād, 230, 249, 369, 371
Faizi, poet, 58
Faizullah Khān, Rohila, 236, 245, 268
Fake, Corporal, 118
Fakhr-ud-dīn Khān, Shujā'at Jang Bahādur, 183
Falam, 425
Falkland, Lucius Bentinck Viscount, 350, 358
famines, 86, 377, 381-385, 390, 391, 395, 396, 425, 426
Faqīr Nūr-ud-dīn, 347
Faraizes, Muhammadan, 328
Faramuz, Afghān, 387
Farhat Khān, 46
Faria, Francisco de, 57
Farid Khān, 'Abul Muzaffar Sher Khān, 24, 27, 28
Farīd-i-Bukhārī, Shaikh, 51, 65
Faridkot, 347
Farīdūn Jāh Mansur 'Alī, 336, 376-385, 405
Faris, Lieut., 306
Farish, Hon. James, 337
farmāns, 69, 88, 98, 123, 133, 134, 158, 183, 196, 208, 222, 389
Farrah, 330
Farrukh-siyar, Muhammad, emperor, 153-160
Farrukhābād, 287, 367, 368
Fasli reckoning, 36, 89
Fath 'Alī Shāh of Persia, 296, 306
Alī Khān of Sindh, 280
Alī of Khambay, 317
Fath Allah 'Imād Shāh, 2, 7
Haidar, Maisur, 275
Jang of Kābul, 340
Khān of Kashmīr, 3, 8, 9
Khan, Afghān, 66
Khan, Habshi, 82, 85, 87
Khan Barūkhzāī, 283
Khān, Mīr, Tālpuri, 254
Khān of Bahāwalpur, 356, 372
Khān of Pāhlanpur, 300, 305, 311
Muhammad, Jam'adār, Kachh, 257, 266, 281
Shāhi Bahādur of Hatwā, 225
Singh Kāyat, 156
Singh Gaikwād, 227, 232, 237, 243, 244, 250, 260, 262; regent, 307, 311
Singh Bhonsla of Akalkot, 314
Fatha Haidar Bahādur, 210
Fathegāon, 307
Fathganj, battle, 271
Fathiābād, battle, 399
Fathigarh, 362, 363, 368, 374
Fathpat, 327
Fathpur, 159, 276, 363, 366
Fathpur-Sīkrī, 47, 52
Fazl Ullat Khān, 221
female infanticide, 357
Ferghāna, 426, 428
Fergusson, Sir James, 403, 405, 410, 411
Ferry, Mons., 409, 411
Fevrier, M., 181
Feyra, Conde de, 67
Fidā-ud-dīn Khān, 178, 183
Fidāī Khān, Nawāb of Bengal, 82
Khān, 'Azim Khān, 120, 121
Field, Capt., 117
Figueyredo, Gomez Yanez de, 51
Filoze, Michel, 272
Finlay, A. S., 334
Firando factory, Japan, 70
Firebrace, Sir Basil, 144
Firishta, Muhammad Qāsim, historian, 16, 71, 326
Firozshāh, battle, 346, 347

Firuz Khān Sūr, 33
Khān of Pāhlanpur, 300
Mulla bin Kawas, 358
Shāh of Bengal, 23, 24
Shāh, prince, 367, 373
Fitch, Ralph, 51, 52, 54
Fitzgerald, Capt., 351
Col. Charles J. Oswald, 414
Sir Seymour, 383, 389
Flacour, Mons., 115
Fletcher, Sir Robert, 223, 238, 239
Fleury, Mons., 283
Flint, Capt., 262
floods, 428-430
Floyd, Col. John, 262
Floyer, Charles, 187, 191
Fonseca, Antonio Pinto de, 70
Forbes, Major David, 283
Ford, Capt. John, 300, 307
Forde, Lieut.-Col. Francis, 207-209
Forsyth, Sir Douglas, 386, 388-390, 393
Fort Harrison,—Sadon, 425
Fort Morton,—Sima, 427
St David—Tegnapatam, 146, 181, 185-195, 204, 206, 208, 211
St George,—Madras, 99-101, 103, 104, 107, 110, 111, 114, 116, 119, 122-125, 128, 136, 145, 146, 165, 186, 188, 208, 243
St Thomas, 16
Stedman,—Maingthauk, 419
Victoria,—Himmatgadh near Bānkot, 201
White, 421, 427
William,—Calcutta, 138, 140, 142, 146, 153, 172, 177, 193, 201, 235, 263, 275, 278
Foulis, Major-General Edward, 331
Fowke, Joseph, 237
Fox, Charles James, 253
Foxcroft, George, 110-112, 116
France, French, 73, 118, 133, 195-198, 201-205, 207-212, 214, 251-253, 256, 267, 269, 274, 275, 283, 409
French East India Co., 64, 68, 72, 95, 110, 113, 114, 131, 151, 154, 155, 161, 162, 182, 206, 227
French Rocks,—Hirodi, 196
Frère, Admiral Ruy, 78, 79
Frere, Sir H. Bartle Edward, 377, 383
Fryer, Sir Fred. Wm. R., 426
Fūlād Khān, 11
Beg Barlās, Mīrzā, 54
Fuller, Mr., Agra, 394
Fullerton, Col. Wm., 253
Furtado, Andre de, 56, 57, 62
Luiz de Mendoza, 107
Fytch, William, 193
Fytche, General Albert, 383

GABRIEL, Mar, Nestorian bishop, 148, 169, 170
Gadhu Rāo, Tanjor, 196
Gadkaris, Kolhāpur, 345
Gāgrūn, 16
Gaillard, M., 198
Gaja Singh of Jodhpur, 77, 91, 94
Singh, *read* Rāja Singh II., 218
Singh of Bikanir, 259
Gajalhatti pass, 262
Gakkhars, 16
Galbraith, General Sir Wm., 419
Gall, Col., 371
Galle, Point de, 92, 94, 100
Galna fort, 86, 287
Gama, Estevão de, 27
Francisco da, 59, 79
João de Saldanha da, 167
Joaquim Manoel Correira da Silva e, 332
Luiz da, 60
Gambier, Robert, 208, 215, 244
Gambhīr Singh of Manipur, 320, 354
Gandāmak, 339, 341, 399, 402
Gandavī, 67
Gandikot, 99
Gangā Rāo of Mārwār, 23
Gangādhar Rāo of Jhānsi, 357
Shāstri, 301, 303
Gangadwāra or Haridwār, 383
Gangaikondān inscription, 35
Gangeri, battle, 367
Ganges, Gangā river, 21, 170, 280, 322, 366, 367, 369, 370, 373, 394
Ganges canal, 358
Gangpara, 306
Ganjām, 211, 331, 333, 421
"Ganj-i-Sawai" ship, 137
Ganpatrāv of Indor, 308
Gaikwād, 350, 360
Ganpura, 37
Gantūr, 37, 260
Garah and Mandla, 181
Garamkonda, 231
Gardhan Pāl, Karaulī, 356
Gardner, Hon. E., 296, 304
Col. William Linnæus, 302, 303
Garey, Capt. Henry, 111
Garhakot, 369
Garhwāl, 330, 430
Garmsīr, 131
Garshāsp, Prince, 83
Gary, Henry, 121
Gatacre, Col. Sir Wm. Forbes, 416
Gāuhati, 112, 318
Gaur, 25, 26, 28, 40, 47, 49, 219
Gaurīnāth Rāja of Āsām, 267
Gāwilgadh, 18, 284
Gawler, Col. John Cox, 376

Gayā Manpur, battle, 216
Gayer, Sir John, 136, 139-141, 143, 144, 146, 147, 149, 151
Geekie, John, 182
Geldria,—Palikāt, 67
George I., 167
III., 301
Georgegarh, 273
Gersappa, 85
Ghafūr Khān, 52
Ghāgrā river, 369, 372, 373
Ghain, Persia, 406
Ghargānw, Āsām, 108
Ghātge, Shirji Rāo, Sakhārām, 272, 273, 279, 289
Ghaus Muhammad of Jaurā, 381
Ghāzi Khān Chakk of Kashmīr, 33, 35, 36, 39, 40, 42
Ghāzī-ud-dīn Khān I., Fīrūz Jang, 151, 153
II., 190, 193, 194, 197, 203
III., Vazīr, 212
Haidar of Audh, 301, 304, 322, 323
Ghāzī-ud-dīn Khān, general, 128, 129, 131, 144, 148
Ghāzīs, fanatics, 340, 370, 372, 402, 403, 419, 423
Ghāzipur, 221, 236, 288, 324
Ghāziuddīnnagar, battle, 362
Ghaznī, 61, 278, 337, 340, 341, 382, 384, 385, 402-404
Ghazni Khān of Kāndesh, 11
Gheria, *see* Vijayadurg
Ghilzāis, 281, 338-340, 400-403, 409, 410, 417
Ghiyās-ud-dīn 'Abul Muzaffar, 38, 40
Khaljī, 1, 3, 5
Mahmud Shah III., 23
Ghodaji II., Rāo of Kachh, 242
Ghodbandar fort,—St Jeronym, 176
Ghosāla fort, 174
Ghovizai, 396
Ghulām 'Alī of Sindh, 280, 292
Bāsit, author, 252
Haidar Khān, Kābul, 359, 406, 417, 419, 420, 428
Husain Khān, Kābul, 401
Husain Khān, Tiba Tibāī, 261, 262
Muhammad, Rohila, 268
Muhammad Ghaus of the Karnātak, 357, 359, 360
Qādir Khān, Rohila, 255, 258-260
Ghurgin Khān, Persian minister, 152, 153
Ghwaja pass, 398
Gibbs, Major-General Sir Samuel, 294
Giesū Khān, 46
Gilbert, General Sir Walter R., 352
Gilchrist, Dr John, 285
Gilgit, 424, 426, 427
Gillespie, Major-General Sir Robert Rollo, 289, 297, 302
Gingen, Capt., 192
Gīr, 375
Girishk, 339, 404, 406
Girvānyuddha Vikrama Sāh, 280, 305
Gladman, Mr, 131
Gnatong, 418
Goa, 10-12, 14-16, 20, 24, 26-28, 30-33, 35, 37-40, 43, 44, 48-55, 57-65, 67, 70, 74, 75, 78, 79, 81, 82, 84, 88-101, 103, 106-108, 110, 121, 124, 129, 133, 139-141, 144, 147, 148, 162, 167, 170, 180, 181, 183, 187, 199, 200, 211, 220, 227, 230, 233, 235, 257, 263, 268, 280, 314-316, 323, 332, 335, 338, 345, 349, 354, 359, 380, 385-388, 392, 397, 406, 413, 415, 416, 422, 425
Goa, Archbishops, 123, 290
Jesuits, 113
Godāvarī river, 21, 59, 193
Goddard, General Thomas, 242-244, 246
Godeheu, M., 197, 198
Godolphin, Sidney, Earl of Godolphin, 151
Godwin, General Sir Henry Thomas, 356
Goens, Rijklof van, 103
Rickhoff, 117
Goes, Benedict B., 63
John, of Leiden, 127
Goghā, 67, 71, 169, 172, 199
Goghanda, battle, 47
Gohad, 224, 244-246, 289, 296
Gohna, landslip, 430
Gokalgarh, 259
Gokhale, *see* Bāpu Gokhale
Golard, M., 178
Golauli, 371
gold coinage, 380
Golden Rock battle, 195
Goldesborough, Sir John, 135, 136
Goldsmid, Maj.-General Sir Fred. John, 389
Golkondā, 29, 32, 37, 50, 54, 63, 67, 68, 72, 79, 80, 87-89, 98, 101, 102, 112-115, 118, 120, 127-131, 133, 179
Gombrūn, 79, 121, 146
Gomm, Field-Marshal, Sir Wm. M. 354
Gondā, rāja of, 373
Gonds, 87, 93, 310, 311
Gonīn battle, 341
Gonzales, Sebastian, 67, 69, 72
Good Hope, Cape of, 1, 4, 270, 274
Gopāl Hari, 210

Gopālpur, 405
Gopālrāv Gaikwād, 392
 Patvardhan, 229
 Singh, Bundelkhand, 296
Gorafar, Mt., 419
Gorākhpur, 302, 326, 368, 370, 372
Goraria battle, 367
Gordon, General Sir Benjamin L., 420, 422
 Major, 223
 General John J. Hood, 406
Gori, 31
Gosain Himmat Bahādur, 284, 286
Gough, General Sir Chas. J. S., 402
 Field-Marshal Lord Hugh, 344, 346-348, 351-353
 General Sir Hugh Henry, 399, 401, 402
Govardhan, 287
Govind Chandra, Kachār, 315, 326
 Pandit, 211, 212
 Rāo of Jalaun, 339
 Singh, last Sikh Guru, 119, 151
Govindrāv Gaikwād, 226, 261, 267, 278, 280
Govindgarh, 353, 354
Govindpur, Calcutta, 138, 140, 143
Gowdie, Major, 264
Graeme, Henry Sullivan, 322
Graham, Col. Thomas, 418, 419, 424
Grant, Lieut., C. J. W., 423
 Sir John Peter, 374
 Sir Robert, 333, 335
 Sir William, 303
Grant-Duff, James C., 310
 Mountstuart Elphinstone, 406, 415
"Granth"—Sikh scriptures, 50
Grantham, Sir Thomas, 127, 128
Gray, Matthew, 113
 Mr, 244
Greathead, General Sir Edward H., 366
Greaves, General Sir Geo. R., 422, 427
Gregory, Syrian, bishop, 110
Grey, General Sir John, 344
 Sir William, 383, 386
Griffin, Sir Lepel H., 403
Griffith, John, 270
Grimwood, Mr and Mrs, 423
Grundler, Mr, 161
Guelemot of Anaksūngai, 159
Gujarāt, 11, 16-19, 21-24, 30, 34, 39, 40, 45, 47-51, 54-58, 61, 67, 68, 72, 74-76, 79, 82, 86, 88, 91, 93, 95, 99, 100, 104, 105, 118, 121, 126, 129, 142, 148, 150, 153-155, 158, 164, 165, 168, 169, 171, 172, 174-176, 178, 180, 183, 187, 192, 250, 278, 307, 327, 429
 Gujarāt, Panjāb, 352
Gulāb Singh, Kashmīr, 347, 348, 365
Gūmsur, 306, 333, 341, 344, 349
Gūmtī river, 369, 373
gunpowder manufactured, 145
Guntūr, 224, 241-244
Gurkhas, 225, 294, 298, 301-304, 353, 368, 369, 418, 423, 424
Guthrie, Lieut.-Col., 283
Gutī, 182, 275
Gwāliar, 5, 15, 36, 61, 87, 92, 103, 104, 106, 107, 217, 244, 248, 285, 289, 322, 329, 330, 338, 342, 344, 362, 366, 367, 372, 373, 391, 413
Gijedde, Capt. Gule, 75, 77
Gyfford, William, 124, 125, 127, 128, 130

HAAS, Mons., 412
 Habīb of Kashmīr, 36, 39
Hāfiz Rahmat, Rohila, 235
Haft Kotal, 341
Haidar 'Alī, 189, 204, 210, 213, 214, 217, 219-231, 235, 238-241, 243-252; 265
 Beg Khān, Lucknow, 239
 Chakk, Sultan, Kashmīr, 34, 51
 Jang, 206
 Mīr Doghlāt, historian, 10, 28, 32
 Qulī Khān, 156, 158, 160, 163, 164, 166
Haidarābād (Bhāgnagar), 42, 54, 119, 127, 150, 151, 164, 166, 200, 206, 207, 243, 281, 283, 286, 293-295, 305, 314, 315, 328, 347, 354, 384, 408, 421
 Sindh, 254, 280, 336, 342, 343
Hailes, Major, 414
Haines, Field-Marshal Sir Fred. Paul, 393
Hājī Hamīd, Turkmān, 167
 Khān, 27
 Khalfa, Mustafī, author, 104
 Mustafa,—M. Raymond, 261
Hājīpur, 17, 26, 47, 54, 213
Hāka, Burma, 421
Hakīm Mirzā, Kābul, 35, 41
 Mehdi, Audh, 327
Hālā, 343
Halicarnassus, Bishop of, 213
Hall, Col. Henry, 316
Halliday, Sir Frederick James, 358
Halliyardurg, 264
Halsey, Mr, 145
Hamīd Khān, 164-166
Hamilton, Lieut., 400
 Sir Robert N. Collie, 344
 William, 153

Hamīr Rānā of Udaypur, 232, 241
Hammans, Major, 427
Hanifī sect, 43
Hankau, 392
Hānsi, 15, 273, 277, 279, 280
Hānsot, 237, 244
Hansrāj of Māndvī, 295, 296
Hanumāngarh or Batner, 8
Harāt,—Herat, 17, 64, 66, 153, 158, 159, 170, 267, 325, 334, 335, 337, 360, 361, 378, 382, 383, 386, 387, 394, 400, 404, 406, 417
Harcourt, Lieut.-Col., 283
Hardinge, Sir Henry, Lord, 345, 347, 350
Hardwar,—Haridwār, 370, 383
Hardiman, General, 308
Hare, David, 305
Hargovind, sixth Sikh Guru, 65, 91
Hariānā, 273, 296
Hariharpur, Orissa, 87
Haripant Phadke, 237, 240, 241, 246, 257, 263, 264
Hari Rām, Ahmadābād, 155
Hari Nārāyan Deva of Sambalpur, 3
Harirāv Holkar, 330, 331, 333, 339, 344
Harishpurgarh, Orissa, 87
Harkisan, eighth Sikh Guru, 106, 110
Harland, Commodore, 148
    Sir Robert, 229
Harpanahalli, 219, 258, 276
Harpur, General, 242
Har-rāi, seventh Sikh Guru, 91, 105, 106
Harris, Bartholemew, 130-132, 136
    General George, Lord, 273, 275
    George F. Robert, Lord, 358, 374
    George R. Canning, Lord, 422
Harrison, Edward, 153, 158
    Lieut., 425
Hartington, Marquis of, 403, 408
Hartley, General James, 244, 249, 261, 262, 275
Harvey, Col. J. J., 419
Hasāji Mohita Hambīr Rāo, 118, 119
Hasan Abdal, Panjāb, 118
    'Alī, Karnātak, 179
    Muqarrab Khān, 69, 77
    Raza Khān, Lucknow, 239
Hasanzāis, 384, 419
Hasti Dal, Almorā, 303
Hastings, Francis, 161, 163
    General Francis Rawdon, Marquis of, 301, 306, 308, 309, 315, 317
    Warren, 172, 191, 218, 219, 228, 230, 233-237, 239, 240, 245, 247-249, 251, 252, 254, 255, 257-259, 269
Hāthras, 306, 366
Havelock, General Henry, 361, 364-367
    Col. William, 351
Hawel, Isaac van den, 127
Hawkins, Capt. William, 65-67, 69
Hay, Mr, 219
Hazāra, 327, 348, 351, 384
Healy, Dr, 354
Heath, Capt., 131, 143
Heber, Bishop Reginald, 316, 322
Hébert, M., 154, 159
Hedges, William, 125-128, 145, 149
Heinzius Huth. of Delf, 127
Helmand river, 153, 404, 406, 410
Henriques, Garcia, 20
    Luiz de Miranda, 113
Henry I. of Portugal, 49
    IV. of France, 64
Herbakhsh Pāl, Karauli, 307
Herbert, Sir Thomas, 82
Herbert (*read* Hébert), Le Chevalier, 151
Heron, Lieut.-Col., 198
Hess, Capt. Hendrik, 78
Hessing, John, 279
Heytesbury, Lord, 332
Hicky, James Augustus, 245
Hidgley,—Ingeli, 130
Higgins, Lieut., 415
Higginson, Nathaniel, 135, 136
Hill, General Sale, 409
Hills, General James, 364, 401
Himmat Khān, 137
Hīmū, General, 35, 36
Hindāl Mirzā, 15, 27-29, 32, 33
Hinde, John, 186, 187
    Col., 368
Hindu College, Calcutta, 305
    girls' school, 353
    temples, Banāras, 86
Hindūpat of Samthar, 323, 380
Hinglājgarh fort, 286
Hingona, 344
Hippins island, Sunda strait, 127
Hippon, Capt., 68
Hīra Singh, Lāhor, 344-346
Hire Chāma Udayār Bola, 45
Hislop, Sir Thomas, 306, 308, 310
Hkama, Burma, 420
Hlall, dākāit, 415 416
Hobart, Lord, 268, 269, 273, 274
    Vere Henry, 388, 393
Hodges, Mr, 211
    Thomas, 225, 229
Hodgson, Brian H., 330
Hodson, Major Wm. S. Raikes, 365, 366, 369
Hoge, Adrigan de Borssele van der, 127
Holcombe, Lieut., 392

Holewell, John Zephaniah, 172, 201, 212, 216
Holkar, 183, 212, 216, 220, 226, 237, 244, 265, 269, 282, 287-291, 295, 298, 300, 304, 307-309
Holland, John, 243, 260
Holland, 49, 67, 318, *see* Dutch
Holmes, Major-General Sir George, 282
  Major-General John, 364, 368
Holt, Col., 416
Homem, Manuel Mascarenhas, 101, 103
Honāwar, 44, 115, 252
Honnali, battle, 326
Honner, General Sir Robert William, 374, 375
Hooke, Rev. Walter, 111
Hooker, Sir Joseph Dalton, 353
Hope, Col. the Hon. Adrian, 370
  Sir Theodore C., 407
Hope-Grant, Brigadier, James, 363, 366-369, 371-373
Hornby, William, 229, 240, 254
Horne, John, 174, 179
Horsford, General Alfred H., 373, 374
Hoskot, 94, 227
Hosūr, 226, 264
Houtman, Cornelius, 57-59
Howard, Major Francis, 420
Hpagyīdoa of Burma, 312, 321
Hsengbyusheng of Burma, 220, 224, 239
Htantabeng, Burma, 319
Hubbard, Mr, 181
Hublī, 117, 416
Hudleston, William, 406
Hudson, Lieut.-General Sir John, 427, 428
Hughes, Rear-Admiral Sir Edward, 249-251, 253
  General Sir Robert John, 401
  Robert, 77
  Major, 372
  William, 375
Hūglī, 26, 85-87, 92, 99, 100, 104, 107, 109, 112, 113, 119, 122, 123, 125-127, 129, 137, 138, 142, 146, 147, 165, 201, 202, 221, 379, 381
Hugo, Hubert, 110
Humāyūn, Emperor, 9, 15, 17, 20, 22-24, 26-29, 31-35
  Jāh, 319, 336
  Shāh, 267
Hume, Mr, of Itāwā, 373
  General Sir Robert, 406
Hunter, Cornet, 307, 310
Hunterman, Sergeant, 210
Husain 'Alī Khān, General, 139
  'Alī Khān, Sayyid, 154, 156, 158-161
  'Alī, 262
Husain Arghūn Shāh, 18-20, 34
  of Kalāt, 337
  Dost Khān, 189
  Husaini, Aghā Khān, 306, 335, 347
  Khān Shāmlū, 64
  Langah I., 6; II., 19
  Nizām Shāh, 33, 37, 39, 41, 80, 87
  Qulī Khān, 47, 48
  Shāh Chakk, 40, 42, 44
  Shāh Sharqī, 3
  Sultān of Persia, 169
Husainpur, 225, 256, 263, 387
Hutchinson, Capt. A., 423

IBRĀHĪM 'ADIL SHĀH I., 24, 25, 29-31, 35, 37
  'Adil Shāh II., 49, 52, 56, 58, 64, 82
  II., Husain Lodī, Dehli, 15, 18, 19
  Husain Mirzā, 42, 45
  Khān Sūr, 34, 36
  Khān II. of Kashmīr, 33, 35
  Khān, 132, 133, 139, 148
  Khān Gārdī, 212
  Nizām Shāh, 56, 58
  Qutb Shāh, 32, 37, 39, 49, 50
Ichalkaranji, 319
Ichhāpur, 165
Īdar, 14, 16, 173
Īdgāh Sarāi, 363
Ikkeri, 80
Ilbert, Sir Courtenay P., 408, 409
"Il Morro"—Korlai fort, 57
'Imād-ul-Mulk Sultāni, 11, 20, 25, 34
"Imām Mahdi," 8
Imām Sāhīb of Golkonda, 179
  ud-dīn, Shaikh, Kashmīr, 348, 351
Imāmiya sect, 377
Immadi Bhairava of Maisur, 43
  Krishna, 171
  Rāja Udayār, 90, 91
Imodi of Sunda, 200
Impey, Sir Elijah, 237, 245, 252, 254
  Edward, 306
'Ināyatullah Khān, 86
  Khān, Vazīr-deputy, 162
Income tax, 389, 414
"Indenture Tripartite," 145
India, Victoria Imperatrix, 393-395, 397, 398
India Council, 414
Indian Navy, 325, 378
Indigo planters, 360
Indor, 272, 279, 286, 291, 298, 308, 330, 331, 333, 363, 367, 368, 417
Indragarh, 373
Indraprastha,—Dehli, 24

Indrapur factory, 146
Indus riv., 25, 329, 330, 332
Ingeli,—Hidgley, 130
Injarām factory, 164, 203
Innes, Col., 318
Innis Khān, 194, 196
Inquisition, 37, 38, 302
Intizām ud-daula Khān Khānān, 195
Īraj Khān, Lucknow, 238
Irāwadī riv., 356, 412, 413, 415, 422
'Īsā Khān, Harāt, 360
Khān Tarkhān, Mirzā, Surat, 93
Qulī, vakīl, 137
Isfahān, 146, 155, 164
Is-hāq Khān, Afghān, 419
of Dīū, 20
Ishvara Chandra Gupta, journalist, 327
Ishvari Singh of Jaypur, 183, 187 [*not* Mewār], 215
Islām Khān, Shaikh, of Bengal, 70
Khān Mashhadi, Nawāb, 86, 90, 91
Shāh Sūr, Sultān, 30, 31, 33
Islāmābād,—Chittagāon, 11
Ismā'īl 'Adil Shāh, 10, 11, 16, 18, 21, 23, 24
Nizām Shāh of Ahmadnagar, 54, 55
Beg, 258-260, 262, 265
Qulī Khān, Gujarāt, 55
Khān of Kashmīr, 35, 36
Ismā'īliah Imāms, 134, 335, 347
Khojās, 338
Istālif, 341
I'timād Khān, Gujarāt, 39, 45, 51; *see* Amānat Khān
I'timād ud-daula—Qamar ud-dīn Khān, Vazīr, 188
Ivy, Thomas, 92

JABALPUR, 295, 308, 366, 368, 369, 386, 421
Jabra Ghāt, 295
Jackson, Coverley, 361
Jacob, Col. John, 343
Jacobābād darbar, 394
Jacobin club, Seringapatam, 272
Jacquemont, Victor, 324
Jādhav-rāi Bhonsla, 84
Jadra earthquake, 34
Ja'far 'Alī Khān (Mīr Ja'far), 185, 203-205, 207, 209, 210, 213, 214, 219, 221, 225
'Alī Khān, Surat, 341
Ja'far Khān, Murshid Qulī, 145, 155
Khān of Nāgar, 424
Jafnapatam, 38, 56, 59, 61, 75, 77, 104, 350
Jagannāth Pūrī, 283, 306, 404
Jagannāth Sankar Seth, Bombay, 381
Jagat Rāi of Bardhwan, 137
Singh I., Rānā, 82, 100; II., 187, 193
Singh of Kāngrā, 93
Singh of Kotā, 95
Singh of Jaypur, 285, 290, 310-312, 405
Jagatjit Singh, Kapūrthala, 396
Jagdalak, 339, 402
Jagdev Rāo, Golkonda, 37
Jagdispur, 184, 365, 371
Jagjivandās, Satnāmi, 126
Jagrāon, 347
Jahān Āra Begam, 71, 94, 111
Jahāndār Shāh, Sultān, 153, 154, 197
Jahāngīr, Sultān, 63, 64, 68-73, 75, 76, 82, 95, 114
Muhammad, of Bhopāl, 323, 333-335, 346
Qulī Khān Beg, Bengal, 26, 27
Qulī Khān Lālah Beg, 66, 67
Jahān Khān, Sardār, Afghān, 203
Shāh, 154, 160
Jailam, Jehlam, or Vyath riv., 34, 81, 352
Jainas, 9, 14, 43, 57
Jaintiā, 318, 322, 329
Jaisalmir, 311, 333
Jaitak fort, 302, 303
Jaitsingh or Jaytsingh, of Mohanpur, 178
Jajhār Singh, Bundela, 87, 88
Jajowan, battle, 149
Jakkatra, Batavia, 76, 81
Jālā, Pandit, Lāhor, 345, 346
Jalāl Khān Lodī, of Bihār, 15, 25, 27
Khān, Islām Shāh, 30
Shāh, Ghiyās ud-dīn I., 38; II., 40
ud-dīn Raushānī, 54, 61
ud-dīn Shāh 'Alam, 212-214, 221, 223
Jalālābād, 177, 340, 398, 402, 403, 408, 428
Jalandhar, 27, 151, 351, 362, 363
Jalandhar Khān, 417
Jalāp-la, 418, 419
Jālnā, 168, 294
Jām Fīrūz, 17, 18
Jesājī, of Nawanagar, 299
Nanda, 8, 17
Jama Bakht, 366
Jamāl Khān, 54, 55
Sāhib, 200
Jambukistna, 194
Jamdat-ul-Mulk Sā'adulla Khān, 99
James I., 64, 67, 72, 74, 75, 78-80
II., 129
James, Commodore Sir William, 198
Rev. John Thomas, Bishop, 322, 324

Jamnā riv., 211, 215, 234, 246, 272, 303, 332
canal, 338
Jamrūd, 122, 334
Jamshīd Qutb Shāh, Golkonda, 29, 32
Jamu, 57, 348, 396
Jang Bahādur, 343, 348, 354, 368, 369, 374, 393
Jangam priests, 116
Jānī Beg Tarkhān, Mīrzā, 51, 52, 55, 56
Janjira Sīddis, 106, 114, 117, 125, 155, 172-174, 215, 217-219, 255, 264
Jānkirām of Pātna, 190, 191
Jankojirāv Sindia, 329, 330, 342
Jānoji Bhonsla, 189, 195, 198, 199, 205, 210, 222, 223, 226, 233
Nimbālkar, 200
Japan, 29, 70, 96, 97
Jāpvo, Mt., 401
Jask, Persia, 78
Janssen, Capt., 297
Jaswan rāja, 351
Jaswantrāv of Dhār, 190, 216
Holkar, 298
Bhāu, 309
Jaswant Singh, 91, 103-105, 115, 119, 122
Jāts, 134, 164, 214, 217, 229, 250, 259
Jataura, 365
Jath, 314
Jatilavarman Srīvallabha Ativarāma, 43
Jauhar, historian, 53
Shāh, Achīn, 312
jauhar, 43
Jaunpur, 38, 236
Jaura-Alīpur, battle, 372
Java, 18, 49, 62, 76, 77, 79, 80, 100, 120, 127, 169, 296
Javān Singh of Udaypur, 323, 336
Jāwad, 309
Jāwad Khān, Nawāb, 188, 194
Mard Khān Bābi, 172, 173, 183, 195
Jawāhir Singh, 219, 222, 224, 226, 227
Singh, Lāhor, 346
Jawākī clan, 396
Jayāji Sindia, 413
Jayjar, 279
Jaymal of Bednūr, 43
Jaynārāyan Singh, 334
Jaypur, 112, 142, 187 (*del.* Mewar), 197, 222, 242, 258, 277, 285, 286, 288-290, 304, 312, 332, 333
Jaysingh, Siwāi, Kachhwāha, 110-112, 142, 150, 154, 159, 160, 164, 168, 173, 181, 183
III., 312, 332
Deva, of Rewā, 299, 300
I., of Udaypur, 125; II., 142, 143
Jaytsingh of Bikanīr, 20
Jehā-Māla, battle, 283
Jehlam riv., *see* Jailam
Jeluk, 418
Jenkins, Sir Francis Howell, 403
Sir Richard, 307, 308, 310
William, 400
Jervis, Capt. E., 382
Jesuits, 53, 63, 67, 85, 102, 143, 152, 170, 181, 199, 226
Jhālāvar, 331
Jhalūr, 267
Jhānsi, 172, 307, 362, 369, 370, 372
Jhīnd, 99, 276, 349, 362, 375
jihād, 322, 327
Jījībāī of Kolhāpur, 219
Jind or Jindān Kuwār, 345, 346, 349
Jinjī, 118, 120, 132-136, 138-140, 143, 180, 190, 191, 194, 214, 216
Jitgarh, 168, 169, 302
Jiyāji Sindia, 344
jizya tax, 41, 123, 124
João IV., of Portugal, 93; V., 171
Joapmī pirates, 313
Jodha Mānak, Wāghar, 375
Jodhpur, 23, 44, 58, 77, 122, 149, 150, 156, 164, 258, 262, 290, 309, 332, 336, 343
Johnson, Capt., 135
Johnstone, Mr, 207, 209
Major-General Sir James, 400
Johor, Malacca, 53, 193
Jones, Sir Harford, 292
General Sir William, 370, 371
Joparra, Malacca, 46
Jotarām, Jaypur, 333
Jotsoma, Nāgā fort, 401
Jourdain, John, 76
Jubilee of Queen Victoria, Empress, 416, 417
Judson, Rev. Adoniram, 321
Jumdat ul-Mulk, 136
Junāgadh, 206
Junnar, 9, 66, 103
Jwāla Prasād, 375

KABBĀLDURG, 171
Kabkalās or Kālusāh, 124, 132
Kābul, 9, 13, 14, 16, 19, 29, 31, 32, 34-36, 41, 48, 50, 52, 54, 57, 58, 66, 96, 99, 111, 119, 149, 177, 179, 234, 267, 274, 292, 294, 295, 311, 330, 335-342, 382, 384, 385, 387, 394, 397-409, 417, 418, 428
Logār, riv., 398, 403
Kachār, 314, 318, 319, 322, 326, 329, 359, 387, 402, 408

Kachaura, 282
Kachh, 55, 191, 266, 281, 303, 304, 312, 313, 316, 331, 410
Kachh Amadan, 405
Kachīn tribes, 409, 411, 418, 420, 425, 427
Kadapā,—Cuddapah, 99, 191, 192, 265, 278, 395
Kadattanād, Malabar, 261
Kadol, battle, 414
Kadūr, in Kūrg, 96
Kāgal, 319
Kājwā, battle, 366
Kākar Pathans or Musa Khels, 410
Kalana, 308
Kalanga or Nalapāni fort, 302
Kalankandan fort, 210
Kalāt, Baluchistān, 331, 337, 338, 358, 378, 389, 394, 428
Kalāt-i-Ghilzai, 380, 401, 404, 406, 417
Kalē, 420, 423
Kālī, goddess, 329
Kālīkata,—Calcutta, 140, 142
Kalim Allah Shāh of Kulbarga, 19
Kālinjar, 30, 44, 85, 281, 298
Kālkā, 354
Kalna inscription, 24
Kālpī, 9, 35, 175, 370-372
Kalūsah or Kabkalās, 124, 132
Kaluttara, Ceylon, 86, 100, 101
Kalyān, 25, 46, 89, 97, 118, 122
Kalyān Singh of Bikanīr, 45
  Singh of Kishnagar, 337
Kalyānī, 103
Kamāl Khān, 10, 11
Kām Bakhsh, prince, 133, 134, 136, 138, 139, 148, 150; 212
Kāma Rājsingh II., of Udaypur, 199
Kāmandurg, 326
Kamāon, 302, 303, 369
Kamboli island, 35, 99, 100
Kamonā fort, 291
Kāmrān Mirzā, 23, 27-29, 31-33
  Mirzā of Harāt, 311, 325, 330, 337, 342
Kamsin, 426
Kanāla fort, 28
Kanara, 115, 122, 148
Kanauj, 28, 366
Kanaund, battle, 265
Kandāhār, Nānder, 85
Kāndesh, 16, 21, 26, 39, 42, 47, 56, 61, 148, 156, 311, 321, 429
Kāndu, riv., 369
Kandy, Ceylon, 32, 56, 59-61, 68, 69, 73, 75, 77, 83, 91, 92, 101, 223, 269, 270, 277, 280, 301, 311
Kāngrā fort, 78
Kanhau chiefs, 423
Kānhoji Angria I., 155, 159, 165
  Angria II., 336, 338
  Gaikwād, 278, 280-282, 299-301
Kanhori, 273
Kaniguram, 406
Kānji, Koli robber, 88
Kanmer, 396
Kannanūr,—Cannanore, 6, 8-10, 20, 22, 40, 42, 108, 114, 254, 262, 271, 275
Kāntāji Gaikwād, 174
  Kadam Bānde, 166-169
Kanthīrava Narasa of Maisur, 106
  Mūkarasu of Maisur, 147, 156
Kāpadvanj, 166, 175, 282
Kāppātt, Malabar, 4
Kapūrthala, 322, 347, 362, 380, 418
Kapuyan, Afghānistān, 397
Karāchī, 381
Karan of Sātāra, 143
Karanjā fort, 70, 110, 117, 125, 176, 178, 236
Karauli, 307
Karda, 269, 271
Karen-ni states, 393, 418, 419
Karez-ī-atta, 406
Kārī, 280, 299
Kārikkāl, 177, 178, 181, 206, 207, 241, 305
Karim fort, 259
Karim Khān, Pendhārī, 308, 309
Kārkala inscription, 43
Karkalu, Āsām, 103
Kārlē, Poonā, 242
Karli, Sāwantwādi, 312
Karna Rānā, of Udaypur, 78, 82
  Singh of Bikanīr, 118
Karnāl, 120
Karnāla fort, 114
Karnātak and K. Nawāb, 119, 131, 151, 152, 156, 167, 179, 180, 182, 184, 185, 189, 195, 198, 199, 202, 210, 218, 220, 221, 225, 226, 230, 239, 244, 245, 249, 252, 256, 257, 262, 265, 269, 278, 279, 292, 357, 360
Karnūl, 192, 278
Kartalab Khān, Muhammad Hādi, 144
Kartārpur, Panjāb, 27
Karunguli,—"Carangoly," 207, 212
Karūr fort, 214, 215, 227, 251, 253, 262, 275, 372
Kārwar, 91, 110, 123, 146
Karwī, Bānda, 372
Kāshghār, 386, 395
Kāshirāv Holkar, 272, 278
Kashmīr, 23, 32-36, 39-45, 48, 49, 51-53, 55, 56, 77, 99, 108, 148, 161, 179, 193, 288, 313, 324, 348, 377, 420, 424, 428

Kāsigāon, battle, 235
Kāsimbāzār, 102, 104, 109, 119, 120, 122, 123, 128, 145, 146, 149, 189, 201, 203
Kāsimkotta, 208
Katak, 49, 184, 185, 191, 207, 246, 283, 284, 305, 306
Katasang, 401
Kāthiāwār, Kāthiāwād, 22, 134, 191, 291
Katir dist., 185
Kātmāndū, 98, 103, 225, 282, 343
Kattiwākkam,—Ennūr, 151
Kattyama Kamayya Nāyyaka, 19
Katuka, Jaina sect, 9
Katula, king of Orissa, 59
Katwā, 181, 184
kaul or *qaul*, grant, 95, 105
Kāvaledurg, 252
Kāvarpāk, 138
Kāverī, Kāverīpuram, 275
Kayankolam, 185
Keane, General Sir John, 336, 337
Keatinge, Col., 237, 295, 297
Kedarji Gaikwād, 187
Keelinge, Capt., 65, 67, 73
Kehri Singh, Nawāb, Bharatpur, 234
Keigwin, Capt. Richard, 124, 127, 128
Keir, General Sir William Grant, 312
Kelly, Dr Ambrose, 400
Kelva-Māhim, 22
Kelve-Katalwāda fort, 178
Kempe Gauda, Bangalor, 91
Kendat, Burma, 413
Kendell, Baron von, 411
Kengarji Bahādur, of Kachh, 398, 410
Kengtung state, 412
Kennaway, Capt. Sir John, 260, 268
Kennedy, General, 406
  Major, 417
Kerman, 335, 338
Kerr, General Lord Mark, 370
  Dr R. H., 290
Kerridge, Thomas, 70, 72, 80
Keshab Chandra Sen, 385
Keyes, General Sir Charles P., 396
Khādim Husain Khān, 213
Khāfī Khān, Muhammad Hāshim, 136, 140, 172
Khagiani tribe, 399
Khaibar pass, 33, 122, 317, 335, 337, 339, 340, 352, 399, 401, 402, 405, 421
Khaim Singh of Jaypur, 405
Khalgāon, 26
khālsā or *khālisā*, governmental, 346, 402
Khambay,—Cambay, 13, 22, 40, 45, 51, 69, 148, 166, 237, 280
Khāmti tribe, 388
Khān Asad Khān, 81
  Bahādur, Bhatti, 296
  Bahādur Khān, mutineer, 362
  Daurān II., Nasrat Jang, 87, 88, 94
  Daurān IV., 'Abdul Samad Khān, 162, 167
  Jahān Lodi, 67, 83-85
  Jahān Bahādur Kokaltāsh, 117, 122, 127, 128, 134
  Khānān, *see* Mun'im Khān, *and* Mirzā 'Abdur Rahīm
  Khānān, Mīr Jumla, 102, 103
  Mīrzā, 17
  Muhammad, Bījāpur, 104
  Singh, Lāhor, 350
  Zamān 'Alī Qulī Shaibānī, 42
  Zamān Bahādur, 87, 89
Khandāla, Poona, 241, 246
  Sātāra, 325
Khānde Rāv, 214
  Rāv, Indor, 289
Khanderāv, son of Malhārrāv, 224, 269
  Dābhāde, 157, 174
  Gaikwād I., 187; II., 360, 386, 392
  Holkar, 339, 344
  Puār, 216, 244
Khanderi island, 123, 124
Khandoji Mānkar, 180, 200
Khands of Gūmsur, 341, 344
Khānuz Zamān, vazīr, Kashmīr, 41
Kharag island, 360
Kharag Singh of Lāhor, 337-339
Kharak Singh of Kapūrthala, 386, 396
Kharkī,—Aurangābād, 68
Khasa Chāma Rāja of Maisur, 238
Khāsi states, 322, 325
Khāsirāv, Indor, 289
Khawās Khān, 26, 30, 32
  Khān, Bījāpūr, 116
Khelna,—Vishālgarh, 145
Khem Sāwant II., 150, 152; III., 199, 285, 291; IV., 316, 329, 335, 383
Khiva, 389
Khizr Khān of Bengal, 28
Khizrpur, 102, 109
Khodadād Khān of Kalāt, 378, 379
Khojās, 347, 354, 377, 378, 382
Khojak pass, 398
Khondamīr, Ghiyās ud-dīn Muhammad, historian, 17, 21
Khonoma, 400-403
Khorāsān, 281
Khost, 398
Khudāganj, 368
Khudāwand Khān Rūmī, 30
  Khān Habshi, 52
Khunza Sultāna, 41

Khurdhā, 286, 306
Khurram 'Alī of Sindh, 280
  Sultān,—Shāhjahān, 71-74, 77
Khushāb pargana, 76
Khushālgarh, 286
Khushk-ī-Nakhud, 404
Khusro Sultān, 63, 65, 68, 79, 82
  Khān, 153, 154
  Turk, Azād Khan, 11
Khusrujī Modi, Poona, 297, 300
Khwāja 'Abdul Hamid Khān, 146
  'Abdullah Khān, 182, 184
  'Alī Shirāzi, Dābhol, 45
  Anwar, 140
  Hadi, 207
  Jahān, 86
  Nāsar, Surat, 69
  Sara 'Abdullah Khān, 79
  Zafar, Gujarāt, 27, 30
Khwāja, battle, 154
Khyrim, Khāsia state, 325
Kidd (or Kyd), Capt. William, pirate, 138, 141, 144
Kidderpur, 317
Killeri, battle, 296
Kim Kathodra, battle, 183
Kimberley, Earl of, 408, 414, 426
Kimedi, 305, 331
Kinarām of Āsām, 267
Kinloch, Capt., 225, 228
  Lieut. Alex. A. A., 400
Kinnear, Major, 194
Kinta, battle, 393
Kirat Singh of Amber, 112, 117
  Singh of Gohad, 285
  Singh of Dholpur, 334, 390
Kīratpur, 105, 106
Kirjean, Mons., 196
Kirkangarhi fort, 178
Kirkī,—Khadkī, battle, 306
Kirkpatrick, General William, 239, 265
Kishenganj, Dehli, 364
Kishm, Persian Gulf, 79
Kishnagar, 310, 337
Kishor Singh I., of Kotā, 104; II., 314-316, 324
Kishwar Khān, Bījāpūr, 42
Kistnāvaram, battle, 193
Kittūr, 258, 319
Kiwām ul-Mulk, 17
Knox, Col., 213
  General Sir Alexander, 280, 282
Kochin, *see* Cochin
Kodkuā, battle, 368
Kodungallūr,—Cranganor, 8, 14, 18, 25, 30, 53, 62, 71, 73, 107, 260, 261, 290
Kohat, 353, 396, 423
Koh-ī-Asmāi, 402
Kohima, Nāgā hills, 400
Koh-ī-nur diamond, 102, 352
Koil, battle, 283
Koilgadi, 198
Koimbatūr, *see* Coimbatur
Koka Fūlād, 40
Kokanāda, —Kakināda, 211
Kolābā, 164, 174, 175
Kolār, 94, 226, 227, 275
Kolattiri, prince, Malabar, 6, 9
Kolhāpur, 89, 102, 154, 155, 169, 190, 220, 232, 259, 266, 285, 313, 315, 316, 319, 321, 322, 344, 345, 377, 386
Kolis, 44, 51, 154, 229, 328
Kollam,—North Quilon, 6, 8, 15, 16, 107, 148; S. Quilon, 292
Kollarun,—Kolladam riv., 249
Komalmer fort, 45
Komaroff, General, 411
Kondāna fort, 110
Kondapalli fort, 37
Kondavīd fort, 14, 49, 192, 209
Kongād dist., 266
Kongal, 278
Konimer,—Kunimēdu, 126
Konkai, 410
Konkan, 35, 38, 51, 97, 102, 126, 177, 244, 307, 399
Kopāl,—Kopāl-durg, 261, 312, 371
Korā, 222, 232-234, 236
Korigāon, battle, 308
Korlai fort, 57
Kōsīr, Red Sea, 324
Koster, Willelm Jacobszoon, 91
Kotā, 81, 103, 104, 156, 165, 175, 217, 288, 308, 315, 316, 318, 331, 363, 366, 370, 382
Kotkai, battle, 419
Kotri, battle, 309
Kotta or Putupatanam, 32, 41, 60
Kottayam, 188, 261
Kovalam,—Covelong, 168, 194
Kovilkonda,—Koilkonda, 37
Krishnadeva Rāya of Vijayanagar, 10-14, 16-18, 22
Krishnā,—Kistna riv., 102, 120, 192, 209, 221, 223
Krishnagīri, Maisur, 226, 264
Krishnāji Bānde, 168
Krishnā Kumārī of Udaypur, 284, 290
Krishna-rāo of Tiyāgar, 207, 210
Krishna Rāja Udayār, 276, 298, 328, 384
Krishnappa of Madura, 67
Kshirgāon fort, 296
Kuār or Kunwar Singh, mutineer, 365, 370

Kūch Bihār, 26, 58, 91, 102, 107, 109, 232
Kudal, 154, 167
Kudalūr,—Cuddalore, 126, 133, 146, 187, 188, 206, 213, 250-253
Kūkās, 388
Kūkīs, Lūshais, 375, 387, 388, 420, 426
Kula Chandra Dhaya Singh, 422, 424
Kulattūr, 390
Kulbarga, 2, 4, 16, 19, 129
Kulina Kula Survasa, play, 360
Kūm, Persia, 306
Kumār Mān Singh, 47, 54
Kumbhakarna of Mewār, 5
Kumbher, 187
Kun Saing, Shān, Sawbwa, 416
Kunch, 175, 371
Kunhāli Marakkār, 59, 60
Kunimēdu,—Konimer, 126
Kunjpura fort, 215
Kunna, battle, 414
Kunwar Sen or Sain, Peshwa, 22
 Rānāji Jand Bahādur, Nepāl, 395
Kunza tribes, 424
Kuppālūr inscription, 12
Kuram valley, 397-399
Kurapotkin, Col., 428
Kurg, 96, 147, 250, 295, 315, 330, 331
Kuru Kuru Timmappa Nāyyaka, 16
Kushāb, 76, 361
Kusk valley canals, 427
Kushtia, Āsām, 382
Kusugal, 261
Kuthar, 231
Kyaikkalo, 319
Kyimyin prince, pretender, 416
Kyimyindaing, 318, 319

LAAN, Joan van der, 106
 Labong, 41
Laccadive—Lākhadiv islands, 38
Lāduba, of Kachh, 312
Lagundi, Sunda strait, 80, 81
Lāhār fort, 244
Laheji sultān, 354
Lāhor, 28, 41, 48, 54, 61, 65, 91, 93, 104, 153, 188, 203, 205, 216, 271, 274, 292, 339, 345, 346, 348, 352, 361, 380, 393, 398, 421
Lakanā or Angad, 2nd Sikh Guru, 27, 33
Lake, Viscount General Gerard Lord, 279, 282-284, 286-288
Lakhairi, battle, 265
Lakhipur, 423
Lakhnauti, 272
Lākhpatji, or Lākhā Rāo, of Kachh, 191, 205
Lakshman Dās, Kashmīr, 420
 Dāwa, Ajaygarh, 294
 Nārāyan of Kūch Bihār, 58
 Sen of Raisin, 23
Lakshmībāī of Sāwantwādi, 285, 291
 of Jhānsi, 362
Lakshmī Rānī of Travankor, 297, 302
Lāl Bāgh battle, Burhānpur, 156
Lāl Dāng treaty, 236
Lāl Mādhu Singh, rebel, 373
Lāl Singh, Lāhor, 346-349
Lalbura, Lūshai, 388
Laliāna, 348
Lalitapattana, inscription, 90
Lally, Thomas Arthur, Count de, 206-210, 212-214, 216, 224, 249-251
Lālsot, battle, 258
Lālu, Buner, 379
Lālujī Lāl, author, 285
Lambe, Mr, 193
Lambert, Commodore, 355, 356
Lamena, battle, 356
Lancaster, Capt. James, 56, 62
 Capt. Jonas, 76
Lancastre, Dom Fernando Martim Mascarenhas de, 133
 Dom Pedro de, 107
Landi Kotal, 405
Lane, General Charles Ed. William, 340
Langford, Capt., 119
Langhorne, Sir William, 112, 114, 116, 119, 122
Lankaranji of Bikanīr, 20
Lanoy, M. de, 180
Lansdowne, Henry C. K .P., Marquis of, 419, 421, 424, 425, 429
Lapa, José Joaquim Jannuario, Visconde de Villa Nova de Ourem, 354
Lara, 50
Lāsalgāon fort, 287
Lashkar Khān, diwān, 195
Laswari,—Nāswāri, battle, 284
Lataband pass, 428
Latīf Khān, Gujarāt, 25
Latīfpur, battle, 248
Lauderdale, James, 8th Earl of, 289
Laungkrek, naval battle, 255
Lauribandar, Sindh, 70
Laval, François de, 62
Lavradio, Conde de, 121
Law, Mr, 161
 Stephen, 179
 Jacques François, 193, 194
 Jean, 200, 216
Lāwa, 381, 383
Lawrence, Maj.-General Stringer, 188, 189, 193-197, 208

Lawrence, Lieut.-General Sir George, 351, 352
Col. Sir Henry M., 340, 348, 361, 363
Lord John L. M., 351, 353, 357, 359, 379, 380, 382-385, 397, 399
Leedes, William, 51
Leeke, Admiral Sir Henry John, 360
Le Fevre, Capt., 306
Legois, Mons., 270
Le Grand, Capt., 370
Leith, Sir George, 279
Lellington, Gregory, 73
Lenoir, Mons., 163-165, 167
Lescke, Rev. William, 73
Leslie, Col., 241
Levant Company, 55
Levant, Father, 196
Levassoult, Mons., 270
Leyā, battle, 350
Lhāsā, 298, 422
Light, Capt. Francis, 257, 263
Lima, Joaquim Lopes de, 338
Limbin, Burmese prince, 412, 416, 417
Lindsay, Sir John, 228, 230
Col., 331
Linga-rāja of Kurg, 295, 315
Lingtu, Sikkim, 418
Linhares, Conde de, 83
Linschoten, John Huygen, 49, 51, 59
Little, Capt., 264
Littleton, Mr, 126, 129
Sir Edward, 142, 143, 147-149
Lockhart, General Sir William S. A., 423, 426, 430
Logarī tribes, 403
Lohāgadh fort, 114
Lohar Chakk, of Kashmīr, 49
London Company of Merchants, 61, 74, 75, 83, 86, 90, 98, 103, 106, 120, 125, 134, 141-144, 151
Longden, Sir James Robt., 395
Lope, Suarez, 8
Lord, Henry, 73
Lorena, Bernardo José de, 290, 305
Louet, Mons., 216
Louis XIII. of France, 72
Low, General Sir John, 335, 356
General Sir Robert C., 415
Lowther, Mr, 173
Lucas, Sir Gervase, 111
Lucknow,—Lakhnau, 21, 100, 126, 146, 223, 272, 276, 335, 361-365, 367, 369, 371-374, 421
Ludhiānā, 188, 296, 330, 336, 347, 362, 388
Ludlow, Major, 302
Ludovico di Varthema, 7
Lugard, General Sir Edward, 370, 371
Lumsden, General Sir Peter S., 410
Lūshais, *see* Kūkīs.
Lushington, Mr, 219
Stephen Rumbold, 323
Lyall, Sir Alfred C., 399, 418
Sir James B., 416
Lytton, Edward R. Bulwer, Lord, 394, 397

MACAO, 33, 96, 97, 294, 345
Macartney, George, Earl of, 247, 251, 253, 256, 257, 274
Macassar, 145, 148
M'Cabe, Robert Blair, 426
Macaulay, Col., 292
Thomas B., Lord, 331
M'Caskill, General Sir John, 341
M'Causland, Col., 369
Macdonald, Major, 389
Mr, 422
Macdonnell, Sir Antony P., 421
Macdowall, Lieut.-General Sir Andrew, 277, 293
Col., 305, 320
Macgregor, General Sir Charles M., 405
Major-General Sir George H., 340
Machai peak, 384, 423
Machari,—Alwār, 299
Macintosh, Sir James, 286
M'Intyre, Capt., 279
Mackenzie, Sir Alexander, 422, 426
Capt. Colin, 424
Col. Humberston, 249
Lieut. K. J., 421
Maclagan, Lieut., 349
Maclaine, Capt., 405
Macleane, Mr, 239
Macleod, Sir Donald F., 386
Brig.-General Norman, 251, 252
Macnab, Lieut., 425
Macnaghten, Sir William Hay, 336-339
Macpherson, General Sir Herbert T., 401-403, 415
Sir John, 256-257
Major Samuel C., 344
Lieut., 354
Col., 423
M'Queen, General Sir John W., 419, 422
Macrae, James, 166, 169
Madagascar, 97
Madakkara island, 114, 174
Madan Pāl of Karauli, 356
Singh, Kotā, 318, 331
Madanpur, 370
Mādhāpolem, 146, 203

Madgīri, battle, 264
Mādhav or Mādhu Singh of Jaypur, 183, 187, 215, 226, 242
Singh of Būndī, 85
Singh of Kotā, 81 ; 318
Mādhavji Bhonsla, 199, 252, 256, 259, 260
Mādhavrāv I., Peshwa, 226, 229, 231
II., 264, 270
Gaikwād, 172
Fadnavis, 330
Sindia, 217, 218, 221, 223, 242, 243
Mādhu Sudan Datta, poet, 353
Madhukēri,—Mercara, Kurg, 331
Madras, 89, 91, 92, 94, 95, 99, 100, 104, 110-112, 120-122, 124, 125, 127, 129, 131-137, 139-141, 143, 145, 146, 150, 165-168, 182-184, 186, 189, 194, 197, 201, 205, 208, 210, 213, 216, 217, 227-230, 235, 238, 240, 244-246, 249, 251-253, 262, 265, 267, 270, 272-275, 279, 290-296, 299, 301, 319, 322, 329-331, 334, 340, 342, 350, 355, 358, 360, 380, 388, 392, 393, 395, 396, 413, 415, 421, 425, 426
Madrasa at Calcutta, 248
"Madre de Dios," ship, 55
Madune Pandar, Colombo, 26, 75
Madura, 16, 18, 20, 22, 25, 37, 40, 46, 63, 65, 67, 81, 92, 106, 128, 135, 148, 177, 192, 198-200, 202, 204, 205, 210, 215, 220, 221, 253, 349
Maetsuyeker, Capt., 97
Magadi, Maisur, 91
Magdala, Abyssinia, 384
Magh chief, 91
Magrath, Lieut., 424
Maguire, Mr, 216
Mah Chuchakk Begam, 36, 41
Mahābaleshwar hill, 325
Mahābat Khān, 66, 69, 79-82, 87, 115
Mahā Bandula, Burman general, 318-320
Mahā-Dhammā Rāja of Burma, 64, 66, 70, 83
Mahā-Dhammā Rāja Dibata, 173
Mahā-Pawāra Dhammā Rāja of Prom, 107, 115
Mahā Thannada, of Burma, 255
Mahād, treaty, 271
Mahādavji or Māloji Gaikwād, 173
Sindia, 229, 241, 242, 246, 250, 255, 256, 268, 273
Mahādanda Bo, Arakan, 153
Māhar riv., 202
Mahārājpur, battle, 344
Mahātadittu, the Khatri, 27
Mahbub 'Alī Khān, Nizām, 385
Khān 'Abdul Nabi, Kashmīr, 161
Mahdī sect, 32
Mahdi Ja'far, 69 ; *read* 'Abdullah Khān Firuz Jang
Mahé, 19, 166, 178, 216, 241, 242, 305, 312
Mahendra Singh, of Patiāla, 378, 394
Mahesh Datt, 256
Maheshāsur,—Maisur or Mysore, 19
Maheshwar, 331
Mahfuz (Muhafiz) Khān, 185, 186, 192, 197-200, 204, 205, 210
Mahī riv., 174, 244
Mahīm, 10, 132, 133, 176-178, 354
Mahīp Nārāyan Bahādur, 247
Mahīpat Rām, rebel, 291
Mahmūd Baiqara of Gujarāt, 2-5, 9, 11, 20, 25, 26
III., of Gujarāt, 27, 30, 31
Mahmūd of Bhakkar, 34
Durānī Shāh, 278, 281
Ghilzāi, 164, 166
Khān Lodi of Bengal, 21, 26, 27
Khān, Gālna, 86
Khān, Kābul, 282
Khān Langāh, of Multān, 6, 19
Shah II. Nāsir Khān, of Gujarat, 20
Shāh II. Bahmani, 2-4, 6, 7, 9 13, 16
Shāh II. Khalji, 11-16, 22
Shāh, Harāt, 267
Shāh, Qandahār, 292
Shāh, Saduzāi, of Harāt, 325
Māhuli, 114
Mahūdra, 374
Maidān, Afghānistan, 341, 402, 419
Maihar, 368
Mailapur, 31, 101, 116
Mainpuri, 368
Maior, Philippe de Valadores Souto, 235
Maissin, Mons., 197, 199
Maisur,—Mysore, 18, 33, 41, 45, 47, 48, 56, 68, 90, 91, 94, 120, 131, 171, 173, 197, 199, 210, 215, 216, 224, 227, 251, 252, 259, 260, 270, 275, 276, 278, 289, 290, 298, 299, 326, 327, 343, 381, 395, 421
Maithāna hill, 430
Maiwānd, 404-406
Majauli, 368
Majendie, Lieut. H. G., 421
Makar, battle, 417
Makin, 430
Makhdum 'Alī, 213

Makka,—Mecca, 12, 30, 31, 33, 39, 56, 137, 147, 305
Makwānpur, 304
Malabar, 38, 40, 49, 106, 118, 119, 127, 143, 145, 146, 148, 224, 250, 263, 265, 266
Malacca, 11, 15, 18, 20, 40, 45-47, 53, 63, 72, 84, 87, 92, 93, 147, 270, 318, 324, 325, 327
Mālāgarh, 366
Malair-kotlā, 388
Malaun, 303
Malay, 19, 80, 97, 318, 328, 393
Malcolm, Sir Charles, 334
General Sir George, 372
Sir John, 274, 277, 292, 296, 308, 309, 312, 323, 324, 327
Māldā, 120, 139, 146
Maldev Rāo of Mārwār, 23, 46
Maldive chief, 96
Malhār-rāv Gaikwād I., 280; II., 386, 389-392
Holkar, 172-174, 176-178, 197, 224
II., 298, 330
Tukāji Holkar, 272
Khuni, Ahmadābād, 187
Puār of Dhār, 330
Rāstia, 229
Māligāon, 311
Malirāv Holkar, 224
Malik Achhi, Kashmīr, 25
Malik 'Ambar, Habshi, 64, 66-69, 72-74, 77, 78, 81, 82
Ayāz of Dīū, 9, 17, 18, 20
Jīwān, Barozāi, 105
Tokan, Dābhol, 48, 49
Malka fort, 379
Malkandi, Orissa, 87
Mālkhed, 117, 129
Malleson, Col. George Bruce, 384
Māloji Bhonsla, 57
Mallū 'Adil Shāh, of Bījāpūr, 24, 52
Malodh fort, Sarhind, 388
Malta, 396
Maltby, Edward, 379
Māltūn pass, 370
Malvalli, battle, 275
Malvana, Ceylon, 86
Mālwa, 15, 16, 22-24, 35, 38-40, 44, 54, 56, 61, 148, 160, 166, 170, 172, 174, 175, 180, 181, 183, 246, 278, 282, 286, 298, 309, 332
Mālwan, 223
Malwat,—Malot, fort, 19
Malwūn, 321
Māma Sāhib, Gwāliar, 342, 344
Māmū-khel, battle, 341
Manaar,—Mannār, 56, 104
Mānaharda hill, 383
Mānāji Āngria, 174, 175, 178
Gaikwād, 260, 261, 267
Morār, 157
Manakadana, 419
Mānakji, Tanjor, 194, 196, 197, 207
Manalgarh, 53
Manappādu, Tinneveli, 97
Mān Singh of Gwāliar, 5, 15
Singh of Amber, 52, 54, 56, 63, 64
Singh of Jalaur, 267
Singh of Jodhpur, 267, 284, 290, 332, 336, 343
Singh of Narwar, 372-374
Manauli dist., 322
Mānbhūm Choars, 328
Mandalē, Burma, 383, 384, 392, 393, 398, 400, 407-409, 411-416, 420-422, 425, 429
Mandangarh fort, 220
Mandasor, 17, 309, 367
Māndil dist., 124
Mandla dist., 181
Mandlēsar, 331
Mandū, 12-15, 22-24, 72, 74, 80, 83
Māndvi, 295, 296
Mangal Singh of Alwar, 391, 426
Mangalūr, 22, 35, 38, 74, 115, 148, 226, 246, 252-254, 273, 274, 279
Mangamāl of Madura, 128, 135, 148
Mangrūl, battle, 315
Manī Begam, of Murshidābād, 231
Manieravare, Ceylon, 86
Mānik Chand Seth, 201
Manikpatam, Orissa, 283
Manipur, 218, 313, 318-320, 322, 330, 345, 354, 400, 422-424
Manjakuppam, Kūdalūr, 185
Manjēri, 353
Mankarwal, battle, 42
Mankot, siege, 36
Manning, Thomas, 298
Mannūr dist., 267
Manor, 36, 170, 176
Manora, 70
Manohar Singh, of Nārwār, 311
Manohargarh, 313, 314
Mānpur, Alī-Rājpur, 408
Manrique, friar, 93
Mansfield, Sir William, Lord Sandhurst, 381, 382
Mansion House relief fund, 390, 396
Manson, Mr, 371
Mansurgarh fort, 84
Manucci, Venetian physician, 98
Manuel, King of Portugal, 18
Manwain, 392

Māppillas, 5, 353, 359, 390, 410, 411, 429
Marakkār, Pate, 26 ; Kunhāli, 59, 60
Marāthās, 78, 121, 122, 124, 134, 135, 138, 139, 143-145, 148, 150, 152, 153, 159, 164, 165, 167, 170-182, 184-186, 188, 189, 191, 193-200, 202, 205, 210, 211, 214-217, 220, 222, 225-227, 229-235, 237, 238, 240, 242, 244, 247, 250, 252, 255, 257, 258, 262, 268, 272, 276, 278, 279, 283, 284, 309
Māraurā fort, 370
Marāvar, 198, 230
Māravarman Sundara Pāndya III., 35
Mardān, 361
Mardes, Dom Manoel José Barao de Candal, 337, 338
Margary, Augustus R., 392
Marghilan, 426, 428
Mari tribe, 405
Maria Theresa of Austria, 238
Markara, a Persian, 112, 114
Marlborough, Earl of, 108
Marley, General, 302
Marmagão, 416
marriage bills, 389, 423
Marsan, Jāt chief, 305
Marshall, General, 308, 310
Marshman, Rev. Dr Joshua, 276
Martāban, 28, 69, 74, 256, 318, 322, 355, 356
Martabar Singh, Nepāl, 343, 346, 348
Mārtānda Varmā, 348, 376
Mārtāndrāv Holkar, 330, 331, 333
Martin, General Claude, 216
  François, 118, 120, 126, 136, 149
Martindell, Lieut.-General Sir Gabriel, 294, 298, 302, 303
Martyres, Dom Francisco de, 98
Mārwār, *see* Jodhpur, 29, 134, 144
Mas riv., 414
Masa'ud Khan, Bījāpūr, 121
Mascarenhas, Francisco de, 44, 45
  Dom Francisco de, Conde de Santa Cruz, 50, 52
  Dom Francisco de, 83, 92
  Giles Yanez, 52
  Hieronymo de, 48, 52
  Dom Luiz, Conde de Alva, 197
  Manuel, 73
  Dom Manuel, 107
  Pedro de, 20, 35
  Dom Philippe, 95
  Dom Vasco de, Conde de Obidos, 99
Mashakai, battle, 417
Mashhd, Persia, 409, 418
Māshik, Manakhel, 406
Mashir ul-Mulk, 269
Masjidia fort, 373
Maskat, Arabia, 32, 79, 97, 128
Massey, William Nathaniel, 381
Master, Streynsham, 102, 114, 116, 119, 120, 122, 124
Masulipatam, 68, 75-77, 83, 87, 88, 114, 119, 122, 123, 129, 132, 142, 146, 195, 200, 209, 241, 294
Mas'ūm Khān Farankhūdī, 50
Malāh, battle, 281
Matheus, friar, 58
Mathews, General, 252, 253
Mathurā,—Muttra, 92, 104, 107, 112, 114, 162, 203, 205, 287, 362
Matiāh sect of Ismā'iliahs, 134
Matūn, 398
Maukmē, 418
Maulāna 'Abdullah, writer, 15
  Ahmad, historian, 55
  Hairāni, author, 4
Maulmain, 388, 412, 417
Maulshobo, battle, 413
Maulvi plotters, 363
  Liakat 'Alī, 387, 389
  of Faizābād, 369, 371
Maung Po-saw, 418
Mauritius island, 145, 207, 246, 272, 274, 297
Maxwell, Col., 262, 264
  Capt., 429
Mayāpur, 201
Mayimama Marakkār, 10
Mayne, Col. William, 357, 358
Mayo, R. S. Bourke, 6th Earl of, 385, 387, 388, 393
Mazagāon fort, 132, 133
Mazar-i-Sharīf, 398, 419
Mazra or Bābā Wali, 404, 405
Meade, General Sir Richard J., 374
Médac, M. René, 223
Medinī Rāi, 14, 15
Medows, General Sir William, 249, 259-262, 265
Mehelati, Persia, 306
Mehidpur, 308, 309
Mehtar of Chitral, 426, 427, 429, 430
Mela, Francisco de, 26
Meliapur,—St Thomé, 116
Mello, Lieut.-Col. Antonio Maria de, 334
  Ayres de Silva de, 60
  Dom Christovão de, 165, 172
  Diogo de, 40
  Dom João José de, 221, 226, 235
  Jorge de, 41
  Pedro de, 176
  Ruy de, 16

Melville, Henry Dundas, 1st Viscount, 267
Membo, Abor fort, 429
Mendāt, Burmese prince, 416, 417
Mendoça, André Furtado de, 67, 68
 João de, 41
Menezes, Archbishop Alexis de, 58, 60, 65
 Diogo de, 48
 Duarte de, 17, 19, 52, 54
 Fernão Telles de, 50
 Dom Francisco de, 72
 Francisco de Cunha e, 257, 266, 268
 Henrique de, 19, 20
 João da Silva Tello de, 93
 Dom Luiz de, Conde de Ericeira, 158, 181, 182
 Dom Martinho da Silveira de, 170
 Vasco Fernandez César de, 154, 158
 Vaso Guedes de Carvalho e, 420, 422
Meng Khamaung of Arakan, 64, 69, 79
Mengdun Meng of Burma, 357, 392, 397, 408, 414, 416
Meng Rādzagyī, of Arakan, 69
Meng rāja—Salīm Shāh, 62
Merchant Adventurers' Company, 101, 103
Mergui, 318, 320
meriā sacrifices, 349, 350
Merv, Persia, 409, 411
Metcalfe, Sir Charles Theophilus, 292, 308, 315, 321, 332-334
Methwold, Mr, Surat, 89, 90
Mewār, 16, 25, 26, 43, 46, 52, 60, 173; (*on* 187 *read* Jaypur)
Mewāt, 266, 268
Mhau, 363
Mherwāra, 316, 333
Miānganj, 369
Mīanī, battle, 343
Michel, Field-Marshal Sir John, 373
Michelborne, Sir Edward, 64
Michni fort, 355, 389
Midagesi fort, 147
Middleton, D., 65
 Lord Francis, 127
 Sir Henry, 64, 68, 69
 Nathaniel, 249
 Bishop Thomas F., 304, 311, 315, 316
Midnapur, 185, 214
Mihrāb Khān of Kalāt, 336
Mildenhall, John, 61, 63, 71
Miller, Major-General William H., 366
Millman, Col., 370
Milne, Capt., 354
Minākshī Ammal of Madura, 174, 181
Mīnbu, 416, 421
Mingyan teak forests, 411, 412
Minhla, 413-416
Minto, Sir Gilbert Elliot, 1st Earl, 289, 290, 295, 297, 301
Mīr 'Abdul Rashīd, author, 100
 'Abdullah of Afghānistān, 157
 Afzal ud-dīn of Surat, 341
 'Alī, Goa, 10
 'Alī Murād Khān of Khairpur, 343
 Asad, Karnātak, 179, 181
 Habīb, 181, 191
 Hasan, poet, 257
 Husain, admiral, 10
 Husain, Qandahār, 164, 175
 Jumla—Mīr Muhammad Saīd, Mu'azzam Khān, 99, 101, 102, 105-109, 111, 114, 118
 Kāsim, *see* Qāsim 'Alī Khān.
 Mahmūd of Afghānistān, 157, 158, 164
 Mahmūd Khān of Kalāt, 428
 Mannū—Mū'in ul-Mulk Rustam Hind, 203
 Mausam Khān, 409
 Mughal, Haidarābād, 217
 Phūlwārī, *see* Najm ud-daula
 Qutb ud-dīn, Surat, 220
 Shāhdād Khān, Sindh, 342
 Sher Muhammad of Mīrpur, 342, 343
 Vais, Ghilzāi, 152-154, 157
Mira Wakar, Shaikh, 314
Miraj, 143
Mīran-Mīr Muhammad Sādiq, 204, 207, 213
Mīrān Husain Nizām Shāh, 54
 Mubārak Khān Fārūqī II., 26, 39, 42
 Muhammad Shāh Fārūqī I., 16, 25, 26; II., 42
Miranda, Fernão de, 50
Mīrānpur Katra, battle, 235
Mīranzāi Mullas, 423
Mirkhond, historian, 17
Mīrpur, 343
Mirta, 140, 162
Mīrzā Ghāzi Beg, 65
 Hakīm 'Askārī, 50
 'Īsā Turkhān, 35
 Jān, 99
 Jawān Bakht—Shāh 'Alam II., 215
 Kāmgār Khān, author, 85
 Khān, *see* 'Abdul Rahīm
 Mehdi, 204
 Muhammad 'Alī—Alahwirdī Khān, *q.v.*
 Muhammad Bāqī, 52

Mīrzā Muhammad Hakīm, 41, 42, 52
 Muhammad Khudā-banda, 67
 Mulī, Nawāb, 98
 Shāhrukh, 56
 Sulaimān of Badakhshān, 41
Mīrzās, 41, 45
Mīrzāpur, 298, 299
Mirzeo, Kanara, 122
Missions, Christian, 140, 141, 149, 161, 167; 191, 198
Mitchell, Arthur Forbes, 279
Miyān Achan, of Surat, 220
 Manju, 58, 64
Mogaung, 409, 418
Mohamdi, 371
Mohamra, battle, 361
Mohan Prasād, 237
 Singh, 368
Mohite chief, 315
Mohkam Singh, Kunwar, 149
Mohmands, 355, 402
Mokand Singh of Kotā, 103, 104
Mokha, 76, 82, 110, 139
Molucca islands, 8, 22, 24, 40, 47, 76
Momain, 384
Mombāsa, 139
Momeit, 422
Momin Khān I., 168; II., 176-178, 180, 183, 199, 205
 Khān III., of Khambay, 229, 230
Momna, Ismā'īliah sect, 134
Mondhis or Satnāmis, 117
Money, Col. Elliot Alexr., 401
 Wm. Taylor, 326
Mongīr, 17, 27, 36, 184, 218, 219
Monomotapa, 45
Monson, Col. the Hon. Geo., 213, 214, 233, 236, 239
 Col. William, 283, 286
Montagne, Edmond, 152
Monteath, Col., 339
Montgomery, Major, 365
Montresor, Col., 291
Moore, Major, 213
Moracin, Mons., 211
Moraes Carneiro, Joaquim Antonio de, 334
Morār, 372
Morārirāv of Gūtī, 180, 182, 194-196, 200, 222, 227
Morasa, 18
Morbudh fort, 96
Morehead, William A., 376
Moreira, Thomé Gomez, 172
Morgan, Capt., 283
Mornington, Earl of, *see* Wellesley
Moroba Phadnavis, 241
Moro Pant Pingla, 115, 118, 119, 123, 124
Morris, Sir John Henry, 401
Morrison, John, 232
 Cornet, 307, 310
 General, 320
Morse, Nicholas, 183
Mortandi Chāvadi—Dupleixpettai, 183
Morung, 292
Mostyn, Thomas, 231
Mounteney, Nathaniel, 89
Mozambique, 121, 391, 392
Mū fort, Kāngra, 93
Muar fort, 15
Mu'azzam, Sultān, *see* Muhammad Mu'azzam
Mubārik Khān Lohānī, 39
 ud-daula, of Bengal, 228, 267
Mubāriz Khān Sūr, 33
 Khān, Haidarābād, 164, 166
 ul-Mulk, 16
Mudāji Bhonsla, 233, 246-248
Mudgiri, 231
Mūdkal, 21
Mūdkī, battle, 346
Mughals, 20, 44, 49, 50, 55-58, 129-133, 176-178, 188, 220
Muhabat Khān, Khān Khānān, 87
Muhabbat Khānji of Junāgadh, 407
Muhāfiz (? Mahfūz) Khān, 185
Muhammad portrait riots, 355, 391
 Shāh of Kashmīr, 3, 8, 9, 25
 Shāh 'Ādil, 33-36
 'Ādil Shāh Sultan, 82, 85, 100, 102, 103
 Akbar Khān, 341
 Akbar, prince, 160
 Alamgir II., 197, 203, 205, 209, 212, 215
 'Alī, Nawāb Wālajah, 190-193, 195-197, 202, 204, 205, 220, 226, 229, 234, 249, 269
 'Alī Khān, Rohila, 268, 269
 'Alī Khān of Tonk, 378, 379, 381, 383
 'Alī Khān, author, 278
 'Alī Shāh of Audh, 335
 'Alī Shāh of Persia, 334, 335
 Amīn, author, 82
 Amīn Khān, Kābul, 111, 114, 118, 121
 Amīn Khān, Vazīr, 152, 158, 162
 A'zam, prince, 121, 124, 146, 148
 A'zam Khān of Kashmīr, 295
 Bahādur Shah II., *see* Bahādur
 Bedar Bakht, prince, 148
 Beg, Hamādāni, 250, 256, 258
 Ghaus, Shaikh, 36
 Hadi, Kartalab Khān, 144
 Hājī Khān of Bāhāwalpur, 357
 Hakīm Mirzā, 48

Muhammad Hasan, 368, 370, 372
Husain Mirzā of Kābul, 9
Husain Mirzā, Sambhal, 41
Husain Khan, Sirdar, 402
Ibrāhīm, prince, 162
Ibrāhīm 'Alī Khān of Tonk, 383
Ismā'īl of Jaura, 381
'Iwaz, Mufti, 304
Jān Wardak, 402, 403
Khān, author, 229
Khān, Ahmadnagar, 59
Khān of Kadappa, 191
Khān of Kohat, 351
Khān of Bhopal, 346, 350, 359
Khān Bangāsh, 168-170, 172
Khān Sūr, 30, 33, 35
Mu'azzam, Bahādur Shāh I., 102, 112, 115, 117, 120, 121, 123, 126, 127, 129, 130, 134, 137; 149-153, 157-160
Mu'azzim, Orissa, 180
Muhabbat Khān Bābī, 206
Qāsim Khān, Mīr-Bahr, 54
Qāsim, writer, 131
Qulī Qutb Shāh, 50, 54, 69
Reza Khān, Arkat, 220, 222, 231, 233
Sādiq, 131
Sākī Musta-idd Khān, author, 153
Shāh II., of Bengal, 1
Shāh III., of Gujarāt, 34
Shāh, Sultān, 160-162, 164, 165, 173, 177, 181, 186, 188; 224, 229, 260
Shāh, Afghān, 341
Turkhān, 18
Zamān Mirzā, 24
Yūsuf, 197, 200, 202, 204, 205, 207-210, 220, 221
Muhī-ul-Millat—Jahāngīr II., 212
Muir, Sir William, 391
Col., 246
Mū'iz ud-dīn Jahāndār Shāh, Sultān, 154
Mū'iz ul-Mulk, Gujarāt, 95
Mukand Deva of Orissa, 42
Mukandwāra pass, 286
Mūk-arasu—Kanthīrava rāja, 147
Mukarram Khān, Bengal, 81
Mukhtar Khān, Gujarāt, 126, 130
Mukhtrāv—Jankujirāv Sindia, 322
Mukwais, 124
Mulakot state, 39
Mulbāgal, 226, 227
Mulhēr, 91
Mulk Murjan, 23
Mulkāpur, battle, 67
mulkgiri taxation, 291
Mullā Husain, Kābul, 336, 337
Muhammad 'Alī of Athva, 171, 172
Mushk-ī-'Alam, Ghilzai, 409
Pāwandā, 430
Shī'ah Ahmad, 53
Mulrāj, Multān, 350-353
Multān, 6, 19, 20, 104, 113, 266, 350-353, 373
Mumtāz Mahall, Nawāb 'Aliā Begam, 76, 85
Munden, Capt., 117
Munghi-Paitān, 37, 179
Mun'im Khān,—Khān Khānān, 36, 46, 47
Khān, Khān Khānān, 153
Khan, Surat, 155, 156, 168
Munīr Muhammad Khān of Bhopāl, 313, 323
Munīr ul-Mulk—Chandu Lāl, 293, 328, 343
Munkirru, 184
Munro, General Sir Hector, 217, 221, 240, 241, 245, 248
Col. John, 293, 297
Sir Thomas, 314, 322
Muntakhab ut-Tawārikh, 59; 312
Muqarrab Khān--Shaikh Hassan, 67, 72, 78
Khān, 132
Murād, Sultān, 56, 58-60
'Alī, Sindh, 280
Bakhsh, prince, 94, 95-101, 103, 104, 106, 107
Murray, Col., 286
Murshid Qulī Ja'far Khān, 145, 147, 150, 159, 162, 180, 181
Murshidābād, 145, 147, 149, 203, 204, 207, 213, 214, 219, 223, 228, 230, 231, 233, 236, 266, 319, 390
Murtazā 'Alī Khān of Vēlūr, 182, 184, 195, 205, 209
Nizām Shāh, 41, 44, 54, 66, 84, 85
Musa-khel Patāns, 409, 410
Muslim riots, 355, 415
Mustafā Khān, 184
Rūmī, 22
Mustafānagar, 204
Mūswē Khan,—Fitrat, 133
Mutta Krishnappa, 63
Virappa, 67
Muzaffar Beg, 207, 209
Husain, Mirza, Safawī, 58
Husain, author, 224
Jang of Arkāt, 188-192, 196
Khān-i-Turbatī, Khwājah, 49
Shāh II. of Gujarāt, 11-20

Muzaffar Shāh III. of Gujarāt, 39, 45, 50, 51, 55, 57
Shāh of Bengal, 1, 3
Muzaffarnagar, 195, 224
Myahtūn, dākaīt, 357
Myauku—Arakan city, 320
Myēdē, 320, 321
Myingaing, prince, 414
Myingun, prince, 408, 410, 414
Mying-an, 413
Mysore, *see* Maisur

NĀBHA, 99, 289, 349, 362
Nabiganj, 229
Nādir Shāh, 170, 176-179, 186; 228
Nādira Begam, 90
Nadīya, 221
Naf riv., 317
Nāgās, 356, 392, 400-403
Nāgama Nāyakka, 37
Nāgapurīya Lampaka sect, 12
Nāgar Brāhmans, 166
Nāgar rāiyats, 326, 327
Nāgar tribes, 424
Nāgari inscription, 5
Nāgoji Manē of Mhaswad, 140
Nāgor, 23, 29, 39, 41, 206
Nāgpur, 199, 222, 308
Nāgūr,—Nagore, 232, 234
Nāhan, 302
Nāhr Singh of Rājpīpla, 313, 316
Naingtaung, 429
Nainī-Tāl, 405
Nainiya Pillai, 159
Nairne, General Sir Charles Ed., 428
Najaf Khān Zulfiqār Khān, 250, 255
Qulī Khān, 259, 265
Najafgarh, battle, 365
Najīb ud-daula, Rohila, 220, 228, 230
Najībullah, Arkāt, 202, 209, 210
Najm Khān of Khambay, 261
Najm ud-daula of Bengal, 222, 223, 225
Nakal-Rām of Kachār, 345, 356
Nalagarh fort, 302
Nalapāni or Kalanga fort, 302
Naldrug, 376
Nāmdār Khān, Pendhārī, 309
Nāna Arjun, 263
Phadnavis, 241-243, 246, 255, 263, 265, 268, 270-272, 277
Sāhib—Dhundhū-panth, 362-365, 367, 373-375, 391
Nānak, 1st Sikh Guru, 27
Nand-Kumār, mahārāja, 221, 222, 231, 237
Nanda Rāja of Maisūr, 217
Nandēr, 85, 151
Nandidurg, 264, 275
Nandurbār, 138, 139
Naning, 327
Nanja Rāja Udayār, 224, 229
Nanjangadh, 116
Napier, General Sir Charles, 341-343, 346, 352-354
Lord Francis, of Merchiston, 382, 388
Field-Marshal Lord Robert C., of Magdala, 372, 373, 383, 384, 393
Napoleon Bonaparte, 296
Nārat pass, 369
Narasa Nāyyaka, 5
Pillai Nāyyaka, 14
Narasa or Narasimha I., of Vijayanagar, 2, 10
Narawara of Burma, 115
Narāyan Singh of Sambalpur, 352
Narāyan Dīn of Ganjām, 211
Narāyanrāv, 5th Peshwa, 232, 234, 235
Narbadā,—Narmadā riv., 80, 176, 183, 244, 324, 332
Narendra Narāyan of Kūch Bihār, 378
Singh of Patiāla, 378
Nargund, 256, 258, 371, 372
Nariād, 280
Narikelbāriā, 328
Narnāl, 165
Narnālā fort, 284
Naroji of Bikanīr, 7
Narpat, or Nirpat Singh, Rādamau, 370
Narsāpur, 192
Narsingh Deo, 62
Pāl of Karauli, 356
Narsinhgarh, 300
Narsingpur, 215
Narwār, 9
Nasanpur, battle, 368
Nash, Lieut., 264
Nāsir Jang, Nawāb Nizām ud-daula, 179, 180, 185, 188, 190-193
Mirzā, of Persia, 178
Nāsir ud-daula, Nizām, 325, 326, 328, 354, 357, 358, 361
ud-dīn Nasrat Shāh of Bengal, 16, 17, 23, 24
ud-dīn of Persia, 409
ud-dīn II. of Mālwa, 5, 11
ud-dīn Haidar of Audh, 323, 325, 327
ud-dīn of Surat, 315
Nasīrābād, 362, 363
Nasīri Khān, 85
Nasīrī battalion, 354
Nasr-ullah of Bokhārā, 341

Nāthdwāra, 315
Native Education Society, 317
    magistrates, 331
Nātsheng of Taungu, 68, 69
Naungdoagyī of Burma, 213, 220
Nau Nihāl Singh, Lāhor, 338
Naushahr, 294
Naushahra, 317, 322, 361, 362
Naval Singh of Bharatpur, 234
Naval Brigade, 366, 367
Navarro, Mr, 132
Nawābganj, battle, 372
Nawanagar, 54, 77, 92 ; 109
Nāyak of Kashmir, 32, 33
Nāyars, 107, 292
Nazar 'Alī Khān, Bharoch, 134
    Muhammad Khān of Balkh, 95, 96
    Muhammad Khān of Bhopāl, 304, 313
Nazarābād,—Maisūr, 259
Nazir Khān of Khairpur, 342
Nazir ud-dīn, Surat, 274, 277
Nē Weng Bureng, 321
Nedham, Mr, 126
Negambo, Ceylon, 92, 94, 270
Negapatam,—Nāgapattan, 105, 106, 180, 186, 206, 248, 249, 251, 377
Negrais, Burma, 199, 203, 211
Neill, Brig.-General James G. S., 362, 364-366
Neko-siyar Sultan, prince, 160
Nelikotta, 198
Nellor,—Nelūr, 202, 207, 395
Nepal, 225, 228, 230, 265, 272, 282, 285, 300-303, 305, 330, 338, 343, 346, 353, 368, 373, 422
Nepāl Taraī, 225, 374
Nepean, Sir Evan, 299
Neri dākaīti, 399
Nestorians, 143
Neutim, or Nivti, fort, 186, 198, 259, 299, 312
Newa fort, 312
Newberie, John, 51
Ngyaungbengzaik, 320
Niāmat-ullah, author, 70
Nicholas, Mr, 70
Nichols, Mr, judge, 117, 119, 121
Nicholls, General Sir Jasper, 302, 304, 340
Nicholson, Admiral, 129
    Brig.-General John, 351, 362, 364-366
"Nicote,"—Ph. de Brito, 62, 64, 68-70
Nieva, Dom Antonio Taviera da, 221
Nihāl Singh of Kapūrthala, 356
    Singh of Dholpur, 390
Nihang Khān, Ahmadnagar, 61
Nikapeti, Singhalese, 74
Nikobar islands, 349
Nīl Darpan, drama, 376
Nīlgiri state, Orissa, 126
Nilt fort, 424
Nīmghāt, 308
Nimla, battle, 296
Nipendra Narāyan of Kūch Bihār, 378
Nīra riv., 132
Nivti fort, 186, 198, 259, 299, 312
Nizām 'Alī Khān of Haidarābād, 206, 207, 217, 218, 220, 222-226, 231, 243, 255, 257, 259, 261, 263-265, 268, 269, 271, 273-276, 278, 282, 283
Nizām Khān Sūr, 33
Nizām Shāh, 74
Nizām ud-dīn Ahmad, historian, 54
    ud-dīn Khān, Surat, 265, 274, 276, 277
    ul-Mulk Ahmadābād, 13
    ul-Mulk, 21, 25
    ul-Mulk, 83, 90
    ul-Mulk, 'Asaf Jāh, 155, 160, 161, 163, 166, 168, 171, 175, 176, 178-185, 188; 189, 192, 194, 210, 217
    ul-Mulk, Chitral, 426, 427, 430
Nizāmat 'Adālat courts, 266
Nizāmat Fund, 358
Nizāmpatam, 68, 117, 122, 146, 192, 209
Noagong, Arakan, 319
Nong-klao, Kāsia, 325
Nong-spung state, Kāsia, 325
Norman, Chief Justice John Paxton, 387
    Lieut.-General Sir Francis B., 402, 413
Noronha, Affonso da, 32
    Dom Affonso de, 78
    Antonio de, 41, 42, 45, 51
    Dom Constantine de Sae, 84
    Diogo de, 33
    Fernando de, 33
    Francisco de, 83
    Dom Garcia de, 27
    Dom Lourenço de, 183
    Dom Pedro Antonio de, Conde de Villa Verde, 135, 141
Norris, John, 87, 88
    Sir William, 142-145
    Judge, 408
North, Lord Frederick, 247
    The Hon. Frederick, 274
Northbrook, Thomas G. Baring, Earl of, 389, 393, 394
North-West frontier, 345

Noton, Capt., 318
Nott, Major-General Sir William, 338-342
Nūr Jahān Begam, 81-83, 95
Nūr Muhammad, Afghān, 395
Nūr Singh of Manipur, 345, 354
Nūrpur fort, 93
Nusting, 325
Nuttal, Maj.-General Sir James M., 387
Nwengal Chins, 427
Nyaung Rām Meng of Burma, 64
Nyaungok, Burmese prince, 404
Nyaungywē, 416

OAKLEY, Sir Charles, 265, 268
Ochterlony, Major-General Sir David, 287, 293, 302-304, 320
Oghi, Hazāra, 384
Oghzlu Sultān, 63
Okhāmandal, 304, 314, 383
Okpho, battle, 428
Oktamā, dākaīt, 416, 421
Olala, or Ullāla, Malabar, 35, 42
Onāu, Audh, 364, 366
Opium Commission, 429
Orakzaīs, 423, 424
Orangal,—Warangal, 14, 151
Orissa, 36, 42, 47-49, 51, 56, 59, 79, 80, 87, 102, 139, 173, 179, 180, 232, 283, 286, 305, 381, 383
Ormuz, 8, 13, 14, 18, 29, 32, 33, 51, 52, 78, 80, 133
Oruzghān Hazāras, 426
Osborne, Col. W., 368
Ostend E.I. Company, 156, 158, 163-165, 167, 168, 170
Oudh, *see* Audh
Ouseley, Sir Gore, 296
Outram, Lieut.-General Sir James, 321, 342, 345, 359-361, 366-369
Oxinden, Sir George, 102, 108, 109, 112
Sir Henry, 118, 121

PACEM, state, 16, 18
Pacheco, Duarte de, 7
Pachim, Sumatra, 17
Padanpalli, 331
Pādapatam fort, 59
Pādra, 386
Padrou, Antonio del, 31
Pagān, 321, 420
Pagan Meng of Burma, 355, 357
Paghman, battle, 402
Pahang, Malacca, 18
Paitan, or Paithan, 37
Paiwār pass, 398
Pakokku, 413, 416
Pālakol, 287
Pālampur, Kāngra, 387
Palandu, Ceylon, 35
Pālanpur, Gujarāt, 158, 305
Palap, 427
Palarūn, 109, 112
Palaspē, Konkan, 399
Pālegārs, 192, 199, 200, 202, 209, 210, 219, 248, 258
Pālghāt, 262, 267
Pālghātcheri, 253
Palha, Joaquim Garcez, 343, 345
Paliār, 131
Pāligarh, 124
Palikāt (Geldria),—Pulicat, 68, 76, 79, 81, 88, 99, 122, 247
Palk, Sir Robert, 196, 220
Palmer, Lieut.-General William, 273
John, & Co., Calcutta, 326
William, & Co., Haidarābād, 314, 315, 320, 328
Col., 340
Pamirs, 428
Palni, 147
Palosi, 419
Panamalī, 131
Panchamal, 263
panchāyats, 301
Pandar, Ceylon, 74
Pandharpur treaty, 299, 303
Pāndu riv., 364
Pāndya, prince, 63
Pāngal, Haidarābād, 37, 263
Panhāla fort, 105, 106, 112, 117, 118, 124, 144, 151, 153, 171, 345
Pānīpat, 19, 215, 216
Panjāb, 16, 41, 47, 60, 84, 105, 151, 191, 193, 211, 225, 277, 288, 347, 349, 352, 361, 375, 388
Panjāb Tenancy Bill, 384
Panjaram of Java, 76
Panjdeh, 411, 414
Panjim—New Goa, 149, 395
Panna, Bundelkhand, 187, 263
Panniār, battle, 344
Pant Sachiv, 156; Mustafā Maherban, 314
Pantalāyini Kollam, 4
Panwāri dist., 296
Pānwel, 246
Pāp Raī, freebooter, 151
Pāpanavaram fort, 293
Papillon, Mr, 141
Parākrama Pāndya Kulashekara, 5
Parashurām Bhāu Patwardhan, 240, 246, 261, 263, 264, 271

Parashurām Bhonsla, 304, 305, 308
Trimbak, Pratinidhi, 134, 150
Parenda, Nāldurg dist., 87
Parijong, 298
Parikshit Rāo of Datiyā, 286, 337
Parindhar Singh, Burma, 316
Paris, Treaty of, 220; with Burmese, 411, 412
Parker, John, 77
Parnāla fort, 43, 134, 144
Parsa, Nepal Tarai, 302
Pārsīs, 328, 355, 359, 391
Paru, Malabar, 71
Pārūr, Malabar, 62
Pārvatī Rānī of Travankor, 297, 302
Parwāndara, battle, 338
Parwīz, prince, 66, 78, 80, 81
Pasachandra, Jaina sect, 14
Passanha, Dom Sebastião de Andrade, 158
Pātan—Anhilwāra, 45, 71
Būndī, 146, 183, 262
Patanī temple, 59
Pathrī, or Patrī, Kāndesh, 20, 306
Patiāla, 99, 223, 289, 347, 349, 362, 367, 375
Patīta, 248
Patli, Murshidābād dist., 203
Pātna, 47, 68, 77, 78, 104, 109, 110, 120, 123, 129, 145, 146, 154, 184, 188, 191, 205, 209, 213, 216, 217, 219, 221, 231, 236, 265, 266, 289, 293, 356, 429
Paton, Major, 303
Patta, 115, 119
Patwardhan jagīrdārs, 299
Paul II., pope, 26; III., 37; IV., 102
Pāwangadh, 244, 283
Pawāra Mahādhamma of Burma, 115
Paya, Jawākī dist., 396
Pāyandah Muhammad Tarkhān, 18
Peach, Col., 226
"peacock throne," 86, 87, 178
Pedda Nāyyak, 105
Venkatādri, 124
Peddapalli — Arjampatnam, Nizampatnam, 68, 75, 117, 122, 146, 192, 209
Peddapur, 208
Peel, Capt. Sir William, 366, 367, 371
Pegu, 16, 27, 40, 41, 60, 62, 163, 179, 201, 203, 237, 318, 356, 357
Peile, Sir James B., 411
Pekin, 298
Pelerino, Order of the, 31
Pellew, Edward, 291
Pelly, Sir Lewis, 392, 394, 395
Pemberton, Capt. Robert B., 320
Penal Code, 377
Penang island, 257, 289, 320, 325
Pendārīs, 295, 298-300, 303-310, 317
Peninsular and Oriental steamers, 342
Penlosor governors, Bhutan, 422
Pennāgaram fort, 264
Pennar riv., 195
Penukonda, 42, 47
"Pepper country," 33; "contract," 266
Perambūr, 152
Pereira, Francisco, 178
Francisco Xavier da Silva, 342
Gonzalo, 24, 42, 46
João, 25
João Vaz, 221
Perez, navigator, 14, 15
Periya Krishnappa, 40, 46
Virappa, 46
Periyāpatna, battle, 275
Permakoil, 251
Permanent Revenue Settlement, 267
Perron, General Pierre, 246, 265, 277, 279, 282-284
Persia, 63, 72, 131, 146, 157, 158, 164, 186, 276, 277, 292, 323, 325, 334, 335, 337, 360, 361, 378, 406, 417
treaty with, 361
Persian Gulf, 79, 97, 296, 313, 315, 360
Perumbākam, battle, 245
Peshāwar, 177, 211, 288, 292, 294, 317, 322, 335, 342, 351, 355, 359-361, 366, 394, 395, 397, 405, 428
Peshbolak, 408
Peshwas, 21; 124, 150, 163, 167, 198, 200, 201, 215-217, 222, 226, 227, 243, 244, 246, 247, 260, 261, 265, 267-269, 277-279, 281, 282, 284, 286, 298-301, 303, 306-313
Pestana, José Ferreira, 345, 354, 380
Petit, Mr, 126
Petlād, 158, 337
Petrie, William, 291
Major, 270
Peyton, Mr, 186
Phaltan Deshmukh, 314
Phayre, Sir Arthur P., 359, 413
General Sir Robert, 389, 391, 392
Mr, 414
Philaur, 347, 348, 361, 362
Philip II. of Spain, 50
Philippine Islands, 219
Phipps, Hon. William, 161, 168
Phond Sāwant II., 152-154, 170, 177; III., 291, 299
Phonda fort, 18, 126, 167, 181, 200, 215, 263
Pichard, Ensign, 197

Pigot, Lord George, 198, 216, 220, 238-240
Pilāji Gaikwād, 160, 165-168, 171, 172
Pimentel, Martin Affonso, 43
Pinhero, Paul de Rego, 63
Piplī, 88, 286
Pīr Muhammad Khān Shirwāni, 39
Piram island, 169
Pirarāja of Kurg, 262
Piro fort, 263, 266
Pishīn, 397, 399, 406, 417
Pitman, Major, 312
Pitt, George Morton, 169, 174
  Consul John, 143, 146
  Thomas, 140, 143-145, 152
  William: his East India Bills, 247, 255
Pleydell, Mr, 216
Plutschau, Rev. Hendrik, 149
Pococke, Admiral Sir George, 204, 205, 208
Plassey,—Palāsī, battle of, 203
Point de Galle, 116
Polarūn, 76, 100, 106, 107, 110, 111
Pollock, Field-Marshal Sir George, 340-342
  Col. John A. Henry, 396
Polor,—Polūr, Karnūl, 210
Polosī, Būnēr, 327
Polwhele, Brigadier, 364
Pombai, 426
Pondicheri, 118, 120, 126, 130, 136, 143, 144, 149, 151, 152, 159, 164, 165, 167, 177-183, 185-187, 189, 190, 192, 196-199, 204, 206, 207, 211-216, 239, 241, 246, 253, 255, 267, 280, 283, 304, 410
Poniapa, interpreter, 197
Ponkān Kachīns, 420
Ponnāni, Malabar, 9, 19, 52, 251, 411
Poona,—Pūna, 106, 109, 190, 191, 201, 216, 217, 226, 231, 236, 237, 239, 240, 242, 255, 256, 263, 265, 269, 271, 272, 277, 278, 281, 282, 287, 297, 300, 301, 306-308, 311, 359, 398, 399, 422, 430
  Treaty of, 286, 306
Popa, Mount, 420
Popham, Lieut.-General William, 244, 248
poppy cultivation, 391
Porca,—Purakkat, 21
Port Blair, 388
  Louis, 297
Porter, Endymion, 88
  W. N., 429
Porto Novo,—Parangipettai, 146, 180, 246, 250, 253
Portman, Rev. Richard, 124
Portugal, Portuguese, 22, 37, 53, 66, 67, 72, 82, 83, 85-95, 100, 115, 129, 139, 143, 154-156; 160, 167, 168, 170, 171, 175, 177, 180, 205, 375, 385, 389
Portugal, Dom Manuel de, 332
  Dom Pedro Miguel de Almeida e, 184
postage, 358
Pottinger, Major Eldred, 335, 339
  Lieut.-General Sir Henry, 350, 358
Powell, Col., 284
  Capt., 366
Prabhās-Pattan or Por-patan, Virāwal, 158
Prāgmalji Bahādur of Kachh, 376, 393
Prahlad Niraji, Pratinidhi, 132
Prasād, Rānā of Amarkot, 28
Pratāp Singh I., or Kīkā, Rānā of Mewār, 117, 118
  Singh II., 193, 199
  Singh of Tanjor, 179, 180, 189, 190
  Singh of Nepāl, 230
  Singh of Jaypur, 242, 259, 285, 310
  Singh of Rājpīpla, 296
  Singh of Sātāra, 292, 296, 309, 310, 313, 325, 337
  Singh, Lāhor, 343
  Singh of Kashmīr, 412
Pratāpgarh, 311, 373
Pratinidhi, 132, 169, 173, 189, 314
Prem Sāgar, 285
Prendergast, Col. Sir Harry N. D., 413, 414
Preston, Capt., 208, 212, 216
Price, Mr, 202
  Major David, 326
  Rev. Dr, missionary, 321
Prideaux, Lieut., 306
Primrose, General James M., 404
Pring, Capt., 76, 77
Prinsep, Geo., 324
Prīthī Narāyan of Nepāl, 230
  Singh of Jaypur, 242
  Singh of Kishnagar, 337
  Singh of Jhālāvar, 394
Pritzler, General Sir Theophilus, 309
Prom, Burma, 28, 66, 107, 312, 320, 356, 357, 415
Provostière, M. de la, 159, 163, 167
Pul-i-Kishti, 411
Pulo Condore island, 145, 146, 148
Punākha, Bhutān, 379

Pūnamallī, Chingalpat, 136
Pūr dist., 124
Puragarh—Mahishāsur, Mysore, 19
Purakkāt,—Poracaud, 21
Pūran Mall, Raisīn, 29
Purandhar, 114, 144, 155, 156, 238, 241
Purandhar Singh, Asām, 329
Puranīya dist., 213, 292, 314
Purenda, 106
Purī,—Jagannāth Purī, 283, 306, 404
Purnaya, of Maisur, 252, 275, 276, 298, 299
Purnem, 259, 278
Putakonda, 322
Putuppattanam or Kotta, 60
Puzan Myang, Burma, 415

QADAM Khān, 39
Qāim Qulī Khān, 180
Qamar ud-dīn Khān, 162, 188
Qandahār, 13, 14, 16, 28, 29, 57, 58, 63, 65, 66, 78, 79, 97-100, 152-155, 164, 175, 176, 187, 267, 274, 278, 292, 334-337, 340, 341, 360, 361, 382, 384, 401-406, 409, 426, 427
Qāsim 'Alī Khān Mīr, or Mir Qāsim, 214, 216-219, 221, 222
Barīd Shāh I., 2, 7
Khān of Bengal, 70, 85, 86
Khān, Mughal general, 137
Qāzī 'Abdullah, Dhāka, 154
Fazīlat, Amīn, 28
Hasan Qazwīn, 57
Quarter Sessions, 167
Qudsia Begam of Bhopāl, 313, 323, 329, 335
Quedā,—Kedah, 257, 263, 279
Quetta or Shālkōt, 394, 405, 410, 417, 420, 425, 428
Quilon, *see* Kollam
Quinton, James Wallace, 423
Qulī Qutb ul-Mulk, 12, 29
Qulij Khān of Kābul, 57
Khān Andajānī, 65
Qutb ud-dīn Khān, Shaikh Khūbū, 65
Qutlū Khān Lohānī, 51
Qutlugh Khān Afkān, 56

RABATA, Kurg, 331
Rachol, 25, 100
Rādamau, 370
Raffles, Sir T. Stamford, 297, 310, 312,
Rafi' ud-Darjāt, 160
ud-daula Shāhjahān II., 160
ush-Shān, 153, 162
Rāghoba Peshwa—Raghunāth-rāv, 198, 205, 217, 218, 220, 221, 223, 224, 226, 231-238, 240, 241, 243, 255
Rāghoji Bhonsla I., 178, 179, 181-184, 190, 195
Bhonsla II., 233, 271, 284, 301, 304
Bhonsla III., 357
Pant, 170, 175
Āngria II., 336, 338
Raghunāth Dās, 193
Nāyyak of Tanjor, 78
Raghugarh, 256
Rahātgarh, 368
Rahīm Gar Muhammad, 372
Shāh Khān, Afghān, 137, 140
Rahīmdād Khān, Tarakzāi, 358
Rāhūn, battle, 151
Rai Barēlī, 305, 316
Rāi Bulchand, trader, 126
Rāi Singh of Bikanīr, 44, 45, 86
Rāi Singh of Nawanagar, 109
Raichūr, 6, 16, 21, 29, 376
Rāidurg, 219
Rāigarh fort, 132, 174, 311
Raila, Nepāl, 303
railways, 346, 357, 360, 377, 384, 399, 405, 420
Raimal Rānā or Rājamalla of Mewār, 2, 10, 14
Rainsford, Col., 104
Raipur Ghāt treaty, 289
Rairī fort, 118, 123, 312
Raisīn fort, 23, 29
Rāj-abhishēk era, 109
Rājabullab, Murshidābād, 207
Rāja-Rām of Kolhāpur, 382, 386
Rāja Sāhib of Kanātak, 193, 210
Rāja Singh of Bikanīr, 259
Singh of Mewār, 100, 125
Rājapur, 90, 117-119, 136
Rājasekhara Vilasa, poem, 103
Rājaur, 82
Rājendra Pratāp Shāhi of Husainpur, 387
Narāyan Kuār of Kuch Bihār, 349
Singh of Patiāla, 394, 395
Singh of Jaintia, 329
Vikrama Sāh of Nepāl, 305
Rājgarh fort, 110, 112, 123, 144, 147, 302, 366
Rāj Guru, Burman, 321
Rājkonda, 12
Rājmahāl, 47, 139, 145, 146, 184, 204, 213
Rājmahendri,—Rājmandri, 195, 204, 208, 224
Rājpīpla, 51, 296, 313, 316

Rājputs, Rājputāna, 21, 23, 43, 122, 123, 178, 214, 275, 276, 309, 332
Rājshāhi, 228
Rāju, Singhalese tyrant, 41
Rākshāsbhuvan, battle, 220
Rāmadeva III., Chikka, of Chandragīri, 71
Rāma Kāmāti, Bombay, 159, 161
Rāmaji Pant, 198, 200
Rāma Rāja I. of Sātāra, 123, 132-134, 138, 140, 142, 143, 152, 154
Rāja II., of Sātāra, 189, 198, 202, 240
Rāya of Vijayanagar, 29, 37, 39, 41-43
Rāmchandra Jādav, 200
Puār of Dhār, 330
Pandit—Rāmchand Pant, 134, 143
Sāwant, 177, 199
Rāmdās, 4th Sikh Guru, 50
Rām-mohan Rāi, 263, 305, 324, 327
Rāmnagar, 67, 112, 159, 247, 338, 351
Rāmnarāyan, Bihār, 191, 204
Tarkaratna, author, 360
Rampa, Godāvari dist., 399, 405
Rāmpur, Rohilkhand, 268
Rāmpura, Rājputana, 286, 309
Rām-rāi, Sikh, 105
Rām Singh of Būndi, 315, 318
Singh I. of Jaypur, 112
Singh II. of Jaypur, 333
Singh of Jodhpur, 195, 234
Singh I. of Kotā, 150
Singh II. of Kotā, 382
Singh of Rājpīpla, 296
Singh, Sikh, 351
Singh, Kūka rebel, 388
Rāmoshīs,—Ramusis, 398, 399
Rāmrī island, 255
Rāmu, Arakan, 318
Ramsay, Andrew, 259
George, 9th Earl of Dalhousie, 326
Rānā Bahādur of Nepāl, 270, 272, 280, 285, 289
Rānā Khān, 260
Rānā Mohan Singh of Narwār, 311, 312
Ranadhīra Kanthīrava Narasu of Maisūr, 91
Ranbīr Singh of Kapūrthala, 386
Singh of Kashmīr, 412
Randatarra, 259
Randhir Singh of Bharatpur, 317
Singh of Kapūrthala, 356, 374
Randhula Khān, 90
Ranga Rāya of Pennakonda, 47
Krishna Muttu Virappa, 128, 135, 148
Krishna Nayyak, 173
Ranga-Rāo, Pālegār, Vizagapatam, 202
Rangarāv Urekur, Dhār, 244
Ranga Rāyal of Chandragiri, 91, 93, 95, 96
Rāngna fort, 106, 150, 313, 345
Rangoji, agent of Damāji Gaikwad, 178
Rangpur, 298, 319, 324
Rangucharlia, dīwān, Maisūr, 408
Rāngūn, 199, 237, 269, 271, 285, 298, 299, 318, 319, 354-356, 368, 388, 393, 403, 407, 410, 413-415, 420, 421, 428-430
Ranier, Peter, 270
Ranjit Rāo, Calcutta, 202
Singh, Bharatpur, 234, 250
Singh of Jaisalmīr, 381
Singh, Lāhor, 274, 287-290, 292, 293, 313, 315, 322, 327-329, 331, 332, 335, 337, 343
Singh of Samthar, 313
Ranjūr Singh, Sardār of Majīthia, 347
Rānmalji of Nauanagar, 109
Rānoji Sindia, 173
Ranthambor, 14, 21, 44
Ranuri, battle, 11
Rāo Sāhib, rebel, 374, 378
Raqia Sultāna, 33
Rārim fort, 186, 198
Ras al Khima, Persian Gulf, 296, 313
Rastell, Thomas, 80, 82
Rasūl—Chilianwālā, 352
Ratansingh,—Ratnasingh, of Bharatpur, 227
Bandhari, 174, 175
of Bikanīr, 356
Ratanpur, 148, 161
Ratnagīri, 413
Ratnasimha Rānā of Mewār, 22, 23
Rattihalli, 12, 221
Raushan Beg, Indor, 308, 309
Raushānīa sect, 54
Rauzat us-Safā of Mirkhond, 17
Rausat ut Tahirin, history, 63
Ravivarmā of Chirakkal, 222
of Kochin, 357, 379
Rāvji Appaji, Baroda, 278
Rāwal Pindī, 343, 411
Rawat Singh of Lāwa, 383
Rawlinson, Col. Sir Henry, 340
Raworth, George, 153
Rāy Singh, 173
Rāyaji Patel, 256
Rāyadhan III. of Kachh, 242, 257, 281
Rāydurg, 258
Rāyakota, 264
Raymond, Mons. M. J. M., 255, 261, 269, 273, 274
Reade, Col., 275
Reay, Lord, 411, 421, 422
Reddi Rāo, accountant, 293

Redonde, Conde de, 74
Red Sea, 138, 326
Reed, General Sir Thomas, 364
Reid, General Sir Charles, 363
 Hon. Lestock Robert, 348
Reinhardt, Walter—"Samru," 219, 221, 242
Renault, Pierre, 202
René, Madec, 232
Rennie, Capt. James, I.N., 356, 361
Renukābāī Daphle of Jath, 314
"Resolution," warship, 277
Revadanda, 23, 180
Revington, Mr, 102
Rewā, 298, 299, 301
Reynolds, Major, 383
Rheede, Hendrik Adrian Darakenstein van, 116
Ribeiro, John, S.J., 145, 163
Richards, Major, 304
 Major-General Sir William, 318, 319
Richelieu, Cardinal Armand J. du Plessis, 94
Richmond, Col., 349
riots, 152, 304, 355, 387, 415, 428, 430
Ripaud, Capt., 272
Ripon, Marquis of, 345, 404, 407, 409, 410
Rivett-Carnac, Sir James, 337
Robert de Nobilibus, 65, 81
Roberts, Gabriel, 146
 Field-Marshal Lord Frederick S., 355, 370, 397, 398, 400, 403-405, 412, 414-416, 425, 427
 Major-General Sir Henry Gee, 347
Robertson, Sir George Scott, M.D., 427
Robinson, Sir Wm. Rose, 390, 393
Rochester, Lord, 127
Rochford, Lieut., 326
Rockingham, Lord, 251
Rodriguez island, 295
Roe, Sir Thomas, 72, 73, 75, 76
Rohan, Banda islands, 73
Rohilas, 185, 189, 191, 211, 217, 230, 231, 234-236, 271, 358, 408
Rohilkhand, 234, 235, 239, 280, 281, 364, 374
Rohtak, 273, 365
Rohtās, 23, 26, 48, 60, 64, 81
Rolt, Mr, 104
Rolte, Hon. Thomas, 121
Roman Catholic Church, 108, 332, 347, 349, 350, 353, 375
Rome, Burmese embassy at, 411
Romer, John, 327
Rose, Lieut., 372
 General Sir Hugh, 368-372, 381; 413
Roshan Akhtar, Muhammad Shāh Sultān, 160-188
Rowcroft, Col., 368, 370, 372, 373
Royal Proclamation, 373
Roz, Francisco, 62
Rūhullāh Khān, 137
Ruiyā fort, 370
Rūjan Singh, Āsām, 325
Rumbold, Sir Thomas, 240, 241, 243, 254
 Sir William, 315
Rūmi Khān, 30
Rundall, Capt. F. M., 423
Rupar, 119, 328
Rūparshi, Nagapurīya Jaina, 12
Rūrkī, 349, 358
Rustam, Bombay broker, 151
Rustam 'Alī, author, 181
 'Alī Khan, 164, 165
 Khān, 44, 52
 Khān of Khairpur, 341
 Zamān, Bījāpur, 105
Russell, George Edward, 333
Russia, 334, 358, 385, 389, 390, 397, 402, 403, 411, 414, 424, 425, 427
 Company, 37
Ryswick, Treaty of, 136

SA, Garcia da, 31
 Sa Henrique da, 40
 Sa Vasco de, 40
Sa e Naronha, Constantine da, 75
Saadābād, 176
Sa'ādat 'Alī I. of Audh, 30
 'Alī II. of Audh, 272, 277
 Khān of Audh, 175
 Khan, Afghān, 355
 Ullāh Khān I. of the Karnātak, 151, 152, 172, 179; II., 184
Sabaji Bhonsla, 233
Sabrosa, Simão Infante de Lacerda Barão de, 335
Sabzalkot, Sindh, 342
Sabzi-mandi, 363, 364
Sādadi inscription, 60
Sādan Khān, rebel, 391
Sādar Malla, Maisur, 326
Sadāshiva of Vijayanagar, 29, 43
Sadāshiv Bhāu, 212, 214-216
 Bhāu Mānkeshwar, 287
 Chimnāji Bhāu, 185
Sadāsukh Dehlavī, Munshi, writer, 312
Sādiq, son of Yāqūb Khān, 85
Sadiq 'Alī, Berār general, 295
 Khān of Bahāwalpur, 356
 Muhammad Khān of Bahāwalpur, 381

Sadīya, Āsām, 429
Sadler, Dr, 366
Sadon or Fort Harrison, 425
Sadras, 97, 196, 247
Sadr Dīwānī 'Adālat court, 230, 244, 245, 251, 266, 323
Sadr Nizāmat 'Adālat court, 231
Sa'dullah Khān, 96
Sadullahpur, battle, 351
Sadusām, battle, 351
Saduzāi tribes, 335
Safavī dynasty, Persia, 164, 166
Safdar 'Alī of Arkat, 179, 181, 182; 189
Jang of Audh, 189, 191, 194, 195, 197
Jang, Qandahār, 340
Khān Bābī, 148, 157
Muhammad Khān, 187, 193
Safi Quli Khān, 159
Sagaing, 416
Sagaing Meng—Hpagidoa of Burma, 312
Sāgar, 4, 306, 324, 329, 368, 369
Sahāranpur, 211, 230
Sāhib Jān, Gilzāi leader, 401
Khān of Mālwa, 12
Sahora, battle, 112
Sāhūjī, *see* Shāhu
Saibana fort, 170
Saïdāpet college, 395
Saif Khān, Muhammad Safi, 80, 91
Saif ud-daula of Bengal, 225, 228
Saighān, battle, 338
St Andrew's church, Bombay, 312
St Barbe, Mr, 400, 414
St David fort, Tegnapatam, 133, 135-137, 140
St George, Fort, 92, 94, 216, *see* Madras
St Helena island, 99, 103, 114, 117, 135, 146
St Iago, Ceylon, 92
St John's church, Calcutta, 157, 176
St John, Dr, 126, 128
St Joseph, Fr. Matheio de, 116
St Leger, Col., 294
St Lubin, Mons., 240
St Theresa, Don Frei Mauricio de, 161
Dom Ignacio de, 165, 172
St Thomas, the apostle, 31
church, Bombay, 159
Mount, 237, 239
St Thomé, 72, 114, 117, 118, 124, 130, 136, 186, 189, 208
Śaka reckoning, 1 *note*, 36
Sakhar bridge, 420
Sakhārām Ghātge Shirji Rāv, *see* Ghātge
Sakraypatna, Kadūr, 96
Sakwārbāī, Sātāra, 189
Salābat Jang, Sūbahdar, 192-196, 198, 200, 206, 209, 210, 217, 218
Khān, 52, 54
Khan Bābī, 172
Khan, Mīr Bakhshi, 94
Sālār Jang, Sir, 384, 385, 408
Sālbāi Treaty, 250, 252, 255, 261
Saldanha, Antonio de, 22
Ayres de, 61
Sale, Major-General Sir Robert Henry, 338-340, 346
Salem, Madras, 226, 407
Burma, 414
Sālēr fort, 115, 116
Salīm Khān—Islām Shāh Sūr, 30
Salīm Mirzā, 44, 62, 64
Salīmgarh, 104, 366
Salīmpur, 369
Salisbury, Marquis of, 391, 392
Salor fort, 58
Salpi Ghāt, 309
Salsette island, 30, 31, 51, 59, 100, 116, 170, 176, 178, 181, 236-238, 243, 250
Salshi mahāl, 150
saltpetre trade, 106, 134
Saluva Timma, Vijayanagar, 18
Salwīn river, 322
Samāchār Darpan, newspaper, 316
Samaji, Sindh, 112
Samāna, 423
Sāmāngadh, 345
Sāmānpur, 302
Samarang, Java, 297
Samarqand,—Samarkand, 4, 385
Sambad Prabhakar, Bengali monthly, 327
Sambaulin, Konkan, 215
Sambhāji I., 111, 112, 123-126, 128, 131, 132; II., 154, 163, 168, 169; 219
Angria, 171, 174, 175, 178-180
Sambhal, 5, 42
Sambhalpur, 289
Sambhar, 165, 174, 176
Sambhu or Abā Sāhib of Kolhāpur, 299
Singh of Udaypur, 377, 381, 391
Sambrooke, Jeremy, 111
Sampayo, Lopé Vaz de, 19-22
e Castro, Dom Francisco José de, 162, 165
Samru, Begam of Sardanha, 259, 266, 268, 270; *see* Reinhardt
Samthar, 218, 307
Samūgarh,—Fathābād, 104
Samvat era, 1 *note*, 36
sanads, 349, 375
Sanda, Arakan, 66

Sanda Thudhammā of Arakan, 105, 128
Sandeman, Sir Robert Groves, 394, 417, 421, 425
Sandoway, 255
Sandūr state, Belāri, 322, 339
Sandwīp, 66, 67, 69
Sangamesvar, 52, 132
Sangamner, 215
Sāngaza or Sānkshi, 28
Sanghī Jotārām, Jaypur, 332
Sangrān: Singh I. of Mewār, 10, 13, 16, 20-22, 26; II., 153, 173
Sangrāmnagar,—Ālamgīrnagar, 111
San-i-jalus years, 102
Sankalapura inscription, 13
"San Philippe" carrack, 53
San Sebastian fort, 42
Sanskrit college, Banāras, 266
Santa Rita, Fr. Constantino de, 334
Theresa, Fr. Maurico de, 155, 156
Santājī Ghorpade, 134, 135, 137, 138, 140
Santo Stephano, Hieronymo de, 3
Sānthāls, rising of, 359
Sarāi fort, 370; ghat, 367
Sarākhs, 410
Sārangpur, 39, 301
Sarbaland Khān, Nawāb Mubāriz ul-Mulk of Pātna, 165-167, 169, 170, 181
Sarceta, 38, 50
Sardaha, Audh, 126
Sardār Khān, Afghān, 188
Singh of Bikanir, 356
Singh, Rānā of Udaypur, 336, 342
sardesmukhī tax, 120, 168, 172
Sarfarāz Khān of Bengal, 179
Sarfoji of Tānjor, 258, 277
Sargujā Rāja, 376
Sarhind, 34, 205, 292, 388
canal, 407
Sarkārs districts, 207, 226, 241, 305
Sarkhej, 51, 157
Sarnāl, 46
Sarup Chand Khatrī, author, 269
Singh of Bikanir, 152
Singh of Udaypur, 342, 377
Sarzora, Konkan, 100
Sāsni, Rohilkhand, 281, 282
Satānatī—Sutānatī, Calcutta, 129, 140, 142
Sātāra, 112, 117, 135, 140-143, 150, 169, 180, 192, 202, 217, 240, 309-311, 313, 314, 325, 350, 375
Sātgāon, 26, 138
satī, 326, 349, 382
satiāsio kal,—S. 1687,—famine, 86
Satlaj riv., 110, 289, 293, 328-330, 346-348, 386
Satnāmīs or Mondhis, Vaishnava sect, 117, 126
Śatrunjaya inscriptions, 76, 77
Satya Prakāsh, Bombay newspaper, 377
Satyamangala, battle, 262
Saubinet, Mons., 207
Saulapā and Saulāwi, Karen-ni chiefs, 418, 420
Saulon, Karen-ni capital, 419, 420
Saunders, Thomas, 191, 198, 199
Saurī, battle, 282
Savandurg, 264
Sāvanūr, 192, 223, 257
Sawālik country, 57; pillar, 19
Sāwantwādi, 108, 150, 152, 170, 199, 278, 291, 298, 300, 312, 313, 329, 335
Saw Maung, Sawbwa, 416, 417
Sayājī of Tānjor, 181, 190
Sayājīrāv Gaikwād I., 226, 227, 261; II., 311, 313, 314, 337, 350; III., 392
Sāyvān fort, 44
Sayyid Achan, Surat, 187
Ahmad, Orissa, 180
Ahmad, Wahhābi, 305, 316, 318, 322, 327
Lashkar Khān, 193
Mīr Bāsha, Miranzāī, 423
Nūr Muhammad, 390
Muhammad of Jaunpur, 8
Muhammad Khān of Arkat, 182, 184
Murtazā Khān, Lucknow, 238
Murtazā Sabzwāri, 52
Shāhjī, Ismā'iliah, 134
Sayyid brothers of Bārha, 154, 155, 160
Schwartz, Rev. Christian Frederich, 191, 243
Scott, Col., 276
Col., 308
Scottish E.I. Company, 74, 138
Missionary Society, 326
Scrafton, Luke, 207, 227
Scudder, Dr John, 313
Seaton, Major-General Sir Thomas, 367, 368
Sebastian, K. of Portugal, 48
Segaulī, 304, 364
Seiwa, 143
Sellebar, 146
Senna, Imām of, 315
Seodan Singh of Alwār, 391
Seogānw, 106
Sequeyra, Diogo Lopes de, 15, 17
Sera district, 202
Serampur—Fredericksnagar, 199, 276, 316, 346
Sergio, Visconde de, 397

Seringapatam, 33, 68, 115, 116, 167, 185, 202, 229, 230, 253, 263, 264, 272, 275, 278, 294
Seton, Capt., 292
Seville, Treaty of, 168
Sewrī, Bombay, 132
Seymour, Sir William, 325
Shadakshara Deva, poet, 103
Shādar, Afghānistān, 105
Shādīpur, 396
Shafto, Capt., 401
Shāh Abbas of Persia, 78, 79, 97
'Alam, *see* Bahādur Shāh I.
Shahbāz, brother of Haidar 'Alī, 189
Khān Kambu of Bengal, 51, 53
Shāh Beg Arghūn, 13-15, 17, 18
Beg Arghūn Khān Daurān, 58, 63, 65, 66, 76
Shāhdaula, battle, 177
Shāhdhara, battle, 152
Shāhgarh, 370
Shāh Husain Arghūn, 19, 20
Husain Safavi, 164
Shāhjahān, Sultān, 71-74, 76-83, 86, 88-91, 95, 97-99, 102-104, 108, 111; 160
Sānī, Rafī'ud-daula, 160
II., Muhī ul-Millat, 212, 215
Shāh Jahān, fanatic, 409, 410
Shāhjahān Begam, Bhopāl, 359, 384, 389
Shāhjahānābād, New Dehli, 92, 104, 205, 212
Shāhjahānpur, 370, 371
Shāhjui, battle, 401
Shāhjī or Shāhūjī Bhonsla I., 57, 77, 82, 84, 86, 87, 89, 90, 98, 109; II., 150, 152-155, 157, 158, 163, 167-169, 189, 190, 197
Shāhū or Abba Sāhib of Sātāra, 292, 310, 337, 350
Shāhujī of Kolhāpur, 315, 316
of Tānjor, 177
Shāh Khalīl-ullāh, Imām, 306
Shāhkōt, 396
Shāh Muhammad, Amīr of Sindh, 343
Shāhnawāz Khān, 90
Khān, Samsām ud-daula, 195, 200
Khān of Kalāt, 337
Shāhpur, 291
Shahryār, Prince, 78, 82, 83
Shāh-rūd, 385
Shāh Safavī Tahmāsp, 29
Zamān of Qandahār, 254
Shaikan tribe, 424
Shaikāwati, 332
Shaikhapura, 349
Shaista Khān, Amīr ul-'Umarā, 89, 92, 96, 99, 106, 109, 111, 113, 120, 121, 123, 125, 128, 132
Shakespeare, Capt. John, 426
Shakhar-khera, battle, 166
Shālkōt or Quetta, 394
Shamānath Khān, 153, 155
Shāmli fort, 272
Shams Khān, Jālandhar, 151
Shams ud-dīn of Firuzpur, 333
ud-dīn of Ghaznī, 341
ud-dīn Muhammad Atgah, vazīr. 39
Shamsābād, battle, 368
Shamshīr Bahādur, Bānda, 281, 285, 317
Khān, Pāhlanpur, 300, 305
Shān states, 225, 416, 422, 427
Shankar Shāh, Gond rāja, 366
Shankarpur, 373
Shāpuri island, 317
Sharaf ud-dīn Husain, 40
Shattankād, village, 151
Shaxton, Capt., 118
Shekhābād, 382
Sheldon, Mr, 149
Sher Afkan 'Alī Qulī Istajlū, 65, 68
'Alī Khān, of Kābul, 378, 380, 382-387, 390, 392, 394, 397, 398, 403, 405
'Alī, assassin, 388
Khān, Gujarāt, 86
Khan, Jinjī, 118, 120
Khan, Kābul, 402
Khan, Bābī, of Junāgadh, 171-173, 206
Khan, Fūlādi, 50
Khan, Wali, Afghān, 404
Muhammad Khān of Kābul, 282, 283, 291
Shāh Afghān, 23-26, 27-30
Khān, Shah II., 36, 38
Singh, Lāhor, 339, 341, 343, 351, 352
Sherdil Khān of Kalāt, 378, 379
Sheridan, Richard Brinsley, 258
Sherpur, Kābul, 400, 402
Sherson, Mr, 292
Shī'ah sect, 29, 43, 152, 282
Shī'ah-Imāmī Ismā'īlias, 306, 382
Shighnān, 426
Shihāb ud-dīn, Khān of Mandū, 12, 13
Shihāb ud-dīn, Ahmad Khān, Gujarāt, 48, 51
Shikarpur, 330, 336
Shikohābād, 176, 283
Shillinge, Capt., 76, 78
Shingarikōta, 226
Shinas, Persian Gulf, 296
Shinwārīs, 408, 428
Shipman, Sir Abraham, 108-111
Shirāz, 146
Shirjirāv Ghātge, *see* Ghātge

Shirley, Sir Robert, 72
Shivgāon, 289
Shiva Prasād, 239
Shivrāv Bhāu of Jhānsi, 286
Shiva Singhji of Sirohi, 311
Shivajī, *see* Sivajī
Sholavandān, 202, 204
Shorapur, 371, 376
Shore, Sir John, Lord Teignmouth, 267, 271-273
Showers, General, 364
Shrīpatrāv, Pratinidhi, 166
Shujā' Shāh, Prince, 91, 92, 96, 98, 102, 103, 105
  Shah, of Kābul, 288, 291, 294, 296, 330, 331, 335-337, 340
Shujā'at Khān, 31 ; 69
  Khān, Kārtalab Khān, 129, 132, 134, 164, 165
Shujā' Mirzā of Afghānistān, 276, 283
Shujā' ud-daula, Vazīr, Nawāb of Audh, 211, 215, 221-223, 230, 231, 234, 236, 248
Shujā' ud-dīn, Amīr Faqīr 'Alī Beg Bahādur, 27
  ud-dīn Khān of Bengal, 165, 166, 173, 178
Shujābād, battle, 350
Shukot Jang of Purnīya, 200, 213
Shuldham, Col., 319
Siālkot, Panjāb, 16, 19, 364
Siam, Siamese, 40, 43, 74, 80, 220, 256, 315, 316, 321, 388
Sībī, dist., 417
Sibindar Narāyan of Kuch-Bihār, 349
Sibley, Capt., 302
Sidasīr Ghāt, 264
Siddis of Janjira, 106, 119, 125, 131, 133, 144, 173, 201, 218, 255
Siddi 'Abdul Rahim, of Janjira, 218
  Ahmad Khān, Surat, 208
  Hāfiz Masa'ūd, 193
  Johār, of Janjira, 106, 255
  Meriam, Janjira, 40
  Miyān Achan, Surat, 208
  Qāsim of Janjira, 119, 120, 123
  Rahman of Janjira, 173, 174
  Sambal, 120
  Yāqūt of Janjira, 114, 132, 137
  Yāqūt Khān, 218, 219 ; 255
Sidney, Earl Godolphin, 151
  Viscount, 255
Sidoji of Tānjor, 177
Sihor, 363
Sikandar 'Adil Shāh, 117, 129
  Begam of Bhopāl, 313, 323, 329, 333, 335, 346, 350, 359, 375, 384
  Jāh, Nizām, 264, 283, 284, 286, 291, 325
Sikandar II., Shāh Lodī, Sultān, 1-3, 5, 7-9, 11, 14, 15 ; 21, 41
  Shāh III., Sūr, 34, 36
  Shāh of Gujarāt, 20
Sikandra, 212, 287
Sikandrabāgh, 319
Sikhs, 27, 65, 105, 151, 152, 157, 216, 259, 271, 273, 274, 277, 293, 322, 327, 334, 335, 346, 347, 350, 351, 365, 368, 378
Sikh Gurus, 27, 33, 46, 50, 65, 91, 106, 110, 119, 151
Sikkim, 303, 305, 332, 353, 376, 418, 422
Sikrāwa fort, 299
Sīkrī, 44
Silak, Asām, 429
Silchar, in Kachār, 408
Silhadī Purbia of Raisin, 23, 29
Silhat, dist., 325, 329, 375
Silva, Bernardo Peres da, 332
  Carlos Eugenio da, 406
  Francisco Teixeira da, 425
  Luiz de Mello de, 38
  Pedro da, 88, 92
  Peres da, 332
Silveira, Dom Rodrigo Sobho de, 101
Sima—Fort Morton, 427
Simla, 390, 394, 400, 404, 407
Simoga, 264
Simon, Mar, Nestorian bishop, 143
Sinanagar, battle, 351
Sinappaiyan, Tanjor, 179
Sinclair, Major, 286
Sindh, 17, 19, 28, 29, 34-36, 46, 55, 56, 104, 105, 191, 205, 254, 276, 300, 314, 328, 331, 332, 336, 338, 341-344, 346, 351
Sindia, 265, 268-272, 277-286, 300, 304, 309, 338, 349
Singarh, 144, 281
Singha of Ceylon, 53, 91, 92, 101, 122
Singhalese, 83, 84, 90, 91
Singussā of Burma, 239, 250
Sipahr Shikōh, Prince, 105, 106
Siprā riv., 308
Siprī, 246, 248, 374
Sīon, near Bombay, 132, 133, 143
Sira, Maisur, 94, 156, 217, 219, 222, 275
Sirāj ud-daula, Mirzā Mahmūd, 189, 190, 195, 200, 201, 203, 204
Sirmūr rāja, 152
Sirohi, 311, 317, 358, 377
Sironj, 175, 246
Sirsa dist., 273, 370
Sirsi, 371
Sirūr, 399
Sīstān dist., 369

Sitāna, 356, 378
Sitārām Rāvji, Baroda, 301
 Rāz of Vizianagaram, 241
Sitawakka, state, 32
Sivājī, 57, 82, 96-98, 103, 105, 106, 108-113, 114, 116-123, 128
 II.,—Shāhujī, 150, 154, 158; 189
 I., of Kolhāpur, 299; II., 336; 377, 382
 of Tānjor, 360
Sivaner, Junnar, 82
Sivāppa Nāyyak of Bednūr, 96, 99
Sivarāv Ghorpade of Sandūr, 322
Sivasingh of Sirohi, 358
Siwāī Rāi Singh of Jaypur, 405
Siwdāshiv Chimnājī, 198
Siwneri, 271
Siyar ul-Matākherīn, 220, 261
Skhardu fort, 99
Sladen, Sir Edward Bosc, 383, 384
slavery, 344, 349, 385
Sleeman, Col. Wm. Henry, 324, 354
Smith, Mr, 124
 Charles, 245
 F. C., 324
 Major-General Joseph, 214, 225-227, 229
 General Sir Harry, 347
 N. H., 292
 Lieut.-General Sir Lionel, 306-310, 315, 319
 Lieut. Manners, 424
 Capt. Stephen, 216
Smyth, Col. Owen Stuart, 423
Soarez de Albergaria, Dom Lope, 14, 15
Sobhdar of Sindh, 280
Sobrāon, battle, 347
Sohāgpur, 305
Sohrāb Khān of Surat, 171, 174
Sojitra, battle, 166
Soldanha, João de, 172
Somatāsh, Shighnān, 426
Sonda, 200
Songadh, 160
Sonpur, Sambalpur, 3
Sorath,—Kāthiāwād, 156
Sosile, Maisur, 275
Soupires, Marquis de, 204, 206
Sousa, Antonio Sergio de, 396, 397
 Dom Frederico Guilherm de, 243, 257
 João de, 42
 Manuel da, 25
 Martim Affonso, 29, 30
Souter, Frank H., 372
Southby, Mr, 211
Spain, 20, 22, 59, 61, 67, 72, 85
Sparkes, Capt., 311
Spencer, Mr, 201, 208
Speult, Capt. Harman van, 79, 81, 82
Spice islands, 75, 98
Spilbergen, Admiral, 62
Srīgāon fort, 178
Srīrangham temple, 194, 196, 199
Srīnagar, Kashmīr, 28, 106, 324, 412, 428
Srīnivasarāv of Arnī, 260
Srīvardhan, Janjira, 150
Stables, Mr., Vizagapatam, 132
Stalker, Major-General James, 360
Standard correspondent, 398
Stanhope, Lieut.-Col., 314
"Star of India," 376, 380, 389
Starkey, Mr, 70
Staunton, Lieut.-Col. Francis French, 308
Steamships,—"Diana," 317; "Enterprise," 319; "Hugh Lindsay," 325
Stedman, Col. Sir Edward, 416
Steel, Richard, 72
Stephens, Thomas, S.J., 49
Stephenson, Mr, 156
Steuart, Lieut.-Col., 331
Stevens, Mr, 99
 Admiral, 205
Stevenson, Col. J. D., 284
 General, 332
Stewart, Field-Marshal Sir Donald Martin, 383, 387, 403, 405, 412
 Capt. James, 242
 General James Calder, 398
Stoddart, Lieut.-Col. Charles, 341
Story, James, 51
Stoletoff, General, 397, 398
Strachey, Sir John, 388, 391, 396
Straits Settlements, 324
Stratton, George, 239, 240
Street, Col., 413
Stringer, Capt., 114
Strutt, Stephen, 157
Stuart, Major-General James, 252, 253, 264, 275
 General Sir Chas. Shepherd, 366, 367, 370
Subhā Singh, 122
Subhān Rāī, author, 148
Suez, 28, 325
Sufi, Shaikh, of Ahmadābād, 69
Suffragam, Ceylon, 73, 74, 86
Suffrein, de Saint Tropez, Pierre André de, 249-253
Sugarloaf Rock, Trichinapalli, 196, 197
Sulaimān Bakhsh, 35
 Kararānī, 40, 42, 45
 Mirzā, of Kābul, 234
 Qirānī, Orissa, 36
 Shikoh, Prince, 103, 106

Sullivan, Sir Benjamin, 280
Sultān Jān, Ghaznī, 341
Sultānpur, 368, 372
Sulu, Sultān of, 267
Sumatra, 17, 31, 59, 62, 72, 135, 146, 159, 161, 318
Sumner, Mr, 216, 222
Sunda Strait, 62, 80, 81, 127, 139, 149, 155, 156, 215, 220, 231, 263, 276
Sundur, p. 339, l. 7,—*read* Sandūr, *q.v.*
Sungrī, Kasia state, 325
Sunnī, Muhammadan sect, 152, 282, 377, 378, 382
Supā, Kānara, 215
Sūra Chandra Singh of Manipur, 422
Surājgarh, battle, 36
Sūrajkund, battle, 351
Sūrajmal Jāt of Bharatpur, 187, 197, 205, 212, 217, 219, 220, 226
of Mārwar, 2
Suraj Singh of Jodhpur, 57, 58, 77
Sura or Kotaldab, battle, 417
Surang, Orissa, 283
Surat, 30, 33, 39, 45, 46, 56, 65-71, 73-76, 80, 82-85, 89, 91, 95, 98, 99, 101, 102, 104, 106, 108, 109, 112-114, 117, 118, 120, 124, 126-133, 135-138, 141-150, 153, 155, 156, 160, 166, 169, 171, 187, 193, 208, 230, 237, 238, 242-244, 261, 389, 408
Surat Singh of Bikanir, 259
Surendranāth Bānarji, journalist, 408
Suriā Jāh-Amjad 'Alī Shāh of Audh, 341
Suribān, vill., 371
Surjan Rāī of Rantambhor, 43, 44
Singh of Mewār, 391
Singh of Urchha, 342
Surji-Anjangāon Treaty, 285, 286
Surkh-pul, 428
Surman, Mr, 156
Sūryaji Piral, Marātha, 132
Sutānatī or Chatānatī, Calcutta, 129, 140, 142
Sutherland, Sergeant, 119
Lord, 127
Col., 279
Col., 336
Suvarnadurg, Ratnāgiri dist., 199
Swally, 24, 69, 71-73, 82, 84, 146
Swan, Capt., 80
Swāt, 356, 378, 379
Swedish East India Company, 171
Syālbet,—Syāl island, 22
Sykes, Mr, 222
Sylveira, Heytor da, 118
John de, 15
Symes, Col. Michael, 269, 281
Symons, General Sir William Penn, 415, 421
Syriac college, 53; language, 290
Syriam, Burma, 62-64, 66, 70, 201, 318
Syrian churches, 30, 59, 101, 109, 163, 169, 170, 290

TABAKĀT-I-AKBARI, history, 57
Tabang Shēwti of Burma, 23, 24, 27, 28, 31
Tabo, Malacca, 327, 328
Tafazzul Khan of Farrukhābād, 373
Tāgor, Dwārkanāth, 348
Tāhir Muhammad bin 'Imād ud-dīn Hasan, historian, 63
Tahmāsp II., Quli Khān Nadir Shah, 169, 170, 175, 186
Taimūr Shāh Durāni, 233, 266, 283
Taimūr-lang,—Tamurlane, 3
Taingda Mingyi of Māndalē, 410, 414
Tāj Khān, 40
Tāj Mahal, Agra, 95
Takaroī or Mughulmārī, battle, Orissa, 47
Takarwutbi of Pegu, 24
Takendrajit Singh, 422-424
Takht-i-Shāh heights, 402
Takht Singh of Ahmadnagar, 343
Talagadh, Kolāba, 174
Talain, Kachār, 318
Talaing, 27, 64, 211
Talāja, Kāthiāwād, 229
Talāpūr, 132
Tal Bahat fort, 370
Talegāon Dabhāde, 242
Tālifū, 384
Tālikōta, battle, 41
Tālpur Mīrs of Sindh, 254, 276, 336, 338, 341, 342
Tamū, Burma, 414, 423
Tāndā or Tāndān near Gaur, 40, 49, 50, 53
Tangassēri, Malabar, 16, 270
Tānjor, 74, 75, 77, 81, 121, 142, 177, 179, 180, 189, 190, 195-198, 206, 207, 209, 218, 221, 229, 232, 234, 238, 239, 253, 267, 360, 377
Tānk, Panjāb, 386, 406
Tantia or Tātya Bhil, robber, 421
Tāntia Jog, 309
Tantia or Tātya Topi, 370-374
Tapeng riv., 225
Tapokara pargana, 266
Tapti or Tāpī riv., 244, 408

Tārābāī of Sātāra, 143, 150-154, 192, 198, 217
Tārāgarh, Nepāl, 93, 262, 302
Tarai, 302, 303
Tārākandā, 151
Tārakzāis, 355, 358
Tārāpur, 22, 23, 176, 178
Tardi 'Alī Katghan of Balkh, 94
Tārīkhi-Alfi, history, 55
-*Badāoni*, 59
-*Haqqī*, 59
-*Faiz Bakhsh*, Afghān history, 239
-*Hindi*, 181
-*Ibrāhīm Khān*, 258
-*Khān Jahān Lodi*, 70
-*Mamālik i-Hind*, 252
-*Muzaffarī*, 278
-*Salīm Skāhi*, 326
Tarleton, Capt., 356
Tartar invasions, 23, 75
Tashi-lhunpo, Tibet, 254
Tāsh-Kargan, 419
Tashon Chins, 420, 421, 425
Taufal Khān, Berār, 43
Taungu, 63, 64, 69, 70, 218, 312
Tavira, Molucca islands, 42
Tavora, Francisco de, 124, 129
Ruy Lourenço de, 27, 48, 67
Tavoy, 318, 320
Taylor, William, Patna, 363
Tazīn pass, battle, 341
Tazkirat ul-Waki'at, history, 53
Teg Bahādur, 9th Sikh Guru, 110, 119
Teghbakht Khān, 172, 173
Tegnapatam, 133, 135; *see* Fort St David
Teherān, Persia, 296, 323, 417
Tehri, Rāja of, 295
Tej Singh of Urchhā, 342
Singh of Lāhor, 346, 347
Tekke Turkomān troops, 411
telegraphs, 357, 381
Telicheri,—Tellicherry, 114, 115, 126, 146, 151, 193, 211, 222, 249, 250
Telingana, 85
Telles, Antonio, 89, 92
Temple, Sir Richard, 388-391, 395, 403
Temudo, Jorge, 38
Tenaserim, 322, 324
Tenkāsi inscriptions, 5, 26, 43
"Tent contract," 293-295
Ternati, — Ternate island, Moluccas, 22, 24, 30, 37, 43, 47-49, 52, 65, 297
Terriagarhi, battle, 80
Teshu Lama, 235, 254
Texeira, Luiz, 77
Thackeray, St John, 319
Thackwell, Lieut.-General Sir Edward J., 351
Thado-Dhamma Rāja of Burma, 83, 97
Thags, 324, 332
Thal-Chotiāli, 409, 410, 417
Thālner, Kandesh, 139, 310
Thān, Kāthiāwād, 134
Thānā, Salsette, 23, 59, 110, 125, 130, 176, 177, 201, 236, 237, 303, 304, 357
Thappa, General Bhimasena, Nepal, 289
Thāttā, Sindh, 17, 18, 20, 35, 36, 52, 53, 55, 76, 82, 112, 113
Thayet-Myo, Burma, 407, 413
Thein-ni, Shān state, 427
Theodore of Abyssinia, 383, 384
Thībau, Wongyi, of Burma, 397, 398, 403, 407, 410, 412-414
Thībaw state, 416, 417
Thirī Thudhamma of Burma, 79
Thirī Thurīya Dhamma of Arakan, 128
Thobal, Manipur, 423
Thomas, George, 270, 272, 273, 276, 277, 279, 280
Mar, Monophisite bishop, 169
Thompson, Sir A. Rivers, 407
Mowbray, 369
Thorne, Robert, 21
Thunbā Wongyi, Pegu, 318
Tibet, 49, 99, 254, 418, 419, 422
Tidor island, Moluccas, 20, 30, 52, 65, 76
Tijāra, Alwār, 266, 268
Tilbegampur inscription, 27
Timak Khān, battle near Ghaznī, 385
Timmappa of Anegundi, 239
Timmarāja of Vijayanagar, 2
Timor island, 345
Tīmūr Shāh, Harāt, 417
Tinneveli,—Tinnevelly, 199, 202, 210, 253, 269, 278
Tipara state, Bengal, 375, 420
Tīpū Sāhib, 239, 245, 246, 249-266, 268, 270, 272-275, 278
Tirakhol,—Terekhol, Sāwantwādi, 186, 205
Tirat Singh of Nunklau, Asām, 322 325
Tirella, battle, 172
Tirhut, dist., 17
Tirohā, Bānda, 296
Tiruchendur, Tinneveli, 97
Tirukkallūr, Malabar, battle, 262
Tirumala of Vijayanagar, Pennakonda, 29, 43, 47, 68
Nāyyaka, of Madura, 80, 106
Tirumalrāo of Maisur, 251
Tirumumpara of Cochin, 6

Tirupati, N. Arkat, 205
Tiruvadi, S. Arkat, 213
Tiruvattūr, N. Arkat, 151, 211, 212
Titu Mīyan, Wahhābi, 328
Tītīya fort, Bundelkhand, 283
Tiyāgar fort, Volkonda, 210, 213, 215, 216, 262
tobacco monopoly at Goa, 119
Todar Mal, 47, 49, 52, 54; 89
Todd, Major Elliot D'Arcy, 337
Togh, Kohat, 396
Tohāwar Jang, 257
Tokā Hindu temples, 217
Tolar state, 44
Tolawē, Singhalese minister, 277
Tombs, Major-General Sir Henry, 363, 380
Tompane, Ceylon, 73
Tongal, general, Manipur, 424
Tongso Penlo, Bhutiya, 379
Tonk state, 332, 373, 378, 383
Tonk-Rāmpura, or Alīgarh Rāmpura, Tonk, 286, 289
Tonquin, 146, 411
Tornā fort, Bor, 96, 144
Towerson, Capt., 79
Traki, Baluchistan, 346
Tranquebar, 73, 78, 81, 142, 149, 161, 185, 186, 191, 206, 215, 346
Travankor, 85, 128, 169, 208, 260-262, 266, 270, 276, 288, 290, 292, 293, 297, 302, 325, 377
Tremlen, William, 91
Trevelyan, Sir Charles Edward, 374, 376, 378, 381
Trevor, Capt., 339
Trichināpalli, 37, 175, 180, 190, 192-197, 199, 202, 203, 207, 230, 234, 262, 322, 377
Trikkalūr, Malabar, 410
Trimbakji Denglia or Dengle, 300, 303, 304, 306, 307
Trimbakrāv Dābhāde, 163, 171
  Māma, 229, 235
Trimliwash, 208
Trimmu Ghat, battle, 364
Trinkomālī, Ceylon, 92, 113, 115, 116, 186, 211, 249-251, 253
Trinomalli or Tiruvannāmalai, S. Arkat, 204, 207, 212, 225
Tiruvadi, S. Arkat, 194
Trivandram, 293
Trivatūr, or Tiruvattūr, N. Arkat, 207
Tronjolly, M., 241
Tsanda Wijaya of Arakan, 153
Tucker, Capt., 297
Tukājī Bhonsla, 177
  Holkar, 224, 269, 272, 278; 344
Tulājī Āngria, 198-201
  of Tanjor, 234, 258
Tulā Rām, Senāpati, Kachār, 345, 358
  Ram, rebel, 326
Tulloch, Major Hector, 426
Tulsībāī of Indor, 291, 298, 308
Tulsi Dās, poet, 47, 80
Tulsipur, Audh, 373
Tungābhadrā riv., 185, 257, 265
Turkey and Levant Company, 50
Turkistān, 386, 395, 398, 402, 427
Turkomans, 409, 418
Turner, Col. Augustus Henry, 427, 430
  Bishop John Mathias, 324
  General Sir Oriel, 410
  Samuel, 254
Tūtakkal, Malabar, 390
Tutikorin,—Tuttukudi, Tinneveli, 85, 97, 103
Tweedale, Marquis of, 342, 350
Tyamong, Sumatra, 146
Tytler, Col., 366

UCHH, Bahāwalpur, 8, 19
Uchitgarh, Konkan, 174
Udayagiri, S. Travankor, 293
Udayampārūr—Diamper Synod, 60, 61
Udaybhanji of Sirohi, 311
Udayār of Maisur, 48, 68, 74
Udaypur, Mewār, 22, 53, 59, 100, 122-124, 143, 150, 153, 183, 187, 193, 199, 262, 276, 305, 309, 323, 348, 376
Uday Singh of Mewār, 26, 46
Udgīr, Bīdar, 89
Udhā-Nalā, battle, 219
Udhambāī Begam, Dehli, 188, 197
Ugargol inscription, 13
Ujjain, Mālwa, 76, 104, 217, 279, 282
Ullāla state, Malabar, 35, 42, 74
Ulubāria, Howrah, 130
Ulugh Mirzā, 24
'Umar Shaikh Mirzā of Farghana, 3
'Umdat ul 'Umarā of Arkat, 229, 269, 279
Umed Singh of Būndī, 183, 189
  Rāo of Būndī, 287
  Singh of Kotā, 308, 314
  Singh of Sirohi, 377
'Umrā Khān of Jāndol, 429, 430
Unā, Hoshiārpur, 351
Underi, or Henery island, 123, 124
"United Company of Merchants," 151, 152
"United English E.I. Company," 170, 180, 185
"United Joint Stock Company," 98

Upton, Col. John, 238, 239
Urchhā, 87, 88, 187
Urmistone, Capt. H. B., 419
'Usmān Lohānī, Khwājah Khān of Bengal, 68, 69
Uttakamand,—Ootacamund, 386, 406, 427
Uttaradurg, 264
Uttattūr, Trichināpalli, 194
Uva, Ceylon, 60, 75, 84
Uzbaks, 40, 42, 96, 159

VADGĀON, 242
Vadnagar, Gujarāt, 166
Vafonrāv, 272
Vaitarnā riv., 36, 38, 44
"Vakil i-Mutālīk," 265
Valdor,—Valdavūr, S. Arkat, 213
Vallabhāchārya Mahārājas, 377
Valle, Pietro della, 80
Valpy, Bishop Thomas, of Lāhor, 396
Van Nec, Dutch sea captain, 60
Vansittart, Henry, 196, 214, 218, 219, 227, 237
Vanchi Mārtānda Perumal of Travankor, 169, 182, 185, 208
Vanspal, Heer, of Tangassēri, 270
Vārīvene, Sindh, 25
Vasco da Gama, 4, 6, 19
Vasconcellos, Dom Francisco de, 182, 183
  Manuel de, 34
  Sancho de, 48
  Correira, Antonio Cesar de, 359
Vasconello, Col. João Casimir da Rocha, 332
Vāsū, raja of Kāngra, 93
Vāsudev Balwant Phadke, 398, 399
Vaughan, Capt., 307
Vazīr 'Alī Khān of Audh, 272, 275, 276
  Asad Khān, 154
  Khān of Bengal, 53
  Muhammad of Bhopāl, 295, 301, 304
  Muhammad Khan of Tonk, 332, 378, 379
Veiga, Tristão Vaz de, 45, 46
Vellāva, Arkat, 193
Vello, Pedro, 53
Vellozo, João Lourenço, 211
V lūr,—Vellor, 120, 172, 195, 249, 275, 289, 290
Venkāji, Sivāji's half-brother, 121
Venkata I., of Vijayanagar, 62
  Nāyyak, 75
Venkatādri, Rāya of Vijayanagar, 29, 43
  Nāyyak of Madura, 56
Venkatagiri, Nellūr, 226
Venkatapati Rāya of Chandragiri, 71, 88, 93
Venkatrāv Ghorpade of Sandūr, 339
Ventura, General, 316
Venūr inscription, 63
Vepery, Madras, 139, 182
Verappoli, Malabar, 290
Verelst, Henry, 225, 228
Verisāl Singh of Rājpīpla, 316
Vernacular Press Bill, 296
Vernon, Sir E., 241
Versova, Salsette, 176
Verulam Tamburan of Kochin, 239
Vesey, Capt., 390
Vicente, Conde de, 111
Victoria, Queen, 372, 373, 390, 416, 417
Vidigueira, Conde de, 82
Vijayadurg or Gheria, 170, 179, 200, 201, 219, 252
Vijayanagar, 2, 6, 8, 11-13, 16, 17, 22, 25, 29, 31, 37, 39, 41-43, 49, 62, 68, 80
Vijayapur, S. Arkat, 126
Vijaya Singh of Mārwār, 259, 262, 267
Vikovich, Capt., 334, 335
Vikramāditya of Mewar, 23, 25
Vikramājit of Gwāliar, 15
Vikrama Singh of Ceylon, 302
Vilapuli, Godāvarī dist., 193
Vilāyati San era, 36
Villanova, Visconde de, 359
Villīnūr, Pondicheri, 213
Villupuram, S. Arkat, 194, 213
Vimala Dharma of Ceylon, 56
Vincent, Friar, 30, 53
  Mathias, 109
Vīra Chāma Udayār of Maisur, 41, 48
Vīrarāja of Kūrg, 329, 331
Viramgām, Gujarāt, 174, 175
Vīrappa Nāyyaka of Madura, 80, 106, 115
Vīravāsaram, Godāvarī dist., 88
Visāji Pandit, 215
Vishālgarh or Khelnā, 117, 140, 144, 145, 151, 345
Vishvanāth Ayār of Madura, 25, 37, 40
Vishvāsrāv, son of Bālāji Bajirāv, 214, 216
Vishvāsrāv Ghātge, 285
Vithoji Holkar, 278, 279
Vizagapatam, 126, 132, 133, 140, 146, 166, 207, 353
Vizianagaram, 202, 209, 241
Volkonda, 192, 194
volunteering, 387
Vriddhāchalam, S. Arkat, 192, 213
Vyāsarpādi vill., Madras, 151
Vypin, Malabar, 38

WAAT in Arabia, 354
Wade, Col. Sir Claude Martin, 337
Wāghars, 303, 314, 375, 383, 384
Waghorn, Thomas, 324
Wahhābīs, 305, 316, 318, 322, 327, 328, 356, 378, 384, 387
Wāī, Sātāri dist., 134, 271
Waite, Sir Nicholas, 142-144, 147, 151
Wajid 'Alī Shāh of Audh, 349, 360, 362
Wake, William, 182
Wākinkhera, 148
Wāla Jāh, Sayyad Ahmad 'Alī Khān, of Bengal, 315, 319
Wales, H.R.H. Edward Prince of, 393
Walī Allah Shāh Bahmanī, 18, 19
Walker, Brig.-General Alexander, 280, 291
Wallace, Col., 287
  Lt.-Col., 345
Waller, Major Robert, 351
  Lieut., 372
Walpole, Lieut.-General Sir Robert, 367, 370
Walsh, Mr, 140
Wanauli, Pūnā, 268
Wandiwāsh, N. Arkat, 131, 203, 211, 212, 246
Wanji Baula Perumāl of Travankor, 208; 276
Wanji or Vanchi (*q.v.*) Mārtānda Perumāl, 208
Wāno, battle, 430
Warangal or Orangal, 226
Ward, Mr., Bombay, 127
  Sir Henry George, 376
Wardhā riv., 284, 310
Wardell, Lieut., 427
Wargāon or Vadgāon, Pūnā dist., 307
Warren, Commodore, 141, 143
wasī riots, 152
Wāsil Muhammad, Pendhārī, 308
Wāsota fort, 310
Watson, Admiral Henry, 200-202, 204, 215
  Commodore John, 223, 236
  Capt., 296
Watt, Capt., 353
Watts, William, 203, 204
Waugh, Col., 331
Waykondān, Trichināpalli dist., 196, 197
Wazīr, *see* Vazīr
Wazīrābād, Panjāb, 352
Waziri tribes, 375, 430
Weddell, Capt., 88, 90
Weldon, Mr, 132
Wellesley, General Sir Arthur (Duke of Wellington), 278, 282-285, 288
Wellesley, Marquis, 274, 275, 278, 280, 288, 290
Wellesley Province, 279
Welsh, Major-General James, 267, 322
Weltevreeden, Java, 297
Wenlock, B. Lawley Lord, 422
Wer, Bharatpur state, 288
West, Sir Edward, 317
Westminster, Treaty of, 100
Wettigan, Burma, 320
Wheeler, Major-General Sir Hugh Massy, 348, 363
Wheeler (*read* Wheler), Edward, 239, 240
Whish, Lieut.-General Wm. Sampson, 351
White, Mr, 120
  Capt., 137
Whitehill, John, 240
  Thomas, 245
Whitlock, Lieut.-General Sir George C., 369, 371, 372
Wild, Brigadier, 340
Wilde, Lieut.-General Sir Alfred Thomas, 384
Wilkinson, Anthony, 37
William III., 132, 136
  IV., 327
Williams, Lieut., 427
Williamson, Major, 413, 414
Willoughby, Major F., 109
  Lieut., 361
Willshire, General Sir Thomas, 337
Wilson, Lieut.-General Sir Archdale, 362, 364
  Daniel, Bishop of Calcutta, 368
  James, 374
  Rev. Dr John, 326
  Capt., 296
Windham, Lieut.-General Sir Chas. Ash, 367
Winter, Sir Edward, 107, 111
Withington, Mr, 70, 72
Wodehouse, Sir Philip Edmond, 389, 395
Wokhā, Nāgās of, 392
Wolseley, Lieut.-General Sir George B., 420, 422-424
Wood, Capt. B., 59
  Sir Charles, 358, 381
  Col. John, 226, 227
  Major-General John Sullivan, 302, 304
Woodington, Major, 281
wreck of the "Eagle Speed," 381
Wuntho, Burma, 416, 423
Wyborne, Sir John, 129
Wyche, Nathaniel, 101
Wyld, Mr, 82

Wymer, General Sir George Petre, 339
Wynch, Alexander, 232
Wyse, Ensign, 353

XAVIER, Francis, 28, 33, 35

YĀDGĀR, rebel in Kashmīr, 56
Yādgār Khān Kashmīri, 175
Yahia Khān, Afghān, 400, 402
Yale, Elihu, 127, 130, 133, 136
Yāma Satrusālya of Nawānagar, 77
Yeman ud-daula—Mīr 'Abdul Nabī Khān, 206
Yanāon or Yanām, Godāvarī dist., 192, 305
Yandabu, Burma, 322, 355
Yanoff, Capt., 424-426, 428
Ya'qūb Beg, Muhammad of Kāshghār, 386, 389-391, 395
Shāh of Kashmīr, 53
Khān, "Shaikhji," pirate, 173, 174
Khān of Kābul, 384, 386, 387, 390, 392, 398-404
Yāqūt Khudāwand Khān, 85
Yār Khān Lati, 203
Khān Alakozāi, Harāt, 342
Yārqand,—Yarkand, Turkistān, 386, 390, 391
Yashodābāī, 270
Yashwantrāv or Jeswant Holkar, 272, 278, 279, 281, 285-287
Yashwantrāv, senāpati, 171
Yate, Col. Charles Edward, 411
Yeola, Nasik dist., 428
Yepu,—Ippoe, Sumatra, 159
Yeshil-kul, Turkistān, 426
Yeshwantgarh, Ratnāgiri dist., 223
Yezd, Persia, 306
Yindowango, Burma, 414
Yokwa Chins, 421
York fort, Sumatra, 130, 146
Young, Henry, 113
Younghusband, Sir Francis Edward, 424, 425
Yule, Mājor, 425
Yūsuf 'Adil Khān Shāh, 2-4, 6, 7, 11
Shāh Chakk of Kashmīr, 48, 51
Yūsufzāīs, 52, 317
Yuthia or Ayodhya, Siam, 31, 40, 43

ZĀBITA Khān, Rohila, 228, 230, 255, 258
Zābulistān, 53
Zafar Khān, Roshan ud-daula, 167
Zafaryab Khān—Aloysius Reinhardt, 270
Zafarābād, Bīdar, 103
Zāhir ud-daula Bahādur of Arkat, 390
Zāhir ud-dīn Muhammad, *see* Bābur.
Zain Khān Koka, 53, 58, 61
Zain ud-dīn Khān, 184
ud-dīn Mahmūd, 200
Zainpur, 40
Zakaria Khān, Afghān, 402
Zālim Singh of Kotā, 267, 308, 314-316, 318; 331
Zamān Khān Abdālī, 187
Shāh, Harāt, 158
Shāh Abdālī, 266, 271, 274, 276-278
Zamīndāwār, Afghānistān, 158
Zamorin of Kochin, 5-9, 11, 12, 19, 26, 27, 32, 36, 40, 45, 46, 52, 60, 71, 134
Zareka island, Persian Gulf, 168
Zemethan, Burma, 414
Zhob, N.W. Frontier, 409, 410, 421, 422
Ziegenbalg, Rev. Bartholomaeus, 149, 161
Zilla Khān, Lāhor, 188
Zimme state, 41
Zinzan, Mr, 128
Ziyā Khān, Surat, 156
Zulfiqār 'Alī of Bānda, 281, 317
Beg, general, 157
Khān of Surat, 72
Khan Nasrat Jang of Arkat, 133-136, 139, 140, 148, 150, 154
Zulfiqār Pass, Afghānistān, 411, 413

Printed at THE DARIEN PRESS, *Edinburgh*